The Effects of Competition

The Effects of Competition

Cartel Policy and the
Evolution of Strategy and
Structure in British Industry

George Symeonidis

The MIT Press
Cambridge, Massachusetts
London, England

© 2002 Massachusetts Institute of Technology

All rights reserved. No part of this book may be reproduced in any form by any electronic or mechanical means (including photocopying, recording, or information storage and retrieval) without permission in writing from the publisher.

This book was set in Palatino in '3B2' by Asco Typesetters, Hong Kong and was printed and bound in the United States of America.

Library of Congress Cataloging-in-Publication Data

Symeonidis, George.
  The effects of competition : cartel policy and the evolution of strategy and structure in British industry / George Symeonidis.
     p. cm.
  Includes bibliographical references and index.
  ISBN 0-262-19468-6 (hc. : alk. paper)
    1. Corporations—Great Britain—History—20th century. 2. Cartels—Great Britain—History—20th century. 3. Strategic alliances (Business)—Great Britain—History—20th century. 4. Competition—Great Britain—History—20th century. 5. Big business—Great Britain—History—20th century. 6. Industrial policy—Great Britain—History—20th century. 7. Prices—Great Britain—History—20th century. 8. Costs, Industrial—Great Britain—History—20th century. I. Title.
HD2845 .S95   2002
338.8'7—dc21   2001044444

Contents

Acknowledgments

The research for this book began several years ago, when I was a graduate student at the London School of Economics, and continued after I took my current post at the University of Essex. My intellectual debt to John Sutton is almost too obvious to be acknowledged. His invaluable advice in the course of many and long discussions has profoundly influenced my work, and I am also grateful to him for numerous insightful comments on various drafts, including those on the penultimate draft of this book.

I have also benefited greatly from discussions with several other people on various aspects of the research presented here. I am especially obliged to V. Bhaskar, Paul Geroski, Tim Hatton, Sajal Lahiri, Stephen Machin, Pedro Marin, Mark Schankerman, Philip Vergauwen, Michael Waterson, and Hugh Wills for their very helpful advice and suggestions at various stages of the project. I also wish to thank seminar audiences at the London Business School; the London School of Economics; Nuffield College (Oxford); the Universities of Athens, Carlos III (Madrid), East Anglia, Essex, Leuven, Maastricht, and Warwick; and at numerous conferences, where parts of this research were presented over the past few years.

I owe a very particular debt to David Genesove and Stephen Martin, both of whom read the entire manuscript and provided very detailed and thoughtful comments. Their suggestions led to significant improvements in the final version.

The financial assistance of the Greek State Scholarships Foundation helped me begin the research reported in this book. Some of this work has appeared in different form in a number of journal articles, and I wish to thank the publishers of *Economica* (Blackwell Publishers and London School of Economics), the *Journal of Industrial Economics* (Blackwell Publishers), and the *Journal of Economics and Manage-*

x

ment Strategy (MIT Press) for permission to use material from these sources. I am indebted to Terry Vaughn, former economics editor at the MIT Press, for his help and encouragement, and I am also thankful to John Covell for dealing very efficiently with the manuscript.

Finally, my warmest thanks go to my parents, Antonis and Niki, and to my wife, Angelina, for their continuous support and encouragement over many years.

1   An Introductory Overview

1.1   A Natural Experiment

This book is a study of the effects of competition on firm strategy, market structure, and industry performance. It combines game-theoretic models of competition with econometric and case-study evidence from a unique natural experiment that occurred in the UK between the late 1950s and the early 1970s. The introduction of the 1956 Restrictive Trade Practices Act led to the registration, and subsequent abolition, of explicit restrictive agreements between firms and the intensification of price competition across a range of manufacturing industries. An equally large number of industries had not been subject to agreements significantly restricting competition, and were therefore not affected by the legislation. A comparison of the two groups of industries over a twenty-year period, using data from both before and after the introduction of the 1956 Act, can provide important insights on the effect of price competition on concentration, firm and plant numbers, profitability, advertising intensity, and innovation.

The introduction of cartel policy in the UK is a very rare opportunity for a systematic and comprehensive empirical analysis of the effects of competition. The most important feature of this natural experiment is that it provides us with a way to bypass two very difficult problems that have been endemic in empirical studies of the effects of competition. The first problem is how to measure the intensity of competition. The second problem is how to unravel the complex links between competition and other variables, such as market structure, innovation, and profitability, given that all these variables may simultaneously affect one another, thus making the identification of one-way causal effects very difficult.

The present setup allows us to bypass these difficulties because a change in the intensity of competition across a wide range of industries was in this case induced by an exogenous and measurable institutional change. Thus there is no need to measure the intensity of competition directly. All that is required is a clear distinction between industries affected by the shift in cartel policy and industries not affected. Moreover, the exogeneity of the institutional change allows us to largely overcome any concerns about potential biases in the estimated impact of competition caused by the existence of complex links between competition and other variables. In other words, the identification of one-way causal effects is a feasible task in the present context.

Several of the issues addressed in this book have been the subject of long-standing debates among economists as well as among policy makers. The present research aims to contribute to a better understanding of these issues and to raise some additional ones. In which industries is collusion more likely? Do cartels raise firms' profits in the long run and do they restrict entry into industries? What is the effect of cartel laws on market structure and profitability across different classes of industries? Is there a link between recent policy changes that have introduced more competition across many national and international markets, and the observed restructuring of a large number of industries? Does competition promote innovation? Do firms advertise less, or do they advertise more, when price competition is tougher? Is higher concentration necessarily associated with higher prices and profits? Finally, what are the constraints on the exercise of merger and antitrust policies? This book examines these issues, and others, using game-theoretic models of oligopoly and a rich data set covering the whole of the UK manufacturing industry.

At a more general level, the analysis of the effects of competition in this book aims to contribute to the recent renaissance of a research program in industrial economics that involves formulating general theoretical predictions and testing them to reveal empirical regularities across industries. This renaissance has come as a response to a rather pessimistic view of the robustness of theoretical and empirical results in industrial economics. According to that view, since the results of game-theoretic models of oligopoly often depend on specific assumptions about a range of factors (some of which are impossible to identify empirically) and the observed empirical outcomes are partly driven by particular and nonsystematic characteristics of industries, "anything can happen in oligopoly." In this book I argue, in line with recent theoretical and empirical work on the determinants of market structure (see Sutton 1991, 1998), that this view is unnecessarily pessimistic. In particular, I analyze a small number of mechanisms, involving observable variables, which operate in a systematic way across industries or for a broad class of industries. Accordingly, the theoretical predictions developed in this book are tested using cross-industry data.

1.2 Key Theoretical Concepts

The empirical analysis of the effects of the 1956 Restrictive Trade Practices Act in this book is firmly based on game-theoretic models in which the intensity of price competition is exogenously determined, while market structure is endogenously determined by means of a free-entry condition. A central feature of these models is the assumption that in long-run equilibrium, net profit is restricted by free entry, irrespective of the type of competition regime facing firms. A change in firm conduct induced by an institutional change, such as the introduction of legislation prohibiting cartels or economic integration, will have little effect on net profit, since it will cause industries to move from one long-run free-entry equilibrium to another. It will, however, have a significant effect on market structure, and it could also affect innovation, nonprice competition, and the labor market. It is precisely through adjustments in these variables, especially market structure, that a new long-run equilibrium will be reached.

This theoretical framework encompasses key insights of the traditional structure-conduct-performance approach, according to which profitability is higher in more concentrated industries because concentration facilitates the exercise of market power by firms. In particular, the present theory allows for a negative effect of entry on profit margins. However, it embeds this in a richer framework that allows for a two-way link between strategy and structure. Unlike the traditional approach, which sees market structure as being largely determined by exogenous "barriers to entry," the present theory emphasizes how changes in firm conduct affect the conditions of entry, and hence market structure.

The unraveling of the two-way link between strategy and structure is carried out by applying a simple distinction between firms' long-run and short-run decisions. Long-run strategic variables include the decision to enter an industry by setting up a plant, and also the expenditures involved in inventing or developing a product, improving a production process, or creating an advertising-based brand image; they may also include the outcome of bargaining with a union over the division of rents. These are considered to be long-run choices because they are relatively difficult to reverse in the short run. On the other hand, short-term decisions are easily reversible and generally involve setting the price of the product or/and the level of output produced in any period. The precise link between long-run and short-run decisions can be summarized as follows. Long-run decisions determine a set of conditions that firms must take as given when making short-run choices. At the same time, firms anticipate, when making their long-run decisions, the way these decisions will affect their own and their rivals' short-run choices, and they act accordingly.

It is firm conduct with respect to the short-run choice variables that is referred to as "intensity of price competition" throughout this book. This should not be confused with the price-cost margin, which is an index of performance rather than of conduct. The difference between the two is important and requires some further clarification.

The Intensity of Price Competition

The concept of the intensity of price competition is intended to capture the idea that, for any *given* market structure and set of long-run variables, profit margins will depend on firms' pricing strategies, which in turn will partly depend on exogenous institutional factors such as the climate of competition policy or the degree of economic integration. Thus, for instance, a switch from collusive to non-collusive pricing behavior represents an increase in the intensity of price competition. On the other hand, a change in the price-cost margin may occur even in the absence of any change in pricing conduct. The key point is that the intensity of price competition refers to the type of pricing behavior, *not* to the level of price-cost margins. It may, in fact, be useful to think of the intensity of price competition as a *functional relationship* between a set of variables that are taken as fixed in the short run, including market structure, and the level of margins. A change in the intensity of price competition will then imply a shift in this functional relationship. For instance, an increase in the intensity of price competition will imply that price-cost margins are lower at any *given* level of concentration.

The attractiveness of this concept for the study of competition in oligopolistic markets stems from the fact that it bypasses the need to specify or observe the determinants of firms' pricing behavior, many of which are unobservable or nonsystematic variables. It may, however, be asked whether we are justified in treating the intensity of price competition (but not the price-cost margin) as an exogenous variable in this book. This is not unreasonable on theoretical grounds, given the well-known multiplicity of equilibria in dynamic game-theoretic models of oligopolistic interaction. In these models, there is a wide range of possible outcomes regarding pricing behavior *for any given set of parameters*, ranging from perfect collusion (i.e., joint profit maximization) to pricing at marginal cost. Moreover, and more important, I would argue that the simplifying assumption of exogeneity of the intensity of price competition is probably justified in the present context for two reasons. First, because cartelization in British manufacturing in the 1950s seems to have been largely a function of exogenous industry-specific factors rather than of endogenous variables such as concentration. Second, because changes in firms' pricing behavior during the 1960s were largely determined by an exogenous institutional change, namely, the shift in cartel policy. Both points will be discussed extensively in later chapters.

Exogenous and Endogenous Sunk Costs

Following Sutton (1991, 1998), an important distinction within the present theoretical framework is between exogenous sunk cost industries, advertising-intensive industries, and R&D-intensive industries. The first of these categories includes industries where the only important sunk cost is the exogenously determined cost of setting up a plant of minimum efficient scale, net of resale value. In such industries there is limited scope, at any given time, for cost-decreasing or quality-increasing investment. The second and third categories include industries in which firms incur, in addition to the exogenous setup cost, significant endogenous sunk costs, such as advertising or R&D, in order to reduce unit costs or increase the consumers' willingness to pay by enhancing product quality or brand image. These costs are sunk before firms set their price or output, and they are endogenous because they can vary depending on each firm's own decisions.

It is, of course, true that firms may make decisions on nonprice variables in all industries. The concept of an exogenous sunk cost industry is simply a useful polar case that captures the fact that in many industries, advertising and R&D are not important strategic considerations. In other words, the general theoretical model throughout this book is one that allows for endogenous sunk costs. But within that model there is a special limiting case which arises when advertising effectiveness and technological opportunity are both very low. In this limiting case, firms spend nothing on advertising or R&D. Thus the equilibria of this limiting-case model coincide with the equilibria of an elementary model in which there is no advertising or R&D, and hence the only sunk cost is the exogenously determined cost of entry. The elementary model can be used to analyze industries with zero or very low advertising and R&D expenditure. On the other hand, the general model is the appropriate model for advertising-intensive and R&D-intensive industries.

The notion that certain costs are sunk is closely related to the distinction between firms' long-run and short-run decisions. At any point in time, some variables are more difficult to change than others. For instance, the decision to enter an industry by setting up a plant is more difficult to reverse, once implemented, than the choice of a price for the product. The reason is that capital stock is difficult to resell and depreciates only gradually, while price setting does not involve any kind of irreversible investment. It follows that the entry decision must be taken as given, and the cost of setting up a plant is largely a sunk cost, when a firm sets a price for its product. A game structure that captures this distinction is that of the multistage game, with the long-run decisions being taken at the earlier stages and regarded as given when the short-run decisions are taken in the late stages of the game.

The simplest structure that can be used to model competition in an exogenous sunk cost industry is a two-stage game where firms decide whether to enter or not to enter at stage 1, then choose a price or a level of output at stage 2. To find the equilibrium of such a game, we have to ask how the entry decision is influenced by the anticipated outcome of short-run price or output competition. Market structure, that is, the number of firms that enter the market and their respective market shares, is endogenously determined as part of that equilibrium.

On the other hand, a three-stage game—with an entry decision at stage 1, choice of advertising and/or R&D expenditure at stage 2, and choice of price or output at stage 3—is the simplest game structure appropriate for endogenous sunk cost industries. The procedure for solving this three-stage game involves asking (1) how the choice of advertising/R&D expenditure is affected by the anticipated outcome of short-run price or output competition, and (2) how the entry decision is influenced by the anticipated outcome of the entire subgame that begins at stage 2. The equilibrium now involves the determination of both market structure and the level of advertising/R&D expenditure.

1.3 Empirical Methodology

The construction of the data set for this book has involved examining a very large number of restrictive agreements registered under the 1956 Restrictive Trade Practices Act. Other sources of information on competition in British manufacturing industry during the 1950s, 1960s, and 1970s were also used. It has therefore been possible to assign all manufacturing industries to one of three groups: those affected by the legislation, those not affected, and those which, for one or the other reason, were difficult to classify. The competition data were matched against data on several other variables, including concentration, firm and plant numbers, profits and profit margins, advertising intensity, and innovation counts, obtained from a variety of official and unofficial sources. Several different samples of industries were constructed and used to analyze a variety of empirical issues. The ambiguous group of industries was excluded from these samples, and the results were based on comparisons between the group of industries with a change in competition regime and the group without such a change.

The time period considered spans a total of more than twenty years, from the mid-1950s to the mid-1970s. For many of the variables, data are available only at roughly five-year intervals during most of this period. In particular, Census of Production data are available for 1954, 1958, 1963, 1968, and then annually from 1970 onward. The years 1954 and 1958 are "before" dates in the natural experiment, the former because the legislation had not yet been introduced, the latter because it had not yet been effectively implemented. Moreover, since the effects of the introduction of cartel policy were gradual and took several years to be fully realized, one should expect to see only the short-run effects of competition by 1963. By 1968 much of the long-run effect should have appeared, and by the early 1970s the full long-run effects of competition had certainly been realized.

The comparisons between industries with a change in competition regime and industries without such a change will rely, for the most part, on the use of panel data econometrics. This has been an obvious choice. By revealing average tendencies in the data, the econometric analysis of the effects of the 1956 Restrictive Trade Practices Act provides results that are fairly general. Moreover, it allows us to control for any measurable factors other than the introduction of cartel policy that had an effect on the endogenous variables of interest during the period examined. It also allows us to control for unobserved time-invariant, industry-specific characteristics, that is, unobservable factors that may be correlated with some of the variables of interest but are more or less constant over time for any given industry. Controlling for these factors implies that they will not blur the key relationships of interest. For all these reasons, most of the empirical analysis in this book is firmly based on the estimation of econometric models.

On the other hand, the econometric analysis, by focusing on the *overall* effects of competition across industries, may not always be appropriate for examining some finer aspects of the theoretical predictions, or for documenting the operation of certain mechanisms, or indeed for illustrating some of the limitations of the theory. Case studies can provide this detail, and they are often a useful complement to econometric work. In this book, therefore, the econometric analysis of the effects of competition is sometimes supplemented by detailed case studies of particular industries.

The Key Identifying Assumption

In recent years, there has been an outburst of work in economics using empirical evidence from natural experiments. Unlike randomized experiments in psychology or other fields, these studies are based on comparisons between experimental groups and control groups that are not randomly constructed. The most frequently used approach is the so-called difference-in-differences method, which consists in comparing the difference between the average change in the variable of interest in the experimental group and the average change in the same variable in the control group. Meyer (1995) provides a critical evaluation of this approach in economics, including a discussion of possible extensions as well as potential limitations.

Since the approach used in the present book is essentially based on the difference-in-differences methodology—although this is applied in the context of regression analysis in order to control more effectively for industry-specific effects, time effects, and changes in other variables—it will be useful to clarify from the beginning the limitations of this methodology. Several potential "threats to validity" are listed in Meyer (1995). These include omitted variables, trends in outcomes, measurement error, simultaneity or selection biases, omitted interactions, and so on. Some of these potential problems apply to a certain extent to all empirical studies; others are more specific to natural experiments, but they are not relevant for the present study or are relatively straightforward to deal with in econometric work; and still others are difficult to deal with in a totally satisfactory manner. As a result, virtually all studies of natural experiments must rely on some identifying assumptions to validate the research design being used. The present book is no exception to this.

The key identifying assumption that I make in this book is that there are no underlying trends in any of the endogenous variables of interest which differ between the experimental and the control group but are unrelated to the 1956 Restrictive Trade Practices Act or any of the other control variables used in the regressions. In other words, I must assume that any difference in the evolution of concentration, profitability, innovations, and so on, following the introduction of the 1956 legislation, between industries with a change in competition regime and industries without such a change—after controlling for changes in a set of relevant and measurable explanatory variables—can be attributed to the effect of the 1956 legislation and is *not* the result of unobserved characteristics that differ between the two groups and cause them to evolve in different ways during the period under study.

Clearly, the validity of this assumption is not immediately obvious in the present context. After all, there must have been some difference in underlying characteristics between those industries that were cartelized in the 1950s and those that were not. The success of the present study therefore depends crucially on being able to argue that this difference does not invalidate the central identifying assumption stated above. Admittedly, as in all studies of natural experiments, it is impossible to test the identifying assumption directly. I believe, however, that a strong case for accepting this assumption can be made on the basis of two sets of indirect tests.

First, as already pointed out above and discussed in considerable detail in later chapters, cartelization in British manufacturing in the 1950s seems to have been largely a function of exogenous factors, including time-invariant, industry-specific characteristics, rather than endogenous variables such as concentration. Second, and more important, later chapters examine the key issue of whether trends in the endogenous variables of interest were different between the experimental group and the control group *before* the effective implementation of the cartel legislation. As it turns out, this evidence suggests that the estimated effects of the intensification of price competition following the introduction of the 1956 Restrictive Trade Practices Act are not biased by any preexisting trends that differ between the two groups.

Further Remarks and Clarifications

Two further remarks on the present research design and the links between theory and empirical testing are in order. Much of the theoretical and empirical analysis in this book abstracts from one potentially important factor, namely, the fact that more intense price competition may affect firms' incentives to reduce their variable costs. This can take the form of increased effort by workers and managers, a relative reduction in wages and salaries, or the adoption of a better technology.

While these are important issues, they are outside the scope of this book. The assumption made here is that any such reduction in variable costs will be largely passed on to prices and will have little effect on price-cost margins. On the other hand, changes in price-cost margins will be largely driven by changes in competition, advertising, and R&D intensity, and the number of firms. Consequently, any potential effects of competition on the labor market and on productivity will not substantially alter the basic links between competition, on the one hand, and market structure, advertising intensity, innovation, and profitability, on the other, which are the subject of this book.

It may also be asked whether the assumption that firms are symmetric and produce one product each, which is made in the theoretical sections of the book, is in fact too restrictive or misleading as to the key mechanisms at work at the empirical level. There are two responses to this. The first is to modify the predictions regarding the equilibrium *levels* of the endogenous variables in order to account for the presence of asymmetric multiproduct firms. This would be in line with Sutton's (1991, 1998) "bounds" approach to the study of market structure.

According to this approach, there is, for any given set of measurable and systematic exogenous factors, a multiplicity of possible outcomes, which is largely due to the presence of asymmetric multiproduct firms. It is then of no use to try to predict a unique outcome on the basis of the observable and systematic characteristics of an industry; the realized equilibrium will also depend on unobservable features of the industry as well as on its history (which is to some extent the product of chance). The bounds approach involves placing bounds on the space of outcomes and thus excluding certain outcomes as impossible or unlikely, while admitting others as possible or likely equilibria. What is the implication of this in the present context? The implication is that the bounds approach would open up the possibility that a change in the competition regime has no effect on certain industries in the long run. This is because such a change would be seen as shifting the bounds that the theory places on the space of outcomes rather than the realized equilibria. Hence, while it would certainly affect industries initially close to the bounds (because the original equilibria would be, after the change in the competition regime, outside the space of possible outcomes), it might or might not affect industries initially well inside the bounds (because the original equilibria would then remain inside the space of possible outcomes).

However, the bounds approach is difficult to apply in the present context, chiefly because of the panel structure of the data. As explained in detail in later chapters, this results in methodological problems with the econometric estimation of bounds. Standard panel regression techniques therefore seem to be the most appropriate approach in the present case.

The second response to the issue of asymmetric multiproduct firms is to argue that the predictions regarding the equilibrium *changes* in the endogenous variables are valid, at least on average, since it is very improbable that the mechanisms identified for the case of symmetric single-product firms would be offset across industries by other mechanisms working in different directions in a more complex setting. In other words, the change in the competition regime will trigger mechanisms that will shift *the realized equilibria* and will be relevant for all industries. While it is conceivable that other influences might operate to mitigate or offset these mechanisms in some cases, any such influences are unlikely to be systematic. In the context of the bounds approach, this is another way of saying that whether an industry is close to the predicted bounds or well inside the bounds is determined by nonsystematic factors; hence, any cases where the change in the competition regime has little or no effect because the industry is well inside the initial bound will be balanced by cases where the effect is disproportionately large because an industry moves from a position close to the initial bound to one well inside the new bound. As a result, we can expect a change in the competition regime to be of relevance for all industries, and any deviations from the general pattern to be due primarily to random factors.

This second response motivates the approach adopted in this book. Its validity must, of course, be tested against the empirical evidence. And it is also important to highlight instances where the presence of asymmetries between firms calls for small modifications to the theoretical predictions obtained from the benchmark case of symmetric firms, which should also be reflected in the evidence.

1.4   Outline of the Book

The core of this book (chapters 4 to 7) consists of a detailed analysis of the effects of competition on market structure, firm strategy, and profitability, combining theory and evidence from British manufacturing industry. Before embarking upon this analysis, however, it is necessary to provide some background information on the evolution of competition in British industry and to discuss the methodological issues involved in defining the two groups of industries: those with a change of competition regime following the introduction of the 1956 Restrictive Trade Practices Act and those without a change in regime.

Cartel Policy and the Evolution of Competition in British Industry

Chapter 2 describes the institutional context of the present study and provides details on the evolution of competition in British manufacturing industry from the early 1950s to the mid-1970s. The purpose of this chapter is to provide the essential background information on the natural experiment analyzed in the book. I therefore begin by describing the structure of the 1956 legislation and its implementation. I explain, among other things, why the large majority of industries registered their restrictive agreements rather than immediately dropping them or secretly continuing them, and why it took more than a decade for the effects of the 1956 Act on competition in British industry to be fully realized. Moreover, rather than assume that the Act had a significant effect on firm conduct, I set out to justify this claim on the basis of the available case-study evidence. The conclusion is that price competition did indeed intensify, following the introduction of restrictive practices legislation, in the large majority of the previously cartelized industries.

A more in-depth analysis of competition and collusion in the 1950s is carried out in chapter 3. In the first part of this chapter I look at the state of competition across British manufacturing industries in the 1950s, and I argue that the existing evidence allows us to distinguish three groups: (1) a group of collusive industries (defined as industries with explicit agreements significantly restricting competition), the large majority of which subsequently experienced a change of competition regime; (2) a group of industries without explicit collusive agreements, which therefore experienced no change in regime; and (3) a residual group of industries for which we are uncertain as to their state of competition. I also describe in some detail the construction of the competition data used throughout the book.

In the second part of the chapter I examine which structural industry characteristics were associated with the occurrence of collusion in the UK in the 1950s. The purpose of this exercise is twofold. On the one hand, it is intended as a contribution to the literature on the factors facilitating or hindering collusion. The significance of this question is rather obvious: attempts by firms to establish price-fixing arrangements are a matter of great concern for public policy, since such behavior is regarded as being against the public interest, and is therefore illegal under most competition laws. On the other hand, the final part of chapter 3 prepares the way for the analysis of the natural experiment by examining the similarities as well as the differences in initial conditions between the two groups of industries. A key result is that the two groups were broadly similar with respect to initial market structure, but rather different with respect to capital intensity or the level of entry costs, advertising effectiveness, and technological opportunity. Thus the occurrence of collusion in British manufacturing industries in the 1950s can be seen as being largely determined by exogenous variables rather than by endogenous variables such as concentration.

The Effect of Price Competition on Concentration, Advertising, and Innovation

Chapter 4 begins by introducing a general theoretical framework for the analysis of the competition-market structure relationship in exogenous sunk cost industries. One of the key results to emerge from the recent literature on the determinants of market structure is that, in exogenous sunk cost industries, an intensification of price competition is expected to cause a rise in concentration. This is the result of a structural mechanism that involves a movement between two free-entry equilibria. The intensification of price competition reduces profit margins, given the initial level of concentration. As a result, firms (or some firms) can no longer cover their sunk costs at the initial free-entry equilibrium: profit margins are too low to generate a normal rate of return on the setup cost incurred in establishing plants. This will inevitably lead to mergers and exit until the gross profit of each remaining firm rises sufficiently to cover sunk costs.

Chapter 4 examines this mechanism in the context of the UK manufacturing industry, focusing on the evolution of concentration over the period 1958–1975. The econometric results, based on a comparison of industries affected by the 1956 Restrictive Trade Practices Act and those not affected, suggest that the intensification of price competition following the termination of price-fixing agreements led to a rise in concentration in exogenous sunk cost industries affected by the legislation. In particular, the results indicate that cartel policy raised, on average, the five-firm concentration ratio by six to seven percentage points in exogenous sunk cost industries. To put this figure in some perspective, note that nearly half of the entire British manufacturing sector was cartelized in the 1950s and the average five-firm concentration ratio across *all* manufacturing industries increased by about eight percentage points between 1958 and 1975, in what was the most significant restructuring of British industry for several decades. The results of chapter 4 suggest that cartel policy was one of the key factors behind this restructuring.

Chapter 5 focuses on advertising-intensive industries. Things are more complicated in this case, because the intensification of price competition is likely to affect firms' incentives to spend on advertising. A first question in this context relates to the link between price and nonprice competition, that is, whether tougher price competition can have a negative or a positive effect on advertising intensity. Moreover, if advertising falls when price competition intensifies, the decrease in the sunk cost that each firm must cover at equilibrium may or may not offset the fall in gross profit due to increased price competition, and hence concentration may decrease or increase.

The first part of chapter 5 introduces a theoretical framework for analyzing these issues, derives general theoretical results, and illustrates these results using a specific model. Given that a decrease in the degree of collusion in the short-run variable can have ambiguous effects on advertising and concentration in industries with high advertising intensity, can we still derive any theoretical predictions about the effects of competition in this class of industries? It turns out that some restrictions can be imposed by theory on the joint behavior of market structure and advertising expenditure following an intensification of price competition. Thus, certain outcomes, such as a fall in concentration together with an increase in advertising expenditure, cannot occur, since they are inconsistent with the requirement that net profits be zero in free-entry equilibrium. Moreover, stronger predictions on the competition-market structure relationship, which are conditional on the behavior of other observable variables, are also derived. Additional insight on these issues is obtained from the analysis of a specific theoretical model.

In the second part of chapter 5, the theoretical predictions are tested using econometric and case-study evidence from British advertising-intensive manufacturing industries from 1954 to 1975. The econometric results indicate that the intensification of price competition following the 1956 legislation caused, on the whole, a rise in concentration in advertising-intensive industries and probably also a fall in advertising intensity. The magnitude of the overall effect on concentration was not any lower in advertising-intensive industries than in exogenous sunk cost industries. On the other hand, the case-study evidence confirms that a fall in concentration, following an intensification of price competition, cannot be ruled out in high-advertising industries. However, more intense price competition must lead to a significant fall in advertising intensity if concentration does not rise—or, conversely, it must cause concentration to rise if advertising falls little or not at all. This is consistent with the theoretical predictions as well as with the overall picture given by the econometric results.

The analysis of the effect of price competition on market structure and technological innovation in R&D-intensive industries is the subject of chapter 6. The chapter begins by adapting the theoretical framework developed in chapter 5 to the analysis of R&D-intensive industries. In contrast with most of the previous literature on the links between market power and innovation—but in line with the empirical evidence on the effect of the 1956 Restrictive Trade Practices Act on market structure—I do not regard concentration as a proxy for market power. In fact, I explicitly treat both market structure and innovation as endogenous variables, while the intensity of price competition is taken as exogenous. The model predicts, first, that the effect of price competition on innovation is ambiguous and, second, that if the effect of price competition on innovation is not negative, then its effect on concentration must be positive.

The empirical results of chapter 6 are consistent with the theory. Using UK data on competition, concentration, and the number of innovations between the early 1950s and the mid-1970s, I find that the intensification of price competition following the 1956 legislation had no significant effect on firms' innovative output and a strong positive effect on concentration in R&D-intensive industries. The magnitude of the overall effect on concentration was at least as high as that estimated for exogenous sunk cost industries. On the other hand, the lack of any overall effect of competition on innovation across industries is not very surprising in light of the mixed theoretical results on this much-debated issue. Perhaps a more promising line of research in this area would be to identify specific conditions favoring a positive or a negative effect of competition on innovation; such an analysis could not be carried out in the present context because of data limitations. It is also interesting to contrast the absence of any overall effect of price competition on innovations with the likely presence of a negative effect on advertising intensity. This raises the question of whether there is a fundamental difference between advertising and R&D in their role as nonprice choice variables in the competitive process that has not been adequately analyzed in existing theories of competition.

Price Competition and Profitability: Are Cartel Laws Bad for Business?

Chapter 7 extends the analysis of the previous chapters by examining the joint effect of price competition on market structure and profitability. If the economic mechanism underlying the observed effect of the 1956 legislation on British industrial structure is the one described above, then one should also expect that there will be no significant change in firms' profits in the long run in exogenous sunk cost industries—and probably also in all classes of industries, given that price competition did not have a very strong overall effect on nonprice variables in the present case. Moreover, one would expect profitability to decline in the short run, that is, before any significant change in market structure occurs, and then be restored or partially restored in the long run through the fall in the number of firms.

Chapter 7 confirms these predictions by examining the joint evolution of market structure variables, such as the number of firms and the number of plants, and profit measures, such as the average firm profit, the average plant profit, and the profit margin, from 1954 to 1973. Two different samples are used in the econometric analysis: a sample pooling all classes of industries and a subsample of exogenous sunk cost industries. In both cases, the results indicate that the 1956 legislation had a negative effect on profitability during the first few years of its implementation, when market structure had not yet fully adjusted. However, the subsequent restructuring of industries affected by the legislation was associated with a recovery of profit margins, so that profitability did not change much in the long run. An interesting implication of these results is that free entry is not incompatible with collusion. In fact, the results suggest that in long-run equilibrium most cartels will result in excess entry rather than excess profits (relative to the absence of collusion), and hence cartel laws will reduce the number of firms rather than their profits. Of course, this crucially depends on entry being unrestricted irrespective of the intensity of price competition. This appears to have been the case in the large majority of cartelized industries in the UK.

Chapter 7 also contains several brief case studies, including the study of an industry where the free-entry condition seems to have been violated before the introduction of cartel policy. It is shown that in this case the theoretical predictions are not confirmed: the breakdown of collusion led to a fall in profitability and no change in concentration. This counterexample can be seen as illustrating the limitations of the present theory, since it suggests that there can be instances where one of the key assumptions of the theory is violated. At the same time, it can be seen as a sharp test of the theory's predictive power. Thus the counterexample confirms the operation of the key structural mechanism driving the theoretical predictions and the econometric results of chapter 7, as well as of much of the rest of the book—namely, the fact that changes in market structure are driven by the relationship between firms' gross profits and sunk costs.

1.5   Policy Implications

Although this book focuses on positive rather than normative issues, there are several policy implications of the results presented here. First, high concentration and mergers may often be a consequence of the intensification of price competition, whether this is brought about by the successful implementation of cartel policy or otherwise. This means that there are important economic constraints on the exercise of merger and antitrust policies. In particular, these policies cannot be used to impose a market structure so fragmented that it is not sustainable in a context of intensified competition. To put this argument slightly differently, some degree of market power is necessary under conditions of increasing returns to scale, since firms must be able to cover their sunk costs. In a context of intensified competition, firms will have to be fewer and bigger (on average) in order to cover their sunk costs, so a stable market structure cannot be achieved if the necessary restructuring is hindered.

The emphasis on structural mechanisms shaping the evolution of market concentration—in particular, the emphasis on the relationship between firms' gross profits and sunk costs—should not, of course, prevent us from recognizing that concentration is also influenced by nonstructural factors, and hence that mergers and the restructuring of industries may go well beyond what is necessary for market structure to be sustainable. The present study in no way suggests a lesser role for merger and antitrust policies; rather, it highlights one of their limitations.

Second, higher concentration need not be associated with higher profit margins, increased allocative inefficiency, and lower welfare, once free entry is maintained. Therefore, concerns with the level of market concentration need not take precedence over the need to ensure that competition remains effective, that is, firms do not engage in collusive practices and no barriers to entry are created. This strengthens the case for a competition policy that focuses more upon the monitoring of conduct than on the regulation of market structure, as has, in fact, always been the approach taken in the UK and the European Union.

Third, the present study has implications for the much-debated issue of the relationship between price and nonprice competition. In particular, it suggests that we need to distinguish between different types of product-specific investments when evaluating the consequences of price competition for expenditure on product "quality" and for innovation. More specifically, while advertising is likely to decrease when price competition intensifies, the effect of price competition on the production of innovations seems to be either insignificant or highly ambiguous. Thus the present study offers support neither for the argument that short-run welfare gains from more price competition are offset in the longer term by a slower rate of technological progress nor for the opposite assertion that innovation is promoted in a context of vigorous price competition. I should also clarify that I am referring here only to innovations *produced* by firms. This book does not examine whether price competition may have an effect on variable costs, and thus on productivity, through increased effort by managers and workers, more efficient internal firm organization, the adoption of better technologies, or otherwise.

Finally, the results of this book imply that the free-entry condition, which has been popular in recent theoretical work but whose policy implications are perhaps not fully appreciated, may be a valid property of long-run equilibria in the majority of industries, at least as an approximation. Of course, this does not mean that free entry can always be relied upon to drive net profits to zero or to maintain effective competition. For one thing, the presence of asymmetries between firms implies that only the marginal firm makes zero profit under free entry. Other firms may well earn higher than normal profits in the long run, not only because of efficiency differences but also because of first-mover advantages. Moreover, the focus on long-run equilibria may be less appropriate in dynamic, innovative industries than in stable, mature ones. Finally, free entry can be compatible with restrictive pricing agreements between firms.

What the results of this book suggest is that the level of excess profits does not depend, in the long run, on firms' pricing conduct, because of forces such as entry and exit that push industries toward the zero-profit equilibrium. It would be misleading to interpret this as suggesting that competition policy has set itself a relatively easy task because, by and large, free entry eliminates excess profits in the long run. Rather, by emphasizing the key role of free entry in restraining higher than normal profits, this book suggests that, in addition to the monitoring of firm conduct, the monitoring of entry conditions into industries is a key priority for competition policy.

2

Cartel Policy and the Evolution of Competition in British Industry

2.1 Introduction

Explicit collusive agreements between firms were widespread in British industry in the mid-1950s: nearly half of the manufacturing sector was subject to agreements significantly restricting competition. Some dated from the 1880s and 1890s, many others had been stimulated by government policies for the control of industry during the two world wars, and still others were the result of the depression of the interwar years (Swann et al. 1974). The agreements were not enforceable at law, but they were not illegal.

The 1956 Restrictive Trade Practices Act required the registration of most classes of restrictive agreements between firms on goods. However, there was no outright prohibition of restrictive practices. Instead, a judicial procedure was adopted for assessing their impact on the public interest, on a case-by-case basis. As it turned out, the hard line taken by the newly created Restrictive Practices Court, especially in its initial judgments, led to the eventual cancellation of the vast majority of agreements. However, this outcome was difficult to anticipate before the first decisions of the Court had been taken. Hence, even though the legislation was introduced in 1956, it had little effect before the late 1950s or early 1960s. Most collusive agreements were abandoned between 1959 (the year the first Court cases were heard) and the mid-1960s.

This chapter begins by describing the key features of the 1956 Act, as well as some amendments made by legislation introduced in the 1960s, and places the Act within the broader context of British competition policy. It then goes on to discuss the nature, extent, and effectiveness of collusion in British manufacturing industry in the 1950s. The final part of the chapter provides a detailed account of the effect of the Act on firm pricing conduct in previously collusive industries during the 1960s. Drawing on existing evidence from case studies and descriptive cross-industry surveys, I examine whether price competition did actually intensify in the large majority of these industries.

2.2   The Origins of British Cartel Policy

Like competition policy in general, UK cartel policy developed gradually over several years since the late 1940s. The first piece of relevant legislation was the 1948 Monopolies and Restrictive Practices (Inquiry and Control) Act, which embodied a case-by-case approach to both monopolies and restrictive practices.[1] The Monopolies and Restrictive Practices Commission was set up to investigate monopolies and collective restrictive agreements referred to it by the Board of Trade on a case-by-case basis. The Commission would normally be asked to determine whether these operated against the public interest and to recommend appropriate remedies if required; the government could then take action on the basis of these recommendations.

There were twenty referrals to the Commission between 1948 and 1950, eighteen of which involved primarily restrictive agreements between members of industrial trade associations. In the large majority of these cases, some or all of the restrictions were found to operate against the public interest. The Commission was generally more hostile toward market sharing, collective exclusive dealing and the collective enforcement of resale price maintenance (which often involved the collective withholding of supplies from retailers selling below the specified resale prices) than toward price-fixing arrangements. In fact, price-fixing was sometimes not condemned as being against the public interest, although the Commission usually recommended in such cases that common prices should be under some outside supervision or control so as to ensure that they remained reasonable.

The impact of the Commission's investigations of specific industries is thought to have been very limited. In several cases an objectionable agreement was replaced by a more acceptable variety, or

---

1. Detailed information on the structure of the 1948 Act, the role and the reports of the Monopolies and Restrictive Practices Commission during the 1950s, and the impact of these reports is contained in Guenault and Jackson (1974), Rowley (1966), Swann et al. (1974), and Mercer (1995), among others.

became subject to government surveillance. Moreover, in some cases the government did not adopt all of the Commission's recommendations. Finally, there was no adequate formal machinery to ensure the implementation of the government's decisions, and "follow-up" action to secure the continued compliance of the industries involved was generally not carried out. For all these reasons, none of the industries investigated by the Commission between 1948 and 1956 experienced any serious shakeout as a result of changes that took place following the investigation.

By the early 1950s the slow progress of the Commission was a cause for some concern. This, together with the fact that the Commission had found certain common types of collective agreements as being against the public interest in almost every investigated industry in which these practices occurred, led to a general reference to the Commission to investigate arrangements involving "collective discrimination." These included, among other things, collective exclusive dealing, the collective adoption and enforcement of resale price maintenance, and the adoption of aggregated rebates and similar discriminatory practices.[2] They did not, however, include price-fixing or market-sharing agreements. The Commission's report, published in 1955, is thought to have been very influential in shaping subsequent developments in cartel legislation. There was, in fact, a split within the Commission. The majority view was that the practices concerned should be prohibited, with provisions made for exceptions on specific grounds. The minority view was that there should be a call for the registration of agreements and a case-by-case examination to decide whether each particular agreement operated against the public interest.

The next stage in the development of legislation on collusive agreements was the introduction of the 1956 Restrictive Trade Practices Act.

2.3 The 1956 Act

The 1956 Restrictive Trade Practices Act required the registration of most types of agreements on goods between two or more firms operating in the UK in which more than one of the parties accepted

---

2. Aggregated rebates are discounts to distributors on the basis of the total quantity purchased from association firms. Collective exclusive dealing is the practice whereby distributors are required to deal only with association firms if they are to be supplied on best terms or at all.

"restrictions," that is, some limitations on the freedom to make decisions. The Act specified that an agreement was registrable when the
restrictions related to prices to be charged or paid, conditions of sale,
quantities and qualities supplied or acquired and processes used,
persons to or from whom goods could be supplied or acquired,
and areas where goods could be supplied or acquired. Thus the Act
adopted a form-based rather than an effects-based approach to cartel
policy: all agreements of a specified form had to be registered, even
if the restrictions had no significant effect on competition. The definition of "agreement" included both formal, written undertakings
and informal, verbal, or even implied (as opposed to expressed)
arrangements. It also included cases in which a trade association
made recommendations to its members. The Act also prohibited the
collective enforcement of resale price maintenance. On the other
hand, agreements on services or relating only to exports, most types
of bilateral vertical arrangements, and agreements to exchange
information on prices, quantities, and so on (so-called information
agreements) were exempted from registration. Finally, individual
resale price maintenance was not prohibited; indeed, the Act provided for its more effective enforcement.[3]

The Economic and Political Background

Several views have been expressed on the politics of the introduction
of the 1956 legislation. For instance, it has been pointed out that the
1956 Act was partly a response to the new conditions of high growth
and the climate of economic liberalism of the 1950s (i.e., it reflected
the view that the economy would be best served by an increasing
reliance on market forces and a strengthening of competition)
and partly a response to business community dissatisfaction with
the administrative approach through the Monopolies and Restrictive
Practices Commission. In fact, the business community preferred a
judicial review of restrictive practices, which is what the Act established. It also seems, however, that the business community was

---

3. Hunter (1966), Swann et al. (1974), and Wilberforce et al. (1966) describe in detail
the structure and the implementation of the 1956 Act. Subsequent developments in UK
cartel legislation until the early 1970s are discussed in Swann et al. (1974) and also in
the various reports of the Registrar of Restrictive Trading Agreements (RRTA, 1961–
1973). The reports of the Registrar also provide details on the implementation of the
legislation over the period 1956–1972, including brief accounts of cases examined by
the Restrictive Practices Court.

little prepared for the strict attitude of the Restrictive Practices Court, which eventually led to the abolition of cartels in Britain.

There is little doubt that the (Conservative) government had to accommodate a lot of pressure from interested parties, especially business, during the period of the drafting of the Bill. Hunter (1966, pp. 85–86) argues that the overall structure of the 1956 Act was a compromise between business interests, public opinion, and the government's eagerness to promote economic liberalism. For instance, he sees the provisions of the Act for more effective enforcement of individual resale price maintenance and for a dilution of the role and power of the Monopolies and Restrictive Practices Commission (which from then on, until the introduction of merger policy in the UK in the mid-1960s, was called simply Monopolies Commission and dealt only with monopolies) as major concessions to business interests. He acknowledges, however, that the structure of the Act also reflected a willingness not to be dogmatic about restrictive practices and the recognition of the potential merits of some restrictive arrangements.

Mercer (1995) provides another interesting, although perhaps more controversial, account of the origins of the 1956 legislation, emphasizing the diversity of interests between different sections of the business community, in particular between large, efficient, internationally oriented firms and smaller, less efficient ones. She argues that the spread of economic liberalism in the 1950s and the growing discontent of the public and the press with restrictive practices were not the only factors behind the passing of the 1956 Act, and that the lack of opposition by larger firms to government plans for the introduction of cartel legislation was also a key factor. Thus Mercer points out that some key concessions to industry, such as those mentioned above, were more likely to benefit larger firms than smaller ones. She also argues, however, that larger firms did not expect that the Act would eventually lead to the abolition of a wide range of restrictive practices. Her argument should not, therefore, be taken to imply that many or most larger firms actually benefited from the introduction of cartel legislation.

Key Provisions of the Act

The Act was based on the principle that restrictive agreements were in general adverse to the public interest unless shown otherwise. A key feature was the adoption of a judiciary procedure for assessing the impact of restrictive practices on the public interest. Central to this procedure was the Restrictive Practices Court, a special judiciary body consisting of High Court judges and qualified lay members. In addition, a new officer within the Board of Trade, the Registrar of Restrictive Trading Agreements, was given responsibility for keeping a register of agreements which was open to public inspection, referring all but insignificant cases to the Court, and investigating for any registrable but unregistered agreements. As it turned out, the process of referring agreements to the Court was gradual and took several years to complete, partly because the Registrar often tried to negotiate with the industries concerned modifications to their agreements that would involve dropping all significant restrictions. The idea was to achieve the purpose of the legislation (as interpreted by the Registrar) without the need for the industries concerned and the Registrar to spend time and money on legal proceedings.

The Act prescribed that registered agreements should be abandoned unless they were successfully defended in the Court by the parties or considered by the Registrar as not significantly affecting competition. Thus there was no outright prohibition of restrictive practices. An agreement could be allowed to continue if the Court was convinced that it had benefits for the public, of a kind defined in the Act, which offset the presumed detriment. In particular, the Act set out a number of headings, known as "gateways," by reference to which an agreement could be defended in the Court. These related to such things as the protection of the public against injury, the need to counteract anticompetitive behavior by other firms, the need to counterbalance monopoly or monopsony power, the avoidance of a serious adverse effect on employment in a specific area, the avoidance of a serious adverse effect on exports, and, more generally, the provision of "specific and substantial" benefits to the public. Thus some of the gateways were sufficiently broad to allow for almost any agreement to be defended in the Court. Provided that an agreement passed through one or more of the gateways, it should then be shown to be in the public interest "on balance" if it was to be upheld.

The Registration of Agreements

By the end of 1959 some 2,240 agreements had been registered, about half of which were of nationwide application. Most of them (approximately 1,800) were between manufacturers, or between manufacturers and distributors. Roughly 970 of the national agreements were thought by the Registrar to be "important," that is, not dealing with trivial restrictions or very small industries. Also, 790 of them contained selling price restrictions, and of these, 730 were agreements made by manufacturers, mostly among themselves rather than with distributors. In the majority of cases, they were agreements between members of trade associations. These figures highlight the prevalence of pricing restrictions in most collusive arrangements. Other types of restrictions, such as market sharing or discriminatory practices, were less common, although this may have been to some extent the result of redrafting and modification of agreements prior to registration, as pointed out below.[4]

An important implication of the procedure set out by the 1956 Act was that the attitude of the Court could not be known until the first Court cases had been heard. Thus the large majority of the existing restrictive agreements were registered rather than being immediately dropped or secretly continued, although in some cases firms redrafted their agreements or even removed some of the restrictions in an attempt to increase the likelihood of a favorable Court decision (see Swann et al. 1974; Hunter 1966). For instance, a reference to "agreed" prices was sometimes replaced by a reference to "recommended" prices, and market sharing was sometimes dropped. It is interesting that in those cases where an agreement was modified prior to registration, firms usually chose to remove those types of restrictions that had been typically condemned in the Monopolies and Restrictive Practices Commission's reports. Thus collective exclusive dealing was sometimes removed, although price-fixing generally was not.

The redrafting of agreements indicates that there was a genuine uncertainty as to how the Act would be implemented and that the large majority of industries perceived the chances of a favorable Court decision as being sufficiently high to make registration worthwhile. The ambiguous attitude of the Monopolies and Restrictive Practices Commission toward price-fixing may have also been a factor in persuading most industries to register pricing agreements.

---

4. The actual number of agreements for any given industry has little significance, for some industries registered only one national agreement covering all or most industry products, while others registered many agreements, each corresponding to a narrowly defined product or to a specific region of the country.

One could add that the respectability of price-fixing was well established among manufacturers and distributors during the interwar years and up to 1956, and, as indicated by various reports of the Commission during the period 1948–1956, many businessmen were bewildered by the argument that price-fixing could be thought of as being against the public interest (see Hunter 1966, pp. 135–136).

That is not to say, of course, that registration was universal: there is evidence that a nonnegligible number of agreements were not registered. Some of these continued secretly, while others were abandoned. For instance, some of the agreements that had been condemned by the Monopolies and Restrictive Practices Commission in its investigations of particular industries were never registered. Since these had attracted a great deal of publicity, they were probably abandoned shortly after the passing of the 1956 Act rather than being secretly continued. Swann et al. (1974, pp. 153–154) mention that out of sixty industries with restrictive agreements listed in the Commission's report on collective discrimination, eight did not register their agreements. This is a nonnegligible percentage, but it has to be borne in mind that in some of these industries the agreements had comprised only the collective enforcement of resale price maintenance or collective exclusive dealing, without any fixing of common prices or market shares. Many of these would normally not be registered, because the 1956 Act contained an outright prohibition of the collective enforcement of resale price maintenance.[5] Once this is taken into account, the incidence of nonregistration of registrable agreements appears to have been rather low.

Implementation of the Legislation

The adoption of a system whereby collusive agreements were not illegal per se, and it was the responsibility of a court to examine possibly complex economic issues in assessing the balance of detriments and benefits on a case-by-case basis, became a subject of considerable debate in the UK during the early years of the implementation of the 1956 Act. However, it did not become a major issue in practice. The hard line taken by the Restrictive Practices Court in its initial

---

5. Moreover, collective exclusive dealing had been consistently condemned by the Commission and was probably dropped by several industries after 1956.

judgments induced most cartels to voluntarily abandon their agreements rather than incur the costs of a Court case with little hope of successful defense. Since the first Court cases were heard in 1959, it was not until that year that industries, on the whole, started abandoning their agreements. Of those agreements that came before the Court and were defended by the parties, only a few were allowed to continue.

Most of the decisions to allow particular agreements to continue sparked a great deal of controversy. Some of these cases involved agreements that were considered by the Court as being beneficial for exports or for technical cooperation and development, with the benefits outweighing the detriment of higher prices. In other cases, the arguments were much more dubious.[6] In fact, after an initial period marked by a series of unfavorable decisions, the attitude of the Court changed somewhat and a greater proportion of agreements brought before it were upheld. By that time, however, the large majority of agreements had been dropped. Most agreements were formally abandoned between 1959 and the mid-1960s, although some were canceled as late as the late 1960s. After the mid-1960s, the attitude of the Court became somewhat tougher again.[7]

One of the most significant cases heard by the Court concerned the agreement between the members of the Yarn Spinners' Association. This provided for a minimum selling price for cotton yarn and for standard terms and conditions of sale. It was the second case to come before the Court, in early 1959, and the size and historical significance of the industry meant that the Court's decision would be of considerable importance for industry in general. Moreover, it would be an indicator of the Court's likely attitude in future cases, given the type of arguments put forward by the parties to the agreement and the general state of the industry. In particular, there was no question of the cartel firms' making any excess profits in this declining in-

---

6. For example, one agreement was allowed to continue partly because it was said to result in cost savings for buyers because there was no need to "shop around." Another was thought to promote product standardization. And still another was allowed to stand because the Court accepted the argument that the restrictions helped keep prices below the competitive level by reducing uncertainty, and hence the return on capital required by firms in the industry.

7. Registration continued during the 1960s and the 1970s. These were mostly agreements of minor significance or agreements that came into operation after the 1956 Act had come into force.

dustry, and the debate largely focused on the issue of the impact of the removal of the minimum price scheme on the structure of the industry, and hence on employment.

The association convinced the Court that the removal of the price restrictions would be detrimental to employment in specific areas of the country. At the same time, the Court accepted the Registrar's view that the agreement had resulted in prices higher than those that would have prevailed under competition, and had allowed the survival of inefficient producers and the maintenance of excess capacity in the industry, all of which were against the public interest. The Court struck down the agreement on the grounds that its beneficial effect on employment was outweighed by the detriments to the public, including the fact that it might have delayed what seemed to be the necessary restructuring of a declining industry. It is generally thought that the decision in the Yarn Spinners' case was an important factor in inducing a large number of industries to voluntarily abandon their restrictive practices.

Another important Court case concerned a series of bilateral agreements between steel firms and a marketing company that these firms had formed to sell basic slag, a by-product of steel manufacture used as a fertilizer. Each of the steel producers appointed one director to the board of the marketing company and had an independent agreement with the company about the terms on which it supplied it with basic slag, including the obligation to sell the whole of its output of basic slag to the company. These bilateral agreements were all identical, and although there was no explicit arrangement between the steel firms, the Court thought that there was an implied arrangement between them, which was registrable under the 1956 Act and against the public interest.

The importance of this case lies not in the economic significance of the product in question, but in the fact that it settled the question of what constitutes an implied arrangement in UK cartel law. The Court pointed out that an arrangement between A and B exists if "(1) A makes a representation as to his future conduct with the expectation and intention that such conduct on his part will operate as an inducement to B to act in a particular way, (2) such representation is communicated to B, who has knowledge that A so expected and intended, and (3) such representation or A's conduct in fulfilment of it operates as an inducement, whether among other inducements or not, to B to act in that particular way."

Information Agreements and Nonregistration

Two other important cases that came before the Court in the mid-1960s involved arrangements to exchange information on prices and price changes. Such arrangements were not registrable under the 1956 Act, unless it could be shown that they were being effectively used as a way to continue a formally abandoned explicit collusive scheme. In the two cases brought before the Court, there had consistently been information exchanges regarding prices and price changes in advance of their coming into effect, and the prices of different firms had always been identical. The Court concluded that these information agreements amounted to the same effect as explicit price-fixing, and found against the parties to the agreements. According to Swann et al. (1974), these Court decisions were instrumental in inducing several more industries with information agreements to cancel them in the mid-1960s.

In fact, the extensive use of information agreements was causing considerable concern among economists and policy makers in the mid-1960s. Early studies of the impact of the 1956 Act showed that in many industries explicit price-fixing agreements had been replaced by informal arrangements to exchange information on prices, price changes, quantities, and conditions of sale, and that in many cases these had serious adverse effects on competition. Thus one of the amendments to the 1956 legislation introduced by the 1968 Restrictive Trade Practices Act was a provision for making certain types of information agreements registrable. It was left to the Board of Trade to decide which types of information exchanges should be targeted, however, and only agreements on the exchange of prices and conditions of sale were subsequently called up for registration. By that time most had already been abandoned.

A second deficiency of the 1956 Act related to the illegal nonregistration of agreements. The Act gave the Registrar of Restrictive Trading Agreements only moderate powers of discovery. For instance, it did not allow unexpected raids and seizing of company documents. In addition, there were no significant penalties for nonregistration. In fact, Hunter (1966, pp. 87–88) has argued that the main deterrent against nonregistration was probably the fear of adverse publicity.

On the other hand, the 1956 Act did provide for penalties in cases of secret collusion when the firms had been parties to an agreement that the Registrar had referred to the Court and the Court had struck down, irrespective of whether the parties had actually defended the agreement in Court. In some such cases considerable fines were imposed. This provision was relevant not only for agreements that had been voluntarily abandoned *after* having been formally referred to the Court and condemned, but also for agreements that had been abandoned *before* being referred to the Court and condemned. In this latter case the referral was a precautionary step taken by the Registrar in order to reduce the likelihood of any future anticompetitive conduct by the firms involved. It is reasonable to assume that these categories contained the majority of the most serious cases of collusion. Still, a large number of abandoned agreements were not referred to the Court, so the provision of the 1956 Act regarding penalties would be irrelevant for firms that had been parties to these (as it would be for firms that had not been parties to any registered agreement). The 1968 Act sought to reduce the incentives for non-registration by allowing injured parties to sue participants to unregistered agreements for damages. This provision was rarely used, and it is difficult to know the extent to which it may have deterred nonregistration.

Resale Price Maintenance

Another important piece of restrictive practices legislation introduced in the 1960s was the 1964 Resale Prices Act. As pointed out above, although the collective enforcement of resale price maintenance was prohibited after 1956, individual enforcement was allowed. Under the 1964 Resale Prices Act individual resale price maintenance was prohibited except for industries exempted by order of the Restrictive Practices Court. The implementation of the legislation was gradual, and by 1967–1968 resale price maintenance had been abolished in all industries except for two that obtained exemptions (pharmaceuticals and books). Most of the industries affected by the 1964 Act were consumer-good, advertising-intensive industries.

An Overall Assessment

The 1956 Act, despite its shortcomings, is generally thought to have been quite effective in breaking down the previously legal cartels in UK manufacturing during the 1960s.[8] It may even be the case that the initial uncertainty about the implementation of the Act contributed to its success. Firms were prompted to register their agreements because they were given the chance (which they perceived as significant) to have them approved by the Court. Once they had registered and then formally abandoned the agreements, it may have been more difficult for them to secretly collude because they were likely to be monitored by the Registrar and/or their customers, and also, in many cases, because of the threat of penalties.

In addition, many of the collusive schemes of the 1950s involved relatively large numbers of firms and were being operated within industrial trade associations. The legality of the agreements and the institutional role of trade associations had greatly facilitated the co-ordination and monitoring of collusion during the 1950s, but this was no longer possible in the 1960s—which may be part of the reason why many firms perceived registration as their best chance of being able to continue their collusion. Several more factors that limited the extent of collusion in the 1960s are discussed in the final section of this chapter. Before examining the effect of the legislation on firm conduct in greater detail, however, it is necessary to have a brief look at the nature of restrictive practices in British industry and to discuss the available evidence on the effectiveness of the cartels.

2.4 Restrictive Practices in the 1950s

Collusion, although not enforceable in the courts, was not illegal in the UK in the 1950s.[9] The agreements registered under the 1956 Act revealed for the first time the extent of cartelization in British manufacturing. Together with information on unregistered agreements reported in a number of other sources on collusion in British industry,

---

8. This is also the view taken in the 1979 comprehensive government review of cartel policy in the UK (SSPCP 1979). Symeonidis (1998) describes subsequent developments in cartel legislation in the UK, including the legislative attack on restrictive practices in the commercial services industries in the 1970s, and also provides a general assessment of the law prior to the 1999 significant restructuring of UK competition policy as a whole.

9. See Political and Economic Planning (1957) and Kuipers (1950) for the details on the legal status of the restrictive agreements. The main point is that associations acting in restraint of trade could not enforce in court agreements between members about conditions on which they transacted business, or agreements to pay penalties. A member who broke such agreements could not be sued.

they allow us to form a quite accurate picture of the state of competition across industries at the time the 1956 Act was introduced. In particular, it is possible to distinguish a group of collusive industries and a group of competitive industries—as well as a residual group of industries for which we are uncertain as to their state of competition. Chapter 3 describes this information in detail. Here I briefly discuss the nature of the agreements before examining the available evidence on their effectiveness.

Nature of the Agreements

A large number of agreements involved important horizontal arrangements, usually between members of trade associations. A typical agreement of this kind contained agreed or recommended minimum or fixed producer prices and standard conditions of sale. Ancillary restrictions, such as collective exclusive dealing or the maintenance of common resale prices, were often used to strengthen the arrangement. In some cases, there was no explicit price-fixing, but the association made recommendations about specified changes in prices following changes in costs. Some agreements also provided for market sharing, either through the operation of quota schemes or by allocating work to parties. In certain cases, especially in some differentiated product industries, prices were individually set but there were common maximum discounts to distributors, resale price maintenance, and sometimes specified conditions of sale or exchange of information on individual prices and price changes.

   In a number of other cases the restrictions were probably of little significance in terms of their impact on competition. Some agreements related only to "conditions of sale"—for instance cash discount terms, delivery charges, formulas for contract price adjustment when costs changed, nonprice matters, and so on—without any apparent regulation of prices or trade discounts, even though such regulation would have been legal under the circumstances. Some other arrangements provided for the maintenance or even the collective enforcement of individual resale prices, but again neither individual prices nor trade discounts were regulated. Finally, in some industries the significance of the restrictions is uncertain, as in the case of agreements providing for the central notification by the parties of inquiries received from customers and for some type of uniform action, other than price-fixing, with respect to these inquiries.

The British cartels were primarily price-fixing bodies. Regulation of nonprice decisions was uncommon. In particular, very few industries were subject to restrictions regarding capital investment, media advertising, or R&D expenditure in the 1950s. In fact, media advertising was not regulated in any advertising-intensive industry, although restrictions relating to sales promotion (such as gifts and coupons to consumers, financial inducements to distributors, publicity in distributors' premises, participation in exhibitions, advertising in trade catalogs, etc.) were far more common.[10] Expenditure on R&D was noncooperatively determined in all but one or two industries. There was some degree of technical cooperation, in the form of exchange of information between firms, in some industries, and sometimes even some joint R&D. Or patent-owning firms had to grant licenses to any other firm participating in the arrangement. But in all but one or two cases these schemes did not amount to anything close to cooperative determination of R&D expenditure.[11]

This was certainly true for joint R&D. In nearly all collusive R&D-intensive industries that performed some joint R&D, such as water-tube boilers, telephone exchange equipment, or electrical machinery, the budget of the joint research department was only a small fraction of the individual firms' research budgets. For most other collusive R&D-intensive industries, there is no mention of any R&D cooperation at all. It would also be misleading to put too much emphasis on the informal exchange of technical information and know-how, for this often occurred in industries that were not technologically progressive or related only to basic research and not to product development. In R&D-intensive industries, on the other hand, the most important form of technical collaboration was patent pooling, that is, the obligation of patent-owning firms to grant licenses to any other firm participating in the arrangement. This was common in several electrical or electronic engineering industries with price-

---

10. The only known case of an industry with restrictions on media advertising was the linoleum industry, a homogeneous-good industry with very low advertising expenditure.

11. Perhaps the only known case of clear and extensive cooperation in R&D was the case of the permanent magnet industry, a small industry with modest R&D intensity and little economic significance.

fixing agreements, including lamps, cables, and telephone exchange equipment.

However, the effect of patent pooling on R&D expenditure is by no means clear. While patent pooling may increase R&D spillovers between firms, its effect on R&D expenditure can be ambiguous and may depend, for instance, on the exact terms under which licenses are granted, including the amount of royalties. It may well be the case that the purpose of the practice was to minimize quality differences between firms, and thus facilitate agreement on price (see chapter 3) rather than to indirectly regulate R&D expenditure. Moreover, there is evidence that patent pooling was practiced in several electronic engineering industries which were not subject to any pricing agreements (see Burn 1958), so it was not necessarily associated with collusion. Indeed, its origins in some electronic engineering industries may be linked to the overall historical context of innovation and international licensing strategies of leading firms in that sector. In any case, and whatever the origins and effects of patent pooling, it has to be borne in mind that it was practiced in only a minority of collusive R&D-intensive industries in the 1950s.

Entry Conditions in Collusive Industries

Was entry restricted in cartelized industries? The evidence from the agreements registered under the 1956 Act, the reports of the Monopolies and Restrictive Practices Commission (cf. Guenault and Jackson 1974, Rowley 1966), and the case studies in Swann et al. (1973) suggests that this was not the general case. Although practices such as collective exclusive dealing and aggregated rebates were often used by the cartels as a way of limiting competition from outside firms, it is not at all clear that these practices also restricted entry. In most industries the agreements were operated within trade associations and there were often no significant restrictions on association membership, so that entry would not be difficult if the entrant was willing to become a party to the agreement. In some industries, on the other hand, the existing association members could reject applications for membership, although they would usually accommodate any powerful nonmember firm. Obviously, rejecting an application for membership would be easier in industries where the association firms had some control over distribution channels, usually through agreements with distributors' associations. Even in such cases, of course, entry into an industry would not be restricted unless the barriers to outside competition were fully effective.

The reports of the Monopolies and Restrictive Practices Commission and the case studies in Swann et al. (1973) also contain information on profitability of firms in collusive industries, and this also supports the view that entry was not restricted in most cases. In particular, two main conclusions can be drawn from this information.

First, profits were more often thought to be "reasonable" than "excessive."[12] Second, there were typically marked variations in costs and profits across firms, and this often meant that the profitability of the less or least efficient was "low," and sometimes even negative in particular lines of production. In fact, it seems that price setting by the cartels often consisted in a compromise between high-cost and low-cost firms, with prices set at a level that allowed the high-cost firms to break even. Of course, it is not clear why cartel firms should not make excessive profits if they could defend the profits against entry. The absence of excessive profits in most British cartels is therefore consistent with a regime of nonrestricted entry.[13]

Were the Agreements Effective?

The lack of excessive profits does not mean that the agreements were not effective. The effectiveness of an agreement depended on two factors: the extent to which the parties conformed to the agreement or accepted the recommendations,[14] and the extent of competition from outside firms, domestic or foreign. Evidence on these issues comes from various sources, including the agreements registered under the 1956 Act; the Monopolies and Restrictive Practices

---

12. Cartelization in many British industries in the 1950s may have been associated with high costs and low productivity rather than high profits. See Broadberry and Crafts (1996) for an econometric analysis of the evolution of labor productivity across British industries over the period 1954–1963 (which includes the first few years of the implementation of the 1956 Act) that provides support for this view.

13. I will return to this issue in chapter 7, where I will present strong econometric evidence consistent with the view that entry was, on the whole, not restricted in cartelized industries.

14. While some of the agreements provided for sanctions such as a fine or expulsion from the association in case of nonconformity, most agreements had no such provisions and were therefore entirely voluntary. The provisions regarding fines were not legally enforceable anyway.

Commission reports; the Political and Economic Planning study of industrial trade associations, carried out just before the Act was passed (Political and Economic Planning 1957), and unpublished background material for this report; and two studies of the impact of the Act, namely Heath (1961, 1963) and Swann et al. (1973, 1974). The evidence indicates that the large majority of the agreements were indeed effective.

In particular, Swann et al. (1974), who conducted case studies of forty industries that had been subject to collusion in the 1950s, emphasize that all but one of these agreements had been operated "honourably" before their cancellation. Much of their evidence on this issue was based on interviews as well as on pricing data over a number of years prior to cancellation. Swann et al. also found that, in the large majority of cases, the parties accounted for at least 75% of the relevant market. Heath (1963) states that 80% of the 159 agreements covered in his questionnaire survey of the short-run impact of the 1956 Act were reported as being effective at the time of cancellation, according to the replies received from firms and trade associations, while, of the rest, only one in five had been ineffective for many years. On the other hand, according to the Political and Economic Planning report on trade associations, some buyers could purchase at prices lower than the agreed collusive prices, either from association firms or from outside firms, in about half of the cartelized industries. It was also pointed out in the report, however, that nonassociation firms were often unable to supply the product in the quantity or quality required.

There were, in fact, a number of factors that limited the effectiveness of outside competition in many industries. The cartels tended to contain most or all of the largest and best-known domestic firms; the outside firms were often not capable of dealing with large contracts, or manufactured a smaller range of products, or had a lower reputation for quality. Moreover, practices intended to limit outside competition—such as aggregated rebates and collective exclusive dealing—were often used. Finally, competition from imports was often limited because of tariffs and quantitative controls (see, for instance, Political and Economic Planning 1959, Milward and Brennan 1996), differing technical standards, transport costs, or international restrictive agreements. Rowley (1966) has even argued that powerful trade associations were frequently afforded protection on balance-of-payments grounds and in order to avoid the development of excess capacity.[15]

The available case-study information on collusive prices also supports the view that the agreements were, in general, effective. Prices of outside firms were typically lower than the cartel prices, although sometimes they were identical or only marginally lower. In some industries, prices were being adjusted according to the extent of outside competition, for instance, in particular segments of the market or for particular contracts. More generally, Swann et al. (1974) found that, although in some collusive industries, prices were being set on the basis of the costs of the more efficient producers, in most cases they were being determined either on the basis of a weighted average of all costs or largely arbitrarily, since no system of relating prices to costs existed or accounting procedures were deficient. The view that prices had been kept, in general, above competitive levels is further strengthened by the evolution of prices and profits after the cancellation of the agreements. It is precisely to this latter issue and other aspects of the impact of the 1956 legislation on competition that I will now turn.

---

15. The limited extent of foreign competition across a range of UK industries in the 1950s is reflected in the low level of import penetration. A rough calculation at the four-digit industry level suggests that, in more than 80% of manufacturing industries, imports accounted for less than 10% of the total value of sales in the domestic market. Even in industries with significant imports—for instance, 50% or more of total sales in the domestic market—the high level of imports does not necessarily reflect competitive pressure. In fact, in many industries with high import penetration, the imported goods were largely complementary to domestic products within the relevant four-digit industry (for example: preserved fruits and vegetables, oils and fats, nonferrous metals, timber). In other cases the industries concerned were subject to quantitative controls or other forms of regulation (thus imports in bacon, iron ore, and other products were very high, but they were a residual source of supply).

Of course, this should not be taken to imply that all UK manufacturing industries were relatively free from foreign competition. Sectors facing a relatively low degree of protection included most food and drink industries, some chemicals, basic metals, clothing and footwear, wood products, publishing, leather and most textile semi-manufactures, and building materials. Note, however, that in several of these industries, foreign competition was limited due to transport costs or international collusive agreements. Sectors with a relatively high degree of protection included the engineering industries, instruments, vehicles, finished metal goods, some chemicals, paper and paper products, furniture, pottery and glass, most finished textile goods, rubber products, and various other finished manufactures. See Political and Economic Planning (1959), Morgan and Martin (1975), Kitchin (1976), and Milward and Brennan (1996) for details on these issues.

2.5   The Impact of the 1956 Legislation on Firm Conduct

The two necessary conditions for a significant effect of the 1956 Act on competition in British industry are (1) that the price-fixing agreements had generally been effective and the parties to them had accounted for a substantial fraction of the relevant markets, and (2) that the explicit agreements were not replaced—at least not in the long run—by informal arrangements having the same effect on competition. In the previous section I discussed the available evidence on the former condition. Here I examine the evidence on the latter.

Some information on the impact of the 1956 legislation on competition is contained in the Registrar's reports (RRTA 1961–1973). In the second report, covering the period 1960–1961, the emphasis was on the "forces of inertia," but in the third, covering the period 1961–1963, the emphasis was different and it was noted that in some industries there was now "keen competition" between the previously colluding firms. Sometimes the breakdown of collusion had been triggered by a specific event, such as a fall in demand or the entry of a new competitor. The fourth report, covering the period 1963–1966, qualified this optimistic view in light of the persistence of information agreements across a range of industries. This concern was replaced in subsequent reports by a more general concern about cases of secret collusion. On the whole, however, the Registrar's reports paint a picture of slow but steady emergence of competition in previously collusive industries.

The Short-Run Effect

There have also been two more systematic studies of the impact of the 1956 Act on competition. Heath (1961, 1963) conducted a questionnaire survey of the short-run consequences of the Act, using a sample of 159 canceled price agreements. The survey was conducted in 1960, only about a year after industries started formally abandoning explicit price-fixing. In only about a third of the cases did the respondents think that competition had intensified. This can be explained by short-term inertia or reluctance to abandon long-standing practices. In fact, the results of the survey seem to strengthen the view that the majority of industries had not anticipated the hard line taken by the Restrictive Practices Court toward cartels, and were not prepared for a more competitive environment in the short run. Heath also noted that many canceled arrangements had been replaced by information agreements.

A more extensive study of the impact of the Act was carried out by Swann, O'Brien, Maunder, and Howe in the early 1970s (Swann et al. 1973, 1974). They conducted case studies of forty industries, including thirty-four with canceled agreements and six with agreements upheld by the Court, and they examined both the short-run and the long-run effects of the legislation. The industries in the sample were chosen to reflect, as the authors pointed out, a wide variety of industrial situations, including producer-good as well as consumer-good industries, capital-intensive as well as labor-intensive industries, and so on.

Regarding the short run, the authors found that price competition increased in about half of the thirty-four industries with canceled agreements. This took the form of a fall in list prices or an increase in discounts to distributors. In particular, price falls of 15% to 25% occurred in six cases. In the other cases the price fall was smaller and/or the increase in competition took the form of an increase in trade discounts. On the other hand, information agreements replaced the former arrangements in at least half of the industries with formally canceled agreements in the sample and were usually, but not always, successful in restricting competition.

The Long-Run Effect

With respect to the long run, Swann et al. found that in many industries with information agreements, price competition emerged after these were abandoned or changed from prenotification into postnotification arrangements in the mid-1960s, following the two decisions of the Restrictive Practices Court on information agreements discussed earlier in this chapter. As a result, price wars occurred in a number of previously collusive industries in the second half of the 1960s, and the final blow came with the provisions of the 1968 Restrictive Trade Practices Act regarding information agreements. Thus in most industries with information agreements, competition emerged about a decade after the introduction of the 1956 legislation.

While the overall picture was one of a gradual strengthening of competition in British manufacturing industries, Swann et al. also noted that in the longer term there were instances of secret collusion or unregistered information agreements in some industries and parallel pricing (i.e., similar and roughly simultaneous price changes) in others. It is necessary to discuss this point in some detail, for it might seem to suggest that in many industries with abandoned agreements, the intensity of price competition may have not increased significantly in the long run. This is not the case. For one thing, the number of cases of detected explicit collusion was small. On the other hand, parallel pricing was quite common: the Monopolies Commission report on parallel pricing (Monopolies Commission 1973) listed approximately sixty industries in which the witnesses thought that parallel pricing occurred. Should this be seen as evidence for the existence of effective (explicit or tacit) collusion in many of these industries?[16] The answer is probably not, and it is based both on case-study evidence and on a more general assessment of changes in the competitive environment facing British firms in the second half of the 1960s.

In particular, evidence from Swann et al. (1973, 1974), Maunder (1972), and various reports of the Monopolies Commission and the National Board of Prices and Incomes on specific industries suggests that in many cases there was competition in discounts and with respect to sales by tender to large buyers, even though list prices tended to move in parallel; and that, in several industries that were reported as being subject to parallel pricing, increases in list prices were not always being followed. Second, the operation of prices and incomes policy since the mid-1960s, while facilitating parallel pricing in some industries, must have prevented excessive increases in profit margins. Third, the progressive opening of the British economy during the 1960s and 1970s must have significantly reduced the scope for effective collusion by domestic firms. And finally, the extent of collusion must have been limited by the operation of the cartel policy itself, including the right of buyers to complain to the competition authorities when they suspected collusion, the powers of the Registrar to investigate, and the provision for penalties to be imposed on colluding firms which had been parties to agreements that the Court had struck down. Swann et al. also mention the lack of moral com-

---

16. The distinction between collusion and parallel pricing implied here is not just one of form, but also one of effect. Thus effective collusion between a given number of firms is assumed to always increase profit margins above "competitive" levels, while this is not necessarily the case for parallel pricing.

mitment compared to the pre-1956 agreements as an additional factor limiting collusion in the 1960s.[17]

2.6   Concluding Remarks

The 1956 Restrictive Trade Practices Act was quite effective in dras-
tically reducing the extent of cartelization in British manufacturing
between the 1950s and the 1970s. In particular, the large majority of
collusive industries registered their explicit restrictive agreements,
and then had to abandon them. The process was slow, and it took
more than a decade for the effects of the law to be fully realized.
Admittedly, there is some uncertainty about the impact of the legislation on competition in each particular industry. Some agreements
may have not been effective at the time they were formally canceled,
and others may have been replaced, even in the longer term, by
secret or tacit arrangements. More generally, the "degree of collusion" can vary, depending on the type of restrictions, the extent of
outside competition, the balance of interests within the cartel, and so
on—and so can the "intensity of competition" in the absence of
any explicit collusion. Is it then legitimate to reduce this continuum
of states to just two competition regimes and interpret the increase
in price competition following the cancellation of agreements as a
change in regime?

A cautious approach would be to say that for an industry that
abandoned an explicit restrictive agreement, there is a high probability that there was, at some point after the cancellation of the
agreement, a change of competition regime induced by the legislation, while this probability is zero for an industry not affected by
the Act. The empirical analysis carried out in this book, based on a
comparison of the evolution of the two groups of industries, would
still be valid under this interpretation. To the extent that some agreements were ineffective in the 1950s and others were replaced by

---

17. Another finding of Swann et al. was that prices or price-cost margins in some of
the industries where competition broke out were restored or partly restored in the long
run. This does not imply, however, a weakening of competition. As described in several of the case studies contained in Swann et al. (1973), this often occurred either after
the number of firms in the industry had decreased, in which case it is perfectly consistent with competition remaining effective (see chapter 7 of this book), or because
prices had fallen to very low levels during a price war or due to a temporary fall in
demand.

undetected secret or tacit collusion in the 1960s and the 1970s, the analysis would, if anything, only somewhat understate the magnitude of the effect of price competition on the endogenous variables of interest, namely, market structure, nonprice conduct, and profitability.

I think, however, that there is no reason to emphasize this more cautious interpretation. The survey and case-study evidence reviewed in this chapter suggests that the large majority of industries that dropped their explicit collusive agreements as a result of the 1956 legislation did experience, sooner or later, an intensification of price competition. Furthermore, the effect was in many cases significant. Hence it is, on the whole, valid to think of this evolution as a change of competition regime induced by an exogenous institutional change. Consequently, a comparison between those industries affected by the 1956 Act and those not affected should provide an accurate assessment of the effects of competition.

3   The Competition Data

3.1   Introduction

The analysis of the effects of competition in this book is based on a comparison of those industries with a change of competition regime following the 1956 Restrictive Trade Practices Act and those without a change in regime. This chapter begins with a detailed description of the available data on competition and collusion across British manufacturing industries in the 1950s and after. The data allow us to distinguish a group of collusive industries, the large majority of which subsequently experienced a change of competition regime; a group of industries without explicit collusive agreements, which therefore experienced no change in regime; and a residual group of industries for which we are uncertain as to their state of competition. The criteria for constructing these groups will be explained in detail, and the issue of potential measurement error or selection bias due to unknown cases of collusion will also be discussed extensively. I will argue that this latter issue is probably not a significant problem for this chapter, and is certainly not a serious difficulty for the analysis carried out in the rest of the book. I will also provide some descriptive statistics on the extent of cartelization across sectors. A detailed survey of restrictive agreements across industries is contained in appendix A.

The final part of the chapter contains an analysis of the structural industry characteristics associated with the incidence of explicit collusion in the UK in the 1950s. Although the analysis relates to explicit collusion, it has to be borne in mind that restrictive agreements in the UK were not enforceable at law, so the issues of coordination and enforcement of agreements were just as relevant as they would be in a context where collusion is tacit. Thus this chapter aims to provide more general insights regarding the factors facilitating or hindering collusion. At the same time, it prepares the way for the study of the effects of the breakdown of collusion in the rest of the book by examining the similarities and the differences in the initial conditions in the two groups of industries, those with explicit restrictive agreements and those without. A key result is that the two groups were quite similar with respect to initial market structure, but rather different regarding capital intensity, advertising effectiveness, and technological opportunity. It seems, then, that the incidence of collusive pricing in British industries in the 1950s was largely determined by exogenous variables, some of which are unobservable industry characteristics, rather than by endogenous variables such as concentration.

3.2   Data Sources on Competition in British Industry

The most comprehensive source of data on competition in British industry in the 1950s and the 1960s is the Register of Restrictive Trading Agreements created under the 1956 Act. This register has always been open to public inspection; in recent years, it has been kept at the Office of Fair Trading in London.

For each agreement in the register, information is available on the products subject to restrictions, the types of restrictions, the names of the parties, the geographical coverage, and the time period during which the agreement was in force after the introduction of the 1956 Act. The amount of detail on the content of any given agreement in the register can vary greatly, depending on what was furnished by the parties and, especially, on how elaborate any given agreement was in the first place. For example, in several cases there are elaborate price lists, covering a large number of different products and specifications, with details on terms and conditions of sale, and possibly also lists of buyers participating in an ancillary scheme of collective exclusive dealing or entitled to carry the products or to receive specified discounts. In many other cases there are again price lists, but they are less elaborate. And in some cases, there is little more than a page containing brief evidence of an agreement to observe certain restrictions, or possibly a simple recommendation by a trade association to its members to raise their prices by a specified amount in order to cover the latest cost increase. In several files, additional information is given in the constitution and by-laws of the relevant trade association, or in the minutes of meetings between the parties.

For those agreements that were brought before the Restrictive Practices Court and were defended by the parties, there is also supplementary, and much more detailed, information in the reports of the Court. These contain detailed accounts of the Court proceedings, and they are often very informative, not only about the exact way in which the agreements were operated but also about the key features of the industries in question, thus allowing for a better understanding of the purpose and significance of particular restrictions. Needless to say, agreements brought before the Court and defended by the parties can safely be assumed to have been effective in the 1950s. As for the rest, there is no guarantee that all registered agreements were indeed fully effective at the time, but the case-study evidence reviewed in chapter 2 suggested that this is a reasonable assumption to make, and that any resulting measurement error should be small; this issue is further discussed below.

The register of agreements and the Court reports contain information on explicit collusion not only in the 1950s but also over the entire period examined in this book. Thus there is information on the dates when the agreements were formally abandoned, on Court decisions to allow explicit collusion to continue in certain industries, and on agreements discovered by the Registrar and his staff during the 1960s and the 1970s.

There is also evidence that some agreements were not registered, either because they were abandoned shortly after the Act was introduced or, in a few cases, because they secretly continued. A number of sources can be used to identify products subject to unregistered agreements. These sources sometimes provide additional information on registered agreements as well, either because some agreements were modified prior to registration or because some sources contain much more detailed information on the industries concerned than the registered agreements. Some of the sources are not as reliable as others, or provide less detailed information.

The reports of the Monopolies and Restrictive Practices Commission before 1956 and those of the Monopolies Commission after that date are entirely reliable and provide significant detail on the industries concerned. It is reasonable to assume that those collusive industries that were investigated before 1956 and did not register their agreements (or registered modified versions of them) must have abandoned them (or abandoned the unregistered restrictions) soon after the introduction of the legislation. It is indeed unlikely that in these much-publicized cases explicit collusion would have secretly continued. The situation with industries investigated after 1956 is slightly more complicated. These were usually investigated because of the presence of a dominant firm or a dominant group of firms. In the majority of these cases, either there is no mention of any restrictive arrangements before or after 1956 or there is a reference to some previously registered agreements. In a few cases, on the other hand, an industry is reported as having had an agreement in the 1950s which either was abandoned, and therefore never registered under the 1956 Act, or was modified before registration. Finally, there are a few cases where the Monopolies Commission uncovered an existing secret collusive agreement during its investigation; information is then provided on the origins of the arrangement.

For the purposes of my classification, all restrictive agreements mentioned in the Commission's reports as having been effective prior to 1956 (or after that date) were treated in exactly the same way as registered agreements—or, more precisely, as registered agreements defended in the Court, since there was no question in those cases of the restrictions not being effective.

Other reliable sources on the state of competition across manufacturing industries in the 1950s include the 1955 Monopolies and Restrictive Practices Commission report on collective discrimination (MRPC 1955), and several industrial case studies undertaken in the mid-1950s as part of an investigation into the structure of British industry and contained in Burn (1958). Various other publications with occasional references to competition in particular industries in the 1950s and the 1960s are mentioned in appendix A. There were only a few agreements reported in these sources and not in any others, and they were treated in the same way as registered agreements for the purposes of my classification.

Finally, two very important but not fully reliable sources are the Political and Economic Planning study of industrial trade associations, undertaken just before the 1956 Act was passed, and the Board of Trade annual reports on the operation of the 1948 Monopolies and Restrictive Practices Act, covering the years 1949 to 1956 (Board of Trade 1949–1952, 1953–1956). These sources provide information on industries alleged to be collusive. Most of these industries registered agreements, but some did not.[1]

More specifically, the Board of Trade annual reports contain lists of products allegedly subject to restrictive practices during the period 1949–1956. This information is not very detailed as to the types of restrictions or the coverage of the alleged agreements. More important, it is based on complaints made by buyers to the Board of Trade, and buyers may wrongly deduce the existence of a price-fixing agreement from parallel pricing, or even from mere price uniformity over a certain time period. It is not very clear to what extent the complaints received by the Board of Trade were subject to some preliminary evaluation before being used to compile the lists of suspect industries, and it is certainly emphasized in the reports that inclusion of a product does not necessarily imply that a restrictive agreement actually exists. On the other hand, it may well be the case that some of the industries that are on the lists and did not register any agreements were in fact collusive. Thus, there is some uncertainty regarding the state of competition for products in the Board of Trade annual reports but not mentioned as being the subject of restrictive agreements in any of the more reliable sources. For this reason, these products were classified as having an ambiguous state of competition in the 1950s. This also implies some ambiguity as to the effect of the 1956 Act in these cases.

Information on restrictive agreements in particular industries is also provided by the Political and Economic Planning (P.E.P.) (1957) study of industrial trade associations. Most of this information is found in the unpublished background material for this study, for the published report provides mostly aggregate data at the sector level. This background material has been deposited in the archives collection of the British Library of Political and Economic Science. Again, much of the information is not very detailed, and comes mostly from buyers (public and private firms, local authorities, etc.). For the same reasons as in the case of the Board of Trade annual reports, this information must be treated with some caution. Hence most industries that were alleged to be collusive in the P.E.P. study, and are not mentioned as collusive in any of the more reliable sources, were

---

1. The reverse is also true: several industries that registered agreements do not appear as collusive in the Political and Economic Planning survey or the Board of Trade annual reports. On the whole, these two sources probably underestimate rather than overestimate the extent of cartelization in British industry in the 1950s.

treated as ambiguous for the purposes of my classification. On the other hand, a fair amount of information in the P.E.P. survey comes directly from firms that were parties to agreements. This information can be treated as reliable and used to identify a few industries that were certainly collusive but failed to register their agreements.

In summary, the above sources allow us to distinguish three groups of products: a group with explicit restrictive agreements, a group without explicit restrictive agreements, and a group with uncertain state of competition in the 1950s. The first of these groups contains all products for which there are registered agreements or which are reported as being subject to collusion in the Monopolies Commission's reports or any of the other fully reliable secondary sources. The second group contains products not mentioned in any of the various sources. And the third group contains products that do not appear in the register or in any of the other fully reliable sources, but may have been subject to explicit or tacit collusion according to the Board of Trade annual reports or the P.E.P. survey.

This classification is based on certain assumptions as to the reliability of the various data sources which seem very reasonable. There is also, however, a more fundamental assumption implicit in this classification: that the existence of a known (i.e., documented) explicit price-fixing agreement is a good overall indicator of collusive conduct in British manufacturing industry in the 1950s. One might raise a number of objections to this, and it is now necessary to discuss these in some detail.

The Reliability of the Competition Data: Tacit versus Explicit Collusion

One possible objection is that the data on British cartels relate to explicit collusion, but not to tacit collusion. Could it then be the case that some of the industries classified as noncollusive actually practiced tacit collusion? One cannot, of course, rule out the possibility that firms in an industry colluded tacitly in the absence of any explicit arrangement. However, it is difficult to understand why colluding firms would not want to enter into an explicit arrangement, given that explicit collusion was legal and widespread in the 1950s. Furthermore, the 1956 Act required the registration of informal and even "implied" understandings as well as formal agreements, and this seems to cover cases of tacit collusion. So tacitly colluding firms would be in little doubt as to their obligation to register. Of course, it is still possible that they might have chosen not to do so—but this is a different issue, to be discussed presently. As far as tacit collusion is concerned, I would argue that, for all the above reasons and given that collusive arrangements of all kinds were not enforceable in the courts, the distinction between tacit and explicit collusion is not very important in the present context.

The Reliability of the Competition Data: The Effectiveness of Agreements

Another possible objection is that some of the agreements may have not been effective at the time they were registered, so classifying these industries as collusive introduces measurement error. There is an even stronger version of this argument: that some of the industries that registered explicit agreements may have done so because collusion was difficult to sustain otherwise. Therefore we may be assigning to the collusive group industries where collusion was actually rather difficult to sustain. This would clearly be worse than measurement error, for it would essentially amount to selection bias. Are the above arguments valid? For one thing, there is little doubt that some of the agreements registered under the 1956 Act may not have been effective. The important question is whether these cases are a large fraction of the total number of registered agreements, and, if so, whether this is likely to result in selection bias. I think that the answer to these questions is in the negative, and I will offer several arguments to support this claim.

First, the case-study evidence discussed in chapter 2 strongly supports the view that the large majority of the agreements had been effective. Recall that only one out of the forty agreements examined in Swann et al. (1974) was thought by the authors to have been ineffective. Second, the Register of Restrictive Trading Agreements is not the only source of information on collusion in British industry. Several industries were investigated by the Monopolies and Restrictive Practices Commission during the 1950s, and several more defended their agreements before the Restrictive Practices Court. The available information, which in these cases is quite detailed, leaves no doubt as to the effectiveness of these agreements, which are a significant part of the total number. Third, all the sources of information on the effects of the 1956 Act, including the Registrar's reports, emphasize that competition was slow to emerge in many industries, and that this was often due to the fact that information agreements replaced the former price-fixing arrangements in the short run. This is not consistent with the view that these arrangements were not effective before 1956.

Fourth, it should be emphasized that a weak agreement could not expect to gain much from a favorable Court decision, because it would still not be enforceable at law. So it is not at all clear why industries with weak agreements would have a strong incentive to register. On the contrary, one might argue that it was industries with strong agreements that had the strongest incentive to register and try to maintain collusion, because of the potentially large cost of a cartel breakdown. And, finally, the evidence from Lydall (1958) and Board of Trade (1944, 1946) discussed below also suggests that there is no serious measurement error or selection bias in the construction of the collusive group of industries in the present study.

The Reliability of the Competition Data: The Issue of Nonregistration

The above discussion suggests that the assumption that the existence of an explicit price-fixing agreement is a good overall indicator of collusive conduct is not an unreasonable one in the present context. There is, however, one final difficulty, which is probably more serious, for it relates to the issue of nonregistration. Again, there is a weaker and a stronger version of the argument. The weaker version is that nonregistration of agreements, if widespread, would lead to serious measurement error. The stronger version is that certain types of industries may have had a stronger incentive to avoid registration than others. Then the failure to take unknown cases of collusion into account could lead to sample selection bias.

There are two possible reasons for nonregistration: firms may suspend an agreement, so that there is nothing to register, or they may switch to secret or tacit collusion. Take, first, the former case. A reasonable conjecture in this case is that very weak agreements would be more likely to be dropped immediately than stronger ones. Even if that were true, we would not be losing much by failing to identify such cases, since we are primarily interested in identifying effective agreements, not ineffective ones. But it is not even clear why the decision to immediately cancel an agreement rather than register it should have occurred in certain types of industries more than in

others, and might therefore be associated with industry characteristics related to the sustainability of collusion: there is not much to
be lost by registering an agreement, even a weak one, when the
alternative is cancellation. In fact, many of the agreements that were
not registered were those that had been condemned by the Monopolies and Restrictive Practices Commission. Clearly, these were not
weak agreements, but the parties may have thought that they had
practically no chance of success in the Court and wished to avoid
further adverse publicity. That leaves us with the second reason for
nonregistration mentioned above. One might argue, for instance,
that industries where tacit or secret collusion would be easier to
sustain or less easily detected after 1956 had less of an incentive to
register. Failure to identify such cases could cause sample selection
bias.

An important thing to note with respect to the issue of nonregistration is the historical context of the introduction of the 1956
Act. As pointed out in chapter 2, there was a great deal of uncertainty about the way the legislation would be implemented. It seems
that industries genuinely thought that they had a good chance of
success in the Court, as evidenced by the fact that many agreements
were redrafted prior to registration and several others were defended
in the Court despite the first few unfavorable Court decisions. The
ambiguity of the attitude of the Monopolies and Restrictive Practices Commission toward certain types of restrictions, including
price-fixing, must have contributed to creating this perception
among firms. Recall also that a comparison of the register with a
list of industries subject to restrictive agreements published in the
Commission's report on collective discrimination in chapter 2 revealed a low incidence of nonregistration of registrable agreements.

To these arguments one could add that the 1956 Act gave the
Registrar powers of investigation. Being an officer at the Board of
Trade, the Registrar would certainly have access to all the complaints
made throughout the 1950s by buyers claiming the existence of restrictive agreements in particular industries. Thus it would be difficult for many industries to collude secretly and go unnoticed for a
long time. For this and all the other reasons mentioned above, it
seems safe to conclude that nonregistration was not a widespread
phenomenon.

Moreover, and most important, in this book I do not rely solely on
information about registered agreements. As pointed out above,

several sources were examined to obtain information on agreements that were not registered. Most of these contain long lists of industries that either were certainly collusive or were alleged to be collusive. The Board of Trade, in particular, was encouraging buyers to come up with information and complaints, which it then used to compile its lists of allegedly collusive industries throughout the period 1949–1956. Although these sources are far from perfect, it would really be surprising if there were a significant number of cases that escaped all of them.

There is also some evidence from a questionnaire survey of competition in UK manufacturing in the 1950s (Lydall 1958) which does not support the view that there may be significant selection bias in the data. The study by Lydall used a sample of 876 manufacturing firms from all sectors. It did not specifically discuss collusive agreements, but some of the information provided suggests that firms that perceived their condition as being characterized by "no strong competition" were primarily in industries which had a high incidence of explicit collusion, according to my classification, while firms that thought that they were facing "strong competition" were chiefly in industries without many agreements. Thus the three sectors with the greatest proportion of firms saying that they faced strong competition were chemicals, food and drink, and textiles. As shown later in this chapter (table 3.1), in these three sectors the number of competitive industries, according to the classification adopted in this book, was much larger than the number of collusive ones.[2] In addition, Lydall mentions engineering, other metal products, and paper and printing as the three sectors with the highest proportion of firms taking part in price-fixing. Again, table 3.1 below reveals that in these three sectors the number of competitive industries, according to my classification, was far smaller than the number of collusive ones.

The final piece of evidence comes from two surveys of cartels and restrictive practices carried out in the mid-1940s by the Board of Trade, one dealing with international cartels in which British firms had some involvement (Board of Trade 1944), the other dealing with internal cartels (Board of Trade 1946). Of course, these surveys were carried out more than a decade before the introduction of the 1956 Act and describe, for the most part, the state of competition across

---

2. It was in fact much larger in chemicals and food and drink, and only slightly larger in textiles. However, the textiles sector is mentioned by Lydall as one with a high proportion of firms acknowledging the existence of price leadership.

manufacturing industries during the 1930s and the early 1940s. Given, however, that most of the British cartels of the 1950s had been active at the time of the Board of Trade surveys (see Swann et al. 1974), a comparison of the information contained in the surveys with my own data on collusion in the 1950s would certainly be interesting.

The two surveys differ somewhat in scope: the one on international cartels was meant to be comprehensive, while the one on internal cartels was conceived as the first part of a wider investigation, and was therefore somewhat less comprehensive, although the industries or sectors chosen spanned the whole spectrum of manufacturing industries, covering capital-good industries as well as consumer-good industries.

Of the two surveys, the one on internal cartels is probably the more useful for my present purposes. The number of industries reported in this survey as being subject to price-fixing and related restrictions is equal to almost a third of the total number of industries classified as collusive in my data set (see table 3.1). In other words, the coverage of the Board of Trade survey was quite large. In spite of this large coverage, a careful reading of the report revealed virtually no cases of industries reported as being subject to restrictive agreements in the late 1930s or early 1940s which were not mentioned as being collusive in any of my primary data sources for this book. Furthermore, nearly all of these industries registered agreements under the 1956 Act.[3]

An Overall Assessment

It seems reasonable to conclude, on the basis of the above discussion, that the issue of potential nonregistration of agreements does not cause any significant bias or measurement error in the present data. Admittedly, it is not possible to back up this claim with anything more than the indirect evidence discussed above. Let me therefore

---

3. The Board of Trade survey of international cartels is less relevant for my present purposes because in many cases only one British firm—usually a dominant firm in the relevant UK industry—participated in the international agreement. Moreover, international cartels often broke down during or after the Second World War. Nevertheless, the report also mentions several agreements in which more than one British firm was a party. Most of these are also reported in my data sources for the 1950s, although a few are not. It is impossible to know whether these agreements were still effective in 1956. Even if they were, this would change my classification of industries in only three cases.

clarify the precise implications of accepting this claim as a maintained assumption for the analysis carried out in the rest of this book.

Except for section 3.4 of the present chapter, which examines the cross section of industries in the 1950s to identify how the incidence of collusion was associated with various structural industry characteristics, this book focuses on the effects of the breakdown of cartels. The key distinction therefore is between industries with a change in competition regime and industries without such a change. Seen from this angle, the issue of potential nonregistration followed by collusion after 1956 is not very important. Any industry that practiced (explicit or tacit) collusion successfully, did not register any agreement, is not mentioned in any of my sources as being collusive, and continued to collude after 1956 would be classified as an industry without a change in competition regime. This is indeed the correct classification: it does not really matter whether the lack of change was due to continuing collusion or to continuing competition.

In other words, all the results reported in chapters 4–7 of this book are not sensitive to the existence of cases of unknown and continuing collusion. The only measurement error in these results can be caused by agreements that were ineffective in the 1950s or agreements that were registered and then replaced by undetected secret or tacit collusion. This can only understate the estimated effects of price competition on the endogenous variables of interest. Bearing this in mind, let me now turn to a detailed description of the competition data.

3.3 The Construction of the Data Set

The approach to modeling the competition effect in this book involves distinguishing between those industries with a change of competition regime following the 1956 Act and those without a change in regime. The first step in this procedure was to assess the reliability of the various sources of information on competition in British industry in the 1950s; this was discussed in the previous section. The next step was to classify all industries according to their state of competition in the 1950s on the basis of three criteria: (1) the reliability of the sources of information on any particular agreement; (2) the types of restrictions; and (3) the proportion of an industry's total sales covered by products subject to agreements and, for each product, the fraction of the UK market covered by cartel firms.

Types of Restrictions

The following types of restrictions were classified as significant with respect to their effect on competition: (1) agreed or recommended minimum or fixed producer prices—possibly complemented by maximum or fixed trade discounts, terms and conditions of sale or contract, resale price maintenance, collective exclusive dealing, and so on; (2) agreed or recommended price changes; (3) agreed maximum or fixed discounts to distributors or users combined with resale price maintenance and terms and conditions of sale— and possibly also prenotification of price or product changes; and (4) quotas, market sharing, or allocation of work to parties.

The following were classified as not significant: (1) terms and conditions of sale or contract, relating to price and/or nonprice matters, without any regulation of prices or trade discounts; and (2) resale price maintenance, individual or collective. Finally, one type of restriction—the reporting of inquiries received from customers leading to some kind of uniform action on terms and conditions, but generally not on prices—was considered as having an uncertain effect on competition.

This classification covers the large majority of the schemes operated by British firms at the time the 1956 legislation was passed. The remaining few cases were intermediate or special, and were usually classified as uncertain (see appendix A for details).

It is necessary to discuss certain aspects of this classification in some detail. Consider, first, agreements that contained maximum or fixed discounts to distributors or users, as well as the maintenance of individually set resale prices, but did not regulate the level of individual prices. Most of these schemes were operated in differentiated-product industries, where the fixing of common prices may have not been practicable. They typically contained elaborate discount structures, which were often supported by ancillary restrictions relating to sales promotion. In some cases, they had succeeded earlier price-fixing agreements that had been modified prior to registration. Finally, case-study evidence suggests that the cancellation of these agreements led to significant increases in trade discounts in some industries. What all this indicates is that this type of restriction was usually a substitute for, or a weaker form of, price-fixing; it was therefore classified as significant.

Second, consider the practice of resale price maintenance in the absence of any agreement between manufacturers specifying either what these maintained prices would be or at least a common set of trade discounts from these prices—other than, possibly, the fixing of *minimum* discounts in order to protect distributors' margins. Sometimes there was an agreement between firms to maintain their resale prices, and sometimes there was no such agreement but resale price maintenance was practiced on an individual basis by most firms in an industry. Also, the enforcement of resale price maintenance could be, until 1956, either individual or collective (for instance, by means of a stop list).[4] These distinctions are not very important in the present context, however, for there are good reasons to believe that, *in the absence of any horizontal arrangement on prices*, resale price maintenance did not significantly affect competition between manufacturers in the industries where it was practiced until it was abolished following the 1964 Resale Prices Act.

The literature on resale price maintenance suggests that the main reason why this practice may reduce competition among manufacturers is that it may help sustain collusion by facilitating the detection of cheating and by minimizing fluctuations of manufacturers' market shares caused by competition among retailers (see Overstreet 1983, Yamey 1966a). This argument is valid in general, but it is probably not very relevant in a context where horizontal price-fixing agreements are widespread and are not illegal. In many industries with agreed common or minimum prices, resale price maintenance may indeed have served as an ancillary restriction to facilitate the monitoring of cheating. But consider an industry without any agreement between manufacturers specifying either what the prices would be or at least a common set of trade discounts. If firms had actually intended to restrict competition among themselves, they would also have explicitly fixed prices or at least maximum trade discounts. The failure to do that in the circumstances of the 1950s can only imply that resale price maintenance was being used in that industry either to protect distributors' margins or as part of an individual pricing strategy.

---

4. Under an agreement among manufacturers to collectively enforce resale price maintenance, a distributor who cut the price of the product of one manufacturer was liable to punishment by all manufacturers. Such punishment often involved a refusal to supply the distributor concerned.

An interesting observation in this respect is that in industries where collective resale price maintenance was practiced without any horizontal pricing arrangement among manufacturers, the agreement to maintain retail prices was usually an agreement between a manufacturers' association and a distributors' association.[5] This is consistent with Yamey's (1966b) view attributing the origins of resale price maintenance in many industries to the pressure exerted on manufacturers by retailers' associations.[6] Moreover, there is evidence (e.g., Board of Trade 1949, Pickering 1966) of unrestricted and even intense competition between manufacturers in several industries where resale price maintenance was practiced, either individually or collectively.

For all these reasons, I have chosen to classify resale price maintenance per se as a nonsignificant restriction in the present context. A possible objection to this is that this practice may in some cases have facilitated tacit or secret collusion in previously cartelized industries *after* 1956. However, it would then, at most, cause only a temporary delay in the emergence of price competition, comparable to that attributed to information agreements. This is because resale price maintenance gradually weakened or broke down in several industries after 1956 and was finally abandoned in almost all industries in the mid-1960s (roughly the same time that information agreements were dropped).

Third, consider those arrangements that related solely to agreed or recommended terms and conditions of sale or contract. This class covers a wide range of restrictions on price and nonprice matters. Examples are the recommendation not to give trade discounts; formulas for contract price adjustment to cover costs when delivery does not take place until some time after the contract is made and costs have changed in the meantime; restrictions on the amount of credit given to customers; agreed or recommended cash discount

---

5. This is in sharp contrast with agreements that contained maximum or fixed discounts to distributors or users in addition to the maintenance of individually set resale prices. These agreements were often among manufacturers only. As mentioned above, I have classified such schemes as significant restrictions on competition.

6. Admittedly, Yamey's view has not been without its critics, partly because of evidence that manufacturers in many industries opposed the abolition of resale price maintenance at the time of the introduction of the 1964 Resale Prices Act. Still, this opposition was attributed by most of these critics to the presumed efficiency gains from resale price maintenance rather than to any potential effect of this practice on competition between manufacturers (see Mercer 1998).

terms, delivery or packing charges, terms of guarantee, arrangements for returns of unsold goods, and so on.

It is difficult to say to what extent such restrictions may reduce competition rather than simply help maintain orderly and stable trading conditions. However, *in the absence of any arrangement concerning prices*, such practices should not affect the state of competition to any significant degree, especially in a context where collusion is not illegal. As in the case of resale price maintenance, one could argue that if firms had actually intended to restrict competition, they would also have explicitly fixed prices. This interpretation is consistent with the fact that several agreements of this kind were allowed to continue, although firms were often required to modify certain restrictions before their agreements were cleared.[7]

Finally, consider those agreements that involved the reporting of inquiries received from customers and uniform action on terms and conditions with respect to these inquiries, but did not provide for price-fixing or the allocation of work. The sharing of information about inquiries from prospective purchasers was not uncommon in industries where the costs of tendering for a job were significant, as was the case in many engineering industries. Often the sharing of information was part of a price-fixing or market-sharing agreement between firms. But in some cases the arrangement did not provide for price-fixing or the allocation of work following the circulation of information about received inquiries. Furthermore, evidence from the Monopolies and Restrictive Practices Commission reports and the P.E.P. survey suggests that such arrangements were not simply the product of redrafting of agreements prior to registration.

There are two reasons why I classified this type of restriction per se as uncertain. In many cases these agreements also provided for the payment by the successful tenderer of a sum of money to be used to compensate other tenderers for the costs of tendering. In some industries the amounts involved were small, while in others they were on a larger scale and may have successfully raised the level of

---

7. The view taken by UK competition authorities, as expressed in the 1980 report of the Director General of Fair Trading (DGFT 1981), was that the recommendation by trade associations of standard terms and conditions of sale or contract—such as terms of guarantee, provisions as to contractual liability for loss or damage, formulas for contract price adjustment, and so on—may often be beneficial to all parties involved and will have no significant effect on competition, provided that the recommended terms and conditions are "fair" to both buyers and sellers, and are clearly stated as being optional rather than compulsory.

prices. However, information on the level of the tendering fee is not always available. More important, these arrangements may have occasionally led to informal understandings about prices or the allocation of work, even if they did not provide for this. Overall, then, it is difficult to assess the extent to which these agreements restricted competition without detailed information on how they were actually operated in each particular case.[8] In the absence of such information, the safest approach was to classify this type of restriction as having an uncertain effect on competition.[9]

Classifying the Industries According to Their State of Competition in the 1950s

Once the various types of restrictions were classified as significant, nonsignificant, or uncertain, the next step was to assign the products that were subject to agreements to the various industry categories used. It was often the case that certain products within a particular industry were subject to significant restrictions while others were not. In this book several different data sets are being used, mainly because the industry definitions used in the published statistics for

---

8. The view expressed here is not inconsistent with the view taken by the Monopolies and Restrictive Practices Commission in its report on electrical machinery (MRPC 1957). Although most sections of the electrical machinery industry had explicit price-fixing agreements in the 1950s, a few had only agreements to report inquiries received from prospective purchasers. The Commission concluded that this practice might be expected to operate against the public interest because of the danger that understandings about prices or allocation of work would follow. Thus the Commission essentially recognized the uncertain effect of such arrangements. In the context of the heavily cartelized electrical machinery industry, however, the Commission was probably justified in stressing the potential for collusion. In other cases, the assessment would have been less straightforward.

9. Note that I have not specifically discussed collective exclusive dealing and other forms of collective discrimination, such as aggregated rebates. The reason is that these were typically used as ancillary restrictions to strengthen a pricing agreement. However, in very few industries collective exclusive dealing was practiced even though the manufacturers did not collude on prices or trade discounts. These cases present something of a paradox: If collective exclusive dealing was being used as an entry barrier, why didn't these firms also attempt to restrict price competition among themselves? Since some of these cases are discussed extensively in reports of the Monopolies and Restrictive Practices Commission, there can be no question of insufficient information about these industries. A possible explanation is that these were instances of *bilateral* collective exclusive dealing, the primary purpose of which was to protect the interests of distributors rather than those of manufacturers. Fortunately, the industries concerned are very few, and either they are not included in the statistical data sources used for this book or they have been classified as ambiguous anyway.

the various endogenous variables are often very difficult to match. Thus different industry categories must be used when analyzing the competition effect on concentration, advertising intensity, innovations, and profitability. Obviously, the use of different industry categories requires creating multiple competition data sets. However, the criteria for constructing these data sets were always the same, and they were obviously independent of the industry definitions used in each case.

In particular, an industry was classified as collusive in the 1950s if the products subject to *significant* restrictions accounted for more than 50% of total industry sales revenue. It was classified as competitive if the products subject to *significant or uncertain* restrictions accounted for less than 10% of industry sales revenue. And it was classified as ambiguous in all remaining cases.[10] Information about the particular products within each industry and the sales revenue of each product was taken from the Census of Production. For agreements of nationwide application, it was assumed that the parties accounted for a substantial fraction of the relevant market (an assumption that is in line with the case-study evidence). For important regional agreements, an estimate of the fraction of industry sales subject to restrictions was made on the basis of the available information on the geographical coverage of the agreements and the regional structure of production in the industries concerned.

Some discussion regarding the use of the 10% and 50% cutoff points is in order. In particular, there are two main questions: First, why choose these particular cutoff points? Second, why use *any* cutoff points?

Clearly, the choice of these particular cutoff points is arbitrary. However, it should be emphasized that most industries classified as competitive were free from any restrictive agreements. Similarly, most industries classified as collusive had agreements covering all industry products. I have used the 10% cutoff point because in some cases secondary industry products were subject to restrictive agreements, although core industry products were not. It was clear, however, that these secondary products did not significantly affect the structure and performance of the industries concerned. Also, I have used the 50% cutoff point because in some cases most core industry

---

10. Products mentioned as being subject to collusion or potential collusion in one of the less reliable data sources, but not in any of the more reliable ones, were treated as products with uncertain restrictions for the purposes of this classification.

products were subject to price-fixing, although some were not. Surely, one would expect a significant effect of the 1956 Act in these industries. In any case, I have also experimented with alternative cutoff points, in particular 20% instead of 10%, on the one hand, and 40% or 70% instead of 50%, on the other. These variations have changed the samples used very little, and in some cases not at all. None of the results reported in this book were significantly affected by variations in the chosen cutoff points.[11]

One might ask why it is necessary to use any cutoff points at all, since an alternative would presumably be to use the information on the exact fraction of sales revenue covered by products with agreements in each industry, on the assumption that the higher this fraction, the more collusive the industry (and thus, all else being equal, the stronger the effect of the Act on competition). However, this approach is impractical, or even misleading, for several reasons.

First, the fraction of sales revenue covered by products subject to agreements in each industry is sometimes difficult to specify other than approximately. This can occur because the information is not sufficiently detailed to allow for this fraction to be estimated very precisely, even though it is sufficient for classifying the industry according to the cutoff points I have used. An additional difficulty is that the exact fraction of sales revenue covered by products with agreements may vary across years. This is not a significant problem when using cutoff points, but it is more serious when trying to construct a continuous measure of competition.

Second, there is no one-to-one link between the fraction of sales revenue covered by products with agreements in each industry and the state of competition across industries in the 1950s. The link between the two is blurred by a variety of factors, including differences across industries regarding the types of restrictions, the extent of

---

11. This also implies that the classification of marginal cases makes little difference to the results. There were, in fact, very few marginal cases (i.e., cases where the fraction of industry sales revenue subject to restrictions was either very close to 10% or 50%, or was higher than one of these cutoff points in one year and lower in another year). These cases were classified on the basis of two criteria. The first was the average or typical value of this fraction over all relevant years. The second was an assessment of which industry products were mainly driving the industry-level values of the endogenous variables of interest in each particular case. For instance, in the case of concentration, I compared the average sales revenue of firms producing regulated products with the average sales revenue of firms producing nonregulated products, the assumption being that the market shares of the larger firms within an industry will largely drive the concentration ratio of the industry as a whole.

outside competition, and the extent to which competition in export markets was regulated (see below). For many of these factors, systematic information is not available. Thus, even though it is clear that an industry with 90% of sales revenue covered by products subject to agreements can be seen as collusive, while one with only 5–10% of sales revenue covered by regulated products can be regarded as competitive, it is not at all easy to compare, say, 90% with 75%, or 40% with 25%.

Third, it is often the case that some products within an industry were subject to significant restrictions in the 1950s, while other products were subject to uncertain restrictions. It is not clear how to deal with such cases if one wants to construct a continuous measure of competition based on the fraction of industry sales revenue under agreements.

Fourth, it is sometimes the case that an industry consists of subdivisions with very different market structures, and although some of these subdivisions were collusive in the 1950s, most were not. The fraction of sales revenue covered by products with agreements is then between 10% and 50%, but it is very difficult to draw any conclusions about the state of competition in the industry as a whole and its effect on other variables. This crucially depends on which industry subdivision is mainly driving the industry-level measures of concentration, profitability, and so on. The use of cutoff points has the advantage of treating such industries for what they really are (ambiguous), rather than trying to fit them into a continuum of states of competition.

Finally, let me again emphasize that the use of cutoff points is actually far less ad hoc than it may seem at first sight, because the majority of industries classified as competitive were essentially free from restrictive agreements and most industries classified as collusive had agreements covering practically all industry products.

Exclusion of Ambiguous Industries

Once all manufacturing industries were classified as collusive, competitive, or ambiguous in the 1950s, according to the criteria set out above, those industries with ambiguous state of competition were excluded from the samples used in this book. The purpose of this was to be able to compare two clearly defined groups, one collusive and one competitive. Treating ambiguous industries as intermediate was not really appropriate, given the heterogeneity of this group, which includes cases with uncertain restrictions, cases for which there is insufficient information, and cases where the regulated products cover between 10% and 50% of total industry sales. The heterogeneity of this group of industries also implies that their exclusion should not lead to any significant selection bias in the results reported in subsequent chapters, since the selection is not done on the basis of any of the endogenous variables of interest.[12]

The Incidence of Collusion in the 1960s and the 1970s

Having classified all industries as collusive or competitive in the 1950s, the final step in constructing the competition data for examining the effect of the 1956 Act in this book was to take into account the available information about cases of collusion in the 1960s and the 1970s. There were no such cases among industries without explicit collusive agreements in the 1950s. On the other hand, although the large majority of industries that were collusive in the 1950s did experience a change of competition regime, there were two kinds of exceptions.

First, as pointed out in chapter 2, a small number of collusive agreements were allowed to continue. In most of these cases, the agreements were still in force in the mid-1970s, so I assigned the industries concerned to the group that was not affected by the 1956 legislation.[13] Second, some illegal restrictive arrangements were

---

12. The potential selection bias due to exclusion of ambiguous industries may be more of a concern for the results on the determinants of collusion presented in the final section of the present chapter. However, as pointed out below, these results were found to be robust to alternative classifications of the industries according to their competitive status in the 1950s.

13. Except when (1) the fraction of the industry covered by the continuing agreement was less than 50% or (2) the fraction of the industry covered by the continuing agreement was more than 50% but another fraction of the same industry, between 10% and 50%, *was* affected by the Act. Such cases were classified as ambiguous. I should also emphasize that the decisions by the Restrictive Practices Court to allow certain agreements to continue do not appear to have been determined by any specific characteristics of the industries involved (see the discussion in chapter 2). Nor was the evolution of these industries similar during the 1960s. Take, for instance, the two collusive industries included in my sample for chapter 4 and assigned to the group that was not affected by the 1956 legislation: cement and glazed tiles. In the cement industry the five-firm concentration ratio increased from 0.86 in 1958 to only 0.89 in 1968, while the price-cost margin increased from 0.25 to 0.29 during the same period. On the other hand, in the glazed tile industry the five-firm concentration ratio increased from 0.65 in 1958 to 0.94 in 1968, and the price-cost margin fell from 0.19 to 0.18 during the same period.

made during the 1960s in previously cartelized industries and were still in force in the early or mid-1970s (before being discovered and referred to the Court). Most of the industries in this group were excluded from the samples used in chapters 4–7 for various reasons—for instance, because the fraction of industry sales revenue covered by products subject to collusion was lower than 50%, or because the agreement was very unstable or the restrictions were not very significant. One has to acknowledge that these industries may not be a random sample, but they are very few anyway. Details on these and other special cases are provided in appendix A.

Export Agreements

A small complication that has arisen with the above method of classifying the industries relates to the operation of export agreements. As mentioned in chapter 2, export agreements were not registrable under the 1956 Act. Thus information on whether any given collusive industry had a restrictive agreement for the export market in addition to the one for the home market is often not available. Furthermore, little is known about whether and when any particular export agreement was abandoned. Now if exports in a collusive industry were never subject to restrictions, or if they were subject to restrictions but remained so after 1958, then the impact of the 1956 legislation on competition in the industry would be smaller than what we would measure it to be under the assumption of no difference between the home market and the export market. Only in the case where the restrictions originally applied to both markets and were subsequently dropped in both markets would we be measuring things correctly.

It could be argued that this is indeed what happened in many, probably most, cases. It is clear from the available information that a large number of agreements covered exports as well as domestic sales. Also, once collusion had broken down in the domestic market, it may have been difficult for firms to maintain it in the export market, especially in the context of intensifying international competition of the 1960s and the 1970s. To this argument one could add that the whole issue is of no importance for industries with insignificant exports.

Still, the issue should not be dismissed so easily. In a few cases, we know that the export market was not subject to collusion, and we can take this into account when calculating the fraction of industry sales subject to significant restrictions in the 1950s. More often, however, either we know that exports were regulated but we do not know for how long, or we have no information at all. In such cases I have assumed that the export market was affected by the 1956 Act in the same way that the domestic market was. Note that the effect of the potential misclassification of industries caused by this assumption can only be an overestimation of the impact of the 1956 Act on competition. In other words, some industries that should really be excluded from the sample as ambiguous may be classified in the group of industries with a change of competition regime in my data set, and some that should be really classified in the control group may be excluded from my data set as ambiguous. Thus the results obtained in chapters 4–7 of the book might understate, if anything, the effect of price competition on the endogenous variables of interest.

However, even this possibility is very remote. To check the *maximum* potential misclassification of industries due to export agreements, I estimated the approximate ratio of exports to total sales in 1958 for all the industries with available concentration ratios for that year, and I reclassified the industries, using the 10% and 50% cutoff points, on the assumption that the export market was *not* affected by the 1956 Act. I found only two industries whose classification changed, which means that the whole issue can be ignored for all practical purposes, at least as long as industries are classified on the basis of cutoff points such as the ones I have used.

Summary of the Classification Criteria

This concludes my discussion of the construction of the competition data. To summarize, an industry in my data was assigned to the group of industries that experienced a change of competition regime if it had been subject to significant collusive agreements in the 1950s covering at least 50% of total sales revenue and these agreements were subsequently abandoned. It was assigned to the control group if less than 10% of the industry was affected by the legislation. Intermediate cases, defined as ambiguous, were excluded.

A Comparison with the Broadberry and Crafts Classification

Broadberry and Crafts (1996, 2000), who have carried out a separate survey of restrictive agreements in British industry in the 1950s, have used somewhat different criteria than the ones that I use here to classify industries as collusive, competitive, or ambiguous in the 1950s. As a result, their categorization of industries is different from mine in several cases, although in almost all of these the difference is by one class (i.e., collusive versus ambiguous, or ambiguous versus competitive). Broadberry and Crafts use the three-digit level of aggregation, while I typically use more disaggregated industry categories. A side effect of this is that the divergence between our respective classifications is smaller than it would have been if I had used the three-digit level of aggregation as well. More specifically, there are three main differences between their classification criteria and mine.

First, Broadberry and Crafts rely heavily on registered agreements, and make relatively little use of other sources on collusion in British industry. For instance, they do not mention the Monopolies and Restrictive Practices Commission reports or the Board of Trade annual reports. They do report some information from the Political and Economic Planning survey, however, although it is not clear how they are using this information when classifying the industries. A comparison of their lists of industries with mine suggests that this factor accounts for part, although not most, of the divergence between our respective classifications.

Second, their two principal criteria for assessing the significance of registered agreements are (1) the existence of a detailed price list with nationwide application, and (2) whether the agreement was referred to the Restrictive Practices Court by the Registrar or at least specifically mentioned in the Registrar's reports as being a pricing agreement. These criteria are somewhat different from the ones that I use to classify the significance of particular types of restrictions (see above). For instance, I do not regard price-fixing agreements that contain a detailed price list as being necessarily more significant or more effective than ones which do not. Clearly, the choice of criteria for assessing the significance of particular agreements is to some extent subjective. As it turns out, however, the difference between the Broadberry and Crafts approach and my approach in this respect does not result in any major discrepancies between our respective classifications of industries, partly because most of the ambiguous cases end up in the intermediate category both in their categorization and in mine. Nevertheless, this factor adds to the divergence between our respective classifications.

Third, it is not clear whether or how Broadberry and Crafts are using the proportion of an industry's total sales covered by products subject to agreements as a criterion in their classification. A comparison of their lists of industries with mine suggests that they have classified as competitive some industries with very low incidence of collusion, just as I have done, but at the same time they have classified as collusive several industries with agreements covering considerably less than 50% of total industry sales. My approach is different, and this also accounts for a good part of the divergence between our respective classifications.

The Incidence of Collusion across Sectors

Table 3.1 summarizes the available information on the occurrence of collusion across manufacturing sectors in the 1950s. The industry definitions used in this table are taken from the official concentration statistics for 1958, as reported in summary table 5 of the *Report on the Census of Production, 1963* (London: H.M.S.O., 1967), and correspond

Table 3.1
Competition and collusion across manufacturing sectors in the 1950s

	No. of industries classified as		
	Collusive	Ambiguous	Competitive
Mining and quarrying	4	0	0
Food, drink, and tobacco	8	8	14
Chemicals and allied products	1	4	8
Basic metal manufacture	12	1	2
Mechanical engineering	6	10	8
Instrument engineering	0	3	2
Electrical engineering	12	2	5
Shipbuilding and vehicles	0	4	2
Other metal products	9	4	2
Textiles	8	9	9
Leather, leather goods, and fur	0	0	4
Clothing and footwear	0	1	11
Bricks, pottery, glass, cement, etc.	8	4	1
Timber, furniture, etc.	1	1	4
Paper, printing, and publishing	5	2	3
Other manufacturing industries	2	3	5
Total	76	56	80

to Census four-digit industries.[14] The 212 industries included in table 3.1 cover most of the manufacturing sector, although certain sectors, such as chemicals or instruments, may be somewhat under-represented, and others, such as basic metals or textiles, may be slightly overrepresented. Since this sample will also be used in the next section to examine the links between the incidence of collusion and other variables, industries without available concentration data for 1958 are not included. However, there is no reason to believe that this causes any significant bias with respect to comparisons across sectors.

On the whole, table 3.1 provides a fairly accurate picture of car-telization in British manufacturing in the 1950s, distinguishing be-tween collusive industries, competitive industries, and industries with ambiguous state of competition. Table 3.2, which uses the same sample of industries as table 3.1, summarizes the evolution of com-petition between 1958 and 1975 across sectors, distinguishing be-tween industries with a change in competition regime and industries not affected by the 1956 Act (and omitting any ambiguous cases).[15] A much more detailed account of the evolution of competition across all manufacturing industries can be found in appendix A.

As can be seen from these tables, collusive agreements were much more widespread in some sectors than in others. In particular, sec-tors with a high or very high incidence of collusion (measured as the fraction of collusive industries in the total number of industries in any given sector) include mining and quarrying, basic metals, other metal products, building materials, and electrical engineering. Sec-tors with a low or very low incidence of collusion include leather goods, clothing and footwear, and instruments. In the case of chem-icals, the relatively low incidence of collusion shown in table 3.1 is to some extent a feature of the particular sample used, since a number

14. In constructing this sample, I have excluded four industries with significant gov-ernment participation or intervention in the 1950s (sugar, ordnance and small arms, aircraft, locomotives), two industries that hardly existed prior to the mid-1950s (syn-thetic rubber, tufted carpets), and one where imports were very much higher than domestic production and were subject to regulation (iron ore).

15. In comparing the two tables, recall that some collusive industries experienced no change in regime, and for others the evolution was ambiguous because of agreements with uncertain effect on competition that were made in the 1960s. Another reason for the discrepancies in the classification of industries across the two tables is that for table 3.1 the 10% and 50% cutoff points are applied to the period 1951–1958, while for table 3.2 they are applied to the period after 1958. The correlations reported in section 3.4 below are based on table 3.1, but this of course is not the case for the results of later chapters.

Table 3.2
The evolution of competition across manufacturing sectors after 1958

	No. of industries with	
	Change in competition regime between 1958 and 1975	No change in competition regime between 1958 and 1975
Mining and quarrying	1	0
Food, drink, and tobacco	8	15
Chemicals and allied products	1	8
Basic metal manufacture	12	2
Mechanical engineering	5	8
Instrument engineering	0	2
Electrical engineering	11	5
Shipbuilding and vehicles	1	2
Other metal products	8	3
Textiles	7	9
Leather, leather goods, and fur	0	4
Clothing and footwear	0	11
Bricks, pottery, glass, cement, etc.	5	3
Timber, furniture, etc.	1	4
Paper, printing, and publishing	3	3
Other manufacturing industries	2	5
Total	65	84

of chemical industries with restrictive agreements are not included in the sample. However, the figures also reflect the absence of agreements in most of the advertising-intensive, consumer-good industries in the chemical sector.

Of the other sectors, paper, printing, and publishing has an above-average incidence of collusion; textiles and mechanical engineering are intermediate; and food and drink, shipbuilding and vehicles, wood products, and other manufacturing have a below-average incidence of collusion. These statistics reveal little about the structural industry characteristics associated with the incidence of collusion in the 1950s, however. This is the subject of the next section.

3.4 The Determinants of Collusion

The data on the British cartels of the 1950s provide a very rare opportunity to examine the impact of several structural industry characteristics on the incidence of collusive pricing, using information which is unusually comprehensive and, as argued above, relatively free from selection bias. An extensive and detailed analysis of the determinants of collusion in British manufacturing industry has been carried out elsewhere (Symeonidis 1999b). Here I will present only some basic statistics that highlight and summarize most of the results obtained, with a focus on results that are particularly relevant as a background for the rest of this book.

In particular, I will discuss how the incidence of explicit collusion is related to a small number of basic structural industry characteristics, namely, capital intensity or the level of sunk entry costs, concentration, and the scope for advertising or R&D. As it turns out, the results reported below are robust to several extensions of the present approach, including the use of econometric analysis, the adoption of a two-stage estimation procedure in order to deal with potential endogeneity issues, the introduction of several more control variables, the use of alternative proxies for some of the variables of interest, and the use of modified criteria to classify industries according to their competitive status in order to check for any potential selection bias (see Symeonidis 1999b).

Theoretical Background

Firms that collude have generally two problems to solve. They must coordinate on a price or a set of prices. And they must ensure that collusion is enforceable, that is, that none of the parties has an incentive to cheat. Thus a common distinction in the literature on the factors facilitating or hindering collusion is between coordination and enforcement of collusive agreements.

Product homogeneity, high industry concentration, the absence of significant cost or size differences between firms, institutional features such as the existence of an industry trade association, and sociocultural characteristics such as "homogeneity of values" and social ties among senior managers are often cited as factors facilitating coordination on a collusive price or set of prices (see, e.g., Scherer and Ross 1990). In addition, coordination must be easier under a permissive climate of competition policy or when collusive agreements are not illegal. While these ideas are intuitively appealing, they have proved difficult to model within a formal game-theoretic framework.

On the other hand, the issue of enforcement of collusive agreements has led to a substantial formal literature on cartel stability. These models can be used to analyze both tacit and explicit collusion when firms cannot legally enforce agreements. They are all formalizations of the basic idea that firms may be able to sustain collusion by threatening to retaliate at a future time in the event of a price cut today. This literature has produced a number of unambiguous predictions regarding the factors that promote cartel stability. These include low uncertainty about demand, conditions that facilitate the monitoring of rival firms, and short retaliation lags (see Tirole 1988, Martin 2002). Another common finding is that high concentration facilitates collusion, although Brock and Scheinkman (1985) have argued that the link may be nonmonotonic in the presence of capacity constraints. Finally, this literature predicts that collusion is hindered by differences in quality or "perceived quality" between firms in vertically differentiated markets (Häckner 1994, Symeonidis 1999a), and will therefore occur less frequently in industries with high advertising effectiveness, and possibly also in industries with high technological opportunity, than in exogenous sunk cost industries.

One problem in much of the theoretical literature on collusion is that market structure is taken as given and entry is not explicitly modeled.[16] It may be argued, however, that any factors that limit the extent of entry (and, more generally, the volatility of market shares) facilitate collusion, because coordination and monitoring are easier when the identity of the principal competitors does not change much over time, and also because the gain from collusion will be less quickly or less easily eliminated by entry. Since capital intensity implies significant sunk costs of entry, this argument can provide a theoretical rationale for a positive effect of capital intensity and the level of sunk entry costs on the likelihood of collusion.

To summarize, the theoretical literature suggests a number of factors that are expected to facilitate or hinder collusion. Some of them are difficult to observe or cannot be tested in empirical work using cross-section data. Of those that are in principle testable, capital intensity or the level of sunk entry costs, and possibly also concentration, are thought to facilitate collusion, while demand uncertainty

---

16. See Fershtman and Pakes (2000) for a recent theoretical approach to collusion that allows for entry and exit.

and the scope for product differentiation, including vertical differentiation through advertising or R&D, are expected to hinder collusion.

Previous Empirical Evidence on the Determinants of Collusion

Despite the rich theoretical literature on the subject, empirical studies of the determinants of cartel formation and sustainability using direct evidence, rather than relying on profitability indices to infer the possible operation of collusive arrangements, are relatively rare. An early study of collusive pricing in the UK in the 1950s by Phillips (1972) did not obtain clear results, partly because of data limitations. Other studies, using US data, have each produced clearer results, but the overall picture is rather mixed. Thus, while the findings by Hay and Kelley (1974) suggest that collusion is less likely under product differentiation, this is not confirmed by Dick (1996a). Collusion is more likely in concentrated industries, according to Hay and Kelley (1974) or Fraas and Greer (1977), but not according to Dick (1996a) or Asch and Seneca (1976). And while Dick (1996a) finds a clear positive link between capital intensity and the likelihood of collusion, Hay and Kelley (1974) find no link between the ratio of fixed to total costs and collusive conduct.[17]

A possible shortcoming of these studies is that the data either originate from antitrust cases, and may therefore be subject to selection bias, or relate to export cartels, which cover only a very small fraction of total economic activity. In contrast, the data on the British cartels of the 1950s provide information which is both comprehensive and, as argued above, relatively free from selection bias.

Data and Variables

I will use a simple but powerful way to model collusion in this chapter, namely a dummy variable, COLL, which takes the value 1 for collusive industries and the value 0 for competitive industries.[18] As pointed out above, an industry was classified as collusive in the

---

17. There is also an empirical literature on the related but different issue of cartel duration (for instance, Jacquemin et al., 1981; Suslow, 1991; Dick, 1996b). Probably the most robust result from this line of research is the negative effect of demand uncertainty on cartel stability.

18. Going beyond this binary classification—for instance, by classifying industries with respect to the "degree of collusion,"—is not possible, given the information available.

1950s if the products subject to significant restrictions accounted for more than 50% of total industry sales revenue, and it was classified as competitive if the products subject to significant or uncertain restrictions accounted for less than 10% of industry sales revenue. All other cases were excluded as ambiguous, leaving a sample of 156 industries.[19]

The concentration measure used here, $C5$, is the share of the five largest producers in the total sales revenue of UK firms, excluding firms with fewer than twenty-five employees. This is the measure that is also used in later chapters. The data for 1958 (a year when the restrictive agreements were still in place) were taken from summary table 5 of the 1963 Census of Production, and correspond to Census four-digit industries.[20] This level of aggregation seems appropriate for the analysis of collusive pricing.[21] However, when competition tends to operate at the regional rather than the national level, these concentration ratios may be a poor measure of market structure. I made an effort to identify such cases and exclude them from the sample. Five industries were thus excluded, bringing the final sample size to 151.

For capital intensity or the level of sunk entry costs, I use two alternative measures: the logarithm of the industry capital-labor ratio, $\ln K/L$, and the logarithm of the industry capital stock divided by the number of plants in the industry, $\ln K/N$. The former is a standard capital intensity measure, while the latter is a measure of the absolute capital requirements for setting up a plant of average scale. The data on the value of the capital stock are estimates rather than primary data, and were taken from O'Mahony and Oulton (1990). See chapter 4 for a detailed description of these data.

Although the capital stock data were at the three-digit level of aggregation (which corresponds to broader industry definitions than

19. Since there were various possible reasons for classifying an industry as ambiguous, it did not seem appropriate to regard these industries as intermediate with respect to the state of competition and include them in the sample, except as a mere robustness check. As discussed in Symeonidis (1999b), this has no effect on the results.

20. These are the only available concentration data for the 1950s that correspond to the industry categories I will be using to analyze the effects of the 1956 legislation on market structure in later chapters.

21. In some cases, a four-digit industry may comprise two or more submarkets which are relatively independent on the demand side. I identified eight such cases in the sample. Three were in the collusive group, and five in the competitive group, so it is unlikely that any bias is caused from this factor.

the four-digit level), it was often possible to derive reasonable approximations of capital stock at the four-digit level by using Census data on the fraction of the three-digit industry investment accounted for by each four-digit industry within any given three-digit industry. In particular, I computed estimates of four-digit capital stock by multiplying the 1958 three-digit capital stock by the ratio of four-digit investment to three-digit investment, averaged over 1954 and 1958.

Data on investment, employment, and plant numbers were taken from the industry reports of the *Report on the Census of Production for 1958* (London: H.M.S.O., 1960–1963), and some adjustments were made to ensure comparability in light of the fact that the O'Mahony and Oulton figures are based on the 1968 Standard Industrial Classification, which is somewhat different from the 1958 S.I.C. Firms employing fewer than twenty-five persons were not taken into account.

Finally, I used advertising-sales ratios (ADS) and R&D-sales ratios (RDS) to classify the industries in the sample. In particular, the industries were split, on the one hand, into low-advertising and advertising-intensive, using the 1% ADS as a cutoff point, and, on the other, into low-R&D and R&D-intensive, using the 1% RDS as a cutoff point. The variable *AD1* was defined as a dummy variable equal to 1 for industries with advertising-sales ratio higher than 1% and 0 otherwise. Similarly, the variable *RD1* was defined as a dummy equal to 1 for industries with R&D-sales ratio higher than 1% and 0 otherwise. The 1% cutoff point was chosen because it is commonly used to classify industries according to advertising or R&D intensity. In addition, it resulted in a not-too-unbalanced split, whereas a higher cutoff point (2%, say) would leave only a small number of industries in the advertising-intensive and R&D-intensive categories. In any case, using the 2% cutoff point gave similar results. Of the 151 industries in the sample, 111 had an ADS lower than 1% and 119 had an RDS lower than 1%.

To construct these ratios for 1958, I combined data from various sources, using an approach similar to that used in later chapters of this book for constructing typical or average advertising-sales ratios and R&D-sales ratios over the entire period 1954–1975. Details can be found in chapter 4 and in Symeonidis (1999b).

There are several reasons why the advertising-sales ratios and the R&D-sales ratios are used here merely to split the industries into groups rather than as continuous variables. First, data limitations made it difficult to construct exact figures, especially for R&D intensity and for advertising intensity in low-advertising industries. Second, a similar approach is used in later chapters, where the analysis is conducted separately for exogenous sunk cost, advertising-intensive and R&D-intensive industries. And third, these binary classifications reflect exogenous industry characteristics, such as advertising effectiveness or technological opportunity, but are relatively robust to other factors that may affect advertising or R&D intensity. Since my primary purpose here is to study the links between the incidence of collusion and some of its potential determinants, the use of the dummy variables $AD1$ and $RD1$ is a way of minimizing the problem of the potential endogeneity of advertising or R&D intensity.[22] Note that the fact that the results were similar when cutoff points of 2% were used instead of 1% strengthens the case for treating $AD1$ and $RD1$ as exogenous, since it suggests that the results are not driven by industries with intermediate advertising or R&D intensity. They are, rather, driven by industries with either very low or very high advertising/R&D intensity, and it is clear that very low or very high advertising/R&D intensity is a largely exogenous feature of industries.

Statistical Evidence

Descriptive statistics, separately for collusive and competitive industries, are given in table 3.3, and simple correlation coefficients between $COLL$ and each of the other five variables are given in table

---

22. The idea is that while the actual level of the advertising-sales ratio and the R&D-sales ratio may depend on many variables, including the intensity of price competition, it is generally exogenous industry characteristics that will determine whether these ratios are above or below 1% (or 2%). Thus, for an industry below the 1% cutoff point, advertising/R&D is not an important strategic variable: in such an industry, advertising is not very effective in raising consumers' willingness to pay or there is little scope for technological innovation from within the industry. On the other hand, in an industry above the 1% cutoff point (and even more in an industry above the 2% cutoff point), advertising/R&D "works." Of course, whether such an industry has an advertising-sales or R&D-sales ratio of 5% or 10% may be largely determined by endogenous factors. However, my binary variables $AD1$ and $RD1$ are not very sensitive to endogenous factors that affect advertising intensity and R&D intensity.

I should also point out that a comparison of advertising-sales ratios and R&D-sales ratios across various years revealed very few instances where an industry had moved from below 1% to above 1% or vice versa; and in most cases this was due to an exogenous institutional change, the introduction of TV advertising in the UK in the 1950s.

Table 3.3
Descriptive statistics for collusive and noncollusive industries, 1958

		Collusive (n = 71)	Noncollusive (n = 80)
$C5$	Mean	0.61	0.52
	Standard deviation	0.20	0.28
	Minimum	0.19	0.08
	Maximum	0.98	0.99
$\ln K/L$	Mean	1.23	0.64
	Standard deviation	0.73	0.86
	Minimum	−0.99	−1.18
	Maximum	3.10	2.38
$\ln K/N$	Mean	0.01	−1.09
	Standard deviation	1.15	1.33
	Minimum	−2.98	−3.60
	Maximum	2.17	3.42
No. of industries with $AD1 = 0$		62	49
No. of industries with $AD1 = 1$		9	31
No. of industries with $RD1 = 0$		59	60
No. of industries with $RD1 = 1$		12	20

Note: n indicates the number of industries.

3.4. There is a strong positive correlation between *COLL* and both $\ln K/L$ and $\ln K/N$, statistically significant at the 1% level, suggesting that capital intensity and the level of setup costs are important determinants of the likelihood of collusive pricing. There is also a positive correlation between *COLL* and *C5*, which is significant at the 5% level but not at the 1% level. As can be seen from table 3.3, the mean level of *C5* is 0.61 for collusive industries and 0.52 for noncollusive industries. Moreover, a test of independence of the respective means of *C5* in the two groups rejects the null hypothesis of independence at the 5% level although not at the 1% level.[23] It should be emphasized, however, that concentration is highly correlated with both $\ln K/L$ and $\ln K/N$ in these data: the correlation coefficient between *C5* and $\ln K/L$ is 0.53, and that between *C5* and $\ln K/N$ is 0.64. Thus it may be the case that the relatively higher level of *C5* in collusive industries simply reflects the higher level of capital

23. A Wilcoxon rank-sum test of the hypothesis that the distribution of *C5* is the same in the two groups also rejects the null at the 5% level but not at the 1% level.

Table 3.4
Correlation coefficients between *COLL* and other variables, 1958

	Correlation coefficient (significance level)
COLL and *C5*	0.19 (0.02)
COLL and ln K/L	0.34 (0.00)
COLL and ln K/N	0.40 (0.00)
COLL and *AD1*	−0.29 (0.0002)
COLL and *RD1*	−0.10 (0.23)

Table 3.5
Advertising, R&D, and collusive pricing, late 1950s

	No. of collusive industries	No. of noncollusive industries
Industries with ADS < 1%	62	49
Industries with 1% < ADS < 2%	6	14
Industries with 2% < ADS < 5%	3	6
Industries with ADS > 5%	0	11
Industries with RDS < 1%	59	60
Industries with 1% < RDS < 2%	5	11
Industries with RDS > 2%	7	9

intensity and setup costs in this group. I will return to this issue below.

Note also the strong and highly significant negative correlation between *COLL* and *AD1*, suggesting that collusion is less likely in advertising-intensive industries than in industries with low advertising intensity, as well as the negative relationship between *COLL* and *RD1*, which is not, however, statistically significant at the 5% or even the 10% level. A more detailed breakdown of industries according to their competition regime, advertising intensity, and R&D intensity is provided in table 3.5. Note that none of the industries in the sample with ADS higher than 5% is collusive.

To check whether there is any (linear) association between concentration and collusion once we control for capital intensity, I have also computed the partial correlation coefficient between *COLL* and *C5*, keeping ln K/L constant. It is equal to 0.007, with a significance level of 0.93. On the other hand, the partial correlation coefficient between *COLL* and ln K/L, keeping *C5* constant, is equal to 0.294, and is significant at the 1% level. Similar results are obtained when using $\ln K/N$ instead of $\ln K/L$. In other words, the association between collusion and concentration in these data virtually disappears when one controls for capital intensity or setup cost, but the association between collusion and capital intensity or setup cost remains strong even when one controls for concentration.

These results are confirmed in Symeonidis (1999b), where the analysis presented here is extended in several ways. In particular, I have run regressions of COLL on C5, AD1, RD1, a measure of demand growth, and a measure of capital intensity or setup cost ($\ln K/L$ or $\ln K/N$), and I have also allowed for a possible nonlinear effect of C5 and the growth variable on COLL. In some specifications I have included among the regressors a proxy for the degree of foreign competition, based on effective rates of protection across industries. I have also included among the regressors a set of sector dummies as a partial check for misspecification due to omitted variables or the presence of industry effects. I have estimated the model using both a standard one-step probit specification and a two-step procedure meant to control for the endogeneity of concentration. I have included a producer-good/consumer-good dummy among the regressors or alternatively I have run regressions separately for producer-good and consumer-good industries. I have also estimated the model using a slightly smaller sample, excluding industries with a high value of imports relative to sales by domestic firms, to confirm that no measurement error is caused by the fact that the concentration ratios are not adjusted for imports.

Finally, and perhaps most important, I have experimented with several different definitions of the variable COLL, using modified criteria to classify the industries as collusive or noncollusive, in an attempt to check for measurement error or selection bias in the classification of industries. For instance, in one of these experiments I have treated all ambiguous industries as intermediate, and in another I have classified as collusive those industries which did not register any agreements but are reported as having been collusive or potentially collusive in the Political and Economic Planning survey or the Board of Trade annual reports.

The results were robust to all these extensions and can be briefly summarized as follows. The strong positive association between capital intensity or the level of setup costs and collusive pricing is confirmed throughout. On the other hand, no clear link between concentration and the likelihood of collusion can be found. In particular, there is no evidence of any linear association, although a nonlinear relationship is present in some regressions, with both very low and very high concentration hindering collusion. There is strong evidence that collusive pricing is less likely in advertising-intensive industries than in low-advertising industries, and weak evidence that it is less likely in R&D-intensive industries than in low-R&D industries. Some of the results indicate that collusion is more likely under conditions of moderate market growth than in a market with declining or stagnant demand, and less likely under fast growth than under moderate growth. Finally, my proxy for the extent of foreign competition is negatively associated with collusion in many regressions, but the effect is relatively weak and not statistically significant once sector dummies are included among the regressors.[24]

Interpreting the Evidence

A possible reason for the absence of any clear link between concentration and the incidence of collusion in the present context is that the coordination and monitoring of collusion must have been greatly facilitated by the fact that the agreements were not illegal and were often operated by members of trade associations. In fact, the administration of collusive agreements was one of the primary functions of British industrial trade associations in the 1950s, and often their main function (see Political and Economic Planning 1957). On the other hand, a nonlinear relationship between concentration and collusion could result from the fact that high levels of concentration are often associated with significant firm asymmetries or the presence of dominant firms, and these factors may hinder collusion.[25]

---

24. Thus, although there is no reason to doubt that the growth of tariffs in the 1920s and the 1930s had greatly facilitated the operation of price agreements, as argued by Swann et al. (1974, p. 197), it is not clear whether tariff protection was an important determinant of the incidence of collusion across industries in the 1950s.

25. One argument which was used by the authors of the 1946 Board of Trade report on British cartels to explain the absence of restrictive agreements in several industries where a single firm controlled a very large part of the market is that in these industries there may be little scope for collusion, since prices are effectively decided by the dominant firm. However, such cases are not very numerous at the four-digit industry level—although they may be more numerous at a lower level of aggregation. Moreover, some industries with dominant firms are not included in the present data set, because their concentration ratio is not reported in the official statistics to avoid disclosure of information about specific firms.

Some remarks on the observed weak negative link between R&D intensity and collusion are also in order, especially when this is compared against the much stronger negative link between advertising intensity and collusion. There are at least two factors that may help explain why the negative link is not stronger for R&D intensity as well. First, a potentially important institutional factor is that public procurement procedures in the UK in the 1950s did little to deter collusion in some R&D-intensive industries, perhaps because their main objective was not to promote competition but to maintain a stable supply by means of a smooth sharing of orders among established firms in these industries.

A second explanation derives from models of cartel stability which predict that quality differences between firms in vertically differentiated markets hinder collusion. Large differences in product quality between firms in R&D-intensive industries are probably not as common as large differences in brand image between firms in advertising-intensive industries. This is because in an R&D-intensive industry, a low-quality firm may find it difficult to compete with a high-quality rival, while in an advertising-intensive industry, heavy advertisers coexist with firms that do not advertise but employ other marketing strategies.[26] Thus collusive pricing should be easier to sustain in R&D-intensive industries than in advertising-intensive industries.

There is in fact some case-study evidence on the British cartels which seems to be consistent with the above interpretation. In some R&D-intensive industries, such as heavy electrical machinery or telecommunications equipment, the collusive agreements were mostly operated by a small number of R&D-intensive firms, which were the only UK producers of the products in question. Hence price collusion was presumably not hindered by large quality differences. Moreover, in several other industries the agreements involved "patent pooling" and exchange of technical information (but not cooperation in R&D). These schemes may have been used to limit quality differences and ensure the success of the pricing arrangements.

Finally, it must be acknowledged that the use of a cutoff point such as an RDS of 1% or 2% to classify industries may not be sufficient for capturing the links between collusion and technological opportunity

---

26. Differences in product quality between firms will also be small in industries with process rather product R&D. This may also weaken any link between R&D intensity and collusion, although it needs to be said that several industries where process R&D is important, such as basic chemicals, are not included in the sample used here.

across industries. As will be discussed in detail in chapter 6, there is indeed evidence of a strong negative relationship between collusion and the number of innovations produced across UK manufacturing industries *within the RDS > 1% class* during the 1950s.

The two most important factors that facilitated explicit collusive pricing agreements in UK manufacturing during the 1950s are low advertising effectiveness and high capital intensity or setup costs. The observed negative link between advertising and the likelihood of collusion is consistent with models of cartel stability that emphasize vertical product differentiation, and also with key insights from the literature on coordination, as opposed to enforcement, of collusive agreements. Note that this negative link cannot be due to a negative effect of collusion on advertising. In chapter 5 I will show that the intensification of price competition following the abolition of cartels in the UK caused advertising intensity to fall. Thus the negative association between advertising and collusion in the 1950s that I find in the present chapter can only mean that collusion is less likely to occur if advertising intensity (and hence advertising effectiveness) is high.

The positive relationship between capital intensity or setup costs and the incidence of collusion is of particular interest because the role of these variables has not been much emphasized in the theoretical literature on collusion. A possible objection to this finding is that capital intensity and the level of sunk costs, both of which are inevitably measured here with some error, may in fact be picking up the effect of concentration in the present sample. To assess the validity of this objection, I have tried using three-digit (unadjusted) $\ln K/L$ and $\ln K/N$. The statistical results were not significantly affected, which implies that they are generally robust to more or less measurement error in these variables. These results suggest that the ease of entry into industries is also a key factor—together with industry characteristics that affect coordination and the enforcement of collusive agreements—in the formation and stability of cartels.

3.5 Concluding Remarks

This chapter has prepared the way for the analysis of the effects of the 1956 legislation in the rest of the book. In the first part, I have described the available data on cartels and competition in British industry from the 1950s to the mid-1970s. I have argued, on the basis of extensive indirect evidence, that there should be no significant measurement error or selection bias in the competition data, and I have also emphasized that any such data problems would not create serious difficulties for the analysis of the effects of the 1956 Act, since the key distinction that needs to be made when carrying out this analysis is between industries with a change of competition regime and industries without such a change. Finally, I have described in detail my methodology for constructing these two groups of industries.

I have then discussed, in the second part, some statistical evidence on the factors facilitating or hindering explicit collusive pricing across British manufacturing industries during the 1950s. The evidence suggests that the most important factors that facilitated collusion were low advertising effectiveness and high capital intensity or setup costs. Let me now conclude this chapter by pointing out some of the implications of this statistical evidence for the rest of the book.

A key implication is that the group of industries with a change in competition regime after 1958 and the group without such a change did not differ significantly with respect to their market structure prior to the introduction of the legislation. This lends some support to a central assumption of this book, namely, that any difference in the evolution of market structure between the two groups after 1958 can be attributed to the effect of the 1956 legislation rather than to any unobserved characteristics that may be correlated with both concentration and collusion.

This argument should not be overemphasized, however. The reason is that the similarity of initial conditions is neither a necessary nor a sufficient condition for establishing the validity of the difference-in-differences methodology in the present context. This is because what matters most is trends, not levels; in other words, the methodology is valid as long as there are no unobserved characteristics that differ between the two groups of industries and cause them to *evolve* in different ways during the period under study. The fact that the two groups did not differ significantly with respect to their initial market structure conditions is only an encouraging indication in that respect. At the very least, it may help dispel a potential concern with the present research design, namely, the possibility that some of the difference that we observe between the two groups after 1958 is due to purely statistical factors (i.e., the simple fact that the scope for an increase in concentration is larger, the lower the initial level of concentration in an industry). Further support for the validity of the difference-in-differences methodology will be provided in later chapters by an analysis of the evolution of market structure in the two groups of industries *before* the effective implementation of the 1956 legislation.

On the other hand, the negative association between advertising intensity, and possibly also R&D intensity, and collusion may seem, at first sight, to complicate the interpretation of some of the results of the next four chapters. However, this is not the case. First, most of the analysis of the effects of the 1956 Act will be performed separately for exogenous sunk cost, advertising-intensive, and R&D-intensive industries. Second, it will be confirmed that these associations are due to more fundamental correlations between the propensity to collude and exogenous industry characteristics, such as advertising effectiveness and technological opportunity, which can be largely controlled for in regression analysis using panel data. And third, further support for the key maintained assumptions of the present study will be derived in later chapters from an analysis of the evolution of advertising intensity and innovative output in the two groups of industries *before* the effective implementation of the 1956 legislation.

4

Price Competition and the Evolution of Concentration in Exogenous Sunk Cost Industries

4.1 Introduction

In this chapter I begin the analysis of the effects of the intensification of price competition in British industry following the 1956 cartel legislation. This chapter focuses on the effect of competition on market structure in exogenous sunk cost industries. In a seminal paper, Selten (1984) predicted that a switch from collusive to noncollusive behavior caused by a toughening of competition policy would cause a decrease in the number of firms in a homogeneous-good industry. The reason for this result is that the number of firms is determined by a free-entry condition which requires that net profit in long-run equilibrium be driven to (almost) zero by entry irrespective of firm conduct. A shift in the competition regime that causes the gross profit of each firm to fall, given the initial industry structure, triggers a process of exit and merger through which gross profit rises again to a level that covers sunk costs. In other words, the zero-profit condition is restored by means of a restructuring of the industry. This framework has been enriched in Sutton's (1991, 1997a, 1998) comprehensive theory of market structure, which distinguishes between exogenous sunk cost, advertising-intensive, and R&D-intensive industries, and examines the links between market size, sunk costs, and concentration in the three types of industries.

This chapter sets out to test the Selten-Sutton prediction of a positive effect of price competition on concentration in exogenous sunk cost industries. I begin by presenting a simple theoretical framework for analyzing competition in exogenous sunk cost industries based on Selten (1984) and Sutton (1991), and I also illustrate the results using a specific theoretical model. This is followed by a detailed discussion of the data set used for the econometric analysis. Since many of the variables used here will also be used in later chapters, this discussion serves as a reference for later chapters as well. Finally, I present the econometric results. They suggest that firm conduct, which is partly determined by exogenous institutional factors, is an important determinant of market structure.

While the idea that more intense price competition might lead to higher concentration is certainly not new, the empirical evidence on this issue has so far been inconclusive. Early attempts to capture this effect by introducing lagged profitability as a regressor in empirical models of the determinants of concentration change have produced mixed results (see Martin 1979a, 1979b). More recently, the literature on economic integration has found some evidence of a positive effect of a reduction of trade barriers on concentration (for example, Caves 1988, Sleuwaegen and Yamawaki 1988). However, since economic integration involves more than just an intensification of price competition, it is not easy to draw clear implications for the competition-concentration relationship from these results.[1] A similar difficulty arises with respect to studies of the effects of deregulation and liberalization on industrial structure and performance: these policy interventions typically involve a reduction or removal of entry barriers as well as an intensification of competition, and it is not easy to separate the two effects.

Studies of the impact of cartel policy on the structure of industry should be more informative in this respect. In Britain, the argument that the breaking up of cartels might lead to higher concentration was used in some Restrictive Practices Court cases by associations defending their agreements and became a topic of debate during the early discussions of the effects of the 1956 Act. However, little evidence was available at the time either for or against this view (Wilson 1962). In later years, the hypothesis of a causal link between the introduction of cartel laws and a rise in concentration was also advanced by economic historians who claimed that differences in the evolution of market structure between the US and the UK could be partly attributed to differences in the competition policy regimes in the two countries (Hannah 1979, Freyer 1992).

In particular, Hannah and Freyer argued that the prohibition of cartels in the US in the 1890s was a key factor behind the great merger

---

1. It is equally difficult to interpret the evidence of a positive link between price competition and concentration in US exogenous sunk cost industries reported by Robinson and Chiang (1996), since their measure of competition was based partly on demand characteristics, such as the degree of product homogeneity, and partly on very specific factors that were assumed to affect firms' conduct, such as the infrequency of orders.

wave of the years 1898–1902. This is a view shared by a number of American historians but rejected by others, for it has proved difficult, in detailed empirical studies, to isolate the effect of competition policy from other influences on mergers, such as the rise of large-scale production, changes in corporation law, or the growth of the stock market (see Nelson 1959, Bittlingmayer 1985). Hannah and Freyer contrasted the US experience with that of the UK, where cartel policy was permissive and market structure remained relatively fragmented until the 1960s. After that date the reversal of cartel policy was associated with the great UK merger wave of the 1960s that closed the gap in industrial organization between the two countries. However, Hannah has also warned of the potential dangers of such broad comparisons by highlighting the case of Germany, where, despite the significant increase in the degree of cartelization in the early twentieth century, the predominance of large firms was more noticeable than in Britain.

More systematic evidence on the impact of the 1956 Restrictive Trade Practices Act on the evolution of market structure in the UK was examined in two studies undertaken in the 1970s. Like the present book, these studies were based on a comparison of industries affected by the 1956 legislation and industries not affected (without distinguishing between exogenous sunk cost, advertising-intensive, and R&D-intensive industries). However, they were both subject to methodological problems and produced conflicting results.

The study by Elliott and Gribbin (1977) is the one closer to the present one, in terms of both the research design and the empirical results. These authors examined restrictive agreements of nationwide application between manufacturers registered before 1960. They found that the rise in the five-firm sales concentration ratio between 1958 and 1968 was, on average, significantly larger in industries with terminated agreements than in industries without agreements, and that most of the differential effect occurred between 1963 and 1968. They also noted, however, that market size was growing faster for industries in the latter group throughout the period, so the cause of the observed difference in the evolution of concentration between the two groups is not clear. Moreover, the criteria they used to classify industries to one or the other group were not made explicit, and no attempt was made to use additional data sources in order to identify unregistered agreements or cases of detected collusion after 1960.

On the other hand, O'Brien et al. (1979) examined merger activity over the period 1959–1972 for a sample of about thirty industries split into four groups: a group with agreements upheld by the Court, another with agreements struck down by the Court, a third group comprising industries which voluntarily abandoned their agreements, and a control group of industries which, according to the authors, had not been subject to collusion prior to the introduction of the 1956 Act. Three different measures of merger activity were used: the ratio of expenditure on acquisitions to total assets, the proportion of firms in an industry taking over other firms, and the proportion of firms in an industry being acquired. The authors found no statistically significant difference in the ratio of expenditure on acquisitions to total assets among the four groups, and they also found that the control group had the highest proportion of both acquirers and acquired firms. They concluded that there was no evidence of any effect of the 1956 Act on merger activity during the period under study. However, their sample may have been too small to be representative. Also, the criteria used to classify industries to the four groups were not always clear.[2]

In summary, the empirical evidence from previous studies of the effect of competition on concentration in the UK, and also in the US, has been inconclusive or mixed. This chapter undertakes a systematic and extensive reexamination of the UK evidence, focusing on exogenous sunk cost industries. Later chapters in the book will examine the evidence for advertising-intensive and R&D-intensive industries. Overall, I extend the previous studies of the effects of the 1956 Act on market structure in several ways. First, I relate my empirical analysis to a theoretical framework, two key elements of which are the distinction between classes of industries and the focus on jointly determined endogenous variables. Second, I look at the impact of the Act over a longer time period, from the mid-1950s to the mid-1970s, and for the whole of manufacturing industry. Third, I use more comprehensive data on competition; in particular, I use information from several sources to identify unregistered agreements and cases of collusion in the 1960s. Fourth, I use explicit criteria to classify industries according to their competitive status. Fifth, I pay much attention to the issue of potential selection or endogeneity bias when interpreting the evidence. And, finally, I perform regression analysis to control

---

2. For instance, some of the industries included in the control group had in fact been subject to restrictive agreements in the 1950s, and one of the industries included in the group whose agreements were upheld by the Court dropped the agreement shortly after the Court's decision.

for other influences on the evolution of market structure, firm conduct, and performance in the UK between the 1950s and the 1970s.

4.2   Theoretical Framework

Consider first an exogenous sunk cost industry producing a homogeneous product. A two-stage game can be used to model competition in such an industry. There are N_0 potential entrants. At stage 1 these firms decide whether or not to enter the industry, and those that do enter, pay an exogenously given sunk cost of entry f. We assume that N_0 is sufficiently large so that at any equilibrium of the game there is at least one nonentering firm. At stage 2 those firms that have entered simultaneously set prices or quantities.

The notion of an exogenous sunk cost industry should be seen as a useful approximation. It attempts to capture two ideas. The first is the idea that firms must operate plants at a level close to minimum efficient scale to be able to compete effectively in the long run. It is in this sense that the setup cost f, defined as the cost of acquiring a plant of minimum efficient scale, net of resale value, is assumed to be exogenously determined by technology. This is, of course, a simplification, for it is well known that plants of suboptimal size can often coexist in an industry along with more efficient plants (see Scherer et al. 1975). Still, the average or typical plant size or capacity in an industry will be largely determined by technology. Hence the cost of successful entry will largely depend on exogenously determined characteristics of the production process.

The second thing that the notion of an exogenous sunk cost industry attempts to capture is the idea that in many industries there is limited scope, at any given time, for investment to decrease cost or to enhance quality or brand image. For this reason, the setup cost f is assumed to be the *only* sunk cost in the two-stage game above. Again this is an approximation, since endogenous sunk costs are unlikely to be zero in any industry.[3] What the structure of the two-stage game tries to capture is that these endogenous sunk costs are very low in

---

3. Advertising and R&D are probably not the only endogenous sunk costs incurred by firms. For instance, the cost of developing a network of contacts or relationships may also be thought of as an endogenous sunk cost. The reason for ignoring it in the present book is twofold. First, it is probably less important (or provides less scope for endogenous investments by firms) than advertising or R&D, at least in the manufacturing sector. Second, it is difficult, if not impossible, to measure in a systematic way across industries.

industries where advertising or R&D is not an important strategic variable, and that this is something largely determined exogenously: advertising effectiveness and technological opportunity are simply very low in certain industries.

In other words, while the general model for analyzing the links between price competition, firm strategy, and market structure must necessarily allow for endogenous sunk costs, there is a special limiting case within that general model which arises when advertising effectiveness and technological opportunity are both very low. The equilibria of this limiting-case model coincide with the equilibria of an elementary model in which there is no advertising or R&D. That is the model of the present chapter.

The Second-Stage Subgame

The equilibrium outcome of the second-stage subgame can be represented by a vector of (gross) profits $\pi_i(S, N, t, c_1, \ldots, c_i, \ldots, c_N)$, where S is market size, an exogenous demand-shift parameter; N is the number of firms that have entered at stage 1; c_i is a vector of parameters specific to firm i (such as marginal cost, capacity, the number of plants operated, and so on); and t is a measure of the intensity of price competition. In particular, t captures the idea that for any given number of firms N, π_i will depend on the firms' pricing behavior, which in turn will depend partly on exogenous institutional factors, such as the climate of competition policy or the degree of economic integration.

The above interpretation of t implies that this variable can be thought of as an inverse measure of the "degree of collusion." A well-known result in oligopoly theory states that under certain conditions, any individually rational and feasible payoff vector can be sustained as an equilibrium of an infinitely repeated game if the players are sufficiently patient (Fudenberg and Tirole 1991). It seems natural, then, to assume that the climate of competition policy or other institutional factors will considerably affect the probability of any particular outcome being realized.[4] For instance, making collusion illegal will make coordination between firms more difficult and will

---

4. Alternatively, one could assume that firms always achieve the highest level of collusion that is sustainable, given a number of parameters taken as exogenous at the "short-run" competition stage. Under this interpretation, a rise in t might correspond to a lower critical discount factor in an infinitely repeated game.

also increase the expected costs of collusion. It should be stressed, however, that, since t refers to the type of pricing *conduct*, it is not equivalent to the price-cost margin, which is a measure of *performance* and can only be treated as endogenous.

Consider now the benchmark case of symmetric single-plant firms. The equilibrium payoff of firm i can be written as $\pi_i(S, N, t)$. Alternatively, one can define a concentration measure C, whose value increases in $1/N$, such as the concentration ratio, and write gross profit as $\pi_i(S, C, t)$. We assume that $\partial \pi_i / \partial S > 0$ and $\partial \pi_i / \partial t < 0$, that is, the equilibrium gross profit of firm i increases with market size and decreases when price competition intensifies (t rises). We also assume that π_i is decreasing in the number of firms N and increasing in the concentration measure C, which is in fact the standard prediction of the traditional structure-conduct-performance approach.[5]

These assumptions are quite plausible, especially in a situation where the total sales revenue in the industry depends mainly on market size S rather than N or t, and the marginal cost curve is relatively flat and not very much affected by S, N, or t.[6] Note also that the key assumption of a negative effect of N on profit per firm is

---

5. According to this approach, concentration increases profitability because it facilitates the exercise of market power by firms; moreover, profits are sustained through "barriers to entry" such as economies of scale, product differentiation through advertising or R&D, and so on. This view has been subject to two main criticisms. One criticism, due to Demsetz (1973), is that high profitability and high concentration in an industry may both be caused by large efficiency differences between firms: since efficient firms have large market shares and make high profits, concentration and industry-level profitability will be correlated even though there will be no causal link between the two. Another criticism is that concentration is itself affected by firm conduct, for instance, by the intensity of competition and by firms' strategies regarding advertising and R&D (which therefore should not be regarded—as is typically the case within the structure-conduct-performance approach—as exogenous barriers to entry).

The view taken in this book is that the structure-conduct-performance approach, although not fundamentally wrong, is incomplete, since it neglects or downplays the endogeneity of market structure and the existence of feedback effects from conduct and performance to structure. The present theory embeds the key result of the structure-conduct-performance approach, namely, the positive effect of concentration on profit margins, in a broader framework that explicitly treats market structure as endogenous. Moreover, the present theory is not inconsistent with the efficiency differences approach, as will be explained below.

6. For instance, in the case of constant marginal cost and unit-elastic demand, these assumptions can be reformulated in terms of some very plausible hypotheses involving price p. In particular, a sufficient condition for $\partial \pi_i / \partial S > 0$ is $\partial p / \partial S \geq 0$; a sufficient condition for $\partial \pi_i / \partial t < 0$ is $\partial p / \partial t < 0$; and a sufficient condition for a negative relationship between π_i and N is that price is nonincreasing in N. Note that this latter condition has received considerable theoretical and empirical support—although the effect of

satisfied under fairly general demand and cost structures in many
oligopoly models, including the Cournot model (see Seade 1980) and
simple models of repeated games (in the latter case the result is for
the maximum sustainable collusive profit).

The Symmetric Equilibrium and Comparative Statics

At stage 1 of the game, firms enter as long as the profit they expect to
make at stage 2 covers the cost of entry. Hence the equilibrium level
of N is given, in the symmetric case, by the largest integer satisfying

$$\pi_i(S, N, t) \geq f, \qquad \forall i. \tag{4.1}$$

Note that the free-entry condition (4.1) is assumed to hold, whatever
the intensity of price competition in the final stage of the game. This
is a key feature of the model, and it is consistent with the empirical
evidence on the British cartels described in chapter 2. We further assume that the equilibrium level of N, as defined by (4.1), is unique;
this will be the case if the average cost curve is either U-shaped or
everywhere declining.

It is then easy to see that an increase in the intensity of competition
t will generally cause a fall in the equilibrium number of firms N^*
and a rise in equilibrium concentration C^*: gross profit, which has
fallen to a level lower than f following the increase in t, can be restored
to a level at least as high as f only through a fall in N by way of exit
or mergers. Note that the free-entry condition (4.1) also implies that
an increase in market size S or a fall in the setup cost f will cause a
rise in N^* and a fall in C^*.

Extensions

Next, consider an exogenous sunk cost industry producing a horizontally differentiated product. Note that this includes the case of

---

entry on price may often be modest (see Bresnahan and Reiss 1991, Geroski 1991,
Sutton 1997a).

To see this, define $S = Npq$, where q is output per firm, and notice that firm profit
can be written as $\pi = (p - c)q = S/N - cq$, where c is marginal cost. Then suppose that
N rises, which implies that pq falls, given S. Now if p is nonincreasing in N, then π
must fall when N rises, whatever happens to q: if q falls, $\pi = (p - c)q$ also falls, while
if q rises, $\pi = S/N - cq$ again falls. A similar argument can be made with respect to
changes in S. As for t, notice that a rise in t (i.e., a movement away from joint profit
maximization and toward the one-shot Nash equilibrium) causes p to fall and q to rise
so that pq remains constant, given S and N; hence $\pi = S/N - cq$ falls.

spatial differentiation. The structure of the game is the same as in the homogeneous-good industry case. In the benchmark case of symmetric single-plant, single-product firms, the equilibrium gross profit of firm i can be written as $\pi_i(S, N, h, t)$, where h is a measure of the (exogenous) degree of horizontal product differentiation, with $\partial \pi_i / \partial h > 0$.[7] The equilibrium number of firms N^* is again the largest integer satisfying the free-entry condition

$$\pi_i(S, N, h, t) \geq f, \qquad \forall i. \tag{4.2}$$

Assuming, as in the homogeneous-good industry case, that π_i is decreasing in N, $\partial \pi_i / \partial S > 0$, and $\partial \pi_i / \partial t < 0$, it is easy to check that N^* is decreasing in t and f and increasing in S and h.[8]

The above framework can be easily extended to exogenous sunk cost industries consisting of multiplant firms, or where the average cost curve becomes horizontal after a certain production level, or where some or all firms produce more than one variety of the (differentiated) product. The only difference is that there now exists a multiplicity of equilibria. The most fragmented equilibrium is the one where each firm operates only one plant, or produces at minimum efficient scale, or produces one variety of the product, whereas more concentrated equilibria, symmetric or asymmetric, can occur if some or all firms operate more than one plant, or produce at a level higher than minimum efficient scale, or produce more than one variety of the product.

Whether the structure of an industry is more fragmented or more concentrated in the presence of multiple equilibria will depend on

---

7. Note that h has a direct equivalent in standard models of horizontal product differentiation: it would be the inverse of the degree of product substitutability in a non-address model of product differentiation, such as Dixit and Stiglitz (1977), or the consumers' unit transport cost (or intensity of preferences) in an address model of product differentiation without choice of location, such as Salop (1979). Both these models can be seen as special cases of the general framework presented here, since h is taken in these models as exogenous and π_i is increasing in h. On the other hand, there is a sharp distinction between horizontal product differentiation and advertising in the present theory—unlike much of the literature following the structure-conduct-performance approach, in which advertising was very often used as a proxy for the degree of product differentiation. Advertising is modeled in chapter 5 as a source of vertical (as opposed to horizontal) product differentiation.

8. See Norman and Thisse (1996) and d'Aspermont and Motta (2000) for an analysis of the positive effect of price competition on concentration using address models of horizontal product differentiation. Section 4.3 below illustrates the positive competition-concentration link in the context of a nonaddress model of product differentiation.

various factors that are difficult to observe or measure across industries. For instance, the presence of economies of scope in setup costs or of first-mover advantages will favor more concentrated equilibria. Note that more concentrated equilibria can also occur with single-plant, single-product symmetric firms with declining average cost curves when part of the fixed cost is incurred at the price competition stage—that is, only if the firm produces positive output (Vickers 1989). Finally, more concentrated equilibria can also occur when the zero-profit condition is violated because of the existence of institutional or other barriers to entry or the use of entry-deterring strategies by incumbent firms (Lyons and Matraves 1996). In all these cases, (4.1) and (4.2) define the *minimum* equilibrium level of concentration as a function of t and the other exogenous variables.

In conclusion, the present theoretical framework provides clear predictions for exogenous sunk cost industries. The next section illustrates these results using a specific oligopoly model. Before analyzing this example, however, several remarks on the general model are in order.

Remarks and Clarifications

To begin with, the use of a two-stage game to model what is essentially a dynamic process of repeated interaction may be seen as a limitation of the present theory. However, this formulation captures the key distinction between short-run and long-run decisions and the notion that long-run decisions constitute a commitment at the time when short-run decisions are being taken. Hence, at any point in time some costs can be thought of as sunk, even though in practice firms incur a continuous stream of expenditures.

It should also be stressed that the capital stock (or any other firm-specific asset created through sunk expenditures) depreciates and has to be renewed. This implies that the mechanism driving the results of the present model—namely, the requirement that gross profit be sufficiently high to cover sunk costs—is entirely appropriate for analyzing the effects of the 1956 Restrictive Trade Practices Act. In other words, the fact that the capital stock was already in place when the exogenous change in the institutional framework (and thus the increase in the intensity of price competition t) occurred in the UK is irrelevant for the long run, because the capital stock has to be replaced periodically. It is, of course, relevant for the short run, for it might imply a relatively weak short-run competition effect on concentration and a relatively slow adjustment to the new long-run equilibrium.[9]

Second, it may be asked why collusion should occur if profits are to be driven to zero by free entry. This may be easier to justify in a context with asymmetric firms, since in that case it is only the marginal firm that makes zero profit. Hence the low-cost firms may gain from collusion in the long run, even though the high-cost firms' profits will be driven to zero. In fact, the evidence from the UK cartels that I have discussed in chapter 2 suggests that price determination was often a bargain between the more efficient and the less efficient cartel members, with prices set at a level that allowed the high-cost firms to break even.

An alternative justification, which is also valid for the case of symmetric firms, is that there are short-run gains from price collusion between a given number of firms, even though these gains are eventually eliminated by changes in market structure. Even when collusion is illegal, these gains may well compensate for any potential losses in case firms are prosecuted for violating the cartel laws, especially if collusion is tacit and therefore difficult to detect and not necessarily, on its own, in violation of the law. In the present context, of course, collusion was not a violation of the law because cartels were not illegal in the UK in the 1950s. Moreover, once price collusion is established, it may persist, even though profits will eventually be driven to zero by entry, because its breakdown will result in short-run losses. The key point in these arguments is that entry and exit do not occur as fast as price or output changes, a feature captured by the model presented here.

Third, the theoretical predictions obtained in this section relate to the minimum rather than the actual level of concentration. Sutton

---

9. The adjustment need not be slow if the cost of the capital investment is spread across many years through interest payments or depreciation allowances. Mergers intended to restore the market power of firms following a rise in the intensity of competition could also speed up the adjustment of concentration to its new long-run equilibrium value. Another factor that could speed up the adjustment is the fact that more efficient firms may acquire less efficient ones soon after competition intensifies to avoid pronounced price-cutting behavior. In turn, less efficient firms, which feel vulnerable once competition intensifies, may prefer to be acquired immediately (i.e., before competition seriously affects their balance sheet position).

(1991, 1998) has proposed a "bounds" approach for testing this class of predictions.[10] However, it is difficult or inappropriate to apply a bounds approach in the present empirical context, for reasons that will be discussed later in this chapter. The alternative is to carry out a regression analysis of the competition effect on market structure, on the implicit assumption that the theoretical results obtained for minimum concentration apply to actual concentration as well. In other words, it will be assumed that the mechanism identified for the benchmark case of symmetric single-plant, single-product firms dominates any other effects that may arise in a more complex setting.[11]

Clearly, the validity of such a claim must be tested against the empirical evidence. However, one remark may be made here. The key issue is whether the symmetry assumption is appropriate in light of the existence of considerable asymmetries between firms in any given industry. These asymmetries often reflect efficiency differences. Now one might expect that once price competition intensifies, high-cost firms (which were previously making zero or almost zero net profit) will be more easily driven out or taken over, while low-cost firms (which were previously making positive net profit) will be more likely to stay in the industry and expand through growth or mergers. At the new long-run equilibrium, the marginal firm will again be making zero or almost zero net profit. Hence, in the absence of any initial negative correlation between firm size and efficiency—which seems quite implausible for the typical industry —concentration should rise. In particular, the expansion of low-cost firms will only reinforce the effect of falling firm numbers on concentration. This story is perfectly consistent with the basic intuition from the symmetric case. In fact, the model presented in this section captures the basic mechanism driving the evolution of market struc-

---

10. The bounds approach, as described in Sutton's work, has mostly focused on analyzing the properties of *lower* bounds to concentration. Recent theoretical work by Nocke (2000) has extended this approach to the study of *upper* bounds to concentration in different classes of industries.

11. A more complex theoretical framework for the analysis of market structure would combine deterministic factors deriving from game-theoretic models of entry (such as the one described in this chapter) with stochastic patterns of firm growth that may account for much of the asymmetry observed in real markets (such as those analysed in Hart and Prais 1956, Simon and Bonini 1958). Sutton (1998) presents an integrated theory of the determinants of market structure that combines the two approaches.

ture in exogenous sunk cost industries, while abstracting from complications that arise from firm heterogeneity.[12]

Finally, the assumption of the exogeneity of the intensity of price competition t is clearly a simplification. However, it is not unrealistic, even on theoretical grounds alone, given the well-known multiplicity of equilibria in models of infinitely repeated games. More important, this assumption is justifiable in the present empirical context for two reasons. First, the key determinant of changes in t during the period under study was an exogenous change in the institutional framework, namely, the introduction of cartel law. In particular, it was shown in chapter 2 that the intensity of price competition increased, following the abolition of price-fixing, in the large majority of the previously cartelized industries. Of course, whether t would change at all depended also on its initial value. The second point therefore is that, as shown in chapter 3, cartelization in the 1950s was largely a function of exogenous industry characteristics rather than of endogenous variables such as concentration. In other words, although in principle the intensity of price competition t should be seen as a function of an exogenous institutional variable T and a vector of other variables $\mathbf{Z}$ (which may include N), in practice the dominant influence on t in the present context was the variable T and some of the exogenous elements in $\mathbf{Z}$. In such a setting, it may be possible to ignore any feedback effects from N on t.

An alternative, although not very different, line of defense of the assumption that t can be taken as exogenous is to say that even if t were made endogenous, it would be possible to derive and test a *conditional* theoretical prediction, provided that t is observable. Suppose, for instance, that we have $t(T, \mathbf{Z})$, where the vector $\mathbf{Z}$ may include N. The free-entry condition can then be written as

$$\pi_i(S, N, h, t(T, \mathbf{Z})) \geq f, \qquad \forall i. \tag{4.3}$$

From (4.3) it is easy to derive a prediction which is conditional on the known change in t, namely, that a change in the institutional variable

---

12. According to a stronger version of the efficiency differences approach, the number of firms need not fall even though concentration should rise following an intensification of price competition. In other words, changes in concentration would be mostly driven by changes in the distribution of market shares rather than by changes in firm numbers. This hypothesis is discussed in detail in chapter 7. However, it is rejected by the empirical evidence reported in that chapter.

T must result in a fall in N if and only if t is larger at the new equilibrium.[13] Having established the increase in t in chapter 2, we are now in a position to test this conditional prediction. In other words, a reduced-form analysis of the effect of a change in the institutional variable T on market structure will be sufficient for testing the theoretical prediction of a positive effect of price competition on market structure.

4.3   A Specific Example: The Linear Demand Model

I will now briefly illustrate the general mechanism described in the previous section using a specific theoretical model. This will also serve as a benchmark, since an extended version of this model will be used in chapter 5 to illustrate some of the results that apply to advertising-intensive industries. Consider an exogenous sunk cost industry producing a potentially infinite number of varieties of a horizontally differentiated product. Competition in the industry is described by a two-stage game as follows. There are N_0 potential entrants, each with the capacity to produce a single variety of the product. At stage 1 they decide whether or not to enter at an exogenously given sunk cost of entry f. At stage 2 those firms that have entered simultaneously set quantities. We assume that N_0 is sufficiently large so that at any equilibrium of the game there is at least one nonentering firm.

There are S identical consumers, and the utility function of each consumer takes the form

$$U = \sum_i (\alpha_1 x_i - \alpha_2 x_i^2) - \alpha_2 \sigma \sum_i \sum_{j<i} x_i x_j + M. \tag{4.4}$$

This is a standard quadratic utility function and it has previously been used, sometimes with small variations, by Spence (1976), Dixit (1979), Vives (1985), Shaked and Sutton (1990), Sutton (1997b, 1998),

---

13. Brander and Spencer (1985) examine a model of a homogeneous-good industry with free entry that allows for a two-way link between the number of firms and a reduced-form competition measure (in particular, a conjectural variations parameter). As expected, they find that a shift in competition policy that makes collusion more difficult for any given number of firms (in my notation, an outward shift of the function $t(T, \mathbf{Z})$) reduces the equilibrium number of firms.

and Symeonidis (2002), among others.[14] The x_i's are the quantities demanded of the different varieties of the product in question, while $M = Y - \sum_i p_i x_i$ denotes expenditure on outside goods. This utility function implies that the consumer spends only a small part of her income on the industry's product (which also ensures that the maximization of U has an interior solution), and hence income effects on the industry under consideration can be ignored and partial equilibrium analysis can be applied.[15] The parameter σ, $\sigma \in (0,2)$, is an inverse measure of the (exogenous) degree of horizontal product differentiation: in the limit as $\sigma \to 0$, the goods become independent, while in the limit as $\sigma \to 2$, they become perfect substitutes. The parameter σ is a basic taste parameter and cannot be influenced by firms in the industry. It can be seen as an industry-specific measure of the degree to which demand is diversified among users with different preferences or requirements. Alternatively, it may reflect the degree of fragmentation of demand caused by transport costs or trade barriers. Finally, α_1 and α_2 are positive scale parameters.

The consumer's inverse demand for variety i is given by

$$p_i = \alpha_1 - 2\alpha_2 x_i - \alpha_2 \sigma \sum_{j \neq i} x_j \tag{4.5}$$

in the region of quantity spaces where prices are positive. Let N denote the number of varieties offered; this is also the number of firms that have entered the industry. Inverting the system of N equations, we derive the consumer's demand function for variety i:

$$x_i = \frac{(\alpha_1 - p_i)[2 + \sigma(N - 2)] - \sigma \sum_{j \neq i}(\alpha_1 - p_j)}{\alpha_2(2 - \sigma)[2 + \sigma(N - 1)]} \tag{4.6}$$

in the region of prices where quantities are positive. It can be easily

---

14. This demand system was introduced by Bowley (1924). A different type of quadratic utility function, which includes the number of firms as a parameter, was proposed by Shapley and Shubik (1969) and was used in slightly different form in Shubik (1980). See Martin (2002) for a detailed comparison of the two models. Sutton (1997b, 1998) provides a comprehensive analysis of a quantity-setting oligopoly using the Bowley demand system. This seems a natural choice in the present context, where the number of firms is endogenous, and hence its inclusion as a parameter in the utility function seems inappropriate.
15. See Shaked and Sutton (1990) for a discussion of how such a utility function can also be derived by aggregating the preferences of heterogeneous groups of consumers.

seen that x_i is linear and decreasing in p_i, and linear and increasing in p_j, $\forall j \neq i$. Since there are S consumers, firm i sells quantity Sx_i. Let each firm have a constant marginal cost of production c, where $c < \alpha_1$.

There are two different ways to model the intensity of short-run "price" competition in the present case. The first is standard and involves comparing the joint monopoly outcome with the Cournot-Nash equilibrium of the second-stage subgame. The second is an attempt to allow for imperfect collusion and involves assuming that at the second-stage subgame each firm maximizes the sum of its own (gross) profit and a fraction λ of the (gross) profit of each of the remaining firms. The parameter λ, $0 \leq \lambda \leq 1$, is then an inverse measure of the intensity of short-run competition, with $\lambda = 0$ corresponding to the Cournot-Nash equilibrium and $\lambda = 1$ corresponding to perfect collusion. Intermediate values of λ represent imperfect collusion and may be justified by reference to some implicit dynamic model of collusion, a reduced-form representation of which is the quantity competition subgame of the present model.[16]

Of course, despite the fact that λ may be a reasonable choice for a continuous collusion parameter, chiefly because of its properties in the final-stage subgame, it remains a rather arbitrary way of modeling collusion. It should therefore be emphasized that this parameter is being used here merely to illustrate the results of the previous section, which are cast in terms of a continuous competition parameter, within the context of the linear demand model. In what follows,

---

16. The parameter λ was first suggested by Edgeworth (1881), who called it the "coefficient of effective sympathy" and applied it to the study of individual behavior. It has been used in oligopoly models by Cyert and deGroot (1973), who named it "coefficient of cooperation," Kuenne (1980), and Shubik (1980), among others. Note that λ is free from some of the theoretical problems encountered in other approaches to modeling the intensity of short-run competition by way of a reduced-form parameter, such as the conjectural variations approach.

What also justifies the use of λ as a reduced-form competition measure is its properties in the final-stage subgame: it can be checked that, for given N, the equilibrium price, price-cost margin, and profit in the second-stage subgame increase and the equilibrium quantity falls as λ rises (the degree of collusion increases). None of the other exogenous variables that affect gross profit, namely, σ or c, have properties similar to those of λ in the second-stage subgame. Of particular interest in this respect are the properties of σ, since this has often been used as a measure of the intensity of competition. It can be checked that a fall in σ (i.e., an increase in the degree of product differentiation) increases both the equilibrium price and the equilibrium quantity of the second-stage subgame.

λ will be treated as a continuous variable, but it will be useful to bear in mind that all the results on the effect of changes in λ on market structure are exactly the same if λ can take only two values, 0 and 1.

Let me again emphasize that treating the intensity of short-run competition as an exogenous parameter is a simplification motivated by the present empirical context. In principle, one could think of λ as a function of an exogenous institutional variable and a vector of other variables, which may include N.[17] The present model would then be appropriate for a situation where the dominant influence on λ is a change in the institutional variable, since in such a setup it would be plausible to assume that the feedback effects from N on λ are small (i.e., $\partial\lambda/\partial N \approx 0$) and can therefore be ignored.

I will now solve for a symmetric subgame perfect equilibrium in pure strategies in the above two-stage game. Using backward induction, I will start by assuming that N firms have entered at stage 1 of the game and solve for the equilibrium of the second-stage subgame. I will then go back to stage 1 to analyze how N is determined, assuming that firms can anticipate, when making their entry decisions, how the second-stage subgame will be played for any given N.

At stage 2, firms compete by setting quantities. Each firm chooses x_i to maximize $\Pi_i = \pi_i + \lambda \sum_{j \neq i} \pi_j$, where

$$\pi_i = S(p_i - c)x_i = S\left(\alpha_1 - c - 2\alpha_2 x_i - \alpha_2 \sigma \sum_{j \neq i} x_j\right)x_i.$$

Solving the system of N symmetric first-order conditions, we obtain the equilibrium value of x in the second-stage subgame as a function of the number of firms N:

$$x(N) = \frac{\alpha_1 - c}{\alpha_2[4 + \sigma(1 + \lambda)(N - 1)]}.$$

The profit of each firm is then given by

$$\pi(N) = \frac{S(\alpha_1 - c)^2[2 + \sigma\lambda(N - 1)]}{\alpha_2[4 + \sigma(1 + \lambda)(N - 1)]^2}. \tag{4.7}$$

It can be easily checked that $\pi(N)$ is increasing in S, decreasing in σ,

---

17. Within this more general formulation, industry A would be defined as being more collusive than industry B if $\lambda^A(N) > \lambda^B(N)$, $\forall N$.

and decreasing in N for $N > 1$. Also, $\pi(N)$ is increasing in λ for all $\lambda \in [0, 1)$ and attains its maximum at $\lambda = 1$. In particular we obtain

$$\frac{\partial \pi(N)}{\partial N} = -\frac{S\sigma(\alpha_1 - c)^2[4 + \sigma\lambda(1 + \lambda)(N - 1)]}{\alpha_2[4 + \sigma(1 + \lambda)(N - 1)]^3}, \tag{4.8}$$

which is negative, and

$$\frac{\partial \pi(N)}{\partial \lambda} = \frac{S\sigma^2(\alpha_1 - c)^2(1 - \lambda)(N - 1)^2}{\alpha_2[4 + \sigma(1 + \lambda)(N - 1)]^3}, \tag{4.9}$$

which is positive for $\lambda \in [0, 1)$ and equal to zero for $\lambda = 1$.

Now at stage 1, the free-entry condition implies that firms enter the industry as long as the profit they can make in the second-stage subgame covers the cost of entry. Assuming, for simplicity, that N is a continuous variable, the free-entry condition implies

$$\pi(N^*) = f, \tag{4.10}$$

where N^* is the long-run equilibrium number of firms. Given (4.8) and (4.9), it is then easy to see from the total differential of equation (4.10) that, for any $\lambda \in [0, 1)$, $dN^*/d\lambda > 0$ (i.e., the equilibrium number of firms increases as the degree of collusion rises). For $\lambda = 1$ (i.e., at the perfectly collusive point), $\pi(N)$ is maximized and, given (4.8) and the exogenously fixed f, so is N^*. Thus more price competition raises concentration in an exogenous sunk cost industry. It is also easy to check that $dN^*/dS > 0$ and $dN^*/d\sigma < 0$, that is, the number of firms increases with market size and falls as the products become less differentiated.

It is straightforward to check that the assumption of quantity-setting firms is innocuous in this model, for similar results are derived for the case of price-setting firms. Moreover, the results do not depend on the assumption of single-product firms either, because similar results are obtained when we allow each firm to produce M varieties, at least for the case where M is exogenously fixed and is the same across firms.

4.4   The Data

The empirical analysis in this chapter essentially involves a comparison of the evolution of concentration after 1958 between those exogenous sunk cost industries affected by the 1956 Restrictive Trade

Practices Act and those not affected—controlling for other factors that may have influenced concentration during the period examined. The industry definitions that I will use in this chapter are taken from the official UK concentration statistics and correspond to the four-digit level of aggregation.[18] The concentration data are available only for 1958, 1963, 1968, and 1975–1977. Since the legislation did not have any significant effect before the first Court cases were heard in 1959, the 1958 observations are all before the natural experiment took place. Moreover, since competition did not break out immediately in several industries, the impact of the Act was felt at least until the late 1960s, and sometimes until the early 1970s. Thus we should expect to see only the short-run effects of competition by 1963, while by 1968 much of the long-run effect should have been realized, and by the early 1970s the full long-run effect had certainly been realized.

This section describes, in considerable detail, the construction of the data set for this chapter. Since many of the variables used here will also be used in later chapters, the discussion in this section is of relevance, and serves as a reference, for data sets used in later chapters as well. Thus the various data sources and the variables used are described below without any particular focus on one or the other class of industries. Readers who would prefer to skip the details of the construction of the data set may go directly to section 4.5, where a summary description of all the variables used in the econometric analysis in this chapter is provided.

Concentration

My concentration measure is the share of the five largest producers in the total sales revenue of UK firms, excluding firms (or plants) with fewer than twenty-five employees. I will use Census-based data at the four-digit (or "product group") level of aggregation for 1958, 1963, 1968, and 1975, taken from three official publications: (1) summary table 5 of the *Report on the Census of Production, 1963* (London: H.M.S.O., 1967); (2) summary table 44 of the *Report on the Census of Production, 1968* (London: H.M.S.O., 1971–1974); and (3) *Statistics of*

---

18. Recall that in the system of Census industry definitions, the industry categories become progressively narrower as digits are added to the industry code. Thus each three-digit industry includes a number of four-digit industries, each of these includes a number of five-digit industries, and so on.

Product Concentration of UK Manufactures for 1963, 1968 and 1975,
Business Monitor PO 1006 (London: H.M.S.O., 1979).[19]

The measurement of concentration presents a number of difficulties
(see Utton 1970). The first of these is the need to use an appropriate
concentration measure. In the present case, the five-firm sales concentration ratio is the only available measure at the four-digit industry level for the period under study.[20] The concentration ratio has
been widely used in the literature on the determinants of market
structure (see Curry and George 1983, Sutton 1991), and it is also one
of the measures recommended by Hannah and Kay in their detailed
comparison of several concentration measures on the basis of a
number of axiomatic criteria (Hannah and Kay 1977). For instance,
Hannah and Kay point out that an important advantage of the concentration ratio is the fact that it is not very sensitive to the number
of small firms, which affects both the degree of inequality of firm
sizes and the overall number of firms, but is not a key feature of
market structure. This is important in the present context not only
because small firms often do not produce core industry products, but
also because the evidence from the various data sources on competition suggests that the British cartels did not usually include all
firms in any given industry, and it was often the smaller firms
that were not cartel members; hence the effect of the 1956 Act on
many small firms in cartelized industries may have been relatively

---

19. The industry categories in the official concentration statistics are defined in accordance to a number of criteria, the most important of which are (1) that they do not
have very low sales, and (2) that they are reasonably homogeneous.

I will also use a few official concentration ratios for 1968 reported in Hart and Clarke
(1980) but not published in the official statistics, and a few concentration ratios for
1975 taken from *Statistics of Product Concentration of UK Manufactures for 1975, 1976 and
1977*, Business Monitor PO 1006 (London: H.M.S.O., 1980). I will not use concentration
ratios for 1976–1977, even though such data are available from the above source and/
or from a list of unpublished concentration ratios for 1976–1977 compiled by officials
at the Office of Fair Trading and kindly made available to me by David Elliott. My
reason for not using the 1976–1977 data in addition to the 1975 data is to avoid creating a panel with a very asymmetric intertemporal structure. I could, of course, use the
1977 (or 1976) figures instead of the 1975 figures. This would barely affect the results,
as can be seen by comparing the results reported here with those reported in Symeonidis (2000a). I have chosen to use 1975 instead of 1977 (or 1976) here for two reasons:
first, because this ensures the maximum possible comparability with other data sets
used in this book, and, second, because in a few cases 1976–1977 concentration data
comparable to those for previous years are not available.
20. For most of the period examined in this book, the plant-level data underlying the
Census of Production are not available, because the individual returns to the Census of
Production have, unfortunately, been destroyed.

weak. Finally, note that the concentration ratio is as appropriate for testing the present theory as any other standard concentration measure, since no presumption is made in the theory about any specific oligopoly model underlying the observed size distribution of firms.[21]

Two other common difficulties with the measurement of concentration are the definition of the relevant market and the treatment of imports. However, these are not very significant problems in the present case. Consider, first, the definition of the relevant market. A typical feature of Census-based concentration ratios is the classification of industries mainly according to supply rather than demand characteristics. For instance, glass containers, metal cans, and plastic containers may be substitutes in demand, but they are classified as parts of three different Census industries. However, this is probably an advantage in the present context, because the British cartels typically operated within industries defined according to their supply characteristics. Thus, to continue with the previous example, producers of metal cans or plastic containers were not parties to the restrictive agreement operated among producers of glass containers. Hence the supply-side classification is appropriate for examining the impact of the 1956 legislation.

Another typical feature of Census-based concentration ratios, the allocation of each plant to a particular industry on the basis of the core products of the plant, does not apply to the present study (except for chapter 7). The UK Census of Production allocates each plant to a "minimum list heading" (MLH) industry, which roughly corresponds to the three-digit level of aggregation. However, the concentration data I will use relate to "product groups," which I refer to as four-digit industries, since the level of aggregation is lower than that of the Census MLH industries and roughly corresponds to the four-digit level. These data have been constructed on the basis of sales of products within each product group by *all* plants employing at least twenty-five persons, irrespective of the Census MLH industry to which any particular plant is allocated.

---

21. Whenever, on the other hand, explicit use is made of the Cournot model of oligopoly, the Herfindahl index may be a more appropriate concentration measure (see Cowling and Waterson 1976). This is not the case here. In any event, the Herfindahl index and the concentration ratio are very strongly correlated. Sawyer (1971), who estimated approximate four-firm concentration ratios and Herfindahl indices for *three-digit* British manufacturing industries in 1963, found a correlation coefficient of 0.94 between the two measures.

Next, consider the treatment of imports. Census-based concentration data typically relate to sales by domestic firms rather than sales in the domestic market, and the data used in this book are no exception. To measure concentration in the domestic market, one would need to subtract exports from and add imports to the sales figures, and make some assumptions about the market shares of importers and the fraction of exports accounted for by the largest domestic firms. Obviously, such an adjustment is subject to serious data limitations, and things are made even more difficult in the present case by changes in the industrial classification used in the foreign trade statistics over time and significant differences between this classification and the one used in the Census of Production during most of the period examined in this book.

Fortunately, however, no such adjustment is necessary for the present study, since the impact of the 1956 Act was usually on competition between UK firms rather than between firms selling in the UK market. In particular, in most cases the membership of the British cartels of the 1950s was confined to UK manufacturing firms. On the other hand, in some cases importers were also parties to the agreements. Even in those cases, however, it is not at all clear that one would want to adjust the concentration ratio for imports, because the foreign producers that supplied the British importers were not subject to the same constraints as the British producers, and hence it may be preferable simply to focus on the competition effect on concentration among British manufacturing firms.[22]

Of course, the concentration data used here are not entirely free from problems. A well-known difficulty with the measurement of concentration in general is the definition of a firm. A firm (or "enterprise") is defined in the UK Census of Production as consisting of all plants under common ownership or control, and control is taken to mean a 50% holding of equity capital. However, effective control may arise with a holding of less than 50%. Another difficulty is that the degree of heterogeneity differs across Census industries, even at the four-digit level of aggregation: some are relatively homogeneous, while others may comprise two or more submarkets which are largely independent. Nevertheless, these factors should not

---

22. Moreover, imports were, on the whole, not significant in the 1950s, but increased during the 1960s and the 1970s. Hence differences across industries in the evolution of the import-adjusted concentration ratio would be influenced by differences across industries in the extent of import penetration.

cause any appreciable statistical bias in a study of market structure using panel data.

I now turn to a discussion of problems associated with the use of the published concentration data. There were two main problems. First, for several industries, data were not available for all years. The main reasons for this were the progressive increase in the number of "product groups" covered and some radical changes in product group definitions over time. For example, data for 1958 were available for some 200 industries, as compared to about 350 for later years. In such cases, there was little that could be done. Second, because of changes in industry definitions over time, the figures were sometimes not comparable over the entire period. In many of these cases, it was possible to construct comparable figures by adjusting the ones published.[23] On the other hand, whenever the change in the industry definition was substantial—in particular, whenever there was a change in industry sales revenue in excess of 20% from one definition to the other—I either discarded the noncomparable figures or, in one or two cases, treated the two definitions as two different industries.[24]

A few observations were excluded because the high level of government participation or involvement in certain industries made the figures meaningless for my purposes. This was the case with locomotives and aircraft throughout the period, and also with the industries affected by the 1967 nationalization of steel (in the latter case only the observations for 1968 and 1975 were discarded). Some observations were excluded because the reported concentration ratio was not the

---

23. In particular, note that summary table 5 of the 1963 Census of Production contains data for 1958 and 1963, while *Statistics of Product Concentration of UK Manufactures for 1963, 1968 and 1975* contains data for 1963, 1968, and 1975. Now noncomparability was usually the result of a small change in industry definition from one table to the other rather than from one year to the next within a single table. Hence concentration (and sales revenue) figures were available for 1963 under both definitions. In such cases, and provided that the change in industry definition was minor, I applied a simple proportional adjustment to some of the published figures to ensure comparability over time. To make sure, in such cases, that the difference in the 1963 figures across tables was due to a change in industry definition rather than to the revision of a figure, I checked the individual Census industry reports.

24. Sometimes the noncomparability was due to a change in industry definition from one year to the next within the same table. Census industry reports were then examined to assess the magnitude of the change. Usually it was minor (less than 10%); concentration ratios were then left unchanged—although sales figures were adjusted on the basis of information from the Census industry reports. Whenever the change was large, the noncomparable figures were discarded.

five-firm concentration ratio.[25] Finally, I excluded a small number of industries for which concentration data were available only for 1968 and 1975, since these were of little relevance for the study of the effects of the 1956 legislation.

Market Size

Market size was defined in section 4.3 as a parameter that shifts quantity demanded at any given price. In practice, however, relative prices change over time for various reasons, including exogenous shifts in demand or marginal cost, changes in product quality, and changes in the product mix within an industry. It may therefore be useful to think of any increase in the profit opportunities in an industry, other than one induced by a change in the intensity of price competition or in endogeneous sunk costs, as an increase in market size. An ideal proxy for market size should therefore capture variations in marginal cost, demand, or the product mix over time, but should be independent of changes in the intensity of price competition or in sunk costs. For instance, the quantity that would be demanded if price were equal to marginal cost is one measure that fits this description, at least for the case where marginal cost is constant and the same across firms.

In practice, there are two possible proxies for market size: sales revenue deflated by the general producer price index, and sales revenue deflated by an industry-specific producer price index. The former does not control for changes in relative prices, while the latter does. It is difficult to say which proxy is better, since this will depend on the particular form of the demand function.[26] Since none of the two proxies is generally superior to the other and neither of the two is independent of the intensity of price competition (as an ideal proxy should be), both will be tried in the empirical model of the next sec-

---

25. Nearly all of these were cases where the total number of firms in the industry (excluding those with fewer than twenty-five employees) was slightly larger than five. In order to avoid the disclosure of information on particular firms, the concentration statistics then report an n-firm concentration ratio equal to 1 (where $n > 5$ is the total number of firms).

26. For example, with a constant-elasticity demand function the total number of profit opportunities in the market is simply proportional to the value of sales, for any given degree of collusion; hence, the first proxy may be preferable. With a linear demand function, however, the second proxy may be preferable, especially when the changes in relative prices are mainly driven by changes in relative marginal costs rather than by shifts in demand.

tion. Using each of these proxies in turn and comparing the results has one further advantage in the present case: it strengthens the case for treating sales revenue as an exogenous variable in these regressions (this point will be further discussed in the next section).

Data on the value of manufacturers' sales at current net producer prices at the four-digit level of aggregation were obtained mostly from the same publications as the concentration ratios, and in some cases from the industry reports of the 1958, 1963 and 1968 Censuses of Production and the 1975 issues of *Business Monitor, PQ series: Quarterly Statistics*. The figures relate to sales by all plants (for 1968 and 1975) or firms (for 1958 and 1963) employing at least twenty-five persons. The exclusion of very small plants is probably a minor issue, since these often produce ancillary rather than core industry products. Moreover, a search through the individual industry reports of the Census of Production did not reveal any serious discontinuities caused by the switch from excluding very small firms to excluding very small plants for any industry in my sample.[27]

A series of general producer price indices was obtained from the *Annual Abstract of Statistics*. Producer price indices for a number of four-digit industries, covering all or part of the period under study, have been published in the *Annual Abstract of Statistics*, in various issues of the *Board of Trade Journal* and *Trade and Industry*, in the *Annual Bulletin of Construction Statistics*, and in *Business Monitor, PQ series: Quarterly Statistics*. For many industries, however, data are not available or are not available for all years, so price indices at a higher level of aggregation or of closely related industries have sometimes had to be used as proxies. An alternative set of price indices can be constructed on the basis of data on the volume of output often reported, along with data on sales revenue, in the individual industry reports of the 1958, 1963, and 1968 Censuses of Production and in Business Monitors.[28]

Both these sets of price indices have shortcomings in addition to the fact that they are often incomplete. Published price indices are calculated largely from information supplied by firms and trade

---

27. Such discontinuities were present in only four industries: granite, limestone, sand and gravel, and ready-mixed concrete. In these industries, firms that employed more than twenty-five persons *and* operated one or more small plants each accounted for a significant fraction of total sales. None of the four industries is included in any of the samples used in this book, however, because they were all classified as ambiguous with respect to their state of competition after 1958.

28. See Nicholson and Gupta (1960) for an early application of this method.

associations on prices of products which are thought to be representative of their respective industries, so they may not always be accurate, especially for earlier years. Also, especially during the 1950s and the 1960s, these indices were calculated on the basis of list prices (i.e., trade discounts were not taken into account at a time when they may have been increasing in many industries, especially those that had previously been cartelized). Finally, the published price indices are based on sales in the domestic market only.

Price indices constructed on the basis of data on the volume of output are subject to more serious problems. These data are usually reported, along with data on sales revenue, for a number of product categories within each four-digit industry, so a price index for the industry can be constructed by using the output volumes of these product categories as weights. To the extent, however, that each of these categories consists of subproducts whose prices or price changes may vary, the overall procedure will result in some measurement error for the four-digit industry indices. The error will be more serious, the more differentiated the products within the industry and the less detailed the breakdown; in fact, some of the data on the volume of output are probably meaningless. A second problem stems from the fact that the volume of output is often not reported for all product categories within a given four-digit industry, and it is difficult to say whether the categories covered are representative. On the positive side, it should be pointed out that since the corresponding data on sales value are at net producer prices, trade discounts are taken into account when price indices are computed on the basis of Census figures on the volume of output; moreover, both domestic sales and exports are covered.

The series of industry-specific price indices that I use in this book were constructed after an evaluation of the likely accuracy of the available figures on a case-by-case basis. For later years, I normally used the published price indices at the four-digit level whenever they were available. For earlier years, I used the output-based figures in some cases, the published price indices in others, and sometimes I took an average. Often the choice depended on data availability: in many cases the output data were incomplete or highly aggregated, while in other cases, published indices at the four-digit level were not available.[29]

---

29. Whenever both these problems were present, the choice usually was between a published index for a three-digit or a two-digit or a closely related four-digit industry,

The problems associated with the use of the published sales data were largely similar to those mentioned above for the concentration data. Thus data were often not available for all years. On the other hand, noncomparabilities caused by small changes in industry definitions were usually dealt with by adjusting some of the published figures.

Competition

The competition data were fully described in chapter 3. Here I focus more specifically on the details of the construction of the key competition variable that is used in this chapter and in the rest of the book. This is a dummy variable, *CHANGE*, which takes the value 1 for industries with a change in competition regime sometime after 1958 and 0 for industries with no change in regime (including a few industries where price agreements continued until the 1970s). Recall that a change in competition regime is defined to correspond to the cancellation of significant restrictive agreements covering at least 50% of sales revenue in an industry. No change in regime implies that less than 10% of an industry was in any way affected by the legislation. Intermediate cases, defined as ambiguous, were excluded. Note that *CHANGE* is an industry-specific variable. The econometric analysis of the competition effect on concentration using *CHANGE* throughout this book will involve interacting this variable with year dummies in order to test whether the time effects on concentration or any other endogenous variable after 1958 are different for the two groups of industries in regressions that also control for other factors, such as market size and setup costs.

Although normally *CHANGE* takes the value 1 for industries with a change of competition regime sometime after 1958 and 0 otherwise, there is also the special case of eight industries that were affected by the nationalization of steel in 1967. All of these industries had restrictive agreements that were abandoned *after* 1963. Now since the

---

on the one hand, and an imperfect output-based price index, on the other. I usually chose the latter approach in the case of sectors where industries are largely heterogeneous with respect to costs (e.g., the food and drink sector), and the former for sectors where a greater degree of homogeneity with respect to costs is present while output figures are often problematic because of the high degree of product differentiation (e.g., the engineering sector). Sometimes I computed both indices and took an average.

nationalization of steel made the concentration figures after 1967 irrelevant, only the 1958–1963 concentration data for these industries
are included in my data set. But during the 1958–1963 period, the
collusive agreements were still in place in these industries. Consequently, I had to choose between dropping these industries from my
sample and classifying them as industries without a change in competition regime after 1958. I chose to do the latter; in any case, the
results reported below are barely affected by these eight industries.

The main feature of the present approach to modeling the competition effect is that it does not impose any structure on the competition data regarding the timing of the impact of the legislation.
As pointed out above, in several industries competition was slow
to emerge. Moreover, there must have been a time lag between the
emergence of competition and the realization of any effect this may
have had on long-run equilibrium concentration or on other variables. For these reasons, there is some uncertainty about the timing of
the impact of the Act in each industry. My approach involves letting
the data reveal how the short-run effect of the legislation compares
with the long-run effect, for manufacturing industry as a whole.[30]

Setup Cost

There are no data for setup costs, so two different proxies were constructed. The first of these was constructed by defining a measure of
minimum efficient scale relative to industry size and multiplying it
by the total value of capital stock in the industry (see Sutton 1991).
I used the simplest possible measure of minimum efficient scale,
namely, the size of the average plant. Divided by industry size, this
becomes equal to the inverse of the number of plants in the industry.
Hence the first proxy used for setup cost is the capital stock of the
average plant. A measure of minimum efficient scale based on the

---

30. An alternative approach to modeling the competition effect was used in Symeonidis (2000a, 2000b). It involved constructing, on the basis of certain plausible assumptions about the timing of the impact of the legislation, an *industry-year-specific* dummy
variable that takes the value 1 for "collusive" and the value 0 for "competitive"
industry-year pairs. This alternative approach imposes more structure on the data and
does not allow for an analysis of the short-run impact of the 1956 Act. On the other
hand, it can take into account some information about dates when particular agreements were abandoned. In any case, the two approaches yield very similar results regarding the long-run effect of the Act on concentration (see Symeonidis 2000a).

size distribution of plants might have been more appropriate, but such a measure could not be used because of data limitations. Even the data on plant numbers and capital stock are only available at the three-digit level of aggregation (i.e., for Census MLH industries). Moreover, the capital stock figures are estimates rather than primary data. As a result of these conceptual and practical problems, this proxy is a rather imperfect one. A further difficulty is that industries differ in the degree to which setup costs are sunk. Ideally, one would want to relate concentration to that fraction of the setup cost which is not recoverable on exit (see Kessides 1990), but estimates of this across industries and over time are not available in the present context.

These difficulties should not be overemphasized, however. For one thing, there are, on average, only about two four-digit industries for each three-digit industry in my sample. More important, if one uses an empirical model of concentration with industry-specific effects, as I will be doing in the next section and in the following chapters, one need not assume that all four-digit industries within any given three-digit industry are similar with respect to setup cost f, or that the capital stock of the average plant is an accurate measure of f, or that all setup costs are sunk costs. All one needs to assume is that the *change* in the capital stock of the average plant is roughly similar for all four-digit industries within any given three-digit industry, that this change is an adequate measure of the *change* in f, and that the degree of "sunkenness" of setup costs is roughly constant for each industry over time (although it can vary across industries). In particular, assume that $K_{it} = \gamma_i K_{Jt}$, $N_{it} = \delta_i N_{Jt}$, and $f_{it} = \theta_i (K/N)_{it}$, where K is capital stock, N is the number of plants, and i denotes a four-digit industry within the three-digit industry J. It then follows that $\ln f_{it} = \ln \theta_i + \ln \gamma_i - \ln \delta_i + \ln(K/N)_{Jt}$. Hence the three-digit $\ln(K/N)$ can be used as an explanatory variable, while the term $\ln \theta_i + \ln \gamma_i - \ln \delta_i$ will be part of the four-digit industry-specific effect, provided that θ_i, γ_i, and δ_i are constant over time for each industry i.[31]

A standard argument against using measures of minimum efficient scale based on the number or the size distribution of plants in empirical models of concentration is that such measures are, by definition,

---

31. In fact, the inclusion of time effects in the empirical specification relaxes even more the assumptions on the parameters θ_i, γ_i, and δ_i, since they are also allowed to change over time, albeit in a uniform way across industries.

correlated with concentration (Davies 1980). To avoid this difficulty, the capital-labor ratio K/L has sometimes been used as a proxy for technical economies of scale. Although it may be more difficult to justify the use of the capital-labor ratio as a proxy for the setup cost f, it seems plausible that the *change* in the capital-labor ratio is a reasonable measure of the *change* in f and is roughly similar for all four-digit industries within any given three-digit industry. The arguments made in the previous paragraph for the three-digit K/N are therefore also valid for the three-digit K/L.

Capital stock was defined as plant and machinery; buildings and vehicles were not included because these are to a large extent recoverable on exit.[32] Estimates of the capital stock (in constant prices) at the three-digit level of aggregation were taken from O'Mahony and Oulton (1990). These authors have computed these estimates from Census investment data using the perpetual inventory method. They have tried various assumptions about asset lives and depreciation rates, and have therefore constructed a number of different capital stock series. Their preferred estimates are the net stock estimates derived on the assumption of fixed and "short" asset lives and exponential depreciation rates. I used these figures for 1958, 1963, and 1968; I also computed figures for 1975 on the basis of their 1973 and 1979 estimates, and on the assumption of a constant annual change in the capital stock between 1973 and 1979.[33]

Overall, the capital stock estimates of O'Mahony and Oulton can be treated as reasonably accurate, although one should also be clear about their limitations. These are caused not only by the fact that the estimates were constructed on the basis of certain assumptions that may not hold in a uniform way across industries, but also by imperfections in the raw data (i.e., the Census investment figures).

---

32. Part of the cost of plant and machinery may also be recoverable on exit. As pointed out above, however, differences across industries in the degree to which setup costs are sunk will be largely captured in panel regressions by the industry effects.

33. A small complication with the 1975 figures has arisen from the fact that the O'Mahony and Oulton (1990) capital stock estimates for 1979 are not adjusted to control for the effect of the apparently considerable amount of premature scrapping of capital assets after 1973. However, the authors provide an estimate for the extent of premature scrapping for all manufacturing industry after 1973. I therefore used this estimate to adjust my 1975 capital stock figures, on the assumption that the extent of premature scrapping was constant for every year between 1973 and 1979 and similar across industries. Since the relevant period for applying this adjustment in my data set is very short, the resulting figures for 1975 are very similar to the unadjusted ones.

There are two main problems with the raw data, both of which are acknowledged by the authors.

The first problem is that the investment data before 1948 are less reliable and are available only at a very high level of aggregation, namely, for eleven industry groups covering the whole of manufacturing. The use of these data to construct capital stock figures for 1954 and later years introduces a potentially significant measurement error, especially for 1954 and 1958. On the other hand, for 1963 and later years the influence of the pre-1948 investment on current capital stock is negligible.

The second limitation relates to the way investment is defined in the Census of Production. The Census figures are for acquisitions minus disposals of capital assets, but the definition of disposals refers only to the selling of assets; it does not include the scrapping of assets either by firms that exit the industry or by remaining firms. Of course, O'Mahony and Oulton assume finite asset lives and allow for depreciation, so ultimately any scrapped assets are eliminated from the capital stock estimates. But this happens with a significant lag, and there may be measurement error induced by the fact that certain industries experience a higher rate of exit or more rapid technological change (leading to the scrapping of assets) than others during a certain period.

The potential effect of these measurement errors on the results of interest in this book is not clear a priori. Fortunately, it may not be very significant in practice, as is suggested by the similarity of results using the benchmark estimates of capital stock to results using somewhat more refined estimates of capital stock whenever such more refined estimates could be constructed (see chapter 7, section 7.4, for a more detailed discussion of this important point).

Data on the number of plants (or Census "establishments") at the three-digit level of aggregation were taken from the Census of Production (various years). There were a number of practical problems in constructing a series of comparable figures for plant numbers, and a brief discussion of these problems is now in order.

First, the total number of plants in an industry is greatly affected by the number of very small plants. These typically account for a very small fraction of industry capital stock and often produce ancillary rather than core industry products. An additional complication in the present context is that the reported number of plants employing fewer than eleven persons for all manufacturing industry showed a 50% increase between 1972 and 1975, while the reported number of plants employing at least eleven persons remained more or less the same between 1972 and 1975, as well as between 1970 and 1977. One cannot help but think that the large increase in the number of very small plants is artificial, whatever the reason. Because of these various problems with very small plants, I did not take into account plants with fewer than twenty-five employees in my constructed figures for plant numbers.

Second, there were some problems with comparability across years. A number of three-digit industries were substantially redefined between 1963 and 1968. While fully comparable figures for the number of plants employing at least twenty-five persons for 1963 and 1968 were published in summary table 1 of the 1968 Census of Production, comparable figures for 1958 are not available. Moreover, the definition of "establishment" was modified between 1968 and 1970, and this caused an artificial decrease in the reported number of larger plants between these two years. In many industries the number fell by up to 20%, and in a few cases by as much as 50%. Clearly, then, the 1968 and 1970 data are not comparable.

A series of comparable figures for all years in my sample was constructed as follows. For 1963 and 1968 I used the data reported in summary table 1 of the 1968 Census of Production. For 1958 I adjusted the figures reported in the 1958 Census of Production to ensure comparability with 1963.[34] Finally, to construct the figures for

---

34. Whenever the 1963 industry definition had not been significantly modified in 1968, I constructed 1958 figures according to the following formula: *Estimated N(1958)* = $[N_1(1958)/N_1(1963)] * N(1963)$, where $N_1(1958)$ is the number of plants with at least twenty-five employees in 1958, as published in summary table 4 of the 1958 Census; $N_1(1963)$ is the number of plants with at least twenty-five employees in 1963, as published in summary table 4 of the 1963 Census; and N(1963) is the number of plants with at least twenty-five employees in 1963, as published in summary table 1 of the 1968 Census (the reference table for the series as a whole).

Whenever the 1963 industry definition had been significantly modified in 1968, it was usually still possible to construct comparable figures for 1958 with the help of more disaggregated data for 1958 and 1963 published in the individual industry reports of the 1963 Census. These were data on the number of plants operated by firms employing at least twenty-five employees, and were used on the assumption that the proportional change in this number over the period 1958–1963 would be equal to the proportional change in the number of plants employing at least twenty-five persons. I therefore computed *Estimated N(1958)* = $[N_2(1958)/N_2(1963)] * N(1963)$, where $N_2(1958)$ and $N_2(1963)$ are the figures from the 1963 Census industry reports.

1975 I proceeded as follows. First, I used the proportional change in the number of employees in plants with at least twenty-five employees between 1968 and 1970 as a measure of the actual proportional change in the number of larger plants over the period 1968–1970. Clearly, this approach is not ideal, but it is certainly much better than using the reported data on plant numbers for 1968 and 1970 to compute the 1968–1970 proportional change in plant numbers. Since the relevant period is very small, this should not cause any significant measurement error in the plant number estimates for 1970 and later years.[35] Then, to derive the estimated number of plants for 1975, I adjusted the figures reported in the 1975 volume of *Business Monitor, PA series: Report on the Census of Production* on the basis of my estimates for plant numbers in 1970 (and I also made some further adjustments because the cutoff points for the plant size distributions changed between 1970 and 1975).[36]

Employment data for three-digit industries were taken from summary table 1 of the 1963 Census, summary table 1 of the 1968 Census, and summary table 2 of the 1975 Census. Again, because of changes in industry definitions between 1963 and 1968, comparable data were sometimes not available for 1958, so they were constructed either by proportional adjustment of the reported figures or with the help

35. In the large majority of industries, the proportional change in the number of employees over the period 1968–1970 was small, while the proportional change in the *reported* number of plants was larger and always negative, which is consistent with what was said above about the noncomparability of the 1968 and 1970 figures for plant numbers. In only a few cases was the reverse true, and I then used the reported figures for plant numbers, on the assumption that the noncomparability problem was not serious in these particular industries.

Note that the use of the proportional change in the number of employees as a proxy for the actual proportional change in the number of plants captures changes in the number of plants caused by the shutdown of plants or the settingup of new ones, since these also affect employment. However, measurement error is induced by the fact that employment in existing plants may also change. But the period 1968–1970 is such a small part of the overall period examined in this book that this should not make much difference to the estimated overall change in K/N across industries.

36. More specifically, I started by computing *Estimated $N(1970) = [L(1970)/L(1968)] * N(1968)$*, where $L(1970)$ and $L(1968)$ are numbers employed in plants with at least twenty-five employees in 1970 and 1968, respectively, and $N(1968)$ is the number of plants with at least twenty-five employees in 1968, as published in summary table 1 of the 1968 Census. Then I computed *Estimated $N(1975) = [N_1(1975)/N_1(1970)] * Estimated N(1970)$*, where $N_1(1975)$ is the number of plants with at least eleven employees in 1975, as published in the 1975 Census industry reports, and $N_1(1970)$ is the number of plants with at least eleven employees in 1970, as published in the 1970 Census industry reports.

of more disaggregated data taken from the 1963 Census industry reports.[37]

Defining the Sample of Exogenous Sunk Cost Industries

This chapter focuses on exogenous sunk cost industries (i.e., industries without significant advertising or R&D expenditures). What constitutes "significant" advertising or R&D is, of course, somewhat arbitrary. It is clear that an industry should be classified as an exogenous sunk cost industry when its advertising-sales ratio and its R&D-sales ratio are both relatively low; but the theory is silent as to what constitutes an appropriate cutoff point. On the other hand, the 1% cutoff point is quite commonly used to classify industries according to their advertising or R&D intensity. This is the approach adopted in this book as well: I will define the group of exogenous sunk cost industries to consist of all industries with an average or typical advertising-sales ratio (ADS) of less than 1% *and* an average or typical R&D-sales ratio (RDS) of less than 1% over the relevant period.

Given this definition, it was necessary to determine the average or typical ADS and RDS for all four-digit industries for which concentration data were available, and then check whether these ratios were higher or lower than 1%. It should be emphasized that ADS and RDS are not to be used in this chapter as explanatory variables in the regressions. They are to be used only to classify industries as exogenous sunk cost, advertising-intensive, or R&D-intensive.

R&D-Sales Ratios

R&D expenditure data for the UK are available for various years since 1964 at a level of aggregation between the two-digit and the three-digit (for about thirty to forty "subsectors"). They have been published in *Research and Development Expenditure*, Studies in Official Statistics no. 21 (London: H.M.S.O., 1973); *Research and Development:*

---

37. In subsequent chapters I also use data on capital stock, the number of plants, and employment for 1954 and 1973. The capital stock data are from O'Mahony and Oulton (1990). Employment figures were taken from summary table 1 of the 1958 Census and from summary table 2 of the 1973 volume of *Business Monitor, PA series: Report on the Census of Production*. Data on plant numbers were taken from the industry reports of the 1958 and the 1973 Censuses. Corrections were made to ensure comparability over time.

Expenditure and Employment, Studies in Official Statistics no. 27 (London: H.M.S.O., 1976); and *Industrial Research and Development Expenditure and Employment*, Business Monitor MO14 (London: H.M.S.O., various years since 1972). Data for years before 1964 have been published in *Industrial Research in Manufacturing Industry: 1959–1960* (London: Federation of British Industries, 1961); *Estimates of Resources Devoted to Scientific and Engineering Research and Development in British Manufacturing Industry, 1955* (London: H.M.S.O., 1958); and *Industrial Research and Development Expenditure 1958* (London: H.M.S.O., 1960). The earlier data are somewhat less reliable, and even for the 1964–1975 period some of the series are incomplete, since the number of subsectors varies slightly from year to year.

A comparison of these various sources suggested that there were no substantial changes in R&D intensity at the sector level or for manufacturing as a whole between the late 1950s and the mid-1970s. Some sectors, such as mechanical engineering, experienced relatively significant fluctuations in R&D intensity over the period, in contrast with other sectors, such as chemicals, but the overall changes were not very large. Hence all the sources were used to classify the industries according to their R&D intensity. This was measured as the ratio of company-funded R&D to sales, where R&D includes all current and capital R&D expenditure by private or public firms, but excludes royalties and government-financed R&D.[38]

As already mentioned, however, these data are at a relatively high level of aggregation. To derive typical R&D-sales ratios for four-digit industries, the UK data were used to determine average or typical R&D intensities at the subsector level; in addition, US data were used as a guide for *relative* R&D intensities of industries within any UK subsector. R&D expenditure data for the US, at a level of aggregation similar to (or sometimes slightly higher than) the UK four-digit industry level, have been published by the Federal Trade Commission for the period 1973–1977 in an *Annual Line of Business Report* for each one of these years. Note that the direct use of the US data to classify British industries according to their R&D intensity would not be ap-

---

38. It is not clear to what extent royalties constitute an endogenous sunk cost. In addition, there are serious data limitations regarding royalties paid and received by UK firms at the industry level. On the whole, royalty payments were probably roughly equal to royalty receipts for UK manufacturing as a whole during the period under study, although payments were greater than receipts in engineering and the reverse was true for chemicals.

propriate, since the absolute levels of R&D intensity reported in the *Annual Line of Business* reports are, on average, much higher than the UK R&D-sales ratios for the same period. The assumption made here is simply that the relative R&D intensities of four-digit industries within any given subsector will tend to be similar in the two countries, which is not unreasonable. Thus the US figures were used as a guide for disaggregating the UK R&D-sales ratios to the four-digit industry level.[39]

In fact, this procedure was sometimes qualified to take into account additional information on R&D intensities in specific British industries, taken from official or unofficial sources, such as the reports of the Monopolies Commission, the reports of the National Board for Prices and Incomes, and case studies contained in Pratten (1971) and Pavitt (1980).

The overall procedure yielded reasonably accurate R&D-sales ratios. In any case, these were used only to classify the industries with respect to R&D intensity, using 1% as a cutoff point. Even if some industries were misclassified, they must be "marginal" cases with typical RDS close to 1%, so the empirical results should not be greatly affected. Finally, there were a few subsectors whose R&D intensity had changed over time in a way that affected the classification of industries. These industries were classified on the basis of what seemed to be their typical status over the relevant period.

Advertising-Sales Ratios

Data on manufacturers' advertising expenditure come from a number of sources. Summary table 9 of the 1963 Census of Production and summary table 4 of the 1968 Census of Production contain data on advertising expenditure for 1963 and 1968, respectively, at a level of aggregation somewhat higher than the three-digit level (ninety "industry groups" are distinguished for 1968, seventy for 1963). Data on press and TV advertising are also available for all years from market research sources: the *Statistical Review of Press Advertising* and the *Statistical Review of Independent TV Advertising*, both published by Legion Information Services, Ltd., until 1963; the *Statistical Review of Press and TV Advertising*, published by Legion Information Services,

---

39. In those cases where the level of aggregation in the *Annual Line of Business* reports was higher than the UK four-digit industry level, the assumption was usually made that all four-digit industries within a particular Line of Business category had the same R&D intensity.

Ltd., from 1963 until the early 1970s; and the *MEAL Monthly Digest of Advertising Expenditure*, published since 1968 by Media Expenditure Analysis, Ltd. These data are reported both for individual brands and for industries, at a relatively low level of aggregation, but they are often not available for low-advertising industries. Also, they relate to the UK market rather than to UK firms. Finally, data on aggregate advertising expenditure by type of advertising have been published by the Advertising Association in *Advertising Expenditure 1960* (London: Advertising Association, 1962) and, subsequently, in *Advertising Quarterly*.

A detailed comparison of these various data sources suggested (1) that the Census figures probably include some expenditures that represent sales promotion rather than media advertising, and (2) that the Legion/MEAL figures are, on the one hand, downward-biased due to incomplete coverage or noncoverage of certain media and, on the other hand, upward-biased because they are estimated by pricing the measured amount of advertising according to published rates, that is, without taking discounts into account (this mainly affects the estimates for TV advertising).

For my present purposes, advertising expenditure is defined as media advertising only, since other selling expenses generally affect marginal cost and are incurred at the price competition stage. The following procedure was therefore adopted for deriving advertising-sales ratios at the four-digit level for industries covered by Legion/MEAL. A minimum ADS was derived using Census sales data, approximately adjusted for net imports according to the *Annual Statement of the Trade of the United Kingdom*, and Legion/MEAL advertising data, adjusted downward to account for discounts from published rates for media advertising. Changes to this minimum ADS across time were checked. Moreover, a maximum ADS was estimated using Census sales and advertising expenditure data. Since these data are available for industry groups and only for 1963 and 1968, estimates at the four-digit level were derived by using the Legion/MEAL figures as a guide for the *relative* advertising intensities of four-digit industries within each industry group and by assuming that changes over time were similar to those of the minimum ADS.

Now as pointed out above, the difference between the two estimates of ADS is due to incomplete coverage or noncoverage of certain media by Legion/MEAL, and probably also to the inclusion of some sales promotion expenditures in the Census figures. Although it is not possible to know the magnitude of these errors in each industry, one can have an approximate idea of these magnitudes for manufacturing as a whole by comparing *aggregate* advertising expenditure figures reported in the various data sources, including figures on aggregate expenditure *by type of advertising* published by the Advertising Association. On the basis of that comparison for manufacturing as a whole, the average of the two estimates of ADS was taken as a good approximation to the true ADS in each particular industry.

Industries for which Legion/MEAL data were not available were usually easy to classify as having ADS < 1%, but sometimes US data from the *Annual Line of Business* reports were used as a guide to relative advertising intensities of four-digit industries within each Census industry group.

The advertising-sales ratios derived by this procedure should be reasonably accurate—and certainly sufficient for the purpose of classifying the industries with respect to advertising intensity. The only complication was that, in a few cases, the advertising-sales ratio changed over time in a way that affected the classification of the industry. These industries were classified on the basis of what seemed to be their typical status.

4.5 Empirical Model and Results

The theoretical analysis in this chapter suggests the following empirical model for concentration in exogenous sunk cost industries:

$Concentration = C(S, f, t, w)$,

where S, f, and t are as defined in section 4.2 and w is a vector of variables, some of which may be nonmeasurable, industry-specific characteristics. Note that the vector w includes the degree of horizontal product differentiation, a variable difficult to measure but unlikely to change significantly for any given industry within a ten-year or a twenty-year period.

Given that the theoretical predictions are for minimum concentration, should one estimate a lower bound rather than a regression line? The estimation of a deterministic lower bound does not allow for disequilibrium low levels of concentration below the bound, so it is probably not appropriate in the present context. On the other hand, estimating a stochastic lower bound by maximum likelihood

methods is possible only when the least squares residuals are positively skewed; otherwise the maximum likelihood estimates are
actually the same as the least squares estimates (see Waldman 1982).
As it turns out, the residuals from the least squares dummy variable
models estimated in this section are negatively skewed. This is due
to the fact that some industries experienced large increases in concentration during the period examined, so the observations for the
early years have large negative residuals. There may, however, be a
more fundamental problem with the estimation of a lower bound in
the present case, which is due to the panel structure of the data. In
particular, it may not be appropriate to control for industry effects
when estimating a bound. On the other hand, the failure to control
for industry effects would essentially reduce the data set to a pooled
time-series cross section, and it would then be very difficult to identify a competition effect on concentration because of the prevalence
of industry effects.

The above discussion suggests that the use of standard least squares
regressions is the most appropriate approach in the present case. Note
that an implicit assumption made under this approach is that the theoretical predictions for minimum concentration also apply to actual
concentration (i.e., that the mechanism driving the theoretical results
in the case of symmetric single-plant, single-product firms dominates
any other effects that may arise in a more complex setting).

The Sample

The basic sample of industries used in this chapter was constructed
from the set of industries with available concentration data as follows. First, since the focus of the chapter is on exogenous sunk cost
industries, all industries with average or typical advertising-sales
ratio (ADS) or R&D-sales ratio (RDS) higher than 1% over the relevant period were excluded. Second, I excluded industries with ambiguous state of competition in 1958 (or, in a few cases, ambiguous
state of competition in the 1960s and early 1970s). Third, I excluded
industries with a switch of competition regime but for which concentration data were not available for at least the three core years
1958, 1963 and 1968 (except for one industry without 1958 data,
which I nevertheless included in the basic sample since it abandoned
its restrictive agreement after 1963). However, I did not exclude industries without a change in regime and with available data for only

Table 4.1
The basic sample of exogenous sunk cost industries

Data available for	No. of industries with change of competition regime after 1958	No. of industries without change in competition regime after 1958
1958, 1963, 1968, 1975	27	34 (of which 2 collusive)
1958, 1963, 1968	9	3
1963, 1968, 1975	1	15
1958, 1963	0	14 (of which 8 collusive)
1963, 1968	0	4
Total	37	70

Notes: (1) The group of industries without change in competition regime after 1958 includes two industries (glazed tiles and cement) in which collusion continued throughout the period and for which data are available for all four years.
(2) The group without change in competition regime also includes eight industries that were affected by the nationalization of steel in 1967. All of these had agreements that were abandoned after 1963. They have been classified in this group because only 1958–1963 data are used for these industries.
(3) One industry with a change in competition regime and data available for 1963–1975 is included in the sample, since this industry abandoned its agreement after 1963.

a subset of the period 1958–1968. This left an unbalanced sample of 107 exogenous sunk cost industries, including 37 with canceled agreements, and 364 observations. In most cases, observations were available for all four years in the sample (1958, 1963, 1968, and 1975). In some cases, however, observations were available for only three years or for only two years. Table 4.1 gives details on the structure of the basic sample, distinguishing between industries with a change in competition regime after 1958 and industries without such a change. The full set of industries and information on key variables are given in appendix B (table B1).

As can be seen from table 4.1, the panel is quite unbalanced. This should not be a problem, but there is also an asymmetry in this sample between industries affected by the 1956 Act and industries not affected. In particular, industries without a full set of observations for at least the core period 1958–1968 are excluded if they are classified as industries having experienced a change in competition regime ($CHANGE = 1$) but not if they are classified as industries not affected by the 1956 Act ($CHANGE = 0$). The idea was to include as much information as possible in the basic sample while avoiding any potential bias in the comparison of the short-run and long-run effects of the legislation. It would also be interesting to check whether

Table 4.2
Concentration in 1958 and competition regime in exogenous sunk cost industries

	Mean C5 in 1958 (st. deviation of C5)
Basic sample	
Industries with change of competition regime after 1958 (n = 36)	0.514 (0.206)
Industries without change of regime after 1958, including 8 industries where collusion was abandoned after 1963 (n = 51)	0.496 (0.281)
More balanced sample	
Industries with change of competition regime after 1958 (n = 36)	0.514 (0.206)
Industries without change of competition regime after 1958 (n = 37)	0.435 (0.277)

Notes: (1) The figures are based on industries with available data for 1958; n indicates the number of industries.
(2) The group of industries without a change in competition regime includes two industries where collusion continued throughout the 1960s and the 1970s.
(3) The group of industries without a change in regime in the basic sample (but not in the more balanced sample) includes eight industries that were affected by the nationalization of steel in 1967. If these industries are excluded, the mean C5 in 1958 for the group without a change in competition regime in the basic sample is 0.455 (and the standard deviation is 0.283).

the results are substantially the same when this asymmetry between the two groups is removed. Thus I have also constructed a second sample, which includes only industries with a full set of observations for 1958–1968; in the large majority of cases, the 1975 observation is also available. This "more balanced sample" contains 73 industries, including 36 with a change in competition regime, and 280 observations.

Descriptive Statistics

Some descriptive statistics on initial levels and changes in concentration are reported in tables 4.2 and 4.3. As pointed out in the previous section, the five-firm sales concentration ratio, C5, is the only available measure of concentration at the four-digit industry level for the period under study. Table 4.2 reports descriptive statistics for C5 in 1958 for industries with and industries without a change in competition regime after 1958. There is little difference between the two groups in the basic sample: the mean of C5 is 0.514 for 36 industries

Table 4.3
Average change in C5, exogenous sunk cost industries: 1958–1968 and 1958–1975

	ΔC5 1958–1968	ΔC5 1958–1968	ΔC5 1958–1975
Industries with CHANGE = 1	0.129 (0.117) n = 36	0.125 (0.123) n = 27	0.164 (0.158) n = 27
Industries with CHANGE = 0	0.087 (0.090) n = 37	0.085 (0.090) n = 34	0.115 (0.121) n = 34

Notes: The figures in the first column are based on seventy-three industries with available observations for both 1958 and 1968. The figures in the second and third columns are based on sixty-one industries with available observations for 1958, 1968 and 1975. The figures in parentheses are standard deviations. n indicates the number of industries.

with $CHANGE = 1$ and 0.496 for 51 industries with $CHANGE = 0$. Note, however, that the latter group includes some collusive industries. Most of these are dropped in the more balanced sample, and although the difference between the two groups increases, it is still not very large.

The fact that average concentration was somewhat higher in the group of collusive industries may seem puzzling if one expects price competition to have a positive effect on concentration. However, the competition effect on concentration will be very difficult to identify in a cross section of industries because of the importance of industry-specific characteristics for concentration. Another factor that blurs the competition effect on concentration in a cross section is the fact that the two variables are also negatively related because of a third variable—capital intensity or the level of setup costs, which has a positive effect on concentration (see the regression results below) but also increases the likelihood of collusion, as discussed in chapter 3. In the more balanced sample of exogenous sunk cost industries, for instance, the mean of 1958 $\ln K/N$ for thirty-eight industries with collusive agreements in 1958 is -0.40 (with a standard deviation of 0.89), while it is -1.30 (with a standard deviation of 1.19) for thirty-five industries without agreements. The respective means (standard deviations) of $\ln K/L$ are 1.11 (0.59) for cartelized industries and 0.57 (0.90) for noncartelized industries. These figures confirm the positive link between capital intensity and collusion in 1958 obtained in chapter 3 for the manufacturing sector as a whole.

Table 4.3 presents statistics on the average change in $C5$ over the periods 1958–1968 and 1958–1975. The table suggests that price competition has a significant effect on market structure in exogenous sunk cost industries. Thus the average change in $C5$ between 1958 and 1975 in twenty-seven industries affected by the 1956 Act and for which observations are available for both these years was 16.4 percentage points. This compares to 11.5 percentage points for thirty-four industries not affected by the legislation. A comparison between industries with a large increase in $C5$ over the period 1958–1975 and industries with a large decrease in $C5$ over the same period is also very revealing. Obviously, the comparison is limited to the sixty-one exogenous sunk cost industries with available data for both these years. Of the five industries with the largest rise in $C5$, four (bread; single yarn of cotton, glass fibers, and man-made fibers; woven cloth of man-made fibers in the loom state; rope, twine, net, and manufactures thereof) are industries with $CHANGE = 1$, and only one (leather, undressed) has $CHANGE = 0$. Conversely, of the five industries with the largest fall in $C5$, four (fiberboard packing cases; men's and boys' tailored outerwear; fish and marine animal oils; bearings, other than ball bearings and roller bearings, and bushes) are industries with $CHANGE = 0$, and only one (metal windows, metal door frames, etc.) has $CHANGE = 1$.

These comparisons, as well as the figures presented in table 4.3, must be interpreted with some caution for two reasons. First, the use of the untransformed concentration ratio alone could be somewhat misleading, to the extent that the change in $C5$ depends, for purely statistical factors, on the initial value of $C5$ (see the discussion on functional form below). Second, changes in some of the other determinants of concentration were not similar in the two groups over the relevant periods. To control for these factors as well as for time effects, I now turn to the econometric analysis of market structure. As it turns out, the econometric results confirm the picture that emerges from the descriptive statistics of table 4.3.

Controlling for Industry and Time Effects

The econometric model that I will use is a panel data model with individual-specific effects. These should control for industry-specific characteristics that are relative stable, and thus unlikely to change significantly for any given industry within a ten-year or a twenty-year period. Three time dummies, for 1963, 1968, and 1975, are also included among the regressors (the benchmark year is 1958). There are good reasons for this. The average five-firm concentration ratio across UK manufacturing industries, which had already been rising throughout the 1950s, increased by eight percentage points—from about 55.5% to 63.5%—between 1958 and 1968, then changed very little between 1968 and the mid-1970s (Hart and Clarke 1980, Hart 1985). Now it was during the 1958–1968 period that the impact of the 1956 Act on competition was mostly realized. If the rise in concentration was partly caused by factors other than the 1956 Act or changes in setup costs and market size, then the estimated coefficients would be seriously biased if the model were specified without time dummies.

Several factors have been cited as having contributed to the rise in concentration during the 1960s. They include changes in the tax system in the mid-1960s that are thought to have encouraged mergers; economies of scale in product development, distribution, and the raising of finance; improvements in the system of transport; the emergence of large retailers with significant bargaining power; and the progressive opening of the British economy. It is very difficult to measure these factors at the industry level, and no such attempt will be made here. However, there is no reason to expect that they would affect the group of industries with a change in competition regime and the control group of industries in different ways. To the extent that their effect has been more or less realized across all industries, it should be largely captured by the time dummies.

The Effect of Foreign Competition

Of all these factors, the one whose omission from my empirical specification is the most regrettable is the intensification of foreign competition caused by the gradual opening of the British economy during the 1960s and the 1970s. Unfortunately, it is difficult to control for this in a more satisfactory way. Ideally, one would need some measure of the extent of foreign competition for each industry across time. Two possible candidates are the import penetration ratio and the rate of effective protection. However, there are serious problems, theoretical and practical, with both of these measures. Estimates of effective rates of protection are available at a high level of aggregation and for only some years in my sample; also, they are often subject to measurement error. The import penetration ratio, on the other hand, is a poor proxy for the extent of foreign competition: it cannot capture the effect of the mere threat of competitive imports, it does not take into account imports by domestic producers (which may not be in competition with domestic products), and it is itself clearly endogenous. Moreover, the industrial classification used in the foreign trade statistics during the period examined in this book has been subject to changes over time and is often difficult to match with the industrial classification used in the Census of Production.

It should be emphasized, however, that there is no reason to think that foreign competition may have had a differential effect across the two groups of industries (i.e., the group with $CHANGE = 1$ and the one with $CHANGE = 0$) after 1958. As pointed out in section 3.4 of chapter 3, a rough test of the link between the extent of foreign competition and the incidence of collusion in the 1950s revealed a negative association, but this was not statistically significant when controlling for sector effects (see also Symeonidis 1999b). Thus there is no strong evidence of any difference in initial conditions between the two groups with respect to foreign competition.

Moreover, although tariff reductions occurred throughout the 1960s and the 1970s, they became more pronounced after 1967, when the Kennedy Round was completed (see Morgan and Martin 1975).[40] This may be part of the reason why Kitchin (1976) was not able to find any overall pattern of falling or rising effective protection between 1963 and 1968 in UK manufacturing. On the other hand, the effect of the 1956 restrictive practices legislation was mostly realized between 1958 and 1968 (i.e., before the first stage of the Kennedy Round tariff cuts).

Finally, there is no evidence that changes in the level of effective protection were any different between industries with a change in competition regime and industries in the control group, at least between 1963 and 1968. Kitchin provides estimates of effective protection for both these years at a level of aggregation between the two-digit and the three-digit industry level. Although these estimates are subject to serious limitations, they are sufficient for a rough comparison. Effective tariff protection increased, according to these figures, in six out of twelve industry groups that I could classify as having experienced a change in competition regime, and decreased

---

40. In contrast, the Dillon Round tariff cuts of 1961 were small and were partially offset by the import surcharge of 1964–1966.

in the other six. For industry groups that I could classify as having experienced no change in competition regime, the respective numbers were eight and ten.

In summary, then, it is not unreasonable to argue that the estimated effect of the 1956 Act in this and in subsequent chapters is not biased by the failure to control for foreign competition.

The Econometric Specification

Since there was no obvious choice of functional form, a number of specifications were tried. An argument often made in empirical studies of concentration is that since the concentration ratio is bounded between 0 and 1, the change in the concentration ratio may depend, for purely statistical reasons, on its initial value. For instance, the concentration ratio cannot increase by much in absolute terms when it is already very high, and it cannot decrease by much when it is already very low. Failure to take this into account could result in heteroskedasticity, and it could even bias the regression coefficients if there is a systematic association between the initial value of concentration in the sample and any of the regressors. In the present case, there may be a weak association, linear or nonlinear, between the value of $C5$ in 1958 and the variable $CHANGE$ (see chapter 3 and table 4.2). To overcome any potential problems from this, it seemed appropriate to complement the results using $C5$ with results using a transformation of $C5$ which is not bounded (see Wright 1978). The logistic transformation, $\text{logit} C5 = \ln[C5/(1 - C5)]$, was therefore tried as an alternative to the untransformed concentration ratio.

Plots of residuals against fitted values and formal tests for heteroskedasticity such as the Koenker test (which is robust to nonnormality of the residuals) and the Breusch-Pagan test were used to compare the two specifications. It turned out that heteroskedasticity was present in both specifications and that, contrary to what is usually expected, it was not more pronounced in regressions using $C5$ than in those using $\text{logit} C5$. Results for both $C5$ and $\text{logit} C5$ will be reported below.

Preliminary regressions were also performed to compare different functional forms for the independent variables. As expected, specifications with log transformations of the exogenous variables were generally preferable on the basis of the properties of the residuals and/or tests for nonnested models.

The above discussion suggests the following specification:

$$Conc_{it} = \alpha_i + \beta_1 \ln Sales_{it} + \beta_2 \ln(K/x)_{it} + \beta_3 Y63 + \beta_4 Y68 + \beta_5 Y75$$
$$+ \beta_6 CHANGE * Y63 + \beta_7 CHANGE * Y68$$
$$+ \beta_8 CHANGE * Y75 + u_{it},$$

where i stands for industries and t for time periods, and α_i is the industry-specific effect. "Conc" is either the four-digit industry five-firm sales concentration ratio, $C5$, or its logistic transformation, logit $C5$. "Sales" is the four-digit industry sales revenue deflated either by the general producer price index (SS) or by an industry-specific producer price index (DS); both of these are measures of market size. "K/x" is either the three-digit industry capital stock of the average plant, K/N, or the three-digit industry capital-labor ratio, K/L; both of these are proxies for setup costs.[41] $Y63$, $Y68$, and $Y75$ are time dummies for 1963, 1968, and 1975, respectively.

Finally, the interaction terms should capture any differences in the evolution of concentration after 1958 between industries with a change in competition regime ($CHANGE = 1$) and industries without such a change ($CHANGE = 0$). Thus the coefficient on $CHANGE * Y63$ measures the effect of the 1956 Act on $C5$ or logit $C5$ between 1958 and 1963, the coefficient on $CHANGE * Y68$ measures the effect between 1958 and 1968, and the coefficient on $CHANGE * Y75$ measures the effect between 1958 and 1975. Obviously, $CHANGE$ is defined here according to the industry categories used for $C5$. As pointed out in the previous section, an attractive feature of the present approach to modeling the competition effect is that it does not impose any structure on the competition data regarding the timing of the impact of the legislation. Rather, it allows the data to reveal how the short-run effect of the legislation compares to the long-run effect for manufacturing industry as a whole.

I should also point out that it is not possible to use a dynamic panel data model (i.e., include lagged values of $C5$ or logit $C5$ among the explanatory variables) in the present context. Such an approach would be motivated by the fact that concentration may adjust grad-

---

41. Recall that since the model includes industry-specific effects, one need not assume that the three-digit industry K/L or K/N is an accurate measure of setup cost at the four-digit industry level. All that is required is that the *change* in K/L or K/N is roughly similar for all four-digit industries within any given three-digit industry, and is an accurate measure of the *change* in setup cost.

ually to its long-run equilibrium level. However, the estimation of a dynamic model involves taking first differences and then using lagged values of the endogenous variable as instruments; to apply this method, one effectively "loses" the first one or two periods in the panel. In the present case, this would amount to losing much of the crucial information captured by the interactions of *CHANGE* with the time dummies.

In any case, it is not clear that a dynamic specification would be a significant improvement over the one used here. For one thing, the years in the panel that I use in this chapter, and also in the panels used in subsequent chapters, are separated by long periods, typically five years or more. Although concentration may take longer than five years to fully adjust to its long-run equilibrium level, much of the adjustment should occur within a few years. Moreover, my econometric specification does not impose any structure on the competition data regarding the timing of the impact of the legislation. In other words, it allows the competition effect on concentration to operate with an arbitrary lag. Of course, this flexibility of the specification does not extend to the other determinants of concentration included in the model, namely, market size and setup costs. Changes in setup costs, in particular, may affect market structure relatively slowly, as firms gradually renew their capital stock. However, recall that setup costs are measured somewhat imprecisely throughout this book. As a result, part of the effect of changes in setup costs is likely to be captured by the time dummies in most regressions. I will return to this issue below, when discussing the regression results. The point I wish to make here is that (1) the use of a weak proxy for setup cost, (2) the intertemporal structure of the panel, and (3) the way in which the competition effect is modeled reduce any potential benefit that might be derived from specifying a dynamic model for concentration in the present context.[42]

A stronger objection to the model used here is that some of the independent variables may be endogenous. This is probably not a serious problem for the market size and setup cost proxies, since the variation in these empirical measures across industries and five-year periods must be mainly driven by the variation in the corresponding

---

42. It could also be argued that if lagged concentration were indeed an important explanatory variable in the model, its omission would show as significant serial correlation in the residuals. But there is no such evidence in the models estimated below.

theoretical variables. In the case of market size, an indirect check of this claim is provided by a comparison of results using ln DS with those using ln SS. For example, consider the argument that changes in sales revenue may be endogenous with respect to changes in the competition regime since an intensification of price competition may raise deflated sales revenue.[43] If that were indeed a serious problem in the data, one would expect the results from regressions using ln DS and those from regressions using ln SS to differ, especially regarding the coefficients on the competition variables. As will be seen below, the results are in fact very similar.

A more serious objection is the potential endogeneity of the variable $CHANGE$. This is an important issue and needs to be discussed in detail.

The Key Identifying Assumption

The principal objection regarding the use of the variable $CHANGE$ is that whatever difference one may observe in the evolution of concentration after 1958 between industries with $CHANGE = 1$ and industries with $CHANGE = 0$ may be to some extent due to unobserved characteristics that differ between the two groups of industries rather than to the 1956 legislation. If this were indeed the case, then the key identifying assumption of this book would no longer be valid (see chapter 1). Unfortunately, it is not possible to test formally for exogeneity because there are no appropriate instruments for $CHANGE$. Those variables that were shown in chapter 3 to be strongly correlated with the incidence of collusion in 1958 cannot be used as instruments: capital intensity is also a key determinant of concentration and is therefore included as an independent variable in the model, while advertising intensity is not relevant for a sample of exogenous sunk cost industries and is itself endogenous.

However, there are several reasons to believe that the potential endogeneity of $CHANGE$ is not a serious problem in the present

43. In fact, it is by no means clear that the breakdown of collusion will lead to a rise in industry sales revenue when the deflator used is the general producer price index for all manufacturing. Whether sales revenue increases or decreases will depend on the elasticity of demand. Although a joint monopoly would operate on the elastic part of the demand curve, its abolition may well move the industry to the inelastic part of the demand curve, so sales revenue may rise or fall relative to its original level. Moreover, collusion need not involve joint profit maximization, so it is not even clear that a collusive industry will be operating on the elastic part of the demand curve.

context.[44] First, table 4.2 suggests that the difference in market structure conditions in 1958 between industries affected by the legislation and those not affected is not very pronounced. This is consistent with the evidence presented in chapter 3, according to which there was no systematic link between concentration and collusion across manufacturing industries in 1958. Admittedly, the relative similarity of initial market structure conditions is not a very decisive argument against the potential endogeneity of *CHANGE* in the present case, because the two groups of industries were operating under different conditions in 1958. Indeed, if one looked at the end of the period under study (i.e., the year 1975), one would find that the two groups had quite different average concentration ratios then. On the other hand, the relative similarity of initial market structure should at least help dispel the concern that some of the difference that we observe between the two groups after 1958, especially in regressions using *C5*, is due to a purely statistical factor, the fact that the change in *C5* may generally depend on the initial value of *C5*.

Second, one could argue that even if *CHANGE* is influenced by certain variables that also affect concentration and are not included in the model, these variables are more likely to be part of the industry-specific effect than of the error term, since the large majority of industries classified as collusive in 1958 were subject to restrictive agreements for many years before the introduction of the 1956 legislation. Such correlations between the industry-specific effects and the endogenous variables, if they exist, will not cause any econometric difficulties, provided that an appropriate specification is used.

Finally, a powerful indirect check of the claim that the potential endogeneity of *CHANGE* is probably not a serious problem would be to examine the evolution of market structure in the two groups of industries *before* 1958. If the two groups were found to be similar in this respect, then it would probably be safe to conclude that any observed difference between them in later periods is due to the legislation. Unfortunately, the available concentration data before 1958 are not comparable with the data used in this book because of changes in industry definitions and the concentration measures used. How-

---

44. Arguments similar to those that I use below, and in subsequent chapters, to defend the key identifying assumption in my analysis of the effects of the 1956 Act have also been put forward in several other recent studies of natural experiments. See, for instance, Chevalier (1995), Eissa (1995), and Eissa and Liebman (1996).

ever, there are comparable figures for firm numbers in both 1954 and 1958 for a large sample of industries. As will be pointed out in chapter 7, where these data are analyzed in detail, there was almost no difference whatsoever in the evolution of firm numbers during the period 1954–1958 between the two groups of industries.[45]

Further evidence can be obtained from a comparison of three-firm employment concentration ratios for three-digit industries in 1951 and 1958. The data are contained in Armstrong and Silberston (1965), and are taken from Evely and Little (1960) and the 1958 Census of Production. Because of changes in industry definitions and other noncomparabilities between the two years, the sample is small. The average change in the three-firm concentration ratio C3 during the period 1951–1958 was 2.5 percentage points for fifteen exogenous sunk cost industries with a change of competition regime after 1958, and 2.0 percentage points for eleven exogenous sunk cost industries without such a change. A test of independence of the respective means of the change in C3 in the two groups could not reject the null hypothesis of independence at the 5% level or, indeed, at the 10% or 20% level. Although this sample is very small and the three-digit level of aggregation is far from ideal, there is clearly no evidence of any differential underlying trend between the two groups.

Econometric Results

The choice of estimation procedure in panel data models depends on whether the individual effects are correlated with the independent variables (Hsiao 1986). If they are not correlated, then a random-effects specification is preferable, since it produces efficient estimates by taking account of the unobserved heterogeneity both between groups and within groups. If the individual effects are correlated with the independent variables, then the random-effects model produces inconsistent estimates, so a fixed-effects model must be used instead. This latter model takes into account only the within-group heterogeneity, and therefore produces estimates that are less efficient, although they are always consistent. In the absence of any prior indication of potential correlation between the individual effects and the

---

45. A four-year period is, of course, rather short. However, the period 1958–1963 is also rather short, and this does not prevent the difference between the two groups (presumably caused by the 1956 Act) from emerging sharply during that period. See chapter 7 for details.

independent variables, a formal test, such as the Hausman test, can be used to choose the preferred model.

In the present case, the Hausman test has given somewhat mixed results, largely depending on what proxy is being used for setup cost: in most regressions using ln K/N the test favors the fixed-effects model, while in most regressions with ln K/L it favors the random-effects model. The two sets of results are very similar with respect to the market size variable and the competition terms, but differ regarding the respective explanatory power of the time dummies and the setup cost proxies. In any case, results from both models are given below for the basic sample: table 4.4 presents results for the fixed-effects specification, and table 4.5 reports results for the random-effects model, using generalized least squares estimation. Results are reported in table 4.6 for a more balanced sample that includes only industries with a full set of observations for 1958, 1963, and 1968. Only results for the random-effects model are presented for the more balanced sample, because the Hausman test now more clearly fails to reject this model. The reported standard errors are heteroskedasticity-consistent, adjusted for small sample bias following MacKinnon and White (1985).[46]

The results from all three tables tell a similar story about the effect of the 1956 Act on concentration in exogenous sunk cost industries. The coefficients on $CHANGE * Y68$ and $CHANGE * Y75$ are both positive and statistically significant at the 1% or the 5% level in all regressions. The magnitude of these coefficients implies that the intensification of price competition following the 1956 legislation raised, on average, the five-firm concentration ratio by about six to seven percentage points in exogenous sunk cost industries. The effect was almost fully realized by 1968. Note that this may understate the impact of price competition on concentration to the extent that there is measurement error in the construction of $CHANGE$ due to ineffective or unregistered agreements. Moreover, the coefficient on $CHANGE * Y63$ indicates that the effect was only partly realized by 1963, presumably because in several industries competition had not yet emerged or its effect on concentration had not yet been fully realized. All these results are not much affected by the choice of de-

---

46. The reported results are all for models without serially correlated disturbances. I also estimated a model with an AR1 error structure, and the results were very similar to those reported here. The estimated coefficient of serial correlation in these regressions was very low (and sometimes even negative): between 0.05 and −0.12 when using the basic sample, and between 0.05 and −0.03 when using the more balanced sample.

pendent variable, $C5$ or logit $C5$, or the choice of proxies for market size and setup cost.

Three other features of the results are worth emphasizing. First, the effect of market size on concentration is everywhere negative and statistically significant at the 1% level, which is consistent with the theoretical predictions of sections 4.2 and 4.3. Moreover, the coefficients on sales revenue are very similar in these regressions, irrespective of whether one uses ln SS or ln DS as a proxy for market size, thus strengthening the case for treating sales revenue as an exogenous variable.

Second, the use of rather weak proxies for setup cost in these regressions results in significant correlation between these variables and the time dummies. In regressions using ln K/N and in random-effects regressions using ln K/L, the time dummies are not statistically significant, but the setup cost proxies are highly significant and have large coefficients. The reverse is true for fixed-effects regressions using ln K/L. Clearly, the impact of the increase in setup costs across industries during the 1960s and the 1970s cannot be very clearly separated from the impact of other factors that are probably captured by the time dummies in these data. This is a fairly general feature of the results reported in this book, but, as can be seen from a comparison across tables in this chapter, it has no significant implications for the results of interest (i.e., those regarding the competition effect and the market size effect).

Third, two different R^2s are reported for each regression in table 4.4. The first is derived from transforming the data to obtain deviations from industry means and applying OLS to the transformed data. The second (denoted R^2_{LSDV}) is obtained from applying OLS to the untransformed data after including a set of industry dummies among the regressors. Thus the difference between the two R^2s is a measure of the explanatory power of the industry effects in these regressions. As can be seen in table 4.4, the industry effects explain about half the variation in the concentration ratio in these data.

4.6 Concluding Remarks

Competition policy on restrictive agreements in the UK has been an important factor in increasing concentration in exogenous sunk cost manufacturing industries. The empirical results of this chapter are consistent with theoretical models that emphasize the endogeneity of market structure and the effect of firm conduct on structure. A key

Table 4.4
Regression results for concentration in exogenous sunk cost industries (fixed-effects estimation)

	Dependent variable: C5				Dependent variable: logit C5			
ln SS	−0.078	—	−0.082	—	−0.30	—	−0.31	—
	(0.016)		(0.017)		(0.10)		(0.10)	
ln DS	—	−0.073	—	−0.073	—	−0.31	—	−0.31
		(0.015)		(0.016)		(0.09)		(0.10)
ln K/N	0.089	0.100	—	—	0.45	0.49	—	—
	(0.023)	(0.023)			(0.14)	(0.13)		
ln K/L	—	—	0.022	0.035	—	—	0.19	0.23
			(0.038)	(0.038)			(0.21)	(0.20)
Y63	0.006	0.004	0.026	0.027	0.07	0.07	0.16	0.16
	(0.012)	(0.013)	(0.014)	(0.014)	(0.08)	(0.08)	(0.08)	(0.08)
Y68	0.038	0.035	0.081	0.078	0.21	0.21	0.39	0.39
	(0.020)	(0.020)	(0.025)	(0.025)	(0.11)	(0.11)	(0.14)	(0.13)
Y75	0.038	0.033	0.100	0.093	0.23	0.22	0.48	0.47
	(0.027)	(0.027)	(0.038)	(0.039)	(0.16)	(0.16)	(0.21)	(0.21)
CHANGE * Y63	0.041	0.040	0.038	0.036	0.09	0.09	0.08	0.07
	(0.020)	(0.020)	(0.021)	(0.021)	(0.12)	(0.12)	(0.12)	(0.12)
CHANGE * Y68	0.062	0.056	0.057	0.050	0.26	0.24	0.24	0.22
	(0.021)	(0.021)	(0.021)	(0.021)	(0.12)	(0.12)	(0.12)	(0.12)
CHANGE * Y75	0.073	0.062	0.067	0.056	0.32	0.27	0.30	0.25
	(0.026)	(0.026)	(0.027)	(0.027)	(0.14)	(0.14)	(0.15)	(0.15)

R^2	0.52	0.51	0.50	0.48	0.45	0.46	0.44	0.44
R^2_{LSDV}	0.96	0.96	0.95	0.95	0.95	0.95	0.95	0.95
No. of industries	107	107	107	107	107	107	107	107
No. of industries with $CHANGE = 1$	37	37	37	37	37	37	37	37
No. of observations	364	364	364	364	364	364	364	364

Notes: Heteroskedasticity-consistent standard errors in parentheses. R^2 is derived from transforming the data to obtain deviations from industry means and applying OLS to the transformed data. R^2_{LSDV} is obtained from applying OLS to the untransformed data after including a set of industry dummies among the regressors.

Table 4.5
Regression results for concentration in exogenous sunk cost industries (random-effects estimation)

	Dependent variable: C5				Dependent variable: logit C5			
ln SS	-0.085 (0.012)	—	-0.076 (0.013)	—	-0.38 (0.07)	—	-0.33 (0.07)	—
ln DS	—	-0.081 (0.012)	—	-0.071 (0.013)	—	-0.38 (0.07)	—	-0.33 (0.08)
ln K/N	0.123 (0.010)	0.124 (0.010)	—	—	—	0.61 (0.06)	—	—
ln K/L	—	—	0.140 (0.015)	0.141 (0.015)	—	—	0.72 (0.08)	0.72 (0.08)
Y63	-0.002 (0.012)	-0.001 (0.012)	0.002 (0.013)	0.003 (0.013)	0.04 (0.07)	0.05 (0.07)	0.05 (0.07)	0.06 (0.08)
Y68	0.020 (0.013)	0.024 (0.013)	0.019 (0.016)	0.022 (0.016)	0.14 (0.07)	0.16 (0.07)	0.12 (0.08)	0.14 (0.08)
Y75	0.008 (0.016)	0.013 (0.016)	-0.006 (0.020)	-0.002 (0.021)	0.10 (0.09)	0.13 (0.09)	0.002 (0.11)	0.02 (0.11)
CHANGE*Y63	0.040 (0.018)	0.040 (0.018)	0.041 (0.018)	0.040 (0.019)	0.09 (0.10)	0.09 (0.10)	0.09 (0.10)	0.09 (0.10)
CHANGE*Y68	0.062 (0.018)	0.055 (0.018)	0.067 (0.020)	0.060 (0.019)	0.26 (0.11)	0.23 (0.11)	0.29 (0.11)	0.26 (0.12)
CHANGE*Y75	0.076 (0.022)	0.064 (0.022)	0.085 (0.023)	0.074 (0.023)	0.34 (0.13)	0.28 (0.13)	0.39 (0.13)	0.34 (0.13)

Constant	1.486	1.443	1.170	1.119	4.46	4.49	2.91	2.89
	(0.129)	(0.133)	(0.133)	(0.138)	(0.76)	(0.79)	(0.77)	(0.80)
R^2	0.51	0.51	0.47	0.47	0.45	0.45	0.42	0.42
Hausman statistic	2.80	0.71	22.29	17.88	3.86	1.45	15.99	12.91
Prob-value	0.95	0.99	0.004	0.02	0.87	0.99	0.04	0.11
No. of industries	107	107	107	107	107	107	107	107
No. of industries with $CHANGE = 1$	37	37	37	37	37	37	37	37
No. of observations	364	364	364	364	364	364	364	364

Note: Heteroskedasticity-consistent standard errors in parentheses.

Table 4.6
Regression results for concentration in exogenous sunk cost industries: more balanced sample (random-effects estimation)

	Dependent variable: C5				Dependent variable: logit C5			
ln SS	-0.084	—	-0.076	-0.067	-0.37	—	-0.33	—
	(0.014)		(0.014)	(0.015)	(0.07)		(0.08)	
ln DS	—	-0.078	—	—	—	-0.37	—	-0.32
		(0.014)				(0.08)		(0.08)
ln K/N	0.122	0.126	—	—	0.61	0.62	—	—
	(0.013)	(0.013)			(0.07)	(0.07)		
ln K/L	—	—	0.124	0.127	—	—	0.68	0.68
			(0.021)	(0.021)			(0.11)	(0.11)
Y63	-0.003	-0.003	0.003	0.002	0.01	0.01	0.02	0.02
	(0.014)	(0.014)	(0.016)	(0.016)	(0.08)	(0.08)	(0.09)	(0.09)
Y68	0.024	0.027	0.033	0.035	0.15	0.16	0.16	0.17
	(0.016)	(0.016)	(0.019)	(0.020)	(0.08)	(0.08)	(0.10)	(0.10)
Y75	0.011	0.013	0.012	0.014	0.11	0.12	0.06	0.07
	(0.019)	(0.020)	(0.025)	(0.026)	(0.10)	(0.10)	(0.13)	(0.13)
CHANGE * Y63	0.042	0.042	0.044	0.044	0.12	0.12	0.13	0.13
	(0.020)	(0.020)	(0.020)	(0.021)	(0.11)	(0.11)	(0.11)	(0.11)
CHANGE * Y68	0.059	0.051	0.062	0.055	0.26	0.23	0.28	0.25
	(0.020)	(0.019)	(0.021)	(0.021)	(0.11)	(0.11)	(0.12)	(0.12)
CHANGE * Y75	0.074	0.062	0.080	0.069	0.34	0.28	0.37	0.32
	(0.023)	(0.024)	(0.024)	(0.025)	(0.14)	(0.14)	(0.14)	(0.14)

Constant	1.469	1.403	1.175	1.080	4.38	4.34	2.87	2.70
	(0.149)	(0.154)	(0.152)	(0.157)	(0.82)	(0.88)	(0.84)	(0.88)
R^2	0.55	0.54	0.51	0.50	0.49	0.49	0.46	0.46
Hausman statistic	1.87	2.91	15.53	12.88	4.81	2.48	12.07	10.43
Prob-value	0.98	0.94	0.05	0.12	0.78	0.96	0.15	0.24
No. of industries	73	73	73	73	73	73	73	73
No. of industries with $CHANGE = 1$	36	36	36	36	36	36	36	36
No. of observations	280	280	280	280	280	280	280	280

Note: Heteroskedasticity-consistent standard errors in parentheses.

prediction of these models is that in exogenous sunk cost industries, an intensification of price competition, brought about by institutional changes such as the introduction of cartel laws or a higher degree of economic integration, will cause a rise in concentration. This basic theoretical insight gets strong support from the evidence presented here. In particular, the results indicate that, on average, cartel policy in the UK raised the five-firm concentration ratio by about six to seven percentage points between 1968 and 1975 in exogenous sunk cost industries. To put this figure in some perspective, note that nearly half of the entire British manufacturing sector was cartelized in the 1950s and that the average five-firm concentration ratio across *all* manufacturing industries increased by about eight percentage points between 1958 and 1975.

Moreover, the view taken in this chapter is that the increase in concentration in previously collusive British industries during the 1960s was the inevitable result of a general structural mechanism. In other words, the initial level of concentration was simply not sustainable once competition intensified, so market structure had to adjust to restore profits in the long run. Additional insight on this mechanism will be provided in chapter 7, which will examine the effect of the 1956 restrictive practices legislation on profitability in the short run and in the long run.

The mechanism driving the theoretical results of this chapter—namely, the requirement that market structure adjusts under free entry and exit to satisfy the requirement that gross profits cover sunk costs—is fully compatible with the view, expressed in Swann et al. (1974, pp. 176–177) and Curry and George (1983), among others, that a toughening of cartel policy would cause firms to try to restore market power through mergers and would thus lead to higher concentration. This view places less emphasis on structural effects than on the pursuit of market power that is assumed to underlie firm behavior in oligopolistic industries. The key difference between a purely behavioral interpretation of the effects of the 1956 legislation and an interpretation that emphasizes the operation of a structural mechanism is that, under the latter interpretation, one must conclude that firms essentially had no choice but to try to restore their market power.

The problem with the purely behavioral interpretation is that it provides no general explanation of how market structure is determined for any given competition regime.[47] Hence it cannot really be seen as an *alternative* theory of the competition-concentration relationship. As a description of managerial behavior, however, it is perfectly consistent with the structural mechanism outlined in this chapter, and it may even help draw attention to an ancillary mechanism that could potentially speed up the adjustment of concentration to its new long-run equilibrium value following an increase in the intensity of price competition. In particular, more efficient or financially stronger firms may try to restore their market power soon after competition intensifies rather than go through a period of reduced profitability while waiting for the exit of the more vulnerable firms—which can take time, especially in industries with slow technological progress and a slow rate of depreciation of the capital stock.

The mechanism that drives the evolution of structure in exogenous sunk cost industries is relatively straightforward. Once we allow for advertising or R&D, however, complications arise. The theoretical predictions are no longer as clear and strong as the predictions for exogenous sunk cost industries. More important, there has to be a partial change of emphasis, from a single variable, concentration, to the joint determination of a pair of variables, concentration and the level of endogenous sunk costs (advertising or R&D). The next two chapters examine the effects of competition in advertising-intensive and R&D-intensive industries. Then the final chapter returns to some of the most central predictions of the present theory, those that relate to the joint determination of market structure and profitability, in a way that highlights some of the basic similarities across classes of industries.

---

47. Another problem with the behavioral interpretation is that it may not always be valid. I will return to this issue in chapter 7, section 7.3.

5   Price Competition, Advertising, and Market Structure in Advertising-Intensive Industries

5.1   Introduction

Chapter 4 provided strong econometric evidence to support the theoretical prediction of a positive effect of price competition on concentration in exogenous sunk cost industries. This chapter continues the search for general theoretical results and empirical regularities on the effects of competition, focusing this time on advertising-intensive industries.

Things are more complicated in this case, because the intensification of price competition may affect the incentive of firms to spend on advertising. The first of two key issues examined in this chapter is therefore the link between price and nonprice competition. The second is the effect of competition on market structure. If more price competition causes firms to spend less on advertising, then the effect on market structure can, in principle, be ambiguous: the decrease in the amount of sunk costs that each firm must cover at equilibrium may or may not offset the fall in gross profits due to increased price competition, so concentration may decrease or increase. Clearly, this ambiguity arises only if more intense price competition is associated with less advertising, a hypothesis that has received some empirical support from case studies of particular industries (see Scherer and Ross 1990, p. 673; Gasmi et al. 1992; Slade 1995), but on which there is no systematic cross-industry evidence.

The objective of this chapter is, then, to analyze the *joint* effect of short-run price competition on advertising and concentration in advertising-intensive industries, combining theory, econometric analysis, and case-study evidence. The game-theoretic analysis brings together and expands on two previous lines of research. The first is the literature on the determinants of market structure. Selten (1984) and Sutton (1991) have examined how price competition affects concentration in exogenous sunk cost industries, but they have not discussed this issue in the context of industries with significant endogenous sunk costs. The second is the literature on the interaction between short-run and long-run decisions in oligopoly. Several authors have examined the effect of anticipated short-run conduct on strategic long-run decisions (e.g., Yarrow 1985, Ireland 1987, Jehiel 1992, Friedman and Thisse 1993, Fershtman and Gandal 1994, Ziss 1994, Fershtman and Pakes 2000). However, in most of these studies, products are homogeneous or horizontally differentiated, and in nearly all of them (the only exception being the study by Fershtman and Pakes) market structure is taken as exogenous. In the model described in this chapter, on the other hand, the product is vertically differentiated (in the sense that there are several varieties of the product, which differ in quality or "perceived quality") and the long-run equilibrium is seen as involving the joint determination of market structure and the level of advertising expenditure or intensity. The exogenous factors in this framework are preferences, technology, and short-run conduct.

In the next two sections I derive a number of theoretical predictions. In advertising-intensive industries, theory places weaker constraints on the space of outcomes than in exogenous sunk cost industries. Nevertheless, it is possible to show that certain outcomes cannot occur within the present framework, since they are inconsistent with the requirement that net profits be zero in free-entry equilibrium, while others, although possible, may be unlikely.

I then test the theory against empirical evidence on the effects of the 1956 Restrictive Trade Practices Act on advertising and market structure in advertising-intensive industries. I use econometric analysis to identify the overall effects of price competition across industries. This is, of course, a powerful test since it provides general results and allows one to control for other factors that may have influenced the evolution of industries during the period under study. On the other hand, this approach may not fully reveal some of the subtle ways in which price competition shapes the evolution of advertising-intensive industries. To shed more light on the specific mechanisms at work in these industries, the econometric analysis is supplemented in this chapter by the analysis of case studies.

5.2 Theoretical Framework

Consider an advertising-intensive industry where each firm produces one variety of a differentiated product. Competition in such an industry can be modeled by means of a three-stage game as follows. At stage 1 each of N_0 potential entrants decides whether or not to enter the industry, and those firms that do enter pay an exogenously given sunk cost of entry f. At stage 2 each firm i chooses to spend an amount A_i on advertising. Advertising increases the consumers' willingness to pay for the firm's variety, either by increasing its perceived quality or by providing information about the variety.[1] Finally, at stage 3 firms set prices or quantities. Note that A_i is a fixed cost which is incurred prior to the price or quantity competition stage; in particular, a higher level of advertising is not associated with any increase in the marginal cost of the firm. N_0 is assumed to be sufficiently large so that at any equilibrium of the three-stage game there is at least one nonentering firm. In what follows, I will characterize a symmetric subgame perfect equilibrium in pure strategies in this three-stage game.

This game structure captures the idea that at any point in time some variables are more difficult to change than others, and are therefore taken as given when making shorter-term decisions. Hence at any point in time some costs can be thought of as sunk, even though firms in practice incur a continuous stream of expenditures. A long-run strategic variable in every industry is the decision to enter or not to enter. In industries where advertising is effective, and therefore nonprice competition through advertising is a key element in the set of competitive strategies employed by firms, an additional long-run strategic variable is the expenditure involved in creating an advertising-based brand image. Note that whether or not advertising should be regarded as a long-run decision has been a matter of some

---

1. In general, advertising will shift the demand function of a "representative" consumer outward, so that the consumer is willing to pay a higher price for a given quantity or to buy a larger quantity at the same price. This is what is meant by the phrase "advertising increases the consumers' willingness to pay." Note that A_i could also be interpreted as purely "informative" advertising if it were assumed to increase market size, in the sense of an increase in the number of consumers, rather than the willingness of any particular consumer to pay. The results of this section would still be valid under such an interpretation, since the only crucial assumption in the present framework is that A_i raises gross profit π_i. The exact way this is brought about is irrelevant.

debate.[2] Much recent work, however, has treated advertising as a long-run decision on the grounds that *brand image* reacts relatively slowly to current expenditure, is probably difficult to modify in the short run, and is in all likelihood more difficult to modify than standard short-run choice variables, such as price or output. This chapter follows this approach.

I assume, for simplicity, that advertising and the entry decision are the only long-run choice variables in the game. It is, of course, true that in some advertising-intensive industries R&D is also important. R&D could also be included in the parameter A_i, in which case the results of this section would be more generally valid for all classes of industries with significant endogenous sunk costs (advertising or R&D). Under this interpretation the parameter A would represent the sum of advertising and R&D expenditure throughout this section.[3]

An alternative approach is to point out that the number of industries where advertising and R&D are both key strategic variables—as suggested by an advertising-sales ratio and an R&D-sales ratio that are both in excess of 2%, say—is in fact very small. Usually one or the other of these two variables is dominant. Hence, in the present chapter A_i can be treated as representing advertising only, on the implicit assumption that the presence of endogenous R&D expenditures in some advertising-intensive industries will not significantly alter the mechanism and the results described. I adopt this approach, although I will provide some further cautionary remarks on this issue at the end of this section. Note that this approach is perhaps justified by the fact that, for several of the key empirical results of this chapter, the sample used consists of industries with typical advertising-sales ratio higher than 2% (rather than 1%, which is the commonly used cutoff point).

The Third-Stage Subgame

The equilibrium of the third-stage subgame can be represented by a vector of payoffs $\pi_i(S, N, h, e, t, A_1, \ldots, A_i, \ldots, A_N, g_1, \ldots, g_i, \ldots, g_N)$,

---

2. Schmalensee (1992) has argued that it is not clear that advertising should be seen as a longer-term decision than price, because advertising depreciates relatively quickly and price, too, can often have durable effects on demand. He also shows, however, that key theoretical results derived from a three-stage game that treats advertising as a sunk cost are robust to alternative approaches to modeling the interaction between advertising and price competition, provided that advertising is treated as a *fixed* cost.
3. This is the approach taken in Symeonidis (2000b).

where S is market size, N is the number of firms that have entered at stage 1, h is a measure of the degree of horizontal product differentiation, e is a measure of "advertising effectiveness," g_i is a vector of parameters specific to firm i and independent of N and the A_i's (such as marginal cost or capacity), and t is a measure of the intensity of price competition.

The interpretation of t is the same as in the previous chapter: for any given N, π_i will depend on the firms' pricing strategies, which in turn will partly depend on exogenous institutional factors, such as the climate of competition policy or the degree of economic integration. Although a change in t will be mainly interpreted in this chapter (as elsewhere in the book) specifically in terms of the degree of collusion, it can be seen more broadly as any change in the gross profit associated with firms' conduct (but not with demand-side or technological parameters such as h or e), for given N and A_i's. For instance, a reduction in manufacturers' margins, for given N and A_i's, caused by pressure from retailers or competition from imports, would represent an increase in the intensity of price competition t. However, as pointed out in chapter 4, t is not equivalent to the price-cost margin, which is treated here as endogenous.

In the benchmark case of symmetric single-plant firms, the equilibrium gross profit of firm i can be written as $\pi_i(S, N, h, e, t, A_i, (A_{-i}))$, where (A_{-i}) denotes the $(N-1)$-tuple $(A_1, A_2, \ldots, A_{i-1}, A_{i+1}, \ldots, A_N)$. Alternatively, one can write gross profit as $\pi_i[S, C(N, A_i, (A_{-i})), h, e, t, A_i, (A_{-i})]$, where C is any concentration measure whose value increases in $1/N$ for given A_i's (and depends only on N when $A_i = A_j$, $\forall i, j, j \neq i$), such as the n-firm concentration ratio. We assume that π_i is everywhere increasing in S, e, and h, and decreasing in t and N. In addition, we make two assumptions about the effect on π_i of changes in own and rival advertising expenditure:

Assumption A1. π_i is increasing and strictly concave in A_i with $d\pi_i/dA_i > 1$ at $A_i = 0$, and there exists a level of A_i such that $d\pi_i/dA_i = 1$ for any given N and set of A_j's.

Assumption A2. π_i is nonincreasing in A_j, $\forall j \neq i$.

For some of the results derived below, a third assumption is also used:

Assumption A3. If $A_i = A_j = A$, $\forall i, j, j \neq i$, and all the A's increase (decrease) by the same amount, π_i cannot fall (rise).

These assumptions are straightforward to interpret and seem rather uncontroversial. The first one says that a firm's *gross* profit is increasing at a decreasing rate in own advertising expenditure, and that there exists a point of the profit function, involving some positive amount of advertising, such that one more extra unit of advertising costs as much as the gross profit it creates.[4] The second assumption says that a firm's gross profit is nonincreasing in any given rival's advertising expenditure. This does not rule out advertising spillovers, but it does imply that any such spillovers are not very large.[5] Finally, the third assumption says that if, starting from a situation where all firms spend the same amount on advertising, all firms equally increase (decrease) their expenditure, then the *gross* profit of each firm will not fall (rise). Essentially this implies that the effect of own advertising on own gross profit is sufficiently strong that it cannot be offset by the joint effect of rivals' advertising, when moving from one symmetric configuration to another.

This last assumption is perhaps somewhat stronger than the first two, so it may be worth pointing out that all three assumptions are satisfied in standard models of vertical differentiation with symmetric firms, such as the isoelastic demand model described in Sutton (1991), and the linear demand model with quality indices described in Sutton (1998) and also discussed later in this chapter. In any case, assumption A3 is required only for propositions 5.2 and 5.3 below, but not for proposition 5.1.

The Second-Stage Subgame

At stage 2 each firm chooses A_i to maximize its net profit $\pi_i - A_i - f$, given the choices of the other firms and the number of firms that

---

4. Note that since $d\pi_i/dA_i > 1$ at $A_i = 0$, firms always find it profitable to advertise. One could also imagine that the function π_i is first convex and then concave in A_i. Although a firm would never optimally choose a point on the convex part of the gross profit function representing a positive amount of advertising, it might choose not to advertise at all, if the net profit from doing so were larger than the net profit at the point where $d\pi_i/dA_i = 1$. Since the focus of this chapter is on advertising-intensive industries, it seems natural to ignore cases that involve zero advertising. I also abstract from the issue of potential threshold effects (in the sense that advertising below a certain level has little impact), since any part of the gross profit function below the threshold would have little relevance for the present analysis.

5. This point is further elaborated in the next chapter, section 6.2, where the issue of spillovers is discussed in more detail in the context of R&D-intensive industries. The key insights from that discussion are relevant for advertising spillovers as well.

have entered at stage 1. The first-order condition is $d\pi_i/dA_i = 1$, $\forall i$. This says that each firm spends on advertising up to the point where the cost of an extra unit of advertising is equal to the profit it creates in the third-stage subgame. At any symmetric equilibrium, we have $A_i = A$, $\forall i$, so the first-order condition for firm i can be written as

$$\frac{d}{dA_i}\pi_i(S, N, h, e, t, A_i, (A_{-i})) = 1 \quad \text{at} \quad A_i = A_{-i} = A. \tag{5.1}$$

Equation (5.1) defines the level of advertising expenditure incurred by firms as a function of the number of firms that have entered at stage 1. Note that the assumption has been made that at stage 2 of the game the A_i's are the Nash equilibrium outcomes of a non-cooperative game, whatever the intensity of price competition at the final stage. In other words, firms do not collude in advertising, either perfectly or imperfectly. This assumption, which is common in the theoretical literature on "semicollusion," is largely motivated here by the empirical evidence, according to which collusion with respect to media advertising is generally rare (see Scherer and Ross, 1990, chapter 16). The present empirical context is no exception to this: collusion with respect to media advertising was certainly very rare in British manufacturing industry in the 1950s, as discussed in chapter 2 of this book.

The Symmetric Equilibrium

At stage 1, firms enter as long as they can make a nonnegative net profit, anticipating equation (5.1). The free-entry condition, which is assumed to hold whatever the intensity of price competition at the final stage of the game (in line with the empirical evidence on the British cartels reviewed in chapter 2), is

$$\pi_i = \pi_i(S, N, h, e, t, A_i, (A_{-i}))|_{A_i=A_{-i}=A} = A + f, \quad \forall i, \tag{5.2}$$

where, for simplicity, N is treated as a continuous variable. This implies that each firm makes exactly zero net profit at equilibrium. The number of firms N^* and level of advertising expenditure A^* at the symmetric equilibrium are defined by the two necessary conditions (5.1) and (5.2). Since I am here concerned with comparative statics results, I will assume that these two conditions define a unique equilibrium with $N^* \geq 2$ and $A^* > 0$.

There are a number of different effects at work following a change in the intensity of price competition (or any other exogenous variable). First, there is a direct effect on gross profit, given the initial levels of A^* and N^*. Second, there is an effect on the firms' incentive to spend on advertising, given N^*, which causes both gross profit and the level of advertising expenditure (i.e., both sides of equation (5.2)) to change. These changes also induce a change in N^* until net profit is driven back to zero. Finally, there are indirect effects of the change in N^* on profit as well as on advertising expenditure. Since the sign and magnitude of these effects can vary, little can be said in general about the comparative statics of A^* and N^* without imposing more structure on the model. Clearly, there is no reason to expect that more price competition will affect the incentive to advertise in any particular way. Moreover, since both sides of the free-entry condition will be affected by a change in t, it is not clear in what direction N^* should change to restore the free-entry condition.

But while the comparative statics properties of the model are ambiguous when A^* and N^* are considered separately, several general results can be derived for the *joint* behavior of A^* and N^* following a change in the intensity of price competition.

The Joint Effect of Price Competition on Advertising and Concentration

I begin with the first of three general results regarding the joint behavior of A^* and N^* (or the concentration ratio C^*) following a change in the intensity of price competition t. Note that analogous results can be derived for the effect of a change in any of the other exogenous variables in the model. Let ΔA^* and ΔN^* (ΔC^*) denote the change in A^* and N^* (C^*), respectively. The following proposition places bounds on the space of outcomes by excluding certain outcomes as not admissible within the theory.

Proposition 5.1. Under assumptions A1 and A2, (1) an increase in the intensity of price competition t cannot simultaneously cause $\Delta A^* \geq 0$ and $\Delta N^* \geq 0$ ($\Delta C^* \leq 0$), and (2) no other outcomes are excluded.

Proof. First consider part (1). The gross profit of firm i at the initial equilibrium can be written as

$$\pi_0^* = \pi(A_i = A_0^* \mid S, N_0^*, h, e, t_0, A_{-i} = A_0^*) = A_0^* + f,$$

while the gross profit at the new equilibrium is

$$\pi_1^* = \pi(A_i = A_1^* \mid S, N_1^*, h, e, t_1, A_{-i} = A_1^*) = A_1^* + f.$$

We will also need to define the profit of firm i at the initial equilibrium values of t and N^* when firm i sets $A_i = A_1^*$ while all other firms set $A_j = A_0^*$:

$$\pi' = \pi(A_i = A_1^* \mid S, N_0^*, h, e, t_0, A_{-i} = A_0^*).$$

The proof is by contradiction. Assume that $N_1^* \geq N_0^*$ and $A_1^* \geq A_0^*$ following a rise in t (i.e., we also have $t_1 > t_0$). From A2 and the fact that π_i is decreasing in N and t, we obtain $\pi_1^* < \pi'$. Moreover, since the function $\pi_i(A_i \mid S, N_0^*, h, e, t_0, A_{-i} = A_0^*)$ is concave in A_i and its slope is equal to 1 at $A_i = A_0^*$, its slope is smaller than 1 at all points between A_0^* and A_1^*. Hence $\pi' - \pi_0^* < A_1^* - A_0^*$. Combining the two inequalities, we obtain $\pi_1^* - \pi_0^* < A_1^* - A_0^*$. This is, however, impossible, since net profit must be zero at equilibrium and therefore we must have $\Delta \pi^* = \Delta A^*$. Hence it cannot be the case that $\Delta A^* \geq 0$ and $\Delta N^* \geq 0$ following a rise in t.

To prove part (2) of the proposition, we only need to show that no other outcomes can be excluded even for a much more structured version of the model. The following set of ancillary assumptions is intended to eliminate some of the indirect effects following a change in t:

Assumption A4. $d\pi_i/dA_i$ is nonincreasing in A_j, $\forall j \neq i$.

Assumption A5. $d\pi_i/dA_i$ is independent of N. This implies that A^* is independent of N at equilibrium.

Assumption A6. π_i is homogeneous of degree zero in the A_i's. This ensures that at equilibrium, when all firms set $A_i = A^*$, the payoff of each firm in the third-stage subgame is independent of A^*.

Consider now the effect of an increase in the intensity of competition on N^* and A^*. We distinguish three cases, depending on the sign of the derivative $d\pi_i/dA_i$ with respect to t. Suppose first that $d\pi_i/dA_i$ is everywhere increasing in t (i.e., that the return to a marginal increase in A_i is higher when competition is more intense). In this case an increase in t causes N^* to fall and A^* to rise. To see this, first notice that when t increases, equation (5.1) no longer holds at the original level of A^*. Assumptions A4 and A5 and the concavity of π_i ensure that the new level of A^* will be higher if (5.1) is to be satisfied. The free-entry condition and assumption A6 then imply that, at the initial level of N^*, the equilibrium payoff of each firm will now be lower than the advertising expenditure incurred. Hence N^* must fall.

Next suppose that $d\pi_i/dA_i$ is independent of t. It is then easy to see that A^* will not change and N^* will fall following an increase in t. Finally, if $d\pi_i/dA_i$ is everywhere decreasing in t, the possibility arises of more competition leading to a decrease in concentration. Equation (5.1) no longer holds at the original level of A^* once competition intensifies. Assumptions A4 and A5 and the concavity of π_i then ensure that A^* falls. This may or may not offset the fall in π_i caused by the increase in t, so the direction in which N^* must change to restore the free-entry condition is not known.   □

The intuition for proposition 5.1 is as follows. Starting from a zero-profit equilibrium, an increase in t has a direct negative effect on net profit. For the zero-profit condition to be restored, net profit must rise. This cannot happen through a joint increase in the number of firms (a fall in the concentration ratio) and advertising expenditure, since this will unambiguously further reduce net profit. The reason is that (1) entry reduces the profit of existing firms; (2) an increase in own advertising has a stronger effect on sunk cost than on gross profit when starting from a long-run equilibrium with $d\pi_i/dA_i = 1$, $\forall i$ (owing to the concavity of the gross profit function); and (3) an increase in rival advertising cannot increase own profit.

Note that proposition 5.1 is a prediction on the joint effect of price competition on firm advertising expenditure and market structure. In empirical work, one often has to focus on industry advertising expenditure or the advertising-sales ratio. What can the present theory say about these variables? Consider first the industry advertising expenditure N^*A^*. The key question is whether we can rule out the case $\Delta(N^*A^*) \geq 0$ and $\Delta N^* \geq 0$ ($\Delta C^* \leq 0$) following an increase in t. This joint outcome cannot result from $\Delta A^* \geq 0$ and $\Delta N^* \geq 0$, because of proposition 5.1. And it is very unlikely to result from $\Delta A^* < 0$ and $\Delta N^* \geq 0$, with the rise in N^* offsetting the fall in A^*, so that N^*A^* rises. The reason is that the only way to obtain $\Delta N^* \geq 0$ following a rise in t is through a significant fall in A^*, as will be explained in more detail below. But since a significant fall in A^* is required for even a small rise (or no change) in N^*, it is very difficult to obtain $\Delta(N^*A^*) \geq 0$ together with $\Delta N^* \geq 0$ ($\Delta C^* \leq 0$) following a rise in t.

Next, consider the advertising-sales ratio. It seems plausible to assume that a rise in the intensity of price competition t will *not* lead, in general, to a fall in industry sales revenue in the long run. Hence, ruling out the joint outcome $\Delta A^* \geq 0$ and $\Delta N^* \geq 0$, as proposition 5.1 does, also implies ruling out a joint increase in the advertising-sales ratio (at the firm or at the industry level) and fall in concentration under plausible assumptions about the effect of the rise in t on sales revenue.

Proposition 5.1 suggests that only weak predictions can be made regarding the effect of price competition on market structure and advertising expenditure in advertising-intensive industries. This contrasts with the case of exogenous sunk cost industries, where the competition effect on concentration is unambiguously positive, as shown in chapter 4. The next proposition implies that while a negative effect of price competition on concentration in advertising-intensive industries cannot be ruled out, it may be unlikely.

Proposition 5.2.   Under assumptions A1–A3, a necessary condition for N^* to rise or remain unchanged (hence for C^* to fall or remain unchanged) following an increase in the intensity of price competition t is that equilibrium advertising expenditure A^* falls, and this fall is at least as large as the fall in gross profit directly caused by the increase in t.

Proof.   Suppose that equilibrium concentration falls or remains unchanged following an increase in t. We know from proposition 5.1 that in this case A^* must fall. We now want to show, in addition, that the fall in A^* must be at least as large as the fall in gross profit which was the *direct* result of the increase in t. To be more precise, let π_0^* denote again the gross profit of firm i at the initial equilibrium and π_1^* the gross profit at the new equilibrium. The profit of firm i following a rise in t at the initial levels of N^* and A^* is given by

$$\pi'' = \pi(A_i = A_0^* \,|\, S, N_0^*, h, e, t_1, A_{-i} = A_0^*).$$

From proposition 5.1 we know that if a rise in t results in $N_1^* \geq N_0^*$, it must be the case that $A_1^* < A_0^*$. Also, the assumption that π_i is decreasing in t implies that $\pi'' < \pi_0^*$. We now want to show that if a rise in t results in $N_1^* \geq N_0^*$, then we must have $A_0^* - A_1^* \geq \pi_0^* - \pi''$.

Assume the opposite, that is, $A_0^* - A_1^* < \pi_0^* - \pi''$, given that equilibrium concentration falls or does not change following a rise in t. From assumption A3 and the assumption that π_i is decreasing in N^*, we obtain $\pi_1^* \leq \pi''$. Combining the two inequalities, we obtain $A_0^* - A_1^* < \pi_0^* - \pi_1^*$, which is impossible, since net profit must be zero at long-run equilibrium and hence we must have $\Delta\pi^* = \Delta A^*$. It follows that if concentration falls or does not change following a rise in t, then it must be the case that $A_0^* - A_1^* \geq \pi_0^* - \pi''$. This completes the proof. Note that the reverse is not true, that is, the condition $A_0^* - A_1^* \geq \pi_0^* - \pi''$ is not sufficient to rule out an increase in concentration following a rise in t. (For instance, concentration may rise if the fall in A^* reduces gross profit below π''.)   □

Proposition 5.2 is driven by the fact that a "small" fall in advertising following a rise in t would not be sufficient to offset the direct negative effect of the rise in t on gross profit, and hence net profit would fall at the initial level of concentration. Thus concentration would have to rise to restore the free-entry condition through a rise in profit. To obtain a fall (or no change) in concentration, the fall in A must be large enough to offset the effect of the rise in t on gross profit, so that net profit rises (or does not change) at the initial level of concentration.

Proposition 5.2 is a conditional prediction on the competition-concentration relationship. Since the prediction is conditional on the behavior of another observable variable, profit, it is empirically testable. In particular, an empirical test of this proposition can take two forms. If concentration does not rise (the number of firms does not fall) in the long run following an intensification of price competition in an advertising-intensive industry, then firm advertising expenditure must have fallen and the fall must be at least as large as the fall in gross profit directly caused by the intensification of competition. Alternatively, if firm advertising expenditure rises, remains unchanged, or falls by less than the fall in gross profit directly caused by the intensification of price competition, then concentration must rise (the number of firms must fall) in the long run.

Like proposition 5.1, proposition 5.2 relates to advertising expenditure at the firm level, but also has indirect implications for industry advertising expenditure. Broadly speaking, the proposition says that if concentration does not rise when price competition intensifies, then it must be the case that firm advertising has fallen a lot. It is then also likely that industry advertising and the advertising-sales ratio will have fallen a lot. On the other hand, if this latter effect is not observed when price competition intensifies, then concentration must rise.

Although proposition 5.2 involves a comparison between endogenous variables, these are related to exogenous industry characteristics. Define p as the fraction of profit that is lost as a direct consequence of the rise in t, that is, $(1 - p)\pi_0^* = \pi''$, where π_0^* has previously been defined as the gross profit at the initial equilibrium and π'' has been defined as the gross profit following the rise in t at the initial levels of A^* and N^*. Recall that $f > 0$ denotes the exogenous element of sunk cost.

Proposition 5.3. Under assumptions A1–A3, a necessary condition for N^* to rise or remain unchanged (hence for C^* to fall or remain unchanged) following an increase in the intensity of price competition t is that the fraction of endogenous sunk costs in total sunk costs at the initial equilibrium is larger than the fraction of gross profit lost as a direct result of the rise in t, namely, that $1 - f/\pi_0^* > p$.

Proof. According to proposition 5.2, if concentration does not rise when t increases, then $A_0^* - A_1^* \geq \pi_0^* - \pi''$. Because of the zero-profit condition $\pi_0^* = f + A_0^*$, the previous inequality implies $\pi'' \geq f + A_1^*$, and therefore $\pi'' \geq f$, which is equivalent to $1 - f/\pi_0^* > p$.   □

In industries where exogenous sunk costs are an important part of total sunk costs, the free-entry condition implies that the profit margin can be significantly larger than advertising intensity. Hence, when price competition intensifies, there may be little scope for a fall in A^* that matches the fall in gross profit. Proposition 5.3 implies that a nonpositive effect of price competition on concentration may be unlikely in industries with substantial exogenous sunk costs and relatively low advertising intensity, unless the intensification of price competition has only a small direct effect on the profit margin.[6]

---

6. A numerical example may help clarify this point. Consider an industry with symmetric firms and unit-elastic demand, so that the industry sales revenue is fixed and equal to S. Let $(p - c)/p$ denote the price-cost margin and NA/S the industry advertising-sales ratio. The free-entry condition implies $(p - c)/p = NA/S + Nf/S$, where f is the exogenous sunk cost.

Suppose that initially $(p - c)/p = 6\%$ and $NA/S = 1\%$. Now if the price-cost margin falls below 5% as a direct result of tougher price competition, concentration must rise because A cannot fall below zero. In other words, at any new equilibrium we must

Remarks and Clarifications

Several remarks on the general results derived above are in order. First, the parameter A has been interpreted throughout this section as expenditure on advertising. Thus the implicit assumption has been made that R&D is not very important in most advertising-intensive industries. Now the number of industries where advertising and R&D are both key strategic variables is indeed small; nevertheless, such cases exist. The question then arises as to how the presence of significant endogenous R&D expenditures in these industries may affect the results presented here. The answer is that propositions 5.1–5.3 would still hold, but the parameter A would have to be interpreted as the total amount of endogenous sunk costs, that is, the sum of advertising and R&D costs. Provided one adopts this interpretation, propositions 5.1–5.3 would be valid as general statements on the links between price competition, endogenous sunk costs, and market structure in industries where one or more types of endogenous sunk costs are significant.

Second, the results of this section have been derived for the benchmark case of symmetric single-product firms. Extending the analysis to the case of asymmetric or multiproduct firms is beyond my present scope. However, it is not clear what other effects may arise in these more complex settings that would offset the mechanisms identified for the benchmark case. Thus it is certainly the case that advertising-intensive industries typically comprise multiproduct firms with very different advertising intensities, including firms that advertise very little or not at all. However, low advertisers usually have low sales, so they do not significantly affect either the concentration ratio or the industry advertising-sales ratio (although they may affect the total number of firms). Moreover, certain choices in-

---

have $NA/S \geq 0$, so the free-entry condition can be restored only through a rise in the price-cost margin and/or a fall in Nf/S, both of which require a fall in N. Note that even with a smaller fall in the price-cost margin, a large proportional change in the advertising-sales ratio is required if concentration is not to rise.

Things are different for high-advertising industries. Thus, for instance, if initially $(p-c)/p = 6\%$ and $NA/S = 4\%$, then a fall of the price-cost margin to 5% can be easily offset by a fall in A, and concentration need not rise. In particular, if the price-cost margin is homogeneous of degree zero in the A_i's, then N will remain unchanged provided that NA/S goes to 3%, which represents only a 25% decrease in the advertising-sales ratio; and it will rise if A falls by more than 25%. If, on the other hand, a fall in A causes a reduction in the price-cost margin, then A will need to fall by more than 25% to keep N constant; but this will still be a modest proportional fall in A.

volving multiple varieties, such as the introduction or promotion of secondary brands by high advertisers, may be treated for some purposes as analogous to advertising choices of single-product firms. Finally, the presence of efficiency differences should not matter more in advertising-intensive industries than in exogenous sunk cost industries, and it has already been argued in chapter 4 that the basic theoretical insights regarding the competition effect on market structure are not substantially modified in the presence of efficiency differences.

In any case, the question of whether the theoretical results derived in this section are indeed those that matter for analyzing the effects of price competition in advertising-intensive industries is ultimately an empirical one. The theory developed will be tested below against econometric evidence as well as against evidence from case studies of particular industries.

Third, the results of this section were derived from a model where advertising increases the consumer's willingness to pay rather than providing information about the product. In the empirical analysis, however, the data used are for total advertising, and no distinction is made between "persuasive" and "informative" advertising. However, this discrepancy is more apparent than real. First, as mentioned above, the basic theoretical results of this section would be valid even if advertising were purely informative. Second, in most brand advertising by manufacturers the "persuasive" element is dominant, especially in consumer-good industries, which represent the bulk of the samples used in this chapter.

Finally, let me point out once again that the assumption of the exogeneity of the intensity of price competition t is a simplification. The arguments developed in chapter 4 are valid here as well. To summarize, the assumption of exogeneity of the theoretical variable t is probably justified in the present case because, first, cartelization in the 1950s was largely a function of exogenous industry characteristics and, second, the key determinant of changes in firms' pricing conduct during the period under study was the exogenous change in cartel policy. Moreover, even if t is seen as endogenous (i.e., as a function of an exogenous institutional variable T and a vector of other variables, possibly including N and A), the results of this section could be restated as predictions on the behavior of N^* and A^* *conditional on the observed change in t*, following a change in the institutional variable T. One can therefore conduct a reduced-form analysis of the effect on market structure and nonprice competition of a change in the main determinant of t during the period under study, namely, the institutional variable T.

5.3 A Specific Example: The Linear Demand Model with Quality

To gain additional insight on the links between price competition, advertising, and market structure in advertising-intensive industries, I now briefly examine a model of vertical product differentiation with endogenous market structure that can be seen as a specific case along the lines of the theoretical framework developed in the previous section. This is in fact an extended version of the linear demand model introduced in chapter 4. It should be emphasized from the outset that some of the results of this model are probably specific to its particular structure and the functional forms used. The interest of the model for my present purposes lies in the fact that, despite its specificity, it is sufficiently flexible to generate several of the possible outcomes of the more general theoretical framework of the previous section. As a result, the model can provide additional insight as to the kinds of factors that determine these outcomes.

The Basic Model

Consider an advertising-intensive industry producing a potentially infinite number of varieties of a differentiated product. Competition in the industry is described by a three-stage game as follows. There are N_0 potential entrants, each with the capacity to produce a single variety of the product. At stage 1 they decide whether or not to enter at an exogenously given sunk cost of entry f. At stage 2 each firm chooses a variety, described by a vertical attribute u that I will call "quality" and, in the case of an advertising-intensive industry, represents brand image. Quality increases the consumers' willingness to pay for the firm's variety, but it comes at a sunk cost—namely, advertising expenditure—which is incurred at stage 2. Finally, at stage 3 firms set quantities. Assume that N_0 is sufficiently large so that at any equilibrium of the game there is at least one nonentering firm.

There are S identical consumers, and the utility function of each consumer takes the form

$$U = \sum_i \left(x_i - \frac{x_i^2}{u_i^2} \right) - \sigma \sum_i \sum_{j<i} \frac{x_i}{u_i} \frac{x_j}{u_j} + M. \tag{5.3}$$

This is the quadratic utility function used in chapter 4, augmented by the quality indices u_i (see Sutton 1996, 1997b, 1998; Symeonidis 2000c). The parameters α_1 and α_2 have been dropped to ease notation; these are scale parameters and do not affect the comparative statics results derived from the model. Recall that σ, $\sigma \in (0, 2)$, is an inverse measure of the (exogenous) degree of horizontal product differentiation. We require that $u_i \geq 1$, $\forall i$; this implies that advertising expenditure takes nonnegative values (see below).

The consumer's inverse demand for variety i is given by

$$p_i = 1 - \frac{2x_i}{u_i^2} - \frac{\sigma}{u_i} \sum_{j \neq i} \frac{x_j}{u_j} \tag{5.4}$$

in the region of quantity spaces where prices are positive, and her demand function for variety i is

$$\frac{x_i}{u_i} = \frac{u_i(1 - p_i)[2 + \sigma(N - 2)] - \sigma \sum_{j \neq i} u_j(1 - p_j)}{(2 - \sigma)[2 + \sigma(N - 1)]} \tag{5.5}$$

in the region of prices where quantities are positive, where N denotes the number of firms that have entered the industry. It can be easily seen that x_i is decreasing in p_i and increasing in p_j, $\forall j \neq i$. Also, it is increasing in u_i and decreasing in u_j, $\forall j \neq i$.[7] Since there are S consumers, firm i sells quantity Sx_i. Let each firm have a constant marginal cost of production c, where $c < 1$.

As in chapter 4, I will use here a continuous reduced-form collusion parameter to model different degrees of competition in the final stage of the game. In particular, I assume that in the final stage each firm maximizes the sum of its own (gross) profit and a fraction λ of the (gross) profit of each of the rival firms. The parameter λ, $0 \leq \lambda \leq 1$, is, then, an inverse measure of the intensity of short-run competition, with $\lambda = 0$ representing the Cournot-Nash equilibrium and $\lambda = 1$ corresponding to perfect collusion.

Although the use of λ is a somewhat arbitrary way to model collusion, it turns out to be very useful in providing insight about the effects of price competition in advertising-intensive industries within

---

7. A nice feature of the present model—and one that distinguishes it from models of "pure vertical differentiation," which do not have this property—is that it gives rise to reduced-form profit functions where profit increases in own quality and decreases in rival quality.

the context of the present example.[8] Note that, as in chapter 4, the assumption of exogeneity of λ is justified here not only by an appeal to well-known theoretical results of a multiplicity of equilibria in models of repeated games, but also by reference to the empirical context of this book: when the principal influence on λ is a change in the institutional framework, it is plausible to assume that any feedback effects from N or the u_i's on λ are small (i.e., $\partial\lambda/\partial N \approx 0$ and $\partial\lambda/\partial u_i \approx 0$, $\forall i$) and can be ignored.

Finally, we need to specify an advertising cost function linking quality u_i to advertising expenditure A_i. Let this function be given by $A_i = \varepsilon(u_i^\beta - 1)$, where ε is a positive constant and β is a measure of the cost of advertising or, alternatively, an inverse measure of the effectiveness of advertising in raising a product's perceived quality.[9] We require that $\beta > 2$; this amounts to assuming that $A(u)$ rises with u more rapidly than gross profit and ensures that the model is well behaved in a sense that will become clear below. (For instance, $\beta > 2$ is a necessary condition for the existence of a symmetric equilibrium in the three-stage game with at least two firms in the market.)[10] Since $u_i \geq 1$, it follows that $A_i \geq 0$. Note that firms are assumed to choose u_i (and hence A_i) at stage 2 of the game to maximize own profit, irrespective of the value of λ.

Firms must also incur an entry cost f at stage 1 of the game. This may include some minimal advertising expenditure that is necessary for producing a product of the lowest quality ($u = 1$). To simplify the analysis, it is assumed in what follows that $f = \varepsilon$, so the total sunk cost incurred by firm i prior to the final stage is $F_i = A_i + f = \varepsilon u_i^\beta$. This simplification is particularly justified for industries with high

---

8. The properties of λ in the final-stage subgame are the same as in the version of the model without quality indices described in chapter 4: for given N and for $u_i = u$, $\forall i$, the equilibrium price, price-cost margin, and profit in the second-stage subgame increase and the equilibrium quantity falls as λ rises. None of the other exogenous variables that affect gross profit, namely, σ or c, have properties similar to those of λ.

9. No attempt is made here to explain what determines β and why it differs across industries. Advertising effectiveness is simply taken as an industry-specific characteristic which is not affected by firms' strategies. This is consistent with the fact that the industries where advertising "works" tend to be fairly similar across countries and over time.

10. As pointed out in Sutton (1998), the economics of this model depends only on the composite mapping from firms' fixed costs to firms' gross profits, rather than on the separate mappings of fixed costs to qualities and from qualities to gross profits. Thus the results would not change if we replaced u with u^γ, $\gamma > 0$, in the utility function and required that $\beta > 2\gamma$.

advertising intensity, that is, when f represents a small fraction of the total sunk cost incurred.[11]

The Symmetric Equilibrium

A symmetric subgame perfect equilibrium in pure strategies in the three-stage game can be computed following the methodology of Sutton (1991). The two necessary conditions for a symmetric equilibrium in which N firms offer goods of quality $v > 1$ are

$$\frac{d\pi_i}{du_i}\bigg|_{u_i=v} = \frac{dF}{du}\bigg|_{u=v}, \qquad \forall i, \tag{5.6}$$

and

$$\pi(v|N, v) = F(v), \tag{5.7}$$

where N is assumed to be a continuous variable. Equation (5.6) determines the equilibrium level of u conditional on N (i.e., the equilibrium of the subgame starting at the second stage of the game), while (5.7) is a free-entry condition. It can be shown that, provided that S is sufficiently large (or ε is sufficiently small) *and* β is sufficiently large, there exists a unique symmetric subgame perfect equilibrium of the three-stage game with $N^* \geq 2$ and $v^* > 1$ (see Symeonidis 2000c).[12] This is defined by equations (5.6) and (5.7) after substituting the values of π and F.

In particular, from (5.6) we obtain

$$(v^S)^{\beta-2} = \frac{S(1-c)^2[E_3(E_1 - E_2) + E_1(E_3 - E_4)]}{\beta\varepsilon[4 - \sigma(1+\lambda)]^2[4 + \sigma(1+\lambda)(N-1)]^2}, \tag{5.8}$$

which defines the equilibrium level of quality conditional on the number of firms, $v^S(N)$, where

---

11. It is easy to check that for any given $f \neq \varepsilon$, $A_i + f \to \varepsilon u_i^\beta$ as u_i increases.

12. When S is not sufficiently large (for given ε), then a symmetric equilibrium in the three-stage game with $v^* > 1$ does not exist. In this case firms enter with the lowest possible quality level $u = 1$ and a symmetric equilibrium is derived from a two-stage game with entry at a sunk cost f at stage 1 and quantity competition at stage 2 (and no endogenous sunk costs). This is the game analyzed in chapter 4. The intuition for this case is that firms do not advertise when market size is small because the gross profit generated is not enough to cover the fixed advertising cost. Note that the model of chapter 4 can also be derived as a special case of the present model when β is very large, that is, advertising effectiveness is very small (and S and ε are kept fixed).

$E_1 = 2[4 + \sigma(1 + \lambda)(N - 2)] - \lambda\sigma^2(1 + \lambda)(N - 1),$

$E_2 = 2\sigma(1 - \lambda)(N - 1),$

$E_3 = 4 + \sigma(1 + \lambda)(N - 2),$

$E_4 = \sigma(1 + \lambda)(N - 1)$

are all nonnegative expressions. From (5.7), and using also (5.8), we obtain

$$E_3(E_1 - E_2) + E_1(E_3 - E_4) = \beta[2 + \lambda\sigma(N - 1)][4 - \sigma(1 + \lambda)]^2, \qquad (5.9)$$

which defines the equilibrium number of firms N^*. Given N^*, (5.8) then gives the equilibrium level of quality in the three-stage game, $v^* = v^S(N^*)$. Note that N^* is independent of S, c, and ε. This is due to the simplifying assumption $f = \varepsilon$. With a more general function $F(u)$, N^* could be positively or negatively related to S, c, and ε. This assumption allows us, however, to focus on the variables of interest, that is, λ, β, and σ.

Comparative Statics

The key comparative statics results of this model, within the range of parameter values for which a symmetric equilibrium with $N^* \geq 2$ and $v^* > 1$ exists, have been analyzed elsewhere (Symeonidis 2000c). They can be briefly summarized as follows.

First, a fall in λ (more intense short-run competition) unambiguously reduces quality, and hence advertising expenditure. This is true whether N is kept fixed—as can be easily checked by differentiating $v^S(N)$ with respect to λ—or is allowed to adjust to its equilibrium value according to equation (5.9). Thus more price competition implies less nonprice competition. While this result may be specific to the linear demand model, it is precisely because of this result that the possibility of an ambiguous effect of a change in λ on N^* arises.

Indeed, the second key result is that a fall in λ may cause either an increase or a decrease in N^*, depending on the values of β and σ and the initial value of λ itself. The ambiguity of the competition effect on concentration in this model stems from the fact that more intense price competition reduces advertising expenditure: since a fall in λ causes both gross profit and sunk cost to decrease, for given N, it is not clear in which direction N^* must change to restore the zero-profit condition.

It is also worth mentioning a third result of the model: a decrease in the degree of horizontal product differentiation (a rise in σ) raises advertising expenditure and reduces the number of firms in long-run equilibrium. In other words, λ and σ affect the endogenous variables of interest in very different ways. Thus a rise in σ and a fall in λ both reduce price and gross profit, for any given N. But the former raises advertising expenditure and lowers the number of firms in the long run, while the latter lowers advertising expenditure and has an ambiguous effect on the number of firms. This is worth emphasizing in view of the fact that σ (or a similar index of product substitutability) is often used as a measure of competitive pressure in theoretical studies, on the grounds that a rise in σ reduces profitability for any given number of firms. The present model suggests that it is important to distinguish between the various sources of competitive pressure when analyzing industries with significant endogenous sunk costs.

For my present purposes, also of particular interest are the comparative statics properties of the model with respect to λ in the neighborhood of the Cournot-Nash equilibrium (i.e., for values of λ close to 0). As it turns out, the effect of a change in λ on N^* can then be either positive or negative. The advantage of focusing on this polar case is that we can compare the two possible outcomes of the model for the same range of values of λ, and thus highlight the role of parameters other than λ, such as σ and β, in determining the sign of the competition effect on market structure.

Proposition 5.4. In the linear demand model with quality indices, an increase in the intensity of competition (a fall in λ) decreases (increases) the equilibrium number of firms N^* in the neighborhood of the Cournot-Nash equilibrium if β is greater (smaller) than $2 + [8\sigma/(4 - \sigma)^2]$.

Proof. From the total differential of (5.9) we can compute $dN^*/d\lambda$ as a function of N^*. Evaluate the resulting expression at $\lambda = 0$. Then substitute into this expression the equilibrium value of N^* for $\lambda = 0$. We obtain

$$\left. \frac{dN^*}{d\lambda} \right|_{\lambda=0} = \frac{(\beta - 2)[-8\sigma + (\beta - 2)(4 - \sigma)^2]}{16\sigma},$$

which, given $\beta > 2$, is positive for $\beta > 2 + [8\sigma/(4 - \sigma)^2]$. By continuity, the condition $dN^*/d\lambda > 0 \Leftrightarrow \beta > 2 + [8\sigma/(4 - \sigma)^2]$ also holds in the neighborhood of the Cournot-Nash equilibrium.   □

Note that the function $g(\sigma) = 2 + [8\sigma/(4 - \sigma)^2]$ is an increasing function of σ in the interval $(0, 2)$. For $\sigma \to 0$, $g(\sigma) \to 2$, while for $\sigma \to 2$, $g(\sigma) \to 6$. Thus, for values of $\beta \geq 6$ the competition effect on concentration is always positive in the neighborhood of the Cournot-Nash equilibrium. For $\beta < 6$ the competition effect on concentration can be positive or negative, depending on the degree of horizontal product differentiation: for any particular value of σ, say σ_0, there is a corresponding value of β, say β_0 (where $\beta_0 < 6$), such that the competition effect on concentration is negative for all $\beta \in (2, \beta_0)$ and positive for all $\beta \in (\beta_0, 6)$. Now recall that the higher the value of β, the lower the effectiveness of advertising in any particular industry. What the above results therefore imply is that, in the neighborhood of the Cournot-Nash equilibrium, a negative competition effect on concentration is possible only in industries with high advertising effectiveness. These are also, other things being equal, industries with high advertising intensity. Moreover, it is precisely in these industries that advertising expenditure falls a lot when price competition intensifies in the neighborhood of the Cournot-Nash equilibrium, as the next result shows.

Proposition 5.5. In the linear demand model with quality indices, an increase in the intensity of competition (a fall in λ) in the neighborhood of the Cournot-Nash equilibrium has a stronger effect on firm advertising expenditure $A^* = \varepsilon(v^{*\beta} - 1)$, the higher the effectiveness of advertising (the lower the value of β).

Proof. Differentiate $A^* = \varepsilon(v^{*\beta} - 1)$ with respect to λ and evaluate the resulting expression at $\lambda = 0$. Then substitute into this expression the equilibrium value of N^* for $\lambda = 0$. This yields

$$\left. \frac{dA^*}{d\lambda} \right|_{\lambda=0} = 2^{(\beta+4)/(\beta-2)} \beta(\beta - 2)(4 - \sigma)^2 \varepsilon \left[\frac{S(1 - c)^2}{\varepsilon} \right]^{\beta/(\beta-2)}$$

$$\times \left[2\sigma + \beta(4 - \sigma) \right]^{-(3\beta-2)/(\beta-2)}.$$

Note that this expression is positive for all values of β and σ in the relevant ranges. Now differentiate this with respect to β to obtain

$$\frac{\partial}{\partial \beta}\left[\left.\frac{dA^*}{d\lambda}\right|_{\lambda=0}\right]$$

$$= \frac{-2^{(\beta+4)/(\beta-2)}(4-\sigma)^2 \varepsilon E_5^{\beta/(\beta-2)}[E_7 + 6\beta E_6 \ln 2 + 2\beta E_6 \ln(E_5/E_6^2)]}{(\beta-2)E_6^{4(\beta-1)/(\beta-2)}},$$

where

$$E_5 = S(1-c)^2/\varepsilon,$$

$$E_6 = 2\sigma + \beta(4-\sigma),$$

$$E_7 = (\beta-2)[(\beta^2 + 2\sigma)(2-\sigma) + 2(\beta-\sigma)^2]$$

are all positive expressions for $\beta > 2$, $\sigma \in (0,2)$. Moreover, it can be checked from equations (5.8) and (5.9) that $(v^*)^{\beta-2}|_{\lambda=0} = E_5/E_6^2$. Since we require $v^* > 1$, we also have $\ln(E_5/E_6^2) > 0$. Hence $(dA^*/d\lambda)|_{\lambda=0}$ is decreasing in β. By continuity, $dA^*/d\lambda$ is decreasing in β in the neighborhood of the Cournot-Nash equilibrium. □

The mechanism driving these results is similar to the mechanism driving propositions 5.2 and 5.3. In industries with low advertising intensity there is little scope for a fall in advertising expenditure that matches the fall in gross profit, when price competition intensifies. So a negative (or nonpositive) effect of price competition on concentration is unlikely in these industries: the fall in advertising following an intensification of short-run competition will probably be too small relative to the fall in gross profit, so that net profit will decrease at the initial level of concentration, and concentration will have to rise to restore the free-entry condition. On the other hand, a negative (nonpositive) competition effect on concentration can occur if advertising expenditure falls a lot relative to gross profit, so that net profit rises (does not fall) at the initial level of concentration. This can happen more easily in an industry where advertising intensity is initially high.

Summary of the Theory and Implications for the Empirical Analysis

To summarize, the linear demand model with quality indices illustrates quite nicely, and develops further, some of the main theoretical results on the effect of price competition on advertising and market structure in advertising-intensive industries. The key theoretical predictions of this chapter are, then, as follows. First, an increase in the intensity of competition cannot simultaneously cause concentration to fall (or not to change) and advertising expenditure to rise (or not to change). Second, no clear results can be derived on the effect of price competition on advertising without imposing a considerable amount of structure on our theoretical models. In one such example, the linear demand model, we have obtained the unambiguous result that more price competition reduces nonprice (advertising) competition. Third, while a negative effect of price competition on concentration cannot be ruled out, it is unlikely, since it can occur only if there is a significant fall in advertising expenditure. If, on the other hand, advertising falls little or does not change or rises following an increase in the intensity of price competition, then concentration must rise.

The theory should now be confronted with the empirical evidence. Several questions can be asked. First, is the evidence consistent with proposition 5.1, that is, is it the case that we do not observe the outcomes that are excluded under this proposition? Second, what was the overall effect of price competition on advertising across industries in the present case? Third, is there any evidence of an unambiguous overall effect of price competition on concentration in advertising-intensive industries despite the inconclusiveness of the theory? Fourth, is the experience of particular industries consistent with the conditional predictions on concentration (propositions 5.2 and 5.3)?

5.4   The Data

The econometric analysis of the effects of price competition in advertising-intensive industries in this chapter makes use of several different samples of industries in separate regressions for concentration and advertising intensity. The reason for using different samples for each of the endogenous variables is that the industry definitions across the various statistical sources are often difficult to match.

Many of the variables and the data sources are the same as those used in chapter 4 and will not be discussed again here. This is the case for the concentration ratio, the setup cost proxies (capital stock divided by the number of plants or the capital-labor ratio), the market size proxies (deflated sales revenue), and the competition variable $CHANGE$. There is a small difference in the definition of sales revenue between concentration and advertising regressions: in the former case

I use sales revenue by UK firms, while in the latter case I use sales revenue in the UK market.

The new variables in this chapter are advertising intensity and a set of variables that capture differences across industries and over time in the fraction of TV advertising in total advertising. To construct these variables, systematic data on advertising expenditure across a range of advertising-intensive industries were required. These data are described in some detail below.

Advertising-sales ratios were constructed for 1954, 1958, 1963, 1968, and 1973. The first four of these years are the only ones during the 1950s and the 1960s for which comparable sales revenue data across industries are available at a fairly disaggregated level. On the other hand, 1973 is the last year before the recession of the mid-1970s, which seems to have caused a temporary but significant fall in advertising expenditure in many industries. The data used in the concentration regressions are, as in chapter 4, for 1958, 1963, 1968, and 1975. Recall that 1954 and 1958 are "before" dates in the natural experiment, 1963 is a year when we expect to see only the short-run effects of competition, 1968 is a year when much of the long-run effect should have been realized, and by 1973 or 1975 the full long-run effects of competition had certainly been realized.

Defining the Samples of Advertising-Intensive Industries

This chapter focuses on advertising-intensive industries, defined as those industries with an average or typical advertising-sales ratio (ADS) of more than 1% over the relevant period. The 1% cutoff point was chosen because it is commonly used to classify industries according to their advertising intensity. In addition, I have defined two subsamples of high-advertising industries, one for the concentration regressions and one for the advertising regressions. Each of these includes industries with average or typical ADS higher than 2% over the relevant period. These subsamples were defined in order to test some of the theoretical results using a group of industries for which advertising is clearly a key strategic variable. This may not always be the case for industries with ADS between 1% and 2%; in fact, industries with medium advertising intensity may have features of exogenous sunk cost industries.

The choice of the 2% cutoff point was the result of a trade-off. On the one hand, the subsamples of high-advertising industries should contain a nonnegligible number of industries with a change in competition regime, and hence the cutoff point should not be set too high. On the other hand, they should be sufficiently different from the ADS > 1% samples, and so the cutoff point should not be set too low. As it turned out, the 2% cutoff point satisfies both these criteria. In addition, it splits the group of advertising-intensive industries used in the concentration regressions into two groups of equal size: of fifty-six industries with ADS > 1%, twenty-eight had ADS > 2%.

For the samples used in the concentration regressions, the classification of industries with respect to these two cutoff points was done in the manner described in chapter 4. Thus I estimated the average or typical ADS of all four-digit industries for which concentration data were available, and then checked whether these were higher or lower than 1% and 2%. For this purpose, advertising expenditure was defined as media advertising, that is, other selling expenses were not included on the grounds that they are generally incurred at the price competition stage and do not create any "goodwill."[13]

For the samples used in the advertising regressions, the classification of industries with respect to their typical ADS using the 1% and the 2% cutoff points was done in a slightly different way. One complication in this case was that the 1954 figures were usually untypical, because many British industries did not fully emerge from the implications of wartime controls until the mid-1950s, and also because TV advertising was not introduced in the UK until 1955. On the other hand, the 1956 legislation did not have any impact prior to 1958 and, in fact, its impact was largely realized between 1958 and 1968. I therefore used only the 1958, 1963, and 1968 advertising-sales ratios to classify the industries according to their typical advertising intensity. I did this by simply taking the average ADS for the three "core" years and comparing it with the two cutoff points.

Constructing Advertising-Sales Ratios

The advertising-sales ratio is used in this chapter not only to classify industries as advertising-intensive (ADS > 1%) or high-advertising (ADS > 2%), but also as an endogenous variable. Constructing this

13. Other selling expenses include "direct selling activities" such as visits by salespersons, which are common in producer-good industries, and "promotional activities" such as coupons to consumers and special terms to retailers, which are common in consumer-good industries.

variable involved matching three different industrial classifications. Data on advertising expenditure in the UK market, separately for press and TV, were obtained from the *Statistical Review of Press Advertising* and the *Statistical Review of Independent TV Advertising*, both published by Legion Information Services, Ltd., until 1963; the *Statistical Review of Press and TV Advertising*, published by Legion Information Services, Ltd., from 1963 until the early 1970s; and the *MEAL Monthly Digest of Advertising Expenditure*, published since 1968. These data are reported both for individual brands and for industries, at a relatively low level of aggregation, but are often not available for low-advertising industries. Data on sales revenue of UK manufacturers at current net producer prices were obtained from the individual industry reports of the Census of Production (various years) and the 1973 issues of *Business Monitor, PQ series: Quarterly Statistics*. These figures relate to UK firms rather than the UK market, however. Sales revenue figures for the UK market were derived by adding to the Census sales revenue figures the value of retained imports in the UK and subtracting the value of exports by UK firms. I also subtracted from the sales figures any amount of customs and excise duties. Import and export data were taken from the *Annual Statement of the Trade of the United Kingdom*.[14]

The choice of industry definitions for the advertising regressions was dictated by theoretical as well as practical considerations. The former included using an appropriate level of aggregation from the point of view of the possible existence of advertising spillovers across different brands of a single firm and also from the point of view of competition. The latter included matching different industrial classifications and ensuring comparability in the light of changes over time in some of the industry definitions used in various data sources. In most cases my industry definitions were based on the categories used in the advertising statistics, which roughly correspond to the

---

14. A minor problem was that while the Census sales revenue data are for plants (for 1968 and 1973) or firms (for 1954, 1958, and 1963) employing at least twenty-five persons, the import and export statistics cover all firms. Since very small firms often produce ancillary rather than core industry products and may spend little on advertising or advertise only locally, the exclusion of very small firms (or plants) is a minor issue for many industries, especially when imports and exports are small. In cases where imports or exports were significant, or very small UK producers accounted for a considerable fraction of total sales, an approximate adjustment of the sales figures was made using published estimates of sales by very small UK firms, often available only at a higher level of aggregation.

four-digit or the five-digit level of aggregation, although these were often modified to exclude secondary products or to ensure comparability across various data sources and over time. In a few cases it was also necessary to split a category or merge two categories into one in order to obtain an appropriate market definition or avoid using an industry with very small sales.

The main factors restricting the size of the samples for the advertising regressions were (1) the very limited availability of advertising data for producer-good industries, (2) the difficulties encountered in matching advertising to sales figures, and (3) the exclusion of industries with ambiguous state of competition. In addition, a few observations were excluded because of government regulation of advertising or competition in particular industries over certain periods.

The advertising figures used are for display advertising in the press and on TV by UK manufacturers and importers. They do not include direct selling expenses or sales promotion expenditure. In a few industries, advertising of manufacturers' brands by accredited dealers, which is often carried out in conjunction with the manufacturer, is also included, although it is only a small fraction of the total. However, I excluded any independent advertising by retailers.

The main problems with the Legion/MEAL figures are (1) the incomplete coverage of press advertising, which causes a downward bias, and (2) the fact that the numbers are estimated by pricing the measured amount of advertising according to the published rates (i.e., without taking discounts into account), which results in an upward bias for TV expenditure in particular. Both biases may vary across industries and years. In the case of press advertising, an additional complication is that the coverage improved during the 1950s and the 1960s and it differs slightly between Legion and MEAL. Finally, the Legion/MEAL data do not include the production costs of advertisements.

To reduce the measurement error from these factors I adjusted the Legion/MEAL figures on the basis of data on aggregate annual expenditure by type of advertising published by the Advertising Association in *Advertising Expenditure 1960* (London: Advertising Association, 1962) and, subsequently, in *Advertising Quarterly*. First, the TV advertising figures were adjusted using estimates of the *average* discount across all industries for each year; these were on the order of 10–17% of the published rates, depending on the year. Second, all press advertising figures were adjusted upward by 10% to account for incomplete coverage of press advertising.[15] Third, to ensure comparability of the MEAL 1973 figures with the Legion 1954–1968 data, I adjusted the MEAL figures proportionally, on the basis of a comparison of Legion with MEAL data for 1968 (a year for which data from both sources are available). And finally, I adjusted the Legion/MEAL figures to take into account production costs of press and TV advertisements. These were remarkably stable throughout the period as a fraction of press space or TV time charges, respectively: about 10% of aggregate expenditure. Hence I applied a uniform 10% adjustment across industries. Advertising in other media, such as posters or cinema, was ignored, since cross-industry data were not available and a uniform adjustment across industries would be inappropriate (these expenditures differ considerably across industries). Note, however, that these expenditures were very small: about 5–10% of total advertising expenditure.

Finally, it is worth pointing out that the sales revenue figures are totals for the combined retail and nonretail market. Distinguishing between the two markets might have been more appropriate, given that advertising is mostly targeted toward the retail market, but such a distinction was not feasible given the data available. However, in most industries the fraction of retail in total sales should not change significantly over a ten-year or a twenty-year period. Moreover, the advertising data generally include trade advertising. Despite the somewhat lower coverage of this type of advertising in Legion/MEAL, it is a considerable fraction of the total in some industries.

---

15. The reason for applying a uniform adjustment of 10% to all press advertising figures is as follows. In the case of press advertising, a large part of the difference between Legion/MEAL and Advertising Association data relates to local advertising by very small firms and to industrial or retail advertising or advertising of services, all of which were not relevant for my present purposes. Also, much of the improvement in Legion press coverage during the 1950s and the 1960s was primarily in these sectors. In fact, I assumed that the improvement was *wholly* in these sectors, which in turn implied that the extent of underreporting of media advertising by larger firms in consumer-good industries was fairly uniform over the period. Hence I applied a uniform upward adjustment to all Legion press figures. The choice of the 10% figure was based on a comparison of Legion with Advertising Association aggregate figures for 1968: the Legion press aggregate was 84% of the Advertising Association aggregate, and much (but not all) of this must reflect incomplete coverage of press advertising by larger firms in consumer-good industries.

Table 5.1
Changes in C5 and *ADS*, 1958–1968

	$\Delta C5 > 0$ $\Delta ADS > 0$	$\Delta C5 > 0$ $\Delta ADS < 0$	$\Delta C5 < 0$ $\Delta ADS > 0$	$\Delta C5 < 0$ $\Delta ADS < 0$	Total
No. of industries with average $ADS > 1\%$ and $CHANGE = 1$	1	4	0	1	6
No. of industries with average $ADS > 1\%$ and $CHANGE = 0$	7	8	2	6	23
No. of industries with average $ADS > 2\%$ and $CHANGE = 1$	1	4	0	0	5
No. of industries with average $ADS > 2\%$ and $CHANGE = 0$	4	4	2	6	16

Notes: The figures in the first two rows are based on twenty-nine advertising-intensive industries with available comparable data for C5 and *ADS* for both 1958 and 1968. The figures in the last two rows are based on twenty-one high-advertising industries with available comparable data for C5 and *ADS* for both 1958 and 1968.

5.5 Econometric Models and Results

The empirical analysis of the effects of competition in advertising-intensive industries in this section is based on a comparison of those industries affected by the 1956 Act with a control group of industries not affected. Some information on the joint evolution of concentration and advertising intensity in the two groups between 1958 and 1968 is given in table 5.1. The figures are based on industries with unambiguous state of competition and available data for the five-firm sales concentration ratio, C5, and the advertising-sales ratio, *ADS*, for both 1958 and 1968. C5 is the only available concentration measure at the four-digit level of aggregation, and *ADS* is used instead of advertising expenditure because of the need to control for changes in sales during this period. Note that although the theoretical results of sections 5.2 and 5.3 are cast in terms of both the number of firms and the concentration ratio, the number of firms is not a very appropriate measure of market structure in advertising-intensive industries in practice, since it is too sensitive to the number of small firms that advertise little or not at all and exist alongside the bigger advertisers in practically all of these industries. On the other hand, small nonadvertising firms have little effect on an industry's total advertising expenditure or intensity or on concentration, which also implies that C5 is an appropriate measure for our present purposes.

The sample of industries for table 5.1 is rather small, mainly because of difficulties in matching the industry categories used in the concentration statistics with those used in the advertising statistics. One small discrepancy remains: the concentration ratios are for UK firms, while the advertising-sales ratios are for the UK market. This does not seriously affect the comparability of the figures, however, because few industries in this table had significant imports or exports in 1958 or in 1968.[16]

It can be seen that there are no industries with a change of competition regime in table 5.1 that experienced a fall in concentration and a rise in advertising intensity between 1958 and 1968. In contrast, all the other outcomes are represented by one or more industries in the table. Note, however, that within the group of industries without a change of regime there are only two for which C5 declined and ADS increased. Hence, while the figures in table 5.1 are consistent with proposition 5.1, they must be interpreted with caution, since the overall trend in the 1960s appears to have been a rise in concentration and a fall in advertising intensity.

Econometric Methodology

Clearly, the intensification of price competition following the 1956 legislation was one of several factors that shaped the evolution of concentration and advertising intensity across UK industries between the mid-1950s and the mid-1970s. To assess the impact of the 1956 Act across industries, it is therefore necessary to use econometric analysis. Under this approach, the theoretical predictions regarding the effect of price competition on the joint evolution of market structure and advertising are tested only on average. The theoretical analysis in sections 5.2 and 5.3 suggests estimating the following reduced-form models:

$Concentration = C(S, f, h, e, t),$

$Advertising = A(S, f, h, e, t),$

---

16. Even in those cases, the comparability of the figures would be affected only if advertising intensity differed considerably between UK products and imported goods or export intensity varied considerably across leading UK firms in each industry.

where the variables are as defined in section 5.2. Time-invariant industry-specific characteristics may also influence advertising or concentration, and their effect will be captured in panel regressions by the industry-specific effects.

Since the two equations include the same explanatory variables, there is no efficiency gain from estimating them jointly. Moreover, the sample would have to be substantially smaller for a joint estimation than for separate regressions, for two reasons. First, it is often difficult to match the industry definitions used in the concentration statistics with those used in the advertising statistics. Second, data for particular industries and years are often not available for one or the other of the two endogenous variables. For instance, concentration data are not available for 1954 and 1973, and advertising-sales ratios for 1975 are somewhat less reliable because of the impact of the recession of the mid-1970s on advertising expenditure. Thus the two models will be estimated separately below. Because of the differences in industry definitions and coverage across statistical sources, different samples of industries will be used for the two sets of regressions.

It may also be asked, as in chapter 4, whether it is appropriate to estimate a regression line or a lower bound for the concentration equation. But once again there are problems, practical and conceptual, with estimating a lower bound. The least squares residuals from the concentration regressions are negatively skewed, due to the fact that some industries experienced large increases in concentration during the period examined. More generally, the estimation of a lower bound may be problematic in the present case because of the panel structure of the data and the fact that most of the crucial information would be lost in a pooled time-series cross section. Thus I will proceed to test the theory using standard least squares regressions, on the assumption that the theoretical predictions derived for the benchmark case of symmetric single-product firms carry over to more complex settings.

Of the variables included in the above reduced-form models, the degree of horizontal product differentiation h is difficult to measure, but it should not change significantly over a period of ten or twenty years in the large majority of industries. The same can be said for some of the factors that determine advertising effectiveness e and are related to product characteristics. Both these and h can therefore be thought of as time-invariant industry effects.

TV Advertising and Changes in Advertising Effectiveness

Not all factors affecting advertising effectiveness in the present case can be thought of as time-invariant industry characteristics, however. An important development, which was associated with an exogenous change in advertising effectiveness, was the introduction of commercial television in the UK in 1955. Since some products are more suitable for TV advertising than others, this substantially increased the effectiveness of advertising, and hence advertising expenditure, in a number of industries in the late 1950s and early 1960s, while in other industries the impact was much smaller. The overall impact was considerable: aggregate expenditure on display (as opposed to classified) media advertising as a percentage of GDP increased from 0.81 in 1956 to 1.08 in 1960, according to the statistics published by the Advertising Association, and most of this increase can be attributed to TV advertising.

To control for this factor, a proxy for the effectiveness of TV advertising must be defined. For the advertising regressions, two proxies will be used. The first is the fraction of TV advertising in total display advertising for each industry-year pair in the sample ($TVTOT$). Total display advertising is here defined as the sum of press and TV advertising, that is, other media are ignored because of data limitations. Note, however, that press and TV consistently accounted for some 90–95% of aggregate display advertising throughout the period. The theoretical argument for $TVTOT$ can be seen by drawing a diagram with TV advertising on the horizontal axis and press advertising on the vertical axis to analyze the allocation of a fixed advertising budget between the two media. In industries where TV advertising is effective, the "indifference curves" between the two media will be steep, while the reverse will be the case for industries where TV advertising is not effective. Starting from a point on the vertical axis (representing zero TV advertising), an industry will move farther down the "isocost" curve (toward more TV in total advertising) the steeper the indifference curves (i.e., the higher the effectiveness of TV advertising).

While $TVTOT$ adequately captures the overall effect of the introduction of commercial television, including the fact that TV advertising expanded gradually over a period of several years in a manner that was not uniform across industries, it may be endogenous. The second proxy, $TVINT$, is a compromise between the need to control for the effect of TV advertising and the problem of potential endogeneity.

TVINT was constructed as follows. All industries were classified into four groups, according to the fraction of TV in total display advertising in the late 1960s, that is, after the effect of the introduction of commercial television had been largely realized: less than 10%, between 10% and 40%, between 40% and 70%, and higher than 70%. These cutoff points were chosen on the basis of a histogram of the fraction of TV in total advertising across all industries in the late 1960s.[17] The four groups were assigned the numbers 0, 0.25, 0.55, and 0.85 (i.e., corresponding to the midpoints of each class except for the first class, which comprised many industries without any TV advertising). This number was therefore an index of the *equilibrium* level of TV advertising effectiveness in each particular industry. *TVINT* was then constructed by multiplying this index by the fraction of *aggregate* TV advertising in *aggregate* total advertising for each year in the sample, in order to account for the gradual expansion of TV advertising.

As expected, *TVINT* is strongly correlated with *TVTOT*, with a correlation coefficient of 0.91 for the full sample of industries used in the advertising regressions. On the other hand, since *TVINT* depends only on the long-run equilibrium TV advertising effectiveness in any given industry (which is largely a function of exogenous industry characteristics) and the time path of the expansion of aggregate TV advertising, it should not be endogenous with respect to the advertising-sales ratio of each industry in each particular year.

For the concentration regressions, data limitations resulting from differences in the industry definitions used in the various statistics mean that advertising expenditures can often be estimated only approximately. Again, two proxies for advertising effectiveness will be used. The first is *TVINT*. The second is *TVCLASS*, a variable taking the value 0, 0.25, 0.55, or 0.85 according to whether the fraction of TV in total media advertising expenditure for each *industry and year* was approximately lower than 10%, between 10% and 40%, between 40% and 70%, or higher than 70%, respectively. Since *TVCLASS* can affect concentration only indirectly, endogeneity is probably not a serious

---

17. In a few cases where there was evidence of a substantial change of this fraction after 1968 or of an unstable allocation between press and TV advertising in general, the average or typical value for the late 1960s and early 1970s was used instead of the 1968 figure.

concern in this case. On the other hand, *TVCLASS* is less likely than *TVINT* to be subject to measurement error with respect to the theoretical variable e, and this is particularly important in the concentration regressions because the variation in e in the sample used in these regressions is relatively low.[18]

Other Influences on Advertising Expenditure

In both the concentration and the advertising regressions, time dummies will be included among the regressors to control for factors that may have affected these variables in a more or less uniform way across industries during the period examined. Several factors that are thought to have contributed to the overall rise in concentration in the UK during the 1960s were mentioned in chapter 4.

Regarding advertising, there were important changes during the 1960s in the distribution of manufactured goods: the abolition of resale price maintenance, the growth of large and powerful retailers, the increased significance of sales promotion,[19] and the rise of retailers' own brands (see Pickering 1974, NBPI 1971, Ward 1973). These changes reduced the relative importance of brand advertising, for two reasons. First, more manufacturers were now eager to produce goods under a retailer's label. Second, consumers may have become more sensitive to prices and product availability in large stores and less responsive to brand image, thus causing manufacturers of advertised brands to become more anxious to make deals with large retailers and less keen to advertise. The changes in distribution may also have put some pressure on manufacturers' margins.

These changes are thought to have contributed to the substantial fall in advertising intensity across UK manufacturing in the late 1960s and early 1970s: aggregate expenditure on display advertising as a percentage of GNP fell from 1.04 in 1963 to 0.93 in 1968 and to 0.84 in 1971, before rising to 0.91 in 1973, the last year before the oil

---

18. The reason for this is twofold. First, many industries in the samples used in the concentration regressions, especially in the sample of high-advertising industries, have a high fraction of TV in total advertising. Second, the first year in these samples is 1958, when TV advertising was already quite established: about 25% of total advertising in 1958 was TV advertising, as compared to zero in 1954 and about 36% in the late 1960s and early 1970s.

19. Unlike media advertising, promotional activities such as gifts and coupons to consumers, and financial inducements to distributors affect price competition rather than increasing perceived quality or providing information about a product.

crisis. Note that time dummies can control for these effects only imperfectly, since the impact of changes in distribution patterns on advertising intensity must have varied across industries. This problem
is relevant mostly for the last two years of the panel used for the
advertising regressions, 1968 and 1973. Other factors that may be
associated with the fall in aggregate advertising intensity in the late
1960s and early 1970s include the operation of prices and incomes
policy, the acceleration of the inflation rate, and the increase in import
penetration.

An additional source of noise in the data, this time during 1954–
1958, is the fact that in many respects British industry did not fully
emerge from the implications of wartime controls until the second
half of the 1950s. Advertising was still low in 1954 compared with
the late 1930s, and it was growing rapidly during the mid-1950s even
before the advent of commercial TV. This evolution can be captured
only partly by a year dummy for 1954, since it was not uniform
across industries.

Price Competition and Concentration: The Samples and Descriptive
Statistics

Two samples of industries are used for the concentration regressions
reported in this chapter. The basic sample includes all industries
with an average or typical advertising-sales ratio of more than 1%
over the relevant period. Since, however, I also wished to focus more
closely on a group of industries for which advertising is clearly a key
strategic variable, I have defined, in addition, a subsample of industries with average or typical ADS higher than 2% over the relevant
period.

To construct the first of these samples, I started by excluding from
the set of industries with available concentration data all industries
with average or typical advertising-sales ratio lower than 1%. Then I
excluded industries with ambiguous state of competition in 1958 (or,
in a few cases, ambiguous state of competition in the 1960s and early
1970s), as well as industries with a switch of competition regime but
for which concentration data were not available for at least the three
core years 1958, 1963, and 1968. However, I did not exclude industries without a change in regime and with available data for only a
subset of the period 1958–1968. This left an unbalanced sample of
fifty-six industries, including ten with cancelled agreements, and 204

Table 5.2
The samples used in the concentration regressions: advertising-intensive industries and high-advertising industries

Data available for	No. of industries with CHANGE = 1 and average ADS > 1%	No. of industries with CHANGE = 0 and average ADS > 1%	No. of industries with CHANGE = 1 and average ADS > 2%	No. of industries with CHANGE = 0 and average ADS > 2%
All four years	10	30	5	16
1958, 1963, 1968	0	1	0	1
1963, 1968, 1975	0	11	0	5
1958, 1963	0	3	0	0
1963, 1968	0	1	0	1
Total	10	46	5	23

observations. In most cases observations were available for all four years in the sample (i.e., 1958, 1963, 1968, and 1975). In some cases, observations were available for only three or two years.

To construct the subsample of high-advertising industries, I then simply dropped all industries with average or typical ADS < 2%. This left twenty-eight industries, including five with canceled agreements, and 104 observations. Table 5.2 gives details on the structure of these samples, distinguishing between industries with a change in competition regime after 1958 and industries without such a change.[20] The full set of industries and information on key variables are given in appendix B (table B2).

Some descriptive statistics on initial levels and changes in concentration are reported in tables 5.3 and 5.4. Table 5.3 reports descriptive statistics for the concentration ratio, $C5$, in 1958 for industries with and industries without a change in competition regime after 1958. There is clearly some difference between the two groups for industries with typical ADS > 1%, but this essentially disappears when we turn to industries with typical ADS > 2%. For this latter class of industries the mean $C5$ is 0.707 for the five industries in the sample with $CHANGE = 1$ and 0.686 for the seventeen industries with

---

20. I have also run regressions using more balanced samples, including only industries with a full set of observations for at least the core period 1958–1968. The results were very similar to those reported below. Recall that the same was true for exogenous sunk cost industries. See Symeonidis (2000a) for a discussion of these results (with the minor qualification that data for 1977, instead of 1975, are used in that paper).

Table 5.3
Concentration in 1958 and competition regime in advertising-intensive and high-advertising industries

	Mean C5 in 1958 (st. deviation of C5)
Advertising-intensive industries	
Industries with change of competition regime after 1958 (n = 10)	0.737 (0.131)
Industries without change of competition regime after 1958 (n = 34)	0.609 (0.270)
High-advertising industries	
Industries with change of competition regime after 1958 (n = 5)	0.707 (0.158)
Industries without change of competition regime after 1958 (n = 17)	0.686 (0.231)

Notes: The figures are based on industries with available data for 1958; n indicates the number of industries.

Table 5.4
Average change in C5, 1958–1968 and 1958–1975, in advertising-intensive and high-advertising industries

	$\Delta C5$ 1958–1968	$\Delta C5$ 1958–1975
Advertising-intensive industries		
Industries with $CHANGE = 1$	0.100	0.130
	(0.075)	(0.101)
	n = 10	n = 10
Industries with $CHANGE = 0$	0.049	0.038
	(0.122)	(0.139)
	n = 31	n = 30
High-advertising industries		
Industries with $CHANGE = 1$	0.136	0.150
	(0.082)	(0.123)
	n = 5	n = 5
Industries with $CHANGE = 0$	0.047	0.031
	(0.098)	(0.113)
	n = 17	n = 16

Notes: The figures in the first column are based on industries with available observations for both 1958 and 1968. The figures in the second column are based on industries with available observations for both 1958 and 1975. The figures in parentheses are standard deviations. n indicates the number of industries.

$CHANGE = 0$ and available data for 1958. As will be seen below, this class is the crucial one for testing the theoretical predictions developed in this chapter.

On the other hand, table 5.4 shows that the average increase in $C5$ after 1958 was much larger for industries affected by the legislation than for industries not affected, whatever the sample used. For instance, for the $ADS > 2\%$ sample, the average change in $C5$ between 1958 and 1968 was 13.6 percentage points for industries with a change in competition regime and only 4.7 percentage points for the control group. For the $ADS > 1\%$ sample, the respective numbers for the average change in $C5$ over 1958–1968 are 10.0 percentage points and 4.9 percentage points. Similar differences are observed for the 1958–1975 period. These differences are so large that they can be expected to persist even when controlling for other variables.

A comparison between industries that experienced a large increase in $C5$ over the period 1958–1975 and industries that experienced a large decrease in $C5$ over the same period is also very informative. The comparison is limited to the forty advertising-intensive industries with available data for both these years. Of the five industries with the largest rise in $C5$, two (biscuits for human consumption; washing machines, electrically operated) are industries with $CHANGE = 1$, and three (corsets and brassieres; television receiving sets; knitted, netted, or crocheted goods: hosiery) have $CHANGE = 0$. However, all five industries with the largest fall in $C5$ (tufted carpets, carpeting, and carpet floor rugs; vegetables, quick frozen; fish and fish products, quick frozen; cutlery; powered industrial trucks and industrial tractors) have $CHANGE = 0$.

Price Competition and Concentration: Econometric Model and Results

The basic econometric model for concentration in this chapter is

$$Conc_{it} = \alpha_i + \beta_1 \ln Sales_{it} + \beta_2 \ln(K/x)_{it} + \beta_3 TVCLASS_{it} + \beta_4 Y63$$
$$+ \beta_5 Y68 + \beta_6 Y75 + \beta_7 CHANGE * Y63 + \beta_8 CHANGE * Y68$$
$$+ \beta_9 CHANGE * Y75 + u_{it},$$

where "conc" is either the four-digit industry five-firm sales concentration ratio, $C5$, or its logistic transformation, $\text{logit } C5 = \ln[C5/(1 - C5)]$; "sales" is the four-digit industry sales revenue deflated either by the general producer price index (SS) or by an industry-specific producer price index (DS); "K/x" is either the three-digit industry capital stock of the average plant, K/N, or the three-digit industry capital-labor ratio, K/L; $TVCLASS$ is as defined above; $Y63$, $Y68$, and $Y75$ are time dummies for 1963, 1968, and 1975, respectively; and the interaction terms should capture any differences in the evolution of concentration after 1958 between industries with a change in competition regime ($CHANGE = 1$) and industries without such a change ($CHANGE = 0$). Thus the coefficient on $CHANGE * Y63$ measures the effect of the 1956 Act on concentration by 1963, the coefficient on $CHANGE * Y68$ measures the effect by 1968, and the coefficient on $CHANGE * Y75$ measures the effect by 1975. The benchmark year is 1958. Note that the arguments put forward in chapter 4 regarding the potential endogeneity of some of the independent variables are valid here as well.

Table 5.5 contains results for industries with typical ADS > 1%, including ten industries with canceled agreements, using a fixed-effects specification.[21] The reported standard errors are heteroskedasticity-consistent, adjusted for small sample bias following MacKinnon and White (1985). The coefficients on $CHANGE * Y75$ are everywhere positive and statistically significant at the 5% or the 10% level, thus providing evidence of a positive competition-concentration relationship in advertising-intensive industries. According to these estimates, the effect of the cartel legislation on market structure in advertising-intensive industries was a rise in the five-firm concentration ratio of about six percentage points. Moreover, the results suggest that this effect was only partly realized by 1963 or even 1968. Recall that in chapter 4 some effect after 1968 was also found for exogenous sunk cost industries, but it was, in that case, quite smaller—and could be simply due to time lags in the adjustment of concentration to its new long-run equilibrium. Such an interpretation seems less plausible for the present sample.

There are several reasons why one should not overemphasize this difference between exogenous sunk cost and advertising-intensive industries. First, and perhaps foremost, the 95% confidence intervals for the coefficients on $CHANGE * Y68$ or on $CHANGE * Y75$ in the two classes of industries largely overlap, so there is no strong evi-

---

21. The random-effects model gives similar results with respect to the market size variable and the competition variables, but it is always rejected by the Hausman test in favor of the fixed-effects model.

dence of any difference in the timing of the impact of the 1956 Act on concentration across classes of industries. Second, a few agreements in advertising-intensive industries continued until late into the 1960s before being abandoned. Third, the effect of the Act after 1968 in advertising-intensive industries appears to be more pronounced in regressions using logit $C5$, and it is precisely in these regressions that heteroskedasticity is also more pronounced, which suggests that these particular results may be disproportionately influenced by a few industries with very high concentration. Fourth, the rise in concentration in previously cartelized industries after 1968 does not appear particularly pronounced when one looks at the descriptive statistics of table 5.4. And, finally, the descriptive statistics in table 5.4, especially when read in conjunction with those in table 4.3, suggest that an important factor in the estimated impact of the 1956 Act over time was the evolution of industries *not* affected by the legislation. In particular, while the average $C5$ increased over 1968–1975 in exogenous sunk cost industries without a change in competition regime, it fell slightly in the equivalent group of advertising-intensive industries.

All this is not to say that any estimated effect of the 1956 Act on concentration after 1968 in advertising-intensive industries is necessarily more apparent than real. One potentially relevant factor in this respect is the widespread use of resale price maintenance in these industries, in contrast with exogenous sunk cost industries. It may be the case that resale price maintenance delayed or hindered the emergence of fully effective price competition among manufacturers in some previously cartelized industries. Its abolition in the second half of the 1960s may therefore be one factor behind the rise in concentration after 1968 in these industries.

Another potential factor is the evolution of advertising. A fall in advertising expenditure in previously cartelized industries may have occurred and helped absorb part of the pressure on net profits for several years after 1958. Once advertising had fallen to very low levels, however, it could not fall any farther, which may be why we see an effect of the Act on concentration continuing after 1968 in some advertising-intensive industries (assuming that competition further intensified after that date).

A final interpretation is that the changes in the pattern of distribution and the consequent fall in advertising across manufacturing industries after the mid-1960s created favorable circumstances for a

Table 5.5
Regression results for concentration for industries with average ADS > 1% (fixed-effects estimation)

	Dependent variable: C5				Dependent variable: logit C5			
$\ln SS$	-0.102	—	-0.102	—	-0.71	—	-0.73	—
	(0.018)		(0.018)		(0.12)		(0.13)	
$\ln DS$	—	-0.085	—	-0.085	—	-0.55	—	-0.57
		(0.022)		(0.022)		(0.14)		(0.15)
$\ln K/N$	0.001	-0.004	—	—	-0.28	-0.31	—	—
	(0.029)	(0.031)			(0.22)	(0.24)		
$\ln K/L$	—	—	-0.012	-0.011	—	—	-0.34	-0.33
			(0.032)	(0.035)			(0.27)	(0.28)
TVCLASS	-0.023	-0.013	-0.024	-0.013	-0.54	-0.44	-0.52	-0.42
	(0.036)	(0.039)	(0.036)	(0.039)	(0.26)	(0.28)	(0.26)	(0.28)
Y63	0.050	0.049	0.053	0.050	0.43	0.41	0.42	0.39
	(0.020)	(0.021)	(0.018)	(0.019)	(0.13)	(0.14)	(0.12)	(0.13)
Y68	0.095	0.094	0.102	0.097	0.81	0.79	0.81	0.76
	(0.029)	(0.031)	(0.027)	(0.029)	(0.22)	(0.23)	(0.21)	(0.22)
Y75	0.114	0.114	0.125	0.120	0.99	0.97	1.01	0.95
	(0.040)	(0.044)	(0.037)	(0.042)	(0.28)	(0.30)	(0.29)	(0.31)
CHANGE * Y63	0.025	0.027	0.025	0.027	0.16	0.17	0.16	0.18
	(0.031)	(0.033)	(0.031)	(0.032)	(0.19)	(0.20)	(0.19)	(0.20)
CHANGE * Y68	0.039	0.046	0.038	0.046	0.29	0.34	0.29	0.34
	(0.032)	(0.032)	(0.032)	(0.032)	(0.21)	(0.21)	(0.21)	(0.21)

CHANGE * Y75	0.064	0.065	0.063	0.064	0.67	0.69	0.67	0.69
	(0.032)	(0.036)	(0.032)	(0.035)	(0.25)	(0.28)	(0.25)	(0.28)
R^2	0.36	0.30	0.37	0.30	0.32	0.25	0.32	0.25
R^2_{LSDV}	0.96	0.95	0.96	0.95	0.93	0.93	0.93	0.93
Hausman statistic	33.0	32.0	30.6	17.7	77.9	41.2	51.6	38.1
Prob-value	0.0001	0.0002	0.0003	0.04	≈ 0	≈ 0	≈ 0	≈ 0
No. of industries	56	56	56	56	56	56	56	56
No. of industries with $CHANGE = 1$	10	10	10	10	10	10	10	10
No. of observations	204	204	204	204	204	204	204	204

Notes: Heteroskedasticity-consistent standard errors in parentheses. R^2 is derived from transforming the data to obtain deviations from industry means and applying OLS to the transformed data. R^2_{LSDV} is obtained from applying OLS to the untransformed data after including a set of industry dummies among the regressors.

fall in concentration. However, these factors may have had a bigger impact on industries *not* affected by the 1956 Act if the fall in advertising expenditure since the late 1960s was more pronounced in these industries than in previously cartelized ones, a fact which could be associated with the effect of the 1956 Act on advertising during 1958–1968. Note that most of these stories involve some analysis of the joint evolution of advertising and market structure, so it is probably best to return to these issues after examining the econometric results on advertising later in this chapter.

A second result from table 5.5 is the negative, large, and statistically significant coefficients on the market size variables, which do not differ much between regressions using $\ln SS$ and those using $\ln DS$. To check whether this may be related to the downward trend in advertising expenditure in UK manufacturing during the late 1960s and early 1970s, I reestimated the model for the period 1958–1968 only. The market size coefficients had almost the same magnitude and again were statistically significant. Finally, note that replacing *TVCLASS* with *TVINT* or dropping this variable altogether does not significantly affect the results.

Price Competition and Concentration: The ADS > 2% Sample

The evidence reported in table 5.5 suggests that the long-run effect of competition and market size on concentration is not significantly different in advertising-intensive industries than in exogenous sunk cost industries. This may be because the 1% cutoff point is too low. In particular, the results in table 5.5 may be driven by industries with medium advertising intensity, and in these industries a positive competition effect on concentration may be due to the fact that advertising cannot fall by much anyway. To obtain more decisive evidence on the present theory, it is therefore necessary to examine the sample of industries with typical ADS > 2%, that is, industries where endogenous sunk costs represent a more significant fraction of total sunk costs.

Results for the ADS > 2% sample using a fixed-effects specification are presented in table 5.6, and results for the random-effects model, using generalised least squares estimation, are reported in table 5.7. The Hausman test is inconclusive in this instance. In any case, the two sets of results are similar, except for the coefficients on the setup cost proxies, which are statistically significant in the random-effects model only.

The first thing to note is that the market size coefficients in these regressions are nowhere statistically significant, suggesting that the concentration-market size relationship breaks down in industries with high advertising intensity. This is consistent with Sutton's (1991) robust prediction that concentration may either rise or fall as market size increases in industries with significant endogenous sunk costs.[22] On the other hand, the competition effect is statistically significant and large, although its magnitude should be interpreted with caution since the number of industries with a change of competition regime in the ADS > 2% sample is only five (and none of these has a very high typical ADS).[23] In any case, the 95% confidence intervals for the coefficients on *CHANGE * Y68* or on *CHANGE * Y75* in these and the previous regression results largely overlap, so there is no strong evidence of any difference in the magnitude of the long-run competition effect on concentration across classes of industries.

To check whether any of the five industries with a change of regime has a disproportionate influence on the results, I reestimated the model, excluding each of the five industries in turn. The coefficient on *CHANGE * Y75* remained significant at the 5% or the 10% level in all cases.

Since *TVCLASS* is a somewhat crude proxy, it may also be interesting to see what happens if it is dropped altogether. In fact, the results are very similar to those in tables 5.6 and 5.7. Finally, using *TVINT* instead of *TVCLASS* again produces results similar to those reported here. The absence of any significant effect of *TVCLASS* or the market size variables on concentration is not inconsistent with the theory of section 5.2: a rise in advertising effectiveness e or market size S causes both advertising expenditure and gross profit to increase, given the initial number of firms, so the effect on concentration is ambiguous. Only the joint outcome $\Delta A^* \leq 0$ and $\Delta C^* \geq 0$ is ruled out. In fact, the lack of any systematic market size effect on concentration is one of the predictions of the specific example presented in section 5.3.

A potential concern with the above results is that none of the industries with a change in competition regime in the samples used had an advertising-sales ratio higher than 5% in 1958, and many had

---

22. Other econometric studies that have confirmed this prediction include Sutton (1991, chapter 5), Matraves (1992), Lyons and Matraves (1996), and Robinson and Chiang (1996).
23. The five industries are biscuits, cocoa products, condensed milk, electric cookers (stoves), and washing machines.

Table 5.6
Regression results for concentration for industries with average ADS > 2% (fixed-effects estimation)

	Dependent variable: C5				Dependent variable: logit C5			
ln SS	0.013 (0.028)	—	0.013 (0.029)	—	−0.21 (0.24)	—	−0.20 (0.25)	—
ln DS	—	0.037 (0.026)	—	0.037 (0.026)	—	0.09 (0.21)	—	0.08 (0.20)
ln K/N	0.002 (0.059)	−0.003 (0.059)	—	—	0.05 (0.32)	−0.01 (0.33)	—	—
ln K/L	—	—	−0.013 (0.069)	−0.018 (0.069)	—	—	0.07 (0.43)	0.07 (0.44)
TVCLASS	0.047 (0.057)	0.057 (0.058)	0.045 (0.057)	0.056 (0.058)	−0.32 (0.49)	−0.15 (0.48)	−0.32 (0.49)	−0.15 (0.48)
Y63	0.022 (0.035)	0.018 (0.035)	0.026 (0.032)	0.021 (0.032)	0.31 (0.22)	0.26 (0.21)	0.31 (0.21)	0.24 (0.21)
Y68	0.034 (0.056)	0.026 (0.055)	0.043 (0.052)	0.034 (0.051)	0.29 (0.32)	0.21 (0.31)	0.29 (0.33)	0.16 (0.32)
Y75	0.007 (0.083)	−0.007 (0.081)	0.023 (0.082)	0.006 (0.079)	0.20 (0.47)	0.05 (0.45)	0.19 (0.52)	−0.02 (0.50)
CHANGE * Y63	0.036 (0.051)	0.035 (0.051)	0.034 (0.051)	0.033 (0.051)	0.14 (0.28)	0.13 (0.28)	0.14 (0.28)	0.14 (0.28)
CHANGE * Y68	0.086 (0.052)	0.083 (0.052)	0.083 (0.051)	0.080 (0.051)	0.61 (0.32)	0.61 (0.30)	0.61 (0.32)	0.63 (0.31)

CHANGE * Y75	0.124	0.127	0.120	0.124	0.96	1.01	0.96	1.03
	(0.059)	(0.058)	(0.060)	(0.058)	(0.44)	(0.45)	(0.47)	(0.48)
R^2	0.29	0.30	0.29	0.30	0.22	0.22	0.22	0.22
R^2_{LSDV}	0.94	0.94	0.94	0.94	0.93	0.93	0.93	0.93
No. of industries	28	28	28	28	28	28	28	28
No. of industries with $CHANGE = 1$	5	5	5	5	5	5	5	5
No. of observations	104	104	104	104	104	104	104	104

Notes: Heteroskedasticity-consistent standard errors in parentheses. R^2 is derived from transforming the data to obtain deviations from industry means and applying OLS to the transformed data. R^2_{LSDV} is obtained from applying OLS to the untransformed data after including a set of industry dummies among the regressors.

Table 5.7
Regression results for concentration for industries with average ADS > 2% (random-effects estimation)

	Dependent variable: C5				Dependent variable: logit C5			
$\ln SS$	-0.019 (0.023)	—	-0.002 (0.023)	—	-0.03 (0.23)	—	0.10 (0.24)	—
$\ln DS$	—	-0.001 (0.021)	—	0.010 (0.020)	—	0.14 (0.19)	—	0.23 (0.20)
$\ln K/N$	0.067 (0.033)	0.057 (0.034)	—	—	0.57 (0.26)	0.49 (0.26)	—	—
$\ln K/L$	—	—	0.083 (0.048)	0.077 (0.048)	—	—	0.70 (0.34)	0.66 (0.34)
TVCLASS	0.064 (0.057)	0.072 (0.055)	0.060 (0.059)	0.067 (0.057)	-0.04 (0.55)	0.04 (0.52)	-0.07 (0.56)	-0.001 (0.53)
Y63	0.007 (0.029)	0.007 (0.029)	0.006 (0.029)	0.005 (0.029)	0.14 (0.20)	0.12 (0.21)	0.13 (0.20)	0.10 (0.21)
Y68	-0.005 (0.035)	-0.005 (0.034)	-0.008 (0.037)	-0.010 (0.037)	-0.15 (0.24)	-0.17 (0.23)	-0.17 (0.25)	-0.21 (0.25)
Y75	-0.052 (0.048)	-0.053 (0.048)	-0.063 (0.055)	-0.068 (0.055)	-0.53 (0.33)	-0.56 (0.32)	-0.62 (0.38)	-0.69 (0.37)
CHANGE*Y63	0.035 (0.051)	0.034 (0.051)	0.041 (0.048)	0.040 (0.048)	0.04 (0.32)	0.03 (0.32)	0.09 (0.29)	0.08 (0.28)
CHANGE*Y68	0.088 (0.041)	0.087 (0.042)	0.094 (0.041)	0.093 (0.042)	0.59 (0.29)	0.56 (0.29)	0.64 (0.27)	0.62 (0.28)

CHANGE * Y75	0.125	0.127	0.136	0.137	1.00	1.01	1.09	1.10
	(0.044)	(0.045)	(0.048)	(0.048)	(0.45)	(0.45)	(0.46)	(0.46)
Constant	0.914	0.725	0.634	0.504	1.95	0.09	−0.39	−1.74
	(0.251)	(0.228)	(0.247)	(0.216)	(2.48)	(2.03)	(2.53)	(2.06)
R^2	0.26	0.21	0.27	0.23	0.20	0.17	0.20	0.19
Hausman statistic	21.7	54.2	8.8	10.4	30.2	14.4	—	8.2
Prob-value	0.01	≈0	0.46	0.32	0.0004	0.11		0.51
No. of industries	28	28	28	28	28	28	28	28
No. of industries with $CHANGE = 1$	5	5	5	5	5	5	5	5
No. of observations	104	104	104	104	104	104	104	104

Note: Heteroskedasticity-consistent standard errors in parentheses.

advertising-sales ratios much lower than that. As pointed out in section 5.2, the effect of price competition on concentration can be negative only when there is scope for a substantial fall in advertising
intensity. Advertising-sales ratios of 2–3% may still be too low in
that respect: if the advertising-sales ratio cannot fall by very much
anyway, it cannot offset the negative effect of price competition on
gross profit, so concentration has to rise. Could, then, the estimated
positive competition effect on concentration in advertising-intensive
industries be specific to the sample used here?

The answer is "probably not." The main reason is that the estimated positive competition effect on concentration is stronger in the
subsample of industries with typical ADS > 2% than in the full
sample of industries with typical ADS > 1%. While this result should
not be overemphasized, given the small number of industries with a
change in competition regime in these samples, it certainly provides
no indication that the competition effect on concentration may be
weakening, on average, as advertising intensity increases. I should
also point out, however, that the econometric results can identify only
overall effects, and do not imply that a negative competition effect on
concentration will never occur in advertising-intensive industries.
This point will be further explored in the context of one of the case
studies presented below. What the econometric evidence seems to
suggest is that a positive competition effect on concentration is the
most likely outcome in advertising-intensive industries.

Price Competition and Advertising Intensity: The Samples and Descriptive Statistics

I now turn to the impact of price competition on advertising intensity. The basic sample of industries used for the econometric analysis
consists of an unbalanced panel of seventy-one industries with average ADS > 1% over the three core years 1958, 1963, and 1968.[24] A
second sample, including fifty-one industries with average ADS >

---

24. One reason why low-advertising industries were excluded from the present analysis is that any systematic effect of price competition on advertising will be more difficult to identify and also less relevant in industries where advertising is not a key
strategic variable. Moreover, large proportional changes in advertising intensity in
low-advertising industries may have an influence on the results which is disproportionate to their economic significance. Finally, note that all the theoretical predictions
in this chapter are for advertising-intensive industries.

Table 5.8
The samples used in the advertising regressions: advertising-intensive industries and high-advertising industries

Data available for	No. of industries with CHANGE = 1 and average ADS > 1%	No. of industries with CHANGE = 0 and average ADS > 1%	No. of industries with CHANGE = 1 and average ADS > 2%	No. of industries with CHANGE = 0 and average ADS > 2%
All five years	12	31	8	23
1954, 1958, 1963, 1968	2	9	1	5
1958, 1963, 1968, 1973	1	0	1	0
1954, 1958, 1963	0	2	0	2
1958, 1963, 1968	1	2	1	2
1963, 1968, 1973	0	6	0	5
1958, 1963	0	2	0	2
1963, 1968	0	3	0	1
Total	16	55	11	40

2% over the three core years 1958, 1963, and 1968, was also constructed. Note that sample selection is essentially done here on the basis of the *average* ADS—which is likely to be largely driven by advertising effectiveness, an exogenous variable—so there is no selection bias. The samples do not include industries with ambiguous state of competition in 1958 (or in the 1960s and early 1970s). Nor do they include industries with available observations only for 1954–1958 or 1968–1973. However, they do include industries with available data for a subset of the period 1958–1968.[25] In most cases observations are available for all five years in the sample (1954, 1958, 1963, 1968 and 1973). The two samples include 306 and 219 observations, respectively. Table 5.8 gives details on their structure.[26] The full set of industries and information on key variables are given in table B3 of appendix B.

Tables 5.9 and 5.10 present descriptive statistics on initial levels and changes in the advertising-sales ratio, *ADS*, separately for in-

25. Industries with a switch of regime and with advertising or sales data available for only a subset of the period 1958–1968 would have normally been excluded, but there were no such cases in these samples.
26. I have also run regressions using more balanced samples, including only industries with a full set of observations for at least the core period 1958–1968. The results were very similar to those reported below.

Table 5.9
ADS, 1954 and 1958, and competition regime in advertising-intensive and high-advertising industries

	Mean ADS in 1954 (st. deviation of ADS)	Mean ADS in 1958 (st. deviation of ADS)
Advertising-intensive industries		
Industries with change of competition regime after 1958 (n = 14)	0.025 (0.023)	0.035 (0.028)
Industries without change of competition regime after 1958 (n = 42)	0.057 (0.067)	0.071 (0.076)
High-advertising industries		
Industries with change of competition regime after 1958 (n = 9)	0.032 (0.027)	0.045 (0.032)
Industries without change of competition regime after 1958 (n = 30)	0.076 (0.071)	0.093 (0.080)

Notes: The figures are based on industries with available data for 1954 and 1958; n indicates the number of industries.

dustries with a change in competition regime after 1958 and industries without a change in regime. Clearly, there is a large difference in initial conditions between the two groups. For instance, in table 5.9 the mean ADS in 1958 is 3.5% for fourteen advertising-intensive industries with CHANGE = 1 and 7.1% for forty-two advertising-intensive industries with CHANGE = 0 (all industries in the latter group were noncollusive in the 1950s). The picture is substantially the same in 1954 and for the subsample of high-advertising industries. How are we to interpret this negative correlation between collusive pricing and advertising intensity? Recall that this issue was discussed in a slightly different context in chapter 3, where I argued in favor of an interpretation that sees the causality as going from advertising effectiveness (an exogenous variable) to the likelihood of collusive pricing. Under that interpretation, collusion on price is more likely to occur in industries with low advertising effectiveness (and therefore also low advertising intensity).

Table 5.10 shows why an alternative interpretation, namely, that price collusion reduces advertising intensity, is not valid. This table compares the evolution of the mean ADS in the two groups over 1958–1968 and also over 1958–1973. In both groups ADS fell, and the

Table 5.10
Percentage change of mean ADS in advertising-intensive and high-advertising industries, 1958–1968 and 1958–1973

	Mean ADS 1958	Mean ADS 1968	Percentage change 1958–1968	Mean ADS 1958	Mean ADS 1973	Percentage change 1958–1973
Advertising-intensive industries						
Industries with CHANGE = 1	0.037 (0.027) n = 16	0.023 (0.016) n = 16	−36.4%	0.037 (0.029) n = 13	0.019 (0.016) n = 13	−47.1%
Industries with CHANGE = 0	0.071 (0.077) n = 42	0.063 (0.069) n = 42	−12.3%	0.084 (0.083) n = 31	0.050 (0.047) n = 31	−40.8%
High-advertising industries						
Industries with CHANGE = 1	0.045 (0.029) n = 11	0.029 (0.017) n = 11	−36.6%	0.045 (0.032) n = 9	0.024 (0.017) n = 9	−47.6%
Industries with CHANGE = 0	0.094 (0.080) n = 30	0.083 (0.071) n = 30	−11.6%	0.108 (0.084) n = 23	0.065 (0.046) n = 23	−39.8%

Notes: The figures in the first three columns are based on industries with available observations for both 1958 and 1968. The figures in the last three columns are based on industries with available observations for both 1958 and 1973. The figures in parentheses are standard deviations. n indicates the number of industries.

fall was actually more pronounced in the previously collusive group. While in 1958 noncollusive industries had an average advertising-sales ratio about twice as high as that of collusive industries, in the late 1960s and early 1970s the mean *ADS* of the control group was nearly three times as high as the mean *ADS* of the previously collusive group.[27] This is certainly not consistent with the view that price competition promotes advertising. In fact, the reverse could be true. Does this difference persist when we control for other variables, and is it statistically significant? To answer these questions, I now turn to the econometric analysis.

Price Competition and Advertising Intensity: Econometric Specification

The econometric model that I will use is a panel data model with industry-specific effects. The basic specification is

$$\ln ADS_{it} = \alpha_i + \gamma_1 \ln SSDOM_{it} + \gamma_2 \ln(K/L)_{it} + \gamma_3 TVINT_{it}$$

$$+ \gamma_4 Y54 + \gamma_5 Y63 + \gamma_6 Y68 + \gamma_7 Y73 + \gamma_8 CHANGE * Y54$$

$$+ \gamma_9 CHANGE * Y63 + \gamma_{10} CHANGE * Y68$$

$$+ \gamma_{11} CHANGE * Y73 + e_{it},$$

where *ADS* is the industry advertising-sales ratio, *SSDOM* is sales revenue in the UK market deflated by the general producer price index, *TVINT* and *K/L* are as previously defined, and *Y54*, *Y63*, *Y68*, and *Y73* are time dummies for 1954, 1963, 1968, and 1973, respectively. As always, the interaction terms should reveal any differences in the evolution of advertising intensity after 1958 between industries with a change in competition regime ($CHANGE = 1$) and industries without such a change ($CHANGE = 0$). In other words, the coefficient on $CHANGE * Y63$ measures the effect of the 1956 legislation on $\ln ADS$ by 1963, the coefficient on $CHANGE * Y68$ measures the effect by 1968, and the coefficient on $CHANGE * Y73$ measures the effect

---

27. Moreover, of the five industries with the largest *percentage* rise in *ADS* between 1958 and 1968, only one (chocolate confectionery) has $CHANGE = 1$, while four (razors and blades; sanitary towels; ice cream and ice lollies (ice pops); margarine) have $CHANGE = 0$. On the other hand, three out of five industries with the largest *percentage* fall in *ADS* between 1958 and 1968 have $CHANGE = 1$ (typewriters; domestic refrigerators and deep freezers; lead pencils), and only two (baby carriages; toilet brushes) have $CHANGE = 0$.

by 1973. The benchmark year is 1958. Moreover, the coefficient on $CHANGE * Y54$ measures whether the evolution of advertising intensity was in any way different between collusive and noncollusive industries during 1954–1958 (i.e., before the implementation of the legislation). Finally, note that $CHANGE$ is defined here according to the industry categories used for ADS, that is, the level of aggregation is sometimes the four-digit and sometimes the five-digit industry level.

The reason for using a log transformation of ADS as the dependent variable is to avoid the difficulties that arise from the fact that ADS is bounded below by zero. Preliminary tests revealed a marked tendency for the residual variances to increase with fitted values in regressions with the untransformed advertising-sales ratio. In addition to heteroskedasticity, the coefficients on the competition variables in these regressions may be biased, given that cartelized industries had, on average, a much lower ADS than noncartelized industries, both in 1958 and throughout the period. In particular, if the general trend during the period under study involved larger absolute changes in advertising intensity in industries with higher advertising than in those with lower advertising, as seems to be the case, then using the untransformed ADS as dependent variable might result in an underestimation of any changes in ADS in previously collusive industries.

An implication of using a log transformation of the dependent variable and of including $\ln SSDOM$ and time dummies among the regressors is that the theoretical distinction between the impact of competition on advertising expenditure and on advertising intensity is blurred in practice: the choice of the dependent variable (advertising expenditure or intensity) does not affect the coefficients and standard errors on the interaction terms or $TVINT$.

As usual, the potential endogeneity of $CHANGE$ may be a cause for concern. At first sight, this could be more serious here than in the concentration regressions because of the difference in initial conditions between collusive and noncollusive industries. However, as shown in tables 5.9 and 5.10, cartelization in the 1950s is negatively correlated with advertising intensity *throughout the period*, not just for 1958 or 1954. This suggests that although collusion seems to be correlated with variables that affect advertising intensity and are not included in the model, these variables are time-invariant, industry-specific characteristics. Any such unspecified variables will be captured in the present model by the industry effects, and there will be no endogeneity bias, provided an estimation method that accounts for the correlation between regressors and industry effects is used.

But this does not fully settle the issue. There could be some unobserved characteristic that differs between the two groups and causes them to evolve in different ways after 1958; then one might wrongly attribute this evolution to the effect of the legislation. For instance, suppose that consumers' experience with a product is inversely related to advertising effectiveness, so that newer products are associated with a higher level of advertising, everything else being equal. Suppose also that newer products are less likely to be subject to collusion. If both these conjectures are true, then the decrease in advertising expenditure after 1958 in previously collusive British manufacturing industries could be partly due to the fact that the products involved were more mature than the products produced in noncollusive industries.

An indirect but very informative check of whether this type of bias is likely to be present in the data is provided by a comparison of changes in *ADS* in the two groups *before* the effective implementation of the legislation (i.e., during 1954–1958). Table 5.9 shows that the mean *ADS* for fourteen advertising-intensive industries with collusive agreements, and subsequently a change in competition regime, was 2.5% in 1954 and 3.5% in 1958, which implies a 40% increase in the mean *ADS* during this period. For forty-two industries in the control group, on the other hand, the mean *ADS* was 5.7% in 1954 and 7.1% in 1958, which corresponds to a 25% increase. Thus *ADS* appears to have been rising somewhat more rapidly, in proportional terms, in collusive advertising-intensive industries than in noncollusive ones during 1954–1958.[28]

Did this pattern continue after 1958? The answer is no. As shown in table 5.10, the mean *ADS* for sixteen advertising-intensive industries with a change in competition regime declined from 3.7% in 1958 to 2.3% in 1968, which represents a 36.4% fall. At the same time, the mean *ADS* for forty-two advertising-intensive industries in the control group fell from 7.1% in 1958 to 6.3% in 1968, a 12.3% fall. In other words, *ADS* fell by much more, in proportional terms, in advertising-intensive industries with a change in regime than in advertising-

---

28. The reasons for looking here at proportional rather than absolute changes in *ADS* are the same as the reasons for using ln *ADS* rather than the untransformed *ADS* as dependent variable in the regressions.

intensive industries without such a change during 1958–1968. This is very different from what was happening before 1958, and so it cannot be attributed to any underlying trend in *ADS* that differed between the two groups.

Price Competition and Advertising Intensity: Econometric Results

Tables 5.11 and 5.12 contain regression results for the two samples. Since industries with a change in competition regime had, on average, a much lower advertising-sales ratio throughout the period than industries in the control group, the competition variable *CHANGE* is probably correlated with the industry-specific effects in the panel data model described above. To obtain consistent estimates, fixed-effects estimation was used throughout.

Preliminary tests suggested the presence of a clear outlier, namely, the 1963 observation for the washing machine industry. The advertising-sales ratio reached a record 12.6% in 1963 in this industry, compared with 4.4% in 1958 and 2.9% in 1968. As described in detail in the following section, this was due to very special circumstances in that industry, namely, the temporary entry of firms that used press advertising as part of their process of distribution. These special circumstances and the fact that this type of advertising was definitely nonstandard justify dropping this observation from the sample. In any case, this affects only the coefficient on $CHANGE * Y63$, which is smaller in absolute value and statistical significance when the observation is included; the other results are not significantly affected.

The two tables report results for the basic model as well as for several alternative specifications. Thus, I report regression results using *TVINT*, and also using *TVTOT*. Recall that the main concern with *TVTOT* is its potential endogeneity. However, this may not be a serious problem after all: in preliminary regressions using *TVINT* as an instrument for *TVTOT*, the Wu-Hausman test always rejected the null hypothesis of a significant effect on the estimated coefficients of the potential endogeneity of *TVTOT* even at the 20% significance level. Moreover, since both *TVINT* and *TVTOT* are at best imperfect controls for the effect of TV advertising, I also report results for a specification that does not include either of these variables. Finally, I have also experimented with a specification including the interaction variables $\ln SSDOM * Y54$, $\ln SSDOM * Y63$, $\ln SSDOM * Y68$, and $\ln SSDOM * Y73$ in order to check whether the negative link

Table 5.11

Regression results for advertising intensity for industries with average ADS > 1% (fixed-effects estimation)

	Dependent variable: ln *ADS*					
ln *SSDOM*	−0.21	−0.33	−0.22	−0.34	−0.21	−0.34
	(0.10)	(0.10)	(0.10)	(0.10)	(0.11)	(0.11)
ln *SSDOM* * *Y54*	—	−0.05	—	−0.06	—	−0.06
		(0.06)		(0.06)		(0.07)
ln *SSDOM* * *Y63*	—	0.10	—	0.09	—	0.11
		(0.05)		(0.05)		(0.05)
ln *SSDOM* * *Y68*	—	0.17	—	0.17	—	0.19
		(0.05)		(0.05)		(0.05)
ln *SSDOM* * *Y73*	—	0.21	—	0.21	—	0.22
		(0.06)		(0.06)		(0.06)
ln *K/L*	−0.11	0.13	−0.04	0.19	0.01	0.25
	(0.18)	(0.18)	(0.17)	(0.17)	(0.17)	(0.17)
TVINT	2.02	1.73	—	—	—	—
	(0.69)	(0.64)				
TVTOT	—	—	0.62	0.59	—	—
			(0.16)	(0.15)		
Y54	−0.09	0.34	−0.13	0.43	−0.35	0.20
	(0.12)	(0.63)	(0.10)	(0.62)	(0.10)	(0.66)
Y63	0.04	−0.99	0.09	−0.90	0.09	−1.07
	(0.08)	(0.50)	(0.08)	(0.49)	(0.08)	(0.49)
Y68	−0.16	−1.94	−0.17	−1.97	−0.11	−2.09
	(0.13)	(0.53)	(0.12)	(0.51)	(0.12)	(0.54)
Y73	−0.50	−2.81	−0.55	−2.89	−0.48	−2.87
	(0.19)	(0.70)	(0.18)	(0.69)	(0.18)	(0.73)
CHANGE * *Y54*	−0.19	−0.14	−0.21	−0.16	−0.14	−0.09
	(0.18)	(0.16)	(0.18)	(0.15)	(0.18)	(0.15)
CHANGE * *Y63*	−0.14	−0.13	−0.17	−0.16	−0.16	−0.14
	(0.12)	(0.11)	(0.12)	(0.11)	(0.12)	(0.11)
CHANGE * *Y68*	−0.30	−0.27	−0.33	−0.30	−0.32	−0.28
	(0.13)	(0.12)	(0.13)	(0.11)	(0.14)	(0.12)
CHANGE * *Y73*	−0.22	−0.24	−0.26	−0.28	−0.21	−0.23
	(0.20)	(0.18)	(0.20)	(0.19)	(0.21)	(0.19)
R^2	0.37	0.43	0.38	0.45	0.33	0.40
R^2_{LSDV}	0.89	0.90	0.90	0.91	0.89	0.90
No. of industries	71	71	71	71	71	71
No. of industries with *CHANGE* = 1	16	16	16	16	16	16
No. of observations	305	305	305	305	305	305

Note: Heteroskedasticity-consistent standard errors in parentheses.

Table 5.12

Regression results for advertising intensity for industries with average ADS > 2% (fixed-effects estimation)

	Dependent variable: ln ADS					
ln SSDOM	−0.24	−0.38	−0.24	−0.37	−0.26	−0.39
	(0.13)	(0.13)	(0.13)	(0.13)	(0.13)	(0.13)
ln SSDOM * Y54	—	−0.12	—	−0.11	—	−0.13
		(0.07)		(0.07)		(0.07)
ln SSDOM * Y63	—	0.15	—	0.14	—	0.16
		(0.05)		(0.06)		(0.05)
ln SSDOM * Y68	—	0.19	—	0.19	—	0.20
		(0.06)		(0.06)		(0.06)
ln SSDOM * Y73	—	0.25	—	0.25	—	0.25
		(0.07)		(0.07)		(0.07)
ln K/L	0.07	0.31	0.12	0.32	0.12	0.34
	(0.22)	(0.21)	(0.22)	(0.21)	(0.21)	(0.20)
TVINT	1.34	0.50	—	—	—	—
	(0.80)	(0.73)				
TVTOT	—	—	0.42	0.31	—	—
			(0.18)	(0.16)		
Y54	−0.11	0.83	−0.13	0.84	−0.31	0.83
	(0.16)	(0.68)	(0.13)	(0.68)	(0.10)	(0.67)
Y63	0.03	−1.43	0.06	−1.34	0.08	−1.46
	(0.11)	(0.56)	(0.10)	(0.57)	(0.10)	(0.56)
Y68	−0.19	−2.09	−0.20	−2.15	−0.12	−2.14
	(0.18)	(0.65)	(0.17)	(0.65)	(0.16)	(0.65)
Y73	−0.54	−3.11	−0.59	−3.19	−0.48	−3.14
	(0.25)	(0.71)	(0.25)	(0.72)	(0.23)	(0.71)
CHANGE * Y54	−0.25	−0.09	−0.28	−0.13	−0.24	−0.08
	(0.23)	(0.15)	(0.23)	(0.15)	(0.23)	(0.14)
CHANGE * Y63	−0.12	−0.16	−0.14	−0.17	−0.12	−0.16
	(0.15)	(0.12)	(0.15)	(0.13)	(0.15)	(0.12)
CHANGE * Y68	−0.32	−0.36	−0.35	−0.38	−0.33	−0.36
	(0.17)	(0.14)	(0.17)	(0.13)	(0.17)	(0.14)
CHANGE * Y73	−0.20	−0.28	−0.24	−0.31	−0.20	−0.28
	(0.24)	(0.20)	(0.25)	(0.20)	(0.25)	(0.20)
R^2	0.36	0.46	0.37	0.47	0.34	0.45
R^2_{LSDV}	0.86	0.88	0.87	0.88	0.86	0.88
No. of industries	51	51	51	51	51	51
No. of industries with CHANGE = 1	11	11	11	11	11	11
No. of observations	218	218	218	218	218	218

Note: Heteroskedasticity-consistent standard errors in parentheses.

between market size and advertising intensity observed in the basic specification is more pronounced in certain years than in others.[29]

On the whole, there is no evidence of any positive effect of price competition on advertising intensity, and there is some evidence of a negative effect. In particular, the coefficient on $CHANGE * Y68$ is everywhere negative and statistically significant at the 5% level. On the other hand, the coefficient on $CHANGE * Y73$ is also negative, but it is not statistically significant. The magnitude of the effect of price competition on advertising is not easy to estimate very precisely. On the whole, the average effect is a fall in the advertising-sales ratio on the order of 20–25%. The coefficients on $TVINT$ or $TVTOT$ and the time dummy for 1973 (in the specification without the interactions of market size with year dummies) have the expected signs and are statistically significant. In particular, they confirm our expectations of a positive effect on ADS of the introduction of TV advertising and of a negative effect on ADS of the structural changes of the late 1960s.

Note also that the coefficient on $CHANGE * Y54$, although negative, is not statistically significant. Recall that this coefficient measures whether the change in ADS during 1954–1958 was different between collusive and noncollusive industries. The negative sign of the coefficient is consistent with the descriptive statistics of table 5.9. However, there is no statistical significance even at the 20% level, which strengthens the argument that the observed difference between the two groups after 1958 is due to the legislation.

Interpreting the Evidence

How should we interpret the results on the effect of the 1956 cartel law on advertising intensity? As we have seen, the coefficient on $CHANGE * Y68$ is negative and statistically significant, while the coefficient on $CHANGE * Y73$ is negative but not statistically significant. I would argue that the evidence is consistent with the view that the intensification of price competition following the 1956 Act probably had a negative effect on advertising intensity across a range of UK industries during the 1960s. There are three different arguments to support this view.

---

29. I also tried replacing ln K/L with ln K/N as my setup cost proxy. The results were very similar to those presented here. They have been omitted, since this variable is not directly relevant in the advertising regressions anyway.

First, recall that the impact of the legislation on competition was mostly realized during 1958–1968. Second, note that the coefficients on $CHANGE * Y73$ are not very much lower in absolute value than the coefficients on $CHANGE * Y68$. It is mostly the standard errors which are higher. This may not be very surprising, since it has been argued above that there is considerable noise in the data for 1968–1973. Third, the coefficients on $Y68$ and especially on $Y73$ indicate a significant fall in ADS throughout manufacturing industry during the late 1960s and early 1970s, which is consistent with the raw statistics of table 5.10. What table 5.10 also shows is that during 1968–1973, the average ADS fell by much more in industries not affected by the 1956 legislation than in industries affected. One reason could be that for industries in the latter group, advertising intensity had already fallen considerably during 1958–1968 and could not fall much farther. For industries in the control group, however, which had not been much affected during 1958–1968, there was significant scope for a fall in ADS after 1968, and this fall actually occurred because of changes in the pattern of distribution or other factors.

Note that this interpretation, although rather speculative, is consistent with the evolution of market structure in the two groups of industries after 1958, as already discussed above. In particular, it is consistent with the fact that during 1968–1975, $C5$ fell slightly, on average, in advertising-intensive industries not affected by the 1956 Act, although it increased, on average, in advertising-intensive industries affected by the Act. How could all these different pieces of evidence fit together?

Suppose that in addition to the effect of the cartel legislation after 1958, which was undoubtedly a major shock, there was an intensification of price competition across advertising-intensive industries after the mid-1960s due to the abolition of resale price maintenance and structural changes in the pattern of distribution. Now consider the following hypothetical account of events after 1958. During a first phase, from 1958 to 1968, the 1956 Act caused price competition to intensify, and hence advertising to fall in previously collusive industries. However, the fall in advertising was not sufficient, on the whole, to offset the fall in profits, and so concentration increased in these industries. During a second phase, from 1968 to 1973, competition intensified in *all* advertising-intensive industries, and perhaps the competitive pressure was again stronger in previously collusive industries because resale price maintenance had until that time hindered the emergence of fully effective price competition. But these industries had already experienced a significant fall in advertising as a result of the cartel legislation, so it was difficult for advertising to fall much farther. As a result, these industries experienced a further rise in concentration after 1968. On the other hand, industries that had not been affected by the cartel legislation responded to the intensification of price competition and the decline in the role of brand advertising in the late 1960s through a fall in advertising expenditure. This largely offset the pressure on profits and prevented concentration from rising in these industries after 1968.

This is not an implausible story, but I should repeat that certain parts of it are somewhat speculative. In particular, I should emphasize two main caveats. First, some of the regression coefficients on which this story relies are not very precisely estimated. Second, the samples used in the advertising and the concentration regressions are not identical, and this may affect the comparability of the two sets of results.

A comparison of the two sets of results, in particular tables 5.5 and 5.6 with tables 5.11 and 5.12, also provides some interesting insights on the explanatory power of the industry-specific effects in the regressions presented in this chapter. In all these tables, two R^2's are reported: the first is derived from transforming the data to obtain deviations from industry means and applying OLS to the transformed data, while the second (denoted R^2_{LSDV}) is obtained from applying OLS to the untransformed data after including a set of industry dummies among the regressors. Thus the difference between the two R^2's is a measure of the explanatory power of the industry effects in these regressions. Clearly, industry-specific characteristics explain much of the cross-industry variation in both concentration levels and advertising intensity. In addition, the concentration regressions have greater explanatory power than the advertising regressions when the R^2 is defined to include fixed industry effects and lower explanatory power when the R^2 does not include industry effects. In other words, the industry-specific effects have relatively more explanatory power for concentration than for advertising intensity.

There are at least two possible reasons for this. First, the use of an imperfect proxy for setup cost in these regressions may imply that industry effects pick up differences in setup costs across industries, and these are more directly relevant to concentration than to advertising. Second, market structure is more difficult to change than advertising (a fact reflected in the structure of the game analyzed in section 5.2), so it is expected to be less responsive than advertising to relatively small changes in exogenous variables.

Let me now summarize the results so far. I have set out to examine four empirical questions in this chapter. The econometric evidence presented in this section has provided answers to three of these questions. First, the evidence is consistent with proposition 5.1, since we do not observe the outcomes that are excluded under this proposition. Second, there is considerable evidence of a negative overall effect of price competition on advertising intensity. Third, there is strong evidence of a positive overall effect of price competition on concentration in advertising-intensive industries. The final question, which concerns propositions 5.2 and 5.3, cannot be answered on the basis of the econometric results. Support for these propositions is provided by case studies, and this is the subject of the next section.

5.6   Two Case Studies

This section provides a brief account of the evolution of two different segments of the UK electrical appliance industry during the 1960s, focusing on the effect of the intensification of price competition on advertising and market structure. The overall trend in the evolution of the electrical appliance industry during the 1960s was an increase in the intensity of price competition, a fall in advertising intensity, and a rise in concentration. This evolution is consistent with the econometric evidence of the previous section. However, even more interesting than the overall trend was the experience of particular markets within the industry over specific time periods. This experience offers several direct tests of the theory developed in this chapter.

The two segments that I will examine are the washing machine industry and the domestic refrigerator industry. Both industries are well documented and particularly suitable as case studies for a variety of reasons. They were relatively concentrated in the late 1950s, although the market shares of the industry leaders were moderate, and they were not subject to any restrictions on entry. Moreover, advertising was a key strategic variable in both industries at the time the restrictive practices legislation came into effect, as indicated by advertising-sales ratios around 4% in both cases. Finally, both industries experienced an increase in the intensity of price competition during the 1960s, but they were not very much affected by the introduction of TV advertising in the UK. Although the intensification of price competition was not the only factor that shaped the evolution of nonprice competition and market structure in the two industries, this evolution is consistent with the theoretical predictions of this chapter.

Both industries were subject to restrictive agreements at the time the 1956 Act came into force (the arrangement on washing machines was actually part of a wider arrangement covering many types of electrical appliances). The agreements provided for retail price maintenance and common maximum discounts to distributors, and also contained ancillary restrictions relating to sales promotion and conditions of sale. The refrigerator manufacturers' agreement also provided for the exchange of price information between the parties. There were no explicit restrictions with respect to individual prices. More important, there were no restrictions on media advertising or on entry, which is consistent with my theoretical model. Most of the important washing machine and refrigerator producers were parties to the agreements. As a result of the 1956 Act, the arrangement on washing machines was abandoned in 1959 and that on refrigerators probably was canceled at about the same time. Resale price maintenance continued to be individually imposed until the mid-1960s, although it was weakening. Eventually this, too, was abandoned following the introduction of the 1964 Resale Prices Act.

Other exogenous influences on the electrical appliance industry during the period under study include the discontinuous growth in demand, the gradual reduction of tariffs and transport costs, and changes in the pattern of distribution. Demand for all types of electrical appliances was growing, but it was subject to considerable fluctuations caused to a large extent by changes in macroeconomic policy (Corley 1966, Hatch 1972). Import penetration was not significant until the mid-1960s, but it subsequently intensified, for washing machines and especially for refrigerators. And the breakdown of resale price maintenance in the mid-1960s led to increased competition among retailers and, together with the growth of large retailers, may have put additional pressure on manufacturers' margins or influenced their advertising strategies. Finally, a factor that did *not* have much impact on the industry was the introduction of TV advertising: press advertising remained by far the most important type of advertising for electrical appliances.

The Washing Machine Industry

The experience of the washing machine industry from the mid-1950s to the late 1960s provides a clear contrast between two different competition regimes. The industry was relatively concentrated in 1958, with the five largest firms accounting for 76% of total sales of UK firms. The largest producer throughout the 1950s was Hoover, whose market share had nevertheless declined from about 50% of total industry sales in the early 1950s to around 35% in 1958. This decline was to a large extent due to the rapid expansion of A.E.I.-Hotpoint, achieved largely through heavy media advertising and despite the fact that the Hotpoint models were among the most expensive in the market (Mayers 1963, Shaw and Sutton 1976). These two firms had a combined market share of around 50% in the late 1950s.

The leading firms avoided price competition in the 1950s and preferred to use advertising to stress product quality, a strategy consistent with the permissive climate of competition policy and also with the fact that their sales efforts were mainly directed toward upper-class and middle-class households. Advertising expenditure in the press and on TV, including production costs of advertisements, increased steadily from 2.5% of total manufacturers' and importers' sales revenue in the UK market in 1954 (when TV advertising had not yet been introduced) to 4.4% in 1958 (with TV advertising accounting for about one-third of total advertising expenditure). Hoover and A.E.I.-Hotpoint accounted for somewhat less than 40% of total industry advertising in the UK market.[30]

The nature of competition in the industry changed dramatically in the early 1960s. The underlying conditions for this change seem to have been the introduction of the restrictive practices legislation

---

30. The advertising data for the whole of this section were taken from the *Statistical Review of Press Advertising*, the *Statistical Review of Independent TV Advertising*, the *Statistical Review of Press and TV Advertising*, and the *MEAL Monthly Digest of Advertising Expenditure*. The figures were adjusted to take into account press undercoverage, discounts for TV advertising, and production costs of advertisements. Advertising by accredited dealers is included, together with advertising by manufacturers and importers, but advertising by the Electricity Council and Electricity Boards (which have been acting as retailers in the market) for own-brand appliances is not. Data on sales revenue of UK producers, the five-firm concentration ratio, and firm numbers were obtained from the Census of Production and *Business Monitor, PQ series: Quarterly Statistics* for various years, and relate to complete machines only. Some data on market shares were also taken from market research sources. Import and export data for various years are from the *Annual Statement of the Trade of the United Kingdom*.

and the emergence of a mass market for washing machines. These underlying conditions should be distinguished from the event that triggered the breakout of price competition, namely, the entry of low-price firms. The most important new entrant was Rolls Razor, a firm that soon came to represent a serious challenge to established producers. Rolls Razor had a three-part strategy (Shaw and Sutton 1976): offering to sell simple twin-tub machines at prices as much as 25% lower than incumbent firms; bypassing the traditional distribution outlets by selling directly to consumers; and engaging in heavy press advertising both to contact customers and to stress its low prices (the advertisements contained reply coupons which potential buyers would use to invite a visit by a salesman). At first, the established firms' response was to increase their advertising expenditure and, in the case of Hoover, also to introduce sophisticated automatic models. By 1962, however, Rolls Razor had a market share of more than 10%, and there was entry of more direct-selling, low-price firms, most notably Duomatic.

Starting in early 1962, the industry leaders cut the prices of their existing models and also introduced new, cheaper models to compete for the emerging mass market. Advertising expenditure, on the other hand, soared: in 1963, the industry spent a record 12.6% of sales revenue in the domestic market on advertising (though if Rolls Razor and Duomatic are excluded, the industry advertising-sales ratio was 7–7.5%). Duomatic and Rolls Razor had a combined market share of 15–18% in 1963, although they accounted for nearly half of total industry advertising expenditure. On the other hand, Hoover and A.E.I.-Hotpoint, whose combined market share was 55% in 1963, accounted for 30% of total advertising expenditure, although they both had a much higher advertising-sales ratio than in the 1950s. Note that advertising by the direct-selling firms was of a different type than that of the established producers, since it was used as part of a radical distribution policy and as a means of stressing rather than relaxing price competition. Still, of course, it was a fixed cost which had to be covered by gross profit.

The fall in the prices of washing machines during the 1960s is reflected in the official producer price index of the industry. This increased by 1.5% between 1958 and 1962, then fell by 5% in 1963 and by a further 5.5% between 1963 and 1968. This should be compared with the evolution of the producer price index for all manufacturing, which increased by 8% over 1958–1963 and by a further

11.5% over 1963–1968. Despite the fall in margins and an increase in advertising outlays that far exceeded the growth in sales revenue, the number of UK producers of washing machines employing at least twenty-five persons increased slightly from twenty-five in 1958 to twenty-six in 1963, according to the Census of Production. In fact, there was hardly any merger activity during this period (Hart et al. 1973), and while some exit of smaller firms did occur during the 1961–1962 slump (Hatch 1970), this almost exactly offset the entry of new firms during the boom of 1959–1960.

Hence the evolution of the industry between 1958 and 1963 seems to correspond to an outcome which is excluded under proposition 5.1: an increase in advertising outlays without a corresponding fall in the number of firms following an intensification of price competition.[31] Proposition 5.1 predicts that such an outcome is not sustainable in the long run because firms can no longer cover their sunk costs when faced both with lower margins and with higher advertising expenditure. Note that the growth in demand during 1958–1963 complicates things somewhat in the present case, but since advertising expenditure increased by much more than sales revenue, thus leading to a very large increase in the advertising-sales ratio, the basic mechanism driving proposition 5.1 still applies.

Events in the washing machine industry after 1963 are consistent with proposition 5.1. The exit of Rolls Razor in 1964, following a significant fall in its sales and market share, was only the beginning of the general restructuring of the industry through exit and merger (see Hart et al. 1973). The number of UK firms employing at least twenty-five persons fell from twenty-six in 1963 to eighteen in 1968. It kept falling after that date, probably because of intensified import penetration as well as changes in distribution, and was as low as seven in 1973. The industry advertising-sales ratio also fell after 1964 and was only 2.9% in 1968, with the downward trend continuing well into the 1970s.[32]

In summary, the evolution of the washing machine industry in the early 1960s is interesting for two main reasons. The first reason is

---

31. The rise of the five-firm sales concentration ratio from 76% in 1958 to 85% in 1963 was mainly due to the 15% market share of Rolls Razor (cf. Hart et al. 1973), and should not conceal the fact that the structure of the industry remained too fragmented for firms to be able to cover their sunk costs.

32. Other factors may also have played a role in the restructuring of the industry, such as the fall in demand between 1963 and 1968, although it must be noted that advertising expenditure fell by much more than sales revenue over that period.

that it helps draw a distinction between long-run effects, which have been the main focus of analysis in this chapter, and short-run disequilibrium states. The second reason is that it confirms proposition 5.1 in a very direct way, namely, by documenting the mechanism that breaks an unsustainable industry configuration: when firms cannot cover their sunk costs, there must be exit or a reduction in endogenous sunk costs or both. More specifically, the short-run disequilibrium appears in this case to correspond to that outcome which is excluded under proposition 5.1, namely, an increase in advertising without a corresponding fall in the number of firms following an intensification of price competition. The evolution of the washing machine industry shows that this outcome can occur in the short run, but it must eventually break down, because it is not sustainable in the longer term.

The Domestic Refrigerator Industry

The evolution of the domestic refrigerator industry since the mid-1950s provides further support for the theoretical results of this chapter, in particular propositions 5.2 and 5.3. Domestic refrigerators can be mechanically operated or heat-operated. The former, which accounted for about 65% of total sales in 1958 and about 75% in 1968, are all electric. Of the latter, which were in decline throughout the period under study and accounted for less than 10% of total sales in 1973, most are electric but some are gas models. The relevant market is the market for all types of refrigerators, because the gas models have always been coproduced with their electric counterparts, and the restrictive agreement of the refrigerator manufacturers covered all types.

The industry was relatively concentrated in 1958, with only nine or ten UK firms employing at least twenty-five persons, although none of these had a market share higher than 20%. A change of competition regime seems to have occurred soon after the 1956 Act came into effect. The emergence of price competition was triggered by the slump of 1961–1962; this left many firms in the industry with considerable excess capacity, some of which had been the result of expansion by established producers or entry of new firms during the boom of 1958–1960. Net producer prices, which had been relatively stable throughout the 1950s, fell by about 20% between 1960 and 1964 (Hatch 1970, Mayers 1963). This is also reflected in the official producer price index of the industry, which fell by more than 25% between 1958 and 1963, while the producer price index for all manufacturing increased by 8% over the same period.

Changes in distribution in the mid- and late 1960s, including the growth of retailers' own brands (Baden-Fuller 1980) may have put further pressure on profit margins. An additional major influence on competitive conditions in the industry since the mid-1960s was the growth of imports. While in the 1950s these were not significant, in 1968 they accounted for more than a quarter of total manufacturers' and importers' sales revenue in the UK market. The producer price index of the industry remained unchanged between 1963 and 1968, at a time when the producer price index for all manufacturing increased by about 11.5%.

Nonprice competition was an important element of manufacturers' strategies in the 1950s, but its significance diminished over the following decade. Advertising expenditure in the press and on TV was 3.7% of total manufacturers' and importers' sales revenue in the domestic market in 1958 and remained high during the early 1960s. The most important advertisers throughout this period were Electrolux, Frigidaire, and, until its closure in 1964, Pressed Steel. These three firms were consistently among the four largest producers of refrigerators in the 1950s. Note that part of the reason for the high advertising-sales ratio of the industry in the early 1960s was a 1962 deal between Rolls Razor and Pressed Steel, whereby Rolls Razor would market Pressed Steel refrigerators. The venture accounted for more than a quarter of the industry's advertising expenditure in 1963, but for only about 7% of sales, and Pressed Steel eventually ceased production. Thus it seems reasonable to regard the high advertising of the early 1960s as a short-run disequilibrium response to the new competitive regime in the industry.

This interpretation is consistent with the fact that the industry advertising-sales ratio collapsed after the exit of Pressed Steel in 1964, reaching 1.1% in 1968 and even lower levels in the 1970s.[33] One reason for this large fall in advertising intensity was the intensification of price competition. Another reason must have been the negative effect of the changes in distribution and the growth of retailers' own brands on the effectiveness of brand advertising by manufacturers.

---

33. Advertising by domestic producers never recovered. A small temporary increase in industry advertising intensity in the early 1970s was largely due to advertising of certain imported brands.

How was the evolution of market structure in the refrigerator industry affected by the described changes in the competition regime
and the role of advertising? Between 1958 and 1968, price competition intensified and advertising intensity fell dramatically. According
to proposition 5.2, these are circumstances where a fall in concentration (a rise in firm numbers) is possible. In particular, if we were to
observe a decline or no change in concentration in the refrigerator
industry between 1958 and 1968, then proposition 5.2 would be
confirmed. This is because the proposition predicts that whenever
concentration does not rise following an intensification of price
competition, then it must be the case that advertising has fallen substantially, everything else being equal. Note that if, on the other hand,
we were to observe a rise in concentration in the refrigerator industry
between 1958 and 1968, proposition 5.2 would not be rejected; one
could always claim that the fall in advertising was not large enough.
However, the empirical relevance of proposition 5.2, and more generally of the idea that a negative competition effect on concentration
is possible in advertising-intensive industries, would be seriously
questioned, since it would then be difficult to see under what plausible industry conditions we may get an outcome different from the
standard positive competition effect on concentration.

There is also a slightly different way to think of this particular
experiment, which makes use of proposition 5.3 as well. The refrigerator industry was one of a handful of industries with an initial
advertising-sales ratio higher than 3% that experienced a significant
increase in the intensity of price competition in the 1960s. A high
advertising-sales ratio implies that there is scope for a significant
reduction in advertising, and thus for a negative effect of price
competition on concentration. Of all the industries in this class, the
refrigerator industry experienced one of the largest falls in the
advertising-sales ratio during the 1960s. If the hypothesis of a potentially negative competition effect on concentration in industries with
high advertising effectiveness is to have any empirical relevance,
one should see this effect in this particular industry.

In fact, one does see a negative competition effect on concentration, and a positive effect on the number of firms, in the refrigerator
industry between 1958 and 1968. Changes in market size and other
factors complicate somewhat the interpretation of the evidence in
terms of our theoretical predictions, but the basic mechanisms at

work should still be reflected in the evidence.[34] Thus the number of domestic firms did not change significantly over 1958–1968. According to the Census of Production, the number of UK manufacturers of mechanically operated domestic refrigerators employing at least twenty-five persons was nine in 1958, and this number was the same in 1963 (despite the considerable entry and exit of firms over 1959–1963; see Hatch 1970) and in 1968. These figures do not include foreign firms selling in the UK market. Given that imports were far higher in 1968 than in 1958, the number of foreign firms with sales in the UK must have been higher in 1968 than in 1958, and hence the same must also have been the case for the total number of firms (excluding those with fewer than twenty-five employees) with sales in the UK. Note that the years 1958, 1963, and 1968 are all broadly comparable with respect to demand conditions.

Moreover, evidence from market research suggests that the four-firm concentration ratio in the UK market for domestic electrical refrigerators as a whole (including imports) declined from about 60% in the late 1950s to 45% in 1967 before rising to 55% in 1969 (see Baden-Fuller 1980). Note that much of the rise in concentration between 1967 and 1969 was due to the 1967–1968 A.E.I.-G.E.C.-English Electric mergers, which were not carried out with the specific objective of merging the electrical appliance divisions of these firms.[35] One reason for the fall in concentration during the 1960s was a shifting of market share away from the two leading domestic firms, something not really captured by the model of this chapter (which assumes symmetry). However, another reason was the growth of imports, so the fall in concentration is also linked to the evolution of firm numbers and thus can be attributed partly to the forces identified in the theoretical model.

---

34. The effect of market growth is to create a "bias" toward a rise in firm numbers and a fall in concentration to the extent that the exogenous component of sunk costs is significant. However, this may not be true in a high-advertising industry, since market growth will then induce an escalation of advertising expenditure, all else being equal (see Sutton, 1991). Moreover, other factors may influence concentration upward and firm numbers downward, as is likely to have happened in the present case—see the discussion in chapter 4 on the various factors that contributed to the overall rise in concentration in the UK during the 1960s.

35. These mergers had a much smaller impact on concentration in the washing machine industry than in the refrigerator industry because of the low market share of G.E.C. in washing machines and a 1965 agreement whereby A.E.I.-Hotpoint took over English Electric's washing machine division and English Electric took over A.E.I.-Hotpoint's stove division (see Hart et al. 1973).

It should be pointed out that the concentration data are not strictly comparable with the data on firm numbers described above. The former refer to sales of all electrical refrigerators in the UK market; the latter refer to sales of mechanically operated refrigerators by UK producers employing at least twenty-five persons. Nevertheless, both pieces of evidence point in the same direction. Moreover, the stability, or even increase, of firm numbers and the apparent fall in concentration in the refrigerator industry between 1958 and 1968 should be seen in the context of the overall substantial fall in firm numbers and the increase in concentration in British manufacturing as a whole during the 1960s. As pointed out in chapter 4, Hart and Clarke (1980) report a rise of eight percentage points in the average five-firm sales concentration ratio among UK producers at the four-digit industry level between 1958 and 1968. My own calculations suggest that most of this can be attributed to a fall in firm numbers, since the number of UK firms employing at least twenty-five persons fell during the same period by about 25–30% in the average industry (see chapter 7 of this book). Compared to this benchmark, the refrigerator industry experienced a relative rise in firm numbers and a relative fall in concentration during 1958–1968, even if foreign firms are not taken into account.

Interestingly, this is not the end of the story for the refrigerator industry. Competitive pressure continued to intensify after 1968, as shown by the fact that the producer price index of the industry increased by only 9.5% over 1968–1973, while the producer price index for all manufacturing increased by 37% over the same period. Several factors may have caused price competition to intensify further, and one of them was certainly import penetration: imports increased from 25% of total sales in the UK in 1968 to almost 50% in 1973. Now advertising was already low in 1968, so it could not fall much farther. Proposition 5.2 would then predict that during 1968–1973 the number of firms should have fallen, everything else being equal, since the pressure on margins could no longer be offset by any significant reduction in sunk costs. This is indeed what happened: according to Business Monitors, there were only six UK producers of all types of domestic refrigerators still in operation in 1972–1973.

In summary, the experience of the refrigerator industry during 1958–1968 shows that a negative competition effect on concentration is not just a theoretical oddity. This was a high-advertising industry that experienced a significant increase in the intensity of price competition and a large fall in advertising expenditure during the 1960s. These are the conditions that can lead to a fall in concentration, and in this case they did. Furthermore, both phases in the evolution of the refrigerator industry seem to be consistent with proposition 5.2. The experience of the industry during 1958–1968 suggests that an increase in the intensity of price competition must lead to a substantial fall in advertising if the number of firms does not fall (and concentration does not rise), as predicted by the proposition. The experience of the industry during 1968–1973, on the other hand, suggests that an intensification of price competition must cause the number of firms to fall (and concentration to rise) if advertising falls little or not at all, which is again consistent with proposition 5.2.

5.7 Concluding Remarks

In advertising-intensive industries, tougher price competition will affect both the incentive of firms to spend on advertising and market structure. The theoretical predictions on the effects of competition in this class of industries are weaker than the corresponding results for exogenous sunk cost industries. The theory is in general silent as to whether advertising expenditure will rise or fall when price competition intensifies. Moreover, if advertising rises, then concentration must also rise. But if advertising falls, then the decrease in the sunk costs that firms must cover at equilibrium may or may not offset the fall in gross profits due to increased price competition, and so concentration may decrease or increase.

In the first part of this chapter a theoretical framework was introduced to deal with these issues. The focus was on deriving predictions on the *joint* effect of price competition on advertising and market structure. Two general results were derived. The first of these places a bound on the space of outcomes by excluding certain outcomes as not admissible within the theory. In particular, a fall in concentration together with an increase in advertising expenditure, following an increase in the intensity of price competition, cannot occur. The second result, which further restricts the space of outcomes, is a prediction on the competition-concentration relationship which is conditional on the behavior of other observable variables. The key implication of this result is that more price competition must lead to a significant fall in advertising intensity if concentration does not rise, or, conversely, it must cause concentration to rise if advertising falls little or not at all. Taken together, the theoretical results indicate that a positive effect of price competition on concentration is the most likely outcome in advertising-intensive industries, since the reverse can occur only in the event of a significant fall in advertising expenditure.

In the second part of this chapter, the theory was tested against econometric and case-study evidence on the evolution of advertising-intensive manufacturing industries following the introduction of cartel legislation in Britain in the late 1950s. The econometric results indicate that the intensification of price competition following the introduction of the legislation caused, on the whole, a rise in concentration of about six percentage points in advertising-intensive industries, and probably also a fall in advertising intensity on the order of 20–25%. The case-study evidence confirms that a negative effect of price competition on concentration cannot be ruled out in high-advertising industries. However, a necessary condition for this to occur is that tougher price competition leads to a significant fall in advertising intensity. On the other hand, if advertising falls little or not at all when price competition intensifies, then concentration will rise, which is consistent with the theoretical predictions as well as with the econometric results.

6

Price Competition, Innovation, and Market Structure in R&D-Intensive Industries

6.1 Introduction

The relationship between market power and innovative activity has been a much-debated issue ever since Schumpeter's pioneering work. On the one hand, large firms in concentrated markets are often seen as the main engines of technological progress, for reasons that relate to the optimal scale for R&D and innovation, appropriability conditions, and the presence of financial constraints. For instance, one argument along these lines is that in the presence of capital market imperfections, firms with market power can more easily finance R&D from own profits and are therefore more likely to undertake R&D projects, which are inherently risky and often involve significant sunk costs. Another argument is that firms with market power can more easily appropriate the returns from innovation, and therefore have better incentives to innovate.

On the other hand, it is often argued that the lack of competitive pressure may lead to inertia and managerial slack, and hence to a reduced level of innovative activity. In its simplest version, this view essentially implies that managers and workers of firms with market power can capture some of the monopoly rents in the form of slack or lack of effort. More recent versions of this idea have focused on the fact that competition may improve the ability of firms' owners to provide appropriate incentive schemes to managers.

The view of competition as a stimulus to innovation is probably the majority position among policy makers today. This represents a significant shift in opinion from the days when promoting national champions was regarded by many as the best way to encourage innovation. But although this latter position seems to be in decline, the theoretical and empirical support for the view that competition is generally beneficial for innovation is far from clear. In fact, despite the very extensive literature on the subject, the issue of the links between market power and innovation is still not settled.

A Long-Standing Debate

The theoretical literature on competition and innovation consists of several strands. One line of research has focused on the interaction between short-run and long-run decisions in oligopoly. Although some of these studies have found that less short-run competition may result in, or be associated with, more investment in the long-run variable (such as R&D expenditure), others have shown this result to depend on particular functional forms or the specification of the collusive technology (see Yarrow 1985, Fershtman and Gandal 1994, Ziss 1994, Fershtman and Muller 1986, Davidson and Deneckere 1990, Fershtman and Pakes 2000).[1] Another strand of the theoretical literature has analyzed endogenous growth models of innovation. These studies have also produced mixed overall results, although they have succeeded in identifying specific conditions that may determine whether competition is associated with more or less innovation. Thus, for instance, a negative competition effect on innovation has been obtained in models with profit-maximizing firms and leap-frogging technological progress, while a positive effect can occur if firms are non-profit-maximizing or technological progress is step-by-step (see Aghion and Howitt 1997, 1998; Aghion et al. 1999). Note that strong predictions regarding the effect of competition on innovation are generally more difficult to derive in models with asymmetric firms, since the response of each firm to intensified competition may then depend on the relative efficiency levels (see Boone 2000). Finally,

---

1. A common assumption in this context is that firms cannot collude in the long-run variable, whatever their short-run conduct. This is often justified in theoretical studies by a reference to the fact that long detection and retaliation lags hinder the stability of collusion. Since long-term decisions take time to implement, the reaction to rivals' behavior is relatively slow (i.e., there are relatively long retaliation lags); hence collusion in long-run variables will be relatively difficult to achieve. In the case of R&D, an additional argument is that deviations from agreed levels of R&D expenditure are difficult to observe, at least as long as R&D cooperation does not take the form of a joint venture; in other words, detection is also problematic, and this further hinders collusion on R&D.

the theoretical literature on the effects of competition on managerial incentives has provided only weak support for the view that competition improves managerial performance (see Nickell 1995 for a survey).

On the empirical side, a number of surveys (e.g., Cohen 1995, Symeonidis 1996) suggest that there is no strong general relationship between market power and innovation, and that industry characteristics such as appropriability conditions, demand, and especially technological opportunity explain much more of the cross-industry variation in R&D intensity and innovation than market power or market structure. It is therefore all the more interesting that the results from a number of UK studies of innovation seem to be less ambiguous. In particular, both Geroski (1990) and Blundell et al. (1995) have found evidence of a positive link between competition and innovation in British industry.

One of the main methodological problems in the empirical literature on the determinants of innovation has been the relative neglect, until recently, of the endogeneity of market structure. Thus an implicit assumption in many empirical studies has been that market power is greater in concentrated markets. This assumption implies that to analyze the effect of market power on innovation, one can simply examine the effect of concentration or firm numbers on innovation. This approach, however, is not justified in a context where market structure is seen as endogenous. Within the theoretical framework of this book—which centers on the idea that more intense price competition will generally lead to higher concentration—an approach that considers high concentration as a proxy for high market power is simply wrong. Moreover, the empirical evidence presented in chapters 4 and 5 suggests that this criticism should be taken seriously.

More specifically, there are two main implications of the theoretical and empirical analysis of previous chapters of this book for the study of the links between market power and innovation. First, market structure cannot be taken as a proxy for market power in cross-industry studies. Second, both innovation and market structure should be seen as jointly determined endogenous variables, a view which is consistent with much recent work on technological change and the evolution of market structure in R&D-intensive industries (see Utterbach and Suarez 1993, Klepper 1996, Klepper and Simons 1997, Sutton 1996, 1998, among others).[2]

There have been numerous attempts to address one or the other of these issues in econometric work. Thus some authors have examined the determinants of innovation using measures of competitive pressure or market power other than market structure, such as import penetration; some of this work will be reviewed below. Others have tried to address the endogeneity issue by using instrumental variable techniques or by estimating simultaneous equation systems, with rather mixed results (see, e.g., Farber 1981, Lunn 1986, Levin and Reiss 1988).[3] However, none of these studies has explicitly modeled innovative output and concentration as jointly determined by some exogenous measure of competition (as well as by other variables). This is the approach that will be taken here.

Before describing my methodology in more detail, I will briefly discuss a number of previous empirical studies of the determinants of R&D or innovation that have used measures of market power other than market structure. Taken as a whole, these studies provide little evidence of a negative effect of competition on innovation, and only weak evidence of a positive effect.

This is certainly the conclusion from a comparison of two studies of the effects of import competition on R&D or innovation. The first is a detailed study of R&D-spending reactions of US firms to increased high-technology import competition over the period 1971–1987, carried out by Scherer and associates (see Scherer 1992, Scherer and Huh 1992). The authors found that the response varied considerably across firms, and that most of this variation was unsystematic.

---

2. This recent literature consists of two main strands. One line of research has focused on developing stylized theories of the life cycle of R&D-intensive industries and testing them against evidence from industry case studies. See Klepper and Simons (1997) for a comparison of different theories. A second approach has questioned the generality of any particular evolutionary path, and has focused instead on a small number of mechanisms that are likely to work across a broad range of industries. This is the approach of Sutton (1996, 1998).

3. Innovation may affect market structure directly or indirectly, and in various and contradictory ways. For instance, it may increase or decrease the minimum efficient scale of production, and it may facilitate or hinder the entry of new firms. So it is perhaps not surprising that the econometric literature on this issue has been inconclusive. For instance, while Farber (1981) and Levin and Reiss (1988) found a positive effect of R&D on concentration, Mukhopadhaya (1985) found a negative effect of R&D on concentration change, and Geroski and Pomroy (1990) found a negative effect of innovation counts on concentration change.

If anything, rising import competition had, on average, a negative but statistically insignificant effect on R&D intensity in the short run. In the longer term, no overall effect either way could be identified, partly because of data limitations. On the other hand, Bertschek (1995) found a positive and statistically significant association between the import penetration ratio and the introduction of innovations in a panel of German firms over the period 1984–1988. This study focused on short-run reactions only, and left open the question of the long-run effect of changes in the competitive environment on innovation. More generally, a difficulty with studies of the effects of import penetration is the potential endogeneity of imports and the possible presence of reverse causality between import penetration and innovative activity.

A more long-run view was taken in Geroski's (1990) study of the determinants of innovations used (as opposed to innovations produced) at the three-digit industry level in the UK during the 1970s. Geroski split the 1970s into two five-year periods, and exploited the resulting panel structure to control for technological opportunity and other time-invariant industry-specific characteristics. He included six different measures of market power among his independent variables: the extent of market penetration by entrants, the number of firms with fewer than ninety-nine employees as a fraction of the total number of firms, the market share of exiting firms at the year of exit, the five-firm concentration ratio, the change in the concentration ratio, and import penetration. The coefficient on import penetration was negative but not statistically significant. The coefficients on the other five variables, however, suggested that more competitive conditions favored the use of innovations by firms, although only in the case of the concentration ratio and the change in the concentration ratio was the effect statistically significant.

While Geroski found evidence of a positive effect of competition on the use of innovations across British manufacturing industries in the 1970s, a more recent study by Broadberry and Crafts (2000) found no evidence of any link between the two variables in the 1950s. The measure of competition used by Broadberry and Crafts was based on the incidence of collusive pricing in the 1950s, and their results were robust to different ways of classifying industries as collusive or competitive. A potential limitation of their analysis derives from the use of cross-section data. As will be pointed out in section 6.3, the available innovations data are subject to measurement errors, which may make their use in cross-section regressions—but not in panel regressions—

somewhat problematic. Furthermore, it is generally very difficult to unravel the two-way link between competition and innovation using cross-section analysis. These difficulties can, however, be avoided by examining the evolution of the two variables over time—in particular, by examining the evolution of innovative activity across industries following the enactment of the 1956 restrictive practices legislation.

The Present Study

This chapter focuses on industries where R&D and technological innovations are important for competition. The theoretical framework used to analyze these industries has much in common with that developed in chapter 5 for analyzing advertising-intensive industries. Equilibrium in R&D-intensive industries is seen here as involving the joint determination of market structure, R&D expenditure, and innovative output. As elsewhere in the book, the intensity of price competition can be thought of as an inverse measure of the degree of collusion, and is taken as exogenous.

I will begin by adapting the general theoretical framework of chapter 5 to the analysis of R&D-intensive industries. The model is sufficiently general to allow for a variety of possible outcomes regarding the effect of price competition on innovation. This approach is motivated by the idea that strong results on this question can be obtained only by imposing a considerable amount of structure on theoretical models. Such results are often of limited generality or depend on features of the model that are difficult to observe or measure across industries. My approach is also motivated by the inconclusiveness of much of the existing literature on the links between market power and innovation. Instead, I will focus on weaker predictions that can be derived from a more general model and relate to the joint behavior of innovation and market structure following an intensification of price competition in industries with significant R&D expenditures.

In the second part of the chapter, I will examine the econometric evidence on the effect of price competition on concentration and the production (rather than the use) of innovations in the UK following the introduction of the 1956 Restrictive Trade Practices Act. Although the effect of the 1956 Act on innovation has often been discussed (see, e.g., Wilson 1962, Swann et al. 1973, 1974), this chapter provides the first systematic analysis of this issue.

My empirical methodology differs from that of previous empirical studies of the links between market power and innovation. In particular, I model market structure and innovative output as endogenous variables in reduced-form equations derived from a game-theoretic model. I make no attempt to analyze the interaction between innovation and market structure using a simultaneous-equation system, since the available data are simply not sufficient for obtaining proper identification of the equations in such a system. I use the panel structure of the data to control for industry-specific effects as well as for key determinants of innovation, such as technological opportunity, which are likely to be correlated with measures of competition but are relatively stable over time. Moreover, I explicitly focus on long-run effects, although I also compare these to short-run effects. Finally, and perhaps most important, I bypass the need to measure or proxy the intensity of price competition, since I use information on a major exogenous institutional change that significantly affected the competitive environment facing UK firms in several industries.

6.2   Theoretical Framework

Consider an R&D-intensive industry where each firm produces one or more varieties of a differentiated product. A three-stage game can be used to model competition in such an industry. At stage 1 firms decide whether or not to enter the industry at an exogenously given cost of entry f. At stage 2 each firm i chooses to incur a cost R_i, which represents expenditure on process or product R&D. The results of R&D are measured by an index of "innovative output" I_i, which is also realized at stage 2 of the game. A rise in I_i enhances product quality (and thereby increases the consumers' willingness to pay) or reduces the marginal cost of production; either way, it affects the firms' objective functions in the final-stage subgame. Finally, at stage 3 firms simultaneously set prices or quantities. I will be looking, in what follows, for a symmetric subgame perfect equilibrium in pure strategies in this game.[4]

---

4. The structure of the model analyzed in this section is similar to the structure of the linear demand model of section 5.3. The competition measure t is the equivalent of the inverse of the parameter λ of the linear demand model. The innovation index I is the equivalent of the quality index u, and the basic technological relationship between I_i and R_i is similar to that between u_i and F_i in the linear demand example. Finally, assumptions R1–R3, made below, are all satisfied in the linear demand example. Of course, the present model is much more general.

The structure of this game reflects the fact that (1) decisions on R&D expenditure involve significant sunk costs and (2) product or process characteristics cannot be changed as easily or as quickly as price choices, although they are still more flexible than entry decisions. However, I abstract from issues of uncertainty regarding the outcome of R&D projects, as do, in fact, many models within the general class of "nontournament" models of R&D rivalry, of which the present model is an example.[5] The key underlying assumption of these models, as opposed to the literature on patent races, is that each firm can achieve product or process improvements through its R&D expenditure without preventing other firms from obtaining equivalent benefits from their own R&D.

The Third-Stage Subgame

The equilibrium of the third-stage subgame can be represented by a vector of gross profits $\pi_i(S, N, h, t, I_1, \ldots, I_i, \ldots, I_N, k_1, \ldots, k_i, \ldots, k_N)$, where S is market size, N is the number of firms that have entered at stage 1, h is a measure of the degree of horizontal product differentiation, k_i is a vector of parameters specific to firm i and independent of N and the I_i's, and t is a measure of the intensity of price competition.[6] The interpretation of t is the same as in previous chapters: for any given N, gross profit π_i will depend on the firms' pricing behavior, which in turn will depend partly on exogenous institutional factors. For instance, t can be thought of as an inverse measure of the degree of collusion.

In the benchmark case of symmetric firms, the equilibrium gross profit of firm i can be written as $\pi_i(S, N, h, t, I_i, (I_{-i}))$, where (I_{-i}) denotes

---

5. Previous studies using nontournament models of R&D competition in which market structure and the level of R&D are jointly endogenous variables include Dasgupta and Stiglitz (1980), Motta (1992), and Sutton (1996, 1997b, 1998).

6. In R&D-intensive industries the degree of horizontal product differentiation depends not only on demand characteristics, such as the extent of diversification of users' preferences and the level of transport costs, but also on technological factors—namely, the availability of alternative research paths leading to different varieties of the product or associated with different submarkets within the industry, as well as the extent of scope economies in R&D across the various research paths (see Sutton 1998). For our present purposes, it will be sufficient to subsume all these influences—which can be regarded as exogenous—within the concept of horizontal product differentiation. This is not inconsistent with Sutton's emphasis on the trade-off between spending on R&D to enhance the quality of existing products and spending to develop new products, and the implications of this trade-off for market structure in technologically progressive industries. In the present model, the incentive to provide variety increases (and the equilibrium level of concentration should normally fall) as h rises.

the $(N-1)$-tuple $(I_1, I_2, \ldots, I_{i-1}, I_{i+1}, \ldots, I_N)$. Alternatively, one can write gross profit as $\pi_i[S, C(N, I_i, (I_{-i})), h, t, I_i, (I_{-i})]$, where C is any concentration measure whose value increases in $1/N$ for given I_i's (and depends only on N when $I_i = I_j$, $\forall i, j$, $j \neq i$), such as the concentration ratio. I will assume that π_i is everywhere increasing in S and h, and decreasing in t and N. Moreover, I will make two assumptions about the effect on π_i of changes in own and rival innovative output:

Assumption R1. π_i is increasing and strictly concave in I_i.

Assumption R2. π_i is nonincreasing in I_j, $\forall j \neq i$.

The first of these assumptions says that a firm's gross profit is increasing and strictly concave in its own innovative output, while the second says that a firm's gross profit is nonincreasing in any given rival's innovative output.

The Second-Stage Subgame

At stage 2 each firm chooses R_i to maximize its net profit $\pi_i - R_i - f$, given the choices of the other firms and the number of firms that have entered at stage 1. Now assume, for simplicity, that the choice of a level of expenditure R_i by firm i entirely determines the innovative output of that firm, given the fundamental (and exogenous) technological characteristics of the industry. That is, let innovative output I_i be determined by the innovation production function $I_i = I(r, R_i)$, where r is a measure of technological opportunity (hence I_i is strictly increasing in r for any given value of $R_i > 0$). Note that this function implies that I_i is independent of R_j, $\forall j \neq i$ (i.e., that there are no R&D spillovers). This assumption is made for simplicity and could be relaxed without changing the key results of the model, provided that spillovers are not very large, so that the gross profit π_i remains nonincreasing in R_j, $\forall j \neq i$.[7]

---

7. To see this, note that the R&D of firm j has two opposing effects on the gross profit of firm i. On the one hand, an increase in the R&D of firm j raises its innovation index, and thus increases its market share and gross profit at the expense of firm i's market share and gross profit. This negative R&D externality is always present in the model. On the other hand, when there are positive R&D externalities (spillovers), there is also another effect: an increase in the R&D of firm j raises the innovation index of firm i, and thus causes the gross profit of that firm to increase at the expense of firm j's own gross profit. The results of the model are not altered as long as this second effect does not dominate the first (i.e., as long as spillovers are not too large). It is interesting in this respect that Geroski (1994) found no evidence of significant R&D spillovers in British industry during the period that I analyze in this book.

Another implicit assumption, which is probably more difficult to relax without modifying the results, is that the "efficiency" of firms in carrying out R&D projects does not depend on the intensity of price competition. In other words, for any given level of R_i, I_i does not depend on t. Finally, the function $I_i = I(r, R_i)$ also abstracts from any stochastic influences on innovative output. This may seem like an oversimplification, but it merely reflects the fact that uncertainty does not play an important role for the issues examined here.

A key implication of the above innovation production function is that R and I are essentially interchangeable choice variables. In other words, it makes no difference whether the equilibrium of the second-stage subgame is defined in terms of a set of conditions for the optimal choice of the R_i's or in terms of a set of conditions for the optimal choice of the I_i's. Finally,

Assumption R3. I_i is increasing and weakly concave in R_i, with $dR_i/dI_i < d\pi_i/dI_i$ at $R_i = 0$, and there exists a level of R_i such that $d\pi_i/dI_i = dR_i/dI_i$ for any given N and set of R_j's.

The weak concavity of the innovation production function is actually a stronger condition than what is required, but it is consistent with the empirical evidence, which provides strong support for the presence, on average, of constant or diminishing returns to scale in the production of innovations (see, e.g., Kamien and Schwartz 1982, Bound et al. 1984, Hausman et al. 1984, Crepon and Duguet 1997). The results of this section would not change if the innovation function were convex, provided that gross profit π_i remained strictly concave in R_i.[8] The second part of assumption R3 ensures that there exists a level of $R_i > 0$ such that one more unit of R&D costs as much as the gross profit it creates (i.e., $d\pi_i/dR_i = 1$, $\forall i$). This is a necessary condition for the existence of an interior solution to the firm's problem of choosing the optimal innovation index (or the optimal level of R&D expenditure).

The first-order condition for the optimal choice of I_i by firm i is $d\pi_i/dI_i = dR_i/dI_i$. This says that for any given N and set of I_j's, each

---

8. The requirement that $dR_i/dI_i < d\pi_i/dI_i$ at $R_i = 0$ ensures that firms will choose to carry out some R&D at equilibrium. The assumption of a continuous innovation production function is, of course, a simplification. A more general formulation would allow for the presence of indivisibilities in R&D projects, especially since in some industries the absolute size of the typical R&D project may be large. However, the existence of indivisibilities does not significantly alter the basic analysis of the incentives to conduct R&D.

firm spends on R&D up to the point where the cost of an extra unit of R&D is equal to the profit this creates in the third-stage subgame through the corresponding rise in innovative output. At any symmetric equilibrium, we have $I_i = I$ (and hence $R_i = R$), $\forall i$, so the first-order condition for firm i can be written as

$$\frac{d}{dI_i}\pi_i(S, N, h, t, I_i, (I_{-i})) = \frac{d}{dI_i}R_i(r, I_i) \qquad \text{at} \quad I_i = I_{-i} = I. \qquad (6.1)$$

Equation (6.1) defines the level of R&D expenditure incurred by each firm, and the level of innovative output, as a function of the number of firms that have entered at stage 1. Note that at stage 2 of the game the I_i's and R_i's are the Nash equilibrium outcomes of a noncooperative game, whatever the value of t at the final stage. This assumption is standard in many theoretical models of semicollusion, and it is also consistent with the empirical evidence presented in chapter 2 of this book, according to which collusion with respect to R&D was rare in British manufacturing in the 1950s, even in industries where firms colluded on price.[9]

The Symmetric Equilibrium

At stage 1 firms enter as long as they can make a nonnegative net profit, anticipating equation (6.1). The free-entry condition, which—as in previous chapters—is assumed to hold whatever the value of t may be at the final stage of the game, is given by

$$\pi_i = \pi_i(S, N, h, r, t, R_i, (R_{-i}))|_{R_i = R_{-i} = R} = R + f, \qquad \forall i, \qquad (6.2)$$

where, for simplicity, N is treated as a continuous variable. Note that the gross profit has been written as a function of the R_i's and r (rather than the I_i's) in equation (6.2). This way of expressing the profit

---

9. It is, of course, true that firms may find it easier to collude on R&D when R&D cooperation takes the form of a joint venture. However, as pointed out in chapter 2, there was hardly any R&D cooperation of that form in British industries that practiced price-fixing in the 1950s. More generally, allowing for collusion on R&D in the present model would probably increase the likelihood that a breakdown of collusion (affecting all choice variables) leads to a rise in R&D and innovations. A rise in R&D in this case might also imply a rise in the net profit of each firm, for a given number of firms. Proposition 6.1 below, which is a prediction on the joint effect of price competition on innovations and market structure, would have to be modified to take that possibility into account. If, however, a breakdown of collusion had no effect on R&D in the more general model, proposition 6.1 should still hold unambiguously.

function will often be convenient in the present analysis. Concentration C^*, the number of firms N^*, R&D expenditure R^*, and innovative output I^* at the symmetric equilibrium are defined by the two necessary conditions (6.1) and (6.2). Since I am here concerned with comparative statics results, I will assume the existence of a unique equilibrium with $N^* \geq 2$ and $R^* > 0$, $I^* > 0$.

As in the case of advertising-intensive industries analyzed in chapter 5, little can be said in general about the comparative statics of I^*, R^*, and C^* individually without imposing more structure on the model. In particular, an intensification of price competition can lead to more, less, or no change in R&D expenditure and innovative output. This is because a rise in t can increase, decrease, or leave unchanged the incentive to spend on R&D.

More specifically, a firm's incentive to spend on R&D depends on the total derivative $d\pi_i/dR_i$, and the effect of a rise in t on this derivative is ambiguous. To see this, consider a decomposition of the overall effect of a change in t on $d\pi_i/dR_i$ based on writing $\pi_i = (p_i - c_i)x_i$, where p_i, c_i and x_i denote here, respectively, the *equilibrium* price, the *equilibrium* marginal cost, and the *equilibrium* output of firm i in the final-stage subgame. The decomposition reveals four different effects, two of which work in opposite directions for any reasonable form of the profit function. To see this, note first that a rise in R_i should generally cause both $p_i - c_i$ and x_i to increase, which is why π_i will also increase as a result. Now, on the one hand, the higher the value of t, the higher the level of output sold, and hence the larger the profit to be made by a unit increase in the price-cost margin following a rise in R_i. This effect would imply that the higher the value of t, the higher the value of the derivative $d\pi_i/dR_i$. On the other hand, the higher the value of t, the lower the price-cost margin, hence the smaller the profit to be made by a unit increase in output following a rise in R_i. This second effect would imply that the higher the value of t, the lower the value of the derivative $d\pi_i/dR_i$. Therefore, provided that a rise in R_i causes both $p_i - c_i$ and x_i to increase, as has been assumed here, the overall effect of a change in t on $d\pi_i/dR_i$ is ambiguous in general.

Not only is the effect of price competition on innovation ambiguous, but the effect on market structure can be uncertain. This is because both sides of the free-entry condition will be affected by a change in t, so it is not clear in what direction C^* should change to restore the free-entry condition.

The Joint Effect of Price Competition on Innovations and Concentration

It is, however, possible to derive general results regarding the *joint* behavior of I^* and C^* following a change in the intensity of price competition t. The following proposition, which is analogous to proposition 5.1 in chapter 5, excludes certain outcomes as not admissible within the theory. In particular, the proposition provides a sufficient condition for a rise in concentration following an increase in t.

Proposition 6.1. If an increase in the intensity of price competition t causes either an increase or no change in R^* (and therefore also in I^*), then concentration C^* must rise.

Proof. It will be convenient to write gross profit directly as a function of the R_i's in what follows. From assumptions R1 and R3, we know that π_i is strictly concave in R_i. Moreover, from R2 and R3, π_i is nonincreasing in R_j, $\forall j \neq i$. The gross profit of firm i at the initial equilibrium can be written as

$$\pi_0^* = \pi(R_i = R_0^* \mid S, C_0^*, h, r, t_0, R_{-i} = R_0^*) = R_0^* + f,$$

and the gross profit at the new equilibrium is

$$\pi_1^* = \pi(R_i = R_1^* \mid S, C_1^*, h, r, t_1, R_{-i} = R_1^*) = R_1^* + f.$$

Also, the profit of firm i at the initial equilibrium values of t and N^* when firm i sets $R_i = R_1^*$ while all other firms set $R_j = R_0^*$ is

$$\pi' = \pi(R_i = R_1^* \mid S, C_0^*, h, r, t_0, R_{-i} = R_0^*).$$

The proof is by contradiction. Assume that $C_1^* \leq C_0^*$ and $R_1^* \geq R_0^*$ following a rise of t from t_0 to t_1. Since π_i is decreasing in N, decreasing in t, and nonincreasing in R_j, $\forall j \neq i$, we obtain $\pi_1^* < \pi'$. Also, since the function $\pi_i(R_i \mid S, C_0^*, h, r, t_0, R_{-i} = R_0^*)$ is concave in R_i and its slope is equal to 1 at $R_i = R_0^*$, its slope is smaller than 1 at all points between R_0^* and R_1^*. Hence $\pi' - \pi_0^* < R_1^* - R_0^*$. Combining the two inequalities, we obtain $\pi_1^* - \pi_0^* < R_1^* - R_0^*$. This is, however, impossible, since net profit must be zero at equilibrium, and therefore we must have $\pi_1^* - \pi_0^* = R_1^* - R_0^*$. Hence it must be the case that C^* falls if R^* rises or does not change following a rise in t. $\qquad\square$

The intuition for proposition 6.1 is as follows. Starting from a zero-profit symmetric equilibrium, an increase in t unambiguously reduces net profit below zero, for given C and R_i's. For the zero-profit condition to be restored at a new symmetric equilibrium, net profit must rise. Now suppose that the increase in t has also caused all firms to spend more or exactly the same on R&D. This cannot increase net profit because (1) an increase in own R&D has a stronger effect on sunk cost than on gross profit when starting from a long-run equilibrium with $d\pi_i/dR_i = 1$, $\forall i$ (owing to the concavity of the gross profit function with respect to R_i), so it reduces gross profit; (2) if own R&D does not change, it has no effect on profit; and (3) an increase or no change in rival R&D cannot increase own profit. In these circumstances, then, there is only one way net profit can increase, through a rise in concentration.

Note that proposition 6.1 is a sufficient, but not necessary, condition for a positive competition effect on concentration in R&D-intensive industries. A positive competition effect on concentration can occur even if the R&D expenditure and the innovative output of each firm fall, provided that this fall is not too large and therefore does not offset the direct negative effect of the rise in t on gross profit. Formal theoretical results capturing this insight are easy to obtain, and they are comparable to results obtained in section 5.2 of chapter 5 for advertising-intensive industries. The key implication is that in R&D-intensive industries, a nonpositive effect of competition on concentration, although not impossible, may be unlikely.

Finally, note that proposition 6.1 is a prediction on the joint effect of price competition on *firm* innovation and market structure. The question arises as to whether anything can be said about the joint effect of price competition on *industry* innovation and market structure. In particular, an interesting question is whether it is possible to rule out the case $\Delta(N^*I^*) \geq 0$ and $\Delta N^* \geq 0$ ($\Delta C^* \leq 0$), where ΔI^*, ΔN^*, and ΔC^* denote the change in I^*, N^*, and C^*, respectively. This joint outcome can occur in one of two ways: either through $\Delta I^* \geq 0$ and $\Delta N^* \geq 0$; or through $\Delta I^* < 0$ and $\Delta N^* \geq 0$, with the rise in N^* offsetting the fall in I^*, so that N^*I^* rises. The former case is ruled out by proposition 6.1. The latter case cannot be ruled out on the basis of the assumptions we have made, but it does seem very improbable. To obtain $\Delta N^* \geq 0$ following a rise in t, R^* needs to fall considerably; if it falls by only a small amount, it will not offset the direct negative effect of the rise in t on gross profit, so N^* will fall. But since a significant fall in R^* is required for even a small rise (or no change) in N^*, it is very difficult to obtain $\Delta(N^*I^*) \geq 0$ together with $\Delta N^* \geq 0$ ($\Delta C^* \leq 0$) following a rise in t.

Discussion

The implications of the above model for the empirical analysis of innovation at the industry level are, then, as follows. First, if industry innovative activity increases or does not change following a rise in the intensity of price competition, then it is very likely that concentration has risen. Second, if we actually observe that more price competition causes a joint effect *other than* $\Delta(N^*I^*) \geq 0$ and $\Delta C^* \leq 0$, then proposition 6.1 will have been confirmed, since the joint outcome $\Delta(N^*I^*) \geq 0$ and $\Delta C^* \leq 0$ is a necessary condition for the joint outcome $\Delta I^* \geq 0$ and $\Delta C^* \leq 0$. The empirical results on the evolution of industry innovation and market structure in section 6.4 can therefore be used both to test proposition 6.1 and to examine whether it is possible to establish an empirical regularity which implies a slightly stronger constraint on the space of outcomes than proposition 6.1.

I will close this section with two brief remarks that draw on points already raised in previous chapters. (I will omit, however, the usual arguments regarding the exogeneity of the intensity of price competition t.) First, the assumption has been made throughout this section that R&D and the entry decision are the only long-run choice variables in the game. This was motivated by the fact that the number of industries where advertising and R&D are both key strategic variables is small. Hence it may be, on the whole, legitimate to assume that the presence of endogenous advertising expenditures in some R&D-intensive industries will not significantly alter the mechanism and the results described in this section.[10]

Second, while the present results have been derived for the benchmark case of symmetric single-product firms, it is not clear what other effects might arise in a more complex, asymmetric setting that would offset the mechanisms identified here regarding the competition effect on innovation and market structure. On the other hand, there is a potential complication with respect to the link between market size and concentration. In particular, it is possible that the variance of the firms' growth rate within any given industry is bigger in R&D-intensive industries than in other industries because of large asymmetries between firms in exploiting profit opportunities through

---

10. An alternative approach would be to interpret R as the total amount of endogenous sunk costs and I as an index of product quality or brand image. The results of this section would then be valid for all classes of industries with significant endogenous sunk costs (advertising or R&D).

successful innovation.[11] Now the larger this variance, the more likely
it is that an increase in market size will have a positive effect on
concentration, other things being equal. Of course, this is only one
potential mechanism through which market size may affect concentration, and there are many others. The point is, however, that the
presence of potentially large asymmetries in the growth of firms in
R&D-intensive industries may cause a positive "bias" in the observed
market size effect on concentration relative to the benchmark prediction for the symmetric case. Such a bias could be much more pronounced in R&D-intensive industries than in other industries.

The theory should now be confronted with the empirical evidence.
The first question to be asked is what was the effect of the 1956 Act
on innovations in British industry. This is a question on which the
theory developed in this section is deliberately silent. Provided that
we observe a nonnegative effect, the next question will then be whether
concentration did indeed rise, as suggested by the present theory.

6.3   The Data

To analyze the effects of price competition in R&D-intensive industries, I will use several different samples of industries in separate
regressions for concentration and innovation counts. The reason for
using different samples is that the industry definitions across the
various data sources are often difficult to match. Many of the variables and the data sources are the same as those used in chapter 4.
This is the case for the concentration ratio, the setup cost proxies
(either the capital-labor ratio or capital divided by the number of
plants), the market size proxies (sales revenue deflated either by the
general producer price index or by industry-specific price indices),
and the competition variable CHANGE. The data used in the concentration regressions are, as in previous chapters, for 1958, 1963,
1968, and 1975.

The only new variable in this chapter is the number of innovations
produced by firms in each industry over time. Note that there is a
significant difference between innovations produced and innovations
used, and that I employ the first of these measures. This reflects the
fact that the focus of this chapter is on the determinants of innovative
output that is the result of own R&D, not the determinants of firms'

---

11. There is considerable evidence that the size distribution of the profit outcomes
from innovation is highly skewed. See, for instance, Scherer et al. (2000).

incentives to adopt innovations produced in other industries or by other firms in the same industry.

The innovations database that I will use in this chapter is the only available source of systematic information on innovative activity across British manufacturing industries for the entire period examined in this book. Systematic data on other measures of innovative output, such as patents, are not available prior to the 1960s. There are, of course, well-known problems with measures of innovative output such as innovation counts or patents. Attempts to count the number of "significant" innovations are subject to some arbitrariness and even possible biases in the evaluation procedure. Moreover, even "significant" innovations differ in their economic value or the R&D expenditure incurred. Patent counts are subject to even greater problems, since patents are even more heterogeneous than significant innovations with respect to their economic significance or the amount of R&D involved. In addition, the propensity to patent innovations varies considerably across industries. Despite their shortcomings, however, measures of innovative output such as innovation counts and patents have been used extensively in studies of innovation. When panel data are available, as in the present case, many of these shortcomings are much less serious, as will be discussed in detail below.

Defining the samples of R&D-intensive industries

Although I will focus mostly on R&D-intensive industries, defined as industries with an average or typical R&D-sales ratio (RDS) of more than 1% over the relevant period, I also constructed several additional samples.

For the concentration regressions, I constructed a subsample of high-R&D industries, defined as industries with average or typical RDS higher than 2% over the relevant period. The objective was to confirm that the results obtained from the full sample are not driven by industries with medium R&D intensity (which may have features of exogenous sunk cost industries). In other words, the idea was to construct a subsample of industries for which R&D is clearly a key strategic variable. The choice of the 2% cutoff point leaves a nonnegligible number of industries with a change in competition regime in the high-R&D subsample, and at the same time it ensures that this subsample is sufficiently different from the RDS > 1% sample. In addition, the 2% cutoff point splits the group of R&D-intensive industries used in the concentration regressions into two groups of roughly equal size: of sixty-one industries with RDS > 1%, twenty-seven had RDS > 2%. The classification of industries with respect to these cutoff points was done in the manner described in chapter 4.

For innovation, it was not possible to use a similar subsample of high-R&D industries, since there were very few industries with a change in competition regime and average or typical RDS higher than 2% over the period in the basic sample used in the innovation regressions. In any case, given the results obtained from the innovation regressions using the basic sample of industries with typical RDS > 1% (see below), it seemed more important to check the robustness of these results using a larger group of industries than a smaller one. To this end, I constructed a slightly enlarged sample, including, in addition to those industries contained in the basic R&D-intensive group, several industries with average RDS < 1% but with a relatively high number of innovations in the database during the period under study.[12] This effectively amounts to using slightly modified criteria for selecting the group of technologically progressive industries.

The Innovations Data: General Features

The innovations data used in this chapter come from a major survey of significant innovations commercialized by UK firms during 1945–1983. The survey was carried out by researchers in the Science Policy Research Unit (SPRU) at the University of Sussex over a period of several years and covers a total of 4,378 innovations. The data were collected in three waves over a fifteen-year period: a first survey was conducted in 1970 for the period 1945–1970 and identified 1,304 innovations; a second, in 1980, covered the period 1970–1980 and identified a further 848 innovations; and a third, carried out in 1983, covered the whole period 1945–1983 and added another 2,226 innovations.

---

12. In particular, three groups of industries with typical RDS < 1% were initially included in the enlarged sample: (1) industries in the nonferrous metal sector, whose R&D-sales ratio was close to 1% for much of the period; (2) all industries with RDS < 1% in the five core R&D-intensive sectors (chemicals, mechanical engineering, instruments, electrical and electronic engineering, and vehicles); and (3) four more industries with a large number of innovations in the database (iron and steel, glass other than containers, paper, and plastic products). Some of these were later dropped because of their ambiguous state of competition.

An innovation was defined, for the purposes of the SPRU survey, as "the first successful commercial introduction of a significant new product, process, material or system into British manufacturing industry or services." This definition excludes mere inventions, organizational innovations, unsuccessful innovations, and the process of diffusion. An explicit attempt was made by the researchers to exclude all incremental innovations from the database.

The researchers asked nearly 400 industry experts to identify significant technical innovations successfully commercialized in the UK since 1945 in their sector of expertise, to name the firm or other organization responsible for each innovation, and to provide some basic information for each innovation.[13] The innovating firms were then contacted, whenever possible, and asked to confirm the information given by the experts and to provide additional and more detailed information on a range of variables. Thus the database contains, for each innovation, a brief description of the innovation; the date of its introduction; the industrial classification and the "technical class" of the innovation; the name, size, and status of the "innovating unit" (for instance, whether an independent firm, a subsidiary, a public body, etc.); the country of origin of the innovation; the industrial classification of the innovating unit and of the first user of the innovation; and information on a number of other variables. The SPRU database is deposited in electronic form in the Data Archive at the University of Essex.

The SPRU data have been extensively described and discussed by Townsend et al. (1981), Robson et al. (1988), and Geroski (1994). More than two-thirds of the total number of innovations are drawn from five core sectors: chemicals, machinery and mechanical engineering, instruments, electrical engineering and electronics, and vehicles. These sectors are also the most R&D-intensive sectors in manufacturing. Most of the remaining innovations come from four other sectors: basic metals, shipbuilding and marine engineering, building materials, and rubber and plastic goods. The remaining sectors innovate very little, which is consistent with the fact that they spend very little on R&D. Of the total number of entries in the database, about 75% are product innovations and 25% are process innovations—although, as pointed

---

13. Each sector was covered by several experts who were drawn from research and trade associations, academic institutions, government departments, trade and technical journals, individuals and consultants, as well as from firms.

out in Robson et al. (1988), the definition of what is a process innovation in an industry, rather than a product innovation by suppliers, is often somewhat arbitrary. The prevalence of product innovations in the SPRU data implies that most of these innovations were not first used in the sector that produced them. An implication of this is that a classification of innovations by user industry would differ considerably from the classification by producer industry that I use in this chapter.

There was a general upward trend in the number of innovations introduced in the UK over 1945–1983, which corresponds to a similar upward trend in the index of industrial production. Geroski (1994, chapter 2) points out that the two series appear to be co-integrated (i.e., that there seems to be a stable long-run relationship between them). Nevertheless, the number of innovations in the data appears to be relatively low relative to industrial production during the first few years covered by the survey, and again during 1981–1983. In both cases, this may be partly a consequence of the data collection procedure.[14] These potential inconsistencies in the data do not affect my analysis, however, since neither the very early period nor the period after 1980 is included in my data set of innovation counts for this chapter.

One feature of the data that is worth mentioning, although it is not directly relevant for the present study, is the large number of innovations in the SPRU database that have been produced by small firms.[15] Moreover, it is worth bearing in mind that a large fraction of the innovations in the database do not appear to have been the result of very expensive R&D projects. This observation will turn out to be useful when choosing an appropriate innovation lag for these data (see below).

---

14. The low numbers of innovations during the early period may be partly due to the difficulty of finding in 1970 experts who had been active during that period. And the decline in innovation counts after 1980 may be due to the fact that this period was covered in only one wave of data collection, while all the other years were covered in two waves.

15. The share of innovations produced by larger firms is much lower than their share of R&D expenditures, while the reverse is true for smaller firms (see Geroski 1994, chapter 2). There may be various reasons for this, including underreporting of R&D by small firms, overrepresentation of some low-concentration industries in the SPRU database, failure to take into account links between small and large firms in the production of innovations, and differences in the type of projects undertaken by larger and smaller firms. Whatever the reasons, the SPRU data are certainly free from any potential large-firm bias.

The Innovations Data: Problems and Solutions

As pointed out above, any attempt to count the number of significant innovations is subject to some arbitrariness and possible biases in the evaluation procedure. Fortunately, in the case of the SPRU data, these biases seem to affect the comparability of innovative activity across industries more than the comparability over time for any given industry.

One feature of the data stands out in this respect. Although the industries that contribute the most to the production of innovations in the SPRU database are, on the whole, those that have high R&D intensity, there is also considerable overrepresentation of some industries and underrepresentation of others. This clearly occurs to an extent far greater than what can be justified by the fact that the ranking of industries by R&D intensity is not necessarily the same as the ranking of industries by innovative output (measured either by innovation counts or by patents).[16] The problem has been recognized by the SPRU researchers themselves, and it is probably due to the fact that experts in different sectors had different views on what constitutes a "significant" technical innovation. However, these inconsistencies do not affect the analysis of the determinants of innovative activity carried out in this book. This is because I use panel data, so differences across industries in the measurement of innovative output become part of the industry-specific effects and do not affect the results of interest.

Although the most important inconsistencies in the SPRU data are across industries, there are also some problems affecting the comparability of innovation counts over time in some industries. An inspection of the raw data reveals that for several low-innovation industries, there is overrepresentation of the period 1945–1970 and underrepresentation of the period 1970–1980.[17] On the other hand, for at least two high-innovation industries, textile machinery (MLH 335) and scientific and industrial instruments (MLH 354), there is

---

16. Examples of industries with a disproportionately large number of innovations in the database are textile machinery and mining machinery. Examples of industries with a disproportionately small number of innovations in the data are toilet preparations, polishes (both of which do not have even one innovation), and aerospace.

17. Examples include the entire sector of leather and leather goods, with more than fifteen innovations during 1945–1970 and none thereafter, several food industries, cement, and others.

the opposite problem: overrepresentation of the period 1970–1980, as is recognized by the SPRU researchers themselves (Townsend et al. 1981). These inconsistencies are probably due to the fact that the data were collected in waves, so the same experts were not necessarily contacted in each wave. None of the industries with obvious time inconsistencies were included in the samples used for the innovation regressions of this chapter. Low-innovation industries were not included anyway, since I have chosen to focus on R&D-intensive or innovation-intensive industries only. In addition, I explicitly excluded textile machinery and instruments.

The inconsistencies that originate from the data collection procedure are not the only problems with the SPRU data, however. Perhaps the most important problem for my present purposes stems from the way in which the innovations are assigned to the various industries. In addition to a short description of each innovation and an indication of its "technical class," the data report the *principal* industry classification of the innovating firm or organization,[18] the industry classification of the innovation, and the industry classification of the first user of the innovation. None of these is satisfactory for my purposes.

The classification by first user industry is simply not relevant, since I am interested in the production, not the use, of innovations. The principal industry classification of the innovating firm may be misleading in the case of diversified firms. Thus, for example, an innovation by the detergent division of a firm such as Unilever would be classified in the food sector, since this is the principal industry classification for Unilever. Since many firms in chemicals and engineering (which form the bulk of the population of innovating firms) are diversified, this is a significant problem. Finally, the industry classification of the innovation is misleading in the case of process innovations, which, as pointed out above, are a considerable part of the total in the SPRU data. For example, the industry classification of a process innovation by the National Coal Board involving the use of new or improved machinery would be "mining machinery," although this is clearly not an innovation by firms in the mining machinery industry.

To minimize the measurement error from the misclassification of innovations across industries, I reclassified all the innovations in the

---

18. In cases where the innovating unit is a subsidiary of another firm, the data report the principal industry classification both of the subsidiary and the parent firm.

SPRU database according to the industry where each innovation was produced. Broadly speaking, this involved classifying product innovations according to the industry of the innovation and process innovations according to the industry in whose production process the innovation was made. Thus, in the examples mentioned above, I classified product innovations by the detergent division of Unilever in the soap and detergent industry and process innovations involving new or improved mining machinery by the National Coal Board in the coal industry. The reclassification was not always straightforward, however, and I often had to make use of the descriptions of innovations given in the SPRU database or of independent information regarding the industrial activities of specific firms.[19] Since the focus of the present study is on company-financed noncooperative R&D, innovations by public research establishments and industrial research associations were excluded; their number was small, anyway. However, innovations by public firms were included.[20]

---

19. The most common difficulty was the following. Suppose that the principal industry classification of the innovating firm/unit is A, the industry classification of the first user of the innovation is again A, and the industry classification of the innovation is B. It is then not always easy to tell whether this is a process innovation in industry A or a product innovation in industry B by a division of that particular innovating firm/unit.

Clearly, in such a case it is helpful to know the exact description of the innovation and whether the firm in question has a plant in industry B. Information on the latter question for the year 1968 is contained in a detailed Directory of Business published as part of the Census of Production of that year. Although this directory is obviously less useful for innovations introduced in the 1950s than for those introduced in the 1960s and early 1970s, and its coverage is not complete, it often provided the key information required for classifying particular innovations. In other cases, my classification was based on more subjective criteria. For instance, cases in which industry A in the above example was iron and steel and industry B was instruments were classified as process innovations, since it seemed unlikely that steel firms would have divisions producing instruments. On the other hand, cases where both A and B were electronic engineering industries were usually classified as product innovations, since firms in that sector tend to be diversified into related industries.

20. There is also a second problem with the way the innovations are assigned to the various industries in the SPRU database, which applies especially to low-innovation sectors, such as food and drink, textiles, and clothing. In these sectors, the innovations are very often assigned to the sector rather than to any particular industry. In fact, they are assigned to the first "minimum list heading" (MLH) industry in each of these sectors, which is, of course, very misleading. In most of these cases, it was possible to reclassify the innovations to the appropriate industries. In any case, since my empirical analysis focuses on R&D-intensive or innovation-intensive industries, the sectors that were subject to serious measurement errors of this kind are not included in the samples used in this chapter. Note that MLH 411, man-made fibers, which is the first MLH industry in the textile sector, is R&D-intensive. This industry was also dropped from my samples, however, because of ambiguous state of competition in the 1950s.

The level of aggregation used in the SPRU database is the three-digit (or MLH) industry level, which is lower than the four-digit industry level used in the concentration statistics. However, I was often able to classify the innovations in the data according to more disaggregated industry categories, roughly corresponding to the four-digit industry level or to a level between the three-digit and the four-digit. These were usually the MLH industry subdivisions indicated in Central Statistical Office, *Standard Industrial Classification* (London: H.M.S.O., 1968), although sometimes two or more such subdivisions were merged either to avoid creating industry categories with very few innovations or because it was impossible to achieve a very detailed industry breakdown of the innovation counts or of the sales data. In other cases, it was not possible or not necessary to go beyond the three-digit industry level, because the descriptions of the innovations were not sufficiently detailed or the three-digit industry was itself a relatively homogeneous market—both in terms of the possible existence of R&D spillovers across products and from the point of view of competition. One industry, aircraft, was excluded because of heavy government involvement throughout the period.

Innovation Lags

Although the SPRU data record the number of innovations for every year between 1945 and 1983, it is necessary to group the innovation counts into somewhat longer periods, so that they can be matched with Census-based figures on sales revenue and other variables that are available only at roughly five-year intervals during the 1950s and the 1960s. Using five-year periods to group the innovations is therefore an obvious choice, but this still leaves open the question of exactly which periods to use.

Data on sales revenue, capital stock, employment, and so on are available for 1954, 1958, 1963, 1968, and then annually from 1970 onward. Data for 1953 are not available, but I constructed estimates for 1953 sales revenue on the assumption that the proportional change of the deflated sales revenue in any given industry over 1953–1954 was equal to the average yearly rate of change of the deflated sales revenue in that industry over 1954–1958. I used the same method to construct estimates for the 1953 capital-labor ratio and the ratio of capital stock to the number of plants in each industry. Now it is reasonable to assume that the sales revenue in any given year t is a measure of average market size between years $t - 2$ and $t + 2$. It is also reasonable to assume that R&D expenditure in any given year is influenced by market conditions (such as market size or the intensity of price competition) in that year. It follows that the sales revenue in year t can be thought of as a determinant of R&D spending between years $t-2$ and $t+2$. The key question is What is the time lag between R&D spending and the commercialization of innovations?

It is well known that the time lag between the beginning of a research project and the commercialization of innovations varies greatly, depending on the nature and significance of the innovations. Estimates of the *average* lag across industries will also depend on the criteria used to compile any particular survey of innovations. In fact, such estimates range from one to four years (see Mansfield et al. 1971, Pakes and Schankerman 1984, Acs and Audretsch 1988). In addition, there is evidence, at least for the UK, that R&D expenditure tends to increase in the last year or years of a research project (Schott 1976).

The simplest way of linking R&D spending to innovation counts in a cross-industry study is to hypothesize that the bulk of R&D spending for innovations commercialized in year t takes place at a certain year $t-x$, where x is an average across industries and types of innovations. This is the approach typically taken in the empirical literature on the determinants of innovative activity, and this is also the approach that I will follow. What should be the value of x? If the average lag between the beginning of a project and the commercialization of innovations is one to four years, then the average lag between the bulk of R&D spending and the commercialization of innovations should be one to two years. On the assumption of a one-year lag, the number of innovations commercialized in year t is determined, on average, by market conditions in year $t-1$. Thus sales revenue in year t (which, as already pointed out, is a measure of average market size between years $t-2$ and $t+2$) should be matched with the number of innovations commercialized between years $t-1$ and $t+3$.[21]

---

21. An alternative way of linking R&D spending to innovation counts would be to assume that the number of innovations in any given year t is a function of R&D expenditures from year $t-4$ to year t, with appropriate weights applied for different years. This approach is not very practical, however, when sales revenue data are available only at five-year intervals. Besides, in the absence of any systematic information on innovation lags in each particular industry, this approach is still only a rough approximation to the actual innovation lags across industries and types of innovations.

The time periods chosen for grouping the innovations data in this chapter are therefore 1952–1956, 1957–1961, 1962–1966, 1967–1971, and 1972–1976. These were matched with data on sales revenue (and capital intensity) for 1953 (my estimates), 1958, 1963, 1968, and 1973, respectively. Note that these time periods are also very convenient in the present case because focal-point years, such as 1955, 1960, 1965, and so on are not borderline between any two consecutive periods. This is important because the experts and the firms consulted for the construction of the SPRU database may have used focal-point years whenever they were uncertain about the exact date of the introduction of an innovation. The fact that focal-point years are close to the midpoints of the time periods that I use here to group the innovations should practically eliminate any errors resulting from imprecise dating of innovations in the SPRU database.

These time periods are also convenient from the point of view of the evolution of competition in British manufacturing. The number of innovations commercialized in any given industry during 1952–1956 was clearly determined by market conditions prior to the introduction of the 1956 restrictive practices legislation. Innovative output during the next period, 1957–1961, was driven by market conditions during 1956–1960, which covers the last few years of cartelization as well as the first two years after industries had started to formally abandon price-fixing. But because of the fact that in many R&D-intensive industries price-fixing agreements continued until the early or even the mid-1960s, the period 1956–1960 can be seen, on the whole, as a time when competition had not yet emerged to any significant scale. The next period in the innovations data, 1962–1966, is one in which we expect to see the short-run effect of competition on innovation. In the final two periods, 1967–1971 and especially 1972–1976, we almost certainly observe the long-run effect of competition.

While the assumption of a one-year innovation lag seems reasonable and has been used in previous studies using the SPRU data (e.g., Blundell et al. 1995), I also experimented with an alternative set of time periods for grouping innovation counts, chosen on the assumption of an average two-year lag between the bulk of R&D spending and the commercialization of innovations. This implied matching innovation periods 1953–1957, 1958–1962, 1963–1967, 1968–1972, and 1973–1977 with sales revenue data for 1953, 1958, 1963, 1968, and 1973, respectively. The choice of a two-year lag is consistent with the evidence from a survey of R&D expenditure and innovations in a sample of firms drawn among the 300 largest firms in British industry in the early 1970s (Schott 1976). Note, however, that the study by Schott focused on large or very large firms. On the other hand, a large fraction of the innovations in the SPRU database are by small firms, and the average R&D project of a small firm is likely to be less expensive than that of a large firm. To the extent that this also implies that smaller firms are generally involved in shorter-term projects than larger firms, a one-year average innovation lag may be an appropriate assumption for the SPRU data.

In any case, I chose to use the assumption of a one-year lag for my basic specification of innovation counts (with dependent variable $INN1$), but I also checked the robustness of the results under the alternative assumption of a two-year average innovation lag (using the alternative dependent variable $INN2$). Both sets of results will be reported below, although they are, in fact, very similar.

Innovations Introduced or Innovations Produced?

A final complication with the SPRU data arises in connection with the precise meaning of the term "introduction" of an innovation. In particular, the introduction of an innovation in the UK by a domestic "innovating" firm (which can be the UK subsidiary of a multinational firm) does not always imply that this firm actually *produced* the innovation. A considerable number of innovations in the database had been imported from outside the UK. Fortunately, the SPRU data report the country of origin for each innovation. But, unfortunately, there are serious doubts regarding the reliability of this information, as pointed out by the SPRU researchers themselves (see Townsend et al. 1981). The main problem seems to be the small number of innovations that are reported as having originated outside the UK.[22]

Despite this difficulty, the country-of-origin indicator can be used to check the robustness of the results to alternative definitions of the dependent variable. If the exclusion of those innovations that are

---

22. Townsend et al. (1981) attribute this feature of the data to a variety of factors, including a potential bias in the collected information. According to these authors, the bias may have resulted from a mixture of technological nationalism, real difficulties in distinguishing innovating firms and countries from imitating firms and countries, and a high rate of import of foreign technology through mechanisms that are not easily observable (such as imitation, reverse engineering, and inventing around patents), as opposed to more measurable mechanisms (such as licensing, or transfers within multinational firms).

reported as having originated outside the UK does not significantly affect the results, one can safely conclude that the presence of imported innovations in the database is not a serious problem. To check this, I constructed the variable INN3, which is based on the population of SPRU innovations reported as being of UK origin. In all other respects, INN3 is similar to INN1, that is, it groups the innovations into five-year periods assuming a one-year innovation lag. Bearing this discussion in mind, I will use the terms "innovations produced" and "innovations introduced" interchangeably for the rest of this chapter.

6.4 Empirical Models and Results

The econometric analysis of the effects of competition in R&D-intensive industries in this section will be based on a comparison of those industries affected by the 1956 Act with a control group of industries not affected. The theory developed in section 6.2 suggests estimating the reduced-form models

$Innovations = I(S, f, h, r, t),$

$Concentration = C(S, f, h, r, t),$

where the variables are as defined in section 6.2. Time-invariant industry-specific characteristics may also influence innovative activity or concentration, and their effect will be captured in panel regressions by the industry-specific effects. The two models will be estimated in separate regressions—given that the two equations include the same explanatory variables and it is also very difficult to match the industry definitions used in the concentration statistics with those used for the innovations data.[23] Once again, because of practical and conceptual difficulties with estimating bounds, the analysis will be con-

---

23. It is also difficult to obtain any meaningful descriptive statistics on the joint evolution of concentration and innovation counts in individual industries (such as those reported for the joint evolution of advertising intensity and concentration in table 5.1). There are two reasons for this. First, innovation counts tend to be volatile, so a rise or a fall in innovation counts between the late 1950s and the late 1960s, say, in any given industry may not in itself be very informative. Second, changes in innovative activity are likely to be correlated with changes in sales, but it is not clear how to control for this when focusing on the evolution of innovation counts in individual industries; for instance, dividing the number of innovations by deflated sales revenue would give a different picture than dividing it by the log of deflated sales revenue.

fined to obtaining regression results, on the assumption that the theoretical predictions derived for the benchmark case of symmetric single-product firms carry over to more complex settings.

In addition to the variables included in the above reduced forms, other factors, including macroeconomic fluctuations, may have affected innovations and concentration during the period examined in a more or less uniform way across industries. As in previous chapters, time dummies will be included among the regressors to control for these factors. One variable that is not explicitly included in the theoretical model, but is generally thought to be an important determinant of innovation, is the degree of appropriability of the outcome of R&D; this is related to the degree of R&D spillovers within an industry. This variable and two others, the degree of horizontal product differentiation h and technological opportunity r, are very difficult to measure accurately over time. However, it is not unreasonable to assume that these variables will be relatively stable over a period of ten or twenty years for the large majority of industries. Hence they will be largely captured by the industry effects in the panel data models estimated below.

As far as technological opportunity is concerned, it is well known that the ranking of manufacturing sectors in terms of R&D intensity tends to be very similar between countries and across time periods, which is consistent with the view that technological opportunity is relatively stable at the sector level. This is certainly less obvious for three-digit industries and even less so for four-digit industries; however, any changes in technological opportunity will only tend to increase the "noise" in the results, as long as they are not correlated with changes in the intensity of competition or other variables.

Price Competition and Innovation: The Samples and Descriptive Statistics

As mentioned in section 6.3, I use two different samples of industries to analyze the determinants of innovation in this chapter. Both are balanced panels, with five periods for each industry. The first one comprises all industries with an average or typical R&D-sales ratio (RDS) of more than 1% over the period from the mid-1950s to the mid-1970s, excluding industries with ambiguous state of competition in the 1950s or later years. This sample contains thirty industries and 150 observations. The second sample includes, in addition, twelve

Table 6.1
Innovation counts in 1952–1956, 1957–1961, 1962–1966, 1967–1971 and 1972–1976

	Mean (st. deviation) of *INN1*				
	1952–1956	1957–1961	1962–1966	1967–1971	1972–1976
Industries with average RDS > 1%					
Industries with CHANGE = 1 (n = 10)	1.8 (2.2)	3.1 (2.7)	1.9 (2.3)	2.5 (2.1)	2.3 (1.1)
Industries with CHANGE = 0 (n = 20)	5.4 (4.9)	7.6 (7.8)	7.7 (6.0)	8.5 (8.3)	7.9 (8.0)
Industries with average RDS > 1% or a large number of innovations in the SPRU database					
Industries with CHANGE = 1 (n = 16)	2.4 (2.7)	3.5 (3.1)	3.3 (3.5)	2.8 (2.1)	2.5 (1.5)
Industries with CHANGE = 0 (n = 26)	5.6 (4.6)	7.5 (7.3)	8.7 (7.2)	9.2 (8.6)	8.3 (7.7)

Note: n indicates the number of industries.

industries with average RDS < 1% but with a relatively large number of innovations in the SPRU database. The full set of industries and information on key variables are given in table B4 of appendix B.

Table 6.1 presents descriptive statistics for innovation counts separately for industries with a change in competition regime and industries without such a change. The figures are based on the near-total number of innovations introduced in British industry and recorded in the SPRU database (i.e., excluding only a small number of innovations produced by public research establishments or industrial trade associations). Perhaps the most striking feature of the data is the significant dissimilarity in initial conditions between the two groups. In particular, the average number of innovations introduced during 1952–1956 was 1.8 for R&D-intensive industries with a change of competition regime in the 1960s and 5.4 for R&D-intensive industries without a subsequent change in regime (all of which were non-collusive in the 1950s).

However, it would be very misleading to interpret this large difference in initial conditions as an indication of a negative effect of collusion on innovative activity. An alternative interpretation, proposed in chapter 3, is that collusive pricing may be more difficult to achieve or to sustain in industries with high technological opportunity. Table 6.1 shows why this alternative interpretation is probably the correct one. The table compares the evolution of innovative activity in the two groups of industries between the early 1950s and the mid-1970s, when competition had been established in previously collusive industries. Clearly, the large dissimilarity in the *level* of innovative activity between the two groups persists throughout the period, despite the trend toward more innovations in the average industry over time. Furthermore, this trend is somewhat more pronounced in industries without a change in competition regime, which is certainly not consistent with the view that collusion has a negative effect on innovation. On the other hand, the observed difference in the *evolution* of innovative activity between the two groups is not large in proportional terms, at least for the basic sample. Moreover, it may be partly due to the fact that industries with $CHANGE = 1$ were growing more slowly than industries with $CHANGE = 0$ during the period under study. To examine these issues in a more powerful way, I now turn to the econometric analysis of the determinants of innovative activity.

Price Competition and Innovation: Econometric Specification

The basic model for innovation counts is

$$Inn_{it} = f(\alpha_i, \beta_1 \ln Sales_{it} + \beta_2 \ln(K/L)_{it} + \beta_3 Y58$$

$$+ \beta_4 Y63 + \beta_5 Y68 + \beta_6 Y73 + \beta_7 CHANGE * Y58$$

$$+ \beta_8 CHANGE * Y63 + \beta_9 CHANGE * Y68 + \beta_{10} CHANGE * Y73).$$

The dependent variable is the total number of innovations produced by firms in any given industry and five-year period, defined in three different ways, as described in the previous section. In particular, *INN1* is defined on the basis of the entire SPRU data set—excluding only innovations by public research establishments or industrial trade associations—and assuming a one-year lag between (the bulk of) R&D spending and the commercialization of innovations. Thus the time periods used for grouping the innovations to construct *INN1* are 1952–1956, 1957–1961, 1962–1966, 1967–1971 and 1972–1976. *INN2* is defined on the basis of the same population of innovations as *INN1*, but this time assuming a two-year innovation lag.

In other words, the time periods for grouping the innovations are in this case 1953–1957, 1958–1962, 1963–1967, 1968–1972 and 1973–1977. Finally, to construct $INN3$ all innovations classified in the SPRU data as having originated outside the UK were excluded, and the innovations were grouped into five-year periods according to a one-year innovation lag.

The independent variables are defined as follows. "Sales" is either total sales revenue by UK firms deflated by the general producer price index (SS) or total sales revenue deflated by an industry-specific producer price index (DS). The level of aggregation for these data is the same as that for the innovation measures and the competition variable $CHANGE$—that is, sometimes it is the three-digit industry level, sometimes it is the four-digit industry level, and sometimes it is between the three-digit and the four-digit industry level. K/L is the capital-labor ratio, defined at the three-digit industry level.[24] $Y58$, $Y63$, $Y68$, and $Y73$ are time dummies corresponding, respectively, to time periods 1957–1961, 1962–1966, 1967–1971 and 1972–1976 when $INN1$ or $INN3$ is used, and to 1958–1962, 1963–1967, 1968–1972, and 1973–1977 when $INN2$ is used.

Finally, the interaction terms should reveal any differences in the evolution of innovation counts since the mid-1950s between industries with a change in competition regime ($CHANGE = 1$) and industries without such a change ($CHANGE = 0$). The benchmark period is 1952–1956 (or 1953–1957), which is clearly before the introduction—let alone the implementation—of the legislation. Thus the coefficient on $CHANGE * Y58$ measures the impact of the 1956 Act on changes in innovative output between the benchmark period and the period 1957–1961 (or 1958–1962); the coefficient on $CHANGE * Y63$ measures the impact of the 1956 Act on changes in innovative output between the benchmark period and the period 1962–1966 (or 1963–1967); and so on.

Four key features of the innovations data have directed the choice of econometric specification. First, the dependent variable takes only integer values, so a count data model must be used. Second, it is evident from table 6.1 that there is very considerable overdispersion

---

24. I also experimented with the capital stock of the average plant, K/N, as a proxy for setup cost. The results were similar to those reported here. Let me also repeat that since the model includes industry-specific effects, one need not assume that K/L or K/N is an accurate measure of setup cost. All that is required is that *changes* in K/L or K/N are plausible measures of the *change* in setup cost.

in the innovations data; in other words, the variance is much larger than the mean. The overdispersion is so pronounced that it will certainly persist in any Poisson regression: the conditional variance of the dependent variable, although somewhat reduced through the inclusion of regressors, will remain larger than the conditional mean. In such circumstances, the standard Poisson model is not appropriate, even if one can partly control for heterogeneity through the inclusion of fixed industry-specific effects (see Cameron and Trivedi 1998, Hausman et al. 1984). On the other hand, both a random-effects Poisson model and a negative binomial model can provide valid results under overdispersion. Third, there is no "excess zeros" problem in the present data: only in 18 out of 150 observations in the basic sample does the dependent variable INN1 take the value 0. And fourth, as shown in table 6.1 and discussed in detail above, cartelized industries had, on average, a much lower average number of innovations throughout the period than noncartelized industries. This implies that CHANGE is probably correlated with the industry-specific effects, so a random-effects model cannot be used. To obtain consistent estimates, the conditional fixed-effects negative binomial specification proposed in Hausman et al. (1984) will be used below.[25]

A potential limitation of my specification for innovation counts is that although it controls for fixed industry effects, it does not allow for any effect of past innovative activity within an industry or by firms in other industries on current innovation. As in previous chapters, a dynamic specification cannot be used here because of data limitations. However, the effect of past innovation on current innovation—unlike the impact of industry-specific characteristics, which is captured by the industry effects—may not be as important in industry-level data as it often is in firm-level data. Moreover, while the production of innovations in an industry may be generally influenced by knowledge generated in other industries, Geroski (1994)—who worked with annual firm-level and industry-level innovations data for much

---

25. This model is of the NB1 form, according to the terminology of Cameron and Trivedi, that is, the conditional variance of the dependent variable is assumed to be a multiple of the conditional mean. In addition to a multiplicative individual-specific fixed effect, the model allows for an individual-specific overdispersion parameter (see Cameron and Trivedi 1998). As pointed out by Blundell et al. (1995), this model requires strict exogeneity of the regressors, an assumption which is not implausible in the present context, where we use industry data and five-year periods. The dynamic model proposed by Blundell et al. cannot be implemented here, since it requires a long panel so that presample information can be used to approximate the fixed effects.

of the period that I analyze in this book—found no evidence of significant cross-industry (or within-industry) R&D spillovers in UK
manufacturing.

Price Competition and Innovation: The Identifying Assumption
Again

As in similar specifications used in previous chapters, the potential
endogeneity of $CHANGE$ is an obvious cause for concern. Put simply, the potential problem is that any difference observed in the
evolution of innovation counts during the 1960s between industries
with $CHANGE = 1$ and industries with $CHANGE = 0$ may be to
some extent due to unobserved characteristics that differ between the
two groups of industries rather than to any effect of the 1956 cartel
legislation. Ideally, one would want to test formally for exogeneity,
but this is impossible here because there are no appropriate instruments for $CHANGE$.

How serious is the problem? At first sight, it may seem rather serious, since the initial conditions regarding innovative activity were
very different in the two groups. As shown in table 6.1, the mean
number of innovation counts during 1952–1956 was considerably
lower in industries with a subsequent change in competition regime
than in industries without such a change. However, table 6.1 also
shows that the picture was still very much the same ten or twenty
years later, when competition had generally been established in previously cartelized industries. This suggests that cartelization in the
1950s is correlated with some variable that strongly influences innovative activity but remains relatively stable over time in any given
industry. An obvious candidate is technological opportunity. This—
as, indeed, any other time-invariant industry-specific characteristic—
is captured in the present model by the industry-specific effects.
Hence there should be no endogeneity bias, provided that one uses a
specification that accounts for the correlation between regressors and
industry effects.

There is an additional indirect check that can indicate whether the
potential endogeneity of $CHANGE$ is likely to be a serious problem
in the data: one can compare the evolution of the two groups of industries between 1952–1956 and 1957–1962. The simplest way this
can be done is by examining the descriptive statistics reported in
table 6.1. Alternatively, one can check the regression coefficient on

CHANGE $* Y58$.[26] Because (1) of the time lag between R&D spending and the commercialization of innovations discussed in section 6.3 and (2) of the fact that in several R&D-intensive industries price-fixing agreements were not abandoned until the early 1960s or even later, any changes in innovative activity between the period 1952–1956 and the period 1957–1962 cannot be attributed to the 1956 Act. If there is an endogeneity problem with CHANGE that may affect the regression results, then there should be evidence that the two groups of industries evolved in different ways during the 1950s.

There is no such evidence from the descriptive statistics in table 6.1. In particular, the mean number of innovations produced in ten R&D-intensive industries with a subsequent change in competition regime was 1.8 during 1952–1956 and 3.1 during 1957–1961. The respective figures for twenty R&D-intensive industries without a change in regime were 5.4 and 7.6. In other words, there is no evidence that innovative activity changed in different ways in the two groups of industries during the 1950s: the increase in innovations between 1952–1956 and 1957–1961 can be attributed to a common time trend. As we will see below, this is confirmed by the regression results: the coefficient on CHANGE $* Y58$ is not statistically significant. We may therefore conclude that any estimated difference between the two groups in later periods should be due to the 1956 legislation. Alternatively, if it turns out that there is no difference between the two groups in later periods, we may conclude that the legislation had no effect on innovation.

Price Competition and Innovation: Econometric Results

Table 6.2 presents results for the basic sample of thirty R&D-intensive industries (i.e., industries with average or typical RDS of more than 1% over the period from the mid-1950s to the mid-1970s). The sample includes ten industries with a change of competition regime. The main reason for focusing on R&D-intensive industries is the expectation that any systematic impact of price competition on the production of innovations may be more difficult to identify or less relevant in industries where R&D is not a key strategic variable. Also, the theory of section 6.2 relates specifically to R&D-intensive industries. In any

---

26. A valid objection to this second type of check is that if CHANGE were indeed endogenous, then the coefficient on CHANGE $* Y58$ would itself be biased. However, this check is intended here as a mere confirmation of the picture that emerges from the descriptive statistics, not as a formal test.

Table 6.2
Regression results for innovation counts in R&D-intensive industries (negative binomial conditional fixed-effects estimation)

	Dependent variable: INN1		Dependent variable: INN2		Dependent variable: INN3	
ln SS	0.27	—	0.19	—	0.25	—
	(0.16)		(0.16)		(0.19)	
ln DS	—	0.17	—	0.11	—	0.23
		(0.14)		(0.14)		(0.17)
ln K/L	0.15	0.07	0.07	0.03	0.28	0.22
	(0.26)	(0.26)	(0.26)	(0.26)	(0.31)	(0.31)
Y58	0.25	0.27	0.33	0.34	0.13	0.13
	(0.16)	(0.17)	(0.17)	(0.17)	(0.20)	(0.20)
Y63	0.19	0.25	0.19	0.23	0.13	0.14
	(0.19)	(0.19)	(0.20)	(0.20)	(0.23)	(0.23)
Y68	0.10	0.20	0.26	0.33	0.20	0.21
	(0.26)	(0.26)	(0.25)	(0.25)	(0.29)	(0.28)
Y73	−0.11	0.04	0.14	0.23	−0.02	−0.01
	(0.33)	(0.33)	(0.32)	(0.32)	(0.38)	(0.37)
CHANGE * Y58	0.25	0.26	0.28	0.29	0.21	0.21
	(0.36)	(0.36)	(0.37)	(0.37)	(0.41)	(0.41)
CHANGE * Y63	−0.26	−0.28	−0.11	−0.12	−0.40	−0.41
	(0.41)	(0.40)	(0.41)	(0.41)	(0.46)	(0.45)
CHANGE * Y68	0.07	0.03	−0.07	−0.09	−0.02	−0.02
	(0.38)	(0.38)	(0.39)	(0.39)	(0.41)	(0.40)
CHANGE * Y73	0.18	0.11	0.07	0.02	−0.02	−0.03
	(0.39)	(0.39)	(0.39)	(0.39)	(0.42)	(0.42)
Constant	−0.80	0.51	−0.16	0.77	−0.85	−0.57
	(1.96)	(1.77)	(2.01)	(1.78)	(2.36)	(2.09)
Log likelihood	−233.0	−233.9	−241.9	−242.3	−202.8	−202.7
No. of industries	30	30	30	30	30	30
No. of industries with CHANGE = 1	10	10	10	10	10	10
No. of observations	150	150	150	150	150	150

Note: Standard errors in parentheses.

case, table 6.3 contains results for a larger sample of forty-two industries, including sixteen with a change of competition regime. This sample includes, in addition to the R&D-intensive group, a number of industries with average RDS < 1% but with a relatively large number of innovations in the SPRU database.

There is no evidence of any overall effect of the intensification of price competition, following the introduction of the 1956 Act, on innovations introduced in British industry. The coefficients on the interaction terms are not statistically significant, even at the 10% or the 20% level, irrespective of the sample used or the form taken by the dependent variable (*INN1*, *INN2*, or *INN3*). In particular, the coefficient on *CHANGE* * *Y63* is everywhere negative, but not statistically significant, while the coefficients on *CHANGE* * *Y68* and *CHANGE* * *Y73* are sometimes positive and sometimes negative. Clearly, the results provide no evidence of any short-run or long-run effect of price competition on innovation in the present context.

An interesting feature of the results presented in tables 6.2 and 6.3 is the almost general failure of the explanatory variables in these regressions. Time-invariant industry-specific characteristics seem to account for much of the cross-industry variation in innovation counts. As mentioned above, one variable that is almost certainly picked up by the industry effects is technological opportunity. In addition, a lot of variation in innovation counts seems to be due to variables difficult to measure or to observe, including random events.

It is somewhat reassuring that the coefficients on the market size proxies, ln *SS* and ln *DS*, are often statistically significant at the 5% or the 10% level in regressions using the larger sample (but not in regressions using the basic sample of R&D-intensive industries). This suggests that the larger amount of information contained in the larger sample increases the efficiency of the estimated coefficients on the market size variables. Note, however, that the magnitude of these coefficients is fairly low, even in the larger sample. Taken at face value, these estimates suggest that a 1% increase in market size causes at most a 0.25% rise in the expected number of innovations.[27]

---

27. The rate of growth has sometimes been used instead of market size as a regressor in empirical models of innovation. To see whether this makes any difference to my results, I estimated a model including $\Delta \ln SS$ or $\Delta \ln DS$ among the regressors, defined for industry i and year t as the change in ln *SS* or ln *DS*, respectively, in the five-year period preceding year t. The coefficients on these variables were everywhere highly nonsignificant, and the rest of the results did not change much. Note that in order to use this alternative specification, the first-year observation for each industry had to be dropped.

Table 6.3
Regression results for innovation counts in the enlarged sample of innovative industries (negative binomial conditional fixed-effects estimation)

	Dependent variable: INN1		Dependent variable: INN2		Dependent variable: INN3	
ln SS	0.27	—	0.19	—	0.25	—
	(0.14)		(0.14)		(0.17)	
ln DS	—	0.18	—	0.13	—	0.25
		(0.12)		(0.12)		(0.14)
ln K/L	0.19	0.13	0.10	0.06	0.17	0.12
	(0.21)	(0.21)	(0.21)	(0.21)	(0.25)	(0.25)
Y58	0.19	0.21	0.24	0.25	0.07	0.08
	(0.14)	(0.14)	(0.14)	(0.14)	(0.17)	(0.17)
Y63	0.22	0.28	0.22	0.26	0.18	0.18
	(0.16)	(0.16)	(0.17)	(0.16)	(0.19)	(0.19)
Y68	0.12	0.20	0.24	0.30	0.23	0.23
	(0.21)	(0.20)	(0.21)	(0.20)	(0.24)	(0.23)
Y73	−0.12	0.01	0.06	0.13	0.03	0.04
	(0.27)	(0.26)	(0.26)	(0.25)	(0.31)	(0.29)
CHANGE ∗ Y58	0.11	0.12	0.33	0.34	0.27	0.27
	(0.27)	(0.27)	(0.27)	(0.27)	(0.30)	(0.30)
CHANGE ∗ Y63	−0.05	−0.07	−0.03	−0.05	−0.07	−0.07
	(0.27)	(0.27)	(0.29)	(0.29)	(0.31)	(0.31)
CHANGE ∗ Y68	−0.17	−0.19	−0.07	−0.09	−0.28	−0.26
	(0.28)	(0.28)	(0.28)	(0.28)	(0.31)	(0.31)
CHANGE ∗ Y73	−0.12	−0.15	−0.16	−0.17	−0.15	−0.12
	(0.29)	(0.29)	(0.30)	(0.30)	(0.32)	(0.32)
Constant	−0.61	0.42	0.06	0.78	−0.48	−0.40
	(1.67)	(1.44)	(1.69)	(1.45)	(1.98)	(1.74)
Log likelihood	−333.9	−334.7	−340.3	−340.7	−294.3	−293.9
No. of industries	42	42	42	42	42	42
No. of industries with CHANGE = 1	16	16	16	16	16	16
No. of observations	210	210	210	210	210	210

Note: Standard errors in parentheses.

Price Competition and Concentration: The Samples and Descriptive
Statistics

I now turn to the analysis of the competition effect on concentration
in R&D-intensive industries. Recall that in the absence of any effect
of price competition on innovation, the theory predicts that concentration should rise. Two samples of industries will be used for the
econometric analysis: a basic sample including all industries with an
average or typical R&D-sales ratio (RDS) of more than 1% over the
relevant period, and a subsample of industries with average or typical RDS higher than 2% over the relevant period. To construct these
samples, I started by excluding from the set of industries with available concentration data all industries with average or typical RDS
lower than 1%. Then I excluded industries with ambiguous state of
competition in 1958 (or, in a few cases, in the 1960s and early 1970s),
as well as industries with a switch of competition regime but for
which concentration data were not available for at least 1958, 1963,
and either 1968 or 1975. This left an unbalanced sample of sixty
R&D-intensive industries and 197 observations. To obtain the subsample of high-R&D industries, I then also dropped all industries
with RDS < 2%; this left twenty-six industries and eighty-four observations. Table 6.4 gives details on the structure of these samples,
distinguishing between industries with a change in competition regime after 1958 and industries without such a change. The list of
industries and information on key variables can be found in appendix B (table B5).

Clearly, these samples are highly unbalanced, mainly as a result of
the fact that concentration data for 1958 are not available for a large
number of R&D-intensive industries. Although there is no reason
to suspect that this feature of the data might bias the results, it is
nevertheless worth checking this presumption using more balanced
samples. To this end, I also constructed a sample that includes only
industries with average or typical RDS higher than 1% and with a
full set of observations for at least the core period 1958–1968; in the
large majority of cases, the 1975 observation is also available.[28] This
sample contains twenty-nine industries and 114 observations.

Some descriptive statistics on initial levels and changes in concentration for R&D-intensive industries are reported in tables 6.5 and

---

28. I also included one industry (industrial engines) with available data for 1958, 1963,
and 1975, but not for 1968.

Table 6.4
The basic samples for the concentration regressions: R&D-intensive industries and high-R&D industries

Data available for	No. of industries with $CHANGE = 1$ and average $RDS > 1\%$	No. of industries with $CHANGE = 0$ and average $RDS > 1\%$	No. of industries with $CHANGE = 1$ and average $RDS > 2\%$	No. of industries with $CHANGE = 0$ and average $RDS > 2\%$
All four years	9	18	4	8
1958, 1963, 1968	0	1	0	0
1958, 1963, 1975	1	0	0	0
1963, 1968, 1975	0	22	0	8
1958, 1963	0	3	0	2
1963, 1968	0	6	0	4
Total	10	50	4	22

Table 6.5
Concentration in 1958 and competition regime in R&D-intensive and high-R&D industries

	Mean C5 in 1958 (st. deviation of C5)
Industries with average RDS > 1% (basic sample)	
Industries with $CHANGE = 1$ (n = 10)	0.704 (0.171)
Industries with $CHANGE = 0$ (n = 23)	0.683 (0.193)
Industries with average RDS > 1% (more balanced sample)	
Industries with $CHANGE = 1$ (n = 10)	0.704 (0.171)
Industries with $CHANGE = 0$ (n = 19)	0.686 (0.196)
Industries with average RDS > 2% (basic sample)	
Industries with $CHANGE = 1$ (n = 4)	0.699 (0.189)
Industries with $CHANGE = 0$ (n = 10)	0.652 (0.246)
Industries with average RDS > 2% (more balanced sample)	
Industries with $CHANGE = 1$ (n = 4)	0.699 (0.189)
Industries with $CHANGE = 0$ (n = 8)	0.639 (0.247)

Notes: The figures are based on industries with available data for 1958; n indicates the number of industries.

Table 6.6
Average change in C5, in R&D-intensive and high-R&D industries, 1958–1968 and 1958–1975

	ΔC5 1958–1968	ΔC5 1958–1975	ΔC5 1958–1968	ΔC5 1958–1975
Industries with average RDS > 1%				
Industries with	0.093	0.122	0.093	0.118
CHANGE = 1	(0.102)	(0.111)	(0.102)	(0.118)
	n = 9	n = 10	n = 9	n = 9
Industries with	0.027	0.034	0.032	0.034
CHANGE = 0	(0.125)	(0.122)	(0.127)	(0.122)
	n = 19	n = 18	n = 18	n = 18
Industries with average RDS > 2%				
Industries with	0.152	0.111	0.152	0.111
CHANGE = 1	(0.087)	(0.096)	(0.087)	(0.096)
	n = 4	n = 4	n = 4	n = 4
Industries with	0.025	0.042	0.025	0.042
CHANGE = 0	(0.092)	(0.110)	(0.092)	(0.110)
	n = 8	n = 8	n = 8	n = 8

Notes: The figures in the first column are based on industries with available observations for both 1958 and 1968. The figures in the second column are based on industries with available observations for both 1958 and 1975. The figures in the last two columns are based on industries with available observations for 1958, 1968, and 1975. The figures in parentheses are standard deviations. n indicates the number of industries.

6.6. Table 6.5 reports descriptive statistics for the concentration ratio, C5, in 1958 for industries with and industries without a change in competition regime after 1958. There is no evidence of any significant difference between the two groups: the mean C5 is 0.704 for the ten cartelized industries in the sample and 0.683 for the twenty-three noncartelized industries with available data for that year. On the other hand, table 6.6 shows that the average increase in C5 after 1958 was much larger for R&D-intensive industries affected by the legislation than for industries not affected. For the former group the average change between 1958 and 1975 was about twelve percentage points, while for the latter group it was only 3.4 percentage points.

A comparison of industries that experienced a large increase in C5 between 1958 and 1975 with those that experienced a large decrease in C5 over the same period is also revealing. The comparison is limited to the twenty-seven R&D-intensive industries with available data for both these years. Of the five industries with the largest rise in C5, three (air and gas compressors; washing machines, electrically operated; electric lamps) are industries with $CHANGE = 1$, and only two (television receiving sets; radio communication equipment) have $CHANGE = 0$. However, all five industries with the largest fall in C5 (cutlery; finished synthetic organic dyestuffs; powered industrial trucks and industrial tractors; finished detergents; soap) have $CHANGE = 0$.

Of course, changes in other potential determinants of concentration may partly account for these differences. To control for these other factors, we need to use econometric analysis.

Price Competition and Concentration: Econometric Model and Results

The basic econometric model for concentration is

$$Conc_{it} = \alpha_i + \gamma_1 \ln Sales_{it} + \gamma_2 \ln(K/x)_{it} + \gamma_3 Y63 + \gamma_4 Y68 + \gamma_5 Y75$$

$$+ \gamma_6 CHANGE * Y63 + \gamma_7 CHANGE * Y68$$

$$+ \gamma_8 CHANGE * Y75 + e_{it},$$

where "conc" is either the four-digit industry five-firm concentration ratio, C5, or its logistic transformation, $\text{logit} C5 = \ln[C5/(1 - C5)]$; "sales" is either SS or DS (see above); "K/x" is either the three-digit industry capital-labor ratio, K/L, or the three-digit industry capital stock of the average plant, K/N; Y63, Y68, and Y75 are time dummies for 1963, 1968, and 1975 respectively; and the interaction terms capture any difference in the evolution of concentration after 1958 between industries with a change in competition regime and industries without such a change. Thus the coefficient on $CHANGE * Y63$ measures the effect of the 1956 Act on concentration by 1963, the coefficient on $CHANGE * Y68$ measures the effect by 1968, and the coefficient on $CHANGE * Y75$ measures the effect by 1975. The benchmark year is 1958. CHANGE is defined according to the industry categories used for C5. Once again, the potential endogeneity of some of the independent variables may be an issue here. The response to this is the same as in previous chapters.

Results for concentration were obtained using both a fixed-effects model and a random-effects model. The two sets of results were very similar, except for the coefficients on the setup cost proxies, which were highly significant in the random-effects model only. Since the Hausman test invariably and clearly failed to reject the random-effects model and—unlike the case of the innovation regressions above—there are no a priori reasons for doubting the validity of the hypothesis that the regressors are not correlated with the industry effects, the results from the random-effects model are presented below. I also report, however, some of the results derived using a fixed-effects specification to facilitate comparisons with previous chapters.

Once again, heteroskedasticity was present in these regressions, and it was more pronounced in regressions using logit $C5$ than in those using $C5$. Although the reported standard errors are heteroskedasticity-consistent, the results from the specifications using logit $C5$ may be subject to the objection that too much weight is placed on a few industries with very high concentration.

Tables 6.7 and 6.8 present results for the basic sample of R&D-intensive industries, while table 6.9 focuses on the more balanced sample of R&D-intensive industries with available observations for at least the three core years 1958, 1963, and 1968. There are ten industries with canceled agreements in these samples. All the results provide clear evidence of a strong positive competition effect on concentration in R&D-intensive industries. In particular, the coefficients on $CHANGE * Y68$ and $CHANGE * Y75$ are everywhere positive and statistically significant at the 5% level. According to these coefficients, the introduction of cartel law caused, on average, a rise in the five-firm concentration ratio of as much as ten percentage points in R&D-intensive industries. This effect was largely realized between 1963 and 1968. On the other hand, there was very little effect between 1958 and 1963 in this class of industries. It should be noted, however, that these samples include three industries where agreements were not abandoned until after 1963, and in two of these competition did not fully emerge until after 1968.[29] Finally, note that the market size effect on concentration breaks down in R&D-intensive industries, as expected: the coefficients on the sales variables have conflicting signs and they are nowhere significant at the 5% level.

These results are not driven by industries with medium R&D intensity. To check that the competition effect persists at high levels of R&D intensity, I also estimated the model using the sample of industries with typical RDS > 2% over the period; the results appear in table 6.10. These results should be interpreted with some caution,

---

29. They also include an industry with a change of regime but for which $C5$ is not available for 1968 although it is available for 1975 (so $CHANGE * 75$ picks up all the effect of the 1956 Act between 1963 and 1975 in this industry).

Table 6.7
Regression results for concentration in industries with average RDS > 1% (random-effects estimation)

	Dependent variable: C5				Dependent variable: logit C5			
ln SS	-0.010 (0.015)	—	-0.006 (0.016)	—	0.15 (0.13)	—	0.23 (0.14)	0.27 (0.14)
ln DS	—	-0.006 (0.014)	—	-0.002 (0.014)	—	0.20 (0.13)	—	—
ln K/N	0.073 (0.016)	0.073 (0.016)	—	—	0.66 (0.15)	0.66 (0.15)	—	—
ln K/L	—	—	0.062 (0.019)	0.063 (0.019)	—	—	0.61 (0.19)	0.62 (0.19)
Y63	-0.014 (0.022)	-0.015 (0.022)	-0.009 (0.022)	-0.011 (0.022)	-0.15 (0.17)	-0.16 (0.17)	-0.15 (0.17)	-0.16 (0.17)
Y68	-0.016 (0.025)	-0.019 (0.025)	-0.008 (0.026)	-0.011 (0.026)	-0.24 (0.20)	-0.28 (0.20)	-0.24 (0.21)	-0.29 (0.22)
Y75	-0.024 (0.029)	-0.027 (0.029)	-0.017 (0.031)	-0.020 (0.031)	-0.38 (0.21)	-0.44 (0.22)	-0.41 (0.24)	-0.48 (0.25)
CHANGE * Y63	0.003 (0.035)	0.002 (0.035)	0.002 (0.035)	0.002 (0.035)	0.06 (0.24)	0.05 (0.24)	0.12 (0.23)	0.10 (0.23)
CHANGE * Y68	0.091 (0.032)	0.092 (0.032)	0.084 (0.033)	0.085 (0.033)	1.10 (0.71)	1.10 (0.71)	1.09 (0.71)	1.09 (0.71)
CHANGE * Y75	0.112 (0.031)	0.113 (0.031)	0.104 (0.034)	0.105 (0.033)	0.90 (0.32)	0.91 (0.32)	0.90 (0.33)	0.91 (0.32)

Constant	0.786	0.740	0.675	0.634	-0.60	-1.04	-2.08	-2.47
	(0.152)	(0.137)	(0.161)	(0.144)	(1.34)	(1.30)	(1.49)	(1.46)
Hausman statistic	7.88	5.50	4.55	4.06	7.30	—	2.33	2.89
Prob-value	0.45	0.70	0.80	0.85	0.50		0.97	0.94
R^2	0.29	0.29	0.19	0.20	0.31	0.31	0.22	0.22
No. of industries	60	60	60	60	60	60	60	60
No. of industries with $CHANGE = 1$	10	10	10	10	10	10	10	10
No. of observations	197	197	197	197	197	197	197	197

Note: Heteroskedasticity-consistent standard errors in parentheses.

Table 6.8
Regression results for concentration in industries with average RDS > 1% (fixed-effects estimation)

	Dependent variable: C5				Dependent variable: logit C5			
ln SS	-0.019 (0.023)	—	-0.019 (0.022)	-0.011 (0.020)	0.27 (0.27)	—	0.29 (0.27)	—
ln DS	—	-0.011 (0.020)	—	—	—	0.36 (0.24)	—	0.36 (0.24)
ln K/N	0.030 (0.029)	0.032 (0.029)	—	—	0.17 (0.29)	0.14 (0.30)	—	—
ln K/L	—	—	0.018 (0.035)	0.022 (0.036)	—	—	0.25 (0.41)	0.21 (0.40)
Y63	0.001 (0.026)	-0.002 (0.025)	0.005 (0.025)	0.002 (0.024)	-0.07 (0.21)	-0.10 (0.21)	-0.07 (0.22)	-0.10 (0.21)
Y68	0.016 (0.033)	0.011 (0.032)	0.025 (0.031)	0.019 (0.031)	-0.02 (0.29)	-0.09 (0.29)	-0.05 (0.34)	-0.11 (0.33)
Y75	0.019 (0.040)	0.014 (0.039)	0.030 (0.039)	0.022 (0.038)	-0.07 (0.35)	-0.17 (0.35)	-0.13 (0.44)	-0.21 (0.42)
CHANGE * Y63	-0.008 (0.035)	-0.007 (0.035)	-0.009 (0.035)	-0.008 (0.035)	-0.01 (0.29)	-0.02 (0.29)	-0.01 (0.29)	-0.02 (0.29)
CHANGE * Y68	0.074 (0.040)	0.076 (0.040)	0.069 (0.040)	0.071 (0.040)	0.97 (0.64)	0.96 (0.63)	0.95 (0.65)	0.95 (0.64)
CHANGE * Y75	0.093 (0.040)	0.096 (0.040)	0.087 (0.041)	0.090 (0.040)	0.80 (0.43)	0.82 (0.43)	0.78 (0.42)	0.81 (0.42)

R²	0.23	0.22	0.22	0.22	0.15	0.16	0.15	0.16
R²_LSDV	0.92	0.92	0.92	0.92	0.82	0.83	0.82	0.83
No. of industries	60	60	60	60	60	60	60	60
No. of industries with CHANGE = 1	10	10	10	10	10	10	10	10
No. of observations	197	197	197	197	197	197	197	197

Note: Heteroskedasticity-consistent standard errors in parentheses.

Table 6.9
Regression results for concentration in industries with average RDS > 1%: more balanced sample (random-effects estimation)

	Dependent variable: C5				Dependent variable: logit C5			
$\ln SS$	-0.007 (0.019)	—	-0.004 (0.019)	—	0.18 (0.18)	—	0.29 (0.18)	—
$\ln DS$	—	-0.002 (0.017)	—	0.001 (0.017)	—	0.21 (0.16)	—	0.30 (0.16)
$\ln K/N$	0.071 (0.023)	0.071 (0.023)	—	—	0.67 (0.19)	0.67 (0.19)	—	—
$\ln K/L$	—	—	0.064 (0.035)	0.065 (0.035)	—	—	0.60 (0.31)	0.59 (0.31)
Y63	-0.001 (0.026)	-0.003 (0.026)	0.003 (0.026)	0.001 (0.026)	-0.08 (0.21)	-0.10 (0.21)	-0.09 (0.21)	-0.11 (0.21)
Y68	-0.009 (0.030)	-0.013 (0.030)	-0.003 (0.032)	-0.006 (0.032)	-0.17 (0.24)	-0.20 (0.21)	-0.17 (0.27)	-0.20 (0.27)
Y75	-0.021 (0.038)	-0.025 (0.038)	-0.018 (0.044)	-0.022 (0.043)	-0.51 (0.29)	-0.57 (0.30)	-0.56 (0.38)	-0.61 (0.39)
CHANGE * Y63	-0.013 (0.037)	-0.013 (0.038)	-0.012 (0.037)	-0.012 (0.037)	-0.04 (0.27)	-0.04 (0.27)	0.03 (0.25)	0.03 (0.25)
CHANGE * Y68	0.082 (0.035)	0.082 (0.035)	0.076 (0.036)	0.076 (0.036)	0.99 (0.74)	0.99 (0.74)	1.00 (0.73)	0.99 (0.73)
CHANGE * Y75	0.106 (0.036)	0.108 (0.036)	0.101 (0.038)	0.103 (0.038)	0.99 (0.34)	1.00 (0.34)	1.02 (0.35)	1.03 (0.35)

Constant	0.772	0.718	0.667	0.618	−0.86	−1.10	−2.61	−2.72
	(0.192)	(0.169)	(0.196)	(0.174)	(1.79)	(1.62)	(1.85)	(1.68)
Hausman statistic	3.79	3.63	2.29	2.11	6.60	7.40	3.82	4.70
Prob-value	0.88	0.89	0.97	0.98	0.58	0.49	0.87	0.79
R^2	0.30	0.30	0.18	0.18	0.32	0.31	0.20	0.19
No. of industries	29	29	29	29	29	29	29	29
No. of industries with $CHANGE = 1$	10	10	10	10	10	10	10	10
No. of observations	114	114	114	114	114	114	114	114

Note: Heteroskedasticity-consistent standard errors in parentheses.

Table 6.10
Regression results for concentration in industries with average RDS > 2% (random-effects estimation)

	Dependent variable: C5				Dependent variable: logit C5			
ln SS	0.006 (0.018)	—	0.011 (0.020)	—	0.16 (0.18)	—	0.39 (0.18)	—
ln DS	—	0.013 (0.016)	—	0.017 (0.018)	—	0.27 (0.16)	—	0.47 (0.18)
ln K/N	0.053 (0.029)	0.053 (0.029)	—	—	0.81 (0.27)	0.80 (0.27)	—	—
ln K/L	—	—	0.044 (0.038)	0.044 (0.037)	—	—	0.76 (0.36)	0.78 (0.36)
Y63	−0.024 (0.032)	−0.028 (0.032)	−0.025 (0.034)	−0.029 (0.033)	−0.24 (0.31)	−0.30 (0.31)	−0.37 (0.33)	−0.44 (0.33)
Y68	−0.010 (0.039)	−0.017 (0.039)	−0.006 (0.042)	−0.013 (0.041)	−0.31 (0.35)	−0.44 (0.36)	−0.45 (0.40)	−0.60 (0.41)
Y75	−0.023 (0.052)	−0.034 (0.053)	−0.021 (0.061)	−0.032 (0.061)	−0.58 (0.40)	−0.77 (0.41)	−0.85 (0.48)	−1.08 (0.51)
CHANGE * Y63	0.0001 (0.055)	0.001 (0.055)	0.002 (0.055)	0.002 (0.056)	0.14 (0.38)	0.13 (0.38)	0.26 (0.39)	0.25 (0.39)
CHANGE * Y68	0.144 (0.041)	0.146 (0.041)	0.134 (0.041)	0.135 (0.041)	2.29 (1.45)	2.29 (1.44)	2.25 (1.42)	2.26 (1.41)
CHANGE * Y75	0.111 (0.056)	0.117 (0.056)	0.101 (0.058)	0.106 (0.057)	0.96 (0.56)	1.04 (0.56)	1.04 (0.57)	1.12 (0.55)

Constant	0.608	0.546	0.517	0.465	-0.82	-1.89	-3.79	-4.61
	(0.183)	(0.161)	(0.219)	(0.197)	(1.79)	(1.63)	(1.87)	(1.92)
Hausman statistic	6.01	6.02	2.26	2.38	8.64	9.85	7.98	1.55
Prob-value	0.65	0.64	0.97	0.97	0.37	0.28	0.44	0.99
R^2	0.28	0.25	0.14	0.13	0.34	0.32	0.19	0.18
No. of industries	26	26	26	26	26	26	26	26
No. of industries with $CHANGE = 1$	4	4	4	4	4	4	4	4
No. of observations	84	84	84	84	84	84	84	84

Note: Heteroskedasticity-consistent standard errors in parentheses.

since the number of industries with a change in competition regime in this sample is only four, all of which are drawn from the electrical engineering sector.[30] The main reason for reporting these results is to show that there is no indication of any weakening of the competition effect on concentration at relatively high levels of R&D intensity.

6.5 Concluding Remarks

This chapter has analyzed the impact of price competition on innovative output and market structure in R&D-intensive industries. The theory suggests that strong predictions on the effect of competition on innovation are difficult to derive in general. On the other hand, it is possible to derive a prediction on the evolution of market structure that is conditional on the behavior of innovative activity following a rise in the intensity of price competition. In particular, if innovative activity does not fall with more price competition, then concentration must rise. In fact, a positive effect of price competition on concentration is the most likely outcome in R&D-intensive industries, since the reverse can occur only in the event of a significant fall in R&D expenditure.

The introduction of the 1956 Restrictive Trade Practices Act provides a rare opportunity for addressing these issues in an empirical context. An econometric analysis based on a comparison between those industries affected by the legislation and those not affected has produced no evidence of any significant overall effect of price competition on innovation at the industry level, and clear evidence of a strong positive overall effect on concentration in R&D-intensive industries. The effect on concentration was at least as large as that estimated for exogenous sunk cost industries. The empirical evidence is therefore consistent with the theory.

The empirical results of this chapter are based on reduced-form econometric equations in which concentration and innovation are treated as endogenous variables, while the intensity of price competition is taken as exogenous. The results are therefore subject to the usual limitations of this type of econometric analysis. The use of reduced-form equations is a powerful way of revealing overall effects,

---

30. The very high coefficients on *CHANGE * Y68* in these regressions may be partly due to "overshooting" of the concentration ratio in electrical engineering industries affected by a series of mergers in the second half of the 1960s, including the 1967–1968 mergers between A.E.I., G.E.C., and English Electric, three of the largest and most diversified UK electrical engineering firms.

but it may fail to capture some potentially interesting interactions between the variables of interest. For instance, it could be the case that innovations are often introduced by new entrants (as argued by Geroski 1994). An increase in the intensity of price competition could then cause innovations to fall by reducing new entry, and thus the pool of potentially important innovators. At the same time, the intensification of price competition could induce existing firms to innovate more in order to avoid bankruptcy and exit. Hence a zero overall effect of competition on innovation could be consistent with a more complex mechanism than the one identified in this chapter. Or it could be the case, as suggested by recent theoretical results on the competition-innovation relationship based on theoretical models of endogenous growth (Aghion and Howitt 1997, 1998), that competition reduces innovation under certain circumstances and increases it under different circumstances. Again, this could be consistent with the zero overall effect suggested by our analysis.[31]

These various possible mechanisms and theoretical predictions from more specific models (or others that focus on potential interactions between innovation and market structure) can be tested only with data far richer and more detailed than those used in this book. But, in any case, our inability to test these hypotheses in the present context does not alter the basic result of this chapter, namely, the lack of any overall effect of price competition on innovation and the presence of a strong competition effect on concentration across R&D-intensive industries following the abolition of restrictive agreements in British manufacturing in the 1960s. The result on concentration confirms similar results in previous chapters. On the other hand, the result on innovations, which is consistent with the Broadberry and Crafts (2000) finding of no significant effect of collusive pricing on

---

31. A third possibility might be that high concentration leads to low (high) innovation, everything else being equal, so that an increase in the intensity of competition, by causing concentration to rise, leads to a fall (rise) in innovations. At the same time, the intensification of price competition could induce firms to innovate more (less) at any given level of concentration. Again the overall effect could be zero, but the interaction of the various factors would be more complex than what is implied by the present analysis.

However, this interpretation does not seem to be consistent with the facts. Because market structure adjusted only gradually in R&D-intensive industries affected by the 1956 Act, as shown in the concentration regressions of this chapter, some insight on the interaction of innovation and market structure can be gained by comparing the short-run effect with the long-run effect of the 1956 Act. The results of tables 6.8 and 6.9, taken as a whole, provide little evidence that the short-run effect of the Act (i.e., the effect before the adjustment of market structure) was different from the long-run effect.

innovation in the 1950s, has interesting implications for the debate on the links between price and nonprice competition.

In particular, we saw in chapter 5 that stronger price competition has probably reduced advertising expenditure in British industry. The results of the present chapter indicate that the production of innovations has been largely independent of the intensity of price competition. Thus there seems to be a fundamental difference between advertising and R&D, which has not been adequately analyzed in existing theories of competition. There are, of course, many obvious and important differences between advertising and R&D. The question is Why would any of these differences imply that price competition should generally have a negative effect on advertising but an ambiguous effect on R&D? This question is outside our present scope, and it is not clear whether it can be fully addressed within the present theory. Nevertheless, one remark may be appropriate here, since it builds on a distinction between advertising and R&D made in chapter 3.

It was pointed out in that chapter that a low-quality firm in an R&D-intensive industry may find it difficult to compete with a high-quality rival, while in an advertising-intensive industry heavy advertisers may face significant competition from firms that advertise little and employ different marketing strategies. Under certain conditions, this will imply that firms may be more inclined to cut back advertising expenditure than R&D expenditure when faced with a change in the competitive environment that causes a fall in gross profit. Now even if that were true, we would still need to explain why this behavior should persist in the long run, and it is here that a potential limitation of the present theory may be coming into focus. Expressed in somewhat general terms, the limitation may be as follows: If history matters, and there is a multiplicity of possible long-run outcomes, then the comparative statics of the long-run equilibria may sometimes depend on the short-run dynamics. In other words, there may be instances where systematic short-run effects persist in the long run and influence the long-run equilibria. The study of these short-run effects might then help narrow down the space of possible (or likely) long-run outcomes.

Chapter 7 returns to one of the strongest mechanisms analyzed in this book. Unlike the present chapter and the two previous ones, it adopts a more unifying approach in order to provide more detail and a richer understanding of the basic mechanism that links competition, market structure, and profitability across all classes of industries.

7

Price Competition and Profitability: Are Cartel Laws Bad for Business?

7.1 Introduction

Recent advances in oligopoly theory have shed new light on the much-debated issue of the links between firms' conduct, market structure, and market performance. Selten (1984) and Sutton (1991, 1998) have shown that under free entry and exit, an intensification of price competition in a homogeneous-good industry will have no significant effect on firms' profits in the long run, although it will cause a decrease in the number of firms. Previous chapters of the present book have described and extended the theory of the competition-market structure relationship to advertising-intensive and R&D-intensive industries, and have also provided several empirical tests of the theory for different classes of industries. The empirical results were indeed consistent with the Selten-Sutton predictions for exogenous sunk cost industries. Moreover, the results suggested that the mechanism that causes concentration to rise when price competition intensifies is so strong that it will only infrequently break down in advertising-intensive or R&D-intensive industries.

There is, however, one aspect of the present theory that has not yet been empirically examined, and that is the effect of competition on profits. This chapter concludes the empirical analysis of the effects of the 1956 Restrictive Trade Practices Act in this book by examining the *joint* effect of price competition on market structure and profitability.

The only previous statistical analysis of the effects of the 1956 Act on profitability is the study by O'Brien et al. (1979). These authors used firm-level data taken from company accounts for a sample of about thirty industries and examined two different measures of profitability: the rate of return on capital and the rate of return on sales. They found a decline in the mean level of profitability between the period 1951–1958 and the period 1958–1967 for their full sample of firms, but could not identify any significant difference in the evolution of profitability between firms in industries affected by the 1956 Act and those in industries not affected. They also found weak evidence of a recovery of the rate of return on capital over the period 1968–1972 in industries affected by the restrictive practices legislation relative to the control group of noncollusive industries, although this was not statistically significant. Moreover, a recovery of the rate of return on capital was also observed for firms in industries with agreements upheld by the Restrictive Practices Court relative to firms in the control group. Thus the results provided no evidence of any effect of the 1956 Act on the profitability of firms. O'Brien et al. (1979) also examined merger activity over the same period, but again found no evidence of any significant difference between industries with a change in competition regime and those without such a change. As mentioned in chapter 4 of this book, the main methodological limitations of the O'Brien et al. study were the use of a rather small sample of industries and the fact that the criteria for classifying industries across groups were somewhat dubious in a few cases.

Despite these limitations, the O'Brien et al. study is one of a few empirical analyses of the links between competition and profitability that has explicitly treated concentration as an endogenous variable and not as a proxy for the degree of market power. The literature on the effects of economic integration on industry performance has sometimes followed a similar approach, using import penetration or the degree of tariff protection as measures of competitive pressure and recognizing the potential effect of changes in these variables on market structure as well as on performance. Many of these studies find a negative effect of import competition on price-cost margins, especially in concentrated industries, which they typically interpret as being consistent with the hypothesis that foreign competition reduces the market power of domestic firms (see, for instance, Jacquemin et al. 1980, deMelo and Urata 1986). There are, however, several important methodological differences between these studies and the present one.

First, some of the profit measures that are relevant in the context of the present theory have not been generally used in the existing literature on the determinants of profitability. Second, economic integration leads to changes not only in firms' conduct but also in product substitutability and market size. Hence it is not easy to draw very clear implications for the competition-profitability relationship from studies of the effects of import competition on industry performance. Third, and most important, none of these studies has examined the interaction between changes in market structure and changes in profitability or compared the short-run and the long-run evolution of profitability following an intensification of competition. These are, however, key issues within the theory developed in this book. As a result, the econometric approach adopted here differs in important respects from that of previous studies. In particular, since the theory's predictions regarding the long-run competition effect on profitability depend on allowing market structure to change to restore the long-run equilibrium, it is important for testing these predictions that one does *not* control for changes in market structure when specifying the profitability equation.

In the remainder of this chapter, I begin with a brief reminder and clarification of the theoretical predictions regarding the impact of price competition on profitability. This is followed by a brief discussion of some case-study evidence from industries affected by the 1956 Act. In particular, I describe two case studies that seem to confirm the theoretical results, then present a counterexample that illustrates the limitations of the present theory and yet at the same time can be seen as a sharp test of the theory's predictive power.

Finally, I provide econometric results on the joint effect of competition on market structure and profitability. My market structure measures in this chapter are the number of firms and the number of plants; this analysis therefore complements the one carried out in previous chapters using the concentration ratio. The main advantage of using firm or plant numbers is that data on these come from exactly the same sources as the profit data. Therefore the samples used for the market structure regressions and the profit regressions in this chapter are identical. I use three different profit measures: the gross profit of the average firm, the gross profit of the average plant, and the industry price-cost margin. My results are in line with the theory, justifying the recent shift of emphasis toward models that endogenize market structure and consequently emphasize the effect of firm conduct on structure rather than on performance.

7.2 Theoretical Issues

The mechanism that I will test in this chapter has been described in previous chapters, so I will provide only a brief summary and some extensions and clarifications in what follows. Let me start again with the benchmark case. Under free entry, the net profit of each of a number of symmetric firms must be zero—or almost zero, taking account of the integer constraint and assuming that the number of firms is not very small—irrespective of firm conduct. An increase in the intensity of price competition, caused by the introduction of cartel laws, economic integration, or some other exogenous institutional change, will cause gross profit and the price-cost margin to fall, given the initial number of firms. As a result, firms will no longer be able to cover their sunk costs at the initial free-entry equilibrium. In an exogenous sunk cost industry, this will inevitably lead to mergers and exit until the gross profit of each firm rises sufficiently to cover its sunk costs, which have remained unchanged. Note that the fact that the capital stock is already in place when competition intensifies is not important in the long run because capital depreciates and has to be renewed. Thus the degree to which setup costs are sunk when competition intensifies and the rate of depreciation of the capital stock will affect only the speed of adjustment to the new long-run equilibrium market structure.

At the new long-run equilibrium, the number of firms (or plants) will be lower, but there will be no significant change in firm (or plant) gross or net profit. More specifically, one would expect profitability to decline in the short run, that is, before any significant change in market structure occurs, and then be restored, or partially restored, in the long run through a fall in firm numbers. This is the basic mechanism that the present chapter sets out to test.

If the integer constraint is taken into account, little can be said about the exact effect of more intense price competition on profit without imposing more structure on the model. In the specific model analyzed by Selten (1984), both total industry net profit and plant (or firm) net profit are more likely to increase than to decrease following a switch from a collusive to a noncollusive regime (see also Phlips 1995, chapter 3). However, in a context where the integer constraint is the only reason for positive net profit, this can be expected to be small in general, at least at the plant or firm level, so any change in profit may be difficult to identify empirically. Since, in addition, there is no clear prediction as to the direction of the change, it seems legitimate to consider a weaker version of the Selten result as the main testable prediction of the theory, namely, that a switch of competition regime has no significant effect on plant (or firm) gross or net profit in the long run.[1]

Two Key Assumptions

Clearly, these results depend on two crucial assumptions. The first is that incumbent firms under a collusive regime cannot prevent entry of new firms into the industry or, more generally, that the scope for entry deterrence is not larger in a collusive equilibrium than in a noncollusive one. If this were not the case, then a breakdown of collusion would reduce net and gross profit and would have an ambiguous effect on the number of firms.

It is, in fact, possible to construct theoretical models of collusion where firms make supranormal profits either by adopting trigger strategies that deter entry (Harrington 1989, 1991) or by adopting a strategy of gradually accommodating entry (Friedman and Thisse 1994). In such models, a decrease in the degree of collusion will reduce net and gross profit and will have an ambiguous effect on the number of firms—assuming that the scope for entry deterrence is smaller in a more competitive equilibrium. Hence an empirical test of the present theory regarding the effect of competition on profits may also be interpreted as a test of alternative theories of collusion.

The second key assumption is the symmetry assumption. However, the typical industry is subject to significant asymmetries, due to a variety of factors, including multiplant or multiproduct firms, or efficiency differences between firms. In previous chapters I have argued that the presence of asymmetries is unlikely to modify the theoretical predictions regarding the effect of price competition on market structure in any significant way. This may not be true for the effect on profitability. In the presence of asymmetries, free entry is consistent with supranormal profits for all but the *marginal* firm in an industry, and it is not clear whether any general theoretical prediction can be derived about the long-run equilibrium effect of more intense price competition on the profit of the *average* firm.

In fact, results from specific models suggest that the effect of tougher price competition on firm profit and even on the price-cost margin may be positive in the presence of efficiency differences, even

---

1. Also, the effect on industry net profit will be ambiguous, although industry gross profit should fall because of the fall in the number of firms.

when no account is taken of the integer constraint (see Montagna 1995). The intuition is that an exogenous shock that reduces prices in the short run drives the less efficient firms out of the industry, so in long-run equilibrium price may fall by less than the marginal cost of the average firm in the industry, and thus the price-cost margin of the average firm may rise. In other words, low-cost firms will expand at the expense of high-cost rivals, and since low-cost firms always have higher margins in an asymmetric industry, the possibility arises that the margin of the average firm will be higher in the new long-run equilibrium despite the increase in the intensity of competition. Of course, this is only a possibility, and it could also be the case that the overall effect is a fall in the margin of the average firm. For my present purposes, it is sufficient to note that in the presence of efficiency differences, the long-run effect of price competition on profitability is ambiguous.

The above discussion suggests that the present theory can accommodate several of the predictions of models that emphasize efficiency differences between firms. However, it is at odds with one potential implication of some of these models, namely, that the number of firms need not fall in the long run when price competition intensifies. The reason why this could happen is as follows.[2] An intensification of price competition would put pressure on price-cost margins and cause low-cost firms to expand at the expense of high-cost firms in the short run; this redistribution of market shares would also raise concentration. Because of the expansion effect, it is possible, if the efficiency differences are sufficiently large, that the gross profit of low-cost firms increases *given the initial number of firms*. This would lead to entry of low-cost firms. Of course, the gross profit of high-cost firms would decrease, thus causing exit of those firms. But this whole mechanism opens up the possibility that the total number of firms does not fall (or, at any rate, does not fall significantly) in the long run, following an increase in the intensity of price competition, even though concentration should rise as a result of the redistribution of market shares among firms. It also opens up the possibility that industry profitability does not fluctuate (i.e., fall in the short run and then rise following changes in market structure). This mechanism, which could be regarded perhaps as a strong version of the

---

2. See Aghion and Schankerman (2000), where this possibility is discussed along with many others that are not inconsistent with the predictions of the present theory.

efficiency differences approach, is clearly incompatible with the theory developed in this book. The empirical evidence presented in this chapter can therefore also be seen as a test of the two competing models.

Endogenous Sunk Costs

I have so far focused on the case of an exogenous sunk cost industry. Things can be more complicated in industries with significant endogenous sunk costs, such as advertising or R&D. A change in the intensity of price competition will affect the incentive of each firm to spend on advertising or R&D, which is part of the total sunk cost incurred. As a result, it may not always be the case that more intense price competition causes the number of firms to fall. On the other hand, the long-run effect on net profit will still be (approximately) zero, although gross profit may change because of the change in advertising/R&D expenditure, and the direction of that change is not predictable in general.

As shown in previous chapters, however, the competition-concentration relationship will only infrequently break down in practice in advertising-intensive or R&D-intensive industries. Thus one should not overemphasize the potential differences across classes of industries in this respect. The same may be true for the effect of price competition on profitability. It is not difficult to show that under plausible assumptions, this effect should be negative in the short run (i.e., before any change in market structure occurs) and can be ambiguous in the long run (i.e., once market structure adjusts) in industries with endogenous sunk costs, just as in exogenous sunk cost industries. To see this, consider two cases.

Suppose, first, that price competition has no significant effect on the nonprice variable at the industry level, as was the case in chapter 6 with innovative output and (presumably) R&D expenditure. Gross profit and the price-cost margin must then fall in the short run when price competition intensifies, given that neither R&D nor market structure has changed. In the long run, both gross profit and the price-cost margin can rise or fall, depending on market structure, total industry sales revenue, and the type and degree of asymmetries between firms. For instance, if firms are symmetric and their number falls and industry sales revenue rises in the long run following an intensification of price competition, the free-entry condition implies that the effect on the price-cost margin can be ambiguous.

Next, suppose that price competition has a negative effect on the nonprice variable at the industry level, as was the case in chapter 5 with advertising expenditure or intensity. In the short run, gross profit and the price-cost margin should decline as a result of more intense price competition—and this effect could be reinforced by the fall in advertising. In the long run, the effect is ambiguous. For instance, if firms are symmetric and their number falls, advertising expenditure or intensity at the firm level can rise or fall, and the free-entry condition then implies that the same is true for profitability.

Summary of the Theory and Implications for the Empirical Analysis

Two main conclusions can be drawn from the above discussion. First, in the presence of asymmetries between firms or endogenous sunk costs, such as advertising or R&D, it is difficult to derive any strong theoretical results regarding the effect of price competition on profitability in the long run. Second, the basic intuition from the benchmark case—that profitability should initially decline following a rise in the intensity of price competition and then be restored, or partially restored, through a change in market structure—emerges as the dominant mechanism driving the joint evolution of structure and performance across classes of industries. The only exception to this can occur in rather special cases where price competition has a particularly strong effect on nonprice variables; however, the evidence from previous chapters suggests that there are very few such cases in the present context. This has two implications for the empirical analysis of profitability in this chapter.

The first implication is that the key testable prediction in this chapter is that profitability should initially decline following an intensification of price competition, and then be restored through a fall in firm numbers. This will be tested against alternative predictions derived from two other theories mentioned above: the theory that cartels deter entry and a strong version of the efficiency differences approach.

The second implication is that there is probably little to be gained from performing separate regressions for each class of industries. On the other hand, there is an important gain from pooling the data, namely, an increase in the efficiency of the estimation. This is important here for several reasons. First, the effect of price competition on firm or plant numbers may be less easy to identify than the effect on concentration, because firm or plant numbers are very sensitive to the number of small firms or plants, and these may have not been affected by the 1956 Act to the same extent as larger firms or plants (see section 7.4). Second, there are few advertising-intensive or R&D-intensive industries with a change in competition regime in the present sample. Given that profit data are inherently "noisy," it is questionable whether any meaningful results can be derived in separate regressions for advertising-intensive and R&D-intensive industries. Third, since one of the key testable predictions in this chapter is that price competition has no significant long-run effect on profit, one should use the largest possible sample to give the data the best possible chance to reveal a nonzero effect. Moreover, another key aspect of the analysis will be the comparison of short-run and long-run effects, and again the difficulty of doing this may increase as the size of the sample used decreases.

In any case, since the theoretical predictions for the effect of price competition on profit are perhaps less clear for advertising-intensive and R&D-intensive industries than for exogenous sunk cost industries, I have also run regressions for the subsample of exogenous sunk cost industries; the results will be discussed below. The main purpose of this is to check that the results for the whole sample are not driven by advertising-intensive or R&D-intensive industries, because that would not be consistent with the theory.

Before presenting the econometric results, however, I will discuss some case-study evidence that illustrates very nicely the central structural mechanism that drives the results of this chapter and of the book as a whole. In fact, part of the interest of these case studies derives from the fact that they can confirm that the observed patterns in the cross-industry data identified in this chapter and in previous chapters are the result of the mechanism proposed in the theory rather than of other factors quite different from those suggested by the theory.

7.3   Case-Study Evidence

Several of the case studies of the effects of the 1956 Restrictive Trade Practices Act discussed in Swann et al. (1973) provide evidence that is consistent with the theory described in section 7.2. Admittedly, the evidence is somewhat sketchy, since the main focus of these case studies is on the effect of the Act on competition—and not on its repercussions on market structure and industry performance. Moreover, it is not always easy to separate the effect of competition from the influence of other factors on profitability and market structure in the industries investigated. Nevertheless, a brief description of the evolution of some of the industries in the Swann et al. sample between the late 1950s and the early 1970s should help provide a better understanding of the mechanisms that drive the econometric results obtained later in this chapter. Two of the best-documented cases are the transformer industry and the glass container industry.

The Electrical Power Transformer Industry

The details on the operation of collusive arrangements in the electrical power transformer industry during the 1950s became widely known even before the implementation of the 1956 Act, since the industry was the subject of a Monopolies and Restrictive Practices Commission inquiry in the mid-1950s, along with several other subdivisions of the electrical machinery industry (see MRPC 1957). Subsequently, the industry registered its agreements and defended the most important of these in the Restrictive Practices Court, which struck it down in early 1961.

The agreement covered the home market and related to all but the smallest sizes of transformers. It provided for common minimum net selling prices, the reporting of inquiries and orders received from customers, and aggregated rebates (i.e., discounts to buyers on the basis of the total quantity purchased from firms who were parties to the agreement). These firms were members of the Transformer Makers' Association, which had always included all the producers of very large transformers. However, there was some competition from a few outside firms for large, as opposed to very large, transformers, and significant competition from outside firms for smaller equipment. It is therefore not surprising that the Monopolies and Restrictive Practices Commission found that the profitability of association firms was lower for the smaller sizes of transformers than for the larger sizes. On the whole, profitability was higher than the average for all manufacturing, but not excessive, according to the Commission. The membership of the association declined somewhat in the late 1950s, so outside competition may have been stronger in 1961 than at the time of the Commission's investigation.

Collusion among members of the association had been effective during the 1950s, and competition was slow to emerge after the agreement was formally abandoned following the Court judgment. Explicit price-fixing was replaced by the exchange of information on prices and tenders, and this helped sustain prices and margins for several years, despite occasional price-cutting (see Swann et al. 1973). Interestingly, several firms that were not members of the association at the time of the Court hearing seem to have adhered to the implicit arrangements after 1961.

Eventually, however, competition was triggered by a combination of events, the most important of which may have been the significant fall in demand after 1964. A second factor was the decision of the Restrictive Practices Court to strike down two information agreements in other industries on the grounds that they had amounted to the same effect as explicit price-fixing (see chapter 2). A third factor was a more aggressive purchasing policy on the part of certain buyers. As a result, prices fell by as much as 25–40% between 1964 and 1968, according to figures reported by Swann et al., while costs slightly increased during the same period. The price fall was more pronounced for medium-sized transformers than for very large equipment.

The main response of the industry to this substantial decline in prices and profits was merger and exit. The evolution of market structure in transformers was, of course, closely linked with developments in other markets for electrical equipment, all of which experienced an intensification of price competition during the 1960s. But nowhere was the change in market structure so pronounced as in transformers. According to figures based on the Census of Production, the five-firm sales concentration ratio in the industry, which had fallen from 50% in 1958 to 45% in 1963, jumped to 76.7% in 1968, an increase of over thirty percentage points in five years. A large part of this increase was due to mergers: Swann et al. (1973) list more than ten mergers between producers of transformers (and other electrical machinery) over the period 1965–1969.[3] Admittedly, this

---

3. Unfortunately, the Census figures on firm numbers in the transformer industry are not comparable over the period 1963–1968, because of changes in the definition of subproducts within the industry.

was probably a case of overshooting, as suggested by the fact that the five-firm concentration ratio declined slightly after 1968, reaching 68.8% in 1975.

By the late 1960s, then, the industry was much more concentrated and the number of firms was much smaller than in the early 1960s or even in 1964, the date when prices started falling. Did prices rise in the late 1960s, as would be predicted by the theory of this chapter? The answer is that they did—indeed, quite sharply. The evidence reported by Swann et al. suggests that prices started to rise in 1969 and were higher in 1971 than in 1963. In fact, price rises of up to 50% were reported for 1969–1970 and 1970–1971. This was attributed by industry experts to the elimination of excess capacity through mergers and exit.

The Glass Container Industry

The experience of the glass container industry has much in common with that of the electrical power transformer industry. As in the case of transformers, collusion had a long history in the glass container industry, and had been facilitated during the 1950s by the steady and moderate growth in demand. The agreement among producers of glass containers came before the Restrictive Practices Court in 1961 and was defended by the parties. Under the agreement, the members of the British Bottle Association, who were responsible for about 80% of the total UK production of glass containers, had to observe common minimum prices and standard conditions of sale, and also offered aggregated rebates to distributors. Competition from outside producers of glass containers was weak, since several nonmembers sold only to specific buyers and/or tacitly observed the association prices. However, there was also competition from producers of containers of different materials, such as paper, tin, and plastic, and this was on the increase at the time the case was heard in the Court.

Swann et al. (1973) report that price competition emerged in the industry soon after the explicit price-fixing agreement was condemned by the Court, despite an attempt to sustain collusion through the operation of an information agreement. Unlike the transformer industry, however, there were no spectacular price falls in glass containers, possibly because demand fluctuations were not very pronounced. Moreover, the price falls that occurred are somewhat difficult to interpret because the cost of materials seems also to have fallen during the first half of the 1960s. The clearest indication of a change in competition regime is therefore the decline in profitability in the industry in the first half of the 1960s, as documented in Swann et al. on the basis of data from company reports.

In particular, the largest firm in the industry experienced a continuous decline in its rate of return to capital, which fell from 18% in 1960 to 5.8% in 1965. For the other firms the evidence is somewhat mixed, but for all of them profitability clearly declined over 1962–1964 (i.e., in the first few years after the emergence of price competition). However, profitability recovered in the mid-1960s. And while the evidence provided by Swann et al. on the profitability of various firms in the second half of the 1960s is rather sketchy, the overall picture is one of sustained moderate profitability for the industry as a whole. At the same time, prices in early 1969 were at roughly the same level as in late 1965, although wages and costs of materials had been rising during that period. Why did the rate of return on capital recover in the mid-1960s, and how was it then sustained despite increases in input prices that were not fully passed on to selling prices?

The answer is probably twofold. First, technical progress in the industry led to increased efficiency during the 1960s and helped to keep unit costs low despite increases in input prices. Second, the recovery and subsequent stability of profits must have been related to the restructuring of the industry, which was partly realized through a series of mergers beginning in 1962 and continuing until the late 1960s. Thus, according to highly disaggregated data from the Census of Production, the number of producers (excluding those with fewer than twenty-five employees) declined by as much as 50% in all the principal product lines within the glass container industry between 1958 and 1968, while the five-firm sales concentration ratio for the industry as a whole increased from about 63.5% in 1958 to 69.5% in 1963, and to 87.3% in 1968, a rise of nearly twenty percentage points in five years.

The two case studies briefly described above provide support for the theoretical predictions of the present chapter. Are they typical examples of the effect of cartel policy on profits and market structure? This question can be answered only by using econometric analysis. Prior to that, however, it is worth discussing a counterexample.

The Secondary Battery Industry

In the case of the secondary battery industry, the predictions of this chapter are not confirmed by the facts. The reason is that a key assumption of the theory, the assumption of free entry under the collusive regime, is violated. In one sense, then, this case study illustrates the limitations of the theory. In another sense, and perhaps somewhat paradoxically, it confirms the present theory, albeit in a different way than the two previous cases. In particular, the evolution of the secondary battery industry between the late 1950s and the early 1970s demonstrates the relevance of a structural interpretation of the effects of the 1956 Act on profits and market structure, as opposed to a purely behavioral interpretation.

The secondary battery industry was investigated by the Monopolies Commission in the early 1960s as part of the Commission's inquiry on various classes of electrical equipment for vehicles (see Monopolies Commission 1963). Detailed information on the evolution of the industry in the 1950s and the 1960s can therefore be drawn both from the Commission's report and from Swann et al. (1973). Sales of secondary batteries fall into one of four main types: automotive batteries sold as initial equipment, automotive batteries sold for replacement, traction batteries sold as initial equipment, and traction batteries sold for replacement. The structure of the industry has always been characterized by a relatively high degree of concentration, especially in the initial equipment market, which was dominated throughout the 1950s and the 1960s by two firms, Lucas and Chloride. In the case of automotive replacement batteries, several smaller firms also were active, and their market share increased during the second half of the 1950s, as we will see below. Overall, the combined market share of Lucas and Chloride was around 70% of total industry sales revenue in 1960.

These two firms were the most prominent members of the British Starter Battery Association, which also included two smaller firms. A number of other firms remained outside the association, either because they chose to do so or because they were refused membership. The agreement between the members related to replacement batteries for motor vehicles and provided for common list prices, common discounts for various classes of buyers, and restrictions on the relationships between manufacturers and buyers. The regulations affecting the distribution of batteries are of considerable interest for our present purposes.

There were several classes of buyers, but a key distinction was between "service agents" and other types of buyers. Each of the four association members had its own network of service agents, who could buy only from that particular manufacturer. Their names, addresses, and total number had to be reported to the association, and no transfer of an agent from one manufacturer to another could take place without the consent of both manufacturers concerned. In addition, the member firms could sell directly to wholesalers, retailers, or fleet operators. There were no *individual* exclusive dealing arrangements for these classes of buyers, but there was *collective* exclusive dealing. In other words, these buyers were required to deal only with association firms if they were to be supplied at all.

In addition to the agreement on replacement batteries, there was a tacit understanding between Lucas and Chloride that they would not canvass one another's customers in the automotive initial equipment market. As for traction batteries, there were occasional discussions on prices among three firms, including Chloride, which were the only significant producers of this type of battery.

The arrangements on initial equipment and traction batteries were terminated when the 1956 Act was introduced, and were never registered. On the other hand, the agreement of the British Starter Battery Association was revised and then registered. The main changes were the abandonment of common list prices and the abolition of collective exclusive dealing; clearly, the purpose of the changes was to make the agreement more acceptable to the Court. The revised agreement provided for maximum trade discounts and retained the individual exclusive dealing arrangements with "service agents." According to Swann et al., the abolition of collective exclusive dealing had a significant impact on the structure of the industry, since smaller firms that had previously found it difficult to enter the industry or expand due to the lack of distribution outlets could now emerge as legitimate competitors in the replacement market. As a result, the combined market share of nonassociation firms in the replacement battery market doubled within a few years to reach approximately 50% in the mid-1960s.

In 1960 this revised agreement was replaced by an information agreement. Soon after that, the Monopolies Commission began its investigation of the industry. The principal conclusions of the Commission's report regarding the secondary battery industry were that competition was muted and that the two leading firms, especially Lucas, enjoyed excessive profits, although these came mainly from initial equipment and traction batteries, not from automotive replacement batteries. The Commission thought that resale price maintenance and the operation of the information agreement had contributed to restricting competition in the industry, and recommended that they be abandoned. The information agreement was indeed abandoned shortly afterward, while resale price maintenance continued for a few years before it was dropped as a consequence of the 1964 Resale Prices Act.

The available evidence on prices and profits indicates that by the mid-1960s competition had intensified in the industry and that this trend continued in the following years. In fact, Swann et al. argue that the market power of the leading firms was already being eroded in the early 1960s because of competition from smaller producers of cheap batteries. Between 1963 and 1970, the prices of a leading manufacturer increased by only about 20% while the cost of materials more than doubled. In addition, the large producers had to introduce cheaper types of batteries to protect their market share against smaller firms. According to Swann et al., firms in the industry were able to reduce unit costs through technical improvements and better organization in the 1960s. Still, there is little doubt that profit margins fell. Although profit data are not readily available, the report of the National Board for Prices and Incomes on prices of secondary batteries (NBPI 1968) states that the profitability of the larger firms was by no means excessive in 1968, and that the increase in the cost of materials during that year could not be absorbed without an increase in prices.

While price-cost margins appear to have fallen during the 1960s, there was no significant change in market structure. No exit of important firms and no major mergers occurred in the industry in the 1960s. According to the Census of Production, the number of domestic producers of automotive batteries (which is the major product of the industry) employing at least twenty-five persons fell from fifteen in 1958 to eleven in 1963, then increased to sixteen in 1968, while the overall rate of growth of demand during this period was not much different from the rate of growth of demand for manufacturing as a whole. The fluctuations in firm numbers were probably driven by the entry and exit of smaller firms. Unfortunately, separate concentration data for this industry are not available. However, the concentration ratio for the battery industry as a whole, including primary and secondary batteries, increased by about six percentage points between 1958 and 1968, which is slightly less than the average for all manufacturing (eight percentage points). This relatively modest change is consistent with the conclusion that the 1956 Act did not have a major effect on market structure in the secondary battery industry.

In summary, the industry experienced an intensification of price competition, a fall in margins (with no subsequent recovery), and no significant change in market structure during the 1960s. What explains this evolution, which is so different from that of the transformer industry or the glass container industry—or of several other industries affected by the restrictive practices legislation? The answer is certainly not to be found in any substantial fall in endogenous sunk costs. Both advertising and R&D were moderate in this industry, on the order of 1%, and did not change very much during the 1960s.

Rather, the answer has to do with the initial conditions in the industry, and particularly the existing barriers to entry. In the replacement battery market, the system of collective exclusive dealing seems to have acted as a barrier to entry by smaller firms. In the initial equipment market, the market power of the two leading firms had been based both on their ability to offer better products and on the existence of long-standing relationships between the battery producers and the car manufacturers. Because of these various entry barriers, the incumbent firms were probably earning excess profits in the 1950s. Hence the reduction in profits brought about by the intensification of price competition could be absorbed without the need for a major restructuring of the industry.

It remains to be seen whether the experience of the secondary battery industry was indeed exceptional among industries affected by the 1956 Act and therefore cannot undermine the key assumptions of the theory set out in the introduction to this chapter. If that is the case, it can be regarded as a counterexample that essentially confirms the mechanism driving the theoretical predictions of this chapter, and of the book as a whole.

This is because the evolution of the secondary battery industry clearly illustrates the difference between a structural and a purely behavioral interpretation of the effects of the 1956 Act on market structure. Recall that according to a purely behavioral interpretation, the introduction of cartel laws would cause firms to try to restore market power through mergers. As I argued in the concluding section of chapter 4, this may well be true in most cases, but it cannot be regarded as a theory of the competition-market structure relationship because it does not explain how equilibrium market structure is determined. Furthermore, the purely behavioral interpretation is not always valid, as the evolution of the secondary battery industry shows. On the other hand, a structural interpretation emphasizes the fact that changes in market structure are driven by the relationship between firms' gross profits and sunk costs. This interpretation is confirmed by the experience of the secondary battery industry.

7.4   The Data

As in previous chapters, the econometric analysis below will be based on a comparison of industries affected by the 1956 Restrictive Trade Practices Act with a control group of industries not affected. I will use data on profits and firm/plant numbers for five different years: 1954, 1958, 1963, 1968, and 1973. The first four of these years are the only ones for which such data are available between the early 1950s and the late 1960s, and 1973 is the last year before the oil crisis. As discussed in detail in previous chapters, the Act had little effect before the first Court cases were heard in 1959, and continued to have an effect on British industry until at least the late 1960s, and in some cases until the early 1970s.

The industry definitions used in this chapter are sometimes at the three-digit level of aggregation and sometimes at the four-digit level. In particular, in most cases they are the "principal products" within any three-digit "minimum list heading" (MLH) industry, as defined in the individual industry reports of the UK Census of Production. Whenever an MLH industry was not further subdivided into principal products or the subdivisions changed a lot over time, the MLH industry was used as the industry definition for this chapter. Because of changes over time in the Census industry or principal product definitions, the panel is unbalanced. This section describes the construction of the data set for this chapter. Once again, readers who would prefer to skip the details on the data may well do so, since a summary description of all the variables is given in section 7.5.

Industry Definitions

Several of the remarks made in chapter 4 with regard to the concentration data are also valid for the data used in this chapter.[4] However, the data used here differ from the data used in chapters 4–6 in one respect. The data used in chapters 4–6 were constructed on the basis of sales of products within each industry or product group by *all* plants employing at least twenty-five persons, irrespective of the Census MLH industry to which any particular plant was allocated. In this chapter, however, the data are constructed on the basis of sales of plants (or firms) classified to any given principal product or MLH industry.[5] While this may be a matter of some concern in cross-industry studies, it is far less important in studies using panel data, such as the present one.

As mentioned above, the industry definitions used in this chapter are sometimes MLH industries and sometimes "principal products." Whenever an MLH industry was not further subdivided in the Census reports, there was little choice but to use it as an industry definition. Most MLH industries are further subdivided into principal

---

4. Thus the classification of industries mainly according to supply rather than demand characteristics is appropriate in the present context because the British cartels typically operated within industries defined according to their supply characteristics. Also, the fact that the data cover only UK firms is not a serious problem to the extent that the impact of the 1956 Act was mostly on competition between UK manufacturers rather than between manufacturing firms selling in the UK market.

5. Let me clarify this point. The UK Census of Production, like the Censuses of Production in many other countries, allocates each plant to an MLH industry (roughly corresponding to the three-digit level of aggregation) on the basis of the core products of the plant. MLH industries often are further subdivided into principal products, and each plant is allocated to a single principal product on the basis of the core product of the plant. When computing figures for the net value of output, wages and salaries, firm numbers, and so on, all the products produced in a certain plant are classified to the industry that the plant is assigned to according to its core product. This means that the reported net output for the principal product "coffee," for instance, is not the actual net output for coffee, but the total net output of all plants whose principal product is coffee. Sales of coffee by plants classified to other industries are excluded, while sales of products other than coffee by plants whose principal product is coffee are included. Obviously, the profit figures, the figures for firm numbers, and so on are all subject to the same problem.

Note that this occurs only in the data set used in the present chapter, not in any of the data sets used in previous chapters of this book (except for the two variables that are defined at the three-digit level in previous chapters, K/N and K/L). For instance, the sales concentration ratio, the advertising-sales ratio, the value of sales, and so on for coffee are derived on the basis of the total sales of coffee by all plants in manufacturing industry.

products, but there are several complications that may arise with this. I will mention only the most important ones.

One complication is that the 1973 Census of Production, like all Censuses of Production after 1968, contains no information for principal products; all the figures are for entire MLH industries. Hence, in some cases I had to decide whether to use the figures for a certain MLH industry for 1954–1973 or the figures for principal products within that MLH industry for 1954–1968. In practice, the decision to use principal products was often imposed by the fact that several MLH industries were ambiguous with respect to the state of competition, while some of their principal products were not. Whenever there was a real choice, I usually preferred to use principal products, since the gain from working with more numerous and more disaggregated industry categories more than offset the loss of information for 1973, a year not so crucial for my purposes.[6]

Second, the definitions of principal products often change across years, so in several cases the figures are not comparable over the entire period 1954–1968 (excluding minor noncomparabilities that can be dealt with by making small adjustments). For instance, there could be a choice between using an entire MLH as the relevant industry category, with data for all five years, and using, say, two principal products within that MLH, with data for 1954–1963 only. In such cases, I normally chose to use the entire MLH as my industry definition, unless the MLH as a whole would be classified as ambiguous with respect to its state of competition, while some of its principal products would not.

A third complication arises when the definition of an MLH industry changes over time. In some of these cases, it was possible to construct comparable figures by adjusting the ones published. In others, I could make use only of the subset of years with comparable

---

6. Thus, whenever the industry definition that I use is at the four-digit level (i.e., a principal product) rather than at the three-digit level (i.e., an entire MLH industry), the 1973 observation is not available. Does this lead to any bias in the results regarding the effect of the 1956 Act by 1973? A bias could be introduced only if MLH industries were systematically different from principal products in some respect, for instance, in the degree of homogeneity. But there is no evidence to support such a claim: there are several fairly heterogeneous industries which are not subdivided into principal products, and hence do have a 1973 observation in my data, just as there are many homogeneous industries which are not subdivided into principal products. Moreover, even if it were the case that industries with an available 1973 observation were different in some respect from industries without a 1973 observation, this would probably affect only the estimated *time effect* for 1973, not the estimated effect of the 1956 Act.

data or use one or more principal products with comparable data within the MLH industry.

Finally, some principal product categories have very low sales or do not correspond to any meaningful market because they contain mostly secondary or unspecified products. To deal with this, I merged a few small principal products into larger ones, and I also excluded some categories altogether from the sample.[7]

More generally, my principal aim was to maximize the relevant information in the data set, and this broadly involved maximizing the number of meaningful industry categories with comparable figures for the core period 1958–1968. As in previous chapters, some industries were excluded, either entirely or for part of the period, because of heavy government participation or involvement (locomotives, aircraft, and several industries in the steel sector).

Data Sources and Variables

Several profit measures will be used in the econometric analysis of section 7.5: the industry gross profit divided by the number of firms, the industry gross profit divided by the number of plants, and the price-cost margin. All these were constructed using data on net output at current net producer prices, wages and salaries, firm numbers, and plant numbers from the industry reports of the Census of Production (various years) and from the 1973 issues of *Business Monitor, PQ series: Quarterly Statistics*. The figures are for all firms employing at least twenty-five persons.[8] Certain figures were adjusted to ensure comparability over time. Usually this involved only minor corrections, although for plant numbers more elaborate corrections had to be made. All these adjustments were similar to those applied to the data used for the concentration regressions (see chapter 4, section 4.4).

Industry gross profit was defined as the net value of output minus wages and salaries, and it was deflated using either the general producer price index, obtained from the *Annual Abstract of Statistics*, or industry-specific price indices, constructed in the manner described in chapter 4. Note that my definition of gross profit includes fixed

---

7. In some cases, however, industry categories described as "other" or "remainder" consist primarily of a small number of well-specified products; these were included.
8. In fact, the figures for 1963 and later years are for all firms operating plants that employ at least twenty-five persons rather than for all firms that employ at least twenty-five persons, but the measurement error this causes is negligible.

costs, such as capital costs, advertising expenditure, royalties, and R&D expenditure (other than salaries of R&D personnel). Unfortunately, it also includes some variable costs, the most important of which are "other labor costs," including employers' national insurance contributions, employers' contributions to pension funds, and so on. Data on these are not available for most years, and the implicit assumption was made that these costs were a constant fraction of total variable costs within each industry over the time period considered, or that any changes in these costs were uniform across industries and will therefore be picked up by time effects.[9] More generally, it is well known that Census-based profitability data are not very precise, but this problem is greatly alleviated by the use of panel data.

In addition to being used to construct profit measures, the number of firms and the number of plants were used as dependent variables in some regressions. A limitation of using these variables as measures of market structure is that they are sensitive to the number of small firms (or plants). It is well known that small firms often do not produce core industry products. For instance, most engineering industries contain a large number of firms that produce only parts and accessories. Moreover, the British cartels did not usually include all firms in any given industry, and it was often the smaller firms that were not cartel members. Hence the effect of the 1956 Act on many small firms in cartelized industries may have been relatively weak. These problems are alleviated somewhat by the fact that very small firms (firms with fewer than twenty-five employees) are excluded from my data. Other measures of market structure, such as concentration measures, are not available for the industry categories used in this chapter.

Market size can be measured either by the net value of output or by sales revenue, deflated either by the general producer price index or by an industry-specific producer price index. Perhaps net output more accurately reflects the extent of profit opportunities in an industry, and is therefore a better proxy for market size. However, its use in profit equations is not very appropriate because of potential endogeneity problems. Industry-specific prices may also be endoge-

---

9. Some statistics on labor costs in UK manufacturing as a whole, as well as in selected sectors for 1950–1967, were published in the October 1968 issue of *Economic Trends* (pp. 25–33). They show that throughout that period changes in "other labor costs" mirrored almost exactly the changes in wages and salaries.

nous, and this is likely to be a more serious problem in profit equations than elsewhere in this book. On the other hand, a drawback of the general producer price index is that it does not control for changes in the relative prices of materials. This discussion suggests using sales revenue deflated by the general producer price index as a proxy for market size in profitability regressions in order to minimize any potential endogeneity problems, while at the same time checking the extent to which the results are robust to choosing different proxies for market size.

The competition data were fully described in chapter 3, and the construction of the competition variable $CHANGE$ was described in chapter 4. Recall that $CHANGE$ takes the value 1 for industries with a change in competition regime and 0 otherwise (the latter group includes three industries—salt, glazed tiles, and cement—with agreements continuing throughout the period).[10] An econometric analysis of the competition effect on any endogenous variable y can then be performed by testing whether the time effects on y after 1958 are different for the two groups of industries in regressions that control for other factors affecting y.

As in previous chapters, I use here the capital-labor ratio, K/L, or the capital stock of the average plant, K/N, as proxy for the cost of setting up a plant of minimum efficient scale (net of resale value). I use either one of these proxies in regressions with the price-cost margin as dependent variable. However, in regressions where the number of firms or plants is the dependent variable or directly enters into the definition of the dependent variable, I use only K/L, since the use of K/N would not be appropriate.[11]

---

10. The data set also contains four industries that were affected by the nationalization of steel in 1967 and had restrictive agreements that were abandoned *after* 1963. Since the nationalization of steel made the figures on firm numbers and profitability after 1967 irrelevant, only the 1954–1963 observations for these industries were included in my data. During this period the collusive agreements were still in place in these industries, so I chose to classify them as industries with no change in competition regime. Note that the results are barely affected if these industries are dropped from the sample. I also treated in the same way a fifth industry, telecommunications equipment (MLH 363), where collusion continued until 1963 and then fully broke down only in some sections of the industry. Thus I included only the 1954–1963 observations for this industry in my data set.

11. Recall that since all the empirical models estimated in this book include industry-specific effects, one need not assume that K/L or K/N is an accurate measure of setup cost. All that is required is that *changes* in K/L or K/N are accurate measures of the *change* in setup cost, which does not seem implausible.

Estimates of net capital stock, defined as plant and machinery, are available from O'Mahony and Oulton (1990) at the three-digit level of aggregation (i.e., for Census MLH industries). Recall that in previous chapters my approach was to use these three-digit figures on the assumption that changes in K/L and K/N over time would be roughly similar for all four-digit industries within any given three-digit industry. In fact, in previous chapters there was no alternative but to make this assumption, because of data limitations. In the present chapter there is an alternative, namely, to adjust the capital stock estimates on the basis of Census data on the fraction of investment on plant and machinery accounted for by each "principal product" within any given three-digit MLH industry.

A very simple adjustment was applied: the three-digit industry capital stock was in each case multiplied by the ratio of principal product investment to MLH industry investment, averaged over two years. For example, my estimate for the 1963 capital stock in the principal product "coffee" was the 1963 capital stock of the MLH industry "miscellaneous food products" multiplied by the ratio of investment in coffee over total investment in the MLH industry averaged over 1958 and 1963.[12] These estimates of capital stock were then matched with employment data or with data on plant numbers at the same level of aggregation. The figures on investment, employment, and plant numbers were taken from the Census of Production (various years). Again, minor corrections were made to some of these figures to ensure comparability over time.

The adjustment applied here to the capital stock figures is admittedly rough. However, it should produce reasonable approximations of capital stock, or at least of *changes* in capital stock, at the four-digit industry level. As it turns out, the regression results are largely similar whether I use the three-digit industry estimates of K/L and K/N, as in previous chapters, or my more refined four-digit industry estimates of K/L and K/N derived using the procedure outlined above. The only significant difference between the two sets of results is that the use of the adjusted data results in larger coefficients and t-statistics on the setup cost proxy itself. This suggests (1) that the adjustment is

---

12. For 1954, the first year in the sample, it was not possible to average relative investment over two years. Therefore the three-digit industry capital stock was multiplied by the ratio of principal product investment to MLH industry investment for 1954.

in the right direction and (2) that any further refinement of the capital stock estimates would not affect the results for the variables of interest, namely, those capturing the competition effect.

Note that an additional important implication of these comparisons is that any measurement error in the three-digit industry estimates of K/L and K/N used *in previous chapters* has not significantly affected the results for the variables of interest. The results reported in section 7.5 are those obtained using the adjusted capital stock data.

Of course, one should be aware of the limitations of these data. These originate not only from my own rough procedure for deriving estimates at the four-digit industry level, but also from imperfections in the Census investment figures and the O'Mahony and Oulton methodology for constructing the three-digit industry capital stock estimates. These limitations have been discussed in detail in chapter 4, section 4.4. As a result, O'Mahony and Oulton are somewhat cautious about the accuracy of their estimates of the *level* of capital stock in different years, and tend to rely more on their estimates of the *change* in capital stock across years.

Finally, a remark on the interpretation of the capital-labor ratio in profit equations may be in order. This variable, or the capital-output ratio, has often been used in profitability studies to control for the fact that the endogenous variable, namely, the price-cost margin or the rate of return on capital, includes the gross return to capital. In the present study, the capital-labor ratio is seen as a proxy for setup cost. This is not a real difference, however, since the setup cost is essentially the cost of installing capital (plant and machinery).

Union power has often been found to have a positive effect on profitability in empirical studies of the effects of unions, and this result is consistent with theoretical models of firm-union bargaining. I therefore include in this chapter a proxy for union power among the regressors in some specifications. The measure used is union density, defined as the number of unionized employees over the total number of employees. Data on this variable for the period examined here are available at a level of aggregation between the two-digit industry and the three-digit industry level, and were taken from Bain and Price (1980).

A potential objection to including a proxy for union power among the regressors is that this variable could be endogenous. For instance, the prospect of plant closures following an increase in the intensity of competition might lead to a reduction of union power, to the extent that this prospect represents a bigger threat for the welfare of workers than for that of shareholders or managers. While this argument may be correct under many circumstances, it is less obvious that the same objection applies to union density, which is the proxy used here: union membership will not necessarily fall when the bargaining power of the union decreases as a result of changes in the competitive environment.[13] Essentially, union density is seen here as a variable that picks up primarily exogenous influences on union power. In any case, because of measurement and potential endogeneity problems, results are reported below both with and without union density as one of the regressors.

This chapter presents results for a basic sample, pooling exogenous sunk cost, advertising-intensive, and R&D-intensive industries, as well as for a subsample of exogenous sunk cost industries, defined as industries with an average or typical advertising-sales ratio of less than 1% *and* an average or typical R&D-sales ratio of less than 1% over the relevant period. The procedure used to determine these ratios was essentially the same as the one used in previous chapters; details have been given in chapter 4. The only significant new complication was the generally low advertising-sales ratios for 1954, sometimes even for industries with high advertising intensity in later years. Since the 1954 advertising levels are often not typical, I largely ignored them and used mostly the advertising-sales ratios during the period 1958–1968 (or 1958–1973 whenever relevant) to classify the industries according to their typical advertising intensity.

7.5 Empirical Models and Results

To study the joint effect of price competition on market structure and performance, in this section I estimate reduced-form equations derived from the theory sketched in section 7.2. According to this theory, market structure and profits are both endogenous and determined by the same set of exogenous variables. These include market size, the level of setup costs or scale economies, the intensity of price competition, union power, and various time-invariant industry-

---

13. For instance, it may be the case that although the monetary benefits from union membership decrease when the union's bargaining power in wage negotiations declines, many workers also think that being union members could reduce their chances of being laid off.

specific characteristics (such as the degree of product differentiation or the elasticity of demand).

Some of the theoretical predictions of this chapter would best be tested using data for net profit (i.e., gross profit minus fixed costs). Unfortunately, it is not possible to construct measures of net profit with the data available. As pointed out above, the capital stock figures are estimates, and while the estimated proportional changes in capital stock over time in any given industry are reasonably accurate, the estimated levels should be treated with caution. As a result, only measures of gross profit can be used. While this is a limitation of the present analysis, it should be emphasized that the theory also provides several predictions regarding gross profit.

Thus a key prediction is that the industry gross profit divided by the number of plants should not change significantly following an intensification of price competition. This will not be true if, contrary to what the present theory maintains, cartels generally deter entry in long-run equilibrium. Moreover, a key insight of the present theory is that profitability should initially decline following a rise in the intensity of price competition, and then be restored, or partially restored, through a fall in firm numbers. None of the alternative theories discussed in section 7.2 can accommodate this prediction. Finally, if it can be shown that the long-run effect of cartel laws on the industry price-cost margin is not significant, on average, across industries, then total industry gross profit will not fall in the long run—under the plausible assumption that industry output does not fall as a result of more intense price competition. Provided that total industry sunk costs do not rise as a result of more intense competition—which, in a model with exogenously determined setup costs, is equivalent to saying that the number of plants does not rise—total industry *net* profit will not fall in the long run: cartel laws, in this case, definitely will not be bad for business.

The Samples and Descriptive Statistics

The basic sample of industries for this chapter contains 201 industries and 760 observations. I excluded industries with ambiguous state of competition in 1958 (or, in a few cases, in the 1960s and early 1970s), as well as industries without at least two available observations for the core period 1958–1968 (i.e., industries with data available only for 1954–1958 or 1968–1973). The sample of exogenous

Table 7.1
The samples used in the econometric analysis

Data available for	No. of indus-tries with $CHANGE = 1$	No. of indus-tries with $CHANGE = 0$	No. of exogenous sunk cost indus-tries with $CHANGE = 1$	No. of exogenous sunk cost indus-tries with $CHANGE = 0$
All five years	16	30 (1 collusive)	10	15 (1 collusive)
1954, 1958, 1963, 1968	39	49 (1 collusive)	35	32 (1 collusive)
1958, 1963, 1968, 1973	0	2	0	1
1954, 1958, 1963	6	19 (3 collusive)	5	9 (2 collusive)
1958, 1963, 1968	7	1	7	0
1963, 1968, 1973	2	5	2	0
1958, 1963	4	4 (3 collusive)	3	3 (3 collusive)
1963, 1968	3	14	3	9
Total	77	124	65	69

Note: The group of industries without a change in competition regime after 1958 includes three industries where collusion continued throughout 1954–1973 and five industries where collusion continued for the entire period for which I have data in my sample (including four industries affected by the nationalization of steel in 1967).

sunk cost industries was derived from the basic sample by dropping all industries with typical advertising-sales ratio (ADS) or typical R&D-sales ratio (RDS) higher than 1% over the relevant period; it contains 134 industries and 502 observations. One difference between these samples and those used in previous chapters is that I have here included *all* industries with available observations for only two of the three core years 1958, 1963, and 1968—and not just those without a change of competition regime. Table 7.1 gives details on the structure of both samples. The full set of industries and information on key variables can be found in table B6 of appendix B.

Descriptive statistics on initial levels of profit and market structure measures are presented in table 7.2. In particular, the table reports means and standard deviations of five different variables in 1954 and 1958, separately for industries with a change in competition regime after 1958 and industries without such a change. The variables are the number of firms, NFIRMS; the number of plants, NPLANTS; the industry gross profit (i.e., the net value of output minus wages and salaries) divided by the number of plants and deflated by the general

Table 7.2
Initial conditions (1954, 1958) in industries affected by the 1956 Act and in industries not affected

	Mean (st. deviation) of ln NFIRMS	Mean (st. deviation) of ln NPLANTS	Mean (st. deviation) of ln PLANTPROFIT	Mean (st. deviation) of ln FIRMPROFIT	Mean (st. deviation) of PCM
All industries with CHANGE = 1 (n = 55)					
1954	4.17 (0.96)	4.53 (0.93)	4.22 (0.85)	4.57 (0.91)	0.169 (0.063)
1958	4.06 (0.92)	4.47 (0.90)	4.29 (0.89)	4.70 (0.95)	0.170 (0.061)
All industries with CHANGE = 0 (n = 79)					
1954	4.24 (1.16)	4.56 (1.08)	4.09 (1.10)	4.39 (1.23)	0.181 (0.080)
1958	4.10 (1.13)	4.43 (1.08)	4.20 (1.15)	4.51 (1.25)	0.175 (0.078)
Exogenous sunk cost industries with CHANGE = 1 (n = 45)					
1954	4.20 (0.95)	4.54 (0.93)	4.05 (0.77)	4.39 (0.83)	0.168 (0.065)
1958	4.08 (0.90)	4.48 (0.90)	4.08 (0.80)	4.48 (0.86)	0.168 (0.064)
Exogenous sunk cost industries with CHANGE = 0 (n = 47)					
1954	4.55 (1.01)	4.86 (0.94)	3.65 (0.86)	3.95 (1.00)	0.156 (0.050)
1958	4.43 (1.00)	4.74 (0.93)	3.65 (0.84)	3.98 (0.98)	0.144 (0.042)

Notes: The figures are based on industries with available data for both 1954 and 1958. The figures for ln NFIRMS and ln FIRMPROFIT are based on 77 (rather than 79) industries with CHANGE = 0 and 46 (rather than 47) exogenous sunk cost industries with CHANGE = 0. The group of industries without a change in regime includes 8 collusive industries (7 in the exogenous sunk cost sample). n indicates the number of industries.

producer price index for all manufacturing, *PLANTPROFIT*; the deflated industry gross profit divided by the number of firms, *FIRMPROFIT*; and the price-cost margin, *PCM*, defined as the net value of output minus wages and salaries divided by sales revenue. For the first four of these variables a log transformation is used. The figures are based on industries with available data for both 1954 and 1958, and therefore can also provide information on the evolution of profits and market structure across different groups of industries before the implementation of the 1956 legislation.

The first thing to note is that there is little difference in initial conditions between industries affected by the 1956 Act and those in the control group, especially when one looks at the full sample. Note that the price-cost margin is slightly higher for industries in the control group on the basis of the full sample, but lower when focusing on exogenous sunk cost industries. This is partly due to the fact that advertising-intensive and R&D-intensive industries tend to have higher price-cost margins and also are less likely to be collusive than exogenous sunk cost industries.

Even more interesting is the comparison of the 1954–1958 changes in the two groups. The evolution of ln *NFIRMS* and ln *NPLANTS* was very similar in the two groups, especially that of ln *NFIRMS*. Thus, on the basis of the raw data at least, one can argue that any differences observed after 1958 should be attributed to the legislation rather than to any preexisting differential trend in the two groups. This is important not only for this chapter but also for previous chapters, since a key assumption throughout this book has been that the results regarding the competition effect on market structure are not subject to any significant bias caused by the potential endogeneity of the competition variable *CHANGE*.[14]

---

14. It is also interesting in this respect to check the 1954–1958 change of ln *NFIRMS* *specifically* in advertising-intensive and R&D-intensive industries. In each case, there are only a few industries with *CHANGE* = 1, so the results should be interpreted with some caution. Consider first the subsample of R&D-intensive industries with available data for 1954 and 1958. The average value of ln *NFIRMS* decreased from 4.55 in 1954 to 4.45 in 1958 in the six industries with *CHANGE* = 1, while it decreased from 3.47 to 3.36 in the sixteen industries with *CHANGE* = 0. Clearly, there is almost no difference between the two groups.

Next, consider the subsample of advertising-intensive industries with available data for 1954 and 1958. The average value of ln *NFIRMS* fell from 3.84 to 3.73 in the six industries with *CHANGE* = 1, while it fell from 3.80 to 3.67 in the twenty-five industries with *CHANGE* = 0. Again, there is very little difference between the two groups.

On the other hand, the average *PCM* was roughly constant between 1954 and 1958 in industries with *CHANGE* = 1 but declined somewhat in industries with *CHANGE* = 0. This decline was not large, at least for the full sample: about half a percentage point. Moreover, it can be argued that if it turns out that the average *PCM* declined during 1958–1963 in industries with a change in the intensity of competition relative to the control group, then this must surely be the effect of the 1956 legislation, since the trend was, if anything, the opposite before 1958. I will return to these issues when discussing the regression results below.

Table 7.3 presents statistics on the average change in each of the five endogenous variables of interest over 1958–1963 and 1963–1968. (There are considerably fewer observations for 1973 than for 1958–1968, so descriptive statistics for 1958–1973 would be less informative.) In both periods, ln *NFIRMS* and ln *NPLANTS* decreased considerably more, on average, in industries with a change in competition regime than in industries without such a change. For the period 1958–1968 as a whole, the number of firms in the former group fell by about 45%, while it fell by only about 20% in the latter group. Also, the number of plants fell by about 25% in the former group, compared to 8% in the latter. Of course, these comparisons do not control for changes in other variables; still, the differences between the two groups are very large indeed.[15]

With respect to the profit measures, a different picture emerges. Consider the price-cost margin, which is perhaps the "cleaner" of the three measures, since it is not directly affected by the changes in firm and plant numbers. The most interesting figures are those for the whole sample. In both groups of industries the average *PCM* increased over 1958–1963 and over 1963–1968. However, during 1958–1963 the rise was larger for industries with *CHANGE* = 0 by about

---

15. Another interesting comparison is between industries with a large increase in ln *NFIRMS* over 1958–1968 and industries with a large decrease in ln *NFIRMS* over the same period. The comparison is limited to 144 industries with available data for both these years. Of the five industries with the largest rise in ln *NFIRMS*, only one (builders' woodwork and prefabricated timber buildings) has *CHANGE* = 1, while four (tufted carpets, carpeting, and carpet floor rugs; powered industrial trucks and industrial tractors; plastic products; fiberboard packing cases) have *CHANGE* = 0. In contrast, of the five industries with the largest fall in ln *NFIRMS*, three (lime and whiting; bread and flour confectionery; spun cotton yarns) are industries with *CHANGE* = 1, and two (loom state cloth of cotton; tiles, other than of precast concrete and brick-earth) have *CHANGE* = 0.

Table 7.3
Average change in ln $NFIRMS$, ln $NPLANTS$, ln $PLANTPROFIT$, ln $FIRMPROFIT$, and PCM, 1958–1963 and 1963–1968

	Δln $NFIRMS$	Δln $NPLANTS$	Δln $PLANTPROFIT$	Δln $FIRMPROFIT$	ΔPCM
All industries with CHANGE = 1 (n = 62)					
1958–1963	−0.18 (0.24)	−0.09 (0.23)	0.35 (0.30)	0.44 (0.30)	0.024 (0.033)
1963–1968	−0.20 (0.22)	−0.15 (0.22)	0.29 (0.25)	0.33 (0.29)	0.012 (0.035)
All industries with CHANGE = 0 (n = 82)					
1958–1963	−0.09 (0.32)	−0.03 (0.34)	0.40 (0.26)	0.47 (0.28)	0.032 (0.033)
1963–1968	−0.09 (0.22)	−0.05 (0.22)	0.24 (0.31)	0.27 (0.31)	0.004 (0.044)
Exogenous sunk cost industries with CHANGE = 1 (n = 52)					
1958–1963	−0.19 (0.25)	−0.10 (0.24)	0.35 (0.29)	0.44 (0.29)	0.024 (0.030)
1963–1968	−0.22 (0.22)	−0.16 (0.22)	0.28 (0.26)	0.33 (0.30)	0.011 (0.036)
Exogenous sunk cost industries with CHANGE = 0 (n = 48)					
1958–1963	−0.12 (0.24)	−0.07 (0.26)	0.43 (0.22)	0.48 (0.24)	0.033 (0.022)
1963–1968	−0.11 (0.19)	−0.08 (0.19)	0.23 (0.29)	0.26 (0.25)	0.012 (0.038)

Notes: The figures are based on industries with available data for 1958, 1963, and 1968. The figures in parentheses are standard deviations. n denotes the number of industries.

one percentage point, while the exact opposite is the case for 1963–1968. In other words, the average *PCM* in industries with *CHANGE* = 1 *fell* during 1958–1963 by about one percentage point *relative to the control group of industries*, but it recovered during 1963–1968.[16] In exogenous sunk cost industries, on the other hand, we still have a relative fall in *PCM* during 1958–1963 in industries where price competition intensified, but no obvious recovery during 1963–1968. Admittedly, these changes are not large, and it is difficult to draw any conclusions on the basis of these statistics alone. To unravel the link between changes in market structure and changes in profitability in industries affected by the 1956 Restrictive Trade Practices Act, I now turn to the econometric analysis.

The Econometric Model

As in previous chapters, I will use a panel data model with individual-specific effects. These control for industry characteristics that affect market structure and profitability but are relatively stable over time, such as the degree of horizontal differentiation and the elasticity of demand. Time dummies will also be included among the regressors in an attempt to control for other factors that may have influenced the evolution of market structure and profitability over the period examined, such as changes in the tax system in the mid-1960s that are thought to have encouraged mergers; improvements in the system of transport; economies of scale in product development, distribution, and the raising of finance; the progressive opening of the British economy; the UK government's prices and incomes policies between 1965 and 1973; and macroeconomic fluctuations. It is very difficult to measure these factors at the industry level, but it is plausible to assume that their effect would have been more or less realized equally across all industries, or at least that there would not be a systematic

16. Two of the five industries with the largest increase in *PCM* between 1958 and 1968 have *CHANGE* = 1: clay, brick-earth, marl, shale, and chalk; and domestic hollow-ware. The other three are finished thread; electrical equipment for motor vehicles, cycles, and aircraft, excluding accumulators (secondary batteries); and powered industrial trucks and industrial tractors. Similarly, two of the five industries with the largest decrease in *PCM* between 1958 and 1968 have *CHANGE* = 1: cotton waste yarns; and electrical ware of porcelain, earthenware, or stoneware. The other three are British wines, alcoholic cider, and perry (fermented pear juice); photographic and document copying equipment; and margarine.

difference between previously collusive and noncollusive industries
with respect to these factors. Some indirect evidence supporting this
statement for the case of import competition was discussed in chapter 4.

The basic specification for the number of firms is

$$\ln NFIRMS_{it} = \alpha_i + \beta_1 \ln SS_{it} + \beta_2 \ln(K/L)_{it} + \beta_3 Y54 + \beta_4 Y63 + \beta_5 Y68$$
$$+ \beta_6 Y73 + \beta_7 CHANGE * Y54 + \beta_8 CHANGE * Y63$$
$$+ \beta_9 CHANGE * Y68 + \beta_{10} CHANGE * Y73 + u_{it},$$

and similarly for the number of plants. SS is the industry sales revenue deflated by the general producer price index;[17] K/L is the capital-
labor ratio; $Y54$, $Y63$, $Y68$, and $Y73$ are time dummies for 1954, 1963,
1968, and 1973, respectively; and the interaction terms should pick
up any differences after 1958 between industries with a change in
competition regime and industries without such a change. Thus the
coefficient on $CHANGE * Y63$ ($CHANGE * Y68$, $CHANGE * Y73$)
measures the effect of the 1956 Act between 1958 and 1963 (1968,
1973). The benchmark year is 1958, since it is generally accepted that
the Act had little effect on competition before then. The coefficient on
$CHANGE * Y54$ serves as an indirect check of the presumption that
the evolution of market structure during 1954–1958 was not significantly different between the two groups of industries. $CHANGE$ is
defined here (and in the profit regressions below) according to the
industry categories used for the endogenous variables. In some
regressions the variable $UNION$, which denotes union density, is also
included.

The estimated model for each of the three profit measures defined
above is

$$\ln Profit\ measure_{it} = \alpha_i + \gamma_1 \ln SS_{it} + \gamma_2 \ln(K/x)_{it} + \gamma_3 Y54 + \gamma_4 Y63 + \gamma_5 Y68$$
$$+ \gamma_6 Y73 + \gamma_7 CHANGE * Y54 + \gamma_8 CHANGE * Y63$$
$$+ \gamma_9 CHANGE * Y68 + \gamma_{10} CHANGE * Y73 + e_{it},$$

where the "profit measure" is $\ln PLANTPROFIT$, $\ln FIRMPROFIT$ or

---

17. As mentioned in section 7.4, the potential endogeneity of prices, especially in profit
regressions, suggests using the general producer price index for all manufacturing as a
deflator of sales revenue (a measure of market size). Using industry-specific price indices as deflators gave results broadly similar to those reported here.

PCM; "K/x" is either the capital stock of the average plant, K/N, or the capital-labor ratio, K/L; and the other variables are the same as above. Again, *UNION* is sometimes also included as an additional regressor.[18]

This specification is very different from those typically used in "traditional" studies of the link between market structure and profitability (such as Cowling and Waterson 1976, or Hart and Morgan 1977), or in the literature on the effects of economic integration on profitability. In these studies, a measure of market structure is always included among the regressors. My specification, on the other hand, is a reduced-form equation derived from a theoretical model in which market structure and profit are both endogenous. As pointed out in the introduction to this chapter, the model's predictions regarding the effect of a change in the intensity of price competition on profitability depend on allowing market structure to change to restore the long-run equilibrium. It is therefore important for testing these predictions that one does not control for changes in market structure when specifying the profit equation.

Note that a simultaneous-equations approach cannot be used here because it is difficult to find any variable that affects the number of firms and does not also influence profitability. Nevertheless, the reduced-form equations can still provide important insights on the interaction between market structure and profitability through a comparison of short-run and long-run effects of competition, as will be shown later in this chapter.[19]

---

18. The denominator of *PCM* is sales revenue. Some studies (e.g., Hart and Morgan 1977, Conyon and Machin 1991) have used net output as the denominator of *PCM* on the grounds that net output, unlike sales revenue, is not influenced by input prices, duties and subsidies, and the degree of vertical integration within an industry. These arguments are more important for cross-section studies than for studies using panel data. In any case, regressions using this alternative definition of *PCM* gave results similar to those reported here.

19. Let me also point out again that a dynamic panel data model cannot be used in the present context because of data limitations. Since the years in my panel are separated by periods of four to five years, however, it is not clear that there should be any significant effect of lagged values of the endogenous variables because of adjustment lags or for other reasons. Also, some of the other arguments advanced in the context of the concentration regressions of chapter 4 may be of relevance here as well, namely, that the econometric specification used allows the competition effect to operate with a lag, that setup costs are measured somewhat imprecisely anyway, and that there is no evidence of significant serial correlation in the residuals of the models estimated in this chapter.

Estimation Results

The model has been estimated for the whole sample as well as for the
sample of exogenous sunk cost industries and the results are presented
in tables 7.4–7.6. All the results are for a fixed-effects specification.[20]
The reported standard errors are heteroskedasticity-consistent, adjusted for small sample bias following MacKinnon and White (1985).
As in previous regressions using fixed-effects estimation, two different R^2's are reported: the first does not include the fixed industry
effects, while the second does.[21]

Table 7.4 contains regression results for $\ln NFIRMS$ and
$\ln NPLANTS$. Note that in the regressions using the whole sample,
interaction variables are used to control for possible differences between exogenous sunk cost, advertising-intensive, and R&D-intensive
industries with respect to the effect of market size on the number of
firms or plants. In particular, $AD2 * \ln SS$ ($RD2 * \ln SS$) is equal to
$\ln SS$ for industries with typical or average ADS (RDS) higher than
2% over the relevant period and to 0 for industries with ADS (RDS)
lower than 2%.[22]

The results in table 7.4 suggest that the 1956 Act had a strong
and statistically significant negative effect on the number of firms
in the long run. This effect was only partly realized by 1963, and it
was mostly realized by 1968. The magnitude of the coefficient on
$CHANGE * Y73$ implies that the intensification of price competition
following the 1956 Act reduced the number of firms by about 12%
in the average industry between 1958 and 1973. For exogenous sunk

---

20. The Hausman test always rejects the random-effects model. In any case, the results
from this model with respect to the competition effect are similar to those obtained
using fixed-effects estimation.

21. The reported results are for models with standard i.i.d. residuals. I also estimated a
model with an AR1 error structure, and the results were very similar to those reported
here. The estimated coefficient of serial correlation in these regressions was very low
(and often even negative): around 0.05 in market structure regressions, and between
−0.05 and −0.20 in profit regressions.

22. I also experimented with alternative interaction variables—using 1% instead of 2%
as the cutoff point—but these were not statistically significant. In preliminary regressions, I also included such interaction variables for the competition effect, but they
were not statistically significant, either individually or jointly. Note that whether
an industry's typical advertising-sales ratio or R&D-sales ratio over a period of ten or
twenty years is higher or lower than 2% is largely determined by exogenous characteristics such as advertising effectiveness and technological opportunity, so the interaction variables are not endogenous.

cost industries in particular, the effect was even stronger: a fall of about 15% or more. This may understate the impact of competition to the extent that there is measurement error in the construction of CHANGE as a result of ineffective or unregistered agreements.

The effect of competition on the number of plants was somewhat weaker: the coefficients on $CHANGE * Y68$ and $CHANGE * Y73$ in regressions with $\ln NPLANTS$ are negative but smaller in absolute value than the corresponding coefficients in regressions with $\ln NFIRMS$, and usually are not statistically significant at the 5% level. This implies that while much of the structural adjustment in British manufacturing following the 1956 legislation took the form of exit, mergers were also part of the process, and hence the reduction in firm numbers was more pronounced than the reduction in plant numbers. (Recall that the theory developed in this book allows for both exit and mergers as a result of tougher competition.)

Finally, note that the coefficient on the capital-labor ratio is negative and usually statistically significant at the 5% level in these regressions, while that on market size is positive and statistically significant at the 1% level. A comparison with the coefficients on the interaction variables $AD2 * \ln SS$ and $RD2 * \ln SS$ suggests that market size has a positive effect on firm or plant numbers across all classes of industries, although this effect is less pronounced in advertising-intensive industries.[23]

Table 7.5 presents results for $\ln PLANTPROFIT$ and $\ln FIRMPROFIT$. The first of these variables may be the one more closely associated with the theory described in section 7.2. This is because the capital-labor ratio is meant to control for setup costs at the *plant* level. (Note, in this respect, that the coefficient on $\ln K/L$, which is everywhere positive and statistically significant, is larger in regressions with $\ln PLANTPROFIT$ than in regressions with $\ln FIRMPROFIT$.) To the extent that the plant-to-firm ratio increases, gross profit per firm could rise relative to gross profit per plant if there are significant economies of multiplant operation. The results in table 7.5 provide no evidence of any significant impact of the 1956 Act on the gross profit of the average plant, which is consistent with the theory. More-

---

23. It is not surprising that differences across classes of industries with respect to the market size effect on firm numbers are not significant. Numerous small firms in advertising-intensive and R&D-intensive industries spend little or nothing on advertising or R&D, and may produce secondary industry products. The endogenous sunk cost models of chapters 5 and 6 (or of Sutton 1991, 1998) are not relevant for these firms.

Table 7.4
Regression results for ln *NFIRMS* and ln *NPLANTS* (fixed-effects estimation)

	Dependent variable: ln *FIRMS*				Dependent variable: ln *PLANTS*			
	All industries		Exogenous sunk cost industries		All industries		Exogenous sunk cost industries	
ln *SS*	0.582	0.581	0.518	0.515	0.658	0.658	0.605	0.604
	(0.041)	(0.041)	(0.041)	(0.040)	(0.031)	(0.031)	(0.031)	(0.031)
ln *K/L*	−0.065	−0.064	−0.108	−0.110	−0.125	−0.124	−0.138	−0.138
	(0.047)	(0.047)	(0.055)	(0.055)	(0.041)	(0.041)	(0.048)	(0.048)
UNION	—	−0.346	—	−0.514	—	−0.209	—	−0.194
		(0.293)		(0.381)		(0.226)		(0.286)
Y54	0.113	0.119	0.080	0.086	0.100	0.103	0.063	0.065
	(0.024)	(0.025)	(0.030)	(0.030)	(0.024)	(0.024)	(0.028)	(0.029)
Y63	−0.182	−0.177	−0.191	−0.184	−0.102	−0.099	−0.114	−0.111
	(0.022)	(0.022)	(0.026)	(0.026)	(0.021)	(0.022)	(0.025)	(0.025)
Y68	−0.351	−0.340	−0.322	−0.310	−0.234	−0.228	−0.226	−0.222
	(0.034)	(0.034)	(0.041)	(0.040)	(0.032)	(0.032)	(0.039)	(0.038)
Y73	−0.450	−0.408	−0.401	−0.355	−0.381	−0.356	−0.319	−0.302
	(0.051)	(0.059)	(0.061)	(0.067)	(0.045)	(0.052)	(0.053)	(0.056)
CHANGE ∗ *Y54*	0.004	0.005	0.028	0.030	−0.054	−0.054	−0.028	−0.027
	(0.040)	(0.040)	(0.045)	(0.045)	(0.035)	(0.035)	(0.041)	(0.041)
CHANGE ∗ *Y63*	−0.037	−0.035	−0.021	−0.017	−0.025	−0.024	−0.014	−0.012
	(0.031)	(0.031)	(0.035)	(0.035)	(0.029)	(0.029)	(0.034)	(0.033)
CHANGE ∗ *Y68*	−0.095	−0.086	−0.110	−0.090	−0.063	−0.057	−0.062	−0.054
	(0.042)	(0.043)	(0.048)	(0.052)	(0.035)	(0.036)	(0.040)	(0.043)

CHANGE * Y73	-0.133	-0.119	-0.190	-0.155	-0.080	-0.071	-0.128	-0.115
	(0.061)	(0.062)	(0.066)	(0.071)	(0.054)	(0.055)	(0.061)	(0.064)
AD2 * ln SS	-0.305	-0.297	—	—	-0.300	-0.296	—	—
	(0.078)	(0.078)			(0.066)	(0.067)		
RD2 * ln SS	0.087	0.095	—	—	-0.053	-0.048	—	—
	(0.081)	(0.082)			(0.073)	(0.073)		
R^2	0.64	0.65	0.68	0.68	0.65	0.65	0.65	0.65
R^2_{LSDV}	0.98	0.98	0.98	0.98	0.98	0.98	0.98	0.98
Hausman statistic	159.8	162.9	143.6	142.7	127.4	130.9	74.4	70.1
Prob-value	≈ 0	≈ 0	≈ 0	≈ 0	≈ 0	≈ 0	≈ 0	≈ 0
No. of industries	201	201	134	134	201	201	134	134
No. of industries with CHANGE = 1	77	77	65	65	77	77	65	65
No. of observations	758	758	501	501	758	758	501	501

Note: Heteroskedasticity-consistent standard errors in parentheses.

Table 7.5
Regression results for ln *PLANTPROFIT* and ln *FIRMPROFIT* (fixed-effects estimation)

	Dependent variable: ln *FIRMPROFIT*				Dependent variable: ln *PLANTPROFIT*			
	All industries		Exogenous sunk cost industries		All industries		Exogenous sunk cost industries	
ln *SS*	0.441	0.440	0.455	0.453	0.363	0.362	0.365	0.362
	(0.058)	(0.058)	(0.059)	(0.058)	(0.054)	(0.054)	(0.051)	(0.050)
ln *K/L*	0.146	0.147	0.154	0.152	0.200	0.202	0.182	0.179
	(0.055)	(0.055)	(0.065)	(0.065)	(0.052)	(0.052)	(0.059)	(0.060)
UNION	—	−0.532	—	−0.446	—	−0.638	—	−0.767
		(0.389)		(0.421)		(0.316)		(0.361)
Y54	−0.078	−0.070	−0.018	−0.012	−0.068	−0.058	−0.003	0.007
	(0.036)	(0.036)	(0.039)	(0.039)	(0.035)	(0.035)	(0.038)	(0.037)
Y63	0.347	0.354	0.379	0.385	0.268	0.277	0.302	0.314
	(0.031)	(0.031)	(0.036)	(0.036)	(0.031)	(0.030)	(0.036)	(0.036)
Y68	0.524	0.542	0.575	0.585	0.411	0.431	0.481	0.498
	(0.046)	(0.046)	(0.052)	(0.051)	(0.044)	(0.044)	(0.050)	(0.049)
Y73	0.616	0.680	0.694	0.734	0.566	0.641	0.616	0.685
	(0.067)	(0.070)	(0.075)	(0.077)	(0.059)	(0.066)	(0.069)	(0.074)
CHANGE ∗ *Y54*	−0.043	−0.042	−0.085	−0.083	0.017	0.018	−0.026	−0.024
	(0.057)	(0.057)	(0.062)	(0.062)	(0.054)	(0.054)	(0.060)	(0.059)
CHANGE ∗ *Y63*	−0.014	−0.011	−0.031	−0.028	−0.026	−0.022	−0.038	−0.033
	(0.046)	(0.046)	(0.050)	(0.050)	(0.045)	(0.045)	(0.050)	(0.050)
CHANGE ∗ *Y68*	0.069	0.082	0.028	0.045	0.035	0.052	−0.020	0.009
	(0.055)	(0.057)	(0.061)	(0.065)	(0.050)	(0.051)	(0.056)	(0.059)

CHANGE * Y73	0.092	0.114	0.115	0.145	0.012	0.040	0.035	0.088
	(0.086)	(0.090)	(0.086)	(0.094)	(0.079)	(0.081)	(0.087)	(0.094)
AD2 * ln SS	0.250	0.261	—	—	0.242	0.257	—	—
	(0.125)	(0.125)			(0.112)	(0.113)		
RD2 * ln SS	−0.232	−0.220	—	—	−0.096	−0.081	—	—
	(0.114)	(0.115)			(0.110)	(0.112)		
R^2	0.78	0.78	0.80	0.80	0.74	0.75	0.74	0.74
R^2_{LSDV}	0.97	0.97	0.97	0.97	0.97	0.97	0.96	0.96
Hausman statistic	70.3	79.7	64.1	65.5	46.8	60.5	39.1	45.0
Prob-value	≈0	≈0	≈0	≈0	≈0	≈0	≈0	≈0
No. of industries	201	201	134	134	201	201	134	134
No. of industries with CHANGE = 1	77	77	65	65	77	77	65	65
No. of observations	758	758	501	501	758	758	501	501

Note: Heteroskedasticity-consistent standard errors in parentheses.

over, there is no evidence of any significant impact of the Act on firm gross profit either.

An interesting feature of the results in tables 7.4 and 7.5 is the magnitude of the coefficients on the year dummies. After controlling for market size, the capital-labor ratio, union density, the effect of cartel policy, and industry effects, the number of plants or firms in any given industry in 1973 was, on average, about 30–40% lower than in 1958, while the gross profit of the average plant or firm was more than 50% higher. This evolution seems to have continued an existing trend during 1954–1958.

To some extent the high coefficients on the year dummies must be due to the crudeness of the setup cost proxy used here. Since K/L was increasing across industries throughout the period, it is correlated with the time dummies; thus, to the extent that K/L is only an imperfect proxy for setup costs, and these were also increasing, their effect could be partly picked up by the time dummies. Note, in this respect, that K/L is not statistically significant at the 5% level in some regressions for ln $FIRMS$, and that in random-effects specifications its explanatory power is considerably higher while that of the time dummies is somewhat lower. Moreover, the time dummies may be capturing the effect of scale economies not directly associated with the cost of plant and machinery, such as scale economies in marketing or the raising of finance. Finally, some of the apparent explanatory power of the time dummies may simply be due to the unbalanced structure of the panel.

Still, it is difficult to escape the conclusion that much of the fall in firm and plant numbers during this period was due to factors not explicitly included in the present theory. This, of course, does not invalidate the comparison between industries affected by the 1956 Act and industries not affected, to the extent that these other factors are not correlated with the variable $CHANGE$.

While the results in table 7.5 are consistent with the theory, the discussion in the previous paragraph and the fact that the overall changes in ln $PLANTPROFIT$ and ln $FIRMPROFIT$ reflect to a large extent the significant decrease in firm and plant numbers during the 1950s and the 1960s suggest that it is also necessary to consider other profit measures in order to assess the impact of the 1956 Act on firms' profits. A measure not directly influenced by firm or plant numbers, such as the price-cost margin, should be particularly useful.

Table 7.6 reports the results. The first thing to note is that the coefficients on $CHANGE * Y68$ and $CHANGE * Y73$ are small and nowhere statistically significant, even at the 10% level. The failure to detect any long-run effect of price competition on the price-cost margin is consistent with the theory developed in this book. In particular, it justifies the Selten-Sutton emphasis on the effect of firm conduct on market structure rather than on profits. Of the other variables, $\ln K/L$ and $\ln K/N$ have a positive effect on PCM, while union density has a negative effect, as expected. The time dummies may again be picking up some of the effect of scale economies on the price-cost margin, given that $\ln K/L$ and $\ln K/N$ are imperfect proxies for setup cost. These results are hardly affected if the sales variable, which is nowhere statistically significant, is dropped.

It is also very interesting to compare the short-run and the long-run impact of competition. This may be the most decisive test of the present theory, which predicts a particular link between the evolution of market structure and the evolution of profitability in the short run and in the long run. Table 7.4 shows that the effect of the 1956 Act on market structure was modest over the period 1958–1963; on the other hand, it was between 1963 and 1968 that most of the restructuring of previously cartelized industries occurred. Moreover, the overall picture from table 7.6 (despite small differences across regressions) is that price-cost margins declined, on average, between 1958 and 1963 in these industries, before recovering mostly during 1963–1968. Note that the coefficient on $CHANGE * Y63$ is everywhere negative and typically statistically significant at the 5% or the 10% level, while the coefficients on $CHANGE * Y68$ and $CHANGE * Y73$ are sometimes positive, sometimes negative, and nowhere statistically significant.

This is precisely the sort of link the theory predicts between the evolution of market structure and the evolution of profitability in previously collusive industries: a moderate effect on the number of firms by 1963, at which date several industries were in short-run disequilibrium with reduced margins (including industries where the adjustment of concentration to its long-run value was being delayed by a slow rate of depreciation of the capital stock); then a significant negative effect on firm numbers between 1963 and 1968, leading to a rise in price-cost margins in these industries.

The coefficient on $CHANGE * Y63$ in regressions with PCM, although typically significant at the 5% or 10% level, is nevertheless

Table 7.6
Regression results for PCM (fixed-effects estimation)

| | Dependent variable: PCM | | | | | | | |
	All industries				Exogenous sunk cost industries			
ln SS	0.008	0.006	0.008	0.005	0.004	0.002	0.003	0.001
	(0.007)	(0.006)	(0.006)	(0.006)	(0.007)	(0.007)	(0.006)	(0.006)
ln K/L	0.020	—	0.021	—	0.014	—	0.014	—
	(0.007)		(0.007)		(0.008)		(0.008)	
ln K/N	—	0.012	—	0.013	—	0.007	—	0.007
		(0.006)		(0.006)		(0.007)		(0.007)
UNION	—	—	−0.177	−0.176	—	—	−0.186	−0.188
			(0.042)	(0.041)			(0.051)	(0.051)
Y54	0.006	0.005	0.008	0.008	0.010	0.009	0.012	0.011
	(0.004)	(0.004)	(0.004)	(0.004)	(0.005)	(0.005)	(0.005)	(0.005)
Y63	0.029	0.030	0.031	0.033	0.030	0.032	0.033	0.034
	(0.004)	(0.004)	(0.004)	(0.004)	(0.005)	(0.005)	(0.005)	(0.005)
Y68	0.026	0.030	0.032	0.035	0.036	0.040	0.040	0.043
	(0.006)	(0.006)	(0.005)	(0.005)	(0.006)	(0.006)	(0.006)	(0.006)
Y73	0.021	0.030	0.042	0.050	0.040	0.046	0.057	0.062
	(0.009)	(0.009)	(0.009)	(0.009)	(0.011)	(0.010)	(0.010)	(0.009)
CHANGE * Y54	−0.003	−0.003	−0.003	−0.003	−0.005	−0.005	−0.005	−0.005
	(0.007)	(0.007)	(0.006)	(0.006)	(0.007)	(0.007)	(0.007)	(0.007)
CHANGE * Y63	−0.012	−0.012	−0.011	−0.011	−0.011	−0.011	−0.009	−0.009
	(0.006)	(0.006)	(0.006)	(0.006)	(0.007)	(0.007)	(0.007)	(0.007)

CHANGE * Y68	-0.004	-0.004	0.001	0.001	-0.010	-0.010	-0.003	-0.003
	(0.006)	(0.006)	(0.007)	(0.006)	(0.007)	(0.007)	(0.008)	(0.008)
CHANGE * Y73	-0.003	-0.011	0.004	-0.003	-0.008	-0.014	0.004	-0.001
	(0.011)	(0.011)	(0.011)	(0.011)	(0.013)	(0.013)	(0.013)	(0.014)
AD2 * ln SS	-0.013	-0.015	-0.009	-0.012	—	—	—	—
	(0.015)	(0.015)	(0.015)	(0.015)				
RD2 * ln SS	-0.025	-0.026	-0.021	-0.022	—	—	—	—
	(0.014)	(0.014)	(0.014)	(0.014)				
R^2	0.28	0.28	0.31	0.30	0.33	0.32	0.36	0.35
R^2_{LSDV}	0.89	0.89	0.89	0.89	0.88	0.88	0.88	0.88
Hausman statistic	29.6	29.2	39.6	37.5	19.8	17.7	28.9	26.6
Prob-value	0.003	0.004	0.0002	0.0004	0.03	0.06	0.002	0.005
No. of industries	201	201	201	201	134	134	134	134
No. of industries with CHANGE = 1	77	77	77	77	65	65	65	65
No. of observations	760	758	760	758	502	501	502	501

Note: Heteroskedasticity-consistent standard errors in parentheses.

not large: about one percentage point. This is consistent with the evidence from the descriptive statistics of table 7.3. It has to be borne in mind that only a subset of the previously cartelized industries were in short-run disequilibrium in 1963. In several industries competition had not yet emerged, and there must have been several others where competition had emerged and much of the adjustment of market structure had already taken place. Thus the magnitude of the coefficient on $CHANGE * Y63$ should not be taken as a measure of the fall in the price-cost margin following a change of competition regime and prior to any adjustment of market structure; this is likely to be much larger than one percentage point.

Several additional remarks are in order. First, the econometric analysis confirms that the potential endogeneity of $CHANGE$ does not seem to be a source of significant bias in the results. Recall that an indirect check of this claim is to compare the evolution of market structure and profitability between industries with $CHANGE = 1$ and industries with $CHANGE = 0$ *before* 1958. I have already emphasized that the descriptive statistics provide no evidence that the differences between the two groups after 1958 could be attributed to a preexisting differential trend. This is confirmed by the econometric analysis. Thus the coefficient on $CHANGE * Y54$ is nowhere statistically significant, even at the 20% level, suggesting that there was no difference in the evolution of market structure and profitability between the two groups of industries before 1958 (the benchmark year). Moreover, the coefficient on $CHANGE * Y63$ usually has the same sign as the coefficient on $CHANGE * Y54$, which implies that even if a differential trend between the two groups of industries had existed before 1958 for some variables and is imprecisely measured (because the 1954–1958 period is too short, say), this trend was, if anything, reversed during 1958–1963.

Second, a comparison of the R^2's in table 7.4 with those in table 7.6 reveals an interesting feature of the regressions presented in this chapter. In both these tables two R^2's are reported and, as pointed out previously, the difference between the two is a measure of the explanatory power of the industry effects. It can be seen that when the R^2 is defined to exclude fixed industry effects, it is very much higher in regressions with $\ln NFIRMS$ and $\ln NPLANTS$ than in regressions with PCM. On the other hand, when the R^2 is defined to include fixed industry effects, it is only slightly higher in regressions with $\ln NFIRMS$ and $\ln NPLANTS$ than in regressions with PCM. In other words, the industry-specific effects have far more explanatory power for the price-cost margin than for firm or plant numbers. The importance of time-invariant industry-specific characteristics in regressions with PCM is consistent with existing evidence according to which the variation in price-cost margins over time within the typical industry is modest when compared to the between-industry variation (see Geroski 1991). The interesting question therefore is why this is not also the case for firm and plant numbers in the present context. One explanation may be the significant decline in firm and plant numbers throughout the period examined here; this decline is largely picked up by the time dummies and thus raises the R^2 (excluding the industry effects) in regressions with $\ln NFIRMS$ and $\ln NPLANTS$.

Finally, it could be argued that the profit equations estimated above do not adequately control for industry-specific factors that may cause departures from long-run equilibrium. Hence I also ran regressions including among the regressors the variable $\Delta \ln SS$, defined for industry i and year t as the change in $\ln SS$ in the five-year period preceding year t. A disadvantage of this alternative specification was that the first-year observation for each industry could not be used, and this implied dropping all 1954 observations. In any case, the coefficient on $\Delta \ln SS$ was everywhere positive and sometimes statistically significant, but the rest of the results did not change.

7.6 Concluding Remarks

This chapter has examined the joint evolution of market structure variables, such as the number of firms and the number of plants, and profit measures, such as the average firm profit, the average plant profit, and the profit margin, in UK industries over the period 1954–1973. The results support the hypothesis of a negative long-run effect of the 1956 Act on the number of firms and of no significant long-run effect on profitability. The former result is consistent with the finding of a positive overall impact of the Act on concentration in previous chapters. Moreover, the comparison of short-run and long-run effects of competition suggests a link between changes in market structure and profitability: in the short run, when the number of firms has not yet fallen very much, profit margins decline; but they recover in the long run, once the number of firms falls.

These results are consistent with the theoretical framework developed in this book, which has emphasized the effect of price competition on market structure and nonprice competition rather than on profitability. The results say that in long-run equilibrium, most cartels will result in excess entry rather than excess profits relative to the absence of collusion. Legislation prohibiting cartels will therefore reduce the number of firms rather than their profits.[24]

The results also imply that most cartels cannot restrict entry in the long run—or at least they cannot restrict entry to a larger extent than noncolluding firms. There are exceptions to this, as suggested by one of the case studies described in this chapter. When the free-entry condition is violated before the introduction of cartel policy, the breakdown of collusion may lead to a fall in profitability and no significant change in market structure. In this case, a reduction in profits can be absorbed without the need for a major restructuring of the industry, because firms were previously making excess profits. In one sense, this case study illustrates the limitations of the present theory, since it suggests that there can be instances where one of the key assumptions of the theory is violated. But at the same time, it confirms the operation of the structural mechanism driving the theoretical predictions and the econometric results of much of this book, namely, the fact that changes in market structure are driven by the relationship between firms' gross profits and sunk costs.

One thing that has not been much emphasized here is the fact that price-cost margins can change for two different reasons: either because prices change or because unit costs change. Throughout this chapter I have tended to focus on changes in margins as being driven by exogenous factors and to play down the distinction between price changes and cost changes, on the assumption that cost changes are largely passed on to prices, everything else being equal. Nevertheless, I have implicitly attributed the short-run fall in profitability in previously collusive industries to a fall in prices caused by the abolition of price-fixing agreements. On the other hand, the recovery of

---

24. Another interesting implication of the results presented in this chapter is that they confirm that explicit collusion was generally not replaced by tacit collusion in the long run in the large majority of the previously collusive industries. Recall that this is also what the case-study evidence suggests, as pointed out in chapter 2. If explicit collusion had been replaced by tacit collusion, then the profitability of industries affected by the 1956 Act would have increased in the long run relative to the profitability of industries not affected by the legislation, given that the fall in firm numbers was more pronounced in the former group than in the latter. But this is not what we observe.

profitability in the longer term could be due to a recovery in prices or a fall in unit costs or both. Again, I have implicitly attributed much of this recovery to price increases following the drastic fall in the number of firms. But my results are not inconsistent with the view that margins also increased because less efficient firms could not survive in the more competitive conditions of the 1960s, and so the unit cost of the average firm fell. In fact, I have hinted in section 7.2 that such an effect could be part of the story, and in at least one of the case studies discussed in section 7.3 it probably was.

At the same time, it is clear that the fall in firm numbers was a key aspect of the evolution of industries affected by the 1956 Act. In particular, the results of this chapter are *not* consistent with a strong version of the efficiency differences approach, according to which the main effect of more intense price competition would be the expansion of low-cost firms at the expense of high-cost firms (which would also explain why average industry profitability might not fall in the long run) rather than a fall in the total number of firms. The results of this chapter suggest that although the expansion of efficient firms and a fall in unit costs may be part of the explanation for the long-run recovery of profitability in previously collusive industries, this recovery was largely the result of the significant restructuring of these industries through exit and mergers.

It is also worth emphasizing that this chapter does not provide any direct test of the free-entry zero-profit condition. What has been tested here is not whether net profit is approximately zero in the long run for the marginal firm; this is a very difficult task without firm-level data on profits and capital costs. What this chapter has tested is whether a change in firm conduct has any effect on profit in the short run and in the long run. Thus the results presented here would also be consistent with a model that predicts that the net profit of the marginal firm is consistently larger than zero by a nontrivial amount, and that this amount is not much affected by a change in conduct. One mechanism that could account for the existence of supranormal profits for the marginal firm is, of course, strategic entry deterrence. However, it is not clear whether this can be assumed to work across all industries and irrespective of whether incumbent firms collude to fix prices or not. The results presented here seem, therefore, to suggest that the zero-profit condition is a valid assumption, at least as a first approximation, for most industries characterized by free entry.

Still, as pointed out by Scherer and Ross (1990), this approximation may be indeed rough—especially for R&D-intensive industries, where firms' capabilities often change at a rate slower than the rate at which technology and demand conditions shift. In such industries, and perhaps also in others, it may be questionable whether a zero-profit equilibrium is actually achieved at any point in time. Moreover, the presence of asymmetries between firms implies that only the marginal firm makes zero profit under free entry. More efficient firms or firms enjoying first-mover advantages may well earn higher than normal profits in the long run. It is, however, probably safe to suggest, on the basis of the results presented in this book, that in the large majority of industries, the level of excess profits in the long run does not depend on firms' pricing conduct, because of forces such as entry and exit that push industries toward the zero-profit equilibrium. It is mainly in this sense, I think, that the free-entry zero-profit condition is a useful approximation for the study of competition and the determinants of market structure and profitability.

Epilogue

The search for general theories and cross-industry empirical regularities has recently reemerged as a key priority in industrial economics. It has come as a response to the rather pessimistic view that "in oligopoly, anything can happen." It is, of course, true that the results of game-theoretic models of oligopoly often depend on specific assumptions made (including assumptions about unobservables). It is also true that the empirical outcomes we observe are partly driven by particular characteristics of industries (including some which are the product of history or chance). However, the richness of theoretical results and the corresponding variety of empirical outcomes do not imply that "anything can happen." In particular, it is still possible to identify a number of mechanisms, involving observable variables, which operate in a systematic way across industries or for a broad class of industries. This book has set out to analyze some of these mechanisms. Accordingly, the theoretical predictions have been tested using cross-industry data, and a number of cross-industry empirical regularities have emerged.

A Brief Review of the Theory

The most fundamental mechanism analyzed in this book relates to the joint effect of an increase in the intensity of price competition on market structure and profitability in exogenous sunk cost industries. Starting from a free-entry equilibrium, an intensification of price competition—brought about by the introduction of cartel laws, economic integration, or some other exogenous institutional change—will cause profitability to fall, given the initial number of firms. As a result, firms (or less efficient firms) will no longer be able to cover their sunk costs. This will lead to a fall in firm numbers and a rise in concentration until profitability is restored to a level that allows the least efficient firm to cover its sunk costs. This is a clear and strong theoretical result, and one that can be tested against the empirical evidence using econometric analysis as well as industry case studies.

On the other hand, the theory offers no general predictions regarding the effect of price competition on advertising intensity, R&D intensity, and innovative output. Specific results in this area can be obtained only by imposing a considerable amount of structure on theoretical models. In empirical work, one can nevertheless still examine whether any empirical regularities emerge despite the inconclusiveness of the theory.

What of the competition-market structure relationship in advertising-intensive and R&D-intensive industries? Some general results can be derived, although the theory now places only weak constraints on the space of possible outcomes. The most likely outcome will still be a positive effect of price competition on concentration, because a negative effect on concentration can occur only in the event of a substantial decline in advertising or R&D intensity. Similarly, profitability will most likely decline initially, following an increase in the intensity of price competition, before it is restored through a fall in firm numbers. Given these theoretical results, the empirical evidence can be used for two different, but complementary, purposes. First, to confirm that the outcomes we observe on average across industries are indeed the ones which are predicted as being most likely by the theory; this requires the use of econometric analysis. Second, to verify that the outcomes which are predicted as being less likely can still be observed in certain special cases; this requires the use of case studies.

A Brief Review of the Empirical Evidence

The introduction of cartel policy in the UK in the late 1950s was a very rare natural experiment in industrial economics. It has given us the opportunity to analyze the effects of competition in a systematic way without many of the problems that typically arise when we try to define an empirical proxy for the intensity of competition or to unravel the complex interactions between competition, market structure, and performance. In particular, in this book the analysis of the effects of competition following the introduction of cartel policy in the UK was based on a comparison of the evolution of two clearly defined groups of industries: those that experienced a change in competition regime as a result of the legislation and those that were not affected by the legislation.

Previous studies of the effects of the introduction of restrictive practices legislation in the UK include Swann et al. (1973, 1974), Elliott and Gribbin (1977), and O'Brien et al. (1979). Swann et al. (1973, 1974) conducted a series of industry case studies, focusing on the effects of the legislation on competition rather than on its repercussions on market structure and industry performance. Their analysis is a rich source of information on the emergence of price competition in previously collusive British industries during the 1960s. Elliott and Gribbin (1977) provided the first statistical results indicating a significant effect of UK cartel policy on concentration across a wide range of industries. Their results have been confirmed by the present study, which has also extended their analysis in several important ways. On the other hand, O'Brien et al. (1979), who performed a detailed statistical analysis using firm-level data for a modest sample of industries, found no evidence of any significant effect of the legislation either on merger activity or on profitability.

The econometric results reported in this book suggest that the 1956 Restrictive Trade Practices Act, which led to the abolition of restrictive practices across a wide range of industries, was one of the main factors behind the significant increase in concentration in British manufacturing during the 1960s. In particular, the intensification of price competition following the termination of price-fixing agreements caused a rise in the five-firm concentration ratio of at least six to seven percentage points, on average, in industries affected by the legislation. The impact was strong in all classes of industries. A comparison of short-run and long-run effects provides further insight on these events. The legislation had a negative effect on profitability of previously collusive industries during the first few years of its implementation, when market structure had not yet fully adjusted. However, the subsequent restructuring of these industries was associated with a recovery of profit margins, so that profitability did not change significantly in the long run. Thus the evidence is consistent with the theory.

The econometric evidence also suggests that the intensification of price competition following the 1956 Act caused, on the whole, a fall in advertising intensity in advertising-intensive industries affected by the legislation. Moreover, case-study evidence confirms that a fall in concentration, following an intensification of price competition, cannot be ruled out in high-advertising industries. However, tougher price competition must lead to a significant fall in advertising intensity if concentration does not rise or, conversely, it must cause concentration to rise if advertising falls little or not at all, which is consistent with the theoretical predictions as well as with the overall picture given by the econometric results. The negative effect of price competition on advertising can be contrasted with the absence of any overall effect on the number of innovations produced by firms. In particular, there is no evidence of any significant effect of the 1956 Act on firms' innovative output in R&D-intensive industries.

Wider Issues

Some of the wider normative issues regarding competition, such as the effect of different competition regimes on social welfare or the question of how much competition is socially desirable, have not been discussed in this book because they are too difficult to examine empirically. For instance, data limitations have precluded any analysis of the effect of the 1956 cartel legislation on prices. Moreover, no attempt has been made to examine the effect of the 1956 Act on the productive efficiency of firms, since this raises some conceptual and practical issues that are difficult to resolve with the information available. The case-study evidence reported in Swann et al. (1973, 1974), although consistent with the hypothesis of a positive effect of the Act on the efficiency of firms, is rather sketchy. Thus the question of the link between competition and efficiency following the breakdown of cartels in Britain remains open.

Other positive and normative implications of the present study are, however, easier to draw. One implication is that in long-run equilibrium most cartels will result in excess entry rather than excess profits (relative to the absence of collusion), and hence cartel laws will reduce the number of firms rather than their profits. A second implication is that the recent trend toward more competition in national and international markets is likely to increase concentration at both the national and the international level. However, a qualification is needed here for policy interventions that involve a reduction or removal of entry barriers in addition to an increase in the intensity of competition: the effect of such policies on market structure will be ambiguous. A third implication is that competition is probably not a substitute for policies that promote innovation, since the rate of innovation does not appear to be much affected by the degree of price competition.

What about competition policy? If high concentration and mergers are an inevitable consequence of tougher price competition, as the present study suggests, then there are constraints on the exercise of merger and antitrust policies, since these policies cannot be used to maintain or impose a market structure that is not sustainable in the long run. Of course, to the extent that market structure is also influenced by nonstructural factors, competition could lead to excessive restructuring, so merger policy has still an important role to play.

The same is true for competition policy in general, since there is always a real danger that dominant firms in concentrated markets may try to abuse their market power. This brings us to the final implication of the research reported in this book: the link between competition and concentration is complex, and the present study strengthens the case for a competition policy that focuses more on the monitoring of conduct than on the regulation of market structure. Indeed, a central message of this book is that when free entry is maintained, high concentration need not be associated with high profit margins and increased allocative inefficiency, because it may itself be the result of more intense competition.

Appendix A: A Survey of Collusive Agreements in British Manufacturing Industries

This appendix contains a survey of explicit collusive agreements across British manufacturing industries from the early 1950s to the mid-1970s. It reports all the relevant information that I have used to construct the competition data for this book. This information comes from various sources, the most important of which have been described in chapter 3, section 3.2. It will be presented here industry by industry, using the "minimum list heading" (MLH) categories of the UK 1968 Standard Industrial Classification as basic industry categories.* I emphasize that this classification is used here merely as a way of organizing the presentation of the material. The information on restrictive agreements will be reported for products and subproducts within any given MLH category.

The survey will cover only important national and regional collusive agreements. That is, I will not be concerned with local agreements or with agreements containing only trivial restrictions or involving a few producers of some very specific product. Moreover, the survey will cover only agreements between manufacturers. Although there were numerous important restrictive agreements in agriculture and in distribution, and many more between firms in the construction industry, these are not relevant to the present study. On the other hand, the services industries, as pointed out in chapter 2, did not fall within the scope of the 1956 Act.

When describing particular agreements, I will focus on the most important restrictions of each. Thus, whenever there were agreed or recommended prices or agreed quotas, I will usually not give details about ancillary restrictions, such as conditions of sale, quantity discounts, approved lists of distributors, or resale price maintenance. The large majority of price agreements also specified conditions of sale, and I will not be mentioning this in each particular case. Moreover, while a few agreements provided for net producer prices, the large majority specified minimum or fixed "list prices" and complemented these by a set of maximum or fixed discounts to distributors ("trade discounts") and other buyers. I will not be mentioning the provision regarding trade discounts as a separate restriction in each case. Finally, note that neither the distinction between "agreed" and "recommended" prices nor

---

* A glossary of British terms appears at the end of the appendixes.

the distinction between "minimum" and "common" prices carries too much weight—especially in light of the fact that many agreements were redrafted prior to registration. I therefore will often simply use a term such as "pricing agreement" or "price-fixing agreement" or an equivalent expression in what follows. On the other hand, I will always specifically mention any important nonprice restrictions, such as market sharing, collective exclusive dealing, aggregated rebates, and restrictions relating to advertising or R&D.

Whenever a particular agreement did not provide for price-fixing or market sharing, I will elaborate on the types of restrictions that were in force. I will not, however, discuss cases of individual resale price maintenance by firms in an industry, either before or after 1956. These do not constitute agreements under the 1956 Act; more important, as I explained in chapter 3, there is no evidence that resale price maintenance had a significant effect on competition between manufacturers in the absence of any other restrictions.

The question of whether a particular agreement covered the export market in addition to the home market is often not an easy one, so it will not be given much attention here, except for very few cases where the relevant information is both available and important for classifying an industry as collusive, competitive, or ambiguous in the 1950s. Another difficult question concerns the participation of British firms and associations in international cartels. Since this issue is not directly relevant to the present study, it will be, for the most part, left aside. I will report only significant cases of international cartels that are mentioned in the Register of Restrictive Trading Agreements or the reports of the Monopolies and Restrictive Practices Commission. On the other hand, I will report all the available evidence on information agreements—although the lack of systematic data on information agreements poses some serious problems in this respect. Thus my review of information agreements, based on evidence contained in the register or from case studies, will inevitably be incomplete.

The available information on significant restrictions other than pricing restrictions is also less than complete. The main reason is that several agreements were modified before registration, and this sometimes implied removing provisions regarding market sharing, collective exclusive dealing, or aggregated rebates. This difficulty should not be overemphasized, however, since information on such schemes is provided in several data sources other than the register, including the 1955 Monopolies and Restrictive Practices Commission report on "collective discrimination." This report covered the large majority of the most important instances of collective exclusive dealing, aggregated rebates, barriers to entry into distribution, and collective resale price maintenance—although it did not usually specify the exact restrictions that applied to each industry listed, provided little information on coverage, and sometimes used rather broad industry definitions.[1]

---

1. There are four such broad industry definitions in the report: "certain chemicals," "certain electrical products," "groceries," and "hardware"; the last two should be taken to mean "certain groceries" and "certain hardware products."

The following abbreviations will be used for some of the data sources. Rxxx denotes the number (xxx) of an agreement in the Register of Restrictive Trading Agreements. BT denotes the Board of Trade annual reports on the operation of the 1948 Monopolies and Restrictive Practices Act, covering the years 1949 to 1956. PEP denotes the Political and Economic Planning survey of industrial trade associations, including the unpublished background material for this survey. MRPC stands for Monopolies and Restrictive Practices Commission, MC stands for Monopolies Commission, and MMC stands for Monopolies and Mergers Commission (all of which are successive names for the same public body). "Lloyds' report" refers to the 1949 report of the Lloyds' Committee on resale price maintenance (Board of Trade 1949), and CD refers to the 1955 MRPC report on collective discrimination. Finally, the reports of the Restrictive Practices Court, which have been published as *Reports on Restrictive Practices Cases* by the Incorporated Council of Law Reporting, are conventionally cited as LR [volume no.] RP [page no.].

For each product, I will start with the information contained in the Register of Restrictive Trading Agreements and then report any relevant additional information from other sources. To avoid repetition, references to other data sources will be made only when these sources contain *additional* information relative to the register. This is typically the case with the reports of the Monopolies and Restrictive Practices Commission, the reports of the Restrictive Practices Court, the 1955 MRPC report on collective discrimination, and the case studies contained in Swann et al. (1973). It is less often the case with the lists of collusive or allegedly collusive industries in PEP and BT. Hence references to PEP or BT will be made below only (1) for industries which did not register any significant restrictive agreements but are listed as collusive or allegedly collusive in these sources, and (2) for industries whose registered agreements do not seem significant and the detailed evidence contained in PEP confirms that they should be treated as competitive. The BT lists distinguish several types of restrictive practices, including price-fixing, market sharing, and collective discrimination. Unless otherwise stated, "collusion" should be taken to mean price-fixing when a reference is made to the BT lists below.

I will also indicate which agreements were referred to the Restrictive Practices Court. In particular, agreements referred to the Court will be marked with an * next to their number on the register (i.e., Rxxx*). For those that were struck down by the Court without being defended by the parties, no other information will be given.[2] For those that were contested by the firms involved, I will indicate what the outcome was in each case. Brief descriptions of all the agreements that were referred to the Court since the introduction of the 1956 Act and summary accounts of Court proceedings for

---

2. I will not distinguish between agreements abandoned after being referred to the Court (which was the usual case) and agreements referred to the Court after being abandoned (which was a precautionary step sometimes taken by the Registrar in order to reduce the likelihood of any future collusion by the firms involved). This distinction is usually difficult to make on the basis of the available data.

contested cases can be found in the reports of the Registrar of Restrictive Trading Agreements (RRTA 1961–1973) or, after 1973, in the annual reports of the Director General of Fair Trading.

In addition to presenting the "raw" data on collusion, I will provide summary assessments of the effect of the 1956 Act on competition across industries and product groups. This should help clarify the link between the "raw" competition data and my classification of industries according to their competitive status. An industry in my data sets is classified as collusive in the 1950s (or in later years) if the products subject to *significant* restrictions accounted for more than 50% of total industry sales revenue. It is classified as competitive if the products subject to *significant or uncertain* restrictions accounted for less than 10% of industry sales revenue. And it is classified as ambiguous (or the state of competition is classified as ambiguous) in all remaining cases, namely, when the restrictions cover most of the industry but their effect on competition is uncertain, or the data source is not fully reliable, or the collusive products cover more than 10% but less than 50% of total industry sales, and so on.

Furthermore, an industry in my data sets is defined as one with a change of competition regime if in the 1950s it had been subject to significant collusive agreements covering at least 50% of total sales revenue and these agreements were subsequently abandoned. It is defined as an industry without a change in competition regime if less than 10% of the industry was affected by the legislation. And it is defined as ambiguous (or the effect of the 1956 Act on the industry is defined as ambiguous) in all other cases.

My assessments below should be interpreted in relation to my classification criteria. This should be kept in mind especially for cases where an industry is said to have experienced a "change in competition regime." This means that in the 1950s the industry in question had been subject to significant collusive agreements covering at least 50% of total sales revenue and these agreements were subsequently abandoned. In other words, the expression "change in competition regime" should not be taken to imply that competition definitely intensified as a result of the 1956 Act in that particular industry. Such information is available for several industries and will be reported below; in many cases, however, information is simply not available and the maintained assumption—which, as discussed in chapter 2, gets very significant support from survey and case-study evidence—is that competition indeed intensified, sooner or later, in the large majority of the previously collusive industries.

Stone and Slate Quarrying and Mining (MLH 102)

Stone mining and quarrying. About seventy-five regional agreements in dry and coated stone for roadwork, building work, and so on were registered, then formally abandoned between 1959 and 1961. They all comprised agreed prices, and some also provided for market sharing or the allocation of work. There were also agreements between associations to respect each other's arrangements in their respective areas. These regional cartels probably covered more than half of total industry sales. At the national level, the Roadstone Producers Advisory Committee gave recommendations for price increases to cover changes in costs until 1961 (R1717). Swann et al. (1973) provide details on this industry and also argue that competition gradually intensified in the 1960s, although in some areas this had not yet occurred by the late 1960s—partly as a result of information agreements. On the other hand, an official investigation into the industry carried out in the 1970s revealed a large number of regional or local restrictive agreements, many of which had been in operation since the early 1970s, while others had been in operation since the 1960s. These agreements were placed on the register (and most were also referred to the Court), and were abandoned in the late 1970s. All in all, the state of competition in the stone mining and quarrying industry throughout the 1960s and the 1970s must be regarded as ambiguous.

Slate and slate products. A pricing agreement of the North Wales Slate Quarries Association (R400) was abandoned in 1959. Wales accounted for about 80% of the total UK production of slate and slate products in the 1950s. Hence there was probably a change of competition regime in this industry.

Chalk, Clay, Sand, and Gravel Extraction (MLH 103)

Sand and gravel. About thirty regional agreements in sand and gravel were registered, then formally abandoned between 1959 and 1961—although some of them were replaced by information agreements. They all comprised agreed prices, and some also provided for market sharing or the allocation of work. There were also agreements between associations to observe each other's arrangements in their respective areas. The agreements probably covered more than half of total industry sales; this is also the view expressed in PEP. Three of the agreements (R595*, R943*, R1712*) were by Scottish associations that had previously been the subject of an official inquiry—see MRPC, *Report on the Supply of Sand and Gravel in Central Scotland* (London: H.M.S.O., 1956). An official investigation into the sand and gravel industry carried out in the mid-1970s revealed several dozen regional or local restrictive agreements which had been in operation since the early 1970s or even earlier. These agreements were placed on the register (and most were referred to the Court), and were abandoned in the late 1970s. There is some uncertainty about their coverage and effectiveness, however. In summary, the state of competition in the industry during the 1960s and the 1970s should probably be regarded as ambiguous.

Clay. Three national agreements covered all types of clay except fireclay. The China Clay Association recommended price changes and required members to report their individual prices and any intention to change them to the association (R128). The China Stone Association fixed prices and quotas (R190). And the Ball Clay Producers Federation's agreement contained minimum list prices, although it did not regulate trade discounts (R377). All three agreements were abandoned in 1959. In addition, various associations of firebrick producers (listed under MLH 461 below) fixed the price of fireclay until 1959–1961. Overall, there was a change of competition regime in the clay industry.

Other products. There is no evidence of any restrictive agreements.

Iron Ore and Other Metalliferous Mining and Quarrying (MLH 109.1,2)

Iron ore. The case of iron ore is special in several ways. First, imports were far greater than domestic production and they were centrally purchased. Second, the Iron and Steel Board (the regulatory body for the steel industry) had implemented a scheme that may have resulted in price discrimination against users of domestic iron ore. Third, most of the domestic iron ore was mined by steel firms, which were also the principal users. See D. Burn, *The Steel Industry 1939–1959* (Cambridge: Cambridge University Press, 1961) for details. In any case, there is no evidence of any collusive agreements between iron ore producers, and there was no change in competitive conditions between the mid-1950s and the mid-1960s. In 1967 the iron ore industry was radically transformed as a result of the nationalization of steel.

Other metalliferous mining and quarrying. No evidence of any restrictive agreements.

Salt and Other Nonmetalliferous Mining and Quarrying (MLH 109.3,4)

Salt. The salt industry is mentioned as collusive in PEP, and it was also listed in CD; however, no agreement was registered in the 1950s. An investigation of the industry by the MMC in the 1980s revealed an unregistered pricing agreement, which had been in operation for several decades. See MMC, *White Salt* (London: H.M.S.O., 1986). Thus the salt industry was collusive throughout the time period examined in this book.

Other nonmetalliferous mining and quarrying. The British Fluorspar Producers Association fixed prices for fluorspar until 1960 (R477).

Grain Milling (MLH 211)

Flour. Several agreements by various associations and groups of flour millers were registered. Most of them were regional and provided for recommended prices (R175, R176*, R776*, R777, R778, R779, R780, R783*, R969, R1247, R1599*, R1608, R1652*, R2276, R2429, R2443). There were also five important national agreements. Three of them, by the National Association of British and Irish Millers, covered most types of flour and associated products, and comprised recommended prices and a scheme of aggregated rebates for large buyers (R782*, R784*, R844). The fourth, by the Association of Millers of Proprietary Brown Flour, required members to report their individual prices and any intention to change them to the association (R843). The fifth, by the Millers Mutual Association, whose members included all the important producers of flour, comprised a system of quotas (R2154). All the national and regional agreements were abandoned in 1958–1959. Hence there was a change of competition regime in the flour industry. An MMC inquiry found competition in the industry to be effective in the 1970s—see MMC, *Flour and Bread* (London: H.M.S.O., 1977).

Ready-to-eat breakfast cereals. No evidence of collusive agreements.

Other products. An agreement between members of the Lentil Millers Association (R781), containing prices and quotas, and a pricing agreement among producers of soy flour (R1495) were both canceled in 1959.

Bread and Flour Confectionery (MLH 212)

Bread. The price of bread was under government control until 1956. After 1956, it became subject to various agreements by national, regional, and local associations. The three most important agreements were referred to the Restrictive Practices Court and were unsuccessfully contested by the parties (see LR 1 RP 387, LR 1 RP 347). In particular, R962* was a pricing agreement by the Federation of Wholesale and Multiple Bakers, whose members were "plant bakers" in England and Wales. R252*, R981*, and R980* were price agreements by the Wholesale and Retail Bakers of Scotland Association, the Scottish Association of Master Bakers, and a Joint Costing Committee of the two associations, respectively. All these agreements were abandoned in 1959–1960. Regional agreements in the industry (R985, R1048, R1311, R2462, R2469, R2470, R2471, R2478, R2480, R2580, R2599, R2601) were also terminated at that time, as were agreements by associations of "master bakers" (R1542, R1566, R2275) and numerous local collusive arrangements.

Swann et al. (1973) describe the gradual emergence of competition in the bread industry, despite parallel pricing and some information agreements about discounts—for instance, R3061*, which ended in 1965. Further information is contained in MMC, *Flour and Bread* (London: H.M.S.O., 1977). The MMC discovered a large number of agreements between leading firms that had been in operation since the late 1960s or early 1970s. Most of them involved the exchange of information about discounts to particular buyers or about intended increases in discounts. Some arrangements were national, but most were local. All of them were placed on the register (and some were referred to the Court) and were abandoned in the mid-1970s. See the report of the Director General of Fair Trading for 1977 for details. However, it is very doubtful that these arrangements had any significant effect on competition. The view of the MMC was that they were an attempt, largely unsuccessful, to resist pressure from retailers for progressively larger discounts. In fact, discounts kept rising between 1965 and 1975, which suggests that competition was largely effective. Hence the bread industry experienced a change of competition regime as a result of the 1956 Act.

Flour confectionery. This industry was not subject to any national agreements. Some of the regional or local pricing arrangements among bakers covered flour confectionery as well, but most did not. These agreements probably affected more than 10% but less than 50% of total industry sales.

Biscuits (MLH 213)

An agreement by the National Association of Biscuit Manufacturers provided for prices, conditions of sale, and restrictions on sales promotion (R1519); it was abandoned in 1959. Chocolate biscuits were also covered by agreements between chocolate confectionery manufacturers; they ended in the early 1960s (see MLH 217 below). The biscuit industry was also listed in CD, which implies that it was subject to collective discrimination arrangements before 1956. In summary, there was a change of competition regime in this industry. Cereal filling, a secondary product of MLH 213, was also subject to a pricing agreement, which was operated by the Rusk Manufacturers Association and was abandoned in 1960 (R610*).

Bacon Curing, Meat and Fish Products (MLH 214)

Bacon. The British Bacon Agents Association recommended prices for British bacon (R2750). Its members were agents appointed by curers or curers who acted as their own agents. The agreement ended in 1961 and was replaced by an information agreement, which lasted until the early 1970s. However, about a third of the members withdrew from the association in 1962–1963. A pricing agreement by the Association of Scottish Bacon Curers and the Scottish Provision Trade Association was abandoned in 1960 (R1185*). Finally, the register also contains a series of annual contracts for the purchase of pigs between farmers' representatives and the British Bacon Curers Federation or smaller associations of curers (R2301, R2305, R2286). These contracts, which specified prices and terms of purchase, had been a feature of the industry ever since the end of government control of the distribution of fatstock, and continued until the early 1970s. It is unlikely that they had any significant effect on competition between producers of bacon. In conclusion, there was a change of competition regime in this industry.

Sausages and cooked meats. An agreement by the Scottish Association of Cooked Meat Manufacturers, which ended in 1960, contained recommended price changes for sausages and other meat products (R99). However, Scottish producers accounted for less than 10% of the total UK production of sausages and cooked meats, so the industry was largely competitive; this is consistent with the evidence reported in PEP.

Other meat and fish products. An agreement by the Association of British Salted Fish Curers and Exporters, abandoned in 1959, related only to maximum prices for the purchase of imported wet salted fish (R241). An agreement between members of the Salmon Merchants Association of Great Britain, who were curers of raw salmon, was also about buying prices and was abandoned in 1959 (R473).

Milk and Milk Products (MLH 215)

Heat-treated milk. A number of regional and local agreements among processors/distributors of milk were registered, then abandoned between 1959 and 1965. Most of these were market-sharing agreements, but some also contained pricing restrictions. Several were referred to the Court (R2213*, R1222*, R2988*, R2119*, R2198*, R2199*, R2574*). The fraction of the total UK production of heat-treated milk covered by these agreements is difficult to estimate; it may have been less than 50%. The industry was also included in the BT lists of allegedly collusive industries, but no precise information was given on coverage. Adding to the uncertainty regarding the evolution of competition in this industry is the fact that maximum prices and profit margins were regulated by the Milk Marketing Board (the regulatory body for the milk industry) at least until the late 1960s. It is therefore clear that the effect of the 1956 Act on this industry should be seen as ambiguous.

Butter. The register contains two national pricing agreements: R814 by the English Butter Conference and R1047 by the Butter Makers and Packers Association. Both ended in 1959–1960. Hence there was a change of competition regime in the butter industry.

Cheese. The cheese industry comprises two different product categories: processed cheese, which accounted for less than 50% of total industry sales throughout the period, and nonprocessed cheese. There is no evidence of any collusive agreements in processed cheese. In contrast, several types of nonprocessed cheese were subject to collusive pricing. In particular, the Cheshire Cheese Makers Association (R396), the Lancashire Cheese Association (R813), the Company of Scottish Cheesemakers (R285), the Wensleydale Cheese Joint Conference (R580), and the Cheddar and Caerphilly Cheese Makers Association (R424, R2558) recommended or fixed prices of cheese. All these agreements ended in 1959–1960. R396 was replaced for some time by an information agreement. The fraction of the cheese industry affected by the 1956 Act was probably around 40%.

Cream. The National Association of Creamery Proprietors and Wholesale Dairymen recommended minimum prices for fresh cream (R812). The Clotted Cream Makers Association recommended price increases for clotted cream to cover changes in costs (R395). Finally, the Association of Tinned Cream Manufacturers recommended minimum prices of tinned sterilized cream (R582). All these arrangements were canceled in 1959, leading to a change of competition regime in the cream industry.

Condensed milk. The Association of British and Dominion Condensed Milk Manufacturers recommended minimum prices for all classes of condensed milk until 1960 (R585). The abolition of this agreement led to a change of competition regime in the industry.

Milk powder. The Association of British Manufacturers of Milk Powder recommended minimum prices for milk powder until 1960 (R584, R421). Thus the industry experienced a change in competition regime.

Ice cream. No evidence of any restrictive agreements.

Other milk products. An agreement by the Imitation Cream Division of the Bakery Allied Traders Association (R2567) contained recommendations about price changes; it was abandoned in 1960.

Sugar (MLH 216)

Prices, market shares, and profit margins in the sugar industry were under government regulation throughout the period examined in this book. Details can be found in Hart et al. (1973) and in MMC, *S & W Berisford Limited and British Sugar Corporation Limited: A Report on the Proposed Merger* (London: H.M.S.O., 1981). All the registered agreements relating to sugar were among distributors, except one, which was a pricing scheme implemented by the government and the three main manufacturers in 1974 (R3833). It replaced previous schemes in the industry and was discontinued in 1976.

Cocoa, Chocolate, and Sugar Confectionery (MLH 217)

Cocoa and chocolate. The register contains a series of agreements between five (later four) of the largest producers in the industry, covering cocoa, drinking chocolate, chocolate confectionery, and chocolate biscuits (R287*, R2639*, R288). For the first three of these product categories, the restrictions included maximum discounts to distributors, the requirement that each firm enforces its (individually set) retail prices, the prenotification of any changes in individual prices or discounts, and numerous provisions regarding sales promotion. For chocolate biscuits, there were only restrictions on sales promotion. All the arrangements ended between 1960 and 1962.

Another agreement, by the Wholesale Confectioners Alliance of Great Britain and Northern Ireland (R169*), was referred to the Court in 1961 and was unsuccessfully contested by the parties (LR 2 RP 135, LR 2 RP 231). This was an association of wholesalers of chocolate and sugar confectionery. The agreement essentially involved an agreed split between wholesalers and retailers of the total difference between producer prices and consumer prices (which were fixed and maintained by the individual manufacturers). The effect of this on competition between manufacturers is somewhat uncertain, but at least it implies that resale price maintenance and the restrictions on trade discounts were effective throughout the industry. Furthermore, the existence of an effective price notification agreement is confirmed by PEP, and the industry was also listed in CD, which confirms the existence of collective discrimination arrangements before 1956. In conclusion, the industry probably experienced a change of competition regime as a result of the 1956 Act.

Sugar confectionery. The agreement of the Wholesale Confectioners Alliance of Great Britain and Northern Ireland (R169) related to sugar confectionery as well. In this case, however, the arrangements between manufacturers provided only for restrictions on sales promotion and the maintenance of individual resale prices (see R287, R2639, R288, and the Lloyds' report). The industry was also listed in CD. The state of competition in this industry in the 1950s should probably be regarded as ambiguous.

Fruit and Vegetable Products (MLH 218)

There is no evidence of any significant restrictive agreements in this industry.

Animal and Poultry Foods (MLH 219)

Animal feeding stuffs, other than dog and cat foods. No important agreements were registered in the 1950s. (An agreement by the Association of Fish Meal Manufacturers, R1635, related only to delivery charges; besides, fish meal is a minor product of the industry). However, the industry was listed in BT as allegedly collusive. In addition, an official investigation carried out in the 1970s revealed that a collusive agreement between leading producers had been in operation since 1970 (R4556*, R4673*). This was abandoned in 1978. All in all, the effect of the 1956 Act on this industry was ambiguous.

Dog and cat foods. The National Association of Dog Biscuit Manufacturers fixed the price of biscuit powder or dust, biscuit meals, and dog meals (R96). The agreement dealt only with residuals and low-priced dog and poultry food, not with the manufacturers' proprietary brands. Since the whole of the product category "dog biscuits" (including proprietary brands) accounted for only about 10–20% of total sales of dog and cat foods during most of the relevant period, the industry can be seen as essentially competitive.

Vegetable and Animal Oils and Fats (MLH 221)

A pricing arrangement by the Scottish Association of Edible Fat Melters (R1186) ended in 1959. PEP mentions the Raw Fat Melters Association as allegedly collusive. Also, both BT and PEP mention an arrangement whereby the members of the Federation of Bone Users and Allied Trades regulated the prices and allocated the supplies of fat and bones for the production of tallow, grease, and other products (in this case the information in PEP comes from a firm in the industry). The combined share of the products covered by these associations was less than 10% of total industry sales revenue. Thus both MLH 221 as a whole and most of its principal products experienced no change in competition regime as a result of the 1956 Act.

Margarine (MLH 229.1)

There is no evidence of any restrictive agreements in this industry apart from an allegation about collective discrimination arrangements in margarine reported in BT.

Starch and Miscellaneous Foods (MLH 229.2)

Starch and glucose. The British Dextrine Manufacturers Association recommended minimum prices for all dextrins until 1959 (R242). The affected products accounted for about 20% of sales revenue in this product group. Moreover, liquid glucose is mentioned in PEP and BT as allegedly collusive.

Coffee, and coffee and chicory extracts and essences. No evidence of any restrictive agreements.

Self-raising flour. The Self-Raising Flour Association recommended prices for self-rising flour until 1959 (R185). There was therefore a change of competition regime in this industry.

Other products. No evidence of any restrictive agreements.

Brewing and Malting (MLH 231)

Beer. Several brewers took part in regional price-fixing agreements by wholesale bottlers, which were generally abandoned in 1958–1959. The register also contains some regional agreements by groups of brewers. These regulated the relations between brewers and public houses, and sometimes also provided for the prenotification of individual price changes, but did not impose restrictions on individual prices (R45, R1457, R1602, R2239, R2317). The effect of these arrangements on competition between beer producers is difficult to assess. Moreover, the fraction of the UK beer market covered by these agreements, which remained in force until the mid-1960s, was probably between 20% and 50%.

Malt. An annual agreement between various associations of farmers, maltsters, and brewers regarding the price of barley destined for malting was not renewed after 1959 (R1589, R1849, R2382). An agreement by the Maltsters Association of Great Britain, relating to conditions of sale, was partly canceled in 1967 (R199). These are unlikely to have had any significant effect on competition between malt producers, so the industry can be seen as competitive throughout the period.

Soft Drinks (MLH 232)

The register contains many regional price-fixing agreements by various associations of manufacturers/bottlers (R127, R267, R270, R589, R594, R738, R794, R982, R1162, R1199, R1229, R1250, R1300, R1419, R1709, R2284). All ended between 1958 and 1960. The fraction of the total UK soft drinks market affected by these regional cartels is difficult to estimate, because the agreements did not cover national proprietary brands. Also, according to PEP, the agreements were not always effective. As far as national brands are concerned, an arrangement between two leading firms, Schweppes and Lyons, which may have amounted to market sharing, remained in force until the 1970s, because of various technical reasons relating to the form of the agreement (R3679, R3680). See the Registrar's report for the period 1969–1972 and the annual report of the Director General of Fair Trading for 1974 for details. Overall, the effect of the 1956 Act on the soft drinks industry should be seen as ambiguous, although the effect on competition between the large advertising-intensive firms was probably not significant.

Spirit Distilling and Compounding (MLH 239.1)

Spirit distilling. An agreement between members of the Pot Still Malt Distillers Association, relating to prices of malt whiskey sold to blenders, was abandoned in 1956 and was never registered. The information comes both from PEP and from the October 1956 issue of the periodical *Cartel.*

According to PEP, there were no similar arrangements among grain distillers, but intentions to change individual prices were notified. In conclusion, the industry probably experienced a change in competition regime after 1956.

Whisky.   Domestic and export sales of whiskey were officially rationed until 1954. In fact, rationing in the home market continued until the late 1950s (see Hart et al. 1973). Moreover, the firms agreed on *maximum* prices for whiskey, according to CD, PEP, and BT, although no such agreement appears in the register. The effect of rationing and of maximum prices on competition is difficult to determine in general, so the state of competition in this industry in the 1950s should probably be seen as ambiguous.

Other products.   No evidence of any significant restrictive agreements affecting manufacturers. "Wines and spirits" are listed in CD.

British Wines, Cider, and Perry (MLH 239.2)

There is no evidence of significant restrictive agreements affecting manufacturers. "Wines and spirits" are listed in CD.

Tobacco (MLH 240)

The principal sources of information on the tobacco industry are PEP (which, in this case, reports evidence given by a tobacco firm), the Lloyds' report, and especially MC, *Report on the Supply of Cigarettes and Tobacco and of Cigarette and Tobacco Machinery* (London: H.M.S.O., 1961). According to these sources, the most important factor restricting competition in the industry during the early 1950s was the government-controlled allocation of raw materials among producers. This ended in 1954, and was followed by a large expansion in the market share of the two leading firms at the expense of smaller firms. An agreement by the Northern Tobacco Manufacturers Association to set minimum prices of cheaper types of tobacco sold in Scotland and northern England also ended at that time; in any case, the largest firm in the industry had never been a party to that arrangement. After 1954, there were no horizontal agreements on prices, although the industry practiced collective resale price maintenance through the Tobacco Trade Association until 1956 (see also CD and BT). There were also occasional discussions about distributors' margins, but no explicit agreement. The register does not contain any important restrictive agreements among tobacco manufacturers. This evidence suggests (1) that the state of competition in the industry was ambiguous until the mid-1950s because of government control, and (2) that it would probably be safe to classify the industry as one without a change in competition regime between the *late* 1950s and the 1970s.

Coke and Manufactured Fuel (MLH 261)

Coke. The register contains two national and several regional agreements on coke. The price of blast-furnace coke was regulated by an agreement between the British Coking Industry Association, the British Iron and Steel Federation, and the Council of Iron Producers (R649*). The British Coking Industry Association also recommended prices of hard coke and had marketing schemes for various regions (R650*). Both agreements ended in 1964–1965. Further information on the hard coke industry is provided in PEP, in which it is pointed out that the retail prices of hard coke were regulated by the government, while the producer prices fixed by the British Coking Industry Association were implemented as part of a government-approved scheme. What is important for our present purposes is that during 1954–1963, there was no change in the state of competition in the coke industry (hard coke and blast-furnace coke). After the mid-1960s, conditions changed dramatically as a result of the nationalization of the steel industry, since the steel firms produced about half of the total output of coke. The register also contains a series of price agreements for gas coke, which were abandoned in the early 1960s. However, gas coke is not part of MLH 261.

Manufactured fuel. No evidence of restrictive agreements.

Other products. Several agreements in the register related to schemes whereby a number of producers of crude tar entered into similar contractual arrangements with a single refiner, specifying the prices to be charged, amounts to be sold, and so on. Nearly all of these ended between 1958 and 1962.

Mineral Oil Refining (MLH 262)

Several agreements in the register related to the common marketing of various mineral oil refining products by two (initially three) of the largest firms in the industry, Shell and BP (R1139, R3717, R1150, R1350, R1708). This continued until 1976. Further information on the industry is contained in PEP, BT, and MC, *Petrol* (London: H.M.S.O., 1965). Several principal products of MLH 262, such as petrol (gasoline), fuel oil, and diesel oil, were listed as allegedly subject to collusive pricing and other restrictions in BT and/or PEP, and the industry was also listed in CD. The Monopolies Commission took a more favorable view on the industry, arguing that there was no evidence of price-fixing in petrol after 1953, despite the existence of parallel pricing. (Before 1953, the price of petrol was under government control.) Instead, there was intense competition for outlets, partly through price incentives to retailers. Moreover, the MC did not consider the common marketing arrangements between Shell and BP to be significant restrictions on competition. Finally, the MC noted that price competition intensified after 1960, but it attributed this to the entry of new firms. All in all, the effect of the 1956 Act on competition in the mineral oil refining industry was ambiguous.

Lubricating Oils and Greases (MLH 263)

The register contains agreements about the common marketing of lubricating oils by two (initially three) of the largest firms in the industry, the same as in MLH 262 (R1133, R3718). This continued until 1976. A price agreement by the White Oils Association, covering certain types of lubricating oils, ended in 1960 (R2161). Very few of the members of this association were refiners; most were distributors who cleaned, mixed, and packed the oils purchased from the large refiners. Thus the agreement was of limited relevance for competition among manufacturers. Also, the products covered accounted for a small fraction of total industry sales. Hence the 1956 Act probably had no significant effect on this industry.

General Chemicals, Inorganic (MLH 271.1)

An arrangement for the common buying of sulfur by members of the National Sulphuric Acid Association was referred to the Court, contested by the parties, and allowed to continue (R123*—see also LR 4 RP 169, LR 6 RP 210). It remained in force until at least the late 1970s, but its effect on competition among producers of sulfuric acid is not clear—partly because about half of the total output of sulfuric acid was produced from other raw materials and partly because the agreement was a response to the existence of an export cartel among foreign suppliers of sulfur. On the other hand, according to a case study of the chemical industry, written by W. B. Reddaway and published in Burn (1958), some regional sections of the association had agreements on selling prices before 1956. None of these was registered.

There are four other agreements under MLH 271.1 in the register. The producers of copper sulfate had a common selling organization, the British Sulphate of Copper Association (R134). Their agreement, which prescribed that the parties should sell all their production through the company, ended in 1960. The Potassium Carbonate Association regulated the purchase and distribution in the UK of potassium carbonate until 1959 (R785). The Scottish Soda Crystal Manufacturers Association operated as a common selling agency for the soda crystal produced by its members (R1331). Until 1959, it fixed prices and required that members sell all their production through the association. On the other hand, an agreement by the British Acetylene Association related only to conditions of sale and was allowed to continue without a Court hearing, since it was not regarded as restrictive (R1959). Finally, two other products of MLH 271.1 are listed in BT as potentially collusive: sodium metasilicate, and salt and sodium sulfide. The fraction of total industry sales in MLH 271.1 accounted for by collusive or allegedly collusive products was probably around 25–35%.

General Chemicals, Organic (MLH 271.2)

Products of coal tar distillation. Almost all the products in this industry were subject to collusion. The Association of Tar Distillers recommended prices for road tar and bitumen tar mixtures, coal tar fuels, and certain creosote oils (R1033). The agreement was canceled in 1960 and replaced by an information agreement, which ended in 1965. Refined tar was also subject to regional agreements until 1960 (R1417, R1458). The Anthracene Producers Committee of the Association of Tar Distillers fixed prices of anthracene until 1965 (R3126, R3127). Prices of creosote oil for hydrogenation were regulated until 1958 (R3153). Crude tar acids were subject to various pricing agreements between tar distillers and refiners until 1961–1962 (R222, R753, R177, R178, R179). Finally, sales of briquetting pitch were regulated by a common selling organization, the Pitch Pool of the Association of Tar Distillers, until 1974 (R3154). All in all, there was a change of competition regime in the long run in this part of MLH 271.2.

Other organic chemicals. The Phenol Producers Association fixed the prices of phenol, orthocresol, and phenol-cresol mixtures (R219*, R220). R219* was contested by the parties in the Court and was struck down (LR 2 RP 1). Both agreements were abandoned in 1960, although R219* may have been replaced for some time by an information agreement. The Cresylic Acid Refiners Committee recommended minimum prices for cresylic acid and various mixtures until 1960 (R221). Crude and refined benzole (benzene) were sold through a common selling organization, Benzole Producers (R1025, R2081, R3090). The agreement, which prescribed that the parties should sell all their production through the company, continued until the 1970s. Finally, the Naphthalene Producers Committee of the Association of Tar Distillers recommended prices of naphthalene for standard buyers until 1961 and fixed prices for large buyers until 1966 (R2826, R2678, R2679). All these products accounted for a small fraction of total sales in this part of MLH 271.2, however, so the effect of the 1956 Act on competition was not significant.

General Chemicals, Other Than Inorganic and Organic (MLH 271.3)

A pricing agreement between producers of case-hardening compounds ended in 1959 (R62). An agreement between two sellers and five buyers of petroleum-cracking catalysts, providing for cooperation in production, joint sale, and exclusive supply arrangements, was canceled in 1962 (R1502, R1521). These are very minor products of MLH 271.3, which can therefore be regarded as a competitive industry.

Pharmaceutical Chemicals and Preparations (MLH 272)

Pharmaceutical chemicals.   A restrictive agreement between two producers of insulin (R950), providing for cooperation in production and for the joint sale of insulin, was canceled in 1961. See also MRPC, *Report on the Supply of Insulin* (London: H.M.S.O., 1952). Insulin is a very small part of the industry, which was therefore essentially competitive.

Pharmaceutical preparations.   The agreement of the Chemists Federation (R1027*) was the first to be referred to the Restrictive Practices Court and to be contested by the parties in late 1958. The membership of the federation consisted of manufacturers of proprietary medicines, wholesale chemists, and retail chemists. The agreement, which imposed restrictions designed to prevent the sale to the public by anyone except retail chemists (whether or not members) of proprietary medicines manufactured by members, was condemned by the Court (LR 1 RP 75). However, it is not clear why this agreement should have had any significant effect on competition between manufacturers. The same remark can be made about the activities of the Proprietary Articles Trade Association, whose membership consisted of manufacturers and distributors of medicines and toiletries: the association collectively enforced resale prices and set *minimum* distributors' margins until 1956, but it did not regulate the manufacturers' individual prices. See the Lloyds' report for details (the industry was also listed in CD). An agreement of the Proprietary Association of Great Britain, which remained in force throughout the period examined in this book, related only to a code of conduct (R3259). On the other hand, a pricing agreement between three UK and several foreign manufacturers of quinine and quinidine (R3111, R3112), which ended in 1963, covered a very specific product and was of little importance for competition in the industry as a whole.

In contrast, an agreement by the Association of the British Pharmaceutical Industry, which ended in 1960, contained recommended prices for nonproprietary medicines for the home retail and hospital trade (R1134). The agreement did not affect (1) branded proprietary drugs and (2) export sales. According to a case study of the industry, written by C. J. Thomas and published in Burn (1958), roughly a third of total sales of drugs in the mid-1950s were export sales; another third were home sales of branded and unbranded drugs through the National Health Service (either to hospitals or supplied on prescription), and about 70% of those were sales of branded drugs; another third were publicly advertised proprietary medicines, drugs sold without prescription, and veterinary and horticultural medicines. These figures suggest that sales of unbranded drugs in the home market, either through the NHS or without prescription, did not account for more than 10–15% of total industry sales revenue in the mid-1950s, and they probably accounted for less than 10% in the 1960s. Since the only products affected by the agreement of the Association of the British Pharmaceutical Industry were unbranded drugs sold in the home market, the industry should probably be seen as largely competitive.

Toilet Preparations (MLH 273)

A registered agreement by the Hairdressing Manufacturers and Wholesalers Association (R482) specified conditions of sale and *minimum* trade discounts for hairdressers' articles. Most of the restrictions were abandoned in 1959. According to the Lloyds' report, this association was also responsible for the collective enforcement of manufacturers' individual resale prices (until 1956). Similarly, the Proprietary Articles Trade Association enforced resale prices and set *minimum* distributors' margins for other toilet preparations until 1956. The industry was also listed in CD. It is not clear why these arrangements would have had a significant effect on competition between manufacturers. (Note that the membership of both associations consisted of manufacturers and distributors.) Thus both the industry as a whole and all its principal products should be seen as competitive.

Paint (MLH 274)

Paint. Each of the two associations in the paint industry, the Society of British Paint Manufacturers and the National Federation of Associated Paint, Colour and Varnish Manufacturers of the U.K., registered a restrictive agreement (R1920, R1896). A third agreement was registered by the British Paint Advisory Council, which had been set up by the two associations (R385). All three agreements provided for the maintenance of the manufacturers' (individually set) resale prices, and specified trade discounts for various classes of buyers and various types of products, quantity discounts, and terms and conditions of sale. The industry was also listed in CD. The agreements were canceled in 1959. Although the evidence from PEP suggests that these agreements may have not been fully effective, the paint industry should be regarded as one with a change of competition regime.

Other products. A price-fixing agreement by the National Association of Putty Manufacturers (R643), relating to putty and building mastics, was canceled in 1959. It was replaced by an information agreement, which was abandoned in the early 1970s.

Soap and Detergents (MLH 275)

Soap. No evidence of restrictive agreements.

Detergents. No evidence of restrictive agreements in the 1950s. An agreement by the two leading firms, Unilever and Procter and Gamble, was in operation between 1960 and 1968 and was essentially an attempt to resist an ongoing trend toward higher promotional expenditure in the industry (R2983). According to MC, *Household Detergents* (London: H.M.S.O., 1967), promotional expenditure was still excessive in the mid-1960s, although it may have declined subsequently. In any case, there is no evidence of any significant change in the state of competition in the industry between the 1950s and the 1970s.

Other products. An agreement by the U.K. Glycerine Producers Association comprised prices for crude and refined glycerine (R640*, R641). It was abandoned in 1960.

Synthetic Resins and Plastics Materials, and Synthetic Rubber (MLH 276)

Synthetic resins and plastics materials. The register contains evidence of informal discussions about prices by manufacturers of polyester resin in the 1970s (R5043). Moreover, polystyrene molding powder was listed in BT as allegedly collusive in the 1950s. The share of these products in total industry sales revenue was probably less than 10%.

Synthetic rubber. No evidence of restrictive agreements.

Cellulose film. No registered agreements, although this product was listed in BT as allegedly collusive.

Dyestuffs and Pigments (MLH 277)

Dyestuffs. No evidence of any major restrictive agreements. The British Tanning Extract Manufacturers Association set the prices of tanning extracts sold to the leather industry until 1959 (R755). This is a very minor product, however, so the dyestuff industry as a whole was not significantly affected by the 1956 Act.

Pigments. The register contains several agreements covering specific products. The U.K. White Lead Convention fixed the price of white lead (R786). The prices of zinc oxide (R2045*), aluminum red oxide (R2479), "helio fast red" pigment (R555), "persian gulf red" pigment (R592), and various chromium pigments (R756) were also fixed. All these agreements were abandoned in 1959–1960. An international market-sharing agreement in lithophone, involving two UK firms, ended in 1964 (R2989). The combined share of all these products in total industry sales revenue was about 25% in the 1960s.

Finally, according to CD, lead oxide was subject to certain forms of collective discrimination, such as aggregated rebates, before 1956.

Fertilizers (MLH 278)

The register contains three agreements. The British Sulphate of Ammonia Federation fixed the price of sulfate of ammonia, in agreement with one large producer outside the federation, until 1963 (R415*, R416*). A selling organization for basic slag, British Basic Slag, had a series of bilateral agreements with its parent firms, requiring each of these firms to sell the whole of its production of basic slag through the joint company (R1024*, R2865*). The Court recognized that this was effectively an arrangement between the slag producers, and was therefore registrable under the 1956 Act (LR 3 RP 178, LR 4 RP 116); it was abandoned in 1964. Finally, the Phosphate Rock Agency, a common buying organization for phosphate rock, registered and later abandoned an agreement specifying that members should purchase phosphate rock only through the agency (R132). The products affected by these agreements accounted for about 10% of total sales of fertilizers.

Additional information on the industry is contained in MC, *Report on the Supply of Chemical Fertilisers* (London: H.M.S.O., 1959). The price of fertilizers was under government control until 1953. At that time, firms in the industry were charging common prices and the two principal associations, the Superphosphate Manufacturers Association and the Fertiliser Manufacturers Association, recommended trade discounts and conditions of sale. According to CD, the industry was also subject to collective discrimination arrangements. There was no agreement on common prices after 1953, however, and all recommendations on discounts and conditions of sale ceased in 1956. In conclusion, the state of competition in the fertilizer industry was ambiguous in the early 1950s because of government regulation; in the late 1950s, only a fraction of the industry was subject to collusive agreements.

Polishes (MLH 279.1)

There is no evidence of restrictive agreements in this industry.

Formulated Adhesives, Gelatine, Glue, Size, etc. (MLH 279.2)

In a series of agreements between its members and with associations in the leather industry, the Hide, Gelatine, and Glue Section of the Federation of Gelatine and Glue Manufacturers regulated the buying price of gluestock and probably also allocated supplies among its members (R538, R1181, R1182). The buying price of shredded rabbit pelt was also regulated (R1183). The details of the allocation scheme for gluestock are not clear. On the other hand, both BT and PEP mention an apparently different agreement whereby the members of the Federation of Bone Users and Allied Trades regulated the prices and allocated the supplies of fat and bones for the production of glue and other products. The products affected by all these arrangements accounted for about 15% of MLH 279.2 in 1963, but for less than 10% in 1968 and in the 1970s. Because of a substantial change in the definition of the industry between the 1958 S.I.C. and the 1968 S.I.C., the pre-1963 figures are not comparable with the post-1963 figures. Hence it is sufficient, for our present purposes, that the industry can be seen as one without a change in competition regime after 1963.

Explosives, Fireworks, and Matches (MLH 279.3)

Explosives.   No evidence of restrictive agreements.

Fireworks.   An agreement of the British Pyrotechnists Association required members to enforce their (individually set) resale prices and specified trade discounts and conditions of sale (R561). The agreement was canceled in 1959, and the association was dissolved in 1962. An agreement by its successor, the British Firework Manufacturers Safety Association, which lasted until 1970, related only to conditions of sale and safety standards (R3214, R3591). Hence there was a change of competition regime in the fireworks industry.

Matches.   There is no evidence of restrictive agreements between UK firms, although there was an arrangement, involving prices and quotas, between the dominant UK firm and a foreign competitor. See MRPC, *Report on the Supply and Export of Matches and the Supply of Match-making Machinery* (London: H.M.S.O., 1953).

Formulated Pesticides and Disinfectants (MLH 279.4)

There is no evidence of significant restrictive agreements in this industry.

Printing Ink (MLH 279.5)

The register contains an agreement by the Society of British Ink Manufacturers, relating to settlement discounts for sales of printing inks other than news inks (R1376). The agreement also made vague references to attempts by the association to raise the level of net prices by reducing discounts, and the industry was also mentioned as potentially collusive in PEP. It is perhaps best to consider the ink industry as ambiguous.

Surgical Bandages, etc., and Sanitary Towels (MLH 279.6)

Surgical and medical dressings.   The Surgical Dressings Manufacturers Association fixed prices for various types of dressings (R149). This formally ended in 1959, but the member firms established an information agreement and subsequently went through a prolonged period during which price wars alternated with renewed, and partly successful, attempts to collude (R3213, R3608). These attempts seem to have ceased after 1969. Swann et al. (1973) provide full details. A second association in the industry, the Medical and Surgical Plaster Makers Conference, fixed prices for adhesive bandages and dressings until 1959 (R1078). According to CD, the surgical dressing industry was also subject to collective discrimination arrangements before 1956. In the long run, then, the industry experienced a change in competition regime.

Sanitary towels.   No evidence of restrictive agreements.

Photographic Chemical Materials (MLH 279.7)

A price agreement between members of the Federation of Engineers' Sensitised Material Manufacturers ended in 1959 (R554). It was replaced by an information agreement, which lasted until 1966. The products covered in the arrangement, sensitized paper and cloth, accounted for about 30% of total industry sales. However, an official investigation into the industry carried out in the 1970s revealed several collusive agreements on reprographic chemicals, diazo copying materials, and drafting film, which had been in operation since the late 1960s or the early 1970s. See MMC, *Diazo Copying Materials* (London: H.M.S.O., 1977) for details. These agreements, which again covered only a fraction of MLH 279.7, were placed on the register (and were also referred to the Court), and were abandoned in the late 1970s. In summary, the state of competition in the industry throughout the period examined in this book can only be classified as ambiguous.

Iron and Steel, General (MLH 311)

Wrought iron.   The British Wrought Iron Association recommended prices for wrought iron until 1965 (R380*). This is a very minor product of MLH 311.

Ferromanganese.   The register contains a number of pricing agreements involving producers of ferromanganese (R1232, R2049*, R2773*). R1232 ended in 1958, and the other two were abandoned in 1963. This is a secondary product of MLH 311.

Steel products.   The register contains more than seventy price-fixing agreements by various associations and groups of steel producers, covering virtually every product of the steel industry. Some of these products also appear in CD. Rather than listing the individual agreements, which would be very tedious, I will provide here a summary for the industry as a whole and for its principal products.[3]

One of the principal functions of the Iron and Steel Board (the regulatory body for the steel industry) was to set maximum prices for a wide range of steel products. For products covered by these controls, the agreements of the steel producers essentially specified or recommended that the maximum prices set by the Board be treated as fixed prices. For products free of government controls, the prices were set by the relevant associations. The agreements typically specified trade discounts and conditions of sale as well. A few also provided for the reporting of inquiries received from customers, which could sometimes lead to the sharing of orders.

Most agreements in the steel industry were referred to the Court, and two were contested by the parties but struck down by the Court. The first (R1092*) was a pricing agreement by three associations representing manufacturers of heavy steel plates, sections, and joists—about 25% of all steel products (LR 5 RP 33). The second (R1091, R2445*) was between the National Federation of Scrap Iron, Steel and Metal Merchants and the British Iron and Steel Federation, and imposed pricing and other restrictions on the market for steel scrap (LR 4 RP 299). While the vast majority of the registered agreements were between British firms, the register also contains evidence that the British Iron and Steel Federation participated in an international restrictive agreement on steel products, at least during 1962–1965 (R2835).

Most agreements were terminated in 1964–1965, but some were abandoned before 1963. The most important products covered by agreements abandoned before 1963 were steel castings, steel forgings, and tinplate. All the other products were covered by agreements canceled after 1963. This distinction is important in the present context because the steel industry was nationalized in 1967; hence the only relevant period for our present purposes is the period 1954–1963. Whenever an agreement ended *after* 1963, the product in question can be classified as one that experienced no change in competitive conditions over the relevant period. Whenever an agreement ended *before* 1963, however, the product in question must be classified as one with a change in competition regime.

Permanent magnets. A price-fixing agreement by the Permanent Magnet Association (R999, R1000, R1001, R1935*) was contested in the Court and

---

3. I report here, for the record, the numbers of all the significant restrictive agreements between steel manufacturers contained in the register. Brief descriptions of those that were referred to the Court can be found in the Registrar's reports. Referred to the Court: R213*, R245*, R256*, R414*, R864*, R913*, R976*, R1079*, R1081*, R1084*, R1085*, R1092*, R1093*, R1098*, R1100*, R1101*, R1104*, R1105*, R1106*, R1109*, R1111*, R1112*, R1113*, R1121*, R1122*, R1123*, R1125*, R1128*, R1129*, R1130*, R1131*, R1243*, R2445*, R2801*, R2802*, R2803*, R4094*. Not referred to the Court: R861, R862, R863, R1082, R1083, R1086, R1091, R1099, R1102, R1103, R1107, R1108, R1110, R1114, R1116, R1117, R1118, R1119, R1120, R1124, R1126, R1127, R1202, R1203, R2430, R2431, R2432, R2835, R3271, R5069, R5074.

was allowed to continue (see LR 3 RP 119, LR 3 RP 392, Swann et al. 1973). The agreement provided also for joint research, exchange of technical information, and patent pooling. This is a secondary product of MLH 311.

Steel Tubes (MLH 312)

An agreement between the two largest producers of steel tubes, Stewards and Lloyds and Tube Investments, providing for the demarcation of their respective activities and for common prices for certain classes of tubes that both firms produced, ended in 1959 (R1187). A similar agreement between Stewards and Lloyds and a smaller firm was abandoned in 1962 (R1032). A third agreement of this kind, between Stewards and Lloyds and one of the largest steel producers, was abandoned in 1959 (R2519).

Moreover, an agreement by the Large Tube Association fixed, until 1963, the prices of various types of steel tubes and provided for the allocation of orders received from customers (R677). The Association of Electric Steel Conduit Manufacturers fixed the prices of steel electric conduits until 1960 (R795, R1161); steel conduits were also listed in CD. The Conduit Fittings Manufacturers Association set the prices of electrical conduit fittings and accessories until 1959 (R76). The Cased Tube Association set prices and quotas for cased tubes until 1957 (R276). Finally, a pricing agreement by a group of producers of steel pipe fittings ended in 1960 (R1026, R2614). On the other hand, an agreement by the British Hot Finished Tube Conference, which ended in 1967, related only to standard conditions for government contracts (R1029). I should also mention a pricing agreement between two producers of seamless steel tubes, which came into force in 1973 and was abandoned in 1979 (R5073*, R5078*). In summary, both MLH 312 as a whole and its constituent principal products experienced a change of competition regime as a result of the 1956 Act.

Iron Castings, etc. (MLH 313)

Pig iron. Several agreements, covering all types of pig iron, were registered. The Basic Pig Iron Producers Association (R1016, R1097*), the National Association of Hematite Pig Iron Makers (R1094*, R1095), the Foundry Pig Iron Producers Association (R474*) and the Cylinder and Refined Iron Association (R1087, R1088) all set the prices of their respective products or recommended that the maximum prices set by the Iron and Steel Board be treated as fixed prices. Some of these agreements were superseded by others or ended in the late 1950s. Those that were in force in the early 1960s, covering more than 90% of total industry sales, were abandoned in 1964–1965. Thus there was no change in competitive conditions during the period 1954–1963 in the pig iron industry. After the mid-1960s, the industry was radically transformed as a result of the nationalization of steel.

Marine and engineering iron castings. The National Federation of Engineering and General Ironfounders made recommendations for price increases in marine and engineering castings to its thirteen member associations, who then circulated the recommendations to their members (R282, R2791). In fact, until 1962 several regional associations took a more active part in price setting, but after 1962 they merely forwarded the recommendations of the federation and, in a few cases, operated information agreements (see R138, R207, R236, R373, R397, R399, R411, R420, R529, R545, R587, R731, R1583, R1672). The recommendations ceased after 1965.

Other iron castings. Several price-fixing agreements covered nearly all of the more specific types of iron castings. In a series of agreements between its members and with various outside firms, the British Ironfounders Association set prices for cast iron rainwater and soil goods, cast iron drain connections, general builders' castings, and domestic solid-fuel cooking and heating appliances (R2797*, R2798*, R2799*, R2800*). See MRPC, *Report on the Supply of Cast Iron Rainwater Goods* (London: H.M.S.O., 1951) for details of these arrangements, which initially also involved collective exclusive dealing, aggregated rebates, and collective resale price maintenance. The registered agreements were abandoned in 1963. The British Bath Manufacturers Association set minimum prices for cast iron porcelain enameled bathtubs until 1960 (R548*). Note that the bathtub industry is also listed in CD. According to Swann et al. (1973), the abolition of the agreement was followed by a prolonged period of very intense competition that lasted throughout the 1960s. The British Malleable Tube Fittings Association set prices for malleable tube fittings and was also a party to international agreements until 1960 (R661, R664, R1805, R1806, R1807, R1937, R2500). According to BT, it may also have been engaged in collective discrimination arrangements.

Other price-fixing bodies included the National Ingot Mould Association (R997), the Cast Iron Pressure Pipe Association (R475), the Range Boiler Makers Association (R182), the Cast Iron Chair Association (R828), the Cast Iron Axlebox Association (R893), and the Cast Iron Segment Association (R918, R919). All these associations abandoned their respective agreements between 1958 and 1962. According to CD and BT, cast iron heating boilers and radiators were also subject to collective discrimination arrangements before 1956. In summary, both the iron casting industry as a whole and nearly all of its principal products experienced a change in competition regime as a result of the 1956 Act.

Aluminium and Aluminium Alloys (MLH 321)

The register contains restrictive agreements from all three sections of the industry: smelters, fabricators, and founders. The Federation of Light Metal Smelters fixed prices for certain types of ingots until 1958 (R192), although these were "maximum" prices, at least according to the registered agreement. The Light Metal Founders Association recommended price increases to cover changes in costs in the castings industry until 1961 (R419), and operated an information agreement for some time after that date (Swann et al. 1974). The British Aluminium Foil Rollers Association fixed prices for aluminum foil until 1959 (R1074), and operated an information agreement after that date. Finally, seven leading fabricators were parties to a collusive arrangement for aluminum semimanufactures, which was not initially registered and therefore continued until 1967 (R3045*, R3046). See also MC, *Aluminium Semi-manufactures* (London: H.M.S.O., 1967). The arrangement provided for discussions about prices, the occasional allocation of large orders between the parties, and restrictions imposed on distributors for sales of imported goods. In the long run, then, there was a change of competition regime for the aluminum industry as a whole and for most, if not all, of its principal products.

Copper, Brass, and Other Copper Alloys (MLH 322)

Collusive agreements were widespread in this industry, covering its three sections: smelters, fabricators, and founders. The main data source for the semimanufactures section of the industry is MRPC, *Report on the Supply and Export of Certain Semi-manufactures of Copper and Copper-based Alloys* (London: H.M.S.O., 1955). This report described the collusive activities of more than ten associations of fabricators, covering virtually all copper and copper alloy semimanufactures: plate, sheet, strip, rods, and tubes (and also wire, which is not part of MLH 322). The associations imposed agreed prices, aggregated rebates, and, in several cases, collective exclusive dealing. Several were also involved in international collusive agreements. Most of the associations investigated by the MRPC did not register their agreements. Presumably they abandoned them in 1956, in light of the fact that they had been severely criticized by the MRPC. Thus the register contains only agreements by the Rod Rollers Association (R1553), the Cadmium Copper and Bronze Association (R1554), and the High Conductivity Copper Association (R508*). All three ended between 1957 and 1959. It seems that R1554 and R508* were replaced by information agreements for part of the 1960s.

The register also contains one agreement between smelters and another between founders. The British Bronze and Brass Ingot Manufacturers Association recommended prices of bronze and brass ingots until 1962 (R2732). After that date, it operated an information agreement, which seems to have continued until the 1970s. The Merseyside Non-Ferrous Founders Association fixed prices for copper and copper alloy castings until 1959 (R586). Finally, an agreement by the British Non-Ferrous Metals Federation, which was dropped in 1957, related only to recommended conditions of sale (R410). In summary, the 1956 Act caused a change in competition regime for MLH 322 as a whole as well as for most, if not all, its principal products.

Miscellaneous Nonferrous Metals (MLH 323)

Lead manufactures. The Lead Sheet and Pipe Association specified minimum prices for lead sheet and pipes (R1052*). According to CD, it also engaged in certain forms of collective discrimination, including aggregated rebates, before 1956. The agreement was formally canceled in 1962. Until that date the association was also a party to an agreement with two smelters regarding maximum buying prices of scrap and remelted lead (R803). Moreover, between 1962 and 1965 several members of the association operated an effective information agreement (R3075). The register also contains a pricing arrangement of the Association of Lead Sellers, whose membership consisted of manufacturers and merchants of lead sheet and pipes in Scotland (R908), and an arrangement among three smelters for the price of scrap and remelted lead (R1399). Both of these ended in 1962. Lead sheet and pipes accounted for 15–20% of total sales of lead manufactures in the 1960s.

Nickel manufactures. No evidence of any restrictive agreements.

Tin manufactures. No evidence of any restrictive agreements.

Zinc manufactures. A price agreement between producers of zinc strip is mentioned in MRPC, *Report on the Supply and Export of Certain Semi-manufactures of Copper and Copper-based Alloys* (London: H.M.S.O., 1955). This product accounts for less than 10% of total sales of zinc manufactures, however, so the effect of the 1956 Act on the industry was not significant.

Other products. The Collapsible Tube Association fixed prices for all types of collapsible tubes made from nonferrous metals until 1958 (R1258). An agreement between two leading producers of various ferrous alloys, High Speed Steel Alloys and Murex, relating to prices, allocation of products, and some profit-sharing (R1374, R2675), ended in 1962.

Agricultural Machinery, Except Tractors (MLH 331)

An agreement by the Agricultural Engineers Association, whose membership consisted of manufacturers and wholesalers of agricultural machinery and tractors, provided for recommended discounts by manufacturers and wholesalers to various classes of customers and for conditions of sale (R860). The agreement was abandoned in 1957. In addition, the manufacturers practiced resale price maintenance, and there were also, until the late 1960s, agreements between dealers to maintain the manufacturers' prices (R789*, R2846). The industry was also listed in CD and BT for operating collective discrimination arrangements. The effect of all the above schemes on competition between manufacturers is rather uncertain, however. There was no agreement on retail prices, which therefore were individually set. Moreover, each manufacturer appointed a number of distributors and dealers in any given area (both before and after 1957), and the discounts given by different manufacturers to their designated distributors and dealers were not regulated by the agreement—in fact, they varied considerably and were the product of direct negotiations.

The register also contains a series of agreements between two leading manufacturers of agricultural machinery and tractors, Ford Motor and Ransomes Sims and Jeferries, relating to the joint production and/or distribution of certain types of machinery (R2775, R840, R3197). Some of these agreements were abandoned in the early 1960s, while others continued until the early 1970s. Finally, the register contains two price agreements, one by the Agricultural Machine Parts Association (R921) and one by the Milking Machine Manufacturers Association (R1714). The first of these seems to have been a regional arrangement. Both were abandoned in the late 1950s. All in all, the effect of the 1956 Act on the agricultural machinery industry should probably be regarded as ambiguous.

Metalworking Machine Tools (MLH 332)

Metal-cutting and metal-forming machine tools. The register contains an agreement involving six machine tool manufacturers who had formed a "holding company" and accepted restrictions as to the types of machine tools each could produce (R678). Some of them were among the largest firms in the industry. The arrangement was abandoned in 1959. According to a case study of the machine tool industry, written by M. E. Beesley and G. W. Troup and published in Burn (1958), the existence of "exclusive agencies" and the specialization of production within agencies was a common feature of this section of the industry. Each agency comprised several manufacturers, but each manufacturer belonged to a single agency. Without detailed information on how these agencies operated, their effect on competition can only be regarded as uncertain. PEP also mentions an agreement by the Machine Tool Trades Association, which, however, apparently related only to conditions of sale.

Welding and flame-cutting equipment. No evidence of any restrictive agreements.

Pumps, Valves, and Compressors (MLH 333)

Pumps. A registered agreement by the British Pump Manufacturers Association, which was abandoned in 1967, related only to conditions of contract (R425, R1418). However, the association is mentioned in PEP as allegedly collusive. Moreover, a group of firms in the industry were parties, until 1960, to the "pump notification scheme" (R426). This covered relatively large pumping equipment and provided for the reporting of inquiries received from customers, uniform action on terms and conditions with respect to these inquiries, and the payment by the successful tenderer of a fee to unsuccessful tenderers for inquiries that needed a great amount of preparatory work. However, the scheme did not explicitly provide for price-fixing or the allocation of work. As I have explained in chapter 3, the effect of such schemes on competition is not clear.

The register also contains a pricing arrangement among three producers of semirotary wing pumps (R603*, R1727). This ended in 1959. Two other registered agreements should probably be classified to MLH 333. The Hydraulic Association operated a notification scheme for hydraulic plant and also specified conditions of sale (R232). The agreement was modified in 1966, but it was not entirely abandoned. Also, a group of three firms were parties, until 1960, to the "hydraulic machinery agreement," which covered hydraulic turbines and associated hydraulic mechanical equipment, and provided not only for the reporting of inquiries received from customers but also for discussions about prices (R700). The overall picture for the pump industry is one of uncertainty: those agreements that were clearly restrictive covered only certain parts of the industry, while those that clearly covered large sections of the industry contained restrictions with an uncertain effect on competition.

Valves. No agreements for valves were registered, but the industry was mentioned in PEP as allegedly collusive.

Compressors. The Portable Air Compressor Association specified minimum prices for portable air compressors until 1959 (R1301*). The agreement also provided for the exchange of technical information in basic research, although not in product development. In addition, a group of firms were parties to the "centrifugal and axial flow blower and compressor agreement," which regulated prices and tendering fees until 1961 (R717). The combined share of the products covered by these two agreements in the total sales revenue of the compressor industry was about 50% in the 1960s. Hence the 1956 Act caused a change of competition regime in this industry.

Fluid power equipment. No evidence of any restrictive agreements.

Industrial Engines (MLH 334)

Internal combustion engines. Four agreements, covering various types of compression ignition engines and providing for the notification of inquiries and for agreed prices, were abandoned in 1961–1962 (R926, R927, R928, R929). Also, a price agreement for steam engines (R686) was canceled in 1959. There was, then, a change of competition regime in this part of MLH 334.

Other prime movers. The register contains several agreements relating to turbines and condensing plant (some of these also covered products classified to MLH 361). The agreements comprised the notification of inquiries and orders, prices, provisions regarding the payment of fees by subcontractors to main contractors, and often design specifications. The "small turbine agreement" (R705), the "small condenser agreement" (R715) and the "small turbine and small condenser inter-contracting agreement" (R1842) ended in 1961. The "large turbine and large turbo-type alternator inter-contracting agreement" (R1932*) and the "large turbine and large condenser inter-contracting agreement" (R1933*) were abandoned in 1962. Finally, the "large turbine price agreement" (R704*) and the "large condenser price agreement" (R685*) were canceled in 1967. Thus this part of MLH 334 also experienced a change of competition regime as a result of the 1956 Act.

Textile Machinery and Accessories (MLH 335)

The only price agreements for complete machines were the ones registered by the British Jacquard Engineers' Association (R515) and the Lace Machine Builders and Allied Trades Association (R1479). Both were abandoned in 1959–1960. A third agreement, by the British Knitting Machine Builders Association, comprised only conditions of sale and ended in 1964 (R297). On the other hand, most parts and accessories of textile machinery were subject to price fixing until 1959 (R57, R110, R259, R260, R383, R384, R432, R534, R537, R1427, R1451, R1507). The combined share of jacquard machines and lace machines in the product category "complete textile machinery" (which is the one used for the concentration regressions in this book) was probably around 5%. Even if parts and accessories are taken into account, the collusive products covered at most 10–15% of total sales revenue of MLH 335. Hence both the product category "complete textile machinery" and MLH 335 as a whole can be seen as largely competitive.

Construction and Earth-Moving Equipment (MLH 336)

An agreement by the Excavator Makers Association (R83) provided for the reporting of inquiries and tenders, maximum discounts to "resale merchants" and the prenotification of price changes. However, neither individual list prices nor commissions to appointed agents were regulated. The Concrete Mixers Manufacturers Association specified minimum prices and commissions to agents and merchants (R958*, R2373*). The members of the Road Roller Manufacturers Association accepted minimum prices (R880*). The agreement of the Well Drillers Association comprised the reporting of inquiries and minimum prices for tenders (R567). Finally, the Rammer Manufacturers Association set prices for power rammers (R24). All these agreements were canceled in 1959. The affected products accounted for 20–30% of total industry sales.

Mechanical Handling Equipment (MLH 337)

Conveyors, Aerial Ropeways, etc., and Lifting and Winding Devices. An
agreement by the Mechanical Handling Engineers Association (R225) provided for the reporting of inquiries received from customers and for tendering fees in connection with a wide range of mechanical handling equipment.
An agreement by the Aerial Ropeways Association (R226) may have been
somewhat more restrictive, since it also contained a reference to "uniform
action where necessary" following the reporting of inquiries; however, it
covered only aerial ropeways. Both arrangements were abandoned in 1965.
A price agreement in reels and winches, which are secondary products of the
industry, was abandoned in 1959 (R868, R1304). Overall, the effect of the
1956 Act on competition in this industry was ambiguous.

Cranes. Until 1963, the agreement of the Association of Crane Makers
(R2578*) provided for the reporting of inquiries and for discussions between
interested members about the terms and conditions for particular tenders
(but not about prices). There were also occasional attempts to allocate work.
After 1963, the agreement comprised the reporting of inquiries, the reporting
of the terms and conditions set by each individual member for any given
inquiry, and the payment of tendering fees. The arrangement was discontinued in 1967. In conclusion, while there is some evidence of significant
restrictions on competition in this industry, it is probably not overwhelming.

Lifts and escalators. An agreement by the National Association of Lift
Makers contained recommendations about installation and maintenance
charges, conditions of sale, restrictions on sales promotion, and the requirement not to carry out the maintenance of a new lift (elevator) installed by
another member for one year after installation (R1043). Most restrictions
were canceled in 1963. The 1956 Act probably caused a change of competition regime in this industry.

Powered industrial trucks and industrial tractors. No evidence of any restrictive agreements.

Office Machinery (MLH 338)

The register contains an agreement by the Typewriter and Allied Trades
Federation of Great Britain, whose membership consisted of manufacturers,
importers, and distributors of various types of office machinery (R665). The
products covered by the agreement accounted for about 40–50% of total
sales of the office machinery industry. As registered, the agreement provided
for the reporting of individual list prices and trade discounts to the association, the maintenance of manufacturers' individual resale prices, restrictions

on sales promotion, and minimum charges for the renting and maintenance of typewriters and calculating machines in particular. Most of these restrictions were canceled in 1957, but those involving the exchange of information remained. BT also reports allegations of collective discrimination arrangements in typewriters and typewriter components.

Further details on the industry are provided in CD and PEP (in the latter case the information comes from a manufacturer of typewriters). It seems that the original agreement was more restrictive than the one registered, at least for typewriters: it provided for the collective enforcement of resale prices and may also have regulated individual prices. On the other hand, PEP also confirms that many products of the industry were not regulated. The effect of the 1956 Act on the office machinery industry as a whole was therefore ambiguous. There is also evidence that there was a change of competition regime for typewriters in particular.

Mining Machinery (MLH 339.1)

An agreement by the Coal Preparation Plant Association provided for the reporting of inquiries and recommended terms and conditions for contracts with the National Coal Board (R889). This agreement was allowed to continue without a Court hearing, since it was not regarded as restrictive. The Skip Plant Association also had a reporting agreement, which made vague references to uniform action (R1824). The restrictions in question were dropped in 1960. The products covered by R1824, skip plant and mine car handling plant, accounted for less than 10% of total industry sales. Two other agreements by associations in the industry, relating to terms and conditions for contracts with the National Coal Board, were also allowed to continue without a Court hearing (R510, R890). In summary, the industry was probably competitive, a view confirmed by evidence given by the National Coal Board and reported in PEP.

Printing, Bookbinding, and Paper Goods Making Machinery (MLH 339.2)

There were no significant registered agreements. BT reports allegations of collusion in printing blocks, a secondary product of the industry.

Refrigerating Machinery, Except Domestic-type Refrigerators (MLH 339.3)

An agreement by the British Refrigeration Association (R824), covering both commercial refrigerating machinery and domestic refrigerators, provided for the maintenance of the (individually set) manufacturers' prices and the exchange of price information between the parties, and also contained maximum trade discounts, conditions of sale, and restrictions on sales promotion. See also the Lloyds' report for details. The agreement was abandoned, possibly in the late 1950s, leading to a change of competition regime in this industry.

Space-Heating, Ventilating, and Air-Conditioning Equipment (MLH 339.4)

There is no evidence of significant restrictive agreements in this industry.

Food and Drink Processing Machinery (MLH 339.7)

An agreement by the Mineral Water Engineers Association and the Brewery Equipment Section of the Food Machinery Association provided for resale price maintenance, maximum trade discounts, and conditions of sale for mineral water machinery and brewing machinery (R530). The Dairy Engineers Association had a similar arrangement for dairy machinery (R1540). The products affected by these agreements, both of which ended in 1958–1959, accounted for 20–25% of total industry sales.

Miscellaneous Nonelectrical Machinery (MLH 339.5, 6, 8, and 9)

Portable power tools.   The Pneumatic Tool Association specified minimum prices for various types of pneumatic tools until 1959 (R308*). The Pneumatic Metal Working Tool Association also fixed prices until 1959 (R307). The products covered by these agreements accounted for about 20–30% of total industry sales. The industry was also mentioned in PEP as allegedly collusive.

Rolling mills.   An agreement by the Steel Works Plant Association (R227) provided for the reporting of inquiries above a certain value, uniform action on terms and conditions (but not on prices) with respect to these inquiries, and tendering fees. Several of the restrictions were abandoned in 1964. The register also contains an interreporting agreement between the Steel Works Plant Association and the Hydraulic Association, which was canceled in 1961 (R1359), and an arrangement about commissions between members of the Steel Works Plant Association and a group of manufacturers of electrical parts for rolling mills (R698), which ended in 1960. The effect of these agreements on competition in the rolling mill industry is uncertain.

Lawn mowers.   Electric mowers were covered by an agreement of the Associated Manufacturers of Domestic Electric Appliances, which ended in 1959 (R107). The details are described under MLH 368. Electric mowers accounted for about 10% of total sales of mowers, so the effect of the 1956 Act on the industry as a whole was probably not significant.

Other nonelectrical machinery. An agreement by the Society of Laundry Engineers and Allied Trades (R1145) provided for resale price maintenance and conditions of sale, including the requirement not to give discounts to certain types of buyers, but did not specify prices or trade discounts in general. It was abandoned in 1965. An agreement by the Garage Equipment Association, whose membership consisted of both manufacturers and distributors, comprised arrangements for collective exclusive dealing, resale price maintenance, agreed discounts, and conditions of sale (R793*); the industry was also listed in CD. The agreement was abandoned in 1960, and was replaced by an information agreement, which remained in force until 1972. BT also reports allegations of collusion in fire sprinkler equipment.

Industrial (Including Process) Plant and Steelwork (MLH 341)

Boilers and boilerhouse plant. An agreement by the Water-Tube Boilermakers Association comprised a procedure for tendering that effectively resulted in the sharing of orders between member firms (R509*). It was referred to the Court, contested by the parties, and allowed to continue (LR 1 RP 285). Several other agreements, relating to conditions of contract with the Central Electricity Generating Board (the main buyer of water-tube boilers), remained in force throughout the 1960s and early 1970s (R1593, R3728, R1486, R3121). On the other hand, a price-fixing agreement by the Association of Shell Boilermakers was abandoned in 1957 (R391). Although water-tube boilers were the main product of the industry, shell boilers accounted for about 20% of total industry sales in the late 1960s.

Other industrial plant, including process plant. An agreement by the Gasholder Makers Association provided for the reporting of inquiries and minimum prices for larger types of gasholders and gasholder tanks (R1073). The prices of furnaces and kilns were fixed in accordance with the "electric resistance furnace agreement" (R818*) and the "electric melting furnace agreement" (R819), both of which also provided for the reporting of inquiries. All three agreements were abandoned between 1958 and 1960. The affected products accounted for more than 20% but less than 50% of total industry sales.

Constructional steelwork and ironwork. A price-fixing agreement by the British Constructional Steelwork Association (R210*, R229) was abandoned in 1959. A separate agreement, providing for the reporting of inquiries and orders and specifying conditions of sale, continued throughout the 1960s and the 1970s (R3151). An agreement by the Bridge and Constructional Ironwork Association, which contained recommendations about price increases to cover changes in costs (R228), was canceled in 1959, and an interreporting arrangement between the two associations ended in 1960 (R1600). Hence there was a change of competition regime in this industry.

Other fabricated ironwork and steelwork.   An agreement by the Tank and Industrial Plant Association in connection with storage tanks and pressure vessels provided for the reporting of inquiries received and orders placed, the payment of tendering fees, and, in some cases, the allocation of work (R304). The last of these provisions was withdrawn in 1960, and the payment of tendering fees was discontinued in 1965. Additional information from PEP (provided, in this case, by a firm in the industry) suggests that the association's reporting procedure was designed to achieve "fair prices" and to resist "auctioning" by buyers. Hence it is probably fair to say that the 1956 Act caused a change of competition regime in this industry.

Ordnance and Small Arms (MLH 342)

There is no evidence of any significant restrictive agreements in this industry.

Other Mechanical Engineering Not Elsewhere Specified (MLH 349)

Ball and roller bearings.   No agreement was registered, but both PEP and BT mention this industry as allegedly collusive.

Rolls of iron and steel.   The National Forgemasters Association recommended prices for forged rolls until 1962 (R1122*). Also, until 1962, the Roll Makers Association fixed the prices of cast iron and steel rolls (R476). Informal discussions and occasional agreements on prices between some of the leading firms in the cast roll section of the industry continued until the late 1970s (R5075). There is some uncertainty about the effectiveness of these arrangements, however, especially after the nationalization of the steel industry in 1967 (which created a dominant buyer for cast rolls). Thus, although the iron and steel roll industry was collusive in the 1950s, the effect of the 1956 Act on the industry during the period examined in this book must be regarded as ambiguous.

Other products.   Producers of gears reported inquiries and fixed prices in accordance with the "turbine reduction gear agreement" (R692) and the "heavy reduction gear agreement" (R706) until 1960–1961. The Railway Cast Bearings Association allocated orders among its members until 1958 (R1030); this agreement covered only a small part of the bearing industry, however. A price-fixing agreement by the Tuyere Makers Association (R91*) was abandoned in 1959. An agreement by the British Oil Burner Manufacturers Association, relating only to conditions of tender and trading, ended in 1964 (R1144). Piston rings may have been subject to collective exclusive dealing, according to BT. Finally, four other price-fixing agreements in the register should probably be classified under MLH 349: R53, between producers of gas governors; R683, by the Gedges Drawback Hook Manufacturers Association; R920, by the Buffer Rod Makers Association; and R1530*, by the

Pressed Bowl Makers Association. The first three of these ended in 1959, and R1530* was canceled in 1964.

Photographic and Document Copying Equipment (MLH 351)

There is no evidence of collusion in the 1950s. However, a number of price agreements relating to diazo copying machines and drawing office equipment were discovered by the MMC in the course of its inquiry into the diazo copying materials industry (R4077*, R4084*, R4085*). See MMC, *Diazo Copying Materials* (H.M.S.O., 1977) for details. These agreements were apparently in operation for a limited period, from 1969 to 1972, so the industry can probably be classified as one without a change in competition regime between the 1950s and the 1970s.

Watches and Clocks (MLH 352)

Watches. No evidence of any significant restrictive agreements.

Clocks. The British Impulse Clock Manufacturers Association recommended prices for various types of electrical impulse clocks until 1959 (R745). PEP also reports allegations of a collusive agreement between members of the British Synchronous Clock Conference (which may be the predecessor of B.I.C.M.A.) The share of electric clocks in the total sales of MLH 352 was about 20%. According to CD, the mechanical clock industry was subject to collective discrimination arrangements before 1956.

Surgical Instruments and Appliances (MLH 353)

Medical, surgical, dental, and veterinary instruments and appliances. The register contains several agreements on surgical appliances. The Surgical Appliance Manufacturers Association set minimum prices for surgical supports and surgical elastic hosiery until 1963 (R2827). The British Surgical Trades Association recommended price increases for a wide range of surgical appliances, including elastic hosiery and surgical footwear, until 1963 (R2816*). The Scottish Surgical Instrument Manufacturers Association also recommended prices for surgical appliances, including elastic hosiery and surgical footwear, until 1967 (R3160*). A group of manufacturers of balloon catheters fixed prices until 1963 (R2751*). Finally, the Chemists Sundries Association fixed the prices of various pharmacists' and hospital sundries manufactured in earthenware until 1959 (R955). The share of the products covered by these agreements in total industry sales was about 30%. I should also mention an agreement by the Association of Dental Manufacturers and Traders of the United Kingdom, which provided for collective exclusive dealing and the collective enforcement of resale price maintenance, but did not regulate the manufacturers' prices or trade discounts. See the Lloyds' report and MRPC, *Report on the Supply of Dental Goods* (London: H.M.S.O., 1950) for details.

Spectacles and lenses.   Prices for spectacles, frames, and lenses were set by four different associations: the Ophthalmic Prescription Manufacturers Association (R672), the British Metal Spectacle Manufacturers Association (R673), the Plastic Spectacle Manufacturers Association (R674), and the British Ophthalmic Lens Manufacturers Association (R675). All four agreements were abandoned in 1959–1960, leading to a change in competition regime in this industry.

Scientific and Industrial Instruments and Systems (MLH 354)

Optical instruments.   No evidence of any restrictive agreements.

Other scientific and industrial instruments and systems.   The Meter Manufacturers Association set minimum prices for electricity meters (R483, R484). This agreement was formally abandoned in 1960 and was replaced by an information agreement (R3161*), which apparently was successful in reducing competition in the industry until 1970. See also MMC, *Electricity Supply Meters* (London: H.M.S.O., 1979). The Summation Meter Manufacturers Association set minimum prices for summation meters until 1965 (R878*, R1492*). The prices of various other types of instruments for measuring electrical magnitudes were regulated by the "subsidiary power instrument agreement" (R694) and the "patterns group agreement" (R691) until 1958–1960. In addition, the Commercial Instruments Conference fixed the prices of certain types of ammeters and voltmeters until 1961 (R708). Finally, the prices of gas meters were set, until 1957, by the Gas Meter Makers Conference (R669). The share of all the products affected by these agreements in total sales of scientific and industrial instruments and systems (excluding optical instruments) was about 10%. This was, then, a largely competitive industry.

Electrical Machinery (MLH 361)

Generators and turbines.   The agreements in generators and turbines comprised prices, the reporting of inquiries and orders, the payment of fees by subcontractors to main contractors, and sometimes design specifications or exchange of technical information. Before 1956 they also provided for certain forms of collective discrimination, such as aggregated rebates. The "large turbo-type alternator price agreement" (R688*) was canceled in 1967. Five other agreements—the "generator price agreement" (R702), the "small turbine-driven alternator and generator agreement" (R716), the "small turbine and turbine-driven alternator and generator inter-contracting agreement" (R1843), the "alternator price agreement" (R713), and the "marine turbo-generator agreement" (R703)—ended in 1960–1961. In addition, many of the agreements reviewed under MLH 334 are also relevant here (especially R705, R1842, R1932*, R1933*, and R704*). An arrangement between the Steam Turbine and Associated Plant Manufacturers and the Central Electricity Authority (the largest buyer of electrical machinery), regarding discounts for various types of machinery, ended in 1967 (R728). Finally, the "gas turbine generating plant agreement" (R2793) was canceled in 1969. Further details on the operation of these and other agreements in the electrical machinery industry, including some that involved only the reporting of inquiries, can be found in MRPC, *Report on the Supply and Exports of Electrical and Allied Machinery and Plant* (London: H.M.S.O., 1957). In conclusion, this part of MLH 361 experienced a change of competition regime as a result of the 1956 Act.

Transformers. The principal agreement for transformers and related equipment was operated by the Associated Transformer Manufacturers and provided for minimum prices, the reporting of inquiries and orders, and aggregated rebates (R707*). It was referred to the Court, defended by the parties, and struck down in 1961 (LR 2 RP 295, LR 7 RP 202). A second agreement, covering smaller transformers, was abandoned in 1958 (R690), as was an ancillary arrangement involving one firm which was not a member of A.T.M. (R2245). See MRPC, *Report on the Supply and Exports of Electrical and Allied Machinery and Plant* (London: H.M.S.O., 1957) for details on these agreements, and Swann et al. (1973) for an account of the emergence of competition in the industry following the collapse of an information agreement in the mid-1960s. The register also contains a number of annual agreements/contracts between manufacturers of large transformers and the Central Electricity Generating Board (the successor to the Central Electricity Authority), relating to the Board's requirements of very large transformers during the period 1970–1975 (R3616, R3700, R3746). All in all, there was a change of competition regime in this industry.

Switchgear. The register contains two agreements that covered all but the smaller sizes of switchgear (R689*, R711*). They comprised prices, the reporting of inquiries and orders, and design specifications. They were canceled in 1965–1967. A third agreement, which related to mining-type switchgear, ended in 1959 (R722). On the other hand, smaller switchgear was subject to an agreement that involved the reporting of inquiries and conditions of sale, but did not regulate prices (R695); the arrangement was nevertheless canceled in 1960. The register also contains several agreements between manufacturers and the Central Electricity Generating Board, regarding prices to be paid for particular orders of heavy switchgear (R2904, R3077, R3673, R3693). These continued until the mid-1970s, but it is doubtful whether they restricted competition to any significant extent. In any case, heavy switchgear accounted for a relatively small part of total industry sales in the 1970s. Thus the 1956 Act caused a change of competition regime in this industry.

Motors. Several restrictive agreements, covering various types of motors, were registered and then abandoned between 1958 and 1965: the "large electric machine agreement" (R697), the "fractional horsepower motor agreement" (R693*), the "dynamo and motor agreement" (R714), and the "marine motor and generator agreement" (R709). R697 and R709 also covered generators. Some of these were replaced for some time by information agreements. See MRPC, *Report on the Supply and Exports of Electrical and Allied Machinery and Plant* (London: H.M.S.O., 1957) for details on the collusive agreements of the 1950s, and Swann et al. (1973) for a description of the emergence of effective competition in the industry in the 1960s. There was a change of competition regime in the electric motor industry.

Other electrical machinery. Nearly all other types of electrical machinery were subject to collusion: control gear for motors (R701, R720), small switch and fuse gear (R668), electrical parts for rolling mills (R712), electrical equipment for winding or haulage engines (R699), electrical power distribution equipment (R658), railway traction electrical equipment (R2120), electrical equipment for diesel/electric main line locomotives (R2121), mercury arc rectifiers (R687), and protective transformers, relays, and accessories (R696). All these agreements ended between 1959 and 1961. Finally, an agreement on installation charges between the electrical machinery sections of the British Electrical and Allied Manufacturers Association and the Central Electricity Authority and the Area Electricity Boards ended in 1974.

Insulated Wires and Cables (MLH 362)

Collusive agreements were widespread in this industry, covering all types of electric cables. In fact, few industries were as tightly regulated as this one. The agreements provided for common prices, quotas, collective exclusive dealing, aggregated rebates, collective resale price maintenance, and patent pooling. There were also international agreements limiting imports. See MRPC, *Report on the Supply of Insulated Electric Wires and Cables* (London: H.M.S.O., 1952). The agreements were registered, although some restrictions—such as quotas, aggregated rebates, and collective exclusive dealing—were dropped after the publication of the MRPC report or before registration. In particular, the register contains agreements by the Mains Cable Manufacturers Association (R1462), the Mains Cable Manufacturers Association (Super Tension) (R1461*, R2859*), the Telephone Cable Makers Association (R798, R1555, R1556, R1685), the Rubber and Thermoplastic Cable Manufacturers Association (R1541), the Covered Conductors Association (R1523), the Independent Cable Makers Association (R750), the Association of Plastic Cable Makers (R1042), and the Switchboard Cable Association (R1557). Most of the agreements were abandoned between 1959 and 1961, except for those on supertension mains cables and accessories, which were finally canceled in 1969. Supertension mains cables accounted for about 15% of total sales of mains cables (and less than 10% of sales of all cables) in the late 1960s.

Swann et al. (1973) describe the evolution of competition in the industry during the 1960s. Despite parallel pricing and information agreements, competition emerged first for general wiring cables, then for mains cables, and finally, after 1969, for supertension mains cables. On the other hand, Swann et al. thought that the information agreement in telephone cables was relatively more effective in reducing competition. An official investigation into the industry in the 1970s reached similar conclusions, and in fact revealed a number of collusive arrangements between producers of telephone cables, which had been in operation since the 1960s—although they are unlikely to have had an effect comparable to that of the tight cartels of the 1950s. See MMC, *Insulated Electric Wires and Cables* (London: H.M.S.O., 1979). These agreements (R3850*, R3851*, R3852*, R3853*) were abandoned in 1974–1975. In summary, there was a change of competition regime for the industry as a whole and also for most types of cables. The only exception was the telephone cable section of the industry, where competition did not fully emerge during the period examined in this book.

Telegraph and Telephone Apparatus and Equipment (MLH 363)

The evolution of competition in this industry is summarized in Hart et al. (1973). The dominant buyer throughout the period examined in this book was the Post Office. Until 1969, sales of telephone installations to the Post Office were regulated by an agreement between manufacturers and the Post Office, which provided for the sharing of orders between the firms and specified the prices to be paid and conditions of sale. An ancillary arrangement provided for the exchange of technical information and patent pooling (R3376). Telephone installations are the main product of MLH 363. Another principal product is line apparatus for long-distance communication. Sales of line apparatus to the Post Office were similarly regulated, but only until 1963. After 1963 the Post Office gradually introduced more competition in the tendering process. These agreements were not registered, because the Crown (and hence the Post Office) was not bound by the provisions of the 1956 Act (see LR 3 RP 98, LR 3 RP 462). On the other hand, the register contains several agreements relating to sales to other buyers or agreements to which the Post Office was not formally a party: R406, R807, R954, R1135, R1136, R1452, R2210, R2249, R3813, R3961, R4036, R4097. The register also contains agreements to which the Post Office was a party and which were made from the mid-1960s onward (R3377, R3378, R3721). Rather than describing each particular agreement, I will provide a summary of the evidence contained in the register.

First, the evidence confirms that collusion continued well into the 1960s with respect to sales of telephone installations to the Post Office (R3377, R3378). Second, all agreements relating to sales to other buyers were formally abandoned between 1958 and 1960. Third, an agreement between two leading firms on line apparatus (R2249) was canceled in 1965 (i.e., soon after the Post Office introduced competitive tendering for that product). Finally, R3721 was a restrictive agreement between manufacturers and the Post Office, made in the early 1970s and relating to sales of telephone installations to the Post Office. This suggests that competition emerged slowly in this section of the industry after 1969, a point also made by Hart et al. (1973). In conclusion, one can perhaps distinguish two main stages in the evolution of competition in this industry between the 1950s and the 1970s. Before 1963, both MLH 363 as a whole and all its principal products were collusive and did not experience any significant change in competitive conditions—given that the bulk of industry output was sold to the Post Office. After 1963, and until at least the mid-1970s, the state of competition in MLH 363 as a whole and in telephone installations in particular can only be regarded as ambiguous. However, it is probably fair to say that there was a change of competition regime for line apparatus.

Radio and Electronic Components (MLH 364)

Electronic valves, cathode ray tubes, and other active components.   The main association in this industry was the British Radio Valve Manufacturers Association, which consisted of producers of electronic valves and cathode ray tubes for broadcasting or TV receivers. The association members agreed on common prices for "maintenance valves" (which accounted for about 10–15% of the total market for valves in the late 1950s) and common discounts for sales of "equipment valves" to smaller buyers (which accounted for about 20% of total sales of equipment valves). They also practiced collective exclusive dealing, enforced resale prices, and imposed some restrictions on imports and the introduction of new products. See the Lloyds' report, CD, and especially MRPC, *Report on the Supply of Electronic Valves and Cathode Ray Tubes* (London: H.M.S.O., 1957). Following the introduction of the 1956 Act, the restrictions on common prices and the collective enforcement of resale price maintenance were withdrawn, and the rest of the agreement was registered (R313*). It was abandoned in 1959. A pricing agreement by the Association of Tube Rebuilders, relating to rebuilt cathode ray tubes, also ended in 1959. The share of products covered by the pricing restrictions (other than resale price maintenance) in total industry sales revenue was probably about 20%.

Passive radio and electronic components.   No evidence of restrictive agreements.

Broadcast Receiving and Sound Reproducing Equipment (MLH 365)

Gramophone records and tape recordings.   BT reports allegations of collusive pricing and collective discrimination arrangements in this industry, although the only registered agreements date from the late 1960s and relate mostly to sales promotion. However, there are some vague references in one of these agreements to past restrictive practices in the industry, although neither the nature nor the coverage of these is very clear (R3306, R3650). The effect of the 1956 Act on competition in this industry was ambiguous.

Other broadcast receiving and sound reproducing equipment.   The agreement of the Typewriter and Allied Trades Federation of Great Britain (R665), which was described under MLH 338, covered dictating machines as well. In addition to collective resale price maintenance and the reporting of individual prices and trade discounts, R665 provided for minimum prices for the renting and maintenance of dictating machines, and maximum discounts for sales of dictating machines to radio and TV retailers. Most of these restrictions were canceled in 1957, although those involving the exchange of information remained. Sales of dictating machines were only a small part of total sales of broadcast receiving and sound reproducing equipment. The register also contains an agreement by the British Radio Equipment Manufacturers Association, relating to the use of components produced outside the UK and to participation in exhibitions (R2115*). This ended in 1961, but its restrictions were not very significant. The industry as a whole was competitive.

Electronic Computers (MLH 366)

There is no evidence of any restrictive agreements in this industry.

Radio, Radar, and Electronic Capital Goods (MLH 367)

An agreement by the Electro-medical Trade Association, which comprised the requirement not to give discounts to buyers of certain types of electro-medical and allied apparatus, was abandoned in 1959 (R117). A pricing arrangement between producers of flameproof electrically operated gate end boxes ended in 1958 (R721). An agreement by two firms regarding technical collaboration and market sharing in vehicle-actuated traffic signal equipment was canceled in 1968 (R145). Finally, an agreement among three manufacturers, the Central Electricity Authority, and the South of Scotland Electricity Board for the manufacture and installation of indicating equipment, specifying the division of business among the three firms (R37, R684), expired in 1969. The combined share of these products in total industry sales revenue was less than 10%. Hence the effect of the 1956 Act on MLH 367 as a whole was not significant.

Electric Appliances Primarily for Domestic Use (MLH 368)

An agreement by the Associated Manufacturers of Domestic Electric Cookers (R106*), covering electric cookers (stoves) and accessories, comprised agreed increases to individual list prices, maximum discounts to distributors, the maintenance of individual retail prices, the prenotification of any changes in individual prices, and provisions regarding sales promotion. It was abandoned in 1959. An agreement by the Associated Manufacturers of Domestic Electric Appliances (R107)—covering washing machines, electric heaters, vacuum cleaners, electric lawn mowers, and several smaller appliances—provided for maximum discounts to various classes of distributors, the maintenance of individual list prices, and restrictions on sales promotion. The agreement ended in 1959. The Associated Manufacturers of Domestic Electric Water Heaters fixed prices until 1957 (R258). Domestic refrigerators were covered by the agreement of the British Refrigeration Association (R824), described under MLH 339.3, and were also listed in CD. The register also contains price agreements for electric ceiling fans (R718) and desk and bracket-type electric fans (R719), both of which ended in 1960. Finally, BT reports allegations of collective discrimination arrangements in electric appliances. All in all, there was a change of competition regime in the industry as a whole, as well as for most types of electric appliances (especially larger appliances). More details on the evolution of competition in washing machines and refrigerators have been given in chapter 5, section 5.6.

Miscellaneous Electrical Goods (MLH 369)

Electrical equipment for motor vehicles, cycles, and aircraft, excluding accumulators. No agreements were registered in this industry. According to MC, *Report on the Supply of Electrical Equipment for Mechanically Propelled Land Vehicles* (London: H.M.S.O., 1963), there was, until 1956, an agreement between two of the largest firms in the industry, Smith and Lucas, which provided for the demarcation of the firms' respective activities. It dated from the 1930s and also covered products in other engineering industries. However, it was probably of little significance in the 1950s, since the two firms had by then established their respective products. The MC report also described various pricing arrangements between manufacturers of spark plugs, in addition to the collective enforcement of individual retail prices (which ended in 1956). These arrangements apparently covered only a fraction of the total sales of spark plugs. This product was also listed in BT as allegedly collusive, but no information was given on coverage. In any case, spark plugs accounted for less than 10% of the total market for electrical equipment for motor vehicles, cycles, and aircraft. Hence the 1956 Act had no significant effect on the industry as a whole.

Primary batteries. No agreements were registered, but the industry was reported in PEP as allegedly collusive, and was also listed in CD and BT as being subject to collective discrimination arrangements.

Secondary batteries (accumulators). The main sources of information for the evolution of competition in this industry are MC, *Report on the Supply of*

Electrical Equipment for Mechanically Propelled Land Vehicles (London: H.M.S.O., 1963) and Swann et al. (1973). The British Starter Battery Association fixed prices for automotive replacement batteries, practiced collective exclusive dealing, and generally regulated the relations between manufacturers and buyers; the industry was also listed in CD. A modified version of this agreement was registered (R655), then abandoned in 1960. It was, however, replaced by an information agreement, which lasted until the mid-1960s. The MC report also mentions an understanding between the two leading manufacturers, Lucas and Chloride, relating to prices and market shares in the automotive initial equipment market, and an informal pricing arrangement on traction batteries, both of which presumably were terminated in 1956 and were never registered. On the other hand, the register contains an agreement between Chloride and a large manufacturer of primary batteries relating to the demarcation of their respective activities and to prices for selling one another's products (R3743). It also contains several two-party agreements between producers of train, marine, and commercial vehicle batteries, relating to terms for selling one another's products (R3744, R3789, R3790). These arrangements were revised several times before they were finally canceled in the 1970s. All in all, there was a change of competition regime in the secondary battery industry.

Electric lamps. This industry was tightly regulated in the 1950s. The agreement of the Electric Lamp Manufacturers Association provided for common prices, quotas, collective exclusive dealing, aggregated rebates, the collective enforcement of resale price maintenance, patent pooling, and restrictions on granting licenses to nonmember firms. There were also international agreements limiting imports. See the Lloyds' report, CD, and especially MRPC, *Report on the Supply of Electric Lamps* (London: H.M.S.O., 1951). Some of these restrictions were dropped either as a result of the MRPC inquiry or before registration, and so the registered agreement contained only common trade discounts and the exchange of information on individual prices (R1548, R2487). These were formally abandoned in 1959. However, various arrangements in the industry continued throughout the 1960s, including a price information agreement which led to tacit understandings about changes in prices and discounts (R3725) and the prenotification of any new product introductions (R3134, R3283). The industry was officially investigated for a second time in the late 1960s, and the report concluded that although competition had increased somewhat since 1956, it was still not very effective. See MC, *Electric Lamps* (London: H.M.S.O., 1968). Following the investigation, the restrictive arrangements apparently ended. In conclusion, the emergence of competition in the electric lamp industry was gradual and slow, but by the early 1970s the industry had probably experienced a change of competition regime.

Electric light fittings, wiring accessories, etc. A pricing agreement by the Electric Light Fittings Association was abandoned in 1960 (R579*, R1718).

According to CD, the association also practiced collective exclusive dealing before 1956. An agreement by the Association of Manufacturers of Electric Wiring Accessories, relating to the maintenance of individual list prices and common trade discounts and conditions of sale, was canceled in 1959 (R667). Finally, an agreement by the Electric Sign Manufacturers Association, containing some pricing restrictions, was abandoned in 1962 (R1620). In summary, the 1956 Act caused a change of competition regime in this industry.[4]

Shipbuilding and Marine Engineering (MLH 370)

Shipbuilding.   No evidence of restrictive agreements.

Boatbuilding.   The register contains agreements by the Ship and Boat Builders' National Federation (R2854*) and the Marine Traders Association (R2792*), covering boats and marine equipment. The agreements specified whether trade discounts should or should not be given to particular classes of buyers, but did not regulate the discount rates. Although they were both abandoned in 1964, they were not particularly restrictive. A third agreement, by the Fishing Boats Builders Association (R2311), provided for minimum prices, but it covered only Scotland; it ended in 1963. On the basis of this information, it seems that the bulk of the industry was not subject to significant restrictive agreements in the 1950s.

Marine engineering.   No evidence of restrictive agreements.

Ship repairing.   A price-fixing agreement by the North East Coast Ship Repairers Association seems to have continued throughout the 1960s (R1597). An agreement by the Dry Dock Owners and Repairers Central Council was mainly about terms and conditions of contract, but it also contained, until 1966, some minor price restrictions (R1416). The state of competition in this industry should probably be regarded as ambiguous.

Wheeled Tractors (MLH 380)

Tractors were covered by several of the agreements described under MLH 331: R860, by the Agricultural Engineers Association, and also R2775, R840, and R3197. Moreover, resale price maintenance was practiced in this industry. The effect of the 1956 Act on the tractor industry must be regarded as ambiguous.

---

4. I should also mention an agreement among several electrical engineering associations that formed the British Electrical Industry Fair Trading Council (R788). The agreement specified maximum discounts for various classes of buyers, and was terminated in 1960. It covered a wide range of products, mostly from MLH 368 and MLH 369. See also the Lloyds' report for details.

Motor Vehicles (MLH 381)

Cars and commercial vehicles. An agreement by manufacturers and importers of cars and commercial vehicles was referred to the Court in 1960, and was unsuccessfully contested by the parties (R1811*; see also LR 2 RP 173). Its main restrictions were the maintenance of individual resale prices and specified discounts to fleet users. However, neither individual prices nor discounts to buyers other than fleet users, including discounts by each manufacturer to his franchised dealers, were regulated. According to the Court report, about 5–10% of all cars and 25–40% of all commercial vehicles were sold to fleet users. The register also contains an agreement by the Society of Motor Manufacturers and Traders relating to leasing terms and credit sale terms for motor vehicles (R1077); this also ended in 1960. Before 1956, the main organization of the industry, the British Motor Trade Association, collectively enforced the resale prices of cars, commercial vehicles, and motor accessories, and imposed barriers to entry into distribution; however, it did not influence individual prices or trade discounts. Details can be found in the Lloyds' report, CD, and PEP. On the basis of this evidence, the car industry can be regarded as largely competitive, while the commercial vehicle industry should probably be seen as ambiguous.

Motor bodies, engines, and other parts and accessories of motor vehicles. The only agreement in the register is a price agreement by the Bus Seat Frame Association (R957), which was abandoned in 1959. Bus seats are a very minor product of this industry, which was therefore essentially competitive. Parts and accessories of motor vehicles were also covered by the collective discrimination arrangements operated by the British Motor Trade Association; these did not influence the manufacturers' individual prices or trade discounts.

Trailers and caravans. The register contains an agreement by the National Caravan Council, providing for fixed trade discounts, the maintenance of individual resale prices, conditions of sale, and collective exclusive dealing (R1075*). It was abandoned in 1960. Caravans accounted for about 40–60% of total sales revenue in the trailer and caravan industry between the mid-1950s and the early 1970s. Moreover, producers of caravans were generally fewer and of larger average size than producers of trailers. This implies that the concentration ratio for the industry as a whole should be influenced more by the caravan section than by the trailer section, while the reverse should be the case for the number of firms.

Motorcycles, Tricycles, and Pedal Cycles (MLH 382)

An agreement by the British Cycle and Motor Cycle Industries Association, whose membership consisted of manufacturers and importers, provided for common discounts to different types of distributors, the maintenance of the firms' individual retail prices, the prenotification of any changes in individual prices or any new model introductions, conditions of sale, and various restrictions on sales promotion (R531, R533, R2457*, R2789*). Many of these restrictions covered both bicycles and motorcycles (and accessories), but some of the most important ones (such as the fixing of trade discounts) apparently covered only motorcycles. Bicycles were also the subject of an agreement by the Cycle Trade Union, relating to resale price maintenance, sales promotion, and conditions of sale (R532*). Additional information on these arrangements prior to 1956 can be found in CD and in the Lloyds' report. Until 1956, these associations also practiced various forms of collective discrimination, including the collective enforcement of resale price maintenance and collective exclusive dealing. All significant restrictive arrangements ended between 1962 and 1964.

The register also contains an agreement between the two leading bicycle manufacturers, Tube Investments and Raleigh, which related, among other things, to the demarcation of their respective activities with respect to bicycle tubing and certain bicycle accessories, and to prices charged for these products to one another and to other manufacturers of bicycles (R1184). This agreement ended in 1960, but its implications for competition in bicycles (as opposed to bicycle parts and accessories) are not clear. In conclusion, there is sufficient evidence of a change in competition regime for motorcycles. The situation for bicycles is somewhat more uncertain. The share of bicycle sales in total sales of the bicycle and motorcycle industry was about 50–60% for most of the relevant period.

Aerospace Equipment Manufacturing and Repairing (MLH 383)

The main source of information on this industry is the *Report of the Committee of Inquiry into the Aircraft Industry* (London: H.M.S.O., 1965). According to this report, competition was not very effective, especially for aircraft and airframes, partly because of the heavy government involvement in the industry. In particular, competition in aircraft and airframes was being reduced by government procurement procedures that reflected a wish to share the available work among the firms. Competition in aero-engines was more pronounced, at least in the design stage. In the later stages of projects, competition was affected by the existence of production-sharing arrangements, which the government had approved. These were not registered; in fact, the only agreement in the register relates to propellers (R41), which is a minor product of MLH 383. This agreement ended in 1959. On the whole, the 1956 Act had little effect on this industry. Nevertheless, aircraft in particular was not included in any of the samples used in this book.

Locomotives and Railway Track Equipment (MLH 384)

The register contains several agreements between private manufacturers of locomotives, all of which provided for the reporting of inquiries and orders and/or specified terms and conditions of contract: R1455, R1827, R1828, R1829, R2894 and R2895. These were agreements by various sections of the Locomotive and Allied Manufacturers Association, and were revised or abandoned between 1961 and 1967. This industry was excluded from my samples because government establishments accounted for more than two-thirds of total output during the 1950s and the 1960s.

Railway Carriages, Wagons and Trams (MLH 385)

An agreement by the Railway Carriage and Wagon Building Association contained prices, the allocation of work, and terms and conditions of contract (R1558, R2671). It was abandoned in 1962. This industry, too, was excluded from my samples because government establishments accounted for more than two-thirds of total output during the 1950s and the 1960s.

Engineers' Small Tools and Gauges (MLH 390)

The register contains price-fixing agreements by the Twist Drill Association (R478*), the Milling Cutter and Reamer Association (R479), the Flexible Back Bandsaw Manufacturers Association (R413), the Tubular Frame Saw Association (R904), the Short Saw and Crosscut Saw Association (R948), the Circular and Long Saw Association (R977), the British Hacksaw Makers Association (R1497, R1670), the British Hard Metal Association (R1041), the High Speed Steel Tool Bit Association (R1080*), the High Speed Steel Drill Rod Association (R1115*, R2488*), the Welded Tool Manufacturers Association (R417), the Screw Thread Tool Manufacturers Association (R481), and by a group of producers of thread gauges (R896). Several of these agreements will also be listed under MLH 391, since they seem to have covered products in both industries. All the agreements were abandoned in 1959–1960, except for R1080* and R2488*, which lasted until 1965. According to CD, some of these associations also operated collective discrimination arrangements before 1956. Despite the number of agreements, the combined share of the affected products was only about 40–50% of total industry sales revenue—or less, if at least some of the agreements did not cover the export market, which was important in this industry.

Hand Tools and Implements (MLH 391)

The register contains price agreements by the Association of UK Plier Manufacturers (R121), the File Trade Association (R485), the Light Edge Tool and Allied Trades Association (R486*), the Scythe, Sickle and Hook Manufacturers Association (R487), the Precision File Association (R905), the Edge Tool Manufacturers Association (R1559), the Flexible Back Bandsaw Manufacturers Association (R413), the Band Saw Association (R888), the Tubular Frame Saw Association (R904), the Short Saw and Crosscut Saw Association

(R948), the Circular and Long Saw Association (R977), and the British Hacksaw Makers Association (R1497, R1670). Some of these agreements were also mentioned under MLH 390. According to CD and BT, some products of this industry were subject to collective discrimination arrangements before 1956. All the price agreements were abandoned in 1959, leading to a change of competition regime in the hand tool industry.

Cutlery, Spoons, Forks, and Plated Tableware, etc. (MLH 392)

Razors and blades.   No evidence of restrictive agreements.

Knives, tableware, etc.   The Machine Knife Manufacturers Association set prices for guillotine paper knife blanks until 1959 (R947). According to a case study of the industry, written by H. Townsend and published in Burn (1958), there were also pricing arrangements for certain other semifinished goods, but not for finished goods. The affected products accounted for about 10–20% of sales revenue in this product category.

Bolts, Nuts, Screws, Rivets, etc. (MLH 393)

A large number of agreements were registered, covering nearly all the products of the industry. In particular, the register contains price agreements by the Heated Bolt Association (R350*), the Bright Bolt and Nut Manufacturers Association (R408*), the Black Bolt and Nut Manufacturers Association (R351*), the Aircraft Bolt and Nut Manufacturers Association (R348*), the Stainless Steel Bar Products Association (R87), the Rubber Thread Screw Association (R289), and various other associations of producers of rivets (R280, R290, R607, R382), washers (R291), cotter pins (R306), and tacks, nails, and related products (R375, R382, R492, R1066, R1069, R1070, R1071). There were also agreements between some of these associations to observe each other's prices, and agreements between manufacturers and distributors, relating mostly to trade and quantity discounts. According to CD, some products of MLH 393 were subject to collective discrimination arrangements before 1956. All price agreements ended at various dates between 1959 and 1968, except R351*, which was contested by the parties and was allowed by the Court to continue (LR 2 RP 50, LR 2 RP 433, LR 3 P 43, LR 6 RP 1).

To summarize, the industry was collusive in the 1950s, and the combined share of the products with terminated agreements in total industry sales revenue was probably higher than 50%. On the other hand, black bolts and nuts accounted for more than 20% of industry sales revenue, so the state of competition in the industry as a whole was somewhat uncertain in the 1960s and the 1970s. Not only did the price agreement in black bolts and nuts continue until at least the mid-1970s, but the firms involved were also members of several other associations with formally abandoned agreements. The continuation of an explicit price agreement in one market may have reduced competitive pressure in other, closely related, markets. For these reasons, the effect of the 1956 Act on MLH 393 during the period examined in this book should probably be seen as ambiguous.

Wire and Wire Manufactures (MLH 394)

Wire and wire manufactures of iron and steel. A large number of price agreements by various associations and groups of wire manufacturers were registered, covering all types of iron and steel wire and wire manufactures. Most of these covered specific types of wire or wire manufactures, so it would be rather tedious to give details on each here.[5] According to CD, several also provided for collective discrimination. Three agreements were contested in the Court and struck down (see LR 5 RP 146): R867*, by the Locked Coil Ropemakers Association; R869*, by the Wire Rope Manufacturers Association; and R993*, by the Mining Rope Association. Most agreements in this part of MLH 394 were abandoned between 1959 and 1962, although some, including R867*, R869*, and R993*, were canceled in 1964–1965. In some cases, information agreements were in operation in the 1960s. The slow emergence of competition in wire ropes is described in Swann et al. (1973) and in MC, *Wire and Fibre Ropes* (London: H.M.S.O., 1973). On the whole, the 1956 Act caused a change of competition regime in this part of the wire industry in the long run.

Wire and wire manufactures of copper, brass, and other copper alloys. The main source of information for this part of MLH 394 is MRPC, *Report on the Supply and Export of Certain Semi-manufactures of Copper and Copper-based Alloys* (London: H.M.S.O., 1955). This report described the collusive activities of several associations of producers of copper and copper alloy semi-manufactures, including wire and wire manufactures. See the discussion under MLH 322. Most of the associations investigated by the MRPC did not register their agreements. However, the agreements of the Cadmium-Copper and Bronze Association (R1554) and the High Conductivity Copper Association (R508*) were registered and ended in 1959; both covered certain types of wire. The register also contains two agreements on electric cable wire (R630 and R634), both abandoned in 1962. To summarize, the 1956 Act caused a change of competition regime in this part of the wire industry.

---

5. They are the following: R66, R67, R88, R148, R368, R369, R616, R623, R624, R627, R628, R629, R631, R632, R633, R635, R636, R637, R638, R659* (by the Mild Steel Wire Manufacturers Association), R866, R867*, R869*, R945, R993*, R995, R996, R998, R1004, R1005* (by the Patented Steel Wire Association), R1031* (by a group of manufacturers of wire nails), R1067, R1068* (by the Reinforcement Conference), R1072* (by the British Wire Netting Manufacturers Association), R1190, R1198, R1281, R1303, R1314, R1377, R1389, R1436, R1845, R1846, R2313, R2981, R3072 (the last of these was an effective information agreement of the Federation of Reinforcement Fabric Makers). Some of these may also cover wire and wire products of copper, brass, and other copper alloys.

Cans and Metal Boxes (MLH 395)

A price agreement on milk cans by members of the Can Manufacturers Association was abandoned in 1958 (R815). This is a minor product of MLH 395, however. PEP mentions that the Tinbox Manufacturers Association operated an agreement for buying prices of tin scrap, but it is not clear why this should significantly affect competition between manufacturers in the product market. Finally, an agreement between the largest producer of metal boxes, Metal Box, and the largest producer of crown corks, Crown Cork, specifying that each firm would not enter the industry of the other, ended in 1963 (R3110). Since this was not an agreement between manufacturers of metal boxes, however, the industry can probably be regarded as competitive for our present purposes.

Jewellery and Precious Metals (MLH 396)

There is no evidence of any restrictive agreements in this industry.

Metal Furniture (MLH 399.1)

Until 1960, the Metal Bedstead Association fixed minimum prices for metal bedsteads, wire and spring mattresses, and other associated products (R1226*). Moreover, the Bedstead Fittings Association set the prices of bedstead fittings until 1959 (R1251). These products accounted for less than 10% of the metal furniture industry throughout the 1960s and the 1970s. Office furniture was subject to some agreements that will be discussed under MLH 472; none of them was particularly restrictive. Hence the metal furniture industry can be seen as competitive.

Drop Forgings, etc. (MLH 399.5)

The National Association of Drop Forgers and Stampers made recommendations for increases in the price of drop forgings until 1965 (R114*, R115). Certain products of MLH 399.5 were also covered by the pricing agreement of the National Forgemasters Association (R1122*). This ended in 1962, and it is not clear whether R2801*, R2802*, and R2803*, which essentially replaced R1122* until 1965, covered products of MLH 399.5. In any case, there was a change of competition regime in the long run in this industry.

Metal Hollow-ware (MLH 399.6, 399.7)

Domestic hollow-ware. The register contains price agreements by the British Aluminium Hollow-ware Manufacturers Association (R204), the Wrought Hollow-ware Trade Employers Association (R262), the Galvanised

Hollow-ware Association (R541), and the Dustbin Association (R639, R2321). All the agreements were abandoned in 1959–1960, but R541 was replaced by an information agreement, which ended in 1965. This industry experienced a change of competition regime.

Industrial hollow-ware. A price-fixing agreement by the Association of Steel Drum Manufacturers, covering steel drums and kegs, was canceled in 1960 (R135*); it was replaced by an effective information agreement, which lasted until 1965. See Swann et al. (1973) for details on the evolution of competition in this industry. A price agreement between members of the Galvanised Tank Association (R354*), covering galvanized tanks, cisterns, and cylinders, was abandoned in 1959. According to CD, the association also practiced collective exclusive dealing before 1956. After 1959, the industry operated an information agreement, which was referred to the Court in 1965 and was found to have amounted to the same effect as the former explicit pricing arrangement (LR 5 RP 315). The information agreement ended in 1965. All in all, the 1956 Act caused a change of competition regime in this industry.

Miscellaneous Metal Goods (MLH 399.2, 3, 4, 8, 9, 10, 11 and 12)

Metal windows and door frames. The British Metal Window Association fixed the prices of metal windows, door frames, and associated products (R835, R2618*). In its original form, the agreement also provided for some allocation of work. See Swann et al. (1973) and MRPC, *Report on the Supply of Standard Metal Windows and Doors* (London: H.M.S.O., 1957). The agreement weakened somewhat in the late 1950s and early 1960s, because the market-sharing provisions were dropped and the leading producer of metal windows resigned from the association. It was referred to the Court in 1962, contested by the parties, and allowed to continue (LR 3 RP 198). However, it was voluntarily abandoned shortly afterward. The register also contains a price agreement by the Patent Glazing Conference (R836), which ended in 1959. Hence there was a change in competition regime in this industry.

Safes, locks, latches, and keys. The register contains price agreements by the British Lock and Latch Manufacturers Association (R119) and the Cylinder Lock Manufacturers Association (R187). They covered keys, locks, and latches, and were abandoned in 1958–1959. Also relevant is the price agreement of the National Brassfoundry Association, which covered a wide range of brass goods, including locks and latches, and was canceled in 1960 (R349). The 1956 Act caused a change of competition regime in this industry.

Springs. A price agreement by the Spring and Interior Springing Association, covering mattress and upholstery springs, was abandoned in 1960 (R1132*). Two other price agreements covering railway springs, by the Heavy

Coil Spring Association (R994*, R1321) and the Laminated Railway Spring Association (R1002*, R1003), respectively, were abandoned in 1965. The combined share of these products in total industry revenue was probably higher than 50% (at least on the basis the 1968 S.I.C. definition of the industry, which excludes springs for motor vehicles). Hence there was a change of competition regime in this industry.

Needles, pins, and other metal small ware. The register contains price agreements by the Pin and Allied Trades Association (R390), the Metal Skewer Association (R202), the Machinery Belt Fastener Manufacturers Association (R2948) and two groups of producers of pins and similar articles (R2292, R2641). All the agreements were abandoned between 1958 and 1962, although R390 was replaced for some time by an information agreement. BT also mentions slide fasteners (zippers) as an allegedly collusive product. The combined share of the affected products was about 30% of total industry sales revenue. Several products of the industry were also listed in CD.

Domestic gas appliances. The register contains an agreement between the Society of British Gas Industries (representing manufacturers of most types of domestic gas appliances) and the Gas Council (representing the Area Boards, the principal buyers of appliances) (R823). Under the agreement the Boards were to sell domestic gas appliances at the list prices published by the manufacturers, and the manufacturers were to grant to the Boards specified discounts and not to give wholesalers and retailers discounts higher than those given to the Boards. The agreement ended in 1960. However, its implications for competition in the particular circumstances of an industry with a dominant buyer are not clear. In fact, the agreement seems designed to protect the interests of the Area Boards as much as those of the manufacturers. Moreover, the long-run effect of the abolition of the agreement is uncertain. An official investigation into the gas appliance industry carried out in the late 1970s revealed several restrictive agreements, relating mainly to discounts, the exchange of price information, and conditions of sale, which had been in operation for various dates since the early 1970s (R4951, R4956–R4967). Further information is contained in MMC, *Domestic Gas Appliances* (London: H.M.S.O., 1980). Those arrangements that were still in force were abandoned in the late 1970s. In conclusion, the state of competition in this industry was probably ambiguous in the 1950s and/or the 1960s and 1970s.

Metallic closures. The register contains an information agreement among three important firms in the crown cork industry, which resulted in occasional informal understandings about price changes (R3131). It is not clear how long the agreement had been in force and whether it was a replacement for a formal price-fixing scheme. The information agreement was discontinued in 1968. Crown corks accounted for about 25% of the total sales of metallic closures in 1963.

Metal finishing. The register includes price-fixing agreements by the Association of London Galvanisers (R205), the Vitreous Enamellers Association (R792), the Association of Galvanised Steel Gutter and Pipe Manufacturers (R831), the Guild of Metal Perforators (R609), the Association of Scottish Galvanisers (R604), and the Sheffield District Annealers and Heat Treaters Association (R1310). All of these were canceled in 1959–1960. They probably covered about a third of total sales of the industry. PEP also reports (on the basis of evidence given by a trade association of galvanizers) some local pricing agreements on zinc galvanizing.

Other metal goods. A price agreement by the National Brassfoundry Association, covering a wide range of brass goods and including "engineers' and mechanicians' goods," was abandoned in 1960 (R349). A price-fixing agreement by the Stockless Anchor Association ended in 1959 (R1636); however, stockless anchors represented less than 10% of total sales of the product category "anchors and chains." The register also contains price agreements by the Steel Hinge Makers Association (R1028*, R2259), the Scottish Association of Manufacturing Coppersmiths (R901), the Umbrella Components Association (R1006), the Hook and Band Manufacturers Association (R2506), the Ships Ordinary Sidelights Association (R480), and groups of producers of metal clips and brackets (R1496), corrugated joint fasteners (R1353), and hammerlock struts (R2664). All these agreements were canceled between 1959 and 1961. CD also reports that copper cylinders and boilers, radiator blocks, flushing cisterns and copper balls, curtain rods, and other hardware products were subject to collective discrimination arrangements before 1956.

Production of Man-Made Fibres (MLH 411)

No agreements were registered in this industry. The evolution of competition during the 1950s is, however, described in MC, *Man-made Cellulosic Fibres* (London: H.M.S.O., 1968). In the viscose section (about 40% of total industry sales revenue in 1958), discussions on prices between the dominant producer, Courtaulds, and a number of smaller firms were discontinued in 1956. In the acetate section (about 10% of total industry sales revenue in 1958), price discussions were less effective than in viscose. Moreover, the two significant producers, Courtaulds and British Celanese, merged in 1957, so the 1956 Act would have little effect after 1958 anyway. Finally, in nylon, the only producer was British Nylon Spinners, a firm jointly owned by Courtaulds and the chemical giant I.C.I. The monopoly position of B.N.S. was protected by an agreement whereby the parent firms would produce nylon only through B.N.S. and, in return, B.N.S. would produce only nylon. See also D. C. Coleman, *Courtaulds: An Economic and Social History*, vol. 3 (Oxford: Clarendon Press, 1980). The implications of the agreement between Courtaulds and I.C.I. are not clear, however. Since there was only one firm producing nylon, there could be no collusion specifically in nylon. Even if one looks at the market for man-made fibres as a whole, the fact that Cour-

taulds had a 50% share in B.N.S. complicates any assessment of the consequences of the Courtaulds-I.C.I. agreement for competition and for the
structure of the industry. Courtaulds was also a party to a number of international collusive agreements since 1950; these are not, however, relevant for
our present purposes.

In conclusion, only the viscose section of the industry can be regarded as
unambiguously collusive. The share of viscose sales in total industry sales
was less than 50% in the late 1950s, and declined in the 1960s.

Spinning and Doubling on the Cotton and Flax Systems (MLH 412)

Single yarn of cotton, glass fibres and man-made fibres. An agreement
by the Yarn Spinners Association contained minimum prices for cotton yarn
(R79*). The agreement was abandoned in 1959, after being unsuccessfully
contested in the Restrictive Practices Court (LR 1 RP 118). A price agreement
by the Rayon Staple Spinners and Doublers Association, covering yarn of
man-made staple fibers, ended in late 1958 (R1137). There was therefore a
change of competition regime in this industry.

Doubled yarn of cotton, glass fibres, and man-made fibres. The Cotton
Yarn Doublers Association set minimum prices for doubled cotton yarn until
1959 (R269*). And the Rayon Staple Spinners and Doublers Association
regulated the price of doubled yarn of man-made staple fibers until 1958
(R1137). However, the price of doubled yarn of man-made continuous fila-
ment apparently was not regulated. The combined share of the products
covered by the two agreements in total industry sales revenue was about
50% in 1958, but only 35% in 1963 and 25% in 1968.

Finished thread. The Linen Sewing Thread Manufacturers Association
specified quotas for sales of linen thread to government departments and
nationalized industries, and also set minimum prices for certain qualities of
linen thread (R422). According to the association, the pricing restrictions
covered a relatively small fraction of total sales of linen thread. The agreement ended in 1960, and was replaced by an information agreement, which
continued to operate until the early 1970s. Total sales of linen thread
accounted for slightly more than 10% of total sales of finished thread in the
late 1950s and early 1960s, but for less than 10% in the late 1960s and the
1970s. The finished thread industry should probably be seen as competitive.

Flax. An agreement by a group of Scottish flax spinners fixed the prices of
flax line and tow yarns until 1958 (R251). Scotland accounted for less than
40% of the total UK production of flax yarns in the 1950s.

Other products and work done. Until 1959, the Precision Winding Association fixed the charges for electrical-type winding of yarn (R916). A group

of silk spinners allocated supplies of silk waste through a common buying organization until 1960 (R568). Finally, an agreement by the Soft Hemp and Tow Spinners Association, comprising prices for soft hemp and hemp tow, was abandoned in 1960 (R1221). PEP also mentions the Silk Throwsters Association as a potentially collusive body.

Weaving of Cotton, Linen, and Man-Made Fibres (MLH 413)

Woven cotton cloth in the loom state. The register contains three agreements, all of which related to minor products of the industry. An agreement by the Ventile Fabrics Association of Great Britain, whose membership consisted of spinners, doublers, weavers, and finishers, required members to deal with each other only (R403); this was discontinued in 1960. A similar agreement by the Cotton Velvet Council, whose membership consisted of manufacturers and finishers, was canceled in 1957 (R92). Finally, the Window Holland Association, which consisted of manufacturers and finishers, set prices and also operated an exclusive dealing arrangement between the members until 1959 (R78, R1253). All these were secondary products of the industry, however, so the influence of these agreements on the industry as a whole would have been small. According to evidence given by a cotton weaver and reported in PEP, attempts to reach an agreement between firms covering the main products of the industry had consistently failed.

Woven cloth of man-made fibres in the loom state. An agreement by the Rayon Weaving Association provided for minimum prices and recommended price increases for woven cloth of rayon until 1959 (R1138). The affected products covered more than 50% of industry sales revenue. In other words, the 1956 Act caused a change of competition regime in the industry.

Woven cloth of flax or hemp in the loom state. The Association of Flax Canvas Weavers set the prices of certain categories of flax and/or hemp canvas (R680). In three separate agreements, certain groups of weavers agreed upon prices of flax canvas for sale to government departments (R679, R1487, R1851). These agreements ended in 1959–1960. The products affected accounted for more than 20% but less than 50% of total industry sales.

Other products. The Cotton Canvas Manufacturers Association specified minimum prices for rayon tire cord and for cotton canvas fabrics (R31). An agreement by the Canvas Hose Manufacturers Association specified prices for canvas hose (R560). The Book Cloth Association set prices for book cloth (R103). All these agreements were abandoned in 1959–1960. Moreover, until 1958, the Silk Trade Employers Association fixed the prices of certain types of silk fabrics (R244). The Association of Cleaning Waste Manufacturers operated a market-sharing agreement until 1959 (R2113). After 1959, this was replaced for some time by a quantity information agreement. Finally, an agreement by the British Fabric Federation, relating only to conditions of sale for woven and knitted fabric for wearing apparel, was abandoned in 1967 (R2993*).

Woollen and Worsted (MLH 414)

Wool and other animal hair sorted, blended, scoured, or carbonized. A price-fixing agreement by the Wool Carbonisers and Scourers Federation continued until 1969 (R3148*). The parties to this agreement were firms that specialized in the scouring and carbonizing of wool. As pointed out by Hart et al. (1973), this type of specialized activity was common in the past, but over time vertical integration in the woolen and worsted industry resulted in a substantial shift of market share away from independent scourers and toward integrated topmaker-combers. Specialist firms accounted for much less than 50% of total sales revenue in the industry in the late 1960s (i.e., at the time when the federation abandoned its agreement).

Combing of wool tops. There is no evidence of any significant restrictive agreements among integrated topmaker-combers, who were responsible for most combing of wool in the 1960s. Thus the 1956 Act had no effect on this section of the industry. On the other hand, the register contains two price-fixing agreements by associations of commission combers, the Commission Woolcombers Association (R1177) and the Commission Recombers Association (R1176). Both agreements were abandoned in 1959, leading to a change of competition regime in this (much smaller) section of the wool combing industry.

Yarn of wool, hair, and man-made fibres spun on the worsted system. An agreement by the Branded Knitting Wool Association, abandoned in 1960, comprised discounts for hand-knitting wool (R1926). A registered agreement by the Worsted Spinners Federation, relating only to terms of contract and settlement discounts, was allowed to continue without a Court hearing (R1569). According to PEP, however, the federation recommended minimum prices in the 1950s.

Yarn of wool, hair, and man-made fibres spun on the woollen system. An agreement by the Scottish Woollen Spinners Association, containing some minor pricing restrictions, was canceled in 1960 (R218). Neither this nor the agreement of the Branded Knitting Wool Association described above (R1926) must have had any significant effect on the industry as a whole: in both cases the restrictions were minor and the fraction of total in-dustry sales covered was small. The same can be said about the agreements on yarn for the Harris Tweed industry (see below). Hence the woolen yarn industry was essentially competitive.

Woven worsted fabrics. No evidence of any significant restrictive agreements. According to PEP, the Woollen and Worsted Manufacturers Association only specified discounts.

Woven woollen fabrics. The Hebridean Spinners Advisory Committee and the Harris Tweed Industry Consultative Committee set the prices of yarn and Harris tweed until 1964 (R1223*, R2760*). This is a minor product of the industry, however, so the influence of these agreements on the industry as a whole would have been small. The same is probably true for an agreement between a small group of manufacturers of woolen cloth and serge cloth, which specified prices to be charged to government departments (R737). This industry was therefore largely competitive.

Blankets. An agreement by the Blanket Manufacturers Association specified a minimum price for a basic quality of woolen blankets (R801*). The agreement was abandoned in 1959, after being unsuccessfully contested in the Court by the parties (LR 1 RP 208). The effect of the agreement on competition in the industry is not clear, however, since the price restriction covered only a certain type of blanket and—as pointed out in the Court report—no sales were actually being made at the minimum prices. Hence the effect of the 1956 Act on the blanket industry was ambiguous.

Other products and work done. The British Paper Machine Felt Association set the price of felt for industrial machines (R1534). This agreement was discontinued in 1959, and was replaced by an information agreement. The Lancashire Mechanical Cloth Manufacturers Association fixed the price of cloth for industrial machines until 1960 (R917). The Moquette Manufacturers Association fixed the prices of moquettes for the railways until 1959 (R590). Finally, the Bradford and District Waste Pullers Association specified charges for wool shoddy until 1966 (R3032).

Jute (MLH 415)

The register contains a series of price agreements covering all the main sections of the jute industry: spinners, weavers, merchants, and importers. In particular the agreements covered jute yarn (R1340*), jute cloth (R1339*), hessian (burlap) piece goods (R1337*, R1338*), and jute carpets (R1345*). The industry was also listed in CD. The first four of these agreements were unsuccessfully contested in the Court. All were abandoned in 1963, but they were replaced by information agreements, which were effective for some time (see Hart et al. 1973, Swann et al. 1974). There was, however, a change of competition regime in the long run in the jute industry.

Rope, Twine, and Net (MLH 416)

The main products of this industry were subject to tight collusion in the 1950s. According to MRPC, *Report on the Supply of Hard Fibre Cordage* (London: H.M.S.O., 1956), this involved common prices, market sharing, aggregated rebates, collective exclusive dealing, collective resale price maintenance, and international agreements limiting imports. The industry was also listed in CD and BT. Only watered-down versions of the original collusive arrangements in the industry were registered. In particular, the register contains price-fixing agreements by the Hard Fibre Rope Manufacturers Association (R617*), the Trawl Twine Manufacturers Association (R618*), the Hard Fibre Cord and Twine Manufacturers Association (R619*), the Synthetic Cordage Manufacturers Association (R622), the Agricultural Twine Manufacturers Association (R626*), the Plaited Cordage Association (R1231), the Twine Manufacturers Association (R1563, R1797), the Scottish Net Manufacturers Association (R1356, R2736), and a group of producers of combined wire and fiber rope (R865, R1302). All these agreements were abandoned in 1959–1960. According to MC, *Wire and Fibre Ropes* (London: H.M.S.O., 1973), competition in the early 1970s was not fully effective in all markets within the industry. Competition further intensified as a result of action taken after the publication of the MC report. All in all, there was a change of competition regime in MLH 416.

Hosiery and Other Knitted Goods (MLH 417)

Knitted, netted, or crocheted fabrics. The Silk and Rayon Trade Protection Society, whose membership consisted of weavers, finishers, and merchant converters of various types of fabric, recommended minimum prices for warp-knitted fabrics and also for certain finishing processes until 1961 (R1637). The affected products accounted for more than 10% but less than 50% of the knitted fabric industry. A price agreement by the Stockinette Manufacturers Association was abandoned in 1959 (R1448); it covered only a secondary product of the industry, however. Finally, the agreement of the British Fabric Federation described under MLH 413 (R2993*) covered products of MLH 417 as well, although it was not particularly restrictive.

Hosiery. No evidence of any restrictive agreements. An agreement by the National Hosiery Manufacturers Federation contained only conditions of sale and was allowed to continue without a Court hearing (R1200).

Underwear, shirts, and nightwear, knitted, netted, or crocheted. No evidence of any restrictive agreements.

Other clothing, knitted, netted, or crocheted. No evidence of any restrictive agreements.

Lace (MLH 418)

The Madras Manufacturers Association specified prices for madras goods until 1959 (R430). This is not, however, a major product of the lace industry. More important, the manufacturers of leaver's lace agreed to sell all their output through a common selling organization, which set minimum prices (R3163*). These restrictions lasted until 1970. Leaver's lace accounted for about 10–25% of total sales of the lace industry during the period examined here.

Carpets (MLH 419)

Woven carpets, carpeting, and carpet floor rugs. A series of agreements by the Federation of British Carpet Manufacturers provided for minimum prices for certain types of woven carpets, notification of price changes, trade and quantity discounts, conditions of sale, and resale price maintenance (R1316*, R1317*, R1318*, R1319*, R1320*). The industry was also listed in CD. The most important of these agreements were contested in the Court and were struck down (LR 1 RP 472). According to Swann et al. (1973), competition intensified in the 1960s despite parallel pricing and the exchange of price information. The 1956 Act caused a change of competition regime in this section of the carpet industry.

Tufted carpets, carpeting, and carpet floor rugs. No evidence of any restrictive agreements.

Other carpets, carpeting, and carpet floor rugs, and pile fabric rugs. Some products that fall into this category were covered by the agreements of the Federation of British Carpet Manufacturers described above. Moreover, until 1961 a series of registered agreements by the Association of Manufacturers of Mohair and Pile Floor Rugs and Mats provided for specified trade discounts, the maintenance of manufacturers individual prices, agreed prices for comparable qualities, and no changes in individual prices without prior discussion with other members (R557, R1831–R1835).

Narrow Fabrics (MLH 421)

Elastic and elastomeric goods. The register contains a price agreement by the British Elastic Braid Manufacturers Association, which was canceled in 1959 (R143). The affected products accounted for 10–20% of total sales revenue in elastic and elastomeric goods.

Woven machinery belting and other narrow fabrics. An agreement by the Tape Manufacturers Association specified minimum prices for standard cotton and electrical tapes until 1962 (R562*). These products accounted for 10–20% of total sales revenue in this part of MLH 421. In addition, BT reports allegations of collusion between manufacturers of conveyor belting and collective exclusive dealing in the brace webbing industry.

Made-Up Household Textiles and Handkerchiefs (MLH 422.1)

The register contains two agreements, neither of which seems particularly important for the industry as a whole. The first was a market-sharing agreement between five suppliers of rented linen goods; it was abandoned in 1967 (R3104*). The second was a pricing agreement by the Traced Art Needlework Manufacturers Association, which ended in 1961 (R188). The evidence reported in PEP confirms that MLH 422.1 was a competitive industry.

Canvas Goods and Sacks and Other Made-Up Textiles (MLH 422.2)

Canvas sacks and bags. Jute sacks and bags were covered by the agreements between producers of hessian (burlap) piece goods described under MLH 415 (R1337*, R1338*). In addition, the Jute Sack and Bag Manufacturers Association recommended charges for the sewing, stamping, and bundling of jute sacks and bags (R1336*). Merchants and importers were also parties to the pricing arrangements (R1334*, R1335*). All these agreements were contested in the Court, struck down, and abandoned in 1963. Although they were replaced for some time by information agreements, the industry experienced a change of competition regime in the long run as a result of the 1956 Act.

Made-up goods of sailcloth, canvas, and the like. An agreement by a group of producers of canvas freight car covers, relating to prices and the allocation of work, ended in 1961 (R2680). The affected products probably accounted for 10–20% of total sales revenue in this part of MLH 422.2.

Textile Finishing (MLH 423)

The register contains about thirty restrictive agreements by various associations and groups of textile finishers, covering all types of textiles and finishing processes. I will not provide details on each of these agreements here.[6] All of them were mainly about prices, and some had originally comprised additional restrictions, such as market sharing—see MRPC, *Report on the Process of Calico Printing* (London: H.M.S.O., 1954). All were abandoned be-

---

6. Their numbers in the register are as follows: R75, R170, R200, R277, R284, R367, R393* (by the Dyers and Finishers Association), R402, R682, R830, R838, R942, R979, R1160, R1245, R1315, R1324, R1531, R1533, R1535, R1567, R1568, R1582, R1606, R1612, R1637, R1705, R1800, R1801, R2212, R2600.

tween 1958 and 1962, although several were initially replaced by information agreements, some of which lasted until 1970. There was therefore a change of competition regime in MLH 423 as a result of the 1956 Act.

Asbestos Manufactures (MLH 429.1)

The evolution of competition in this industry is described in MC, *Asbestos and Certain Asbestos Products* (London: H.M.S.O., 1973). Prior to 1956, the industry operated price-fixing agreements in most major products, such as asbestos textiles, jointings and related products, brake and clutch linings, and asbestos insulation products. (Brake linings were also listed in BT as allegedly collusive.) For some products there were market-sharing provisions as well. These agreements were not registered. Informal discussions on prices and discounts continued until the late 1960s, although they were not necessarily as effective as the agreements of the 1950s. Some of these arrangements were discovered in the late 1960s and were placed on the register (R3774, R3708). By the early 1970s, all restrictive arrangements apparently had ended. Although the emergence of competition in this industry was delayed for over a decade after the introduction of the 1956 Act, by the mid-1970s the industry had probably experienced a change in competition regime.

Miscellaneous Textiles (MLH 429.2)

A price agreement by the British Mat and Matting Manufacturers Association, covering coir mats and mattings, was abandoned in 1959 (R253). An agreement by the Kapok Processors Association specified minimum prices for pure kapok and kapok mixtures until 1957 (R51). BT also reports allegations of collective exclusive dealing in processed kapok. The products covered by the two agreements accounted for somewhat less than 20% of total sales revenue of MLH 429.2 as a whole.

Leather (Tanning and Dressing) and Fellmongery (MLH 431)

Leather, undressed. The register contains an agreement by the Pigskin Tanners Federation, whose membership consisted of seven Scottish tanners (R2682*). The agreement related to buying prices and buying quotas for pigskins and hogskins, and was abandoned in 1963. This was a regional agreement on a specific product. The 1956 Act had no significant effect on the leather tanning industry as a whole.

Leather, dressed. No evidence of important restrictive agreements, other than allegations of collective discrimination arrangements reported in BT.

Fellmongery. The register contains a number of agreements between two regional associations of sheep hide and skin sellers and two regional associations of fellmongers (buyers of sheep hide and skin) (R2690, R2691, R2695). Under the agreements, each sellers' association should not sell outside its territory and each buyers' association should buy all the sheepskins offered to it at specified prices. The agreements were abandoned between 1959 and 1961, but they are unlikely to have had any significant impact on competition between fellmongers. The fellmongery industry was essentially competitive.

Manufactures of leather not elsewhere specified. The Buffalo Picker Manufacturers Association set prices for buffalo hide pickers until 1959 (R431).

Leather Goods (MLH 432)

There is no evidence of restrictive agreements in this industry.

Fur (MLH 433)

There is no evidence of restrictive agreements in this industry.

Weatherproof Outerwear (MLH 441)

There is no evidence of any significant restrictive agreements in this industry. An agreement by the Clothing Manufacturers Federation of Great Britain, which covered several clothing industries (including MLH 441), is discussed under MLH 443.

Men's and Boys' Tailored Outerwear (MLH 442)

There is no evidence of any significant restrictive agreements in this industry. An agreement by the Clothing Manufacturers Federation of Great Britain, which covered several clothing industries (including MLH 442), is discussed under MLH 443.

Women's and Girls' Tailored Outerwear (MLH 443)

The register contains agreements by the Clothing Manufacturers Federation of Great Britain (R546*), the British Mantle Association (R2464*), and the Apparel and Fashion Industry's Association (R1341*). The three agreements were similar. All three contained a restriction that fixed the seasonal dates at which women's outerwear could be sold at reduced prices. In addition, R546* and R1341* required that members not grant any discounts to buyers other than settlement discounts, and contained a few more minor conditions of sale. R2464* was canceled in 1964, while R546* and R1341* were abandoned in 1968. It is unlikely, however, that these agreements had any significant effect on competition. This view is supported by evidence provided in the 1950s by firms in the clothing industry and reported in PEP: according to one firm, the restrictions on discounts and conditions of sale of the Clothing Manufacturers Federation were not observed; according to another, the restrictions on discounts and conditions of sale of the Apparel and Fashion Industry's Association were observed, but competition was nevertheless very intense.

Overalls and Men's Shirts, Underwear, etc. (MLH 444)

There is no evidence of any significant restrictive agreements in this industry.

Dresses, Lingerie, Infants' Wear, etc. (MLH 445)

There is no evidence of any significant collusive agreements in this industry. The agreement of the Apparel and Fashion Industry's Association, described under MLH 443, covered this industry as well, but, as pointed out above, it did not contain any significant restrictions on competition. Another agreement, by the Light Clothing and Allied Trades Association, comprised settlement terms, delivery charges, and sample discounts (R652, R625). It ended in 1964, and was also of little significance for competition.

Hats, Caps, and Millinery (MLH 446)

The register contains agreements by the South of England Hat Manufacturers Federation (R275), the London Wholesale Millinery Manufacturers Association (R804), the Millinery Guild (R1971*), and the Millinery Distributors Association (R312*). The four agreements covered women's hats only. R1971*, which contained restrictions about sales promotion and the seasonal dates at which goods could be supplied to retailers at reduced prices, continued until 1968. The other three agreements were somewhat interrelated. They provided for collective exclusive dealing, fixed distributors' margins, and conditions of sale and resale; see also CD. In addition, R275 comprised recommendations for price increases, and R312* provided for minimum prices of hats produced by wholesalers. All three agreements were abandoned in 1961. Given that the two manufacturers' associations involved in these agreements were regional and sales of ladies' hats accounted for about half of total sales of MLH 446 in the 1960s, one can conclude that the agreements affected a fraction of total industry sales between 10% and 50%.

Corsets and Miscellaneous Dress Industries (MLH 449.1)

Corsetry. An agreement by the Corsetry Manufacturers Association about settlement and sample discounts was allowed to continue without a Court hearing (R542). This industry was clearly competitive.

Miscellaneous dress industries. An agreement by the Tie Manufacturers Association, relating to trade discounts, as well as to prices for certain qualities of ties, was abandoned in 1968 (R547*). The products covered by the agreement accounted for 40–50% of total sales revenue in this product group.

Gloves (MLH 449.2)

There is no evidence of restrictive agreements in this industry.

Footwear (MLH 450)

Leather footwear. No evidence of restrictive agreements.

Rubber footwear. The agreement of the Rubber Footwear Manufacturers Association related to prices charged for rubber boots and certain other standardized products, trade discounts, the maintenance of manufacturers' resale prices, and collective exclusive dealing. See MRPC, *Report on the Supply of Certain Rubber Footwear* (London: H.M.S.O., 1956) for details. The industry was also listed in CD. The agreement presumably was abandoned in 1956, since it was not registered. Thus the industry experienced a change in competition regime following the introduction of the 1956 Act.

Parts of shoes and work done. The Shoe Tip Association fixed the prices of heel tips and toe plates until 1961 (R168). An agreement by a group of manufacturers of cut leather soles provided, until 1959, for specified trade discounts and aggregated rebates (R1825). Finally, BT mentions allegations of collective exclusive dealing arrangements in boot and shoe repairing.

Bricks, Fireclay and Refractory Goods (MLH 461)

Refractory goods. The register contains price-fixing agreements by the Welsh Silica Association (R69), the Sheffield Ganister and Compo. Association (R224), the National Silica Brickmakers Association (R342), the Fireclay Grate Back Association (R343), the Stourbridge Firebrick Association (R409, R2650), the Woodville District Firebrick and Fireclay Association (R882), the Yorkshire Firebrick Association (R833), the Scottish Firebrick Association (R983*), the Magnesite and Chrome Brickmakers Association (R1625), and a group of firebrick producers (R1089, R1090). In addition, a national organization, the National Firebrick Conference, made recommendations for price increases in firebricks, fireclay, and fireclay refractories to cover changes in costs (R341). All these agreements were abandoned between 1959 and 1961. In some cases, they were replaced for some time by information agreements

(Swann et al. 1974). Bricks were also listed in CD. In summary, there was a change of competition regime in this industry.

Building bricks. The register contains price-fixing agreements by several regional associations of brick producers (R58, R151, R215, R489, R599*, R1422). These registered agreements did not cover most areas. This is consistent with the view expressed in a case study of the building materials industry, written by B. R. Williams and included in Burn (1958). On the other hand, according to PEP, most areas were covered by restrictive agreements in the mid-1950s. In addition, there were national pricing agreements for specific types of bricks: by the Pressed Brick Makers Association (R1277), which covered fletton bricks; by the Stock Brick Manufacturers Association (R938); and by the Enamel Association (R642). According to PEP, R1277 and R938 were effective primarily in the London area. All these agreements were abandoned between 1958 and 1961. Given that fletton bricks accounted for some 40% of total industry output in the 1950s and a significant part of the rest of the industry was also cartelized, it is probably fair to say that the 1956 Act caused a change of competition regime in the building brick industry. An official inquiry into the industry carried out in the 1970s found that competition was effective at the time of the inquiry; see MMC, *Building Bricks* (London: H.M.S.O., 1976).

Sanitary ware of fireclay, etc. The British Sanitary Fireclay Association fixed prices and aggregated rebates for sanitary fireclay ware until 1958 (R1446). The Scottish Fireclay Pipe Association fixed prices for fireclay pipes, drainage goods, and related products until 1960 (R1565, R1808). A pricing agreement by the South Wales and Mon. Sanitary Pipe Association was abandoned in 1960 (R1044, R1789). The industry was also listed in CD. Swann et al. (1973) describe the emergence of competition following the termination of collusive agreements. The 1956 Act caused a change of competition regime in this industry.

Other products. Most other products of MLH 461 were subject to collusion in the 1950s. In particular, the register contains price agreements by the Salt Glazed Conduit Association (R885); the National Clayware Federation, covering a wide range of clayware goods (R877); the Bridgewater Roofing Tile Manufacturers Association, covering roofing tiles of clay and fittings (R1646); the South Eastern Brick and Tile Federation, covering clay bricks and roofing tiles (R58); the Clay Block Association (R194); the Floor Quarry Association (R573); and the National Horticultural Pottery Manufacturers Association (R68). All these agreements ended in 1958–1959. Finally, according to the case study of the building materials industry in Burn (1958), there was also a price agreement for earthenware pipes. PEP also reports complaints that the National Salt Glazed Pipe Manufacturers Association operated a price-fixing agreement, and the salt glazed pipe industry was also listed in CD and BT.

Pottery (MLH 462)

Glazed earthenware tiles. A price-fixing agreement by the Glazed and
Floor Tile Manufacturers Association (R574, R2434, R2652*) was contested in
the Court in 1964 and was allowed to continue (LR 4 RP 239). The agreement, which also provided for some degree of technical cooperation, covered
all types of ceramic wall, fireplace, and floor tiles, and was still in force in the
mid-1970s. According to CD and BT, the industry was also subject to collective discrimination arrangements before 1956. Swann et al. (1973) provide
details on the evolution of the industry from the 1950s to the early 1970s. The
glazed tile industry was collusive throughout the time period examined in
this book.

Sanitary earthenware. The British Sanitary Earthenware Manufacturers
Association fixed the prices of sanitary earthenware until 1958 (R254). According to CD and BT, it also operated collective discrimination arrangements before 1956. Thus the 1956 Act caused a change of competition regime
in this industry. An official inquiry carried out in the 1970s found that despite the occurrence of parallel pricing, competition was effective at the time
of the inquiry; see MMC, *Ceramic Sanitaryware* (London: H.M.S.O., 1978).

Other china and earthenware. A series of price agreements by members
of the Earthenware Association and between the association and a group of
outside firms, covering a wide range of items of earthenware, were abandoned in 1958 (R733, R791, R829). The British Teapot Manufacturers Association fixed prices for teapots, jugs, and associated items of earthenware until
1962 (R894). The English China Manufacturers Association fixed prices for
bone china until 1958 (R1785). A case study of the pottery industry, written
by B. R. Williams and published in Burn (1958), mentions several other
associations of producers of china and earthenware with collusive agreements in the 1950s, and notes that some of the agreements in this industry
were not as effective as the agreements in other sections of MLH 462. Nevertheless, the china and pottery industry should be regarded as one with a
change of competition regime.

Electrical ware. An agreement by the British Electro-ceramic Manufacturers Association, covering die-made electroceramics for electrical insulation, provided for prices and the reporting of inquiries (R956). It was canceled
in 1959. Hence there was a change of competition regime in this industry.

Glass (MLH 463)

Plate glass. A single producer, Pilkington Brothers, was responsible for the
entire production of plate glass. This firm participated in a number of restric-

tive agreements with distributors of plate glass, which were abandoned before or in 1956. After 1958, it was a party to an international market-sharing arrangement. See CD and especially MC, *A Report on the Supply of Flat Glass* (London: H.M.S.O., 1968). Unprocessed plate glass is the main product of this part of MLH 463. Another important product is processed plate glass. The register contains a price agreement by the Plate Glass Association, whose membership consisted of processors and dealers in plate glass (R821*). This agreement was abandoned in 1959, and was replaced by an information agreement, which ended in 1965. The register also contains price-fixing agreements by the Glass Benders Association (R837*), the Scottish Glass Merchants and Glaziers Association (R1188) and the N. Ireland Plate Glass Association (R827), all of which were cancelled in 1958–1960. R837* and R1188 were replaced by information agreements, which lasted until the mid-1960s. The share of processed plate glass in the total sales revenue of the plate glass industry was 15–30% in the 1960s.

Safety glass. An agreement between two of the biggest producers of safety glass, Pilkington and Triplex, relating to the demarcation of their respective activities and exclusive cross-licensing, was abandoned in 1958 (R347). The effect of this agreement on the industry as a whole is not clear.

Glass containers. The agreement of the Glass Bottle Association set minimum prices for glass containers (R660*, R1681, R1682). It was contested in the Court and struck down in 1961 (LR 2 RP 345). Swann et al. (1973) provide details on this case. The 1956 Act caused a change of competition regime in this industry.

Illuminating glassware. No agreements were registered in this industry. However, the 1968 MC report on electric lamps provides some relevant information. The principal product of the industry in the 1950s was glass bulbs for electric lamps. There were three major producers, one of which was a joint subsidiary of the other two. Nothing is known about restrictive agreements between these firms, but it is difficult to see this industry as competitive. During the 1960s, the share of glass bulbs for electric lamps in total sales of illuminating glassware declined substantially. Because of this change in product mix and the ambiguity regarding the initial competitive conditions in the industry, there is considerable uncertainty about the evolution of competition in illuminating glassware.

Other glass products. Competition in the laboratory glassware industry was regulated by the activities of two associations: the British Chemical Ware Manufacturers Association, whose membership consisted of manufacturers of laboratory glassware, and the British Laboratory Ware Association, which represented distributors that provided "technical service" and acted as agents. An agreement between the two associations provided for collective exclusive dealing and specified trade discounts (R374). Moreover, an agreement by the distributors' association provided for common prices for unbranded goods and the maintenance of individual prices of branded goods (R654). The laboratory ware industry was also listed in CD and BT. These agreements ended in 1959. The register also contains a price agreement by the Stourbridge Glass Manufacturers Association, which was abandoned in 1959 (R2507).

Cement (MLH 464)

The agreement of the Cement Makers Federation (R77*), which provided for common prices and aggregated rebates, was contested in the Court in 1961, and the price restrictions were allowed to continue (see LR 2 RP 241 and the report of the Director General of Fair Trading for 1974). The agreement was still in operation in the late 1970s. Swann et al. (1973) describe the evolution of the cement industry from the 1950s to the early 1970s. Collusion continued in the industry throughout the period examined in this book.

Abrasives (MLH 469.1)

No agreements were registered, but PEP mentions the Abrasive Industries Association as allegedly collusive.

Miscellaneous Building Materials and Mineral Products (MLH 469.2)

Asbestos cement goods. According to MC, *Asbestos and Certain Asbestos Products* (London: H.M.S.O., 1973), there was a price agreement in the industry before 1956. The agreement was abandoned after the introduction of the 1956 Act and was not registered. The industry was also listed in both BT and PEP as being subject to collusive pricing and other restrictions. The MC report also stated that competition was generally effective after 1956. Hence there was a change of competition regime in the asbestos cement industry.

Precast concrete goods. The register contains several agreements between members of regional associations. They all contained price restrictions, and some also provided for the reporting of inquiries and the allocation of work between the parties; there were also agreements between associations to observe each other's arrangements in their respective areas (R196, R197, R198, R203, R268, R511, R512*, R521, R539, R540, R909, R910, R1036, R1037, R1242, R1244, R1276, R1352, R1463, R1490, R1671, R1795, R2606). These agreements covered a variety of precast concrete goods: paving slabs and curbs were usually covered, and sometimes partition blocks, pipes and tubes, and other products as well. All the agreements were abandoned in 1958–1960. Two important national agreements ended in 1959: R305, which was operated by the Federation of Building Blocks Manufacturers and contained prices for building blocks, and R951*, which was operated by the British Concrete Pipe Association and provided for minimum prices and the allocation of work for concrete pipes, tubes, and related products in England and Wales. Overall, the largest part of the industry was probably cartelized in the 1950s.

The state of competition in the 1960s and 1970s is less clear. A price agreement by the North East Concrete Producers Association was referred to the Court and was abandoned in 1970 (R3140*). R951* was referred to the Court in 1965, although it had been formally canceled in 1959. Several other collusive agreements in precast concrete goods were in operation at various dates during the 1970s. The most important of these were two national agreements in concrete pipes and manhole components, both of which were discontinued in 1978 (R4556* and R4758*). Finally, according to MMC, *Concrete Roofing Tiles* (London: H.M.S.O., 1981), competition in concrete roofing tiles was muted in the 1970s. The products affected by these arrangements accounted for about 20–30% of total industry sales in the 1970s.

Ready-mixed concrete. The register contains a very large number of local agreements in ready-mixed concrete that operated at various dates during the 1960s and the 1970s (although, oddly, it contains no agreements for the 1950s). The vast majority of these were discovered during an official investigation into the industry carried out in the 1970s. They were placed on the register (and most were also referred to the Court), and were abandoned in the late 1970s. Details can be found in the annual reports of the Director General of Fair Trading for 1978 and 1979 and in MMC, *Ready Mixed Concrete* (London: H.M.S.O., 1981). According to the MMC, however, the agreements were of limited scope and were not always observed. Thus the state of competition in this industry throughout the period examined in this book should be regarded as ambiguous.

Lime and whiting. The register contains price agreements by the Southern Lime Association (R1248), the South West of England Lime Association (R2268), and the British Whiting Federation (R1259). The lime industry was also listed in CD. All agreements were abandoned in 1959, leading to a change of competition regime in this industry.

Roofing felts. A pricing agreement by the Built-up Roofing Council, whose members were manufacturers and/or contractors of built-up bituminous felt roofing materials, was canceled in 1959 (R841). The roofing felt industry was also listed in PEP and BT as allegedly collusive; PEP reported complaints that the Association of British Roofing Felt Manufacturers was a price-fixing body. According to CD and BT, there were collective discrimination arrangements for damp courses before 1956, at least in certain regions. The register also contains two agreements between asphalt and felt roofing manufacturers that suggest price-fixing and the allocation of work may have continued, at

least to some extent, during the 1960s: a regional agreement that was in operation until 1967 (R2818), and an agreement by some of the largest firms in
the industry with respect to a particular tender for a government contract in
1966–1967 (R3106). This evidence suggests that it may be best to classify this
industry as ambiguous.

*Manufactured bituminous asphalt and emulsions, coated roadstone, and
coated slag.* The Asphalt Roads Association (R216) and the British Tar-
paviers Federation (R118) specified standard schedules of charges until 1958.
The Scottish Hot Road Binder Manufacturers and Spraying Association fixed
prices until 1962 (R895). Several other groups or regional associations of asphalt manufacturers and contractors abandoned their collusive agreements
between 1958 and 1961 (R440*, R952, R1192, R1252, R1628, R1934). An agreement by the Mastic Asphalt Employers Federation contained prices for labor
and materials and conditions of contract (R578). Some of the price restrictions were dropped in 1961, while others continued until 1969. A price-fixing
agreement by the Scottish Road Emulsion Association ended in 1958 (R598),
but most of the member firms continued to participate in a collusive arrangement for cold bituminous emulsion until 1967 (R3272). Bituminous
emulsion was also mentioned in both PEP and BT as a potentially collusive
industry, and road-surfacing materials in general were also included in the
BT lists of allegedly collusive products.

An official investigation into the road-surfacing materials industry carried
out in the 1970s revealed a large number of regional or local restrictive agreements, which had been in operation since the early 1970s or earlier. These
agreements related to hot rolled asphalt and coated slag. They were placed
on the register (and most were also referred to the Court), and were abandoned in the late 1970s. See the 1979 report of the Director General of Fair
Trading for details. Their coverage and effectiveness are, however, not very
clear. All in all, the state of competition in this industry throughout the 1960s
and the 1970s must be regarded as ambiguous.

Other building materials and mineral products. Most other products of
MLH 469.2 were subject to collusion in the 1950s. In fact, the only important
products for which there is no evidence of any price agreements are gypsum,
plaster, and plasterboard. However, plasterboard was listed in CD, which
implies that it was subject to collective discrimination arrangements before
1956; according to BT, these probably involved restrictions on entry into
distribution. Gypsum was also listed in BT, probably for the same reason.

The register contains restrictive agreements by the Granite Kerb Conference (R386, R2226, R2227, R2228), the National Tile Fireplace Makers Association (R112), the Architectural Cornish Granite Association (R293, R294,
R295), the Slag Wool Association (R1249), and various associations of manufacturers or engravers of memorials and related goods (R1520, R1543,
R1575*, R2105, R2485). Memorials and fireplaces were also listed in CD or BT

as being subject to collective discrimination arrangements. All agreements were abandoned in 1959–1960, except for some restrictions of R1575* that continued until 1965. R386 was replaced for some time by an information agreement. Moreover, an agreement by the Mica Trade Association, whose membership consisted of manufacturers, importers, and dealers, required members to deal with one another only (R311); this ended in 1959. The members of the Glazed Cement Manufacturers Association agreed on charges and conditions of contract until 1964 (R559). A pricing agreement of the Plaster Ventilators Manufacturers Association continued until 1968 (R3064*). Finally, PEP mentions allegations of collusive pricing by the Association of Wood Wool Manufacturers and the Association of Paving Manufacturers (producers of paving flags and curbs).

Timber (MLH 471)

Sawn, planed, dressed, or further processed hardwood and softwood. The register contains several price-fixing agreements by regional associations of sawmillers, which must have covered more than 20% but less than 50% of the total market (R86, R513, R517, R676, R1194, R937). They were all abandoned in 1958–1959.

Plywood and textured boards. No evidence of any restrictive agreements.

Wood chipboard. No evidence of any restrictive agreements.

Builders' woodwork. The English Joinery Manufacturers Association recommended price increases until 1959 (R191). According to PEP, standard types of joinery were under price control; special types were not. The Scottish Joinery and Door Manufacturers Association also abandoned its pricing agreement in 1959 (R946). Hence the industry probably experienced a change of competition regime as a result of the 1956 Act.

Other products and work done. The Kiln Owners Association set a schedule of charges for kiln drying of timber and plywood until 1958 (R520).

Furniture and Upholstery (MLH 472)

An agreement by the British Furniture Trade Confederation, whose membership consisted of both manufacturers and distributors, required that members deal only with one another and provided for the maintenance of retail prices (R1288*). This agreement covered products of MLH 472, MLH 473 and MLH 399.1. It was abandoned in 1963, but it does not seem to have been very restrictive, especially in light of the very large membership of the confederation. A similar agreement by the Scottish House Furnishers Association also ended in 1963 (R1329*). An agreement by the British Furniture Manufacturers Federated Associations related mainly to settlement discounts and other conditions of sale (R1454*); most of the restrictions were dropped in 1963. Two other agreements on discounts and conditions of sale, by the Association of Folding Furniture Makers (R1464*) and the National Association of Manufacturers and Distributors of Office Equipment (R1790), were canceled in 1963–1964. These agreements are unlikely to have restricted competition between manufacturers to any significant degree. This is confirmed by PEP, where the furniture industry is regarded as competitive. Finally, the register also contains a pricing arrangement between the members of the Chair Frames Association (R4860), which apparently continued until the late 1970s. In any case, this is a minor product of the industry. All in all, the evidence suggests that the furniture industry was essentially competitive.

Bedding and Soft Furnishings (MLH 473)

The National Bedding Federation, which was a member of the British Furniture Trade Confederation, had an agreement similar to the agreement of the latter (see above, under MLH 472). In particular, members were to deal only with one another and distributors were to maintain the manufacturers' retail prices (R1686*). A separate agreement of the federation provided for quantity discounts to be allowed by manufacturers on mattresses sold directly to hotels (R173*). Both agreements ended in 1962–1963. A price agreement by the National Association of Upholstery Fibre Processors, covering upholstery and mattress pads, was abandoned in 1958 (R671). This was a secondary product of the industry, however. Thus the bedding and soft furnishings industry was largely competitive.

Shop and Office Fittings (MLH 474)

A price agreement by the Shopfront Moulding Manufacturers Association was abandoned in 1959 (R463). The scope of this agreement seems to have been limited, however: the membership of the association consisted of only eleven firms, while the total number of firms with more than twenty-five employees in MLH 474 was at least 200 in the late 1950s. The register also contains an agreement by the National Association of Shopfitters, whose membership was large (R467). Unfortunately, it is not clear what the restrictions were in this case and when they were abandoned. It seems that the association originally specified profit margins for contracting work and conditions of sale. But there is no information about the time period during which the restrictions were in force: they may have continued until the 1970s or they may have been abandoned sometime after 1956 or they may have been ineffective ever since the agreement was registered. This industry is not mentioned as collusive in any other data source. It is probably best to regard it as ambiguous.

Wooden Containers and Baskets (MLH 475)

The Shive Manufacturers Association fixed prices until 1959 (R2304). This is a minor product of the industry. Neither this agreement, nor some local price agreements on packing cases, abandoned at various dates between 1957 and 1967, could have had any significant effect on competition for the industry as a whole.

Miscellaneous Wood and Cork Manufactures (MLH 479)

Cork manufactures. No evidence of any restrictive agreements.

Wood manufactures. The register contains pricing agreements by the Association of Wood Block Manufacturers (R1053), the Wood Handle Manufacturers Council (R566), the Brush Wood Turners Association (R551), and the Underwood Products Association, which consisted of producers of chestnut fencing and related products (R1323). The first three agreements ended in 1959, and the fourth appears to have continued until 1972. The affected products accounted for more than 10% but less than 50% of this product category. PEP also mentions allegations of collusion between manufacturers of coffins.

Paper and Board (MLH 481)

Paper, uncoated or coated. A large number of price-fixing agreements by various associations and groups of paper manufacturers, covering nearly all types of paper, were registered. Most of these agreements covered specific types and grades of paper, so it would be tedious to give details on each here.[7] Nearly all were abandoned in 1958–1960, but a few were abandoned in 1962–1963 and some were replaced by information agreements that lasted until the mid- or late 1960s. According to CD, parts of the industry were subject to collective discrimination arrangements before 1956. In the case of newsprint, where prices were under government regulation until 1956 and were then fixed by the Association of Makers of Newsprint between 1956 and 1960 (R1328), there were also, until 1958, international agreements limiting imports (R2433). Finally, two agreements by the British Paper and Board Makers Association, relating to minimum buying prices of waste paper from local authorities (R925*) and minimum and maximum buying prices of waste paper from merchants (R71*), were contested in the Court and struck

---

7. They are the following: R497, R498, R499* (by the Association of Makers of Wood Free Papers), R500, R501, R502, R503, R504, R505, R506, R507, R556* (by the Association of Corrugated Paper Makers), R923, R978, R1237, R1238, R1239, R1240, R1241, R1265, R1266, R1267, R1268, R1282, R1328, R1361, R1364, R1365, R1366, R1367, R1368, R1370, R1456, R1501, R1735, R2224, R2635.

down in 1963 (LP 4 RP 1, LR 6 RP 161). To summarize, there was a change of competition regime for all the principal products of the paper industry. However, a 1967 official report on the price of newsprint made allegations about the existence of an international cartel in this product, involving British and foreign producers. See National Board of Prices and Incomes, *Prices of Standard Newsprint* (London: H.M.S.O., 1967).

Board, uncoated or coated. The register contains pricing agreements for intermittent board (R924), fourdrinier chipboard (R1238, R1370), and certain types of coated board (R1267). They were all abandoned in 1960. The share of these products in the total sales of board was probably between 10% and 50%. On the other hand, the agreements by the British Paper and Board Makers Association on waste paper discussed above are unlikely to have had any major effect on competition in the product market. Finally, BT reported allegations about collective discrimination arrangements in hardboard and fiber building board. According to PEP, however, there was no evidence that sales of building board were regulated.

Cardboard Boxes, Cartons, and Fibre-Board Packing Cases (MLH 482.1)

Paper boxes. No evidence of any significant restrictive agreements. The British Paper Box Federation specified only conditions of sale (R1406).

Cartons. No evidence of any significant restrictive agreements. The British Carton Association specified only conditions of sale (R1404).

Fibreboard packing cases. An agreement by the Fibreboard Packing Case Manufacturers Association contained only a recommendation not to offer discounts (R1230). The industry was basically competitive.

Other products. No evidence of any restrictive agreements.

Packaging Products of Paper and Associated Materials, Other Than Board (MLH 482.2)

A price agreement by the British Paper Bag Federation fixed prices for paper bags until 1965 (R1235). Moreover, the Royal Hand and Grocery Bags Association set prices for soda bags and sugar bags until 1960 (R1369). Paper bags accounted for about 30% of total sales revenue in the whole of MLH 482.2 and for about 45% of total sales revenue of the product category "paper bags and sacks" in the 1960s.

Manufactured Stationery (MLH 483)

A price agreement by the Envelope Makers and Manufacturing Stationers Association, covering envelopes, account books, and personal stationery, was abandoned in 1959 (R987). A price agreement by a group of producers of various types of stationery for use by local authorities also ended in 1959 (R209). The products affected by these agreements accounted for some 30–40% of industry sales revenue in the 1960s. According to the Lloyds' report, the Stationers Proprietary Articles Trade Association, whose membership consisted of both manufacturers and distributors, practiced resale price maintenance and set *minimum* distributors' margins in the stationery industry until 1956, but it did not regulate the manufacturers' individual prices. The stationery industry was also listed in CD.

Miscellaneous Manufactures of Paper and Board (MLH 484)

Wallpaper. The members of the Wallpaper Manufacturers and Employers Association agreed upon the retail prices of wallpaper distributed by specialist merchants, but they did not regulate the prices of wallpaper sold through retail shops (R201). According to CD and BT, they also engaged in collective discrimination arrangements, including collective exclusive dealing, until 1956. The pricing restrictions were terminated in late 1957. The "price-controlled range" accounted for about 50% of total sales of wallpaper in the late 1950s, but this fraction declined in the 1960s. See MC, *Report on the Supply of Wallpaper* (London: H.M.S.O., 1964).

Other products. The Association of Lace Paper Makers (R495), the Association of Makers of Paper Serviettes (R496), the Society of Crepe Paper Makers (R491), and the Federation of Paper Tube Manufacturers (R183) fixed prices for their respective products until 1959. A price agreement by the Vulcanised Fibre and Leatheroid Association ended in 1958 (R1076).

Printing, Publishing of Newspapers and Periodicals (MLH 485, 486)

Newspapers. An agreement between the Newspaper Proprietors Association and the National Federation of Retail Newsagents, Booksellers and Stationers contained provisions that restricted the entry of new retailers into newspaper distribution (R97*). This is probably the reason why the newspaper industry was listed in CD. The agreement was contested in the Court and was struck down in 1961 (LR 2 RP 453).

More significant with respect to competition between publishers was a series of agreements between newspaper proprietors, including proprietors of London daily and Sunday newspapers, relating to common retail price increases and agreed trade discounts (R2001, R2002, R2718, R2719, R2720*,

R2721, R2722, R2805*, R2909, R2965*). Most of these agreements were discontinued in 1964–1966, although in a few cases agreements on price
increases were made as late as 1970 (R3590*). Several other regional agreements provided for the prenotification of price increases and restrictions on
sales promotion; in fact, in most cases the firms involved were required not
to change the prices of their newspapers without prior discussion with the
other parties (R2611*, R2394–R2420). All these ended in 1960–1962. Other
agreements between publishers, mostly regional, comprised conditions of
sale (including a requirement not to sell newspapers before a certain time of
the day), sales promotion, or restrictions on the entry of retailers, and ended
at various dates between 1957 and 1964 (R1653*, R2003, R2004, R2299,
R2300, R2387, R2388, R2422, R2610, R2612). Finally, a series of agreements
between publishers regulating the distribution of newspapers and providing
for agreed trade discounts and conditions of sale were abandoned in the late
1960s or the early 1970s (R2385*, R2386, R2604, and many others similar in
form to those three).

In summary, the industry was probably collusive in the 1950s. It experienced a change of competition regime as a result of the 1956 Act, although
the effect of the Act was probably not fully realized until the 1970s.

Periodicals.   No evidence of any significant restrictive agreements affecting
publishers. Two agreements by the Periodical Proprietors Association,
abandoned in 1961–1962, related only to conditions of sale and restrictions
on the entry of retailers (R871, R875), which probably explains why the industry was listed in CD.

General Printing, Publishing, etc. (MLH 489)

Published books.   No evidence of any significant restrictive agreements affecting publishers. An agreement between publishers relating to the maintenance of individual resale prices (R1586*, R1587*; see also CD and the Lloyds'
report) was contested in the Court in 1962 and was allowed to continue (LR 3
RP 246). This did not greatly affect competition between publishers, however, which, as the Court pointed out, was intense. The register also contains
agreements on discounts and conditions of sale for special kinds of books,
such as educational books, condensed books, and book club editions (R1650,
R2514, R2781). Most of the restrictions in these agreements were dropped in
the early 1960s, although some remained. In summary, this was a largely
competitive industry.

Other published products.   An agreement by the Music Publishers Association, comprising various pricing restrictions, continued until 1973 (R3641,
R3642, R3643). An agreement by the Diary Publishers Association, which
provided for maximum trade discounts, the maintenance of individual list
prices, and conditions of sale, ended in 1961 (R820, R1619, R2283, R2520,

R2608*). PEP also mentions the Greeting Card and Calendar Association as potentially collusive.

General printing, etc. work. The register contains price-fixing agreements by the Ceramic Printers Association (R70), the British Cinema and Theatre Printers Association (R73), the British Embroidery Transfer Manufacturers Association (R171), the Federation of Master Process Engravers (R278*), the Photo-Litho Reproducers Association (R372), the National Association of Engravers and Die-Stampers (R526), the Law Stationers Association (R1225), the Association of Northern Master Electrotypers and Stereotypers (R1254), the Society of Photo Printers (R1445), the Small Offset Association (R1929), the London Trade Typesetters Association (R2444), and the Electrotyping and Stereotyping Employers Federation (R2747*). In the case of the Fine Art Trade Guild (R822), the arrangement originally provided for price-fixing, collective exclusive dealing, and the collective enforcement of resale prices (see CD). Many of these agreements covered preparatory or nonstandard printing work. All were terminated in 1958–1959, except for R2747*, which ended in 1965. A price agreement between the British Federation of Master Printers and the Society of Parliamentary Agents covered only the printing of parliamentary documents (R1038, R1333); it was canceled in 1960. The effect of the 1956 Act on the printing industry as a whole should be seen as ambiguous, although it caused a change of competition regime in specific sections of the industry.

Rubber (MLH 491)

Tyres and tubes. The agreement of the Tyre Manufacturers Conference provided for common prices for "replacement" tires, discussions about price changes in the case of "original equipment" tires, collective exclusive dealing, aggregated rebates, collective resale price maintenance, and restrictions on sales promotion. There were also international agreements limiting imports. See MRPC, *Report on the Supply and Export of Pneumatic Tyres* (London: H.M.S.O., 1955). A modified version of this agreement was registered (R964*, R966, R967, R1327) and then abandoned in 1961. It was replaced by an information agreement, which was referred to the Court in 1965 and was found to have amounted to the same effect as the former explicit pricing arrangement. The information agreement ended in 1965.

The register also contains a series of agreements between the Tyre Manufacturers Conference and associations of distributors, which effectively restricted entry into tire distribution (R963*, R965, R2272, R2273, R2274, R2436, R2509*, R2632, R2633). These agreements were unsuccessfully contested in the Court in 1963 (LR 3 RP 404). Finally, the MRPC report also mentions that the Retread Manufacturers Association recommended prices to its members for retreaded tires; the registered agreement of this association contained conditions of sale only (R2828). All in all, the 1956 Act caused a change of competition regime in the tire industry in the long run. According to Swann et al. (1973), competition between manufacturers was intense in the early 1970s.

Rubber belting. No agreements were registered. However, the industry was listed as allegedly collusive in both BT and PEP.

Rubber hose and tubing. No agreements were registered. However, the industry was listed as allegedly collusive in PEP.

Other rubber goods and work done. Price agreements by the Rubber Proofers Association (R914*), the Screw Stopper Makers Association (R1355), and a group of producers of insulated, varnished, nonadhesive cambric or silk cloth and tape (R710) were abandoned in 1957–1959.

Linoleum, Plastics Floor Covering, Leather Cloth, etc. (MLH 492)

The agreement of the Linoleum Manufacturers Association comprised prices, some form of profit pooling, collective exclusive dealing, aggregated rebates, and restrictions on media advertising. In addition, the association was a party to an international collusive arrangement in linoleum. See MRPC, *Report on the Supply of Linoleum* (London: H.M.S.O., 1956); the industry is also listed in CD. A revised version of the agreement was registered (R729*), and unsuccessfully contested in the Court in 1961 (LR 2 RP 395). Following the Court's decision, the registered agreement was replaced by a watered-down version, which continued until 1963. A price agreement between manufacturers of felt base was canceled in 1965 (R2839*). Finally, a price agreement between manufacturers of leather cloth ended in 1959 (R670). The products affected by these agreements accounted for more than half of total industry sales. Thus the 1956 Act caused a change of competition regime for this industry as a whole, as well as for most of its principal products.

Brushes and Brooms (MLH 493)

There is no evidence of any restrictive agreements in this industry.

Toys, Games, Children's Carriages, and Sports Equipment (MLH 494)

Toys and games. No evidence of any significant restrictive agreements.

Children's carriages. No evidence of any significant restrictive agreements.

Sports equipment. The register contains a pricing agreement on cricket and hockey balls, which ended in the late 1960s or early 1970s (R3048, R3098). According to PEP, there were price-fixing arrangements in certain other sports goods as well (this information comes from a trade association in the industry). Tennis balls were perhaps a case in point. The share of all the regulated products in total industry sales revenue was probably larger than 10%. According to CD, some sports goods were subject to collective discrimination arrangements before 1956.

Miscellaneous Stationers' Goods (MLH 495)

Pens and mechanical pencils. No evidence of any restrictive agreements affecting competition between manufacturers. According to the Lloyds' report, the Stationers Proprietary Articles Trade Association practiced resale price maintenance and set *minimum* distributors' margins in the stationery industry (until 1956), but did not regulate the manufacturers' individual prices. The stationery industry was also listed in CD.

Lead Pencils. The Pencil Makers Conference fixed the prices of cheaper pencils, although not the prices of the more expensive varieties (R1426). This may be seen as a minimum-price agreement. Hence the pencil industry probably experienced a change of competition regime as a result of the 1956 Act.

Other stationers' goods. No evidence of any restrictive agreements affecting competition between manufacturers.

Plastics Products (MLH 496)

A price agreement between manufacturers of polyethylene tubing ended in 1962 (R272). On the other hand, the register contains evidence that manufacturers of PVC pressure pipes engaged in discussions about prices and discounts until 1972 (R3167*, R3215, R3731*, R3732*, R3733*), while producers of polyethylene pipes were parties to a collusive arrangement during 1974–1980 (R5072*). A restrictive agreement on plastic door furniture (knobs, locks, latches, etc.) by the Plastics Hardware Association ended in 1959 (R302). A pricing arrangement between the members of the Flushing Cistern Association continued unregistered until 1971 (R3671*), and was contested in the Court (but struck down). An agreement by the Lampshade Manufacturers Association, abandoned in 1959, comprised only conditions of sale (R360), and the same was the case for an agreement by a group of producers of plastic moldings, which ended in 1972 (R1322). Finally, a pricing agreement by a group of manufacturers of adhesive tapes was abandoned in 1965 (R2970*, R2962*). The products affected by all these agreements represented less than 10% of MLH 496. Hence the 1956 Act had no significant effect on the industry as a whole and on most of its principal products.

Miscellaneous Manufacturing Industries (MLH 499)

Musical instruments.   A restrictive agreement by the Federation of Master
Organ Builders (R1180) ended in 1959. Organs accounted for less than 10%
of total sales of musical instruments. The register also contains an agreement
by the Association of Musical Instruments Industries, specifying maximum
trade discounts and conditions of sale (R3749). This agreement apparently
was abandoned in 1974. Thus there was no change of competition regime in
the musical instrument industry during the period examined in this book.

Other products.   The Briar Pipe Trade Association set minimum prices until
1959 (R600). An agreement by a group of producers of peat moss litter, relating to prices and the allocation of work, ended in 1961 (R799). Finally, BT
reports allegations about a restrictive association in casein buttons, although
it does not specify the types of restrictions. This may refer to an exclusive
dealing arrangement between sellers of casein plastic and producers of
casein buttons, also reported in CD.

Appendix B: Datasets

Table B1
Data set for chapter 4

Industry	Year	C5	SS	DS	K/N	K/L	CHANGE
Clay, brick earth, marl, and shale	1958	0.726	13066	12745	0.51	4.91	1
	1963	0.821	17827	15996	0.74	7.21	1
	1968	0.910	32001	32001	1.25	11.72	1
	1975	0.966	33165	26369	1.91	17.21	1
Iron ore and ironstone	1958	0.789	13502	10856	1.49	7.68	0
	1963	0.884	12748	11475	1.88	11.26	0
White flour for breadmaking	1958	0.715	121751	123922	0.77	4.60	1
	1963	0.792	113211	119913	1.14	6.45	1
	1968	0.808	110439	110439	1.56	9.50	1
	1975	0.895	135726	108612	2.29	13.20	1
Bread	1958	0.315	184559	238086	0.46	2.57	1
	1963	0.714	214081	245906	0.58	2.47	1
	1968	0.773	236006	236006	0.86	2.93	1
	1975	0.823	207525	212485	0.92	3.42	1
Bacon and ham, cured and smoked	1958	0.308	90730	86486	0.21	1.43	1
	1963	0.474	74194	78009	0.31	1.70	1
	1968	0.569	67902	67902	0.55	2.44	1
	1975	0.532	102384	74775	0.66	3.60	1
Sausages and sausage meat	1958	0.505	44575	44238	0.21	1.43	0
	1963	0.522	52110	52719	0.31	1.70	0
	1968	0.562	59218	59218	0.55	2.44	0
	1975	0.565	62598	58139	0.66	3.60	0

Preserved fruit, other than marmalade and jams	1958	0.308	23915	19305	0.46	1.95	0
	1963	0.377	20428	19915	0.86	2.99	0
	1968	0.457	23267	23267	1.28	4.28	0
	1975	0.444	18855	18775	2.12	6.33	0
Vegetable and seed oils	1963	0.823	85828	84149	1.11	7.75	0
	1968	0.843	80519	80519	1.36	10.85	0
	1975	0.869	122108	86560	2.28	16.85	0
Fish and marine animal oils	1958	0.949	12364	5893	0.93	6.31	0
	1963	0.928	14080	9922	1.11	7.75	0
	1968	0.929	14129	14129	1.36	10.85	0
	1975	0.913	20553	12343	2.28	16.85	0
Oilseed cake and meal, meat meal, bonemeal, etc.	1963	0.804	27226	26755	1.11	7.75	0
	1968	0.726	21508	21508	1.36	10.85	0
	1975	0.817	34060	34840	2.28	16.85	0
Malt	1958	0.534	24538	17595	0.81	3.78	0
	1963	0.551	30607	25993	1.36	5.31	0
	1968	0.651	30347	30347	3.03	8.41	0
	1975	0.724	62701	54227	7.20	16.76	0
Coke	1958	0.619	162360	154766	6.02	21.34	0
	1963	0.653	153464	149435	9.73	28.18	0
Steel ingots	1958	0.842	55246	45286	7.54	11.35	0
	1963	0.766	48954	45106	12.15	17.26	0
Steel blooms, billets, and slabs	1958	0.722	258111	223065	7.54	11.35	0
	1963	0.696	203506	187510	12.15	17.26	0

Table B1 (continued)

Industry	Year	C5	SS	DS	K/N	K/L	CHANGE
Steel arches, etc.	1958	0.636	27664	23575	7.54	11.35	0
	1963	0.692	21136	19474	12.15	17.26	0
Hot rolled coil, etc.	1958	0.688	135593	116048	7.54	11.35	0
	1963	0.728	174121	160434	12.15	17.26	0
Steel plates, uncoated, 3 mm thick and over	1958	0.789	159323	131141	7.54	11.35	0
	1963	0.724	130471	120215	12.15	17.26	0
Steel plates and sheets, uncoated, under 3 mm thick	1958	0.911	173290	145342	7.54	11.35	0
	1963	0.942	166268	153199	12.15	17.26	0
Wrought tubes, manipulated, fabricated, etc.	1958	0.858	33584	32245	2.25	4.92	1
	1963	0.733	30886	30007	3.21	7.29	1
	1968	0.793	35437	35437	3.68	8.03	1
Pig iron	1958	0.547	125126	107090	0.61	3.57	0
	1963	0.673	97637	89962	0.97	4.82	0
Iron castings	1958	0.250	225786	222694	0.61	3.57	1
	1963	0.329	266582	259289	0.97	4.82	1
	1968	0.422	272333	272333	1.21	5.65	1
Aluminium and aluminium alloys, and manufactures thereof	1958	0.504	177881	162181	1.39	4.22	1
	1963	0.542	218852	220888	1.55	5.02	1
	1968	0.509	282354	282354	2.22	7.32	1
	1975	0.541	299943	316371	4.24	15.30	1

	Year						
Copper and manufactures thereof	1958	0.746	149102	265497	1.23	5.05	1
	1963	0.741	179616	307212	1.35	5.80	1
	1968	0.798	254943	254943	1.64	6.71	1
	1975	0.830	150489	239120	1.94	7.76	1
Nickel and nickel alloys, and manufactures thereof	1963	0.954	55743	66342	1.83	7.17	0
	1968	0.970	63786	63786	2.13	9.81	0
Tin and tin alloys, and manufactures thereof	1958	0.913	42598	60224	1.74	6.99	0
	1963	0.893	36996	45224	1.83	7.17	0
	1968	0.916	60136	60136	2.13	9.81	0
	1975	0.978	41179	38656	2.69	15.48	0
Zinc and zinc alloys, and manufactures thereof	1958	0.686	28233	35841	1.74	6.99	0
	1963	0.690	37667	41810	1.83	7.17	0
	1968	0.713	44085	44085	2.13	9.81	0
	1975	0.734	29847	18562	2.69	15.48	0
Track-laying tractors	1958	0.902	8315	9536	1.29	3.43	0
	1963	0.980	18749	18488	1.58	3.64	0
Lifts, escalators, and passenger conveyors	1958	0.625	12422	12452	0.29	1.41	1
	1963	0.616	15513	14986	0.33	1.56	1
	1968	0.641	20256	20256	0.41	1.91	1
	1975	0.751	29538	28427	0.53	2.44	1
Mining machinery	1958	0.362	36573	36848	0.51	2.09	0
	1963	0.422	43586	42979	0.56	2.38	0
	1968	0.591	38306	38306	0.70	2.81	0
Space-heating, ventilating, and air-conditioning equipment (1958 S.I.C.)	1958	0.233	45635	45978	0.37	2.13	0
	1963	0.241	78532	77438	0.36	2.06	0

Table B1 (continued)

Industry	Year	C5	SS	DS	K/N	K/L	CHANGE
Fans and ventilating units, industrial (1968 S.I.C.)	1963	0.737	15938	15716	0.36	2.06	0
	1968	0.604	19641	19641	0.41	2.41	0
	1975	0.566	21960	20764	0.50	3.31	0
Bottling, packing, canning, packeting, and labeling machinery	1963	0.553	17937	17687	0.49	2.23	0
	1968	0.567	21958	21958	0.59	2.82	0
	1975	0.592	22718	22118	0.71	3.84	0
Automatic slot machines	1963	0.903	2604	2567	0.49	2.23	0
	1968	0.721	15305	15305	0.59	2.82	0
	1975	0.724	8305	8173	0.71	3.84	0
Pulpmaking, papermaking, and boardmaking machinery	1958	0.840	10981	11063	0.42	2.07	0
	1963	0.938	22077	21770	0.49	2.23	0
	1968	0.833	16208	16208	0.59	2.82	0
	1975	0.825	13125	12916	0.71	3.84	0
Ordnance and small arms	1958	0.712	51490	51877	1.61	2.58	0
	1963	0.625	40566	40001	2.42	3.45	0
	1968	0.766	55543	55543	3.16	5.08	0
Bearings, other than ball and roller bearings, and bushes	1958	0.847	16338	16461	0.76	3.48	0
	1963	0.739	26617	26246	0.73	3.62	0
	1968	0.866	26012	26012	0.92	3.95	0
	1975	0.822	30512	28849	1.07	5.36	0
Gaskets and jointings	1963	0.762	8337	8221	0.73	3.62	0
	1968	0.806	16709	16709	0.92	3.95	0
	1975	0.904	11250	10636	1.07	5.36	0

Category	Year						
Electric cables, other than for telecommunication	1958	0.533	106228	114259	3.00	4.28	1
	1963	0.680	137090	154163	2.84	4.68	1
	1968	0.818	149872	149872	3.75	5.42	1
Electric light fittings, wiring and accessories, etc.	1958	0.381	41734	37492	0.49	1.72	1
	1963	0.380	61029	60668	0.63	2.03	1
	1968	0.473	67898	67898	0.98	2.68	1
	1975	0.470	84145	81542	1.43	4.13	1
Trailers and caravans	1958	0.370	24164	24469	3.47	6.46	1
	1963	0.435	36093	36472	3.49	5.81	1
	1968	0.442	71277	71277	3.71	6.49	1
	1975	0.346	79799	73079	3.78	6.78	1
Hand tools and implements	1958	0.286	30391	32426	0.29	1.92	1
	1963	0.333	38833	39194	0.35	2.34	1
	1968	0.376	39526	39526	0.41	2.73	1
	1975	0.522	45951	39840	0.55	3.62	1
Iron and steel wire	1958	0.561	73452	70269	0.60	3.42	1
	1963	0.577	80919	78527	0.71	4.15	1
	1968	0.573	82320	82320	0.95	5.27	1
	1975	0.655	87046	68175	1.20	6.26	1
Manufactures of iron and steel wire	1958	0.417	59268	59338	0.60	3.42	1
	1963	0.445	76581	77202	0.71	4.15	1
	1968	0.512	86233	86233	0.95	5.27	1
	1975	0.483	131816	122915	1.20	6.26	1
Wire of brass and other copper alloys, and manufactures thereof	1958	0.690	11496	17529	0.60	3.42	1
	1963	0.752	14570	18442	0.71	4.15	1
	1968	0.829	18604	18604	0.95	5.27	1

Table B1 (continued)

Industry	Year	C5	SS	DS	K/N	K/L	CHANGE
Copper wire and manufactures thereof	1958	0.698	41459	72366	0.60	3.42	1
	1963	0.724	23503	43499	0.71	4.15	1
	1968	0.869	38609	38609	0.95	5.27	1
Cans, metal boxes, and other small metal containers	1958	0.869	91347	80517	0.84	2.98	0
	1963	0.904	109910	104299	1.47	4.07	0
	1968	0.908	126711	126711	2.24	6.04	0
Precious metals, refined	1963	0.954	83585	105953	0.36	2.56	0
	1968	0.965	138771	138771	0.68	4.10	0
Jewellery and plate (1958 S.I.C.)	1958	0.218	25559	22731	0.30	2.23	0
	1963	0.263	34946	29945	0.36	2.56	0
Jewellery and plate (1968 S.I.C.)	1963	0.336	23130	19820	0.36	2.56	0
	1968	0.495	27497	27497	0.68	4.10	0
	1975	0.441	63290	49942	0.82	4.95	0
Metal furniture	1958	0.241	42492	41095	0.29	2.47	0
	1963	0.276	57570	57230	0.27	1.87	0
	1968	0.225	66030	66030	0.33	2.24	0
	1975	0.249	64974	63022	0.42	3.23	0
Drop forgings of steel and iron, and steel stampings and pressings	1963	0.583	103497	89132	0.41	2.40	1
	1968	0.612	104139	104139	0.50	2.99	1
	1975	0.650	115994	95893	0.58	3.72	1
Metal hollowware, domestic and industrial	1958	0.252	61627	68700	0.33	2.14	1
	1963	0.335	66378	71636	0.41	2.40	1
	1968	0.327	67972	67972	0.50	2.99	1
	1975	0.412	60195	54461	0.58	3.72	1

Category	Year						
Metal windows, metal door frames, etc.	1958	0.705	26531	27460	0.33	2.14	1
	1963	0.583	30510	30294	0.41	2.40	1
	1968	0.610	33217	33217	0.50	2.99	1
	1975	0.509	52420	34309	0.58	3.72	1
Safes, locks, latches, keys, etc.	1958	0.687	9517	12377	0.33	2.14	1
	1963	0.764	15224	18296	0.41	2.40	1
	1968	0.743	18948	18948	0.50	2.99	1
	1975	0.753	21861	19916	0.58	3.72	1
Single yarn of cotton, glass fibres, and man-made fibres	1958	0.319	188803	159023	0.74	3.39	1
	1963	0.372	134557	132227	1.22	5.22	1
	1968	0.503	123935	123935	1.81	7.46	1
	1975	0.756	82616	78395	2.58	11.05	1
Finished thread for sewing, embroidery, etc.	1958	0.851	26988	22009	0.74	3.39	0
	1963	0.818	23737	22278	1.22	5.22	0
	1968	0.879	27491	27491	1.81	7.46	0
	1975	0.879	27080	25558	2.58	11.05	0
Woven cotton cloth in the loom state	1958	0.116	157737	145988	0.46	3.25	0
	1963	0.193	83641	86041	0.75	4.80	0
	1968	0.313	52050	52050	1.08	7.22	0
	1975	0.437	27205	25111	1.44	9.85	0
Woven cloth of man-made fibres in the loom state	1958	0.211	99105	78882	0.46	3.25	1
	1963	0.358	91010	81405	0.75	4.80	1
	1968	0.519	84540	84540	1.08	7.22	1
	1975	0.636	59521	60036	1.44	9.85	1

Table B1 (continued)

Industry	Year	C5	SS	DS	K/N	K/L	CHANGE
Wool tops or slubbings	1958	0.301	121031	96334	0.39	2.49	0
	1963	0.340	120401	86844	0.50	2.98	0
	1968	0.547	86161	86161	0.73	4.37	0
	1975	0.642	44690	52171	1.06	6.97	0
Yarn of wool, hair, and man-made fibres spun on the woollen system	1958	0.237	52506	46333	0.39	2.49	0
	1963	0.230	72396	65786	0.50	2.98	0
	1968	0.339	68272	68272	0.73	4.37	0
	1975	0.370	59914	63038	1.06	6.97	0
Woven worsted fabrics	1958	0.173	109476	100736	0.39	2.49	0
	1963	0.267	100029	93473	0.50	2.98	0
	1968	0.311	79842	79842	0.73	4.37	0
	1975	0.438	50733	50160	1.06	6.97	0
Woven woollen fabrics	1958	0.177	103410	99048	0.39	2.49	0
	1963	0.151	88506	86576	0.50	2.98	0
	1968	0.240	79218	79218	0.73	4.37	0
	1975	0.268	44284	43274	1.06	6.97	0
Jute yarn, cloth, and other manufactures of jute	1958	0.508	36494	42969	0.94	4.09	1
	1963	0.592	40097	43219	1.07	4.01	1
	1968	0.689	38728	38728	1.24	4.97	1
	1975	0.734	12990	15466	2.27	9.30	1
Rope, twine, net, and manufactures thereof	1958	0.477	29692	26886	0.34	2.30	1
	1963	0.648	33161	27166	0.45	2.86	1
	1968	0.732	24197	24197	0.77	4.24	1
	1975	0.821	21168	17356	1.30	6.82	1

Description	Year						
Knitted, netted, or crocheted goods: underwear, shirts, and nightwear	1958	0.256	40530	31566	0.60	4.26	0
	1963	0.395	46060	37270	0.68	4.23	0
	1968	0.531	48760	48760	0.86	4.92	0
	1975	0.504	41022	46169	0.99	5.81	0
Knitted, netted, or crocheted goods: other clothing	1958	0.150	88309	93221	0.60	4.26	0
	1963	0.212	113456	105789	0.68	4.23	0
	1968	0.332	139594	139594	0.86	4.92	0
	1975	0.402	125522	163748	0.99	5.81	0
Woven carpets, carpeting, and carpet floor rugs	1958	0.412	80749	77717	0.83	2.96	1
	1963	0.423	84798	80025	0.91	3.16	1
	1968	0.575	81014	81014	1.24	3.80	1
Bedding other than wool blankets	1963	0.446	28247	27350	0.08	0.76	0
	1968	0.513	37014	37014	0.14	1.30	0
	1975	0.555	49565	49447	0.24	2.37	0
Other made-up household textiles	1963	0.271	28631	27722	0.08	0.76	0
	1968	0.266	26181	26181	0.14	1.30	0
	1975	0.474	25377	21230	0.24	2.37	0
Canvas goods and sacks	1958	0.252	33245	26594	0.10	0.94	1
	1963	0.280	27742	24382	0.12	1.15	1
	1968	0.249	21177	21177	0.14	1.43	1
	1975	0.313	17515	16040	0.14	1.73	1
Asbestos manufactures other than asbestos cement goods	1958	0.774	41279	37379	1.81	3.28	1
	1963	0.824	49883	47653	2.12	3.59	1
	1968	0.862	58645	58645	2.89	4.45	1
	1975	0.867	52739	60991	4.33	6.23	1

Table B1 (continued)

Industry	Year	C5	SS	DS	K/N	K/L	CHANGE
Leather, undressed	1958	0.382	24405	25969	0.20	1.98	0
	1963	0.453	16743	17306	0.24	2.34	0
	1968	0.556	13845	13845	0.36	3.28	0
	1975	0.763	11320	12061	0.49	4.50	0
Leather, dressed	1963	0.225	63802	66350	0.24	2.34	0
	1968	0.217	75429	75429	0.36	3.28	0
	1975	0.339	62049	70324	0.49	4.50	0
Fellmongery	1958	0.461	8928	7496	0.20	1.98	0
	1963	0.427	16260	11909	0.24	2.34	0
	1968	0.422	10523	10523	0.36	3.28	0
	1975	0.506	8753	9210	0.49	4.50	0
Manufactures of leather or leather substitutes	1958	0.213	19570	20523	0.04	0.42	0
	1963	0.208	26438	26747	0.06	0.58	0
	1968	0.203	28918	28918	0.07	0.70	0
	1975	0.245	31140	32183	0.09	1.01	0
Skins and furs, dressed, etc., and manufactures thereof	1963	0.377	11243	10495	0.10	0.82	0
	1968	0.495	10252	10252	0.14	1.13	0
	1975	0.635	7938	9554	0.16	1.59	0
Weatherproof outerwear	1963	0.223	50884	45994	0.08	0.74	0
	1968	0.306	42361	42361	0.10	0.93	0
	1975	0.298	40485	50254	0.12	1.08	0

Men's and boys' tailored outerwear	1958	0.350	148333	129315	0.07	0.34	0
	1963	0.380	158776	146296	0.09	0.47	0
	1968	0.377	158184	158184	0.13	0.67	0
	1975	0.283	144680	168807	0.17	0.99	0
Women's and girls' tailored outerwear	1958	0.152	82374	75103	0.05	0.53	0
	1963	0.167	86343	82575	0.06	0.59	0
	1968	0.201	85066	85066	0.09	0.78	0
	1975	0.177	99846	123790	0.10	0.87	0
Industrial and heavy overalls, aprons, and jeans	1958	0.241	18897	18872	0.06	0.47	0
	1963	0.261	22866	22522	0.08	0.65	0
	1968	0.274	22717	22717	0.12	0.91	0
	1975	0.326	33242	33321	0.14	1.11	0
Women's and girls' light outerwear	1958	0.082	83327	75540	0.03	0.40	0
	1963	0.129	76555	72727	0.05	0.52	0
	1968	0.166	95702	95702	0.08	0.74	0
	1975	0.160	133928	187785	0.09	0.92	0
Lingerie other than corsetry and brassieres	1958	0.202	35242	33001	0.03	0.40	0
	1963	0.265	34980	33304	0.05	0.52	0
	1968	0.414	37978	37978	0.08	0.74	0
	1975	0.453	30193	38132	0.09	0.92	0
Infants' wear	1958	0.177	16519	15026	0.03	0.40	0
	1963	0.153	17190	16046	0.05	0.52	0
	1968	0.297	20488	20488	0.08	0.74	0
	1975	0.288	17143	25685	0.09	0.92	0

Table B1 (continued)

Industry	Year	C5	SS	DS	K/N	K/L	CHANGE
Gloves, other than sport, knitted, and rubber gloves	1958	0.284	11629	11687	0.06	0.67	0
	1963	0.327	12894	12642	0.06	0.73	0
	1968	0.414	10734	10734	0.08	0.92	0
	1975	0.485	9125	9222	0.13	1.47	0
Tiles, other than of precast concrete and brick earth	1958	0.648	12642	12407	0.40	1.59	0
	1963	0.702	16120	15331	0.54	1.98	0
	1968	0.936	17562	17562	0.73	2.48	0
	1975	0.932	17522	18289	0.94	2.97	0
Sanitary ware of earthenware	1958	0.641	6972	6327	0.40	1.59	1
	1963	0.663	11399	11138	0.54	1.98	1
	1968	0.951	12733	12733	0.73	2.48	1
	1975	0.939	14665	15067	0.94	2.97	1
China, earthenware, etc., domestic and ornamental	1958	0.274	37170	43571	0.40	1.59	1
	1963	0.317	40657	43386	0.54	1.98	1
	1968	0.484	46653	46653	0.73	2.48	1
	1975	0.576	72952	69921	0.94	2.97	1
Electrical ware of porcelain, earthenware, or stoneware	1958	0.769	8289	8289	0.40	1.59	1
	1963	0.808	11521	11092	0.54	1.98	1
	1968	0.857	12014	12014	0.73	2.48	1
	1975	0.754	11610	10957	0.94	2.97	1
Glass containers	1958	0.632	51899	47427	0.83	2.65	1
	1963	0.696	60251	60456	1.41	3.68	1
	1968	0.873	70260	70260	2.13	5.45	1
	1975	0.876	84865	77991	2.89	8.70	1

Category	Year						
Cement	1958	0.855	77393	71133	2.71	10.58	0
	1963	0.890	90038	84136	3.79	14.40	0
	1968	0.890	101579	101579	6.26	23.88	0
	1975	0.930	126930	111057	6.83	25.60	0
Asbestos cement goods	1958	0.983	19849	19923	0.46	3.39	1
	1963	0.942	24842	25524	0.63	4.58	1
	1968	0.986	24510	24510	0.81	6.12	1
	1975	0.982	17075	15740	1.19	8.86	1
Plywood and veneers	1963	0.336	17458	20244	0.16	1.32	0
	1968	0.444	35998	35998	0.18	1.52	0
Textured boards and wood chipboard	1963	0.555	8768	8538	0.16	1.32	0
	1968	0.544	19395	19395	0.18	1.52	0
Builders' woodwork and prefabricated building structures of timber	1958	0.192	51985	58608	0.13	1.17	1
	1963	0.184	83526	89132	0.16	1.32	1
	1968	0.240	125719	125719	0.18	1.52	1
	1975	0.329	126038	125619	0.27	2.66	1
Office, school, and other furniture	1958	0.225	31472	31313	0.10	0.78	0
	1963	0.243	37553	37858	0.12	0.93	0
	1968	0.257	40945	40945	0.19	1.38	0
	1975	0.284	43702	38301	0.33	2.36	0
Wooden containers and baskets	1958	0.116	33083	32711	0.09	0.91	0
	1963	0.162	36207	36717	0.10	1.05	0
	1968	0.176	36502	36502	0.13	1.33	0
	1975	0.217	33061	30625	0.15	1.80	0

Table B1 (continued)

Industry	Year	C5	SS	DS	K/N	K/L	CHANGE
Paper, uncoated	1958	0.526	250871	218468	2.74	8.72	1
	1963	0.566	261650	260101	3.23	9.61	1
	1968	0.548	262225	262225	4.91	13.74	1
Paper and board, coated	1958	0.407	39023	31856	2.74	8.72	1
	1963	0.536	52930	46615	3.23	9.61	1
	1968	0.632	62511	62511	4.91	13.74	1
Paper and board, oiled, waxed, and other waterproof wrappings	1958	0.519	18681	16651	2.74	8.72	1
	1963	0.603	16882	16401	3.23	9.61	1
	1968	0.647	17131	17131	4.91	13.74	1
Boxes and cartons of paper and cardboard	1958	0.314	78812	81573	0.49	3.21	0
	1963	0.303	98159	95149	0.62	3.64	0
	1968	0.387	113954	113954	0.81	4.27	0
	1975	0.385	142961	116943	1.10	6.30	0
Fibreboard packing cases	1958	0.736	61670	52442	0.49	3.21	0
	1963	0.655	91999	84586	0.62	3.64	0
	1968	0.675	119657	119657	0.81	4.27	0
	1975	0.631	149089	114461	1.10	6.30	0
Rubber cellular products	1958	0.863	12392	10971	1.27	3.80	0
	1963	0.774	11688	10815	1.54	4.06	0
Carbons and other office machinery requisites	1958	0.633	10662	9709	0.29	1.63	0
	1963	0.642	14472	13871	0.43	2.33	0
	1968	0.749	17506	17506	0.56	3.41	0
	1975	0.792	17211	18894	0.81	5.56	0

Components, accessories, and semimanufactured goods of plastics	1963	0.120	48989	37990	0.33	2.24	0
	1968	0.164	84334	84334	0.55	3.60	0
	1975	0.136	113173	125688	0.82	5.96	0
Domestic, catering, and furnishing goods of plastics	1963	0.235	19127	14833	0.33	2.24	0
	1968	0.299	31250	31250	0.55	3.60	0
	1975	0.254	45655	52945	0.82	5.96	0
Packaging materials of plastics	1963	0.443	37290	28918	0.33	2.24	0
	1968	0.411	75053	75053	0.55	3.60	0
	1975	0.302	116905	139264	0.82	5.96	0
Musical instruments	1958	0.454	5356	5929	0.16	1.38	0
	1963	0.501	6643	6642	0.21	1.63	0

Notes: C5 is the five-firm sales concentration ratio.
SS is sales revenue (in £1000) deflated by the general producer price index.
DS is sales revenue (in £1000) deflated by industry-specific producer price indices.
K is the value of capital stock of the corresponding MLH industry in 1980 prices (in £ million).
L is employment of the corresponding MLH industry (in 1000).
N is the number of plants with at least 25 employees of the corresponding MLH industry.
CHANGE takes the value 1 for an industry with a change in competition regime and 0 otherwise.

Table B2
Data set for the concentration regressions of chapter 5

Industry	Year	C5	SS	DS	K/N	K/L	TVCLASS	ADTYPE	CHANGE
Flour, other than white flour for breadmaking	1958	0.639	36139	33254	0.77	4.60	0.55	1	1
	1963	0.716	42927	41191	1.14	6.45	0.55	1	1
	1968	0.672	41609	41609	1.56	9.50	0.85	1	1
	1975	0.816	44699	37173	2.29	13.20	0.85	1	1
Cereal breakfast foods	1963	0.977	37469	34156	1.14	6.45	0.85	2	0
	1968	0.935	43215	43215	1.56	9.50	0.85	2	0
	1975	0.914	55558	51992	2.29	13.20	0.85	2	0
Biscuits for human consumption	1958	0.479	136106	127902	1.47	2.63	0.55	2	1
	1963	0.655	140957	137413	2.19	3.69	0.55	2	1
	1968	0.710	146946	146946	3.13	4.30	0.85	2	1
	1975	0.789	169005	155520	4.27	4.92	0.85	2	1
Fish and fish products, quick-frozen	1958	0.932	9978	11186	0.21	1.43	0.85	1	0
	1963	0.917	25958	24769	0.31	1.70	0.85	1	0
	1968	0.911	35375	35375	0.55	2.44	0.85	1	0
	1975	0.781	73511	56958	0.66	3.60	0.85	1	0
Condensed milk	1958	0.909	24067	20038	0.62	3.65	0.25	2	1
	1963	0.934	25072	21001	0.74	4.74	0.25	2	1
	1968	0.944	23911	23911	0.92	5.81	0.85	2	1
	1975	0.889	23228	20122	1.35	8.27	0.85	2	1
Milk powder	1958	0.737	14686	12692	0.62	3.65	0.25	1	1
	1963	0.889	15051	13633	0.74	4.74	0.55	1	1
	1968	0.847	18692	18692	0.92	5.81	0.85	1	1
	1975	0.753	38195	23339	1.35	8.27	0.85	1	1

Ice cream and ice lollies	1958	0.942	22392	18076	0.62	3.65	0.55	2	0
	1963	0.931	14079	15895	0.74	4.74	0.85	2	0
	1968	0.912	19276	19276	0.92	5.81	0.85	2	0
	1975	0.909	49483	30115	1.35	8.27	0.55	2	0
Cocoa products	1958	0.732	176041	163309	0.84	2.42	0.55	2	1
	1963	0.823	171639	166754	1.40	3.40	0.85	2	1
	1968	0.834	180991	180991	2.22	4.64	0.85	2	1
	1975	0.836	218224	184031	3.27	6.72	0.85	2	1
Marmalade and jams	1958	0.629	36118	34021	0.46	1.95	0.55	2	0
	1963	0.729	34564	33391	0.86	2.99	0.55	2	0
	1968	0.756	31488	31488	1.28	4.28	0.55	2	0
	1975	0.689	30137	25043	2.12	6.33	0.85	2	0
Vegetables, etc., preserved (1958 S.I.C.)	1958	0.649	45235	35897	0.46	1.95	0.55	1	0
	1963	0.672	47825	42912	0.86	2.99	0.55	1	0
Vegetables, etc., preserved (1968 S.I.C.)	1963	0.653	65177	58482	0.86	2.99	0.55	1	0
	1968	0.667	73798	73798	1.28	4.28	0.85	1	0
	1975	0.703	101902	95830	2.12	6.33	0.85	1	0
Vegetables, quick-frozen	1958	0.986	7340	8287	0.46	1.95	0.85	1	0
	1963	0.933	24913	23826	0.86	2.99	0.85	1	0
	1968	0.971	35911	35911	1.28	4.28	0.85	1	0
	1975	0.817	58919	62240	2.12	6.33	0.85	1	0
Pickles, sauces, and relishes	1963	0.680	28206	27342	0.86	2.99	0.25	2	0
	1968	0.715	30293	30293	1.28	4.28	0.55	2	0
	1975	0.679	41689	42479	2.12	6.33	0.55	2	0

Table B2 (continued)

Industry	Year	C5	SS	DS	K/N	K/L	TVCLASS	ADTYPE	CHANGE
Soups	1958	0.911	25732	21650	0.46	1.95	0.55	2	0
	1963	0.925	39165	34385	0.86	2.99	0.55	2	0
	1968	0.904	39560	39560	1.28	4.28	0.85	2	0
	1975	0.865	44952	43104	2.12	6.33	0.85	2	0
Dog and cat foods	1958	0.861	24539	20935	0.42	2.77	0.55	2	0
	1963	0.943	38669	40458	0.59	3.88	0.85	2	0
	1968	0.941	58155	58155	0.89	6.16	0.85	2	0
	1975	0.944	74677	78807	1.34	9.66	0.85	2	0
Margarine	1958	0.881	50183	36611	1.46	7.58	0.55	2	0
	1963	0.928	42188	36814	1.91	9.57	0.85	2	0
	1968	0.938	31784	31784	2.89	10.59	0.85	2	0
Compound fat	1958	0.833	22975	15888	1.46	7.58	0.55	1	0
	1963	0.848	21280	19094	1.91	9.57	0.55	1	0
	1968	0.826	16498	16498	2.89	10.59	0.55	1	0
	1975	0.884	27612	19640	3.78	13.51	0.55	1	0
Coffee, and coffee and chicory extracts and essences	1958	0.979	22897	30630	0.63	3.82	0.55	2	0
	1963	0.984	31801	34494	0.96	5.27	0.55	2	0
	1968	0.937	46642	46642	1.67	8.07	0.85	2	0
	1975	0.927	51875	62435	2.51	9.78	0.85	2	0
Alcoholic cider, perry, apple pectin, and British wines	1958	0.812	20540	21770	0.67	3.46	0.55	2	0
	1963	0.972	20075	22784	1.20	4.86	0.55	2	0
	1968	0.916	30004	30004	1.39	5.68	0.55	2	0
	1975	0.902	46976	55645	2.75	7.55	0.55	2	0

	Year								
Cigarettes	1963	0.997	1198822	1258907	4.46	4.84	0.55	2	0
	1968	0.999	1236281	1236281	7.47	7.69	0.00	2	0
Other manufactured tobacco	1963	0.980	145500	158625	4.46	4.84	0.55	2	0
	1968	0.981	129145	129145	7.47	7.69	0.25	2	0
	1975	0.988	94571	119509	12.36	10.25	0.55	2	0
Lubricating oils and greases	1963	0.695	86247	82575	0.80	6.01	0.25	1	0
	1968	0.716	93079	93079	1.28	10.93	0.25	1	0
	1975	0.740	138734	135633	1.68	12.95	0.55	1	0
Pharmaceutical preparations	1958	0.286	119871	89003	1.33	4.10	0.55	2	0
	1963	0.287	168815	138163	1.68	4.93	0.55	2	0
	1968	0.349	221326	221326	2.67	7.55	0.55	2	0
	1975	0.393	341185	474269	4.73	11.40	0.55	2	0
Hair preparations	1958	0.670	16860	18822	0.41	2.02	0.55	2	0
	1963	0.542	26510	27535	0.48	2.03	0.55	2	0
	1968	0.570	31731	31731	0.92	2.96	0.55	2	0
	1975	0.607	46032	60769	1.50	5.06	0.55	2	0
Dental preparations	1963	0.944	13587	12347	0.48	2.03	0.85	2	0
	1968	0.874	14450	14450	0.92	2.96	0.85	2	0
	1975	0.803	21586	24625	1.50	5.06	0.85	2	0
Other toilet preparations	1958	0.420	33779	37708	0.41	2.02	0.25	2	0
	1963	0.373	50961	52931	0.48	2.03	0.25	2	0
	1968	0.405	70585	70585	0.92	2.96	0.25	2	0
	1975	0.421	99401	111633	1.50	5.06	0.55	2	0

Table B2 (continued)

Industry	Year	C5	SS	DS	K/N	K/L	TVCLASS	ADTYPE	CHANGE
Soap	1958	0.832	59413	60862	2.27	7.35	0.55	2	0
	1963	0.809	53272	53019	3.53	9.14	0.85	2	0
	1968	0.801	48123	48123	4.44	14.43	0.85	2	0
	1975	0.764	52683	49235	4.34	14.57	0.85	2	0
Finished detergents	1958	0.904	45542	36105	2.27	7.35	0.55	2	0
	1963	0.845	55501	48629	3.53	9.14	0.85	2	0
	1968	0.799	61265	61265	4.44	14.43	0.85	2	0
	1975	0.828	90114	99083	4.34	14.57	0.85	2	0
Polishes	1958	0.671	17337	18133	0.36	2.20	0.25	2	0
	1963	0.796	17901	18436	0.47	3.04	0.25	2	0
	1968	0.809	17249	17249	0.85	4.29	0.55	2	0
	1975	0.849	14138	18195	1.31	7.31	0.85	2	0
Pesticides, disinfectants, and household deodorisers	1958	0.424	29238	22616	0.41	2.96	0.55	2	0
	1963	0.520	34655	31491	0.68	4.56	0.55	2	0
	1968	0.534	44697	44697	1.28	7.49	0.55	2	0
	1975	0.533	73971	80699	2.57	13.13	0.55	2	0
Powered industrial trucks and industrial tractors	1958	0.698	9424	10001	0.29	1.41	0.00	1	0
	1963	0.764	16297	15212	0.33	1.56	0.00	1	0
	1968	0.555	42182	42182	0.41	1.91	0.00	1	0
	1975	0.607	71547	66984	0.53	2.44	0.00	1	0
Lawn mowers	1963	0.940	9840	9703	0.49	2.23	0.00	1	0
	1968	0.882	18368	18368	0.59	2.82	0.00	1	0
	1975	0.852	19401	19091	0.71	3.84	0.00	1	0

	Year									
Photographic and cinemato-graphic apparatus, and appliances, and document copying equipment	1963	0.706	14917	15978	0.54	3.10	0.25	2	0
	1968	0.843	38812	38812	1.02	2.87	0.25	2	0
	1975	0.787	54097	63083	1.78	7.28	0.25	2	0
Television receiving sets	1958	0.528	78964	81098	0.53	1.10	0.00	1	0
	1963	0.816	66324	72215	0.55	1.00	0.00	1	0
	1968	0.927	86103	86103	1.01	1.98	0.00	1	0
	1975	0.850	135769	201970	1.22	2.80	0.25	1	0
Radio receiving sets	1963	0.579	23118	25140	0.55	1.00	0.00	1	0
	1968	0.747	11556	11556	1.01	1.98	0.00	1	0
	1975	0.835	4939	7389	1.22	2.80	0.25	1	0
Cooking apparatus and appliances, electric	1958	0.651	20221	16031	1.18	2.55	0.00	2	1
	1963	0.600	26332	22655	1.18	2.27	0.25	2	1
	1968	0.859	40547	40547	1.43	3.00	0.25	2	1
	1975	0.791	41854	52480	2.14	4.34	0.25	2	1
Washing machines, electrically operated	1958	0.764	34924	25410	1.18	2.55	0.25	2	1
	1963	0.852	55575	44969	1.18	2.27	0.25	2	1
	1968	0.869	36915	36915	1.43	3.00	0.25	2	1
	1975	0.981	44509	52813	2.23	4.79	0.25	2	1
Batteries and accumulators	1958	0.782	42602	48030	0.49	1.72	0.25	1	1
	1963	0.787	52821	56933	0.63	2.03	0.25	1	1
	1968	0.841	66757	66757	0.98	2.68	0.55	1	1
	1975	0.908	74751	76167	1.43	4.13	0.55	1	1
Electric lamps	1958	0.744	23666	18932	0.49	1.72	0.25	1	1
	1963	0.717	35084	29795	0.63	2.03	0.25	1	1
	1968	0.866	40308	40308	0.98	2.68	0.25	1	1
	1975	0.941	35415	41413	1.43	4.13	0.25	1	1

Table B2 (continued)

Industry	Year	C5	SS	DS	K/N	K/L	TVCLASS	ADTYPE	CHANGE
Cars	1958	0.901	521809	471432	3.47	6.46	0.00	1	0
	1963	0.912	752514	685258	3.49	5.81	0.00	1	0
	1968	0.992	853240	853240	3.71	6.49	0.00	1	0
	1975	0.982	690957	648622	3.78	6.78	0.00	1	0
Cutlery	1958	0.658	22897	20524	0.24	1.75	0.55	2	0
	1963	0.669	29222	26752	0.39	2.20	0.55	2	0
	1968	0.709	33214	33214	0.56	3.42	0.85	2	0
	1975	0.560	25796	27019	0.60	4.41	0.85	2	0
Knitted, netted, or crocheted goods: hosiery	1958	0.214	81626	55153	0.60	4.26	0.25	1	0
	1963	0.201	82066	66593	0.68	4.23	0.25	1	0
	1968	0.433	91573	91573	0.86	4.92	0.25	1	0
	1975	0.455	58546	91096	0.99	5.81	0.25	1	0
Tufted carpets, carpeting, and carpet floor rugs	1958	0.720	8129	7823	0.83	2.96	0.25	1	0
	1963	0.507	24855	23456	0.91	3.16	0.25	1	0
	1968	0.518	61323	61323	1.24	3.80	0.25	1	0
	1975	0.450	101350	131887	1.93	6.23	0.25	1	0
Men's and boys' shirts, underwear, and nightwear	1958	0.191	50765	50194	0.06	0.47	0.55	1	0
	1963	0.254	54607	52636	0.08	0.65	0.25	1	0
	1968	0.355	54724	54724	0.12	0.91	0.25	1	0
	1975	0.400	51410	56144	0.14	1.11	0.25	1	0
Corsets and brassieres	1958	0.308	31864	31902	0.14	0.85	0.25	2	0
	1963	0.380	40321	38997	0.13	0.91	0.00	2	0
	1968	0.590	40537	40537	0.15	1.06	0.55	2	0
	1975	0.632	32675	39991	0.17	1.32	0.85	2	0

Product	Year								
Men's and boys' footwear (1958 S.I.C.)	1958	0.222	65714	61826	0.11	0.67	0.25	1	0
	1963	0.303	72032	67606	0.15	0.87	0.25	1	0
Women's and girls' footwear (1958 S.I.C.)	1958	0.239	90546	85189	0.11	0.67	0.25	1	0
	1963	0.289	98844	92770	0.15	0.87	0.25	1	0
Footwear, other than rubber footwear (1963 S.I.C.)	1963	0.242	183223	171964	0.15	0.87	0.25	1	0
	1968	0.316	175642	175642	0.20	1.15	0.55	1	0
	1975	0.400	160203	180788	0.30	1.52	0.25	1	0
Domestic and fancy glassware	1958	0.741	8502	8153	0.83	2.65	0.25	1	0
	1963	0.721	11943	11346	1.41	3.68	0.00	1	0
	1968	0.805	15646	15646	2.13	5.45	0.00	1	0
	1975	0.777	20237	21335	2.89	8.70	0.00	1	0
Upholstered furniture	1958	0.186	50918	50660	0.10	0.78	0.00	1	0
	1963	0.173	61289	61786	0.12	0.93	0.00	1	0
	1968	0.173	70492	70492	0.19	1.38	0.00	1	0
	1975	0.276	95909	102033	0.33	2.36	0.25	1	0
Domestic furniture, other than upholstered	1963	0.160	91765	92509	0.12	0.93	0.00	1	0
	1968	0.151	119446	119446	0.19	1.38	0.00	1	0
	1975	0.217	184705	193848	0.33	2.36	0.25	1	0
Upholstered divan beds, mattresses, and other bedding	1958	0.399	32714	31871	0.19	1.38	0.00	1	0
	1963	0.418	32665	32174	0.17	1.37	0.00	1	0
	1968	0.451	38611	38611	0.15	1.32	0.55	1	0
	1975	0.515	44476	41789	0.18	1.52	0.55	1	0
Published books	1958	0.311	62287	58950	0.32	2.48	0.00	1	0
	1963	0.339	80119	78913	0.38	2.86	0.00	1	0
	1968	0.322	106922	106922	0.49	3.85	0.00	1	0
	1975	0.328	143567	134590	0.61	5.21	0.00	1	0

Table B2 (continued)

Industry	Year	C5	SS	DS	K/N	K/L	TVCLASS	ADTYPE	CHANGE
Tyres and tubes, other than retreaded tyres	1958	0.932	112412	94782	1.27	3.80	0.25	1	1
	1963	0.945	144054	130074	1.54	4.06	0.25	1	1
	1968	0.928	184836	184836	2.39	5.90	0.55	1	1
	1975	0.964	190550	199087	2.68	7.51	0.55	1	1
Brushes and brooms	1958	0.301	17362	19193	0.19	1.43	0.25	1	0
	1963	0.380	18904	17959	0.26	1.78	0.55	1	0
	1968	0.425	18763	18763	0.35	2.45	0.25	1	0
	1975	0.455	18479	17809	0.42	3.39	0.85	1	0
Toys and indoor games	1958	0.469	37626	36656	0.19	1.17	0.25	2	0
	1963	0.477	42598	41860	0.27	1.57	0.25	2	0
	1968	0.582	65106	65106	0.44	2.10	0.55	2	0
	1975	0.453	93046	85285	0.54	2.69	0.55	2	0

Notes: C5 is the five-firm sales concentration ratio.
SS is sales revenue (in £1000) deflated by the general producer price index.
DS is sales revenue (in £1000) deflated by industry-specific producer price indices.
K is the value of capital stock of the corresponding MLH industry in 1980 prices (in £ million).
L is employment of the corresponding MLH industry (in 1000).
N is the number of plants with at least 25 employees of the corresponding MLH industry.
TVCLASS is a measure of the importance of TV advertising in total media advertising (see text).
ADTYPE takes the value 1 for an industry with typical or average advertising-sales ratio between 1% and 2%, and the value 2 for an industry with typical or average advertising-sales ratio higher than 2%.
CHANGE takes the value 1 for an industry with a change in competition regime and 0 otherwise.

Table B3
Data set for the advertising regressions of chapter 5

Industry	Year	ADS	SSDOM	K/L	TVTOT	TVINT	ADTYPE	CHANGE
Cigars	1954	0.062	1659	2.36	0.00	0.00	2	0
	1958	0.108	2353	3.13	0.37	0.14	2	0
	1963	0.228	4077	4.84	0.43	0.18	2	0
Cigarettes	1958	0.027	172726	3.13	0.39	0.14	2	0
	1963	0.051	205131	4.84	0.45	0.18	2	0
Tobacco	1958	0.039	21991	3.13	0.24	0.14	2	0
	1963	0.054	25720	4.84	0.38	0.18	2	0
Spirits, other than whisky and gin	1954	0.077	6591	2.64	0.00	0.00	2	0
	1958	0.088	9233	2.80	0.15	0.06	2	0
	1963	0.098	13271	4.45	0.13	0.08	2	0
	1968	0.080	16827	6.24	0.19	0.09	2	0
	1973	0.057	38074	9.42	0.26	0.09	2	0
Wines	1954	0.077	16507	4.05	0.00	0.00	2	0
	1958	0.096	19474	3.46	0.28	0.14	2	0
	1963	0.106	31933	4.86	0.23	0.18	2	0
	1968	0.097	41033	5.68	0.43	0.20	2	0
	1973	0.045	96514	7.02	0.49	0.20	2	0
Cider and perry	1954	0.052	5038	4.05	0.00	0.00	2	0
	1958	0.119	10156	3.46	0.45	0.14	2	0
	1963	0.121	6975	4.86	0.63	0.18	2	0
	1968	0.113	10258	5.68	0.65	0.20	2	0
	1973	0.057	15741	7.02	0.66	0.20	2	0

Table B3 (continued)

Industry	Year	ADS	SSDOM	K/L	TVTOT	TVINT	ADTYPE	CHANGE
Soft drinks	1954	0.017	54884	2.71	0.00	0.00	2	0
	1958	0.028	76984	2.91	0.52	0.21	2	0
	1963	0.025	84746	3.04	0.47	0.27	2	0
	1968	0.017	109050	3.89	0.69	0.31	2	0
	1973	0.017	188960	4.79	0.74	0.31	2	0
Margarine	1954	0.037	41207	5.65	0.00	0.00	2	0
	1958	0.060	37644	7.58	0.42	0.21	2	0
	1963	0.088	31576	9.57	0.75	0.27	2	0
	1968	0.113	22486	10.59	0.84	0.31	2	0
	1973	0.083	35703	14.72	0.88	0.31	2	0
Biscuits	1954	0.007	102953	1.75	0.00	0.00	2	1
	1958	0.021	105596	2.63	0.47	0.21	2	1
	1963	0.021	108920	3.69	0.58	0.27	2	1
	1968	0.017	110530	4.30	0.91	0.31	2	1
	1973	0.021	123231	5.27	0.98	0.31	2	1
Cereal foods	1963	0.106	31031	6.45	0.80	0.27	2	0
	1968	0.104	35810	9.50	0.84	0.31	2	0
	1973	0.084	42952	12.10	0.85	0.31	2	0
Canned meat and poultry	1954	0.001	75672	1.33	0.00	0.00	1	0
	1958	0.008	73115	1.43	0.44	0.21	1	0
	1963	0.017	75367	1.70	0.68	0.27	1	0
	1968	0.013	97236	2.44	0.80	0.31	1	0

Canned fish	1954	0.008	17726	1.33	0.00	0.00	1	0
	1958	0.011	40190	1.43	0.36	0.21	1	0
	1963	0.012	30510	1.70	0.22	0.27	1	0
	1968	0.006	41185	2.44	0.89	0.31	1	0
Meat and fish pastes	1954	0.039	5240	1.33	0.00	0.00	2	0
	1958	0.041	6913	1.43	0.52	0.21	2	0
	1963	0.015	7432	1.70	0.78	0.27	2	0
Canned vegetables	1954	0.013	51854	1.63	0.00	0.00	1	0
	1958	0.015	61018	1.95	0.55	0.21	1	0
	1963	0.017	68976	2.99	0.44	0.27	1	0
	1968	0.017	78895	4.28	0.86	0.31	1	0
Frozen foods	1954	0.010	8693	1.48	0.00	0.00	2	0
	1958	0.030	18688	1.67	0.71	0.21	2	0
	1963	0.030	58854	2.26	0.74	0.27	2	0
	1968	0.025	91278	3.23	0.83	0.31	2	0
Ice cream and ice lollies	1954	0.017	14817	3.72	0.00	0.00	2	0
	1958	0.028	19234	3.65	0.63	0.14	2	0
	1963	0.051	13726	4.74	0.77	0.18	2	0
	1968	0.057	16717	5.81	0.72	0.20	2	0
	1973	0.014	44027	7.34	0.57	0.20	2	0
Canned milk	1954	0.032	12178	3.72	0.00	0.00	2	1
	1958	0.038	16747	3.65	0.35	0.21	2	1
	1963	0.039	18249	4.74	0.35	0.27	2	1
	1968	0.026	18820	5.81	0.81	0.31	2	1
	1973	0.014	20198	7.34	0.99	0.31	2	1

Table B3 (continued)

Industry	Year	ADS	SSDOM	K/L	TVTOT	TVINT	ADTYPE	CHANGE
Potato crisps	1963	0.028	19905	2.99	0.94	0.27	2	0
	1968	0.024	26886	4.28	0.87	0.31	2	0
Table jellies	1954	0.034	7042	1.63	0.00	0.00	2	0
	1958	0.036	7170	1.95	0.83	0.06	2	0
	1963	0.015	6411	2.99	0.62	0.08	2	0
	1968	0.013	7101	4.28	0.12	0.09	2	0
Jams and marmalade	1954	0.010	38432	1.63	0.00	0.00	1	0
	1958	0.010	39126	1.95	0.45	0.14	1	0
	1963	0.027	38412	2.99	0.51	0.18	1	0
	1968	0.016	34622	4.28	0.63	0.20	1	0
Sauces, pickles, and salad creams	1954	0.022	19178	1.63	0.00	0.00	2	0
	1958	0.027	20709	1.95	0.40	0.14	2	0
	1963	0.023	24460	2.99	0.21	0.18	2	0
	1968	0.027	26367	4.28	0.42	0.20	2	0
Soups	1954	0.051	11652	1.63	0.00	0.00	2	0
	1958	0.043	23580	1.95	0.49	0.21	2	0
	1963	0.057	33115	2.99	0.45	0.27	2	0
	1968	0.048	33233	4.28	0.76	0.31	2	0
Coffee and coffee extracts	1954	0.044	12625	2.88	0.00	0.00	2	0
	1958	0.074	19922	3.82	0.48	0.21	2	0
	1963	0.084	27602	5.27	0.63	0.27	2	0
	1968	0.024	40452	8.07	0.74	0.31	2	0
	1973	0.040	53582	9.64	0.84	0.31	2	0

	Year							
Cocoa and drinking chocolate	1954	0.071	5796	1.95	0.00	0.00	2	1
	1958	0.116	4625	2.42	0.40	0.21	2	1
	1963	0.081	4442	3.40	0.63	0.27	2	1
	1968	0.057	4415	4.64	0.90	0.31	2	1
	1973	0.059	3652	5.90	1.00	0.31	2	1
Chocolate confectionery	1954	0.014	131442	1.95	0.00	0.00	2	1
	1958	0.024	122200	2.42	0.57	0.21	2	1
	1963	0.059	123018	3.40	0.77	0.27	2	1
	1968	0.060	134432	4.64	0.98	0.31	2	1
	1973	0.045	160991	5.90	0.95	0.31	2	1
Adhesive dressings	1954	0.081	2309	1.42	0.00	0.00	2	1
	1958	0.077	2276	2.01	0.31	0.21	2	1
	1963	0.069	3906	3.92	0.36	0.27	2	1
	1968	0.039	5330	6.07	0.86	0.31	2	1
	1973	0.021	4879	6.26	0.97	0.31	2	1
Sanitary towels	1954	0.019	8015	1.42	0.00	0.00	2	0
	1958	0.013	9331	2.01	0.00	0.00	2	0
	1963	0.027	10474	3.92	0.00	0.00	2	0
	1968	0.031	11941	6.07	0.00	0.00	2	0
	1973	0.060	11898	6.26	0.00	0.00	2	0
Dental preparations	1954	0.241	6445	1.98	0.00	0.00	2	0
	1958	0.224	8703	2.02	0.54	0.21	2	0
	1963	0.274	11123	2.03	0.87	0.27	2	0
	1968	0.167	11713	2.96	0.81	0.31	2	0
	1973	0.165	17081	4.27	0.85	0.31	2	0

Table B3 (continued)

Industry	Year	ADS	SSDOM	K/L	TVTOT	TVINT	ADTYPE	CHANGE
Hair preparations	1954	0.287	10239	1.98	0.00	0.00	2	0
	1958	0.324	13267	2.02	0.50	0.14	2	0
	1963	0.258	22605	2.03	0.40	0.18	2	0
	1968	0.179	26631	2.96	0.47	0.20	2	0
	1973	0.139	42914	4.27	0.63	0.20	2	0
Toilet soap	1954	0.105	12406	6.78	0.00	0.00	2	0
	1958	0.155	15296	7.35	0.39	0.21	2	0
	1963	0.190	15777	9.14	0.87	0.27	2	0
	1968	0.139	15878	14.43	0.93	0.31	2	0
	1973	0.066	24723	15.69	0.87	0.31	2	0
Other toilet preparations	1954	0.140	21117	1.98	0.00	0.00	2	0
	1958	0.145	27282	2.02	0.28	0.06	2	0
	1963	0.114	44477	2.03	0.26	0.08	2	0
	1968	0.110	62266	2.96	0.27	0.09	2	0
	1973	0.091	96613	4.27	0.51	0.09	2	0
Razors and blades	1954	0.071	5294	1.47	0.00	0.00	2	0
	1958	0.087	6007	1.75	0.51	0.21	2	0
	1963	0.115	6923	2.20	0.53	0.27	2	0
	1968	0.222	7024	3.42	0.74	0.31	2	0
	1973	0.117	7462	4.19	0.75	0.31	2	0

Toilet brushes	1954	0.060	2946	1.21	0.00	0.00	2	0
	1958	0.090	2458	1.43	0.33	0.14	2	0
	1963	0.039	3291	1.78	0.44	0.18	2	0
	1968	0.027	3262	2.45	0.55	0.20	2	0
	1973	0.020	4258	2.99	0.68	0.20	2	0
Paper handkerchiefs and facial tissues	1963	0.080	5449	4.84	0.45	0.18	2	0
	1968	0.044	7833	6.08	0.84	0.20	2	0
	1973	0.016	10665	7.90	0.43	0.20	2	0
Paper towels	1963	0.042	2670	4.84	0.03	0.18	2	0
	1968	0.038	5455	6.08	0.66	0.20	2	0
	1973	0.023	9012	7.90	0.85	0.20	2	0
Toilet paper	1963	0.039	12292	4.84	0.46	0.18	2	0
	1968	0.009	17165	6.08	0.19	0.20	2	0
	1973	0.008	28020	7.90	0.68	0.20	2	0
Domestic brushes and paintbrushes	1954	0.008	11114	1.21	0.00	0.00	1	0
	1958	0.016	12261	1.43	0.27	0.06	1	0
	1963	0.016	13675	1.78	0.49	0.08	1	0
	1968	0.012	13171	2.45	0.10	0.09	1	0
	1973	0.009	14023	2.99	0.28	0.09	1	0
Paint	1954	0.008	115533	2.64	0.00	0.00	2	1
	1958	0.019	127330	3.19	0.24	0.14	2	1
	1963	0.026	125338	3.64	0.39	0.18	2	1
	1968	0.021	119802	4.37	0.56	0.20	2	1
	1973	0.021	165041	5.52	0.63	0.20	2	1

Table B3 (continued)

Industry	Year	ADS	SSDOM	K/L	TVTOT	TVINT	ADTYPE	CHANGE
Soap and detergents	1954	0.083	59746	6.78	0.00	0.00	2	0
	1958	0.138	65331	7.35	0.56	0.21	2	0
	1963	0.132	67721	9.14	0.89	0.27	2	0
	1968	0.095	73928	14.43	0.98	0.31	2	0
	1973	0.067	92137	15.69	0.99	0.31	2	0
Cleansers	1954	0.268	3561	6.78	0.00	0.00	2	0
	1958	0.337	6919	7.35	0.49	0.21	2	0
	1963	0.337	9979	9.14	0.88	0.27	2	0
	1968	0.333	8940	14.43	0.87	0.31	2	0
	1973	0.167	11041	15.69	0.94	0.31	2	0
Floor and furniture polishes	1954	0.068	6596	1.69	0.00	0.00	2	0
	1958	0.105	7478	2.20	0.45	0.21	2	0
	1963	0.132	6927	3.04	0.43	0.27	2	0
	1968	0.123	7791	4.29	0.75	0.31	2	0
	1973	0.104	8024	5.95	0.96	0.31	2	0
Shoe polishes	1954	0.088	2508	1.69	0.00	0.00	2	0
	1958	0.080	2864	2.20	0.23	0.06	2	0
	1963	0.140	3186	3.04	0.23	0.08	2	0
	1968	0.066	2909	4.29	0.57	0.09	2	0
	1973	0.035	2512	5.95	0.01	0.09	2	0

Disinfectants and household deodorisers	1954	0.080	5768	2.54	0.00	0.00	2	0
	1958	0.071	8564	2.96	0.54	0.21	2	0
	1963	0.051	8194	4.56	0.58	0.27	2	0
	1968	0.045	10840	7.49	0.80	0.31	2	0
	1973	0.019	17517	14.92	0.81	0.31	2	0
Insecticides and pesticides	1954	0.024	7879	2.54	0.00	0.00	2	0
	1958	0.026	11365	2.96	0.26	0.06	2	0
	1963	0.034	11360	4.56	0.16	0.08	2	0
	1968	0.029	12445	7.49	0.24	0.09	2	0
Dog and cat foods	1954	0.051	11133	2.38	0.00	0.00	2	0
	1958	0.068	22702	2.77	0.53	0.21	2	0
	1963	0.101	35482	3.88	0.86	0.27	2	0
	1968	0.101	52577	6.16	0.98	0.31	2	0
	1973	0.042	70972	8.81	0.95	0.31	2	0
Lawn mowers	1954	0.034	3030	1.87	0.00	0.00	2	0
	1958	0.034	4448	2.07	0.03	0.00	2	0
	1963	0.025	6908	2.23	0.00	0.00	2	0
	1968	0.024	13963	2.82	0.03	0.00	2	0
	1973	0.017	22309	3.65	0.04	0.00	2	0
Rubber gloves	1963	0.038	2469	0.73	0.00	0.27	2	0
	1968	0.025	3337	0.92	0.98	0.31	2	0
	1973	0.011	4424	1.20	0.99	0.31	2	0
Sewing machines	1958	0.137	2750	2.07	0.00	0.06	2	0
	1963	0.117	2913	2.23	0.04	0.08	2	0
	1968	0.094	3630	2.82	0.32	0.09	2	0

Table B3 (continued)

Industry	Year	ADS	SSDOM	K/L	TVTOT	TVINT	ADTYPE	CHANGE
Notepaper	1958	0.053	3122	1.76	0.02	0.00	2	1
	1963	0.028	3907	2.58	0.19	0.00	2	1
	1968	0.027	3050	3.36	0.00	0.00	2	1
Pens and mechanical pencils	1954	0.076	6633	1.77	0.00	0.00	2	0
	1958	0.068	7969	1.63	0.29	0.06	2	0
	1963	0.047	7925	2.33	0.00	0.08	2	0
	1968	0.047	11423	3.41	0.18	0.09	2	0
	1973	0.037	13506	5.18	0.26	0.09	2	0
Lead pencils	1954	0.009	1495	1.77	0.00	0.00	1	1
	1958	0.018	1787	1.63	0.00	0.00	1	1
	1963	0.014	1764	2.33	0.00	0.00	1	1
	1968	0.006	1402	3.41	0.00	0.00	1	1
Toys and games	1963	0.015	40090	1.57	0.34	0.18	1	0
	1968	0.020	59518	2.10	0.55	0.20	1	0
	1973	0.016	95030	2.72	0.67	0.20	1	0
Baby carriages	1954	0.008	5616	0.94	0.00	0.00	1	0
	1958	0.017	6052	1.17	0.47	0.00	1	0
	1963	0.011	6965	1.57	0.11	0.00	1	0
	1968	0.003	5963	2.10	0.00	0.00	1	0
	1973	0.001	5771	2.72	0.00	0.00	1	0

	Year							
Typewriters	1954	0.031	3978	2.83	0.00	0.00	2	1
	1958	0.034	5091	2.64	0.03	0.00	2	1
	1963	0.019	7315	3.14	0.01	0.00	2	1
	1968	0.009	10096	4.48	0.00	0.00	2	1
Tape recorders	1958	0.038	3531	1.10	0.03	0.00	2	0
	1963	0.024	9505	1.00	0.00	0.00	2	0
	1968	0.023	6023	1.98	0.00	0.00	2	0
Radio and TV sets	1954	0.020	73585	0.97	0.00	0.00	1	0
	1958	0.024	82120	1.10	0.04	0.00	1	0
	1963	0.019	84998	1.00	0.04	0.00	1	0
	1968	0.011	95841	1.98	0.05	0.00	1	0
	1973	0.006	307292	2.32	0.13	0.00	1	0
Office furniture	1963	0.016	20428	1.87	0.00	0.00	1	0
	1968	0.010	26308	2.24	0.00	0.00	1	0
Electric lamps and fluorescent lighting	1954	0.011	18503	1.64	0.00	0.00	1	1
	1958	0.017	19963	1.72	0.29	0.06	1	1
	1963	0.013	30653	2.03	0.12	0.08	1	1
	1968	0.015	35515	2.68	0.32	0.09	1	1
	1973	0.008	35630	3.71	0.04	0.09	1	1
Mattresses, divan beds, pillows	1954	0.008	45563	1.31	0.00	0.00	1	0
	1958	0.008	45168	1.38	0.08	0.14	1	0
	1963	0.010	37459	1.37	0.02	0.18	1	0
	1968	0.011	47437	1.32	0.50	0.20	1	0
	1973	0.010	59478	1.39	0.46	0.20	1	0

Table B3 (continued)

Industry	Year	ADS	SSDOM	K/L	TVTOT	TVINT	ADTYPE	CHANGE
Car batteries and accumulators	1954	0.016	22165	1.64	0.00	0.00	1	1
	1958	0.012	21927	1.72	0.15	0.06	1	1
	1963	0.011	26945	2.03	0.15	0.08	1	1
	1968	0.009	34531	2.68	0.32	0.09	1	1
	1973	0.002	45027	3.71	0.40	0.09	1	1
Tyres and tubes	1954	0.017	68407	2.88	0.00	0.00	1	1
	1958	0.021	72141	3.80	0.17	0.14	1	1
	1963	0.017	97444	4.06	0.22	0.18	1	1
	1968	0.016	146660	5.90	0.40	0.20	1	1
	1973	0.012	148535	7.87	0.47	0.20	1	1
Motorcycles, scooters, and mopeds	1954	0.012	12564	4.57	0.00	0.00	1	1
	1958	0.023	16998	5.13	0.13	0.00	1	1
	1963	0.023	10312	7.06	0.00	0.00	1	1
	1968	0.014	7847	8.08	0.00	0.00	1	1
	1973	0.015	15697	7.74	0.00	0.00	1	1
Cars	1954	0.011	180093	6.68	0.00	0.00	1	0
	1958	0.012	255515	6.46	0.01	0.00	1	0
	1963	0.012	415130	5.81	0.01	0.00	1	0
	1968	0.010	537892	6.49	0.03	0.00	1	0
	1973	0.012	906758	6.44	0.09	0.00	1	0
Industrial trucks and tractors	1963	0.021	10006	1.56	0.00	0.00	1	0
	1968	0.014	30320	1.91	0.00	0.00	1	0

Category	Year							
Men's shirts, collars, and pyjamas	1954	0.006	46871	0.29	0.00	0.00	1	0
	1958	0.014	48898	0.34	0.41	0.06	1	0
	1963	0.014	54609	0.47	0.18	0.08	1	0
	1968	0.012	55695	0.67	0.19	0.09	1	0
	1973	0.004	69034	0.87	0.00	0.09	1	0
Women's hosiery	1954	0.026	20947	3.76	0.00	0.00	1	0
	1958	0.017	47937	4.26	0.09	0.06	1	0
	1963	0.011	53552	4.23	0.09	0.08	1	0
	1968	0.010	58079	4.92	0.18	0.09	1	0
	1973	0.008	41551	5.91	0.30	0.09	1	0
Corsetry	1954	0.034	21044	0.88	0.00	0.00	2	0
	1958	0.062	27406	0.85	0.18	0.14	2	0
	1963	0.047	35272	0.91	0.03	0.18	2	0
	1968	0.048	35927	1.06	0.46	0.20	2	0
	1973	0.033	36739	1.21	0.84	0.20	2	0
Footwear	1954	0.009	199319	0.58	0.00	0.00	1	0
	1958	0.010	184301	0.67	0.14	0.06	1	0
	1963	0.010	214995	0.87	0.14	0.08	1	0
	1968	0.011	214349	1.15	0.40	0.09	1	0
	1973	0.006	269970	1.47	0.20	0.09	1	0
Domestic refrigerators and deep freezers	1958	0.037	14120	2.55	0.20	0.00	2	1
	1963	0.032	16587	2.27	0.27	0.00	2	1
	1968	0.011	22095	3.00	0.01	0.00	2	1
	1973	0.022	31393	4.06	0.16	0.00	2	1

Table B3 (continued)

Industry	Year	ADS	SSDOM	K/L	TVTOT	TVINT	ADTYPE	CHANGE
Washing machines	1954	0.025	19213	2.19	0.00	0.00	2	1
	1958	0.044	26214	2.55	0.22	0.06	2	1
	1968	0.029	29250	3.00	0.33	0.09	2	1
	1973	0.008	52081	4.06	0.26	0.09	2	1
Electric cookers and heaters	1954	0.016	18198	2.19	0.00	0.00	2	1
	1958	0.033	24089	2.55	0.08	0.00	2	1
	1963	0.042	44342	2.27	0.14	0.00	2	1
	1968	0.018	52265	3.00	0.05	0.00	2	1
	1973	0.009	61866	4.06	0.14	0.00	2	1

Notes: ADS is the advertising-sales ratio.

SSDOM is sales revenue in the UK market (in £1000) deflated by the general producer price index.

K is the value of capital stock of the corresponding MLH industry in 1980 prices (in £ million).

L is employment of the corresponding MLH industry (in 1000).

TVTOT is the fraction of TV advertising in total media advertising.

TVINT is an alternative measure of the significance of TV advertising (see text).

ADTYPE takes the value 1 for an industry with average advertising-sales ratio between 1% and 2%, and 2 for an industry with average advertising-sales ratio higher than 2% over 1958–1968.

CHANGE takes the value 1 for an industry with a change in competition regime and 0 otherwise.

Data Sets

Table B4
Data set for the innovation regressions of chapter 6

Industry	Period	INN1	INN2	INN3	SS	DS	K/N	K/L	RDTYPE	CHANGE
Lubricating oils and greases (MLH 263)	1952–56	3	4	3	58551	63111	0.49	4.03	1	0
	1957–61	2	1	2	71533	74920	0.70	4.88	1	0
	1962–66	0	0	0	74886	74886	0.80	6.01	1	0
	1967–71	2	2	2	80197	83787	1.27	10.86	1	0
	1972–76	0	0	0	103190	108339	1.60	11.97	1	0
General chemicals, organic, other than coal tar products (part of MLH 271.2)	1952–56	0	0	0	98593	81489	5.00	21.25	2	0
	1957–61	4	5	0	166999	143385	8.25	27.23	2	0
	1962–66	4	3	3	240323	240323	9.66	25.75	2	0
	1967–71	3	4	3	312446	354349	16.29	49.23	2	0
	1972–76	3	2	1	420695	551838	25.05	68.45	2	0
General chemicals, other than inorganic and organic (MLH 271.3)	1952–56	5	5	1	85966	71052	2.40	10.10	1	0
	1957–61	4	3	2	143114	122877	3.99	12.84	1	0
	1962–66	4	4	2	168424	168424	4.67	17.77	1	0
	1967–71	3	3	2	215759	244695	6.47	25.04	1	0
	1972–76	5	9	2	280777	363533	7.59	26.70	1	0
Pharmaceutical chemicals and preparations (MLH 272)	1952–56	7	6	4	119569	81112	0.84	3.40	2	0
	1957–61	19	22	7	141742	120695	1.32	4.10	2	0
	1962–66	15	9	7	194889	194889	1.68	4.93	2	0
	1967–71	12	14	7	244569	300118	2.67	7.55	2	0
	1972–76	12	16	8	363509	525543	4.46	11.30	2	0

Table B4 (continued)

Industry	Period	INN1	INN2	INN3	SS	DS	K/N	K/L	RDTYPE	CHANGE
Paint (MLH 274)	1952–56	4	4	3	116353	109907	0.40	2.69	1	1
	1957–61	6	8	2	132779	128358	0.57	3.19	1	1
	1962–66	2	1	1	136354	136354	0.71	3.64	1	1
	1967–71	4	4	4	128602	144445	0.92	4.37	1	1
	1972–76	4	3	4	171899	193160	1.19	5.52	1	1
Soap and detergents (MLH 275)	1952–56	3	1	2	98982	104347	1.74	6.64	1	0
	1957–61	3	3	0	111817	108659	2.27	7.41	1	0
	1962–66	4	4	2	118241	118241	3.53	9.14	1	0
	1967–71	3	3	1	128165	137219	4.44	14.43	1	0
	1972–76	1	1	1	156682	173380	3.81	15.69	1	0
Synthetic resins and plastics materials and synthetic rubber (MLH 276)	1952–56	9	8	1	109462	68260	4.66	13.02	2	0
	1957–61	11	14	3	171822	135849	5.12	12.18	2	0
	1962–66	14	12	4	258679	258679	6.90	16.68	2	0
	1967–71	8	8	5	366558	446994	7.90	19.17	2	0
	1972–76	8	7	5	399964	610834	10.76	31.98	2	0
Dyestuffs and pigments (MLH 277)	1952–56	6	5	4	80988	77745	3.56	8.44	2	0
	1957–61	11	11	5	72350	68237	4.79	9.73	2	0
	1962–66	3	3	2	82818	82818	5.79	12.00	2	0
	1967–71	11	11	7	89178	90339	10.71	20.56	2	0
	1972–76	6	8	4	139149	157244	13.75	26.88	2	0

Formulated adhesives, gelatine, glue, size, etc. (MLH 279.2)									
1952–56	1	1	0	18435	16138	0.52	4.18	2	0
1957–61	0	0	0	19423	18319	0.70	5.57	2	0
1962–66	2	2	1	25493	25493	0.96	7.22	2	0
1967–71	3	3	2	32410	31232	1.39	7.99	2	0
1972–76	3	3	2	37579	36640	1.98	11.33	2	0
Formulated pesticides and disinfectants (MLH 279.4)									
1952–56	0	0	0	20028	16106	0.37	2.27	2	0
1957–61	2	3	2	25051	21331	0.40	2.72	2	0
1962–66	2	1	1	30600	30600	0.68	4.56	2	0
1967–71	2	2	2	38867	42791	1.28	7.49	2	0
1972–76	6	9	6	52194	72446	2.69	14.92	2	0
Surgical bandages, etc., and sanitary towels (MLH 279.6)									
1952–56	0	0	0	25749	19997	0.28	1.31	0	1
1957–61	1	2	1	23513	20804	0.55	2.01	0	1
1962–66	4	3	1	31660	31660	1.16	3.92	0	1
1967–71	2	2	0	37314	36288	2.12	6.07	0	1
1972–76	1	1	0	45700	42215	2.47	6.26	0	1
Aluminium and aluminium alloys (MLH 321)									
1952–56	8	6	8	143074	160803	1.05	3.23	0	1
1957–61	11	11	10	152853	158305	1.39	4.27	0	1
1962–66	7	6	6	192061	192061	1.55	5.02	0	1
1967–71	7	7	4	247753	232792	2.22	7.32	0	1
1972–76	5	4	5	279127	266303	4.66	15.66	0	1
Copper, brass and other copper alloys (MLH 322)									
1952–56	0	0	0	301232	225263	0.92	4.44	0	1
1957–61	0	1	0	241120	265403	1.26	5.22	0	1
1962–66	2	1	0	301753	301753	1.35	5.80	0	1
1967–71	2	3	2	420605	243113	1.64	6.71	0	1
1972–76	1	0	1	417250	220994	1.87	7.31	0	1

Table B4 (continued)

Industry	Period	INN1	INN2	INN3	SS	DS	K/N	K/L	RDTYPE	CHANGE
Miscellaneous nonferrous metals (MLH 323)	1952–56	4	4	4	140387	134577	1.56	6.21	0	0
	1957–61	2	2	1	143488	150113	1.74	6.70	0	0
	1962–66	2	2	1	174836	174836	1.83	7.17	0	0
	1967–71	0	1	0	233154	178420	2.12	9.81	0	0
	1972–76	2	2	0	207510	155632	2.63	14.65	0	0
Welding and flame-cutting equipment (part of MLH 332)	1952–56	1	2	1	12134	13683	0.65	3.06	1	0
	1957–61	5	4	4	18226	18627	0.80	3.54	1	0
	1962–66	6	6	3	23137	23137	0.77	3.26	1	0
	1967–71	2	2	0	30380	30802	0.96	4.02	1	0
	1972–76	4	5	2	31123	29274	1.02	5.08	1	0
Industrial engines (MLH 334)	1952–56	0	0	0	62369	58111	2.03	3.86	1	1
	1957–61	1	1	1	67277	56870	2.79	4.07	1	1
	1962–66	0	0	0	85543	85543	3.02	4.11	1	1
	1967–71	0	1	0	101817	96445	3.53	4.74	1	1
	1972–76	3	3	3	104037	92112	5.10	6.08	1	1
Powered industrial trucks and industrial tractors (part of MLH 337)	1952–56	0	0	0	8102	10043	0.22	1.13	1	0
	1957–61	0	0	0	11145	12673	0.29	1.41	1	0
	1962–66	2	2	2	17838	17838	0.33	1.56	1	0
	1967–71	1	2	1	46045	49343	0.41	1.91	1	0
	1972–76	2	1	1	70049	70136	0.57	2.44	1	0

Category	Period									
Mining machinery (MLH 339.1)	1952–56	11	8	7	36875	41582	0.49	2.10	0	0
	1957–61	10	14	8	53516	54693	0.50	2.09	0	0
	1962–66	28	28	21	63789	63789	0.56	2.38	0	0
	1967–71	24	25	18	71840	72838	0.70	2.81	0	0
	1972–76	17	13	13	86122	82165	0.98	3.50	0	0
Printing, bookbinding, and paper goods making machinery (MLH 339.2)	1952–56	3	3	3	29191	32917	0.30	1.91	1	0
	1957–61	2	3	2	25392	25951	0.38	2.15	1	0
	1962–66	8	14	5	35795	35795	0.49	2.43	1	0
	1967–71	22	18	16	44586	45206	0.67	2.98	1	0
	1972–76	13	10	7	50969	49067	0.92	4.10	1	0
Space-heating, ventilating, and air-conditioning equipment (MLH 339.4)	1952–56	4	6	4	31097	35067	0.26	1.76	0	0
	1957–61	7	8	4	44873	45860	0.37	2.13	0	0
	1962–66	12	10	9	77232	77232	0.36	2.06	0	0
	1967–71	4	3	1	95937	97270	0.41	2.40	0	0
	1972–76	5	5	4	125158	120486	0.54	3.11	0	0
Packaging and bottling machinery (MLH 339.8)	1952–56	1	1	1	7929	8942	0.30	1.85	0	0
	1957–61	1	1	1	16473	16835	0.42	2.07	0	0
	1962–66	2	5	2	19260	19260	0.49	2.23	0	0
	1967–71	6	5	4	24115	24450	0.59	2.82	0	0
	1972–76	4	4	4	30092	29197	0.65	3.65	0	0
Miscellaneous machinery, other than rolling mills (part of MLH 339.9)	1952–56	11	13	8	93720	105683	0.30	1.85	0	0
	1957–61	17	15	12	113597	116097	0.42	2.07	0	0
	1962–66	19	21	9	138562	138562	0.49	2.23	0	0
	1967–71	18	16	14	154218	156362	0.59	2.82	0	0
	1972–76	12	17	11	228744	221406	0.65	3.65	0	0

Table B4 (continued)

Industry	Period	INN1	INN2	INN3	SS	DS	K/N	K/L	RDTYPE	CHANGE
Constructional and other fabricated ironwork and steelwork (part of MLH 341)	1952–56	2	2	1	91924	103659	0.55	2.49	0	1
	1957–61	4	6	4	140853	143952	0.64	2.50	0	1
	1962–66	9	7	8	139156	139156	0.70	2.60	0	1
	1967–71	1	1	1	170178	172544	0.77	2.80	0	1
	1972–76	1	2	1	242387	233340	0.80	3.31	0	1
Photographic and document copying equipment (MLH 351)	1952–56	5	8	4	7762	6920	0.30	2.86	2	0
	1957–61	5	3	4	8318	7941	0.66	3.29	2	0
	1962–66	3	2	2	12804	12804	0.54	3.10	2	0
	1967–71	5	7	2	41956	39170	1.02	2.86	2	0
	1972–76	8	6	2	57154	57442	1.51	5.64	2	0
Machinery for generating, transmitting and distributing electric power (part of MLH 361)	1952–56	7	9	6	82325	73401	0.91	1.64	2	1
	1957–61	7	5	7	99031	94553	1.12	1.87	2	1
	1962–66	4	7	4	120070	120070	1.10	1.98	2	1
	1967–71	4	1	4	151267	157054	1.28	3.04	2	1
	1972–76	3	3	3	145302	153358	1.35	3.76	2	1
Switchgear and controlling gear for motors (part of MLH 361)	1952–56	1	1	1	80736	71984	0.91	1.64	2	1
	1957–61	3	3	3	118969	113589	1.12	1.87	2	1
	1962–66	2	3	2	139233	139233	1.10	1.98	2	1
	1967–71	5	4	5	144897	150440	1.28	3.04	2	1
	1972–76	2	2	2	115723	122139	1.35	3.76	2	1

Category	Period									
Other electrical machinery (part of MLH 361)	1952–56	2	2	2	68706	61258	0.91	1.64	1	1
	1957–61	7	8	6	89776	85716	1.12	1.87	1	1
	1962–66	6	4	4	89770	89770	1.10	1.98	1	1
	1967–71	2	2	2	99909	103731	1.28	3.04	.1	1
	1972–76	1	2	1	99076	104570	1.35	3.76	1	1
Insulated wires and cables, other than telecommunication cables (part of MLH 362)	1952–56	5	5	2	101215	90243	1.93	3.22	0	1
	1957–61	4	4	3	112680	107585	3.00	4.25	0	1
	1962–66	1	1	1	148034	148034	2.84	4.68	0	1
	1967–71	3	5	2	171854	152860	3.75	5.42	0	1
	1972–76	6	4	6	188044	169877	5.12	7.57	0	1
Radio and electronic components (MLH 364)	1952–56	19	23	6	74132	66096	0.44	1.62	2	0
	1957–61	32	30	13	112946	107839	0.53	1.80	2	0
	1962–66	19	19	7	151737	151737	0.60	1.63	2	0
	1967–71	28	28	15	220987	229441	0.85	2.40	2	0
	1972–76	23	30	16	353699	373310	1.36	3.35	2	0
Broadcast receiving and sound reproducing equipment, except gramophone records (part of MLH 365)	1952–56	12	11	8	81867	72992	0.44	0.99	1	0
	1957–61	10	11	8	101267	96688	0.53	1.10	1	0
	1962–66	10	12	9	104905	104905	0.55	1.00	1	0
	1967–71	10	8	4	108476	112625	1.01	1.98	1	0
	1972–76	2	2	1	262529	277085	1.39	2.32	1	0
Electronic computers (MLH 366)	1952–56	8	11	8	5305	4717	1.58	4.40	2	0
	1957–61	8	9	4	7433	7097	1.84	4.83	2	0
	1962–66	9	8	4	40141	40141	1.80	4.68	2	0
	1967–71	7	6	5	100799	104655	2.30	4.21	2	0
	1972–76	12	13	8	206781	218246	2.67	4.59	2	0

Table B4 (continued)

Industry	Period	INN1	INN2	INN3	SS	DS	K/N	K/L	RDTYPE	CHANGE
Radio, radar and electronic capital goods (MLH 367)	1952–56	7	9	6	50556	45075	1.30	2.80	2	0
	1957–61	13	14	8	51668	49332	1.56	3.10	2	0
	1962–66	21	20	17	127298	127298	1.37	2.80	2	0
	1967–71	24	28	23	157694	163727	1.37	3.32	2	0
	1972–76	28	31	26	218401	230510	1.65	3.64	2	0
Electric appliances primarily for domestic use (MLH 368)	1952–56	1	1	1	89989	73899	0.64	2.11	1	1
	1957–61	4	4	4	133477	118774	1.18	2.55	1	1
	1962–66	0	1	0	200274	200274	1.18	2.27	1	1
	1967–71	1	0	1	202937	227281	1.43	3.00	1	1
	1972–76	1	1	0	231079	289800	2.18	4.06	1	1
Electrical equipment for motor vehicles, cycles, and aircraft (part of MLH 369)	1952–56	2	2	1	60573	61414	0.41	1.64	1	0
	1957–61	3	3	2	71395	77665	0.49	1.68	1	0
	1962–66	8	7	5	84342	84342	0.63	2.03	1	0
	1967–71	3	3	2	108498	109530	0.98	2.68	1	0
	1972–76	0	1	0	130750	134105	1.56	3.71	1	0
Primary batteries and accumulators (part of MLH 369)	1952–56	0	0	0	38407	37471	0.41	1.64	1	1
	1957–61	1	1	0	39663	41494	0.49	1.68	1	1
	1962–66	0	0	0	49182	49182	0.63	2.03	1	1
	1967–71	1	1	0	60498	56122	0.98	2.68	1	1
	1972–76	1	1	1	71920	64716	1.56	3.71	1	1

Electric lamps, electric light fittings, and wiring accessories (part of MLH 369)									
1952–56	2	1	2	58326	51798	0.41	1.64	1	1
1957–61	0	1	0	70465	64431	0.49	1.68	1	1
1962–66	5	5	3	97992	97992	0.63	2.03	1	1
1967–71	6	6	6	110277	116044	0.98	2.68	1	1
1972–76	3	4	3	136861	148468	1.56	3.71	1	1
Marine machinery (part of MLH 370)									
1952–56	5	3	4	109362	123322	0.43	0.98	1	0
1957–61	3	5	1	78298	80021	0.59	1.25	1	0
1962–66	7	5	6	65119	65119	0.86	1.96	1	0
1967–71	2	3	2	71559	72553	0.98	2.11	1	0
1972–76	1	0	1	78174	76500	1.36	2.68	1	0
Motor vehicles and parts, except trailers and caravans (part of MLH 381)									
1952–56	12	11	9	824394	899139	2.72	6.72	1	0
1957–61	16	18	13	1172390	1186438	3.47	6.46	1	0
1962–66	14	14	8	1612064	1612064	3.49	5.81	1	0
1967–71	19	23	16	1820051	1869719	3.71	6.49	1	0
1972–76	21	23	19	2049130	2012628	4.01	6.43	1	0
Motorcycles (part of MLH 382)									
1952–56	1	0	1	35061	31387	1.50	4.44	1	1
1957–61	1	1	1	27233	21586	1.81	5.13	1	1
1962–66	0	0	0	16224	16224	2.84	7.06	1	1
1967–71	1	1	1	18871	17139	3.65	8.08	1	1
1972–76	2	3	0	16263	14118	3.34	7.74	1	1
Paper and board (MLH 481)									
1952–56	6	6	4	293269	269608	1.66	5.83	0	1
1957–61	5	8	5	321880	296653	2.74	8.74	0	1
1962–66	11	8	10	350074	350074	3.23	9.61	0	1
1967–71	5	6	3	377973	390695	4.91	13.74	0	1
1972–76	3	3	3	396899	408918	6.13	17.72	0	1

Table B4 (continued)

Industry	Period	INN1	INN2	INN3	SS	DS	K/N	K/L	RDTYPE	CHANGE
Tyres and tubes (part of MLH 491)	1952–56	0	0	0	93731	99189	0.92	2.69	1	1
	1957–61	1	1	0	96312	89924	1.26	3.80	1	1
	1962–66	0	0	0	123440	123440	1.54	4.06	1	1
	1967–71	1	3	1	158386	175366	2.39	5.90	1	1
	1972–76	3	1	3	162691	182942	3.03	7.87	1	1
Plastic products (MLH 496)	1952–56	7	8	5	41734	35482	0.23	1.66	0	0
	1957–61	6	6	4	65580	60985	0.26	1.86	0	0
	1962–66	9	9	7	146583	146583	0.33	2.24	0	0
	1967–71	18	24	15	249666	321945	0.55	3.60	0	0
	1972–76	17	11	13	397786	574061	0.82	5.26	0	0

Notes: The classification according to MLH industries follows the 1968 Standard Industrial Classification.

INN1 is the number of innovations for time periods 1952–56, 1957–61, 1962–66, 1967–71, and 1972–76.

INN2 is the number of innovations for time periods 1953–57, 1958–62, 1963–67, 1968–72, and 1973–77.

INN3 is the number of innovations, excluding those reported as originating outside the UK, for time periods 1952–56, 1957–61, 1962–66, 1967–71, and 1972–76.

SS is sales revenue (in £1000) deflated by the general producer price index for the years 1953, 1958, 1963, 1968, and 1973.

DS is sales revenue (in £1000) deflated by industry-specific producer price indices for the years 1953, 1958, 1963, 1968, and 1973.

K is the value of capital stock in 1980 prices (in £ million) of the corresponding MLH industry for the years 1953, 1958, 1963, 1968, and 1973.

L is employment (in 1000) of the corresponding MLH industry for the years 1953, 1958, 1963, 1968, and 1973.

N is the number of plants with at least 25 employees of the corresponding MLH industry for the years 1953, 1958, 1963, 1968, and 1973.

RDTYPE takes the value 0 for an industry with typical R&D-sales ratio lower than 1%, 1 for an industry with typical R&D-sales ratio between 1% and 2%, and 2 for an industry with typical R&D-sales ratio higher than 2%.

CHANGE takes the value 1 for an industry with a change in competition regime and 0 otherwise.

Table B5
Data set for the concentration regressions of chapter 6

Industry	Year	C5	SS	DS	K/N	K/L	RDTYPE	CHANGE
Lubricating oils and greases	1963	0.695	86247	82575	0.80	6.01	1	0
	1968	0.716	93079	93079	1.28	10.93	1	0
	1975	0.740	138734	135633	1.68	12.95	1	0
Blacks, mineral and carbon	1963	0.984	10142	8622	7.33	27.33	1	0
	1968	0.971	12250	12250	8.60	33.66	1	0
Organic chemicals: acids (carboxylic), acid anhydrides, and acid halides	1963	0.632	16869	15955	9.66	25.75	1	0
	1968	0.648	23035	23035	16.29	49.23	1	0
Organic chemicals: alcohols (monohydric)	1963	0.946	51182	43596	9.66	25.75	2	0
	1968	0.980	48608	48608	16.29	49.23	2	0
Organic chemicals: esters	1963	0.864	11326	9036	9.66	25.75	1	0
	1968	0.825	18389	18389	16.29	49.23	1	0
Organic chemicals: halogenated derivatives of hydrocarbons	1963	0.974	29000	25566	9.66	25.75	2	0
	1968	0.969	43843	43843	16.29	49.23	2	0
	1975	0.999	57312	73666	23.40	70.00	2	0
Organic chemicals: aliphatic hydrocarbons	1963	0.774	26560	20123	9.66	25.75	2	0
	1968	0.993	39191	39191	16.29	49.23	2	0
Additives for liquid fuels and lubricating oils	1963	0.901	30588	26966	4.67	17.77	1	0
	1968	0.807	41886	41886	6.48	25.04	1	0
	1975	0.904	60214	62292	7.49	25.59	1	0
Bleaching materials	1963	0.816	14602	15129	4.67	17.77	1	0
	1968	0.840	15215	15215	6.48	25.04	1	0
	1975	0.880	12900	15281	7.49	25.59	1	0

Table B5 (continued)

Industry	Year	C5	SS	DS	K/N	K/L	RDTYPE	CHANGE
Chemicals and preparations mainly for PVC processing	1963	0.773	19818	17453	4.67	17.77	1	0
	1968	0.871	24061	24061	6.48	25.04	1	0
	1975	0.750	32430	33732	7.49	25.59	1	0
Food and perfume materials	1963	0.710	20616	18854	4.67	17.77	1	0
	1968	0.811	26590	26590	6.48	25.04	1	0
	1975	0.768	31028	30866	7.49	25.59	1	0
Rubber-processing chemicals and preparations	1963	0.985	13418	11250	4.67	17.77	1	0
	1968	0.940	17118	17118	6.48	25.04	1	0
	1975	0.979	16830	16585	7.49	25.59	1	0
Surface active materials	1963	0.668	13815	13960	4.67	17.77	1	0
	1968	0.551	21260	21260	6.48	25.04	1	0
	1975	0.687	23122	24279	7.49	25.59	1	0
Pharmaceutical chemicals	1963	0.539	52708	42369	1.68	4.93	2	0
	1968	0.610	60624	60624	2.67	7.55	2	0
	1975	0.660	67767	67286	4.73	11.40	2	0
Pharmaceutical preparations	1958	0.286	119871	89003	1.33	4.10	2	0
	1963	0.287	168815	138163	1.68	4.93	2	0
	1968	0.349	221326	221326	2.67	7.55	2	0
	1975	0.393	341185	474269	4.73	11.40	2	0
Hair preparations	1958	0.670	16860	18822	0.41	2.02	2	0
	1963	0.542	26510	27535	0.48	2.03	2	0
	1968	0.570	31731	31731	0.92	2.96	2	0
	1975	0.607	46032	60769	1.50	5.06	2	0

Dental preparations	1963	0.944	13587	12347	0.48	2.03	2	0
	1968	0.874	14450	14450	0.92	2.96	2	0
	1975	0.803	21586	24625	1.50	5.06	2	0
Other toilet preparations	1958	0.420	33779	37708	0.41	2.02	2	0
	1963	0.373	50961	52931	0.48	2.03	2	0
	1968	0.405	70585	70585	0.92	2.96	2	0
	1975	0.421	99401	111633	1.50	5.06	2	0
Soaps	1958	0.832	59413	60862	2.27	7.35	1	0
	1963	0.809	53272	53019	3.53	9.14	1	0
	1968	0.801	48123	48123	4.44	14.43	1	0
	1975	0.764	52683	49235	4.34	14.57	1	0
Finished detergents	1958	0.904	45542	36105	2.27	7.35	1	0
	1963	0.845	55501	48629	3.53	9.14	1	0
	1968	0.799	61265	61265	4.44	14.43	1	0
	1975	0.828	90114	99083	4.34	14.57	1	0
Synthetic resins, thermosetting	1963	0.528	27759	20436	6.90	16.68	2	0
	1968	0.487	40393	40393	7.90	19.17	2	0
Plastics materials other than synthetic resins, thermosetting	1963	0.787	27581	24240	6.90	16.68	2	0
	1968	0.768	30576	30576	7.90	19.17	2	0
	1975	0.794	27783	31102	8.22	28.64	2	0
Plastics materials other than synthetic resins, thermoplastic	1963	0.745	32007	25633	6.90	16.68	2	0
	1968	0.665	54709	54709	7.90	19.17	2	0
Synthetic rubber	1958	0.917	2841	1641	5.12	12.18	2	0
	1963	0.994	27581	21292	6.90	16.68	2	0
	1968	0.994	37863	37863	7.90	19.17	2	0
	1975	0.919	47882	40493	8.22	28.64	2	0

Table B5 (continued)

Industry	Year	C5	SS	DS	K/N	K/L	RDTYPE	CHANGE
Finished synthetic organic dyestuffs	1958	0.971	29134	26262	4.79	9.73	2	0
	1963	0.937	36627	36242	5.79	12.00	2	0
	1968	0.904	40970	40970	10.71	20.56	2	0
	1975	0.877	52043	59336	12.16	30.25	2	0
Polishes	1958	0.671	17337	18133	0.36	2.20	1	0
	1963	0.796	17901	18436	0.47	3.04	1	0
	1968	0.809	17249	17249	0.85	4.29	1	0
	1975	0.849	14138	18195	1.31	7.31	1	0
Gelatine, glue, size, and other adhesives	1963	0.488	28641	29712	0.96	7.22	2	0
	1968	0.461	36415	36415	1.39	7.99	2	0
	1975	0.442	48031	44083	1.86	11.61	2	0
Explosives and fireworks	1958	0.897	47722	46778	1.77	3.58	1	0
	1963	0.864	38202	37976	2.84	5.62	1	0
	1968	0.835	36778	36778	4.09	7.59	1	0
Pesticides, disinfectants, and household deodorisers	1958	0.424	29238	22616	0.41	2.96	2	0
	1963	0.520	34655	31491	0.68	4.56	2	0
	1968	0.534	44697	44697	1.28	7.49	2	0
	1975	0.533	73971	80699	2.57	13.13	2	0
Welding and flame-cutting machines	1963	0.638	11802	11638	0.77	3.26	1	0
	1968	0.501	14590	14590	0.96	4.02	1	0
	1975	0.630	18124	15254	0.87	4.85	1	0

Air and gas compressors and exhausters	1958	0.415	17780	17914	0.63	2.37	1	1
	1963	0.481	24848	24502	0.71	2.72	1	1
	1968	0.572	33439	33439	0.77	2.89	1	1
	1975	0.719	36671	33365	1.03	3.98	1	1
Internal combustion engines, industrial	1958	0.740	44160	39449	2.79	4.07	1	1
	1963	0.677	55144	58265	3.02	4.11	1	1
	1975	0.889	85484	79010	6.04	7.22	1	1
Textile machinery	1958	0.647	51270	51656	0.53	2.42	1	0
	1963	0.603	73907	72878	0.66	2.59	1	0
	1968	0.592	101346	101346	0.72	2.97	1	0
	1975	0.619	93273	88189	0.95	4.15	1	0
Powered industrial trucks and industrial tractors	1958	0.698	9424	10001	0.29	1.41	1	0
	1963	0.764	16297	15212	0.33	1.56	1	0
	1968	0.555	42182	42182	0.41	1.91	1	0
	1975	0.607	71547	66984	0.53	2.44	1	0
Printing, bookbinding, paperworking, etc. machinery	1958	0.446	20260	20413	0.38	2.15	1	0
	1963	0.491	28556	28159	0.49	2.43	1	0
	1968	0.491	33563	33563	0.67	2.98	1	0
	1975	0.440	39662	37500	0.75	3.55	1	0
Rubber and plastics working machinery	1963	0.563	16686	16453	0.49	2.23	1	0
	1968	0.506	24158	24158	0.59	2.82	1	0
	1975	0.508	19540	19228	0.71	3.84	1	0
Photographic and cinematographic apparatus and appliances, and document copying equipment	1963	0.706	14917	15978	0.54	3.10	2	0
	1968	0.843	38812	38812	1.02	2.87	2	0
	1975	0.787	54097	63083	1.78	7.28	2	0

Table B5 (continued)

Industry	Year	C5	SS	DS	K/N	K/L	RDTYPE	CHANGE
Optical instruments and appliances	1963	0.507	9436	10108	0.36	1.35	2	0
	1968	0.570	14143	14143	0.51	1.86	2	0
	1975	0.572	20023	23349	0.68	3.11	2	0
Transformers for lighting, heating, and power	1958	0.499	43892	38349	1.12	1.87	2	1
	1963	0.450	60208	55061	1.10	1.98	2	1
	1968	0.767	55120	55120	1.28	3.04	2	1
	1975	0.689	38395	38395	1.28	3.78	2	1
Starting and controlling gear for electric motors	1958	0.613	33487	29258	1.12	1.87	1	1
	1963	0.479	39976	36558	1.10	1.98	1	1
	1968	0.526	44871	44871	1.28	3.04	1	1
	1975	0.556	46821	46821	1.28	3.78	1	1
Switchgear and switchboards	1958	0.616	79351	69329	1.12	1.87	2	1
	1963	0.609	96849	88570	1.10	1.98	2	1
	1968	0.774	100001	100001	1.28	3.04	2	1
	1975	0.664	70307	70307	1.28	3.78	2	1
Line apparatus for long-distance communication	1958	0.939	11364	10457	2.04	2.08	2	1
	1963	0.962	23632	22753	3.22	2.81	2	1
	1968	1.000	40143	40143	2.77	3.28	2	1
	1975	0.949	31233	34038	3.39	3.62	2	1
Passive components	1963	0.353	76422	73580	0.60	1.63	1	0
	1968	0.335	125370	125370	0.85	2.40	1	0
	1975	0.355	130312	133557	1.44	4.39	1	0

Product	Year							
Television receiving sets	1958	0.528	78964	81098	0.53	1.10	1	0
	1963	0.816	66324	72215	0.55	1.00	1	0
	1968	0.927	86103	86103	1.01	1.98	1	0
	1975	0.850	135769	201970	1.22	2.80	1	0
Radio receiving sets	1963	0.579	23118	25140	0.55	1.00	1	0
	1968	0.747	11556	11556	1.01	1.98	1	0
	1975	0.835	4939	7389	1.22	2.80	1	0
Gramophones, record players, and tape recorders	1958	0.680	29788	25884	0.53	1.10	1	0
	1963	0.553	35794	34463	0.55	1.00	1	0
Electronic computers	1963	0.733	46845	45102	1.80	4.68	2	0
	1968	0.872	117633	117633	2.30	4.22	2	0
	1975	0.864	213692	232886	2.38	5.18	2	0
Radio communication equipment	1958	0.646	14442	13289	1.56	3.00	2	0
	1963	0.638	38064	36648	1.37	2.80	2	0
	1968	0.808	44742	44742	1.37	3.32	2	0
	1975	0.894	61650	67188	1.55	3.75	2	0
Radar and electronic navigation aid equipment	1958	0.783	21413	19704	1.56	3.00	2	0
	1963	0.722	64096	61712	1.37	2.80	2	0
	1968	0.746	82918	82918	1.37	3.32	2	0
	1975	0.807	86093	93826	1.55	3.75	2	0
Electronic measuring and testing instruments	1958	0.467	11790	10849	1.56	3.00	2	0
	1963	0.369	18071	17399	1.37	2.80	2	0
Washing machines, electrically operated	1958	0.764	34924	25410	1.18	2.55	1	1
	1963	0.852	55575	44969	1.18	2.27	1	1
	1968	0.869	36915	36915	1.43	3.00	1	1
	1975	0.981	44509	52813	2.23	4.79	1	1

Table B5 (continued)

Industry	Year	C5	SS	DS	K/N	K/L	RDTYPE	CHANGE
Electrical equipment for motor vehicles, cycles, and aircraft, excluding accumulators	1958	0.747	83330	89751	0.49	1.72	1	0
	1963	0.701	98189	97269	0.63	2.03	1	0
	1968	0.740	125913	125913	0.98	2.68	1	0
	1975	0.807	123426	134512	1.43	4.13	1	0
Batteries and accumulators	1958	0.782	42602	48030	0.49	1.72	1	1
	1963	0.787	52821	56933	0.63	2.03	1	1
	1968	0.841	66757	66757	0.98	2.68	1	1
	1975	0.908	74751	76167	1.43	4.13	1	1
Electric lamps	1958	0.744	23666	18932	0.49	1.72	2	1
	1963	0.717	35084	29795	0.63	2.03	2	1
	1968	0.866	40308	40308	0.98	2.68	2	1
	1975	0.941	35415	41413	1.43	4.13	2	1
Marine machinery	1963	0.346	56700	49781	0.86	1.96	1	0
	1968	0.574	60135	60135	0.98	2.11	1	0
	1975	0.457	55276	56078	1.36	2.89	1	0
Cars	1958	0.901	521809	471432	3.47	6.46	1	0
	1963	0.912	752514	685258	3.49	5.81	1	0
	1968	0.992	853240	853240	3.71	6.49	1	0
	1975	0.982	690957	648622	3.78	6.78	1	0
Internal combustion engines for motor vehicles	1963	0.931	80452	78340	3.49	5.81	1	0
	1968	0.970	85532	85532	3.71	6.49	1	0
	1975	0.914	48412	45773	3.78	6.78	1	0

	Year	C5	SS	DS	K	L	RDTYPE	CHANGE
Aero-engines	1958	0.940	152178	157306	2.24	2.32	2	0
	1963	0.971	108523	107012	3.00	2.58	2	0
Cutlery	1958	0.658	22897	20524	0.24	1.75	1	0
	1963	0.669	29222	26752	0.39	2.20	1	0
	1968	0.709	33214	33214	0.56	3.42	1	0
	1975	0.560	25796	27019	0.60	4.41	1	0
Tyres and tubes, other than retreaded tyres	1958	0.932	112412	94782	1.27	3.80	1	1
	1963	0.945	144054	130074	1.54	4.06	1	1
	1968	0.928	184836	184836	2.39	5.90	1	1
	1975	0.964	190550	199087	2.68	7.51	1	1

Notes: C5 is the five-firm sales concentration ratio.

SS is sales revenue (in £1000) deflated by the general producer price index.

DS is sales revenue (in £1000) deflated by industry-specific producer price indices.

K is the value of capital stock of the corresponding MLH industry in 1980 prices (in £ million).

L is employment of the corresponding MLH industry (in 1000).

N is the number of plants with at least 25 employees of the corresponding MLH industry.

RDTYPE takes the value 1 for an industry with typical R&D-sales ratio between 1% and 2%, and 2 for an industry with typical R&D-sales ratio higher than 2%.

CHANGE takes the value 1 for an industry with a change in competition regime and 0 otherwise.

Table B6
Data set for chapter 7

Industry	Year	NFIRMS	NPLANTS	SS	PROFIT	PCM	K/N	K/L	UNION	ADTYPE	RDTYPE	CHANGE
Slate and slate products	1954	16	17	2601	498	0.192	0.15	0.64	0.455	0	0	1
	1958	17	18	2249	477	0.212	0.13	0.69	0.408	0	0	1
	1963	16	21	2084	467	0.224	0.12	1.17	0.464	0	0	1
	1968	15	17	2169	528	0.243	0.21	2.35	0.395	0	0	1
Clay, brick earth, marl, shale, and chalk	1954	48	116	9927	3185	0.321	0.26	4.67	0.455	0	0	1
	1958	39	120	10955	3835	0.350	0.31	5.91	0.408	0	0	1
	1963	24	87	16964	5632	0.332	0.63	7.74	0.464	0	0	1
	1968	20	102	30359	15311	0.504	1.01	12.61	0.395	0	0	1
Iron ore and ironstone	1954	19	46	10093	3082	0.305	1.18	7.64	0.455	0	0	0
	1958	19	44	11714	3976	0.339	1.55	9.78	0.408	0	0	0
	1963	11	50	11162	4534	0.406	1.26	11.51	0.464	0	0	0
Salt	1954	8	23	14395	4177	0.290	1.36	6.31	0.455	0	0	0
	1958	8	19	14449	5913	0.409	1.94	8.50	0.408	0	0	0
	1963	6	18	18729	10628	0.567	3.17	15.14	0.464	0	0	0
Nonmetalliferous mining and quarrying other than salt	1954	18	45	8771	1589	0.181	0.41	3.39	0.455	0	0	0
	1958	20	40	7088	1015	0.143	0.45	4.38	0.408	0	0	0
	1963	13	24	5197	1859	0.358	0.73	7.77	0.464	0	0	0
Grain milling (MLH 211)	1954	149	227	322879	30864	0.096	0.53	4.16	0.305	0	0	1
	1958	134	223	306594	44288	0.144	0.65	4.82	0.283	0	0	1
	1963	78	183	278566	46326	0.166	1.04	7.17	0.295	0	0	1
	1968	61	149	283599	54094	0.191	1.50	10.38	0.346	0	0	1
	1973	56	133	275183	44925	0.163	1.87	13.23	0.490	0	0	1

Bread and flour confectionery (MLH 212)	1954	763	1096	241093	34421	0.143	0.32	3.17	0.305	0	0	1
	1958	554	839	293119	45856	0.156	0.43	2.86	0.283	0	0	1
	1963	271	728	364153	62594	0.172	0.54	2.58	0.295	0	0	1
	1968	209	536	381206	71191	0.187	0.84	3.03	0.346	0	0	1
	1973	250	507	421962	77066	0.183	0.98	3.30	0.490	0	0	1
Biscuits (MLH 213)	1954	77	111	115973	20859	0.180	0.88	1.76	0.305	2	0	1
	1958	60	95	122312	21270	0.174	1.51	2.65	0.283	2	0	1
	1963	37	75	133484	31649	0.237	2.28	3.74	0.295	2	0	1
	1968	33	65	149081	35662	0.239	3.22	4.39	0.346	2	0	1
	1973	29	54	149029	26332	0.177	4.42	5.37	0.490	2	0	1
Bacon and ham (cured and smoked), sausages and sausage meat	1954	146	185	176828	10066	0.057	0.26	2.21	0.305	0	0	1
	1958	134	168	146719	14883	0.101	0.33	2.49	0.283	0	0	1
	1963	90	138	157864	14325	0.091	0.50	2.08	0.295	0	0	1
	1968	67	101	166037	18246	0.110	0.80	2.49	0.346	0	0	1
Preserved meat or fish, meat extracts, fish cured, smoked, or salted, etc.	1963	50	74	43787	11967	0.273	0.23	1.57	0.295	1	1	0
	1968	43	65	59556	13788	0.232	0.59	2.89	0.346	1	1	0
Other meat products, offal, lard, etc.	1963	103	173	67826	8308	0.122	0.17	2.22	0.295	0	0	0
	1968	99	130	74425	11179	0.150	0.35	2.85	0.346	0	0	0
Butter	1954	27	46	47012	2728	0.058	0.99	13.15	0.305	0	0	1
	1958	26	42	60707	3308	0.054	1.26	12.16	0.283	0	0	1
	1963	15	33	59916	2701	0.045	1.61	15.83	0.295	0	0	1
	1968	17	38	74121	4327	0.058	1.59	16.08	0.346	0	0	1

Table B6 (continued)

Industry	Year	NFIRMS	NPLANTS	SS	PROFIT	PCM	K/N	K/L	UNION	ADTYPE	RDTYPE	CHANGE
Condensed milk	1954	9	16	24685	1553	0.063	1.67	9.39	0.305	2	0	1
	1958	7	19	36241	2871	0.079	1.73	8.85	0.283	2	0	1
	1963	5	14	31741	5205	0.164	3.37	16.58	0.295	2	0	1
	1968	6	10	29158	4758	0.163	5.86	21.74	0.346	2	0	1
Milk powder	1954	9	15	15664	913	0.058	0.73	7.54	0.305	0	0	1
	1958	5	9	12789	648	0.051	0.94	8.78	0.283	0	0	1
	1963	3	5	7801	887	0.114	2.42	16.35	0.295	0	0	1
Cream and other milk products (1958 S.I.C.)	1954	14	22	20159	2894	0.144	0.97	6.62	0.305	1	0	1
	1958	12	21	19366	3469	0.179	1.25	8.28	0.283	1	0	1
	1963	15	27	27786	3516	0.127	1.56	9.19	0.295	1	0	1
Ice cream	1954	22	28	20749	5140	0.248	1.65	8.97	0.305	2	0	0
	1958	14	22	28054	8143	0.290	4.18	12.27	0.283	2	0	0
	1963	13	22	19029	4039	0.212	3.97	20.86	0.295	2	0	0
Cocoa and chocolate products	1954	58	79	185400	26256	0.142	1.28	2.01	0.305	2	0	1
	1958	53	75	174518	32179	0.184	2.10	2.85	0.283	2	0	1
	1963	41	65	175872	43085	0.245	3.63	4.20	0.295	2	0	1
	1968	30	50	195358	43690	0.224	5.79	5.88	0.346	2	0	1
Fruit and vegetable products (MLH 218)	1954	209	309	152109	21938	0.144	0.29	1.65	0.305	2	0	0
	1958	168	263	190250	30516	0.160	0.44	1.97	0.283	2	0	0
	1963	131	223	248688	51160	0.206	0.88	3.13	0.295	2	0	0
	1968	119	201	286069	60947	0.213	1.29	4.41	0.346	2	0	0
	1973	110	172	369177	76929	0.208	1.96	5.34	0.490	2	0	0

Category	Year											
Dog and cat foods	1954	10	12	9937	2148	0.216	0.43	2.53	0.305	2	0	0
	1958	12	14	20516	4363	0.213	0.58	2.72	0.283	2	0	0
	1963	8	15	30693	9976	0.325	1.05	4.71	0.295	2	0	0
	1968	12	17	44694	9639	0.216	1.67	6.61	0.346	2	0	0
Vegetable and animal oils and fats (MLH 221)	1954	47	74	131158	12767	0.097	0.74	5.15	0.330	0	0	0
	1958	44	76	158533	11888	0.075	0.89	6.15	0.311	0	0	0
	1963	45	76	127451	13258	0.104	1.02	8.43	0.334	0	0	0
	1968	45	77	113298	12776	0.113	1.24	12.30	0.394	0	0	0
	1973	41	65	173956	23076	0.133	1.95	16.13	0.471	0	0	0
Margarine (MLH 229.1)	1954	17	18	68701	6919	0.101	1.73	5.85	0.305	2	0	0
	1958	12	14	62065	6364	0.103	2.81	7.83	0.283	2	0	0
	1963	8	9	52338	3932	0.075	4.47	9.86	0.295	2	0	0
	1968	7	8	40621	2240	0.055	5.43	10.76	0.346	2	0	0
	1973	7	8	59649	5270	0.088	7.18	14.96	0.490	2	0	0
Coffee, and coffee and chicory extracts and essences	1954	7	9	11152	1192	0.107	0.47	4.45	0.305	2	0	0
	1958	7	10	21788	3821	0.175	1.16	6.30	0.283	2	0	0
	1963	9	13	29465	6999	0.238	1.58	6.44	0.295	2	0	0
Spirits, distilled	1958	16	65	85846	4758	0.055	0.34	6.20	0.283	0	0	1
	1963	16	70	72550	6366	0.088	0.67	11.62	0.295	0	0	1
	1968	17	74	118681	9181	0.077	0.89	15.39	0.346	0	0	1
British wines, cider, and perry (MLH 239.2)	1954	18	30	13693	3312	0.242	0.54	4.78	0.305	2	0	0
	1958	18	26	18830	6327	0.336	0.67	4.15	0.283	2	0	0
	1963	7	17	19466	6030	0.310	1.20	5.21	0.295	2	0	0
	1968	10	19	27750	6841	0.247	1.32	5.85	0.346	2	0	0
	1973	9	17	41139	13033	0.317	2.02	7.23	0.490	2	0	0

Table B6 (continued)

Industry	Year	NFIRMS	NPLANTS	SS	PROFIT	PCM	K/N	K/L	UNION	ADTYPE	RDTYPE	CHANGE
Tobacco (MLH 240)	1958	26	62	1053944	65865	0.062	2.24	3.14	0.570	2	0	0
	1963	16	47	1224000	79042	0.065	4.46	4.86	0.673	2	0	0
	1968	12	41	1255888	100639	0.080	7.66	7.73	0.769	2	0	0
	1973	10	34	1134385	117867	0.104	11.65	10.10	0.994	2	0	0
Coke and manufactured fuel (MLH 261)	1954	28	92	166172	15091	0.091	3.24	14.14	0.330	0	0	0
	1958	25	83	214270	22461	0.105	6.02	21.60	0.311	0	0	0
	1963	24	56	198204	12943	0.065	9.21	28.43	0.334	0	0	0
Lubricating oils and greases (MLH 263)	1954	54	82	55148	13252	0.240	0.46	5.15	0.330	1	1	0
	1958	46	73	59879	15703	0.262	0.62	5.92	0.311	1	1	0
	1963	40	67	57484	16006	0.278	0.72	7.31	0.334	1	1	0
	1968	37	61	58883	13796	0.234	1.25	12.75	0.394	1	1	0
	1973	34	54	83814	17366	0.207	1.57	14.06	0.471	1	1	0
Miscellaneous basic chemicals (1958 S.I.C.)	1958	96	182	174748	60730	0.348	5.51	23.47	0.311	0	1	0
	1963	104	207	263477	99773	0.379	6.44	32.45	0.334	0	1	0
General chemicals, other than inorganic and organic (MLH 271.3, 1968 S.I.C.)	1963	97	141	171835	57316	0.334	4.11	18.87	0.334	0	1	0
	1968	88	127	211793	62688	0.296	6.27	27.19	0.394	0	1	0
	1973	91	132	341297	83509	0.245	7.36	28.99	0.471	0	1	0
Pharmaceutical chemicals and preparations (MLH 272)	1954	152	184	136436	45331	0.332	1.00	4.25	0.330	2	2	0
	1958	130	160	169296	57592	0.340	1.45	4.57	0.311	2	2	0
	1963	129	182	227398	89222	0.392	1.64	5.09	0.334	2	2	0
	1968	103	150	279096	111350	0.399	2.81	7.92	0.394	2	2	0
	1973	117	148	414171	153658	0.371	4.70	11.86	0.471	2	2	0

Toilet preparations (MLH 273)	1954	57	60	37424	15031	0.402	0.37	2.03	0.330	2	2	0
	1958	59	64	48508	18264	0.377	0.41	2.09	0.311	2	2	0
	1963	69	77	73365	31103	0.424	0.50	2.19	0.334	2	2	0
	1968	56	67	100269	38634	0.385	1.03	3.17	0.394	2	2	0
	1973	69	69	137667	54393	0.395	1.47	4.58	0.471	2	2	0
Paint (MLH 274)	1954	198	272	128395	29220	0.228	0.39	3.04	0.330	2	1	1
	1958	173	248	141652	32847	0.232	0.53	3.47	0.311	2	1	1
	1963	136	219	148773	38306	0.257	0.64	3.93	0.334	2	1	1
	1968	96	146	143872	39135	0.272	0.97	4.81	0.394	2	1	1
	1973	99	131	173887	54041	0.311	1.25	6.07	0.471	2	1	1
Soap and detergents (MLH 275)	1954	66	82	109731	20591	0.188	1.84	7.24	0.330	2	1	0
	1958	56	73	125164	27885	0.223	2.27	7.91	0.311	2	1	0
	1963	42	55	134478	35697	0.265	3.66	9.78	0.334	2	1	0
	1968	37	48	128781	32399	0.252	4.81	16.03	0.394	2	1	0
	1973	45	58	146130	32968	0.226	4.14	17.43	0.471	2	1	0
Synthetic resins and plastics materials	1954	—	63	94210	21470	0.228	4.29	12.88	0.330	0	2	0
	1958	57	78	146874	28741	0.196	4.38	11.56	0.311	0	2	0
	1963	62	101	194080	46757	0.241	5.08	15.96	0.334	0	2	0
	1968	85	128	324191	82940	0.256	6.92	19.15	0.394	0	2	0
Synthetic rubber	1963	4	4	22560	6632	0.294	27.28	72.01	0.334	0	2	0
	1968	4	5	34617	10825	0.313	24.18	62.64	0.394	0	2	0
Dyestuffs	1954	18	28	73182	15085	0.206	4.21	6.13	0.330	0	2	0
	1958	15	23	58603	13441	0.229	5.10	6.77	0.311	0	2	0
	1963	15	27	71993	18408	0.256	6.56	10.52	0.334	0	2	0
	1968	15	20	79126	22532	0.285	14.04	17.77	0.394	0	2	0

Table B6 (continued)

Industry	Year	NFIRMS	NPLANTS	SS	PROFIT	PCM	K/N	K/L	UNION	ADTYPE	RDTYPE	CHANGE
Polishes (MLH 279.1)	1954	38	50	19930	4925	0.247	0.20	1.93	0.330	2	1	0
	1958	30	38	21543	6875	0.319	0.35	2.51	0.311	2	1	0
	1963	34	46	26856	7891	0.294	0.46	3.35	0.334	2	1	0
	1968	29	37	33787	10921	0.323	0.80	4.70	0.394	2	1	0
	1973	29	33	38620	12772	0.331	1.10	6.52	0.471	2	1	0
Formulated adhesives, gelatine, glue, size, etc. (MLH 279.2)	1963	36	55	26219	5894	0.225	0.84	7.86	0.334	0	2	0
	1968	29	42	39693	9217	0.232	1.39	9.00	0.394	0	2	0
	1973	25	36	44826	11298	0.252	1.98	12.78	0.471	0	2	0
Fireworks	1954	17	21	3280	989	0.302	0.04	0.32	0.330	0	0	1
	1958	15	20	3646	857	0.235	0.06	0.41	0.311	0	0	1
	1963	12	20	3554	1029	0.290	0.11	0.89	0.334	0	0	1
Explosives	1954	9	42	65707	12172	0.185	1.59	1.60	0.330	0	1	0
	1958	9	37	51972	12527	0.241	2.98	3.94	0.311	0	1	0
	1963	9	20	41663	12129	0.291	5.63	6.28	0.334	0	1	0
	1968	6	12	39978	11432	0.286	10.30	8.25	0.394	0	1	0
Formulated pesticides and disinfectants (MLH 279.4)	1954	35	42	18211	3791	0.208	0.31	2.56	0.330	2	2	0
	1958	39	49	22835	5787	0.253	0.34	2.96	0.311	2	2	0
	1963	30	40	27686	8439	0.305	0.62	4.83	0.334	2	2	0
	1968	25	33	32399	7832	0.242	1.20	8.14	0.394	2	2	0
	1973	22	22	65472	19064	0.291	2.44	16.21	0.471	2	2	0
Surgical bandages, etc. and sanitary towels (MLH 279.6)	1963	22	42	35148	11317	0.322	1.13	4.04	0.562	0	0	1
	1968	18	37	42561	14561	0.342	2.00	6.11	0.602	0	0	1
	1973	16	34	53802	16919	0.314	2.32	6.30	0.722	0	0	1

Steel forgings	1958	23	29	13645	2756	0.202	0.52	3.95	0.499	0	0	1
	1963	26	35	24829	3362	0.135	0.92	7.05	0.528	0	0	1
Steel sheets and tinplate	1958	17	34	174834	11601	0.066	4.97	7.54	0.499	0	0	1
	1963	11	19	105977	8763	0.083	7.08	12.96	0.528	0	0	1
Steel manufacture without melting, other than forgings, sheets, and tinplate	1958	130	184	259280	21407	0.083	0.90	4.13	0.499	0	0	0
	1963	99	154	294025	25729	0.088	2.29	7.28	0.528	0	0	0
Steel castings	1958	52	63	45413	9411	0.207	0.84	2.42	0.499	0	0	1
	1963	51	66	47703	9490	0.199	1.19	3.75	0.528	0	0	1
Steel manufacture with melting, other than castings	1958	48	95	897286	142228	0.159	28.73	14.82	0.499	0	0	0
	1963	41	97	822988	127014	0.154	41.75	22.42	0.528	0	0	0
Steel tubing and gas cylinders	1958	22	55	189335	33744	0.178	4.53	5.67	0.499	0	0	1
	1963	23	61	187372	28462	0.152	6.25	8.44	0.528	0	0	1
	1968	30	70	209559	39712	0.190	6.09	9.10	0.567	0	0	1
Steel tubes, manipulated, fabricated, etc.	1958	42	63	23553	4069	0.173	0.25	1.81	0.499	0	0	1
	1963	52	69	31605	6555	0.207	0.38	2.71	0.528	0	0	1
	1968	39	53	34377	7230	0.210	0.71	3.81	0.567	0	0	1
Pig iron	1958	24	24	55198	5607	0.102	2.28	7.12	0.499	0	0	0
	1963	10	13	37820	4241	0.112	4.52	12.46	0.528	0	0	0
Pressure pipes and fittings	1958	21	32	39405	5175	0.131	3.37	7.90	0.499	0	0	1
	1963	15	25	38602	5820	0.151	4.02	8.23	0.528	0	0	1
	1968	11	23	38671	3970	0.103	3.46	5.90	0.567	0	0	1
Iron castings for the building industry	1958	53	71	32110	6252	0.195	0.20	0.89	0.499	0	0	1
	1963	39	57	37901	9914	0.262	0.51	2.02	0.528	0	0	1
	1968	29	42	35835	8025	0.224	1.27	4.22	0.567	0	0	1

Table B6 (continued)

Industry	Year	NFIRMS	NPLANTS	SS	PROFIT	PCM	K/N	K/L	UNION	ADTYPE	RDTYPE	CHANGE
Ingot moulds and bottoms	1958	19	19	16357	2386	0.146	2.17	10.37	0.499	0	0	1
	1963	13	14	15561	3217	0.207	2.64	10.38	0.528	0	0	1
	1968	9	17	18545	3370	0.182	1.86	7.74	0.567	0	0	1
Marine and other engineering castings	1958	321	341	58702	8119	0.138	0.17	1.71	0.499	0	0	1
	1963	258	278	54862	9124	0.166	0.32	3.12	0.528	0	0	1
	1968	183	208	48501	9335	0.192	0.49	4.57	0.567	0	0	1
Aluminium and aluminium alloys: fabricated	1954	23	36	98896	10417	0.105	3.64	4.39	0.509	0	0	1
	1958	27	44	106869	12093	0.113	4.00	5.46	0.499	0	0	1
	1963	35	63	145189	19994	0.138	3.68	6.44	0.528	0	0	1
	1968	38	62	171511	20356	0.119	4.95	9.26	0.567	0	0	1
Aluminium and aluminium alloys: founded	1954	76	91	30411	3534	0.116	0.28	1.91	0.509	0	0	1
	1958	74	91	31342	4292	0.137	0.35	2.39	0.499	0	0	1
	1963	90	115	41397	7470	0.180	0.46	3.07	0.528	0	0	1
	1968	90	120	57766	9736	0.169	0.89	5.17	0.567	0	0	1
Copper, brass and other copper alloys: smelted and refined	1954	24	28	64971	2072	0.032	0.56	4.92	0.509	0	0	1
	1958	23	27	42234	2209	0.052	0.51	5.90	0.499	0	0	1
	1963	31	42	52461	3415	0.065	0.36	3.59	0.528	0	0	1
	1968	20	26	105851	5909	0.056	1.36	10.28	0.567	0	0	1
Copper, brass and other copper alloys: fabricated and founded	1954	169	207	227902	24357	0.107	1.03	4.82	0.509	0	0	1
	1958	136	179	202096	23157	0.115	1.35	5.47	0.499	0	0	1
	1963	126	176	259488	33028	0.127	1.55	6.41	0.528	0	0	1
	1968	116	168	342383	37919	0.111	1.73	7.06	0.567	0	0	1

	Year											
Miscellaneous nonferrous metals (MLH 323)	1954	89	123	165314	16254	0.098	1.40	7.54	0.509	0	0	0
	1958	97	127	175503	16495	0.094	1.52	7.04	0.499	0	0	0
	1963	79	123	199829	22709	0.114	1.74	7.59	0.528	0	0	0
	1968	80	115	310325	32855	0.106	2.11	10.34	0.567	0	0	0
	1973	78	107	283136	42038	0.148	2.60	15.45	0.681	0	0	0
Welding and flame-cutting equipment	1954	29	35	17504	2657	0.152	0.74	4.38	0.509	0	1	0
	1958	31	40	23903	4203	0.176	0.76	4.04	0.499	0	1	0
	1963	31	36	18480	3443	0.186	0.60	3.49	0.528	0	1	0
	1968	33	44	32371	6141	0.190	0.48	2.65	0.567	0	1	0
Industrial engines (MLH 334)	1954	41	58	70673	13542	0.192	2.24	4.00	0.509	0	1	1
	1958	35	55	80071	12064	0.151	2.89	4.17	0.499	0	1	1
	1963	27	50	94382	13903	0.147	3.08	4.17	0.528	0	1	1
	1968	21	44	115623	23716	0.205	3.61	4.77	0.567	0	1	1
	1973	16	30	107459	20053	0.187	5.27	6.12	0.681	0	1	1
Textile machinery and accessories (MLH 335)	1954	266	338	95689	21590	0.226	0.36	1.99	0.509	0	1	0
	1958	189	245	77793	14165	0.182	0.52	2.69	0.499	0	1	0
	1963	148	204	113738	28142	0.247	0.65	2.83	0.528	0	1	0
	1968	146	213	140642	35674	0.254	0.69	3.22	0.567	0	1	0
	1973	123	176	143124	39012	0.273	0.91	4.31	0.681	0	1	0
Lifts and escalators	1954	32	54	10618	2835	0.267	0.04	0.36	0.509	0	0	1
	1958	30	62	15773	3688	0.234	0.05	0.39	0.499	0	0	1
	1963	32	70	29641	7099	0.239	0.18	1.10	0.528	0	0	1
	1968	28	62	38827	11528	0.297	0.33	1.65	0.567	0	0	1

Table B6 (continued)

Industry	Year	NFIRMS	NPLANTS	SS	PROFIT	PCM	K/N	K/L	UNION	ADTYPE	RDTYPE	CHANGE
Powered industrial trucks and industrial tractors	1954	7	9	3884	211	0.054	0.19	1.27	0.509	1	1	0
	1958	6	6	7055	981	0.139	0.32	0.86	0.499	1	1	0
	1963	17	23	19281	3175	0.165	0.22	0.92	0.528	1	1	0
	1968	28	35	36516	9248	0.253	0.51	2.15	0.567	1	1	0
Mining machinery (MLH 339.1)	1954	53	66	41508	8456	0.204	0.50	2.13	0.509	0	0	0
	1958	67	80	60392	11032	0.183	0.52	2.12	0.499	0	0	0
	1963	66	84	68058	15533	0.228	0.57	2.44	0.528	0	0	0
	1968	63	91	85380	16290	0.191	0.70	2.91	0.567	0	0	0
	1973	56	75	99856	22153	0.222	0.97	3.64	0.681	0	0	0
Printing, bookbinding, and paper goods making machinery (MLH 339.2)	1954	81	100	26214	7275	0.278	0.32	1.96	0.509	0	1	0
	1958	71	86	26670	7129	0.267	0.39	2.15	0.499	0	1	0
	1963	66	93	35247	10502	0.298	0.48	2.59	0.528	0	1	0
	1968	71	103	54335	12159	0.224	0.63	3.18	0.567	0	1	0
	1973	72	79	62216	12899	0.207	0.87	4.37	0.681	0	1	0
Space-heating, ventilating and air-conditioning equipment (MLH 339.4)	1954	125	148	30226	6520	0.216	0.13	1.15	0.509	0	0	0
	1958	121	136	39389	7976	0.203	0.15	1.11	0.499	0	0	0
	1963	129	167	64507	16584	0.257	0.25	1.75	0.528	0	0	0
	1968	171	221	96991	24068	0.248	0.38	2.80	0.567	0	0	0
Scales and weighing machinery	1954	17	45	9621	2682	0.279	0.23	1.88	0.509	0	0	0
	1958	15	44	8447	2010	0.238	0.22	1.77	0.499	0	0	0
	1963	14	50	11828	3291	0.278	0.23	1.93	0.528	0	0	0
	1968	18	29	14481	4293	0.296	0.42	2.24	0.567	0	0	0

Pulpmaking and papermaking machinery	1954	11	14	7933	1701	0.214	0.61	2.93	0.509	0	0	0
	1958	16	19	17846	3427	0.192	0.73	2.59	0.499	0	0	0
	1963	11	17	24607	4360	0.177	1.25	4.59	0.528	0	0	0
Packaging and bottling machinery	1963	37	52	19727	4576	0.232	0.27	1.31	0.528	0	0	0
	1968	47	63	29047	7010	0.241	0.67	3.58	0.567	0	0	0
Constructional and other fabricated ironwork and steelwork	1963	292	359	139771	26769	0.192	0.37	2.70	0.528	0	0	1
	1968	406	493	193201	39907	0.207	0.33	2.66	0.567	0	0	1
Ordnance and small arms (MLH 342)	1958	42	75	69364	11952	0.172	1.50	2.78	0.499	0	0	0
	1963	32	46	54281	10584	0.195	2.36	3.49	0.528	0	0	0
	1968	30	40	54619	13273	0.243	2.92	5.16	0.567	0	0	0
	1973	22	35	63398	8966	0.141	4.11	7.30	0.681	0	0	0
Photographic and document copying equipment (MLH 351)	1954	29	36	6965	2032	0.292	0.39	3.63	0.509	2	2	0
	1958	16	19	6710	1886	0.281	0.73	4.11	0.499	2	2	0
	1963	22	25	10814	2433	0.225	0.52	3.62	0.528	2	2	0
	1968	19	25	40611	8106	0.200	1.10	3.19	0.567	2	2	0
	1973	25	35	50657	8313	0.164	1.59	6.27	0.681	2	2	0
Watches and parts of watches	1954	8	13	6157	1364	0.222	1.20	3.49	0.509	2	0	0
	1958	10	12	5312	687	0.129	1.08	3.41	0.499	2	0	0
	1963	7	9	5944	1425	0.240	1.68	4.02	0.528	2	0	0
	1968	10	15	11373	1330	0.117	1.89	4.32	0.567	2	0	0
Spectacles and parts of spectacles	1954	82	129	13735	2438	0.178	0.07	0.89	0.509	0	1	1
	1958	78	117	14775	3497	0.237	0.08	0.96	0.499	0	1	1
	1963	76	123	17241	3081	0.179	0.09	1.13	0.528	0	1	1
	1968	68	97	19438	4225	0.217	0.15	1.58	0.567	0	1	1

Table B6 (continued)

Industry	Year	NFIRMS	NPLANTS	SS	PROFIT	PCM	K/N	K/L	UNION	ADTYPE	RDTYPE	CHANGE
Optical instruments	1954	21	30	9597	2589	0.270	0.39	1.42	0.509	0	2	0
	1958	24	36	7776	1994	0.256	0.28	1.83	0.499	0	2	0
	1963	27	43	14877	3646	0.245	0.33	1.49	0.528	0	2	0
Scientific instruments, other than optical instruments	1954	169	237	70464	17754	0.252	0.31	1.58	0.509	0	2	0
	1958	175	246	88353	22821	0.258	0.35	1.59	0.499	0	2	0
	1963	171	253	125441	32006	0.255	0.51	2.09	0.528	0	2	0
Scientific and industrial instruments and systems (MLH 354)	1963	247	417	200021	52256	0.261	0.34	1.42	0.528	0	2	0
	1968	280	464	285892	79626	0.279	0.49	1.96	0.567	0	2	0
	1973	332	461	267226	67153	0.251	0.65	3.29	0.681	0	2	0
Electrical machinery (MLH 361)	1954	232	353	362912	70609	0.195	0.93	1.72	0.509	0	2	1
	1958	228	373	449783	99582	0.221	1.09	1.92	0.499	0	2	1
	1963	234	393	477502	75169	0.157	1.11	2.03	0.528	0	2	1
	1968	220	401	485879	116319	0.239	1.27	3.13	0.567	0	2	1
	1973	255	388	476458	93072	0.195	1.34	3.87	0.681	0	2	1
Insulated wires and cables (MLH 362)	1954	50	83	163215	17718	0.109	1.95	3.45	0.509	0	1	1
	1958	42	70	167783	20815	0.124	2.79	4.30	0.499	0	1	1
	1963	47	91	226293	38766	0.171	2.72	4.69	0.528	0	1	1
	1968	32	78	313794	46708	0.149	3.75	5.47	0.567	0	1	1
	1973	34	68	328690	41434	0.126	5.12	7.63	0.681	0	1	1
Telegraph and telephone apparatus and equipment (MLH 363)	1954	24	77	94159	19913	0.211	1.45	1.66	0.509	0	2	0
	1958	26	86	109117	17372	0.159	1.85	2.09	0.499	0	2	0
	1963	36	86	153897	33656	0.219	2.85	2.78	0.528	0	2	0

Description	Year											
Radio and other electronic equipment, except valves and semiconductors (1958 S.I.C.)	1954	236	407	227325	40139	0.177	0.54	1.69	0.509	0	2	0
	1958	250	432	297348	45764	0.154	0.62	1.80	0.499	0	2	0
	1963	271	546	492174	128292	0.261	0.65	1.75	0.528	0	2	0
Radio and electronic components, except valves and semiconductors (1968 S.I.C.)	1963	119	179	73362	18597	0.253	0.39	1.45	0.528	0	1	0
	1968	167	256	179345	52172	0.291	0.53	1.85	0.567	0	1	0
Broadcast receiving and sound reproducing equipment, except records and tapes	1963	50	83	131206	22732	0.173	0.48	1.07	0.528	1	1	0
	1968	33	66	109384	19626	0.179	0.73	1.76	0.567	1	1	0
Electronic computers (MLH 366)	1963	11	27	39154	12371	0.316	1.80	4.78	0.528	0	2	0
	1968	20	36	92590	21326	0.230	2.24	4.33	0.567	0	2	0
	1973	35	46	208460	63662	0.305	2.62	4.72	0.681	0	2	0
Radio, radar, and electronic capital goods (MLH 367)	1963	77	168	171326	46895	0.274	1.25	2.87	0.528	0	2	0
	1968	94	195	212221	49073	0.231	1.34	3.42	0.567	0	2	0
	1973	115	201	289685	70163	0.242	1.61	3.75	0.681	0	2	0
Electric appliances primarily for domestic use (MLH 368)	1954	92	140	95030	22944	0.241	0.68	2.24	0.509	2	1	1
	1958	85	115	121328	23091	0.190	1.12	2.60	0.499	2	1	1
	1963	102	142	211018	49486	0.235	1.16	2.32	0.528	2	1	1
	1968	100	153	240736	56430	0.234	1.48	3.07	0.567	2	1	1
	1973	92	119	276881	57904	0.209	2.25	4.16	0.681	2	1	1
Electrical equipment for motor vehicles, cycles, and aircraft, excluding accumulators	1954	33	50	63222	14327	0.227	1.11	1.96	0.509	0	1	0
	1958	29	49	70874	11050	0.156	1.34	2.10	0.499	0	1	0
	1963	33	63	74217	17484	0.236	1.17	2.26	0.528	0	1	0
	1968	31	74	128479	35546	0.277	1.44	2.31	0.567	0	1	0
	1973	31	—	138784	22775	0.164	—	2.87	0.681	0	1	0

Table B6 (continued)

Industry	Year	NFIRMS	NPLANTS	SS	PROFIT	PCM	K/N	K/L	UNION	ADTYPE	RDTYPE	CHANGE
Secondary batteries (accumulators)	1954	14	23	24832	4827	0.194	0.50	1.46	0.509	1	0	1
	1958	16	21	23954	4507	0.188	0.67	1.68	0.499	1	0	1
	1963	13	17	27780	5916	0.213	0.94	1.86	0.528	1	0	1
	1968	18	26	40769	9680	0.237	1.28	3.03	0.567	1	0	1
Electric light fittings, wiring accessories, and other electrical goods	1954	153	187	39233	8962	0.228	0.20	1.48	0.509	0	0	1
	1958	168	195	59906	12937	0.216	0.23	1.38	0.499	0	0	1
	1963	160	192	73950	18626	0.252	0.30	1.79	0.528	0	0	1
	1968	129	163	80961	20199	0.249	0.42	2.29	0.567	0	0	1
Shipbuilding and marine engineering	1954	125	202	360296	35662	0.099	1.17	1.40	0.509	0	0	0
	1958	148	216	384318	37087	0.097	1.23	1.56	0.499	0	0	0
	1963	102	161	285071	32624	0.114	1.71	2.42	0.528	0	0	0
	1968	81	146	223519	26045	0.117	1.56	2.26	0.567	0	0	0
Boatbuilding	1954	59	68	8992	1398	0.155	0.04	0.45	0.509	0	0	0
	1958	54	62	6122	681	0.111	0.03	0.43	0.499	0	0	0
	1963	46	55	7248	1079	0.149	0.02	0.33	0.528	0	0	0
	1968	51	56	11329	2130	0.188	0.06	0.92	0.567	0	0	0
Cars	1954	11	25	401716	55719	0.139	27.41	9.73	0.509	1	1	0
	1958	12	29	662249	75580	0.114	29.64	8.93	0.499	1	1	0
	1963	15	52	1042379	170884	0.164	23.04	7.98	0.528	1	1	0
	1968	11	43	1107976	141402	0.128	37.04	9.47	0.567	1	1	0

Motor bodies	1954	106	145	132935	15479	0.116	1.72	4.27	0.509	0	0	0
	1958	100	131	194393	17912	0.092	2.43	4.92	0.499	0	0	0
	1963	82	117	180054	22467	0.125	3.12	5.95	0.528	0	0	0
	1968	87	124	150358	20159	0.134	2.08	5.09	0.567	0	0	0
Internal combustion engines for vehicles	1954	6	8	36161	5869	0.162	7.57	5.01	0.509	0	1	0
	1958	7	8	41374	3685	0.089	6.91	3.75	0.499	0	1	0
	1963	6	10	59125	9306	0.157	5.47	3.32	0.528	0	1	0
Parts and accessories of motor vehicles, other than engines and motor bodies	1954	169	219	158319	29916	0.189	2.06	7.01	0.509	0	0	0
	1958	142	187	182819	32714	0.179	2.18	6.25	0.499	0	0	0
	1963	142	239	317941	62425	0.196	1.87	4.55	0.528	0	0	0
Hand tools and implements (MLH 391)	1954	150	175	27296	5265	0.193	0.26	2.38	0.509	0	0	1
	1958	121	157	30019	6930	0.231	0.29	2.46	0.499	0	0	1
	1963	105	138	33132	8260	0.249	0.35	2.93	0.528	0	0	1
	1968	94	122	33539	7879	0.235	0.42	3.26	0.567	0	0	1
	1973	86	103	38787	10186	0.263	0.57	4.15	0.681	0	0	1
Razors and blades	1954	4	8	11773	7277	0.618	1.59	3.85	0.509	2	1	0
	1958	5	7	11825	6818	0.577	2.33	5.14	0.499	2	1	0
	1963	4	5	16437	8174	0.497	6.66	6.13	0.528	2	1	0
	1968	4	5	20533	12372	0.603	7.66	10.17	0.567	2	1	0
Wire and wire manufactures (MLH 394)	1954	169	231	133773	15781	0.118	0.53	3.70	0.509	0	0	1
	1958	155	225	165482	18115	0.109	0.60	3.80	0.499	0	0	1
	1963	141	246	184890	24667	0.133	0.72	4.51	0.528	0	0	1
	1968	125	213	186584	24964	0.134	0.98	5.77	0.567	0	0	1
	1973	120	193	236630	42727	0.181	1.25	6.49	0.681	0	0	1

Table B6 (continued)

Industry	Year	NFIRMS	NPLANTS	SS	PROFIT	PCM	K/N	K/L	UNION	ADTYPE	RDTYPE	CHANGE
Cans and metal-boxes (MLH 395)	1954	69	105	70094	8992	0.128	0.67	2.48	0.509	0	0	0
	1958	63	96	82301	12013	0.146	0.89	3.12	0.499	0	0	0
	1963	44	78	101514	12318	0.121	1.58	4.16	0.528	0	0	0
	1968	44	75	116529	16418	0.141	2.36	6.22	0.567	0	0	0
	1973	44	70	138612	15881	0.115	3.05	7.39	0.681	0	0	0
Jewellery and plate (1958 S.I.C.)	1954	199	225	25515	5400	0.212	0.08	1.15	0.509	0	0	0
	1958	153	174	23848	4969	0.208	0.11	1.31	0.499	0	0	0
	1963	139	166	34007	6943	0.204	0.13	1.52	0.528	0	0	0
Jewellery and plate (1968 S.I.C.)	1963	101	118	24399	4602	0.189	0.14	1.94	0.528	0	0	0
	1968	67	75	29107	4800	0.165	0.38	4.45	0.567	0	0	0
Metal furniture	1954	123	142	33109	6239	0.188	0.21	1.84	0.509	0	0	0
	1958	100	116	31832	5703	0.179	0.29	2.54	0.499	0	0	0
	1963	118	146	50613	12094	0.239	0.27	2.01	0.528	0	0	0
	1968	107	138	58593	11913	0.203	0.35	2.47	0.567	0	0	0
	1973	109	133	77913	16159	0.207	0.43	2.84	0.681	0	0	0
Drop forgings of steel and iron, and steel stampings and pressings	1963	87	106	88475	14464	0.163	1.38	5.37	0.528	0	0	1
	1968	62	91	89201	14181	0.159	1.51	5.38	0.567	0	0	1
	1973	65	103	105412	17705	0.168	1.87	7.17	0.681	0	0	1
Domestic hollow-ware	1954	101	117	29105	5797	0.199	0.21	1.50	0.509	0	0	1
	1958	84	93	19498	2363	0.121	0.25	2.03	0.499	0	0	1
	1963	72	84	22866	3964	0.173	0.25	1.88	0.528	0	0	1
	1968	50	61	19697	4876	0.248	0.43	3.57	0.567	0	0	1

Industrial hollow-ware	1954	81	93	27689	4795	0.173	0.32	2.94	0.509	0	0	1
	1958	94	118	44388	6654	0.150	0.39	2.77	0.499	0	0	1
	1963	60	78	32322	4926	0.152	0.66	5.31	0.528	0	0	1
	1968	45	65	31439	5845	0.186	0.75	5.80	0.567	0	0	1
Metal windows and door frames	1954	34	46	26320	3254	0.124	0.46	1.64	0.509	0	0	1
	1958	35	44	32013	5152	0.161	0.48	1.43	0.499	0	0	1
	1963	39	56	33880	6678	0.197	0.41	1.56	0.528	0	0	1
	1968	39	60	35126	8096	0.230	0.36	1.66	0.567	0	0	1
Safes, locks, latches, and keys	1963	39	45	15359	5154	0.336	0.35	1.87	0.528	0	0	1
	1968	32	42	19913	5848	0.294	0.66	2.84	0.567	0	0	1
Engineers' and mechanicians' goods	1963	56	82	32464	7387	0.228	0.73	4.61	0.528	0	0	1
	1968	46	61	43906	9840	0.224	1.08	5.32	0.567	0	0	1
Anchors and chains	1954	37	50	9541	1729	0.181	0.24	2.69	0.509	0	0	0
	1958	30	41	8906	1244	0.140	0.40	4.40	0.499	0	0	0
	1963	27	33	10021	1811	0.181	0.68	7.07	0.528	0	0	0
	1968	19	25	9103	1746	0.192	0.71	7.63	0.567	0	0	0
Spun cotton yarns	1954	136	287	190888	20326	0.106	0.65	2.35	0.752	0	0	1
	1958	102	231	104674	9038	0.086	0.85	3.27	0.720	0	0	1
	1963	51	111	64778	6175	0.095	1.80	6.03	0.790	0	0	1
	1968	40	77	52826	4553	0.086	2.12	7.92	0.810	0	0	1
Cotton waste yarns	1954	48	68	16087	2799	0.174	0.23	2.87	0.752	0	0	1
	1958	45	61	11765	2075	0.176	0.25	2.94	0.720	0	0	1
	1963	31	44	10170	1275	0.125	0.33	3.02	0.790	0	0	1
	1968	19	25	4273	480	0.112	0.40	4.60	0.810	0	0	1

Table B6 (continued)

Industry	Year	NFIRMS	NPLANTS	SS	PROFIT	PCM	K/N	K/L	UNION	ADTYPE	RDTYPE	CHANGE
Spun man-made fibres and mixture yarns	1954	32	40	21005	3105	0.148	0.63	2.54	0.752	0	0	1
	1958	32	42	20354	1263	0.062	0.59	2.32	0.720	0	0	1
	1963	24	37	20716	2470	0.119	1.02	4.11	0.790	0	0	1
	1968	18	36	33794	4877	0.144	1.59	5.15	0.810	0	0	1
Creped, bulked, textured, or stretch continuous filament yarns	1963	26	38	26982	3552	0.132	2.11	11.37	0.790	0	0	0
	1968	27	53	66673	14572	0.219	4.00	13.94	0.810	0	0	0
Finished thread	1954	31	45	30305	4211	0.139	0.65	1.97	0.752	0	0	0
	1958	24	38	24631	3851	0.156	1.19	4.07	0.720	0	0	0
	1963	24	37	23646	3847	0.163	2.18	7.97	0.790	0	0	0
	1968	18	28	29301	9796	0.334	2.77	8.86	0.810	0	0	0
Loom state cloth of cotton	1954	402	556	174219	13237	0.076	0.28	2.19	0.752	0	0	0
	1958	252	362	97130	6347	0.065	0.44	3.30	0.720	0	0	0
	1963	119	164	54511	4164	0.076	0.61	4.59	0.790	0	0	0
	1968	73	99	34264	2872	0.084	0.70	5.64	0.810	0	0	0
Loom state cloth of man-made fibres and mixtures	1954	162	209	77785	7233	0.093	0.52	3.20	0.752	0	0	1
	1958	110	149	56182	4269	0.076	0.62	4.12	0.720	0	0	1
	1963	69	102	62504	4982	0.080	1.24	6.86	0.790	0	0	1
	1968	52	78	52929	5997	0.113	2.33	14.58	0.810	0	0	1
Wool combers (on own account)	1954	10	12	31294	1867	0.060	0.45	1.82	0.320	0	0	0
	1958	14	16	28775	2226	0.077	0.64	3.02	0.314	0	0	0
	1963	18	35	47279	4627	0.098	0.70	4.09	0.310	0	0	0

Wool combers (on commission)	1954	39	59	13443	4497	0.335	0.49	3.00	0.320	0	0	0	1
	1958	34	55	12858	3567	0.277	0.80	4.63	0.314	0	0	0	1
	1963	26	47	14971	4647	0.310	0.93	5.15	0.310	0	0	0	1
Spun woollen yarns	1954	91	103	44201	4728	0.107	0.34	3.78	0.320	0	0	0	0
	1958	85	103	38705	5130	0.133	0.34	3.65	0.314	0	0	0	0
	1963	83	108	61631	11066	0.180	0.46	3.46	0.310	0	0	0	0
	1968	80	108	60494	11362	0.188	0.81	6.05	0.346	0	0	0	0
Woven worsted fabric	1954	222	301	123535	16119	0.130	0.26	1.96	0.320	0	0	0	0
	1958	182	252	96368	10333	0.107	0.28	2.13	0.314	0	0	0	0
	1963	130	229	95805	13226	0.138	0.34	2.23	0.310	0	0	0	0
	1968	83	171	73266	12630	0.172	0.49	3.49	0.346	0	0	0	0
Woven woollen fabric, other than blankets, traveling rugs, etc.	1954	253	324	116771	18863	0.162	0.34	2.08	0.320	0	0	0	0
	1958	217	308	95201	11959	0.126	0.31	1.97	0.314	0	0	0	0
	1963	162	237	78752	15308	0.194	0.36	2.27	0.310	0	0	0	0
	1968	135	200	73924	14532	0.197	0.52	3.23	0.346	0	0	0	0
Mechanical cloth, woven felt, and pressed felt	1954	20	33	15088	1527	0.101	0.54	3.78	0.320	0	0	0	1
	1958	16	27	11508	2611	0.227	0.59	3.90	0.314	0	0	0	1
	1963	13	20	8972	2232	0.249	0.74	4.88	0.310	0	0	0	1
	1968	13	22	11636	3318	0.285	0.97	5.95	0.346	0	0	0	1
Jute (MLH 415)	1954	47	72	43789	6016	0.137	0.86	3.20	0.320	0	0	0	1
	1958	48	74	38026	3252	0.086	0.91	4.14	0.314	0	0	0	1
	1963	32	64	38058	5190	0.136	1.02	4.03	0.310	0	0	0	1
	1968	28	57	39104	6035	0.154	1.24	5.03	0.346	0	0	0	1
	1973	21	40	39220	6997	0.178	1.91	7.67	0.449	0	0	0	1

Table B6 (continued)

Industry	Year	NFIRMS	NPLANTS	SS	PROFIT	PCM	K/N	K/L	UNION	ADTYPE	RDTYPE	CHANGE
Rope, twine, and net (MLH 416)	1954	82	127	32957	4595	0.139	0.21	1.94	0.320	0	0	1
	1958	64	110	27823	4633	0.167	0.28	2.55	0.314	0	0	1
	1963	47	99	31223	5564	0.178	0.34	3.14	0.310	0	0	1
	1968	34	54	23690	4720	0.199	0.70	4.73	0.346	0	0	1
	1973	23	40	22809	4383	0.192	1.09	7.12	0.449	0	0	1
Hosiery	1954	240	321	105983	22583	0.213	0.94	5.85	0.320	1	0	0
	1958	188	248	79577	13304	0.167	1.14	6.98	0.314	1	0	0
	1963	157	202	65001	13436	0.207	1.04	6.92	0.310	1	0	0
	1968	92	148	78294	17925	0.229	1.06	5.36	0.346	1	0	0
Underwear, shirts, and nightwear, knitted, netted, or crocheted	1954	100	144	38471	6014	0.156	0.23	1.59	0.320	0	0	0
	1958	90	139	38043	6165	0.162	0.33	2.20	0.314	0	0	0
	1963	58	114	38649	6750	0.175	0.49	2.81	0.310	0	0	0
	1968	52	101	50444	12221	0.242	0.60	3.00	0.346	0	0	0
Other garments, etc., knitted, netted, or crocheted	1954	326	408	62220	11085	0.178	0.15	1.65	0.320	0	0	0
	1958	293	379	70102	11562	0.165	0.28	2.54	0.314	0	0	0
	1963	257	394	114945	21303	0.185	0.49	3.31	0.310	0	0	0
	1968	245	410	138644	27366	0.197	0.64	4.17	0.346	0	0	0
Woven carpets, carpeting, and carpet floor rugs	1954	52	84	76253	14337	0.188	0.99	2.94	0.320	0	0	1
	1958	54	91	78295	14358	0.183	0.94	2.98	0.314	0	0	1
	1963	42	68	79534	16127	0.203	1.24	3.22	0.310	0	0	1
	1968	32	68	80275	15588	0.194	1.25	3.67	0.346	0	0	1

Industry	Year											
Tufted carpets, carpeting, and carpet floor rugs	1958	5	7	4748	618	0.130	0.90	5.98	0.314	1	0	0
	1963	20	24	21159	3938	0.186	0.85	5.20	0.310	1	0	0
	1968	27	37	56536	6529	0.115	1.44	5.41	0.346	1	0	0
Made-up household textiles and handkerchiefs (MLH 422.1)	1954	215	244	34227	3645	0.106	0.04	0.49	0.320	0	0	0
	1958	204	254	35580	4518	0.127	0.05	0.65	0.314	0	0	0
	1963	190	232	41617	5673	0.136	0.07	0.89	0.310	0	0	0
	1968	147	186	46617	6591	0.141	0.14	1.60	0.346	0	0	0
	1973	120	194	69003	14772	0.214	0.23	2.34	0.449	0	0	0
Canvas sacks and bags	1954	80	115	30866	1582	0.051	0.05	0.90	0.320	0	0	1
	1958	68	95	20322	2217	0.109	0.06	1.15	0.314	0	0	1
	1963	47	71	18744	1247	0.067	0.06	1.11	0.310	0	0	1
	1968	31	39	7558	777	0.103	0.08	1.64	0.346	0	0	1
Textile finishing; yarn	1954	92	111	13542	2238	0.165	0.27	2.93	0.320	0	0	1
	1958	70	87	10760	1835	0.171	0.32	3.67	0.314	0	0	1
	1963	52	68	10634	2594	0.244	0.50	4.86	0.310	0	0	1
	1968	41	56	10861	2770	0.255	0.86	8.49	0.346	0	0	1
Textile finishing; woven fabrics of cotton and man-made fibres	1954	179	241	64563	13743	0.213	0.47	2.61	0.320	0	0	1
	1958	151	220	58328	8681	0.149	0.65	3.58	0.314	0	0	1
	1963	96	167	48969	10003	0.204	0.90	5.04	0.310	0	0	1
	1968	76	123	42515	10183	0.240	1.28	7.39	0.346	0	0	1
Textile finishing; woollen and worsted fabrics	1954	60	71	9624	2534	0.263	0.36	4.44	0.320	0	0	1
	1958	45	52	6744	1836	0.272	0.38	5.50	0.314	0	0	1
	1963	37	45	6617	1658	0.251	0.30	3.64	0.310	0	0	1
	1968	23	29	4783	1282	0.268	0.49	5.84	0.346	0	0	1

Table B6 (continued)

Industry	Year	NFIRMS	NPLANTS	SS	PROFIT	PCM	K/N	K/L	UNION	ADTYPE	RDTYPE	CHANGE
Textile finishing: knitted fabrics and other knitted goods	1954	64	75	10559	2907	0.275	0.36	2.91	0.320	0	0	1
	1958	51	63	10904	2854	0.262	0.52	3.74	0.314	0	0	1
	1963	44	57	15408	4580	0.297	0.87	4.94	0.310	0	0	1
	1968	50	70	23572	7396	0.314	1.08	5.93	0.346	0	0	1
Asbestos manufactures (MLH 429.1)	1954	29	40	42462	9203	0.217	1.18	2.95	0.320	0	0	1
	1958	30	41	45229	11116	0.246	1.59	3.60	0.314	0	0	1
	1963	23	40	55278	13314	0.241	1.80	3.60	0.310	0	0	1
	1968	20	39	66278	15944	0.241	2.24	4.29	0.346	0	0	1
	1973	16	33	65727	14066	0.214	3.01	5.55	0.449	0	0	1
Needle felt and needleloom carpeting	1954	13	17	5514	1168	0.212	0.14	2.20	0.320	0	0	0
	1958	13	21	4734	713	0.151	0.14	2.50	0.314	0	0	0
	1963	15	25	7124	1277	0.179	0.19	2.94	0.310	0	0	0
	1968	14	24	8298	2177	0.262	0.40	5.02	0.346	0	0	0
Leather tanning	1954	72	85	38382	2754	0.072	0.15	1.50	0.330	0	0	0
	1958	49	56	21405	1666	0.078	0.20	2.05	0.323	0	0	0
	1963	29	32	17045	1938	0.114	0.31	2.63	0.318	0	0	0
	1968	22	25	15512	1783	0.115	0.50	4.13	0.284	0	0	0
Leather tanning and dressing, or dressing only	1954	170	194	65312	6249	0.096	0.22	2.33	0.330	0	0	0
	1958	150	172	56692	5827	0.103	0.23	2.43	0.323	0	0	0
	1963	130	156	59245	8234	0.139	0.27	2.82	0.318	0	0	0
	1968	120	140	67775	11078	0.163	0.36	3.63	0.284	0	0	0

Fellmongery	1954	25	27	11148	1103	0.099	0.13	2.48	0.330	0	0	0	0
	1958	22	24	8095	549	0.068	0.16	2.90	0.323	0	0	0	0
	1963	29	37	17194	1588	0.092	0.14	2.68	0.318	0	0	0	0
	1968	20	24	11301	1117	0.099	0.22	3.89	0.284	0	0	0	0
Travel goods of leather or leather substitutes	1954	50	56	8974	1632	0.182	0.06	0.61	0.330	0	0	0	0
	1958	33	38	6808	1247	0.183	0.08	0.81	0.323	0	0	0	0
	1963	31	36	7735	1557	0.201	0.11	0.99	0.318	0	0	0	0
	1968	38	45	10300	1823	0.177	0.11	0.99	0.284	0	0	0	0
Leather goods other than travel goods	1954	157	176	13442	2024	0.151	0.02	0.36	0.330	0	0	0	0
	1958	125	134	11890	2042	0.172	0.03	0.49	0.323	0	0	0	0
	1963	120	131	16553	2965	0.179	0.05	0.75	0.318	0	0	0	0
	1968	110	130	16823	3272	0.194	0.06	0.92	0.284	0	0	0	0
Fur (MLH 433)	1954	72	84	9069	1554	0.171	0.08	1.39	0.330	0	0	0	0
	1958	52	55	8614	1158	0.134	0.11	1.62	0.323	0	0	0	0
	1963	53	65	15239	3253	0.213	0.11	1.49	0.318	0	0	0	0
	1968	46	55	13112	2123	0.162	0.14	2.14	0.284	0	0	0	0
	1973	41	57	11104	2121	0.191	0.15	2.69	0.267	0	0	0	0
Weatherproof outerwear (MLH 441)	1954	—	304	45817	5898	0.129	0.07	0.69	0.337	0	0	0	0
	1958	180	242	35686	4591	0.129	0.08	0.83	0.326	0	0	0	0
	1963	157	232	44065	7353	0.167	0.09	0.82	0.319	0	0	0	0
	1968	118	186	35433	7102	0.200	0.10	1.06	0.333	0	0	0	0
	1973	120	178	34884	6999	0.201	0.12	1.29	0.369	0	0	0	0

Table B6 (continued)

Industry	Year	NFIRMS	NPLANTS	SS	PROFIT	PCM	K/N	K/L	UNION	ADTYPE	RDTYPE	CHANGE
Men's and boys' tailored outerwear (MLH 442)	1954	544	760	168227	21008	0.125	0.05	0.33	0.337	0	0	0	0
	1958	459	652	153941	17986	0.117	0.07	0.39	0.326	0	0	0	0
	1963	352	592	163246	23884	0.146	0.09	0.50	0.319	0	0	0	0
	1968	302	551	161643	27406	0.170	0.12	0.72	0.333	0	0	0	0
	1973	315	513	180010	34679	0.193	0.16	0.93	0.369	0	0	0	0
Women's and girls' tailored outerwear (MLH 443)	1954	521	635	86800	11507	0.133	0.05	0.60	0.337	0	0	0	0
	1958	406	520	74984	9193	0.123	0.06	0.66	0.326	0	0	0	0
	1963	369	465	83662	12967	0.155	0.07	0.75	0.319	0	0	0	0
	1968	279	382	80623	13760	0.171	0.10	1.02	0.333	0	0	0	0
	1973	355	416	87260	18909	0.217	0.10	1.15	0.369	0	0	0	0
Heavy overalls and jeans	1954	95	127	17596	1751	0.100	0.05	0.59	0.337	0	0	0	0
	1958	76	99	16160	1871	0.116	0.07	0.65	0.326	0	0	0	0
	1963	81	114	20516	3469	0.169	0.06	0.66	0.319	0	0	0	0
	1968	73	112	21566	3769	0.175	0.08	0.76	0.333	0	0	0	0
Shirts, underwear, etc. (on own account)	1954	213	273	44879	5099	0.114	0.05	0.44	0.337	1	0	0	0
	1958	181	246	45719	5243	0.115	0.06	0.51	0.326	1	0	0	0
	1963	149	227	52713	7485	0.142	0.09	0.72	0.319	1	0	0	0
	1968	111	183	51955	8750	0.168	0.15	1.06	0.333	1	0	0	0
Women's and girls' light outerwear (on own account)	1954	549	665	68151	8938	0.131	0.03	0.43	0.337	0	0	0	0
	1958	492	611	69599	9010	0.129	0.03	0.46	0.326	0	0	0	0
	1963	329	453	63530	10908	0.172	0.05	0.65	0.319	0	0	0	0
	1968	272	403	86700	14397	0.166	0.07	0.74	0.333	0	0	0	0

	Year											
Women's and girls' underwear and nightwear	1954	148	190	24229	2692	0.111	0.05	0.57	0.337	0	0	0
	1958	146	186	30385	2642	0.087	0.06	0.62	0.326	0	0	0
	1963	122	172	33041	4452	0.135	0.10	0.86	0.319	0	0	0
	1968	118	186	33513	6074	0.181	0.13	1.36	0.333	0	0	0
Infants' wear	1954	127	149	12564	2029	0.161	0.03	0.41	0.337	0	0	0
	1958	119	152	14414	2316	0.161	0.03	0.49	0.326	0	0	0
	1963	94	132	13504	2195	0.163	0.06	0.78	0.319	0	0	0
	1968	93	140	18789	3629	0.193	0.08	1.04	0.333	0	0	0
Corsetry	1954	69	105	21817	4559	0.209	0.20	1.40	0.337	2	0	0
	1958	62	101	28208	6340	0.225	0.22	1.27	0.326	2	0	0
	1963	63	123	36944	8763	0.237	0.19	1.19	0.319	2	0	0
	1968	53	119	40566	10123	0.250	0.20	1.25	0.333	2	0	0
Gloves (MLH 449.2)	1954	120	188	14406	2688	0.187	0.03	0.59	0.337	0	0	0
	1958	89	139	10505	1798	0.171	0.04	0.80	0.326	0	0	0
	1963	76	122	12731	2387	0.187	0.05	0.84	0.319	0	0	0
	1968	55	92	11338	2077	0.183	0.07	1.11	0.333	0	0	0
	1973	55	80	12770	2627	0.206	0.09	1.45	0.369	0	0	0
Footwear (MLH 450)	1954	529	778	192337	28566	0.149	0.09	0.63	0.718	1	0	0
	1958	457	674	176126	25157	0.143	0.11	0.72	0.724	1	0	0
	1963	370	615	206016	37473	0.182	0.15	0.91	0.731	1	0	0
	1968	299	559	207150	38775	0.187	0.20	1.21	0.779	1	0	0
	1973	266	441	238701	47744	0.200	0.29	1.54	0.813	1	0	0
Refractory goods	1954	88	147	33677	5805	0.172	0.25	2.25	0.268	0	0	1
	1958	73	149	37460	6518	0.174	0.42	3.95	0.257	0	0	1
	1963	63	130	40633	8734	0.215	0.63	6.02	0.256	0	0	1
	1968	44	111	52710	12125	0.230	0.71	5.67	0.289	0	0	1
	1973	47	—	60518	16273	0.269	—	6.56	0.385	0	0	1

Table B6 (continued)

Industry	Year	NFIRMS	NPLANTS	SS	PROFIT	PCM	K/N	K/L	UNION	ADTYPE	RDTYPE	CHANGE
Building bricks	1954	309	543	60779	12568	0.207	0.12	1.70	0.268	0	0	1
	1958	224	525	54900	9440	0.172	0.12	1.87	0.257	0	0	1
	1963	179	433	71157	16717	0.235	0.20	2.49	0.256	0	0	1
	1968	109	324	64763	15739	0.243	0.45	5.25	0.289	0	0	1
Sanitary ware of fireclay, etc.	1954	82	97	17909	3339	0.186	0.14	1.15	0.268	0	0	1
	1958	70	85	13784	2066	0.150	0.19	1.75	0.257	0	0	1
	1963	60	81	17383	3606	0.207	0.26	2.34	0.256	0	0	1
	1968	35	72	17796	3823	0.215	0.42	3.88	0.289	0	0	1
Tiles, pipes, and other products of fireclay, etc.	1954	62	84	9536	1714	0.180	0.17	1.91	0.268	0	0	1
	1958	52	96	9312	1384	0.149	0.13	1.96	0.257	0	0	1
	1963	32	51	9728	2302	0.237	0.24	2.53	0.256	0	0	1
	1968	28	37	11420	2728	0.239	0.45	3.79	0.289	0	0	1
Tiles, other than of precast concrete and brick earth	1954	36	44	12799	2808	0.219	0.54	2.36	0.574	0	0	0
	1958	25	32	11454	2234	0.195	0.79	3.17	0.524	0	0	0
	1963	17	28	16758	3863	0.231	1.52	5.04	0.569	0	0	0
	1968	10	22	19210	3499	0.182	2.78	8.09	0.721	0	0	0
Sanitary earthenware	1954	16	21	7719	2117	0.274	0.28	1.33	0.574	0	0	1
	1958	14	17	6663	1502	0.225	0.59	2.34	0.524	0	0	1
	1963	14	18	11562	2818	0.244	0.80	2.46	0.569	0	0	1
	1968	7	14	12762	3348	0.262	0.74	2.20	0.721	0	0	1

Product	Year											
China, earthenware, etc., domestic and ornamental	1954	117	143	30243	6367	0.211	0.29	1.11	0.574	0	0	1
	1958	116	152	32197	6611	0.205	0.26	1.05	0.524	0	0	1
	1963	94	132	35215	7119	0.202	0.26	0.95	0.569	0	0	1
	1968	76	121	40676	9435	0.232	0.32	1.15	0.721	0	0	1
Electrical ware of porcelain, earthenware, or stoneware	1954	14	20	6562	1456	0.222	0.58	1.95	0.574	0	0	1
	1958	12	18	8122	2027	0.250	0.83	2.53	0.524	0	0	1
	1963	13	22	10133	2653	0.262	1.15	3.58	0.569	0	0	1
	1968	10	20	10413	1995	0.192	1.23	3.85	0.721	0	0	1
Glass containers	1954	38	58	41369	7882	0.191	1.22	2.98	0.411	0	0	1
	1958	32	51	48845	9591	0.196	1.69	3.49	0.394	0	0	1
	1963	23	41	56727	10781	0.190	2.27	3.91	0.422	0	0	1
	1968	19	37	62587	13997	0.224	3.02	5.15	0.524	0	0	1
Domestic and fancy glassware	1954	19	26	7062	1858	0.263	0.11	0.47	0.411	1	0	0
	1958	16	20	7544	1563	0.207	0.29	1.00	0.394	1	0	0
	1963	15	18	9446	3088	0.327	0.41	1.32	0.422	1	0	0
	1968	16	24	18584	5410	0.291	0.67	1.67	0.524	1	0	0
Glass fibre and miscellaneous glass products	1954	15	22	6283	1995	0.318	0.55	4.49	0.411	0	1	0
	1958	22	34	10631	3104	0.292	0.43	3.40	0.394	0	1	0
	1963	29	40	14873	4490	0.302	0.66	5.10	0.422	0	1	0
Glass fibre and manufactures thereof	1963	9	12	9683	3334	0.344	2.45	9.56	0.422	0	2	0
	1968	7	10	12907	5270	0.408	3.22	9.15	0.524	0	2	0
Cement (MLH 464)	1954	13	47	68489	19738	0.288	2.52	9.41	0.268	0	0	0
	1958	13	50	70011	17720	0.253	2.71	10.64	0.257	0	0	0
	1963	14	54	83280	26467	0.318	3.79	14.55	0.256	0	0	0
	1968	9	53	89608	25912	0.289	6.26	24.08	0.289	0	0	0
	1973	8	53	127577	39435	0.309	7.45	27.07	0.385	0	0	0

Table B6 (continued)

Industry	Year	NFIRMS	NPLANTS	SS	PROFIT	PCM	K/N	K/L	UNION	ADTYPE	RDTYPE	CHANGE
Lime and whiting	1954	37	45	9671	2038	0.211	0.60	6.71	0.268	0	0	1
	1958	33	49	9989	2392	0.239	0.63	8.74	0.257	0	0	1
	1963	26	35	9999	2776	0.278	0.71	8.92	0.256	0	0	1
	1968	11	17	11626	2421	0.208	2.53	20.61	0.289	0	0	1
Pre-cast concrete goods	1954	258	362	48767	8572	0.176	0.14	2.01	0.268	0	0	1
	1958	206	312	49582	8490	0.171	0.19	2.63	0.257	0	0	1
	1963	201	337	65103	13518	0.208	0.23	3.06	0.256	0	0	1
	1968	229	384	107266	25685	0.239	0.41	5.04	0.289	0	0	1
Asbestos cement goods	1954	8	20	21662	4755	0.220	1.18	3.11	0.268	0	0	1
	1958	7	21	20931	4575	0.219	1.25	3.61	0.257	0	0	1
	1963	8	23	26577	6613	0.249	1.47	3.94	0.256	0	0	1
	1968	8	22	27503	7212	0.262	2.06	5.53	0.289	0	0	1
Builders' woodwork and prefabricated timber buildings	1954	180	202	39392	4570	0.116	0.09	0.89	0.456	0	0	1
	1958	147	173	40900	5089	0.124	0.12	1.11	0.435	0	0	1
	1963	173	208	72485	14250	0.197	0.16	1.38	0.394	0	0	1
	1968	228	282	103423	19090	0.185	0.18	1.70	0.323	0	0	1
Wood chipboard	1963	9	16	6603	1387	0.210	0.78	6.17	0.394	0	0	0
	1968	11	18	11087	2166	0.195	1.04	6.39	0.323	0	0	0
Plywood and textured boards	1963	17	17	7218	569	0.079	0.41	3.17	0.394	0	0	0
	1968	19	24	17348	2560	0.148	0.43	3.41	0.323	0	0	0

	Year												
Domestic furniture, not upholstered, mainly of wood	1954	340	424	90625	12637	0.139	0.11	0.98	0.456	0	0	0	0
	1958	265	389	81017	11896	0.147	0.12	1.06	0.435	0	0	0	0
	1963	238	380	89233	15734	0.176	0.13	1.16	0.394	0	0	0	0
	1968	237	298	111984	25856	0.231	0.24	1.98	0.323	0	0	0	0
Upholstered furniture	1954	207	249	41073	6001	0.146	0.03	0.43	0.456	0	0	0	0
	1958	155	190	41476	5678	0.137	0.05	0.54	0.435	0	0	0	0
	1963	159	195	55426	9830	0.177	0.07	0.70	0.394	0	0	0	0
	1968	162	200	56159	10789	0.192	0.10	1.13	0.323	0	0	0	0
Office, school, and other furniture	1954	174	199	28139	4339	0.154	0.08	0.91	0.456	0	0	0	0
	1958	179	216	36409	5271	0.145	0.10	1.04	0.435	0	0	0	0
	1963	137	162	33916	5949	0.175	0.17	1.73	0.394	0	0	0	0
	1968	112	132	36408	6781	0.186	0.20	1.93	0.323	0	0	0	0
Bedding	1954	108	145	28579	4078	0.143	0.15	1.94	0.456	1	0	0	0
	1958	72	103	26141	3686	0.141	0.19	2.13	0.435	1	0	0	0
	1963	55	53	30032	5471	0.182	0.35	2.06	0.394	1	0	0	0
	1968	53	90	44569	8526	0.191	0.20	1.63	0.323	1	0	0	0
Wooden containers and baskets (MLH 475)	1954	271	332	39675	4607	0.116	0.05	0.87	0.456	0	0	0	0
	1958	192	229	29239	3828	0.131	0.08	1.34	0.435	0	0	0	0
	1963	165	216	30027	4554	0.152	0.09	1.55	0.394	0	0	0	0
	1968	147	197	31349	5388	0.172	0.11	1.92	0.323	0	0	0	0
	1973	160	228	49112	10133	0.206	0.12	2.27	0.340	0	0	0	0
Cork manufactures	1954	19	25	3022	575	0.190	0.10	1.71	0.456	0	0	0	0
	1958	13	18	3348	576	0.172	0.25	3.39	0.435	0	0	0	0
	1963	8	9	3855	1013	0.263	0.59	3.87	0.394	0	0	0	0
	1968	7	10	4116	812	0.197	0.47	3.98	0.323	0	0	0	0

Table B6 (continued)

Industry	Year	NFIRMS	NPLANTS	SS	PROFIT	PCM	K/N	K/L	UNION	ADTYPE	RDTYPE	CHANGE
Paper and board (MLH 481)	1954	186	253	311039	71029	0.228	1.83	6.37	0.367	0	0	1
	1958	167	262	332236	57771	0.174	2.74	8.81	0.361	0	0	1
	1963	144	267	381309	74910	0.196	3.18	9.66	0.377	0	0	1
	1968	111	207	385640	71760	0.186	5.05	13.98	0.403	0	0	1
	1973	92	171	415335	74153	0.179	6.31	18.04	0.481	0	0	1
Rigid boxes	1954	211	252	25264	4885	0.193	0.12	1.54	0.367	0	0	0
	1958	177	216	21835	4041	0.185	0.13	1.65	0.361	0	0	0
	1963	154	188	21606	4474	0.207	0.12	1.50	0.377	0	0	0
	1968	117	147	19616	3891	0.198	0.16	2.05	0.403	0	0	0
Cartons	1954	71	92	42532	7823	0.184	0.79	3.68	0.367	0	0	0
	1958	72	91	52073	7774	0.149	1.07	4.35	0.361	0	0	0
	1963	75	102	66679	10795	0.162	1.25	5.15	0.377	0	0	0
	1968	83	113	90021	16757	0.186	1.32	5.47	0.403	0	0	0
Fibreboard packing cases	1954	27	43	38845	8289	0.213	0.94	4.07	0.367	0	0	0
	1958	26	45	46420	8211	0.177	1.03	4.28	0.361	0	0	0
	1963	46	77	75703	13950	0.184	0.92	3.79	0.377	0	0	0
	1968	49	106	112448	18763	0.167	1.18	4.90	0.403	0	0	0
Composite containers of board and metal	1963	10	12	5046	905	0.179	0.64	4.68	0.377	0	0	0
	1968	8	9	6120	1250	0.204	0.81	3.04	0.403	0	0	0
Packaging products of paper and associated materials other than bags and sacks	1963	18	22	12122	3338	0.275	0.75	5.54	0.377	0	0	0
	1968	22	36	28625	4477	0.156	0.99	5.98	0.403	0	0	0

	Year										
Notepaper, envelopes, and boxed stationery, plain postcards, and letter cards	1954	38	50	23205	5164	0.223	0.50	2.17	0.367	0	0	1
	1958	40	58	31337	6112	0.195	0.52	1.97	0.361	0	0	1
	1963	29	44	30927	7668	0.248	0.91	3.18	0.377	0	0	1
Magazines and periodicals	1954	104	146	107087	23731	0.222	0.43	1.77	0.838	1	0	0
	1958	91	128	127585	24462	0.192	0.66	2.22	0.838	1	0	0
	1963	89	149	151136	38114	0.252	0.69	2.70	0.835	1	0	0
	1968	101	170	149372	37386	0.250	0.75	3.67	0.793	1	0	0
Books	1954	127	139	54363	12424	0.229	0.35	2.10	0.838	1	0	0
	1958	131	151	70757	15928	0.225	0.48	2.44	0.838	1	0	0
	1963	113	149	89774	27755	0.309	0.76	3.91	0.835	1	0	0
Stereotyping, electrotyping, and engraving	1954	132	167	15780	3569	0.226	0.13	1.95	0.838	0	0	1
	1958	141	175	20284	4431	0.218	0.16	2.32	0.838	0	0	1
	1963	141	198	25790	5856	0.227	0.20	2.89	0.835	0	0	1
Cellular rubber products	1954	7	9	11450	1369	0.120	2.14	4.21	0.304	0	0	0
	1958	9	12	11155	1056	0.095	1.58	5.72	0.309	0	0	0
	1963	11	16	15573	2260	0.145	1.18	3.96	0.344	0	0	0
Rubber products other than tyres, hose and tubing, and belting	1963	145	223	138082	28431	0.206	0.75	3.00	0.344	0	0	0
	1968	133	213	156152	38990	0.250	0.94	3.70	0.289	0	0	0
Linoleum, plastic floor covering, leather cloth, etc. (MLH 492)	1954	22	29	50166	8403	0.167	2.12	3.97	0.304	0	0	1
	1958	21	31	47266	8095	0.171	2.25	4.75	0.309	0	0	1
	1963	29	44	77154	17841	0.231	2.27	5.00	0.344	0	0	1
	1968	21	31	71197	17027	0.239	3.81	6.97	0.289	0	0	1
	1973	23	37	91327	25859	0.283	3.72	8.51	0.308	0	0	1

Table B6 (continued)

Industry	Year	NFIRMS	NPLANTS	SS	PROFIT	PCM	K/N	K/L	UNION	ADTYPE	RDTYPE	CHANGE
Brushes and brooms (MLH 493)	1954	116	143	20781	3529	0.170	0.13	1.51	0.304	1	0	0
	1958	85	106	19241	4574	0.238	0.18	1.84	0.309	1	0	0
	1963	66	85	20905	4226	0.202	0.25	2.23	0.344	1	0	0
	1968	50	70	20913	4159	0.199	0.37	3.00	0.289	1	0	0
	1973	60	70	24061	5528	0.230	0.45	3.66	0.308	1	0	0
Toys and games	1954	107	140	35143	6665	0.190	0.22	1.30	0.304	1	0	0
	1958	87	117	35248	7988	0.227	0.29	1.69	0.309	1	0	0
	1963	69	108	39519	10791	0.273	0.40	2.05	0.344	1	0	0
	1968	64	104	57697	17575	0.305	0.66	2.55	0.289	1	0	0
Children's and invalids' carriages	1954	23	25	5818	949	0.163	0.08	0.58	0.509	1	0	0
	1958	17	19	4898	802	0.164	0.12	0.80	0.499	1	0	0
	1963	21	27	7484	1390	0.186	0.15	1.06	0.528	1	0	0
	1968	13	19	8401	1962	0.234	0.33	1.84	0.567	1	0	0
Pens and mechanical pencils	1954	28	35	7560	2110	0.279	0.36	2.93	0.304	2	0	0
	1958	18	23	9454	3147	0.333	0.46	2.36	0.309	2	0	0
	1963	14	18	9709	3428	0.353	0.56	2.86	0.344	2	0	0
Lead pencils, crayons, etc.	1958	12	12	2428	623	0.257	0.24	1.94	0.309	1	0	1
	1963	11	12	2512	614	0.244	0.34	2.97	0.344	1	0	1
Office machinery requisites	1954	18	26	8343	2078	0.249	0.27	1.73	0.304	0	0	0
	1958	19	25	10283	2118	0.206	0.29	1.37	0.309	0	0	0
	1963	18	26	13234	2909	0.220	0.46	2.17	0.344	0	0	0
	1968	21	28	19115	5384	0.282	0.68	3.84	0.289	0	0	0

Plastics products (MLH 496)												
	1954	218	258	45274	8217	0.182	0.22	1.95	0.304	0	0	0
	1958	234	295	65068	11416	0.175	0.25	2.14	0.309	0	0	0
	1963	377	491	145292	33741	0.232	0.32	2.63	0.344	0	0	0
	1968	472	625	251331	62572	0.249	0.57	4.29	0.289	0	0	0
	1973	645	722	394152	97511	0.247	0.85	6.26	0.308	0	0	0
Musical instruments												
	1954	51	63	5719	953	0.167	0.08	1.27	0.304	0	0	0
	1958	39	50	5549	980	0.177	0.08	1.10	0.309	0	0	0
	1963	30	42	6829	1684	0.247	0.08	0.83	0.344	0	0	0
	1968	30	48	8285	1858	0.224	0.12	1.68	0.289	0	0	0
	1973	34	52	13468	3323	0.247	0.14	1.85	0.308	0	0	0

Notes: The classification according to MLH industries follows the 1968 Standard Industrial Classification, unless otherwise stated.

NFIRMS is the number of firms employing at least 25 persons.

NPLANTS is the number of plants employing at least 25 persons.

SS is sales revenue (in £1000) deflated by the general producer price index.

PROFIT is the net value of output minus wages and salaries (in £1000) deflated by the general producer price index.

PCM is the price-cost margin, i.e., net value of output minus wages and salaries divided by sales revenue.

K is the value of capital stock in 1980 prices (in £ million) (my estimate; see text for details).

L is employment (in 1000).

N is the number of plants with at least 25 employees.

UNION is union density (i.e., the number of unionized employees over the total number of employees) of the corresponding industry group.

ADTYPE takes the value 0 for an industry with typical advertising-sales ratio lower than 1%, 1 for an industry with typical advertising-sales ratio between 1% and 2%, and 2 for an industry with typical advertising-sales ratio higher than 2%.

RDTYPE takes the value 0 for an industry with typical R&D-sales ratio lower than 1%, 1 for an industry with typical R&D-sales ratio between 1% and 2%, and 2 for an industry with typical R&D-sales ratio higher than 2%.

CHANGE takes the value 1 for an industry with a change in competition regime and 0 otherwise.

Glossary of British Terms

Appendix A

UK	US
Aluminium	Aluminum
Animal feeding stuffs	Animal foodstuffs
Children's carriages	Baby carriages
Electric cookers	Electric stoves
Fibreboard packing cases	Fiberboard packing cases
Gelatine	Gelatin
Glass fibres	Glass fibers
Gramophone records	Phonograph records
Jewellery	Jewelry
Lifts	Elevators
Made-up textiles	Fully manufactured textiles
Man-made fibres	Man-made fibers
Pedal cycles	Bicycles
Perry	Fermented pear juice
Petrol	Gasoline
Self-raising flour	Self-rising flour
Slide fasteners	Zippers
Spectacles	Eyeglasses
Trams	Streetcars
Tyres	Tires
Wagons	Railway freight cars

Whisky   Whiskey

Woollen   Woolen

Appendix B

UK   **US**

Accumulators   Storage batteries

Aluminium   Aluminium

Carbons   Carbon paper

Children's carriages   Baby carriages

Electric cookers   Electric stoves

Engineers' and mechanicians' goods   Engineers' and mechanics' goods

Fibreboard packing cases   Fiberboard packing cases

Gelatine   Gelatin

Glass fibres   Glass fibers

Gramophone records   Phonograph records

Gramophones   Phonographs

Ice lollies   Ice pops

Invalids' carriages   Wheelchairs

Jewellery   Jewelry

Lifts   Elevators

Made-up textiles   Fully manufactured textiles

Man-made fibres   Man-made fibers

Perry   Fermented pear juice

Potato crisps   Potato chips

Pyjamas   Pajamas

Sanitary towels   Sanitary napkins

Spectacles   Eyeglasses

Tyres   Tires

Whisky   Whiskey

Woollen   Woolen

References

Publications used only as data sources are detailed in the text and are not included here.

Acs, Z. J., and D. B. Audretsch (1988). Innovation in large and small firms: An empirical analysis. *American Economic Review*, 78: 678–690.

Aghion, P., M. Dewatripont, and P. Rey (1999). Competition, financial discipline and growth. *Review of Economic Studies*, 66: 825–852.

Aghion, P., and P. Howitt (1997). A Schumpeterian perspective on growth and competition. In D. M. Kreps and K. F. Wallis, eds., *Advances in Economics and Econometrics: Theory and Applications. Seventh World Congress.* Vol. 2. Cambridge: Cambridge University Press.

Aghion, P., and P. Howitt (1998). *Endogenous Growth Theory*. Cambridge, MA: M.I.T. Press.

Aghion, P., and M. Schankerman (2000). *A Model of Market Enhancing Infrastructure*. CEPR Discussion Paper no. 2462. London: Centre for Economic Policy Research.

Armstrong, A., and A. Silberston (1965). Size of plant, size of enterprise and concentration in British manufacturing industry 1935–1958. *Journal of the Royal Statistical Society*, series A, 128: 395–420.

Asch, P., and J. J. Seneca (1976). Is collusion profitable? *Review of Economics and Statistics*, 58: 1–12.

Baden-Fuller, C. W. F. (1980). *The Economics of Private Brands with Special Reference to the Domestic Appliance Industries of the UK and USA*. Ph.D. thesis, London School of Economics.

Bain, G. S., and R. Price (1980). *Profiles of Union Growth: A Comparative Statistical Portrait of Eight Countries*. Oxford: Basil Blackwell.

Bertschek, I. (1995). Product and process innovation as a response to increasing imports and foreign direct investment. *Journal of Industrial Economics*, 43: 341–357.

Bittlingmayer, G. (1985). Did antitrust policy cause the great merger wave? *Journal of Law and Economics*, 28: 77–118.

Blundell, R., R. Griffith, and J. Van Reenen (1995). Dynamic count data models of technological innovation. *Economic Journal*, 105: 333–344.

Board of Trade (1944). *Survey of International Cartels*. London: Board of Trade.

Board of Trade (1946). *Survey of Internal Cartels*. London: Board of Trade.

Board of Trade (1949). *Report of the Committee on Resale Price Maintenance*. London: H.M.S.O.

Board of Trade (1949–1952). *Monopolies and Restrictive Practices (Inquiry and Control) Act, 1948: Annual Report by the Board of Trade*. London: H.M.S.O.

Board of Trade (1953–1956). *Monopolies and Restrictive Practices Acts, 1948 and 1953: Annual Report by the Board of Trade*. London: H.M.S.O.

Boone, J. (2000). Competitive pressure: The effects of investment in product and process innovation. *RAND Journal of Economics*, 31: 549–569.

Bound, J., C. Cummins, Z. Griliches, B. H. Hall, and A. Jaffe (1984). Who does R&D and who patents? In Z. Griliches, ed., *R&D, Patents, and Productivity*. Chicago: University of Chicago Press.

Bowley, A. L. (1924). *The Mathematical Groundwork of Economics*. Oxford: Oxford University Press.

Brander, J. A., and B. J. Spencer (1985). Tacit collusion, free entry and welfare. *Journal of Industrial Economics*, 33: 277–294.

Bresnahan, T. F., and P. C. Reiss (1991). Entry and competition in concentrated markets. *Journal of Political Economy*, 99: 977–1009.

Broadberry, S. N., and N. F. R. Crafts (1996). British economic policy and industrial performance in the early post-war years. *Business History*, 38: 65–91.

Broadberry, S. N., and N. F. R. Crafts (2000). *Competition and Innovation in 1950's Britain*. Working Paper in Economic History no. 57. London School of Economics.

Brock, W. A., and J. A. Scheinkman (1985). Price setting supergames with capacity constraints. *Review of Economic Studies*, 52: 371–382.

Burn, D., ed. (1958). *The Structure of British Industry*. 2 vols. Cambridge: Cambridge University Press.

Cameron, A. C., and P. K. Trivedi (1998). *Regression Analysis of Count Data*. Cambridge: Cambridge University Press.

Caves, R. E. (1988). Trade exposure and changing structures of US manufacturing industries. In A. M. Spence and H. A. Hazard, eds., *International Competitiveness*. Cambridge, MA: Ballinger.

Chevalier, J. A. (1995). Capital structure and product market competition: Empirical evidence from the supermarket industry. *American Economic Review*, 85: 415–435.

Cohen, W. (1995). Empirical studies of innovative activity. In P. Stoneman, ed., *Handbook of the Economics of Innovation and Technological Change*. Oxford: Blackwell.

Conyon, M., and S. Machin (1991). Market structure and the empirical specification of price-cost margins. *Economics Letters*, 35: 227–231.

Corley, T. A. B. (1966). *Domestic Electrical Appliances*. London: Jonathan Cape.

Cowling, K., and M. Waterson (1976). Price-cost margins and market structure. *Economica*, 43: 267–274.

Crepon, B., and E. Duguet (1997). Research and development, competition and innovation: Pseudo-maximum likelihood and simulated maximum likelihood methods applied to count data models with heterogeneity. *Journal of Econometrics*, 79: 355–378.

Curry, B., and K. D. George (1983). Industrial concentration: A survey. *Journal of Industrial Economics*, 31: 203–255.

Cyert, R. M., and M. H. deGroot (1973). An analysis of cooperation and learning in a duopoly context. *American Economic Review*, 63: 24–37.

d'Aspermont, C., and M. Motta (2000). Tougher price competition or lower concentration: A trade-off for antitrust authorities? In G. Norman and J.-F. Thisse, eds., *Market Structure and Competition Policy: Game-Theoretic Approaches*. Cambridge: Cambridge University Press.

Dasgupta, P., and J. Stiglitz (1980). Industrial structure and the nature of innovative activity. *Economic Journal*, 90: 266–293.

Davidson, C., and R. Deneckere (1990). Excess capacity and collusion. *International Economic Review*, 31: 521–541.

Davies, S. (1980). Minimum efficient size and seller concentration: An empirical problem. *Journal of Industrial Economics*, 28: 287–301.

deMelo, J., and S. Urata (1986). The influence of increased foreign competition on industrial concentration and profitability. *International Journal of Industrial Organization*, 4: 287–304.

Demsetz, H. (1973). Industry structure, market rivalry, and public policy. *Journal of Law and Economics*, 16: 1–9.

Dick, A. R. (1996a). Identifying contracts, combinations and conspiracies in restraint of trade. *Managerial and Decision Economics*, 17: 203–216.

Dick, A. R. (1996b). When are cartels stable contracts? *Journal of Law and Economics*, 39: 241–283.

Director General of Fair Trading (DGFT) (1981). *Annual Report of the Director General of Fair Trading for the Period January 1980 to December 1980*. London: H.M.S.O.

Dixit, A. (1979). A model of duopoly suggesting a theory of entry barriers. *Bell Journal of Economics*, 10: 20–32.

Dixit, A., and J. Stiglitz (1977). Monopolistic competition and optimal product diversity. *American Economic Review*, 67: 297–308.

Edgeworth, F. Y. (1881). *Mathematical Psychics: An Essay on the Application of Mathematics to the Moral Sciences*. London: Kegan Paul.

Eissa, N. (1995). *Taxation and Labour Supply of Married Women: The Tax Reform Act of 1986 as a Natural Experiment*. NBER Working Paper no. 5023. Cambridge, MA: National Bureau of Economic Research.

Eissa, N., and J. B. Liebman (1996). Labour supply response to the earned income tax credit. *Quarterly Journal of Economics*, 111: 605–637.

Elliott, D. C., and J. D. Gribbin (1977). The abolition of cartels and structural change in the United Kingdom. In A. P. Jacquemin and H. W. deJong, eds., *Welfare Aspects of Industrial Markets*. Leiden: Martinus Nijhoff.

Evely, R., and I. M. D. Little (1960). *Concentration in British Industry: An Empirical Study of the Structure of Industrial Production, 1935–51*. Cambridge: Cambridge University Press.

Farber, S. (1981). Buyer market structure and R&D effort: A simultaneous-equations model. *Review of Economics and Statistics*, 63: 336–345.

Fershtman, C., and N. Gandal (1994). Disadvantageous semicollusion. *International Journal of Industrial Organisation*, 12: 141–154.

Fershtman, C., and E. Muller (1986). Capital investments and price agreements in semicollusive markets. *RAND Journal of Economics*, 17: 214–226.

Fershtman, C., and A. Pakes (2000). A dynamic oligopoly with collusion and price wars. *RAND Journal of Economics*, 21: 207–236.

Fraas, A. G., and D. F. Greer (1977). Market structure and price collusion: An empirical analysis. *Journal of Industrial Economics*, 26: 21–44.

Freyer, T. (1992). *Regulating Big Business: Antitrust in Great Britain and America, 1880–1990*. Cambridge: Cambridge University Press.

Friedman, J. W., and J.-F. Thisse (1993). Partial collusion fosters minimum product differentiation. *RAND Journal of Economics*, 24: 631–645.

Friedman, J. W., and J.-F. Thisse (1994). Sustainable collusion in oligopoly with free entry. *European Economic Review*, 38: 271–283.

Fudenberg, D., and J. Tirole (1991). *Game Theory*. Cambridge, MA: M.I.T. Press.

Gasmi, F., J. J. Laffont, and Q. Vuong (1992). Econometric analysis of collusive behavior in a soft-drink market. *Journal of Economics and Management Strategy*, 1: 277–312.

Geroski, P. A. (1990). Innovation, technological opportunity, and market structure. *Oxford Economic Papers*, 42: 586–602.

Geroski, P. A. (1991). *Market Dynamics and Entry*. Oxford: Basil Blackwell.

Geroski, P. A. (1994). *Market Structure, Corporate Performance and Innovative Activity*. Oxford: Clarendon Press.

Geroski, P. A., and R. Pomroy (1990). Innovation and the evolution of market structure. *Journal of Industrial Economics*, 38: 299–314.

Guenault, P. H., and J. M. Jackson (1974). *The Control of Monopoly in the United Kingdom*. 2nd ed. London: Longman.

Häckner, J. (1994). Collusive pricing in markets for vertically differentiated products. *International Journal of Industrial Organisation*, 12: 155–177.

Hannah, L. (1979). Mergers, cartels and concentration: Legal factors in the US and European experience. In N. Horn and J. Kocka, eds., *Law and the Formation of the Big Enterprises in the 19th and Early 20th Centuries*. Göttingen: Vandenhoeck & Ruprecht.

Hannah, L., and J. A. Kay (1977). *Concentration in Modern Industry: Theory, Measurement and the UK Experience*. London: Macmillan.

Harrington, J. E. (1989). Collusion and predation under (almost) free entry. *International Journal of Industrial Organization*, 7: 381–401.

Harrington, J. E. (1991). The joint profit maximum as a free-entry equilibrium outcome. *European Economic Review*, 35: 1087–1101.

Hart, P. E. (1985). *Recent Trends in Concentration in British Industry*. NIESR Discussion Paper no. 82. London: National Institute of Economic and Social Research.

Hart, P. E., and R. Clarke (1980). *Concentration in British Industry 1935–75*. Cambridge: Cambridge University Press.

Hart, P. E., and E. Morgan (1977). Market structure and economic performance in the United Kingdom. *Journal of Industrial Economics*, 25: 177–193.

Hart, P. E., and S. J. Prais (1956). The analysis of business concentration: A statistical approach. *Journal of the Royal Statistical Society*, series A, 119: 150–191.

Hart, P. E., M. A. Utton, and G. Walshe (1973). *Mergers and Concentration in British Industry*. Cambridge: Cambridge University Press.

Hatch, J. H. (1970). *Competition in the British White Goods Industry*. Ph.D. thesis, Cambridge University.

Hatch, J. H. (1972). Stop-go and the domestic appliance industry: A case study. *Bulletin of the Oxford University Institute of Economics and Statistics*, 34: 345–358.

Hausman, J., B. H. Hall, and Z. Griliches (1984). Econometric models for count data with an application to the patents-R&D relationship. *Econometrica*, 52: 909–938.

Hay, G. A., and D. Kelley (1974). An empirical survey of price fixing conspiracies. *Journal of Law and Economics*, 17: 13–38.

Heath, J. B. (1961). Restrictive practices and after. *Manchester School of Economic and Social Studies*, 29: 173–202.

Heath, J. (1963). *Still Not Enough Competition? Business Restrictive Practices Re-examined*. 2nd ed. London: Institute of Economic Affairs.

Hsiao, C. (1986). *Analysis of Panel Data*. Cambridge: Cambridge University Press.

Hunter, A. (1966). *Competition and the Law*. London: George Allen.

Ireland, N. J. (1987). *Product Differentiation and Non-Price Competition*. Oxford: Blackwell.

Jacquemin, A., E. deGhellinck, and C. Huveneers (1980). Concentration and profitability in a small open economy. *Journal of Industrial Economics*, 29: 131–144.

Jacquemin, A., T. Nambu, and I. Dewez (1981). A dynamic analysis of export cartels: The Japanese case. *Economic Journal*, 91: 685–696.

Jehiel, P. (1992). Product differentiation and price collusion. *International Journal of Industrial Organization*, 10: 633–641.

Kamien, I., and N. L. Schwartz (1982). *Market Structure and Innovation*. Cambridge: Cambridge University Press.

Kessides, I. N. (1990). Market concentration, contestability, and sunk costs. *Review of Economics and Statistics*, 72: 614–622.

Kitchin, P. D. (1976). Effective rates of protection for United Kingdom manufacturing in 1963 and 1968. In M. J. Artis and A. R. Nobay, eds., *Essays in Economic Analysis: The Proceedings of the Association of University Teachers of Economics, Sheffield 1975*. Cambridge: Cambridge University Press.

Klepper, S. (1996). Entry, exit, growth, and innovation over the product life cycle. *American Economic Review*, 86: 562–583.

Klepper, S., and K. Simons (1997). Technological extinctions of industrial firms: An enquiry into their nature and causes. *Industrial and Corporate Change*, 6: 379–460.

Kuenne, R. E. (1980). Duopoly reaction functions under crippled optimisation regimes. *Oxford Economic Papers*, 32: 224–240.

Kuipers, J. D. (1950). *Resale Price Maintenance in Great Britain: With Special Reference to the Grocery Trade*. Wageningen: N. V. Drukkerij "Vada."

Levin, R. C., and P. C. Reiss (1988). Cost-reducing and demand-creating R&D with spillovers. *RAND Journal of Economics*, 19: 538–556.

Lunn, J. (1986). An empirical analysis of process and product patenting: A simultaneous-equation framework. *Journal of Industrial Economics*, 34: 319–330.

Lydall, H. F. (1958). Aspects of competition in manufacturing industry. *Bulletin of the Oxford University Institute of Statistics*, 20: 319–337.

Lyons, B., and C. Matraves (1996). Industrial concentration. In S. Davies, B. Lyons, et al., *Industrial Organization in the European Union: Structure, Strategy and the Competitive Mechanism*. Oxford: Clarendon Press.

MacKinnon, J. G., and H. White (1985). Some heteroskedasticity-consistent covariance matrix estimators with improved finite sample properties. *Journal of Econometrics*, 29: 305–325.

Mansfield, E., J. Rapoport, J. Schnee, S. Wagner, and M. Hamburger (1971). *Research and Innovation in the Modern Corporation*. London: Macmillan.

Martin, S. (1979a). Advertising, concentration, and profitability: The simultaneity problem. *Bell Journal of Economics*, 10: 639–647.

Martin, S. (1979b). Entry barriers, concentration, and profits. *Southern Economic Journal*, 46: 471–488.

Martin, S. (2002). *Advanced Industrial Economics*. 2nd ed. Oxford: Blackwell.

Matraves, C. (1992). *Endogenous Sunk Costs, Industry Size and Market Structure: A Four Country Test*. Discussion Paper no. 9224. Economics Research Centre, University of East Anglia (Norwich).

Maunder, P. (1972). Price leadership: An appraisal of its character in some British industries. *Business Economist*, 4: 132–140.

Mayers, J. B. (1963). Management and the British domestic electric appliance industry. *Journal of Industrial Economics*, 12: 20–32.

Mercer, H. (1995). *Constructing a Competitive Order: The Hidden History of British Antitrust Policies.* Cambridge: Cambridge University Press.

Mercer, H. (1998). *The Abolition of Resale Price Maintenance in Britain in 1964: A Turning Point for British Manufacturers?* Working Paper in Economic History no. 39. London School of Economics.

Meyer, B. D. (1995). Natural and quasi-experiments in economics. *Journal of Business and Economic Statistics,* 13: 151–161.

Milward, A. S., and G. Brennan (1996). *Britain's Place in the World: A Historical Inquiry into Import Controls, 1945–1960.* London: Routledge.

Monopolies and Restrictive Practices Commission (1955). *Collective Discrimination: A Report on Exclusive Dealing, Collective Boycotts, Aggregated Rebates and Other Discriminatory Trade Practices.* London: H.M.S.O.

Monopolies and Restrictive Practices Commission (1957). *Report on the Supply and Exports of Electrical and Allied Machinery and Plant.* London: H.M.S.O.

Monopolies Commission (1963). *Report on the Supply of Electrical Equipment for Mechanically Propelled Land Vehicles.* London: H.M.S.O.

Monopolies Commission (1973). *Parallel Pricing: A Report on the General Effect on the Public Interest of the Practice of Parallel Pricing.* London: H.M.S.O.

Montagna, C. (1995). Monopolistic competition with firm-specific costs. *Oxford Economic Papers,* 47: 318–328.

Morgan, A. D., and D. Martin (1975). Tariff reductions and UK imports of manufactures: 1955–1971. *National Institute Economic Review,* no. 72: 38–54.

Motta, M. (1992). Co-operative R&D and vertical product differentiation. *International Journal of Industrial Organization,* 10: 643–661.

Mukhopadhaya, A. K. (1985). Technological progress and change in market concentration in the U.S., 1963–1977. *Southern Economic Journal,* 52: 141–149.

National Board for Prices and Incomes (NBPI) (1968). *Prices of Secondary Batteries.* Report no. 61. London: H.M.S.O.

National Board for Prices and Incomes (NBPI) (1971). *Prices, Profits and Costs in Food Distribution.* Report no. 165. London: H.M.S.O.

Nelson, R. L. (1959). *Merger Movements in American Industry, 1895–1956.* Princeton, NJ: Princeton University Press.

Nicholson, R. J., and S. Gupta (1960). Output and productivity changes in British manufacturing industry, 1948–1954: A study from Census of Production data. *Journal of the Royal Statistical Society,* series A, 123: 427–459.

Nickell, S. (1995). *The Performance of Companies: The Relationship Between the External Environment, Management Strategies and Corporate Performance.* Oxford: Blackwell.

Nocke, V. (2000). *Monopolisation and Industry Structure.* Nuffield College Economics Paper 2000-w27. Oxford University.

Norman, G., and J.-F. Thisse (1996). Product variety and welfare under tough and soft pricing regimes. *Economic Journal,* 106: 76–91.

O'Brien, D. P., W. S. Howe, D. M. Wright, and R. J. O'Brien (1979). *Competition Policy, Profitability and Growth*. London: Macmillan.

O'Mahony, M., and N. Oulton (1990). *Industry-Level Estimates of the Capital Stock in UK Manufacturing, 1948–85*. NIESR Discussion Paper no. 172. London: National Institute of Economic and Social Research.

Overstreet, T. R. (1983). *Resale Price Maintenance: Economic Theories and Empirical Evidence*. Washington, DC: Federal Trade Commission, Bureau of Economics.

Pakes, A., and M. Schankerman (1984). The rate of obsolescence of patents, research gestation lags, and the private returns to research resources. In Z. Griliches, ed., *R&D, Patents, and Productivity*. Chicago: University of Chicago Press.

Pavitt, K., ed. (1980). *Technical Innovation and British Economic Performance*. London: Macmillan.

Phillips, A. (1972). An econometric study of price-fixing, market structure and performance in British industry in the early 1950s. In K. Cowling, ed., *Market Structure and Corporate Behaviour: Theory and Empirical Analysis of the Firm*. London: Gray-Mills.

Phlips, L. (1995). *Competition Policy: A Game-Theoretic Perspective*. Cambridge: Cambridge University Press.

Pickering, J. F. (1966). *Resale Price Maintenance in Practice*. London: George Allen & Unwin.

Pickering, J. F. (1974). The abolition of resale price maintenance in Great Britain. *Oxford Economic Papers*, 26: 120–146.

Political and Economic Planning (PEP) (1957). *Industrial Trade Associations: Activities and Organisation*. London: George Allen & Unwin.

Political and Economic Planning (1959). *Tariffs and Trade in Western Europe*. London: George Allen & Unwin.

Pratten, C. F. (1971). *Economies of Scale in Manufacturing Industry*. Cambridge: Cambridge University Press.

Registrar of Restrictive Trading Agreements (RRTA) (1961–1973). *Report*. London: H.M.S.O.

Robinson, W. T., and J. Chiang (1996). Are Sutton's predictions robust? Empirical insights into advertising, R&D, and concentration. *Journal of Industrial Economics*, 44: 389–408.

Robson, M., J. Townsend, and K. Pavitt (1988). Sectoral patterns of production and use of innovations in the UK: 1945–1983. *Research Policy*, 17: 1–14.

Rowley, C. K. (1966). *The British Monopolies Commission*. London: George Allen.

Salop, S. (1979). Monopolistic competition with outside goods. *Bell Journal of Economics*, 10: 141–156.

Sawyer, M. C. (1971). Concentration in British manufacturing industry. *Oxford Economic Papers*, 23: 352–383.

Scherer, F. M. (1992). *International High-Technology Competition*. Cambridge, MA: Harvard University Press.

Scherer, F. M., A. Beckenstein, E. Kaufer, R. D. Murphy, and F. Bougeon-Maasen (1975). *The Economics of Multi-plant Operation: An International Comparisons Study*. Cambridge, MA: Harvard University Press.

Scherer, F. M., D. Harhoff, and J. Kukies (2000). Uncertainty and the size distribution of rewards from innovation. *Journal of Evolutionary Economics*, 10: 175–200.

Scherer, F. M., and K. Huh (1992). R&D reactions to high-technology import competition. *Review of Economics and Statistics*, 74: 202–212.

Scherer, F. M., and D. Ross (1990). *Industrial Market Structure and Economic Performance*. Boston: Houghton Mifflin.

Schmalensee, R. (1992). Sunk costs and market structure: A review article. *Journal of Industrial Economics*, 40: 125–134.

Schott, K. (1976). Investment in private industrial research and development in Britain. *Journal of Industrial Economics*, 25: 81–99.

Seade, J. (1980). On the effects of entry. *Econometrica*, 48: 479–489.

Secretary of State for Prices and Consumer Protection (SSPCP) (1979). *A Review of Restrictive Trade Practices Policy*. London: H.M.S.O.

Selten, R. (1984). Are cartel laws bad for business? In H. Hauptmann, W. Krelle, and K. C. Mosler, eds., *Operations Research and Economic Theory: Essays in Honor of Martin J. Beckmann*. Berlin and Heidelberg: Springer-Verlag.

Shaked, A., and J. Sutton (1990). Multiproduct firms and market structure. *RAND Journal of Economics*, 28: 605–628.

Shapley, L., and M. Shubik (1969). Price strategy oligopoly with product differentiation. *Kyklos*, 22: 30–44.

Shaw, R. W., and C. J. Sutton (1976). *Industry and Competition: Industrial Case Studies*. London and Basingstoke: Macmillan.

Shubik, M. (with R. Levitan) (1980). *Market Structure and Behavior*. Cambridge, MA: Harvard University Press.

Simon, H. A., and C. P. Bonini (1958). The size distribution of business firms. *American Economic Review*, 48: 607–617.

Slade, M. (1995). Product rivalry with multiple strategic weapons: An analysis of price and advertising competition. *Journal of Economics and Management Strategy*, 4: 445–476.

Sleuwaegen, L., and H. Yamawaki (1988). The formation of the European common market and changes in structure and performance. *European Economic Review*, 32: 1451–1475.

Spence, M. (1976). Product differentiation and welfare. *American Economic Review, Papers and Proceedings*, 66: 407–414.

Suslow, V. (1991). Cartel contract duration: Empirical evidence from international cartels. University of Michigan. Mimeo.

Sutton, J. (1991). *Sunk Costs and Market Structure: Price Competition, Advertising, and the Evolution of Concentration*. Cambridge, MA: M.I.T. Press.

Sutton, J. (1996). Technology and market structure. *European Economic Review*, 40: 511–530.

Sutton, J. (1997a). Game-theoretic models of market structure. In D. M. Kreps, and K. F. Wallis, eds., *Advances in Economics and Econometrics: Theory and Applications. Seventh World Congress*. Vol. 1. Cambridge: Cambridge University Press.

Sutton, J. (1997b). One smart agent. *RAND Journal of Economics*, 28: 605–628.

Sutton, J. (1998). *Technology and Market Structure: Theory and History*. Cambridge, MA: M.I.T. Press.

Swann, D., D. P. O'Brien, W. P. J. Maunder, and W. S. Howe (1973). *Competition in British Industry: Case Studies of the Effects of Restrictive Practices Legislation*. Department of Economics, Loughborough University of Technology.

Swann, D., D. P. O'Brien, W. P. J. Maunder, and W. S. Howe (1974). *Competition in British Industry: Restrictive Practices Legislation in Theory and Practice*. London: George Allen & Unwin.

Symeonidis, G. (1996). Innovation, firm size and market structure: Schumpeterian hypotheses and some new themes. *OECD Economic Studies*, 27: 35–70.

Symeonidis, G. (1998). The evolution of UK cartel policy and its impact on market conduct and structure. In S. Martin, ed., *Competition Policies in Europe*. Amsterdam: North-Holland.

Symeonidis, G. (1999a). Cartel stability in advertising-intensive and R&D-intensive industries. *Economics Letters*, 62: 121–129.

Symeonidis, G. (1999b). *In Which Industries is Collusion More Likely? Evidence from the UK*. CEPR Discussion Paper no. 2301. London: Centre for Economic Policy Research.

Symeonidis, G. (2000a). Price competition and market structure: The impact of cartel policy on concentration in the UK. *Journal of Industrial Economics*, 48: 1–26.

Symeonidis, G. (2000b). Price competition, non-price competition, and market structure: Theory and evidence. *Economica*, 67: 437–456.

Symeonidis, G. (2000c). Price and nonprice competition with endogenous market structure. *Journal of Economics and Management Strategy*, 9: 53–83.

Symeonidis, G. (2002). Cartel stability with multiproduct firms. *International Journal of Industrial Organization* (forthcoming).

Tirole, J. (1988). *The Theory of Industrial Organization*. Cambridge, MA: M.I.T. Press.

Townsend, J., F. Henwood, G. Thomas, K. Pavitt, and S. Wyatt (1981). *Science and Technology Indicators for the UK: Innovations in Britain Since 1945*. SPRU Occasional Paper Series no. 16. University of Sussex.

Utterbach, J. M., and F. F. Suarez (1993). Innovation, competition, and industry structure. *Research Policy*, 22: 1–21.

Utton, M. A. (1970). *Industrial Concentration*. Harmondsworth, UK: Penguin.

Vickers, J. (1989). The nature of costs and the number of firms at Cournot equilibrium. *International Journal of Industrial Organization*, 7: 503–509.

Vives, X. (1985). On the efficiency of Bertrand and Cournot equilibria with product differentiation. *Journal of Economic Theory*, 36: 166–175.

Walshe, J. G. (1991). Industrial organisation and competition policy. In N. F. R. Crafts and N. W. C. Woodward, eds., *The British Economy Since 1945*. Oxford: Clarendon Press.

Waldman, D. M. (1982). A stationary point for the stochastic frontier likelihood. *Journal of Econometrics*, 18: 275–279.

Ward, T. S. (1973). *The Distribution of Consumer Goods: Structure and Performance*. Cambridge: Cambridge University Press.

Wilberforce, R. O., A. Campbell, and N. Elles (1966). *The Law of Restrictive Trade Practices and Monopolies*. 2nd ed. London: Sweet and Maxwell.

Wilson, T. (1962). Restrictive practices. In J. P. Miller, ed., *Competition, Cartels and Their Regulation*. Amsterdam: North-Holland.

Wright, N. J. (1978). Product differentiation, concentration, and changes in concentration. *Review of Economics and Statistics*, 60: 628–631.

Yamey, B. S. (1966a). Introduction: The main economic issues. In B. S. Yamey, ed., *Resale Price Maintenance*. London: Weidenfeld and Nicholson.

Yamey, B. S. (1966b). United Kingdom. In B. S. Yamey, ed., *Resale Price Maintenance*. London: Weidenfeld and Nicholson.

Yarrow, G. K. (1985). Welfare losses in oligopoly and monopolistic competition. *Journal of Industrial Economics*, 33: 515–529.

Ziss, S. (1994). Strategic R&D with spillovers, collusion and welfare. *Journal of Industrial Economics*, 42: 375–393.

Index